Monographs on British Economic
Institutions series

edited by Professor E. Victor Morgan
Professor of Economics, University of Manchester

BRITAIN'S COMMODITY MARKETS

Britain's Commodity Markets

Graham L. Rees
Professor of Economics, University College of Wales, Aberystwyth.

Assisted by R. S. Craig and D. R. Jones

Paul Elek Books
54-8 Caledonian Road London N1 9RN

I
Catherine
a
Gwenllian

ISBN 0 236 31076 3

Published by
Paul Elek Books Limited
54-8 Caledonian Road London N1 9RN

Printed in Great Britain by
Weatherby Woolnough Ltd.
Sanders Road Wellingborough Northants NN8 4BX

CONTENTS

LIST OF TABLES

Chapter

FIGURES

LIST OF ILLUSTRATIONS

Acknowledgements: Firms and Associations

The assistance of the following is very gratefully acknowledged:

Anning, Chadwick & Kiver Ltd — Mr. R. James (jr.)

Bache & Co. (London) Ltd — Mr. D. A. Cowley (Chairman & Managing Director), Mr. Stanley

Edward Barber & Son Ltd — P. S. Barber (Director)

British Broadcasting Corporation

British Federation of Commodity Associations — Mr. L. A. Wilson (Sometime Chairman), Mr. H. D. Carritt (Sometime Chairman), & Mr. F. F. Wolff (Chairman)

British Metal Corporation Ltd — Mr. A. G. Charles

British Non-ferrous Metals Federation — Mr. R. W. Gribbon

British Wool Marketing Board — Mr. N. A. Verrinder, Susan E. Bond

Buxton, Ronald, DuCroz & Co. — Mr. E. G. Larkworthy (Director), Mr. J. R. M. Lees (Secretary)

Coffee Terminal Market Association / Wool Terminal Market Association — Mr. C. C. F. Bickford (Secretary)

Committee of the London Public Fur Sales — Mr. A. F. Frayling (General Manager), Mr. E. W. Henderson (Secretary)

Commonwealth Secretariat — Commodities Division

C. Czarnikow Ltd — Mr. R. E. Liddiard (Director), Mr. R. C. Goodwin, Mr. C. C. Loveless

Financial Times — Mr. R. Reeves (Commodities Editor)

The General Produce Brokers Association of London — Mr. J. L. Bailey (Secretary)

Gill & Duffus Ltd.	Mr. L. Byles, Mr. D. B. J. Whitfield
Hale & Son Ltd	The late Mr. C. W. Gunn
Hicks Bros Ltd	Mr. C. G. Hutchins (Chairman & Managing Director), Mr. L. M. Sloper (Director), Mr. Andrews
A. A. Hooker & Co. Ltd	Mr. A. A. Hooker (Director)
Hull Corn Trade Association	Mr. A. R. Turner (Secretary)
Incorporated Oil Seed Association	Mr. A. E. J. Freeman (Secretary)
International Wheat Council	Mr. L. W. Binkhorst (Chief Economist)
The Liverpool Corn Trade Association	Mr. E. F. Sherrard (Clearing House Manager), Mr. W. H. Mulholland (Secretary)
The Liverpool Cotton Association	Mr. J. Mackie (Secretary)
The London Cocoa Terminal Market Association The Oil Terminal Market Association of London The United Sugar Terminal Market Association of London	Mr. W. Galloway (Secretary)
The London Commodity Exchange	Mr. T. H. Jeffery (Secretary)
The London Cattle Food Trade Association	Mr. G. W. Hawkins (Secretary)
The London Corn Trade Association Ltd The London Grain Futures Association Ltd	Mr. A. W. Burton (Sometime Secretary) Mr. A. E. Saville (Secretary)
The London Corn Exchange Co.	Mr. S. G. Jones (Secretary)
The London Metal Exchange	Mr. R. J. Powell (Secretary)
The London Produce Clearing House Ltd	Mr. Kimmins (Sometime Director), Mr. M. Stockdale (Director), Mr. I. McGaw

The London Provision Exchange	Mr. Barry (Secretary) Mr. Chandler
London Wool Brokers Ltd	Mr. B. M. King (Secretary)
J. Lyons & Co. Ltd	Mr. A. W. Ayling
Mars Ltd	Mr. N. P. Phillips
Nagoya Textile Exchange	Mr. T. Kosada (Managing Director)
Joseph Rank Ltd	Mr. P. A. Metaxa
Rowntree & Co.	Mr. E. G. Marshall
The Rubber Trade Association of London	Mr. H. D. Carritt (Chairman) Mr. T. H. Jeffery (Secretary)
Spillers Ltd	Mr. Jefferys, Mr. N. Tate
Sydney Greasy Wool Futures Exchange Ltd	Mr. M. F. Wright (Secretary)
Tea Brokers Association of London	Mr. J. C. L. Murdock (Secretary)
Tokyo Textile Commodities Exchange	Mr. M. Nishidate (Consultant)
Wilson, Smithett & Cope Ltd	Mr. Lionel Cope
Rudolf Wolff & Co.	Mr. F. F. Wolff (Director, Chairman of the British Federation of Commodity Associations & The London Metal Exchange), Mr. A. Strang

PREFACE

IN WRITING this study it has been necessary to take account both of historical sequence on the one hand, and of the simultaneous development alongside one another of many commodity markets on the other. The appropriate degree of detail in the treatment of the various markets at different periods of their development constituted a further problem, for which the best solution appeared to be to examine them at greatest length for the years which were most significant in the development of their organization and techniques.

The large domestic produce markets are dealt with separately in Chapter 3. The changing functions of various intermediaries within these markets provide valuable insights into parallel processes in the commodity markets. Obviously, the distinction between what are generally known as produce and commodity markets is not completely consistent. Usually, however, the latter have evolved from markets in goods to markets in rights to the commodity. In some cases the evolution of commodity markets stopped at this stage, but in others a further development occurred as traders attempted to deal with the risks—especially those of price changes—associated with trade. Moreover, commodity market transactions not infrequently concern, or are associated with, traffic in produce which does not involve U.K. markets directly at all (i.e. what is sometimes known as 'third country trade'). These markets also serve, or else at one time served, a significant re-export trade. By contrast, though some of the produce markets are large enough to have a nation-wide influence on prices and are very much involved in international commerce, they nevertheless remain essentially regional organizations and are without the transactions in rights which distinguish most commodity markets. It is for these reasons that, though developments in the produce markets have been followed down to the present time, their more recent history has been treated only briefly.

Whereas turnover figures and other data relating to futures markets—usually called terminal markets in London—are readily obtainable, at least for recent years, no figures exist of turnover in 'actuals' markets (i.e. in physical produce). In default of such statistics, tables indicating changes in imports have been given in the text, though these do not purport to do more than provide a general indication of changes in the importance of the relevant commodity over the years. It is possible to give this indication for the U.K. commodity markets because transactions on these markets are almost entirely concerned with imported primary produce. Obviously, this is not a necessary relationship,

York; Dr. K. Wolfensberger, Centre for Economic Research, Swiss Federal Institute of Technology; Professor B. S. Yamey, London School of Economics; Mr. B. Lemer; Dr. E. D. Lewis, Principal of the Glamorgan College of Education; Mr. C. A. G. Savidge, Director, British National Committee, International Chamber of Commerce, and Mr. R. C. Wanigatunga of the Central Bank of Ceylon. Needless to say, the responsibility for the errors and omissions which remain is entirely my own.

This study has suffered many interruptions, and would never have been finished at all but for valuable research assistance from Mr. D. R. Jones and the very considerable amount of work done by Mrs. B. J. A. Cook, especially on the tables, the index and in the general preparation of the typescript for publication. During earlier phases in the writing of this book, Mr. R. S. Craig, now of University College, London, provided impressive research assistance, while Mrs. M. Rimmer was equally impressive as a collector of data for the tables. Inevitably, over a period of some years, the typing has been passed to many hands, and I would like to pay particular tribute to the patience—the cheerfulness even—with which Miss P. James, Mrs. M. Jones, Mrs. J. Pennington and Mrs. E. A. Hutton typed out several drafts. Perhaps the most long-suffering of all those connected with the writing of this book, however, has been my wife. In any case, it was she who persuaded me from time to time that I ought to go on writing it.

Graham L. Rees
Aberystwyth
January 1972

but is partly the outcome of Britain's particular commercial history, and partly the result of its present high degree of specialization as an exporter of manufactures and an importer of food and raw materials.

When imports are used to provide an impression of the size of the market at least two major complicating factors must be borne in mind, namely, that not all imports pass through the markets, and that some parcels of commodities may change hands several times on these markets. Such considerations obviously affect the markets in different ways, for whereas resales increase turnover, when the markets are by-passed their importance is undermined. Even so, it must be remembered that transactions which do not pass through the markets are in all probability concluded with the aid of copyright forms of contract devised and supplied by the trade associations concerned.

Some of the terms used in commodity market transactions may be unfamiliar. These are all defined in the text when first used, and the index carries a reference to each of these definitions.

Britain's currency system was decimalized when this study was being concluded. A reference to the commodity quotations which it affected is provided in the Postscript. The Postscript also quotes a press release which indicates that in 1972 the terminal markets at present accommodated in Plantation House, Mincing Lane, will transfer to a new location nearby; in fact to the former floor—suitably adapted—of the Mark Lane Corn Exchange, which is to move to a newly constructed first floor in the same building.

It remains to acknowledge a massive indebtedness to various individuals and organizations. It seems appropriate to list market organizations separately, together with the names of those associated with these organizations. Without their generous assistance this study could not have been written. Many others have also read and commented upon various aspects of the manuscript. Professor E. Victor Morgan, the general editor of this series, read the manuscript in its entirety and made numerous valuable suggestions, while my colleague Mr. J. H. Morris improved both the style and the punctuation at many points. Professor I. G. Jones and Dr. E. B. Fryde, both of the University College of Wales, Aberystwyth, kindly undertook to read the early chapters, while some of my former colleagues at Swansea, namely Mr. E. J. Cleary, Dr. Ralph Griffiths and Mr. R. O. Roberts, contributed further valuable suggestions. Further afield, my indebtedness extends to Professor J. F. Haccaû of the University of Amsterdam; Dr. M. Hoffmeyer of the Institute of International Economics; University of Kiel; Professor W. Minchinton, University of Exeter, Mr. G. F. Ray of the National Institute of Economic and Social Research; Mr. Rees Davies, University College, London; Dr. Schmahl, The Hamburg Institute of International Economics; Mr. W. A. Thomas, University of Liverpool; Professor J. Wiseman, University of

Chapter One

MEDIEVAL COMMODITY TRADE

1. The alien merchants and their trade

DESPITE the expansion of the Moslems throughout the Mediterranean areas in the eighth century, the pattern of trade of the ancient world had not been obliterated entirely for, three centuries later, Venice, Genoa and Pisa were all trading once more with North Africa and the Middle East. Beyond the Mediterranean littoral, the Italians, forging East behind pioneers such as Marco Polo, eventually opened to the West the markets of Bokhara, Samarkand, India and China, from which a small but steady stream of precious silks, spices, furs and other products was henceforth to flow. Meanwhile, another major nucleus of commercial activity was developing in Flanders, in northern France and along the lower reaches of the Rhine. By the fourteenth century these regions had grown into the industrial hub of north-west Europe, with its financial centre at Bruges, its commerce, like that of London, being almost entirely in the hands of foreigners. In exchange for linen and expensive cloths, the English sent their most notable product across the narrow seas to this early manufacturing centre; but English wool was far from being used only in Flemish fabrics, for the Italians, too, sought eagerly for supplies of what was considered by the twelfth century to be the finest wool in all Europe. In spite of having been described at one time as the 'tin islands' by the Phoenicians, and at another as the 'granary of the north' by the Romans, it was for the quality of the clip from its sheep above all else that this island was noted in medieval times: during the early years of the fourteenth century, export figures of some 40,000 sacks a year were recorded. (Wool was reckoned by the sack for customs purposes, the sack being a standard weight of 364 lbs of shorn wool.)[1] Tin was still being exported in addition to pewter and hides, while grain was sometimes exported, and occasionally imported, according to the luck of the harvest.

In spite of—or perhaps because of—the importance of wool for the Flemish and Italian looms, neither London nor any other English city of the period was of the first rank in European commerce, for the most important axis of international trade naturally lay between the two great centres of industry and enterprise, Flanders and Italy. It was this primacy of Flanders and Italy, together with the hazard of the sea voyage, which led to the development of the land route between

19

these two areas and to the growth of the local fairs, which, even before 1200, particularly in Champagne, had become the nerve centres of international commerce.[2] No regular merchant voyages were attempted, through what we now know as the Straits of Gibraltar, until the later thirteenth century.

In common with most underdeveloped countries both then and since, England saw the incursion of many foreigners in search of important raw materials. Indeed, one of the major economic changes which accompanied the emergence of this country into modern times was the slow chequered process by which foreign trade and marketing were wrested from the hands of aliens by the growing number of native merchants. Eventually the growing use of the sea route between the Italian towns and north-west Europe resulted in the appearance in England in the fourteenth century of an increasing number of merchants and their agents from towns such as Lucca and Florence, as buyers of wool. Even in the thirteenth century they were frequently to be encountered in this country in this rôle, using the proceeds of taxes gathered for the Pope to buy entire wool clips, sometimes for years ahead, directly from the large desmesnes, as well as from middlemen. By the reign of Edward I (1272-1307) the greater mercantile firms such as the Society of the Bardi, the Frescobaldi, Peruzzi and Pulci were well established in this country, and with the increasing use of the sea came the periodic visits of the Genoese carracks and the great 'Flanders Galleys' from Venice. The name 'Flanders Galley', of course, signified the chief destination of the Venetian fleet, and in fact many of these ships at first berthed in England only on the return journey from the Low Countries. Though a fleet sponsored by the Venetian government first appeared in England in 1319, regular visits did not start until the 1390s—many decades after the commencement of regular visits to Flanders.[3] Among the Italians, the Genoese were the first to send ships to England with supplies of woad and alum essential to the woollen industry. Even so, they did not visit English harbours frequently until after 1298. The first Florentine state fleet came in 1425, but unlike the other Italian expeditions, they always visited both Flanders and England because of their interest in procuring wool from the latter country.[4]

Incoming cargoes were handled by the colonies of Venetians established at the ports, who loaded in their place the wool, cloth, skins, tin and pewter, stored in readiness at the warehouse headquarters known as factories (i.e. places of sojourn for factors). Southampton, the chief port used by the Italians and one of the most important in the kingdom after London, seems to have been used as a collecting and exporting centre rather than as a focus for selling imports, for Italian merchants travelled down from London regularly to collect their share of the galley cargoes, which they often accompanied in person on the return journey to the capital.[5] The process was set in motion initially by the merchant in Italy, who customarily sent his London factor the details of merchandise consigned to him for sale. The latter then passed on this intelligence to his Southampton agent, providing him with a letter of credence which authorized him to receive the goods. In return for his one per cent commission, the agent saw to customs dues, local charges (such as wharfage), the employment of lightermen to unload the merchandise from the carracks, the engagement of carriers for the journey to London, and possibly, too, the hire of lofts or cellars for temporary storage.

Though the Italians appear to have been the most numerous of the aliens in England during the thirteenth and fourteenth centuries they were by no means the only ones. Furthermore it is questionable, as Postan points out, whether the import of exotic goods by the Italians was as important (apart from woad and alum) as the bulkier commodities which flowed in from the less hospitable north, for the trade of northern Europe (apart from rare furs), was almost exclusively devoted to the necessities rather than to the luxuries of life.[6] Its source for the most part lay in the lands surrounding the Baltic, and its exploitation came to depend almost entirely upon the Hanseatic League of the towns surrounding the Baltic and of the North Sea ports. Though the major centre of their activities was Bruges, these merchants had developed Danzig, Riga and Reval as trading outlets in the Baltic while their Russian activities extended as far east as Novgorod. The Vikings had, of course, pioneered the Hanseatic trade routes along the Russian river valleys to the Caspian to trade with Byzantium, and following in their wake also, the Hansards had come to England, using such ports as London, Boston and Hull. The Hanse was responsible for the major expansion of the fish, timber, iron, wax and fur exports of Scandinavia, as well as for the movement of northern European grain supplies. The timber, pitch, tar and hemp brought in by these traders was indispensable to the English for construction and shipbuilding, and, from the beginning of the fifteenth century, Prussia became the only important source of timber for English ships, though the import of hulls and even of complete ships was far from uncommon. Their canvas, linen and thread were also essential items for shipbuilding, while the bowstaves which they brought were highly prized both for hunting and for war. In manufacture, too, the ashes imported from the northern forests constituted an important raw material in the making of cloth, as did some of their dyes, such as madder from Westphalia. The Hanse merchants also brought copper from Hungary and high-grade iron from Sweden, though the most important sources of metal goods during this period were France, Spain and Italy. Last, but not least, the Hansards imported beer from Bremen and Hamburg to these islands. On the export side their chief interest in English goods was in cloth, some of which they resold in the Low Countries, and much of this North Sea trade in cloth continued to be carried on by Hanseatic merchants as late as the sixteenth century. Their other most notable exports from this country, especially after the consolidation of the Staple System, were of tin and pewter. H. L. Gray has calculated that in 1480, as much as 40 per cent of England's alien trade was carried on by the Hansards.[7]

These 'Easterlings' established their famous headquarters, known as the Steelyard,[8] in London (on the present area of Cannon Street Underground Station and the Hudson's Bay Company headquarters), following the original grant to them of a 'gildhall' by Henry II. It was common at the time for traders doing business in markets abroad to unite in a *hanse*, or fellowship, in order to negotiate concessions. In addition to the Italians and the Hansards, we find that merchants from the Flemish cities in thirteenth century London were also at one time united in 'la hanse c'on apiele hanse de Londres'.[9] During the thirteenth, fourteenth and early fifteenth centuries there were in fact over twelve Hanseatic establishments in this country, of which the main centres were Lynn, Ipswich and Boston, with the Steelyard in London as the administrative headquarters for the country.

Incredible as it may appear to inhabitants of these islands nowadays, and in spite of the considerable quantity of home-brewed ale drunk by the poor, the Englishman of the period was very much a wine-drinker. This chief import of the realm, both by bulk and value, was very largely in the hands of the Gascons, who shipped about two-thirds of the 20,000 tuns a year imported at the close of the thirteenth century. Gascony was, of course, a possession of the English king from 1154 to 1453, a fact which, together with the wine trade to which it was related, led to the presence of Gascon merchants in strength in England during this period. The wine-selling merchant was a familiar sight far inland from his port of arrival, and Unwin recounts[10] the picture, painted by the *Liber Custumarum*, of the Lorraine merchants who brought in most of the remaining wine imports from the Rhineland. It was their custom as they approached London Bridge, to raise their ensign and sing a 'Kyrie Eleison', after which they were allowed to sell a tun of wine retail at a penny a stoop—a departure from the usual practice (laid down in Edward I's *Carta Mercatoria*) of allowing alien merchants to trade wholesale only. Subsequently, when the Sheriff of the City and the king's Chamberlain had taken their customary proportion of the ship's wine cargo at reduced prices, the Lorraine merchants were free to sell wholesale, first to the nobility, then to the merchants of London, Oxford, and Winchester, and afterwards to other merchants and the general public. The buyers from the general public consisted mostly of well-to-do craftsmen, who often bought their wine in bulk from aliens through brokers appointed by the City, for by the late fifteenth century the broker's functions (which were not, of course, limited to the wine trade), had, according to Arnold, become quite strictly defined. Their duties as sworn officials of the City were set out in the oath which they were required to take upon appointment:

Ye shal swere that ye shall neyther bye nor selle nor none other for you any maner merchandise by fraude or colusion to your owne propre use within the fraunches of this cite ne withoute and that yee nether make nor doo to be made any maner bargayne betwene forayn and forayn or forayn and straunger . . . Also that ye bye no maner merchandise of any persone . . . to no persones use but that ye brynge the seller and the byer together, making a rightful bargayne betwene them yf you be requyre . . . Also ye shalle in noo lyvery with any person noor host any maner straunger or alyen upon payne of lesing of your office for usery. Also ye shal doo all your bargayns that ye shall make betwene any maner of persones to be wreten in a booke and that shall have the same booke redy before the Mair and Aldermen for the tyme beyng at all tymes when ye by them shalbe requyred to testefye the bargayn of usery nor eni other false chevisaunce nor untruew bargayn ne contract nor medil ne concent to the same in any wyse.[11]

The list of aliens associated with English trade in the medieval period is far from exhausted by the above account. In the late fourteenth century, for example, between 200 and 250 merchants were engaged in importing salt into this country, of whom some two-thirds were foreigners, the majority of them Dutch, but Bretons were also important and others came from Portugal and Spain, not to mention the Hansards.[12]

In spite of a considerable domestic production in Cheshire and from the Worcestershire springs, a significant import of salt was required from the continent in medieval times. The bulk of this was used for the cure of herrings, a staple in the diet of the day, while considerable quantities were also needed for salting down meat slaughtered in the autumn, and for preserving butter. Most of the overseas supply came from Bourgneuf Bay, and the largest proportion of the remainder from the Spanish Peninsula. Like the trade in victuals, participation in the salt trade was unspecialized—even the Celys, for example, the renowned wool exporters, who normally specialized in that commodity, bought a Breton ship in 1485 and started to import wine, wood, cloth and salt in it.

When ships arrived at an English port, they were assigned to special quays. In the port of London, for example, Queen's hithe and Billingsgate were important wharfs at which goods were discharged, inspected and sold. Both were located in the Pool of London, the position of which owed a great deal to Peter of Colechurch, for his London Bridge,

built at the beginning of the thirteenth century, had so many arches
that navigation beyond what was virtually a dam was very difficult,
the water level being normally five feet higher above the bridge than
below. The task of unloading ships was carried out by specialist
porters and, after landing, commodities had to be weighed to facilitate
customs assessment; the 'great wares', such as corn, malt, salt and
alum, were weighed on the 'great beam', the 'small beam' being
reserved for more precious goods of smaller bulk, such as silk, while
the 'tron' was frequently used for wool.[13]

2. *The London Merchants and their Trade*

Whereas external trade was largely in the hands of foreigners, the
internal distribution and marketing of goods within the country was
often tightly controlled by the closed companies or 'misteries' of
Englishmen. These livery companies, as they were called, were
generally responsible for many public functions in connection with
trade; the Grocers, for example, acquired the privilege of nominating
both the weigher of the King's Beam and the Garbeller (i.e. cleaner)
of Spices, both lucrative posts, since a charge was levied for each commodity weighed and inspected. Most of the London livery companies
ranged over the whole field of distribution, for, in the course of time
(as Miss Thrupp and others have shown[14]) some companies ceased to
have any real connection with the trades after which they were named.
What does seem clear, however, is that it was the official intention
in fourteenth century London that their function should be limited to
supervision of the different branches of the retail trade, though the
crafts themselves do not always seem to have shared this view.[15] The
attitude of the City, expressed in a petition of the Common Council to
the mayor in 1364, was that

> it seems right that everyone who is enfranchised ought to buy and
> sell wholesale, within the City and without, any manner of
> merchandise on which he can make a profit, but he may keep a
> shop and sell by retail only those goods which belong to his
> particular mistery.[16]

In practice, wholesale dealings were most open in the great staple
commodities such as wool and cloth, foodstuffs, wine, timber, metals
and dyes, for no one company possessed either the power or the
organization to control supplies of necessities or widely demanded
goods. In the wine trade, of course, the King himself, through his
Sheriff, Chamberlain and Butler, was always a dominant figure in the
market, both as a buyer of good vintages and as a seller of the inferior
wines paid as customs, for in spite of its bad keeping qualities, wine
sometimes served as money in the Middle Ages, especially for paying
fines and customs duties. The nobility and the gentry, too, who bought
their wines wholesale, often resold them on a rising market. In fact,

anyone trading abroad would be quite likely to return with wine for sale, and the wealthier members of the Grocers Company sometimes dealt in wine on a very large scale, often importing as many as forty to fifty casks at a time. Nor did the Grocers confine themselves to victuals; they were also conspicuous in the distribution of various dyes (such as woad, madder, scarlet grains, saffron and brazil) from both Southampton and London to the towns and villages of the cloth-producing areas. In this activity it seems that they were joined not only by the Drapers and Mercers, but also by the Fishmongers and the Ironmongers.

As was the case in the dye trade, alum, soap, wax and oil were handled indiscriminately by all merchants, and the Grocers again featured prominently, especially in the soap trade. Amber and ivory, too, lay within the Grocers' province, though they were chiefly imported and distributed by the Mercers. In contrast with these miscellaneous items, spices were regarded for some time as the special province of the Grocers, and after 1386 they tried to assume the right to govern the entire retail trade in this produce.

In the salt trade, the Salters' livery company's connection with the trade became so tenuous that, apart from presenting meters of salt to the mayor of the City of London and keeping the measures of this particular 'mistery', they appear on the whole to have sold less salt than the Mercers and Grocers. Of all improbable things, the Salters' principal concern appears to have been the stocking of textiles, while the Chandlers assumed the task of supplying London with salt.[17] Finally, as far as the internal distribution of Baltic goods is concerned, it is worth noting that there were few prohibitions to inhibit the Hanse merchants during most of the medieval period, for, in spite of the frequent claims of the livery companies to the exclusive right of selling retail the goods which pertained to their 'mistery', the Easterlings had sold their goods directly to consumers as well as to merchant intermediaries ever since their first appearance in England, and assumed the right to continue to do so.

3. *Fairs and Markets*

In addition to the Hanseatic merchants, all manner of foreigners were to be seen at the fairs, for the function of these gatherings was to act as central markets for the exchange of goods. Moreover, while markets tended to be held weekly, or bi-weekly, fairs were frequently annual events only. The former gatherings catered for the sale of local produce, while the distinguishing purpose of the fairs was to provide a venue where merchants could purvey goods from distant parts in wholesale quantities. Britain's largest fairs were held at Boston, Bristol, Edinburgh, Exeter, Stamford, St. Ives (Huntingdonshire) and Winchester, while at the end of the fourteenth century, Stourbridge fair had

developed into a very notable event, and survived, though with much
reduced glory, well into the eighteenth century.

At the fairs most of the restrictions common to the medieval town-
ships were waived, and in the officially declared 'peace of the fair'—
and the sites of these gatherings were often marked with Christian
crosses—all conditions of men, from monks and clerics buying for their
flocks, to shopkeepers and artisans, cattle traders and dealers, traded
with one another. As a further inducement to attend the fairs, exhi-
bitions, plays and religious ceremonies were performed. Some fairs
lasted as long as a month, and they all tended to take place either in
summer, when travel was easiest, or else in the autumn after the harvest; Stourbridge fair, for example, started on 8 September and
continued for three weeks.[18] Though most imported goods would be
available at the fairs, some tended to become specialized. Weyhill and
Burford were well known as sheep fairs, while Yarmouth and Ipswich
became noted as sales centres for fish and butter respectively. Stourbridge fair became one of England's chief centres of trade for Flemish
merchants, while Winchester fair was acknowledged as a centre of
English trade for the Italian, French and Spanish merchants.

In London and a few of the largest cities every day except Sunday
was recognized as a market day, and specialized markets were a feature
at a very early date. Fish was sold at Billingsgate even in Saxon times,
while a fair of sorts was held periodically at Smithfield from as early
as the middle of the thirteenth century. Moreover, after some hard
bargaining, Edward III granted the aldermen of the City of London,
shortly after his accession in 1328, the exclusive right to hold markets
within seven miles of London stone, which was near St. Swithin's, in
what is now Cannon Street.

During the early Middle Ages the charters establishing fairs on the
continent were almost invariably granted to Church authorities, but
after the tenth century this was no longer the case. In Britain the fair
seems to have been largely a Norman importation so that, although
an appreciable number were in the hands of ecclesiastics, others were
granted to towns by royal charter or else were in the hands of the
nobility. Fairs were, of course, very profitable for the towns, religious
houses or whoever secured the revenue from tolls, rents of booths and
so on, to say nothing of the fact that, in attracting trade, they also
attracted money into the area. Stourbridge fair provides a good example
of one which was jointly controlled, in this case by the town and the
University of Cambridge. It was a situation which led to frequent
disputes, though Walford relates that one such quarrel was amicably
concluded in 1534 when 'all dranke together at the Pompe Tavern
and the Unyversyte payd for all'.[19]

During the fairs the municipal authority of the town was entirely
superseded and where, for example, a bishop had control of the fair,

he set up his own justices with the keys and custody of the city gates, as well as the cognisance of all pleas concerning breaches of the law, debts, contracts and even lands and houses in the city.[20] This was the case at St. Giles' fair at Winchester, during which all other trading was prohibited in the city and for seven leagues around. After proclaiming the fair, the bishop's officers could, if they wished, even appoint a temporary mayor, while the city court gave place to the 'Pavilion Court' of the fair. This right of jurisdiction was automatically bestowed with the granting of fairs, the courts being generally known as the courts of piepowder (from *pieds poudrés*, i.e. dusty feet). They were an essential institution for merchants who had come from a distance to the fair, and who could not await the more lengthy processes of the regular courts. Their jurisdiction was supreme during the fair as is shown by the case of the monks of Battle, who were granted a market by William the Conqueror in the following terms: 'Those who resort to the market are to answer to no-one but the abbot and monks; the abbot and monks to no-one but God.'[21] It was also comprehensive in its scope, and 'every sort of case came up for decision—from the finding of harlots in the house of William Redknave to great international disputes about wool that involved the Countess of Flanders'.[22] The law administered was Merchant Law, which differed from Common Law in being less formal and more expeditious. It was also more or less uniform all over Europe, having evolved from a set of practical rules and regulations for the equitable conduct of commerce. This international mercantile law defined terms of contracts for sale, methods of sampling, inspecting, weighing, and delivery, as well as determining the grading of produce, methods of sale, and terms of settlement of disputes.

4. *The Techniques of Trade*
Though German historians have debated extensively whether the Middle Ages possessed a class of traders who could be labelled as wholesalers, goods were in fact often handled in bulk, and sold not to the final consumers but to other merchants, frequently changing hands several times before being retailed; in the process, credit was demanded and allowed at every stage from the importer through to the retailer.[23] The wine trade, which was open not only to Vintners among the city guilds but to all and sundry, as we have already seen, provides a good example of this. The wine was frequently bought on credit from the growers and merchants of Gascony and Poitou, by both English and foreign importers, and sold on credit to retailers or wholesalers. A similar system of credit seemed to hold good for many other commodities in common demand, such as corn, leather and woad, whether sold at fairs or distributed from the larger towns. The same arrangement also existed for goods supplied by other foreign merchants, such as the Drapers from Louvain and Douai, St. Omer and Cambrai,

or the Mercers of Paris. A foreign merchant might supply a shipping order to the value of £30 or more on the security of only one of the larger importing merchants, or he might execute a joint shipping order upon the combined security of some half a dozen small traders. The commonest form of transaction among the Cordwainers and Skinners of London at the end of the thirteenth century was for several of the lesser merchants to combine for the purpose of buying a cargo, thus putting themselves collectively on the same bargaining level as a merchant in a sufficiently big way of business to buy a 'shipping order' himself from a foreign merchant or agent.

To a considerable extent England's import and export trades remained separate during the Middle Ages, a feature which required the establishment of mechanisms to effect international payments, and called forth arrangements of various degrees of sophistication from the different trading interests involved. The simplest solution was to attempt to marry the import and export trades, and in some measure, of course, this is what happened—wine, as we have seen, was brought back by numerous small traders who were primarily exporters, while the Vintners frequently took wheat and fish abroad in order to pay for their purchases. On the Genoa-England route, too, trade was highly specialized and relatively simple; wool in exchange for pastel (i.e. woad) and alum. In London, Southampton, Genoa and other towns, transactions often consisted of an actual exchange of these commodities.[24] Specie payments, too, were often made, especially by the Hansards.

During the later Middle Ages, however, the growing use of gold and silver as currency media gave rise to local shortages in western Europe, especially in Spain, despite the appreciable levels of production achieved in Bohemia and Germany. The chief reason for the growth in England of 'bullionist' policies probably lay in the desire on the part of the king to conserve gold and silver supplies in the country in spite of (or perhaps as a nervous reaction to) declining government revenues. The export of bullion was considered at the time to drain the country's wealth, so the restrictive policies followed quite naturally from this belief. It was also a deliberate feature of English foreign policy during the period, resulting from the wars with France (whose king was overlord of Flanders) and the strained relations with the Papacy. The Italians, as we have seen, frequently acted as the Pope's agents, a circumstance which itself often caused English kings in the fourteenth and fifteenth centuries to prohibit the shipment of bullion from the country by these merchants.

The bill of exchange developed from an embryonic stage as a 'letter of credit' whereby overseas payments of amounts advanced in other currencies were facilitated—though the aim of avoiding charges of usury was also a powerful stimulus to the development of credit operations which permitted interest charges to be hidden in the calculation of exchange rates. The facilities provided by the financial houses of the time, which, after the expulsion of the Jews from England at the end of the thirteenth century, were almost all Italian, enabled merchants to avoid the international transfer of cash. A merchant in London, for example, could purchase from a Florentine firm in London an order to pay a certain sum in florins, which could then be sent to that merchant's factor for use in Florence. Similarly, an Italian merchant wishing to buy English wool could do so by paying a Florentine banker in Italy for an order which could be drawn upon in sterling, at the latter's London branch. By this means actual currency transactions in international commerce were minimized, and, because of the separation of importing and exporting activities, the bills of exchange into which these letters of credit developed tended to be bought and sold, rather than kept to maturity, to meet the demand for means of payment in foreign currencies. In this way a bill market arose which reached its most developed form among the great merchant-banking firms, since it was the transactions in these instruments of commercial credit which constituted one of the chief characteristics of an Italian *piazza*, or banking centre.

Because of the rudimentary state of transport and communications many contracts tended unavoidably to become credit transactions as well. This was true even of some drafts payable on sight, though the period of usance of bills in London was usually from one to three months.[25] The incorporation of interest rates was, as previously indicated, common practice at the time, but this was easily accomplished by financiers who had, after all, invented double-entry bookkeeping, and much else besides.

5. *The Emergence of the English Merchant*
Before the end of the sixteenth century, Italians, Hansards and other alien groups, despite their initial advantages and the control they had exercised in the marketing of imports and exports, had been replaced by native merchants. This change occurred as a merchant class arose in England, and grew in importance. By the end of the period these traders became a class distinct from manufacturers as they secured a growing proportion of the country's trade into their own hands. There was, too, a tendency towards specialization by commodity or by market, and even some buying and selling for forward delivery (i.e. promises to deliver goods at some agreed future date). In fact, so wealthy did the merchants of London become in time, that the king turned more and more in their direction for loans—a process not without reciprocating advantages.

One of the most important causes of changes in the marketing of traded goods in England during the late medieval period was that associated with the economic contraction between about 1320 and 1500. This age of diminished opportunities had important repercussions not only on the volume and character of trade, but also on the very attitude towards commerce. According to Postan, it led to the emergence of a mercantilist outlook and commercial xenophobia. If this was so it might partly explain the increasing hold exercised by English merchants on foreign trade. What is certainly beyond doubt is the remarkable growth of an English merchant class, which gradually monopolized the main items of the country's external trade.

The economic depression appears to have affected all the countries of Western Europe, with the result that merchants sought to increase their monopoly powers whenever this seemed possible. The formal organization of German towns into the Hanseatic League by the latter half of the fourteenth century was clearly a symptom of the onset of more depressed conditions. By the beginning of the fifteenth century, moreover, the League had not only succeeded in controlling the Baltic, but also the trade of Poland, Russia and Scandinavia, driving out English merchants in the process; even a large proportion of the Icelandic trade eventually fell to the Germans after they had won over the King of Denmark, the ruler of Iceland. Quarrels affected English trade in the very important Flanders, Zealand and Brabant markets, while the secession of Gascony in 1453 impeded the exchange of wine against cloth and wheat for some time, though not nearly as much as was at one time supposed.[26] Piracy flourished, restricting the flow both of imports and exports. English privateers were particularly busy during this period, though the seizure of trading vessels was not by any means confined to pirates. The friction between English and Hanseatic merchants was particularly severe, but the latter's espousal of Edward IV's cause subsequently ensured the restoration to the Germans of all their ancient privileges in England. Meanwhile, English merchant shipping succeeded in making considerable headway in the Mediterranean despite the sinking of Richard Sturmy's expedition off Malta in 1457. This success was due in part to Edward IV's use of England's commercial strength in imposing a three year ban upon the export of wool in Italian ships. More recently, however, scholars have tended to the view that though Edward's ban was a culminating factor, the opening of the ports of Pisa to free competition by Florence in 1465 owed a great deal to the defects inherent in the system of galley monopolies inaugurated earlier in the century.[27]

The consequence of the growth of an English merchant class competent to handle the major items of commodity trade was a clash of interests between these native merchants and alien traders, which was exacerbated by the economic contraction. This is nowhere better illustrated than in the attempts of the Vintners' Company, led by merchants of considerable wealth, such as John de Oxenford and

Reynold atte Conduit, to wrest the monopoly of the wine trade from the hands of the Gascons.[28] The Grocers' Company, too, assumed the right after 1356, to govern the entire retail trade in spices, and decreed in 1455 that no member should buy spice from anyone outside the Company except 'atte first hand of the merchante straunger'. Such attempts, however, were ultimately overwhelmed by competitive pressures.

For the English monarch the wool trade, in which foreigners had become interested from at least as early as the twelfth century, represented a potential source of enormous revenue and power. Thus, as soon as native merchants became sufficiently wealthy and experienced to handle the commodity on a large scale, and to provide loans for the crown, the king's co-operation was assured for the establishment of a monopoly sales corporation in the produce. This took the form of a wool 'staple', with the English merchants in charge, funnelling all exports of the commodity through this early species of compulsory marketing board. From 1361 the Staple operated principally from Calais, which was conveniently near the Flanders fairs. The Staple greatly facilitated the raising of taxes and loans from the wool staplers: moreover, it contributed greatly to the credibility of such threats of embargo upon exports as the king might care to make to his enemies. For their part, the English merchants, who had formed themselves into a Fellowship of Merchants of the Staple, were very pleased with a system which put considerable liquid assets at their disposal, and gave them the opportunity to emulate John Philpot of London, the de la Poles of Hull, and others who had amassed considerable fortunes.[29]

As exports of cloth replaced exports of wool, about half the entire trade continued to be controlled by foreigners throughout the fifteenth century, and the rise of the Company of Merchant Adventurers is therefore generally recognized to have been a consequence of competition in a period of contraction—the by-product, as Postan emphasizes, of a defeat.[30] The export of English cloth by the Hanseatic merchants had grown from 4,464 pieces in 1422, to 21,000 by the end of the century. (Woollen cloths were accounted for by number, counted in terms of the standard 'cloth of assize', which measured 24 yards by $1\frac{1}{2}$–2 yards). Despite a continuing xenophobia on the part of the English, culminating in the sack of the Steelyard by the London mob in 1493, it was not until 1552, after the conversion of Sir Thomas Gresham by an anti-Hanseatic group, that the English government felt sufficiently strong to revoke the privileges of the 'Merchauntes of the Stillyard'. The final expulsion did not come until 1598, however, when the Spanish threat to the kingdom had been successfully met.

The process of capturing the large proportion of trade controlled by the Italians was a gradual one. The wool Staplers' monopoly of sale, for example, extended in practice only as far south as the Alps, and the king had the right, which he exercised freely in return for financial consideration, of licensing the export of wool to places other than Calais. The customs accounts of the period show that almost all these authorized shipments were to places east of the Straits of Marrock (i.e. Morocco), to the annoyance of the Staplers, who always coupled the grant of any considerable loan to the crown with a plea that these licences be discontinued. Towards the end of the fifteenth century, though, a number of measures did loosen the Italian hold over a considerable section of English trade, at the same time as the triumph of the Yorkist cause strengthened the protectionist lobby of the English merchant, with whom Edward IV was closely in league. A sumptuary law, regulating the manner of dress of different classes, was passed in 1464, and in order to protect the domestic wrought silk, ribbon and lace industries (the production of which goods, it was pointed out, had the inestimable advantage of keeping young girls out of mischief) their import was forbidden. The order that no-one should sell 'any Lawne, Nyfels, Umple, or eny other manere of kerchiefs, were of the prise of a plight shall excede Xs', was also a blow aimed directly at Italian trade, as was the prohibition of the import of sweet wines in 1365 and 1381, and the restriction to sale in wholesale quantities from 1420. Other laws prohibiting the import of a large number of miscellaneous articles, many of Italian origin, came into force towards the end of the fifteenth century, while further troubles attended Henry VII's attempt in 1490 to establish a wool Staple at Pisa. Yet, in spite of Henry's high-handed seizure of the Venetian galleys for use as troop transports for his army in 1492, they continued intermittently to berth at Southampton until 1532. The cessation of their visits at that date was probably attributable to the troubles which had beset Italian trade in the Mediterranean, with the rising power of the Turks and the entry of the Portuguese into the Indian ocean. Moreover, the trade route itself grew more hazardous as piratical attacks in the Mediterranean mounted, so that greater quantities of English wool and other produce, such as tin, had to be taken overland to Italy.[31] An ever-growing proportion of English trade therefore came to be channelled through the Antwerp mart, which had become the greatest entrepôt in the world. Inextricably bound up with this process, as we have seen, was the evolution of the organization of English overseas trade, which had fallen almost entirely into the hands of native merchants by the end of the Tudor period.

in Plymouth.

For SALE by the CANDLE,
At GARRAWAY's Coffee-Houſe, in Exchange-Alley, Cornhill.

On Wedneſday the 11th Inſtant, at Five o'Clock in the Afternoon,

THE following Goods, being Part of the Cargo of the FORTUNE, Capt. John Brown, taken by the French, and afterwards retaken by the Hawke, Capt. Wilſon, viz.

274 Serons of Alicant Burilla
20 Cheſts of Soap

Catalogues of which will be timely delivered, by

MARK HUDSON, } Brokers.
and
THOMAS FIELDER, }

For SALE by the CANDLE,
At GARRAWAY's Coffee-Houſe, in Exchange-Alley.

On Wedneſday the 11th of June 1760, at Five o'Clock in the Afternoon.

THE following GOODS, viz.

408 Hogſheads } Guadaloupe Sugar
8 Tierces }
5 Barrels }

Samples to be ſeen To-morrow, and the day of Sale, at Mr. James Anſell's, in Water-Lane, where Catalogues may be had at the Place of Sale, and of JOHN and JAMES BRADSHAW, and JOHN WARREN.

For SALE by the CANDLE,
At GARRAWAY's Coffee-houſe, in Exchange

2. 'For Sale by the Candle at Garraway's' advertisement. *The Public Ledger.*

1. Garraway's Coffee House, Change Alley, from a nineteenth-century drawing. (Site of the Hudson's Bay Company's first auction.) *Radio Times Hulton Picture Library.*

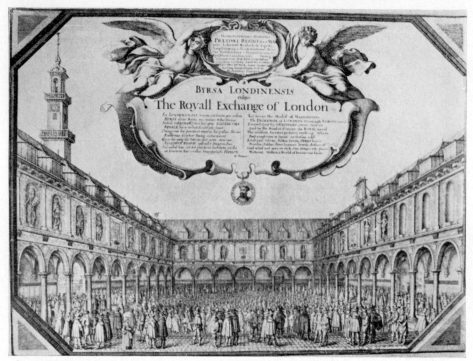

3   The Royal Exchange in the seventeenth century. *The Times*.

4.   *A Sale at East India House* from an aquatint by Stadler after a drawing by Rowlandson and Prigin. From Ackermann's *The Microcosm of London, 1808*.

Chapter Two

THE ROYAL EXCHANGE AND THE COFFEE HOUSES

1. *Early Commodity Exchanges*

THE sightseer in the City of London is unlikely to be there for very
long before he finds himself walking around the cool interior of the
Royal Exchange, to become aware, perhaps for the first time, that the
capital had had a long and varied history before ever it became the
commercial and financial centre of the world. Though London could
boast of important markets as long ago as the fourteenth century, it
is nevertheless fitting that this imposing nineteenth century edifice in
the very heart of the City should now be the symbol of the commercial
development of the capital. A Royal Exchange has stood on this site
ever since Sir Thomas Gresham's original building was opened by
Queen Elizabeth in January, 1571.[1] Before that date Lombard Street
seems to have been the principal haunt of the merchants, while Stow's
account emphasizes the importance of 'Paul's Walk' as a venue where
news might be heard and transactions concluded, payments being made
at the cathedral font.

The first Royal Exchange was destroyed in the Great Fire of 1666,
and almost two centuries later, its successor also went up in flames.
The present building, opened by Queen Victoria in 1844, has witnessed
the era of the City's undisputed world supremacy—though its management, still called the Gresham Committee, is reminiscent of a much
earlier period, its twenty-four members being drawn, at the founder's
wish, equally from the Corporation of the City and from the Mercer's
Company. Very little in the way of commercial activity has taken place
in the Exchange itself since Lloyd's insurance market moved out in
1928, but its history as the cradle of a large number of London's
famous exchanges is extraordinary, since it was here that the Stock
Exchange, the Metal Exchange, and more than a score of other
important markets were once housed. In the 'pepper cellers' beneath
the former Exchange, moreover, the East India Company stored some
of the goods brought back for auction, in the days before Robert
Clive's victories and the growth of trade led to the construction in
the City of more spacious premises, of which the Cutler Street warehouse was the most notable.

The interior of the first two buildings was planned in the same style
as any other market centre, with rows of stalls on either side of 'walks'.
These aisles were named according to the particular group of aliens

33

frequenting that particular section of the Exchange; we read for
example of the 'Italian Walk'. However, upstairs on the first floor, these
paths were often termed 'pawns', either a corruption of the Hanseatic
'bahn', the Dutch 'baan', or possibly[2] a derivation from 'pannus'
meaning cloth, which was commonly pledged on the Exchange.
Certainly, the term was older than the Exchange itself, having been in
use in the form of 'pawnee' in the old Lombard Street market, from the
assembly of the merchants in a place called 'Pawn House' there, as far
back as the time of Edward II.[3] The first floor of the Royal Exchange
was rented out by the Committee to apothecaries, armourers, book-
sellers, goldsmiths and glassware merchants, while the ground floor
was devoted to the necessities and luxuries of the day, such as mouse-
traps, bird-cages, shoeing-horns and lanthorns. These shops served
to provide the rental for the upkeep of the building. Nevertheless, this
retail business was of secondary importance as the main function of the
Exchange was to provide a venue for merchants or brokers for the
negotiation of transactions in bulk. By the eighteenth century the shops
were producing an annual rental of some £4,000, while Addison
describes the merchants 'negotiating, like princes, for greater sums of
money than were formerly to be met with in the royal treasury'.[4]

In spite of the magnificence of the well-known painting by Ernest
Crofts of Queen Elizabeth's opening of the first Royal Exchange (which
hangs in the present building), London's first Exchange was really a
relatively insignificant attempt to imitate the bourse at Antwerp. This
rather improbable township, considerably too far up the Scheldt to
berth the larger ships (which dropped anchor at Arnemuiden[5]), had
nevertheless quietly taken over from Bruges, by the beginning of the
sixteenth century, the position of the leading entrepôt of North-West
Europe. It was here that the Hanseatics found their chief vent for
Baltic and other goods from the North, while the Italians brought fruits
and wine from the Mediterranean, as well as spices from the East—
until they were undersold by the Portuguese after the latter's discovery
of the direct sea route to India, and the sale of their first cargo on the
Antwerp mart, in 1501.[6] In the very cosmopolitan throng at this
'most renowned merchandizing City that ever was in the World', the
English nonetheless held a very special place due, of course, to the
enormous turnover of English broadcloth on that market.

The phenomenon of Antwerp has proved a perennial fascination
for scholars, for while some, such as R. H. Tawney, assert that by the
sixteenth century, 'In its economic organization the machinery of
international trade had reached a state of efficiency not noticeably
inferior to that of three centuries later',[7] others subscribe to the view
that Antwerp was really the 'apotheosis of the medieval fair', its super-
ficial modernity deriving only from its free trade, which made it
resemble nineteenth century markets to some extent. Certainly, some

otherwise very astute dealers on the exchange also normally included astrological considerations in their reckoning, a practice which, as is well known, has now died out completely, even among desperate Chancellors of the Exchequer. Inside the Antwerp Exchange, dedicated *Ad usum mercatorium gentis ac linguae*, a significant proportion of the transactions consisted of bets and lotteries, for the traders and merchant bankers wagered not only on the return of ships from the Indies, but also on any other promising subject, such as the sex of unborn children. It was this spirit which led to the development of marine insurance on the Exchange, and to the emergence of forward dealings in commodities, though these were chiefly confined to the grain trade and not absorbed into the organization of the Exchange in the sixteenth century. Dealings in commodities 'to arrive' (i.e. while still afloat), however, became one of the most notable features of Amsterdam, which very largely succeeded Antwerp as the commercial and financial hub of North-West Europe after Antwerp became engulfed in the political troubles of the third quarter of the sixteenth century. A surprising variety of commodities, including herrings, grain, spices, whale-oil and salt, could be dealt with on the basis of optional contracts by the early seventeenth century. These were a species of futures contract, fixing a price due from buyer to seller for an option upon the purchase of a quantity of, say, herrings at some future time. When the catch did come to market, therefore, the buyer could either take up the agreed quantity, or else pay a previously agreed sum of money should he not wish to take delivery. Malynes describes it as a way

> to make employment with little money, which happeneth upon some sudden advice many times unexpected, whereupon men are very hot either to buy or sell: which is much used in Flanders in buying of Herring, before they are catched, by 'stellegelt', as they call it, that is by a summe of money agreed upon to be paid, if the partie doeth repent himselfe of the bargaine.[8]

By the early eighteenth century, according to contemporary evidence, time dealings in grain, cocoa, saltpetre, and above all in coffee, had assumed considerable importance in the Low Countries. We know too that by 1698 the 'States General had denounced by *plakkaat* a practice which was evidently not uncommon—the sale of large quantities of grain by persons who had none—while the sale of options was also forbidden, 'but continued notwithstanding'.[9] The bear speculator was evidently active on the Amsterdam exchange, therefore, employing a technique which was afterwards used widely only from the second half of the nineteenth century—that is, dealing in promises of future deliveries of produce which were fictitious in the sense that the produce had no specific existence at the time. Such transactions must have necessitated the invention and acceptance of contracts for the purchase and sale of commodities for future delivery. Such a phenomenon of itself, of course, provides considerable justification for Tawney's view, quoted earlier, that the practices of later centuries were not appreciably more advanced than those of the marts of the Low Countries at the height of their fame.

In addition to being the birthplace of speculative practices on a considerable scale, the Low Countries at this period also witnessed the popularization of the auction as the method of sale for colonial and other produce. In the ancient world, auctions had been confined almost entirely to sales of goods which had come into the hands of the state through confiscation or legal process, and were thus the fore-runners of the medieval auctions, which were nearly always a means of repaying creditors arranged at the instance of the judiciary. The only true precursor of the modern auction, therefore, appears to be the Roman voluntary sale, the *bonorum venditio*, a form of selling which re-appeared in commercial use in Venice about the middle of the fourteenth century, and afterwards notably as the method by which the Dutch East India Company organized the bi-annual sale of produce which arrived at irregular intervals, and then usually in considerable quantities. These auctions were often governed by the burning of a portion of candle, the bidding proceeding until the candle had burnt to its allotted length.

Above all else, however, sixteenth-century Antwerp seems to have been notable for the widespread use of instruments of settlement in international commerce. There was very little wholesale buying or selling for cash, and cash customers could exact a discount of up to 30 per cent. There were various forms of credit, but the most common one appears to have been the division of the sum due into three parts, the first payable at the forthcoming fair and the others at the two succeeding ones. Many of the more substantial English merchants were, moreover, switching from trade to finance by lending funds when the market was overstocked and prices were falling. Their usual practice was to discount bills of exchange at two months, on Antwerp, for Staplers or cloth exporters. Two months later, they repatriated their money by advancing it to English traders whose business consisted in buying commodities on the Antwerp mart and elsewhere, for sale in England. Thus, until the 1560s, the bill on Antwerp was the most usual form of commercial currency, while the English Vintners financed their wine imports by means of bills on Lyons, backed by the Italian bankers, who were the backbone of the financial community at that centre, as well as in Antwerp. Transactions among these financiers and merchant bankers eventually became very sophisticated indeed, though according to Tawney,

Till nearly the end of the century, the English cockleshell was towed by the continental leviathans, and the financial resources needed for these grandiose *coups* were not available in London.[10]

2. *The Transactions of the Chartered Companies*

In the meantime, Gresham's Exchange was far from being that great man's only imprint upon Tudor commercial history, for by mid-century he had achieved a remarkable reversal of the fall in the foreign exchange value of sterling. Successive debasements of the pound, especially in the 1540s, had reduced its value from 32s. Flemish at the outbreak of the war in 1522, to 13s. 4d. In order to repay the Crown's debts to the Fuggers and other financiers at Antwerp without turning the exchange rate further against sterling, Gresham proceeded to manipulate the market.[11] He induced the Merchant Adventurers to exchange the receipts from their cloth sales at Antwerp for bills payable in London, and succeeded in delaying domestic importers' purchases of Flemish currency. Sterling exchange rates rose, and Gresham achieved his object, but the process also increased the price of cloth on the Antwerp mart. The boom came to an end as the number of cloths sold dwindled, until, as Fisher points out,

> the opening years of Elizabeth's reign found the cloth trade at a level some 30 per cent below the peak of the boom, a level which was not to be substantially exceeded until the next century.[12]

It proved to be a major turning point, for while the immediate official reaction of the Government was to pass a series of interventionist measures (such as one to keep down the price of wool and another to suspend Hanseatic privileges), its ultimate and most important effect was to launch English merchants upon the quest for other, necessarily more distant, markets. Companies were formed and expeditions financed to open up trade with hitherto unexploited markets, or to chart routes which could be followed in order to trade directly where previously merchants had been content to buy and sell goods on the Antwerp mart.

Almost all the well known trading companies formed in the course of the following half century or so were based, according to Wheeler, upon the Merchant Adventurers' mode of organization.[13] There were clearly reasons for corporate trading in a strength greater, usually, than even the richest individual merchant could muster at the time, for convoys of merchantmen were less vulnerable to piratical attacks and, as a group, more powerful for treating with—or bribing—foreign princes. Such hazards and expenses go far to explain why these true 'merchant adventurers' saw fit to petition for the monopoly of trade to a particular area. The companies were of two sorts to begin with, being either regulated or joint-stock. In the former, each merchant traded as an individual, while in the latter, the members constituted a corporate organization whose profits or losses were shared. The largest of the regulated companies were the Merchant Adventurers themselves, the Eastland, the Russia, and the Levant companies—although the last two, together with the Africa Company, alternated between the two types of organization. The best known of the joint-stock companies were the East India and, at a later date, the Hudson's Bay Company. The regulated form of company served well enough on the whole for trade with countries relatively near England, but most merchants were either not sufficiently wealthy, or else disinclined, to finance more distant trade in the same way. At first, only single ventures were financed by means of the joint-stock form of organization, but it proved difficult to maintain continuity in this way, so that after an intermediate stage of financing a group of ventures as one unit, the continuous joint-stock company came into existence, the transition being complete in the case of the East India Company by about 1660. Though the regulated company survived for some time, the new form of organization gained ground rapidly in the seventeenth century, and finally superseded the other completely.

The Muscovy Company, established in 1553 as a joint-stock venture, was mostly concerned to trade woollen goods for naval stores such as masts, spars, tar, rope, hemp, sailcloth, together with wax, skins, fur, and sometimes corn. In the same year the group of merchants from Southampton, who, in spite of the Portuguese, had already started to trade with parts of Africa, formed an Africa Company and imported ivory, spices and some gold. Not having a charter, however, it possessed no monopoly of the trade, but when, in 1562, John Hawkins captured 300 negroes and sold them in Spanish America, he laid the foundation for the Royal Africa Company which was eventually incorporated in 1660. The ships of this company, as is well known, plied their dismal trade in a triangle, the first leg of which consisted of an outward journey, usually from London, Liverpool or Bristol, with manufactures for West Africa: these were exchanged for slaves there, who were then taken on the notorious 'middle passage' to the New World for sale to sugar, tobacco, and cotton planters. Finally, on the homeward leg, the vessels were frequently laden with cash crops from the plantations, together with some ginger, indigo and logwood.

The expansion of the Levant Company's activities was greatly aided by the decline of Venice and other Mediterranean cities. The company was formed in 1581, and exported mainly woollen goods, together with some tin and lead, in return for citrus fruits, currants, wines of Candia, cotton wool and yarn, silk, spices and drugs. The trade in this last-named group of commodities, having been captured from the Russia Company was, however, destined in turn to be lost to the greatest of the chartered companies, namely the Honourable East India Company, granted a charter on 31 December 1600 to open up the direct sea route with the Orient in defiance of the Portuguese and later the Dutch hegemony in that area. The Company's early imports were mainly spices (the art of charcuterie being still essential at a time when so many animals had to be slaughtered before the winter); 'healthful drugs'—mostly cloves, maces, nutmegs and pepper; indigo for dyeing cloth, cotton yarn, raw silk and calicoes. Last, but very important, imports also included saltpetre, an essential ingredient for making gunpowder. It was not until a later date that coffee and tea were included, imports of the latter, especially, being destined to grow in magnitude beyond anyone's wit to foresee.

Down to 1834, all the tea from China had to pass through the warehouses of the East India Company, whose monopoly as the United East India Company had been confirmed in 1709. The Hudson's Bay Company and the Levant Company also managed to survive the agitation against monopolistic privilege which was a feature of the seventeenth century, but, by 1673, trade with Sweden, Norway and Denmark was freed from this protection: the year 1689 sealed the fate of the Merchant Adventurers and, at the very end of the century, the trade with Africa was liberated, followed by that with Russia and Newfoundland. Even though the State withdrew the charters of privilege from the companies, its interference with the flow of trade was far from being absent: it now took the form of discrimination against foreign carriers instead. During the Civil War, the Dutch had secured command of the provision trade from Europe to the English colonies, and the return of local produce, especially sugar and tobacco.[14] The Navigation Act of 1660 and the Staple Act of 1663 reversed the trend entirely, their effects being to exclude alien-owned and alien-built ships from trade with the colonies, as well as from carrying to England the goods of Asia, Africa and America, and to limit their right to bring in European produce. It is not surprising, therefore, that this policy should have resulted in a considerable growth in the trade of English ports, accompanied as it was by an increase in the island's population, and the suppression of the domestic cultivation of tobacco.

The normal method by which the chartered companies disposed of their imported goods was by auction. Of these, the ones held in the 'Great Hall' of East India House (the site of which was contained by Leadenhall Street, Lime Street, Leadenhall Place and the eastern entrance of Leadenhall Market), were particularly notable. An eyewitness of these sales who set down his impressions at a later date, remarked that:

Those of tea were the most extensive, and they are yet remembered with a sort of dread by all who had anything to do with them. They were held only four times a year—in March, June, September and December; and the quantity disposed of at each sale was in consequence very large, amounting on many recent occasions to 8½ millions of pounds and sometimes much higher: they lasted several days, and it is within our recollection that 1,200,000 lbs have been sold in one day.

This witness also noted that the indigo sales were organized in much the same way.[15] According to Pulling's account,[16] these sales always took place in the presence of the chairman and the directors of the Company and, in the seventeenth century at least, were by the 'ancient mode' of an inch of candle, 'which being lighted, served to limit the period of bidding'. The terms of these auctions were cash; at those of the Royal African Company, for example, a deposit was paid within a day or two of making a purchase, the balance being paid later.[17]

According to figures gathered by Mrs Schumpeter,[18] imports into the United Kingdom rose from some £6 million for 1700, to about £28 million for 1800. Over the same period, however, imports from the East, the West Indies, mainland North America and Ireland had together grown at a much greater rate, from £1.8 million to £15.2 million. 'During the century', as T. S. Ashton remarks,[19] 'England—or rather Britain—had acquired a commercial Empire.' It was one, moreover, in which grocery imports (chiefly sugar, tea, coffee, rice and pepper) had expanded to dominating importance, mainly at the expense of textiles and wine, though the duties upon German linen and French wines had given rise to a thriving clandestine trade in the course of the century.

Percentage of Total Imports[20]

	1700	1800
Groceries	16.9	34.9
Linens	15.6	5.6
Calicoes and piece goods	5.9	4.5
Silk: raw and thrown	6.3	2.4
Flax and hemp	3.0	4.3
Cotton wool	—	6.0
Dye stuffs	1.0	4.2
Timber	4.0	2.1
Wine	10.8	2.4

The period after the Restoration was, of course, most notable for the growth of the re-export trade: about half the grocery imports, for example, were normally re-exported, the proportion of coffee being especially high. It was a trade, furthermore, which together with the general re-orientation of commerce in the direction of the New World, helped to give rise to the phenomenal expansion of the western ports of Bristol, Liverpool, Whitehaven, and Glasgow: in the first named, for example, a well-developed sugar market emerged,[21] while merchants at Whitehaven and the Scottish ports[22] did a considerable business in the re-sale of Virginia tobacco to the French state monopoly in the tobacco business. Liverpool, meanwhile, had stolen a march on the capital by building a wet docks as early as 1710. Altogether, London's share in total imports fell from 80 per cent for 1700 to 63 per cent by 1780.[23]

3. The Coffee Houses

Despite the fall in the proportion of goods which came into the country via the Port of London, the fourfold expansion in the total volume of imports for the country as a whole, which took place during the eighteenth century, represented an enormous influx of produce into the capital. One result of this was to render the Royal Exchange completely inadequate. In London, therefore, in addition to the principal outports, centres of business grew up at the coffee houses which had become popular with the influx of the relatively novel beverages from the colonies and other distant lands. In the city of London, the 'Kingdom of Exchange Alley and its Adjacencies' was evidently an overspill from the Royal Exchange, for almost all the coffee houses were situated immediately behind the Exchange between Cornhill and Threadneedle Street, following the establishment of the first one by a Turkey merchant, Daniel Edward, in 1652. Coffee was probably regarded as an esoteric drink in this country from the reign of James I, following its introduction by merchants of the Levant Company but, in spite of the establishment of a coffee house in Oxford in 1650 by Samuel Jobson and Arthur Tillyard, its preparation was evidently still considered to be sufficiently mysterious two years later to cause Edward to bring with him his Greek servant, Pascue Roffee, to assist in its preparation. After opening initially in George Yard, Lombard Street, they then moved to the churchyard of St. Michael's in Cornhill.

This 'overspill', which was paralleled by the migration of stock-jobbers to Jonathan's Coffee house and the Rotunda of the Bank of England,[24] was not, of course, a mere matter of the inability of the Exchange to afford sufficient accommodation but owed its origin rather to the desire of merchants, with the increase in trade, to get together to discuss business and to have a convenient centre of information. The coffee houses tended in consequence to specialize, and among the dozens which eventually burgeoned in this small area of the City, a few were outstanding for the services which they rendered to the merchants who acknowledged them as the focus of their trading worlds. The Jerusalem Coffee-house, Cowper's-court, Cornhill, for example, was described by Morier Evans as being

> exclusively devoted to the interests of the merchants and others engaged in the trade of China, India, and Australia; and whenever information is required respecting any of these places, or of vessels voyaging to or from or between them, application is only to be made at the bar of the subscription-room, and the most ready and obliging answers are returned. This apartment is well furnished with files of the principal Canton, Hong Kong, Macao, Penang, Singapore, Calcutta, Bombay, Madras, Sydney, Hobart Town, Launceston, Adelaide, and Port Philip papers, and prices

current, besides shipping-lists and papers from the various intermediate stations or ports touched at, such as St. Helena, the Cape
of Good Hope, etc. . . .

. . . The books of East India shipping, including arrivals,
departures, casualties, and all the minutiae, which in their
particular department are kept with all the accuracy distinguishing
the universal record of Lloyd's, afford a ready reference to any
information that may be sought by the public . . .

Between the hours of two and three o'clock p.m., the Jerusalem
Coffee-house can be seen in its full activity of business. The
merchants have about this time left their counting-houses, and
called in to see 'how things are stirring', and meet captains or
others whom they may wish to see before going on 'Change or
leaving the City. If you have the opportunity of going to the
'bar' of the room about these hours, you will find engaged in close
conversation upwards of from one hundred and fifty to two
hundred persons, all of whom are transacting important business,
and who, most assuredly, have the chief of the commerce of the
East in their own hands.[25]

The Jamaica Coffee-house in St. Michael's Alley, as its name implies,
served the West India trade similarly well, its membership—for it was
by means of subscriptions that these places were financed—varying
between 250 to 350 persons. The subscription room was 'exceedingly
commodious', but the Baltic by contrast was a 'very snug little place',
though it was here, rather than at the Jamaica, surprisingly enough,
that the *Daily Journal* of 28 September 1728 advertised the following
item for sale:

To be sold

A NEGRO BOY, aged about eleven years. Inquire at the
Virginia Coffee-House in Threadneedle-Street, behind the Royal
Exchange.[26]

The Baltic in fact started life as the Virginia Coffee-house, or to give
it its full name, the 'Virginia and Maryland', as the result of an exodus
from the Jerusalem owing to the increase in trade with Russia and other
northern European centres,[27] but by 1744 its enterprising proprietor
had re-christened it the 'Virginia and Baltic'. In 1810, when those
traders who were engaged in commerce with the Baltic moved to the
Antwerp Tavern in Threadneedle Street, it finally became known as
the Baltic Coffee House. It was here that the merchants and brokers
who dealt chiefly in tallow, oils, flax, hemp and oil-seeds met for the
auctions, which at one time took place daily, and to examine the 'City
Average Market Letter', which gave prices and imports for the week,
together with a comparative account of the stock and delivery for five
years. Many fortunes were won and lost in the tallow speculations of
the early nineteenth century, for trade in it, together with indigo and

cochineal (which were marketed at Mincing Lane), was a large and expanding one, until they were superseded, in the one case by gas lighting, and in the others by artificial dyes.

At that time the auction rooms at the Baltic, and elsewhere, were lit by candlelight. The notices of sales 'by the candle', still in common use in the early nineteenth century, were by then completely misleading, however, for Tate tells us, in his precise manual, that

> Some public sales are declared to be 'by candle', an expression which now means the public sale of goods in the evening, or by candle light; formerly the expression was 'inch of candle', from the custom of allowing a limited time for bidding; viz., during the time a wax taper was burning an inch, but this method has long been declared obsolete.[28]

Garraway's, as well, was apparently a notable auction centre for the public sale of real estate, the windows of the 'antiquated apartment' being covered with bills advertising these properties. It was, too, the centre for periodic auctions of drugs, mahogany, and timber, while for about fifty years after 1821, Garraway's became the meeting place for the Australian wool auctions. But such a short list does scant justice to the range of other commodities dealt with, from tea to

> part of the Cargo of the FORTUNE, Capt. John Brown, taken by the French, and afterwards retaken by the HAWKE. Capt. Wilson, viz.:
>> 274 Serons of Alicant Barilla
>> 20 Chests of Soap
> Catalogues of which will be timely delivered, by
>> MARK HUDSON
>> and — Brokers[29]
>> THOMAS FIELDER

4. Factors and the Organization of Trade

After both auctions and private treaty sales, the dock warrant played an indispensable role as the means of transferring the claim to the goods being sold. The warrant was known as far back as 1733 in this country in connection with the East India Company's sales, but the development of the warehouse system by the beginning of the nineteenth century gave rise to a considerable extension of its use, the effect of which was that

> the transactions of the merchant are no longer confined within the walls of his own warehouses, but may be equally well conducted on the Exchange, or at the public coffee-houses, where a sort of market is in fact held every day, and property to the value of thousands of pounds sterling changes hands without an original outlay in the shape of duty, etc., of a single farthing, or in fact anything more being done with the goods than getting a proper

transfer made in the dock companies' books, the warrant or
authority for which is become a mercantile instrument, negotiable
for all purposes, whether of sale or exchange, as one of the most
substantial securities which can be afforded.[30]

The proof of ownership of produce when first landed at one of the
ports was (and is) the bill of lading, which constituted a contract
between the shipper of the goods and the transporting company, listing
the goods to be carried and the conditions which limited the liabilities
so incurred. It also stated by whom goods were shipped and to whom
they were to be delivered. Two or three original copies were made
out by the seller, of which the master of the vessel usually carried one.
Another was generally sent by the seller to the buyer as evidence of
shipment, with accompanying invoices. The ship's master had to produce the bill of lading, together with the manifest (i.e., the complete
inventory of the ship's cargo, specifying the value, origin, and destination of each item) at the port of discharge. After the requisite entries
had been made by the customs and the dock companies, the bills were
passed on to the persons named on them. If the goods were for immediate delivery, a *delivery order* was given to a dock's officer, who then
released the goods after having obtained proof of customs clearance.
If the goods had been warehoused, however, either a *dock cheque* or a
dock warrant was given to the owner as a recognition of entitlement to
the goods. Like the bill of lading, the warrant or cheque passed by
mere endorsement and delivery, being watermarked so as to prevent
forgery. Ever since its introduction, this document has continued to be
extensively used as collateral for bankers' loans.

At the simplest level, produce could change hands, especially at the
Royal Exchange, or in the warehouses themselves, directly between
principals to the transaction—that is, between merchants, without the
intervention of brokers, and goods were handed over upon the evidence
of a contract note, a dock warrant or other entitlement. Very frequently, however, merchants were represented by their factors or
agents, who transacted business in their own names, and upon their
own accounts, for a commission which, according to Tate, was

> generally a matter of specific agreement between the two parties.
> . . . In the sales of consignments, the common allowance is 2½%
> . . . When the Agent acts under what is called a *del credere* com-
> mission, or when he undertakes to guarantee the receipt of the
> money for the goods he sells, an extra commission is allowed for
> his risque.[31]

Many of these agents were also merchants, for merchanting (i.e. the
outright purchase of goods for re-sale) was practised side by side with
the acceptance of consignments for sale on commission from the planter
or shipper. The regular factors apparently confined themselves to one
particular branch of trade with the growth of commerce: one early

nineteenth-century writer for example distinguished almost a score of sections in which specialist factors operated.[32] Many of the sugar factors, however, not only sold sugar for the planters, but also acted in practice as purchasers of miscellaneous goods for transmission to the West Indies, including machinery and coal, and on occasion even fulfilled the task of acting as unpaid guardians to planters' children while they were at school in England. All these ancillary activities were usually sustained by the 2½ per cent or so received upon the sale of the sugar consignments, though this might occasionally be bettered.

The factor's responsibilities were normally quite considerable, for in the first instance he had to meet customs duties, freight charges, primage, wharfage, lighterage, warehouse rental, insurance, cooperage and weighing expenses. It was, moreover, the factor's task to sort the produce into grades—and sugar was not, of course, the only commodity which sometimes changed beyond recognition on voyage. It was the factor's decision, too, whether to hold the planter's sugar in the hope of a price sufficiently high to justify the extra warehousing costs, or to sell immediately upon arrival.[33] His problems were in fact very neatly summarized by Richard Pares when he concluded that 'Judgement, rather than activity, was the factor's essential contribution to the sugar market'.[34]

Much of this judgement, of course, involved the range of problems connected with credit transactions. As has been pointed out more than once, the West India factors in particular were to a considerable degree bound to accept deliveries of produce irrespective of the state of the markets, for they often had out on mortgage to the planters large sums, in consideration of which the consignments came.[35] The whole system of making advances on consignments was naturally highly necessary in the conditions of the time, when Britain's requirements of food and raw materials from overseas were mainly being met from what it is now fashionable to call the less-developed countries. It was clearly a widespread system, as the testimony of Charles Turner, a merchant in the East Indies trade, helped to make clear to the Select Committee on Commercial Distress of 1847-48. He speaks of advances made upon oriental produce at that time even 'before it was shipped, and in some cases before it was manufactured'. In answer to later questions, he decried the 'pernicious practice' of hypothecating bills of lading to the East India Company upon produce purchased, in order to obtain money to speculate upon more.[36] Other evidence may similarly be culled from other enquiries of the day, showing how widespread the practice of advancing upon consignments had become. For example, James Cook, a produce broker mostly in the East and West Indies trades, informed the Select Committee of the House of Lords, appointed to inquire into 'the Effect of the Alterations made in the Law regulating the Interest on Money', that Italian silk was sold 'upon bills at four months' date'.[37] The system was in fact universal, and provided the foundation upon which much of the cotton and corn imports of the nineteenth century was based. It was also used widely in the internal trade for financing the movement of butter and provisions, and was enormously important in facilitating the movement of the considerable volume of goods which came from Ireland. In 1823 a Select Committee considered that

> it is proved to the entire satisfaction of Your Committee, not only that the merchants of Great Britain are constantly in the habit of making advances on merchandize consigned to them for sale, to the extent of two-thirds or three-quarters of the value, but that they are also in the habit of obtaining advances themselves from bankers, corn factors, brokers and others, upon the goods so consigned to them, as well as upon their own merchandize. This appears to have resulted necessarily from the great increase of our foreign trade, and is stated by the most respectable witnesses to be practised to such an extent by all classes of merchants (not excepting houses of the highest respectability) that it may be considered essential to the carrying on of trade that it should be continued. . .[38]

It may be guessed that the Committee were not unmindful of the opinion of one of the witnesses who had appeared before it that these credit facilities constituted a very strong inducement to foreigners to make consignments to this country at the time,[39] for the system enjoyed a particular vogue in the entrepôt trade. Advances were made, for example, upon produce coming in from outside the Colonial Empire—such as Brazilian coffee and Cuban sugar—which it was next to impossible to sell in the British market because of the discriminatory duties levied against it. Corn from abroad, too, warehoused until the price of the domestic product rose sufficiently to permit of its release, was also financed in this way, and this could sometimes involve an even longer wait than the considerable periods for which money was immobilized in the East India trade.

By the beginning of the nineteenth century, however, an old established but regrettable legal precedent had been brought to prominence by the increase in trade. This was that though a factor was invested with the actual possession of goods and appeared therefore to be their owner, he had no legal authority to pledge the goods, but only to sell them, regardless of any advances which he might have made to the consignor. The difficulty which the law created was to immobilise the capital advanced by the factor until the goods were sold, or else to subject the party advancing money in return for the factor's pledge of the goods to the risk of loss. The person at risk, in other words, was the pledgee, who stood to lose his money whenever it was not personally redeemed by the factor. As McCulloch argues, it is the business of the principal to satisfy himself as to the conduct and character of the agent or factor he employs; and if he makes a false estimate of them it is more equitable, surely, that he should be made the sufferer than those who have no means of knowing any thing of the matter.[40]

The purchaser was eventually protected, after the law's previous inadequacies had reached scandalous proportions, by the 'Factor's Acts', starting with 4 George IV c.83, described as 'An Act for the better protection of the property of merchants and others who may hereafter enter into contracts or agreements in relation to goods, wares, or merchandise entrusted to Factors or Agents'. It was far from foolproof, however, being amended several times in the course of the century,[41] and finally replaced by the Factor's Act of 1889 (52 & 53 Vict. c.45), the effect of which was to declare the shipper of goods, or the holder of any bill of lading, dock warrant, warehouse or wharfinger's certificate or delivery order, to be the true owner of the goods shipped, or described in such a document, and to entitle the consignee to a lien thereon for the amount of his advances.

5. The Broker

Of the various classes of trader, one of the most commonly threatened by the inadequacies of the law on factors, before the passage of 4 George IV, c.83, was the broker. Unlike a factor, a broker is a person employed as an intermediate or mutual agent who, by avowedly not acting for himself or upon his own responsibility, serves as a witness to the contracts between the two parties.[42] Brokers have had a long history. Even as far back as the reign of Edward I, they were required to be sworn in by the Lord Mayor and Aldermen by the Statute, 13 Edward I c.5, confirmed by 1 James I c.21. Much of the subsequent history of broking is one of spasmodic attempts to curb the activities of the numerous unsworn brokers. There was, for example, an Act for the Regulation of Brokers upon the Royal Exchange in 1673, designed to prevent 'all usurious Contracts and Bargains, false Chevesence and other Corrupt Devices and crafty Deceits'. A further important addition was made to the Statute Book in 1697 with 'An Act to Restrain the Number and ill-Practice of Brokers and Stock jobbers', which proscribed broking in both produce and credit instruments unless the brokers were 'admitted, licensed, approved and allowed by the Lord Mayor and Court of Aldermen', their numbers being at the same time restricted to one hundred. They were provided with a certificate and a silver medal, and required to keep a book in which all transactions were to be noted, and to pay a broker's rent of £5 per annum. The provisions of this act were perpetuated by 6 Ann c.16 and 57 Geo. III c.60, except that in response to numerous petitions from those excluded—opposed with equal vigour by the licensed brokers—their numbers were no longer restricted to one hundred. The names of registered brokers were hung, according to the requirements of the Acts, in a conspicuous place in the Royal Exchange, and it was specifically enacted that

no person shall be licensed to exercise the employment of a broker who shall drive any other trade, and that all persons who have been already admitted brokers, and do use or exercise any trade or calling, shall forthwith leave off and relinquish such trade or calling, or otherwise the court will discharge him or them from the said office.

These and other prohibitions were, however, widely disregarded. Morier Evans for example, after remarking that a broker is restricted by the terms of his bond from speculating on his own behalf, goes on to say that little regard was paid to the supposed injunction, and that scarcely an individual had ever entered the markets who had not infringed the law in this respect.[43] The Economist's leader writer in 1847[44] was equally scathing concerning the need for licensing brokers at all, arguing that the City Corporation were thereby creating a privileged class. Later in the century this attitude snowballed into a more widespread agitation against the licensing system, on the ground that it was a restraint of trade which hampered the expansion of business. Therefore, in spite of the not inconsiderable value of brokers' rents (which amounted to as much as £9,000 in some years) the system was dismantled in 1886, and the register discontinued in 1888.

For a long time before this date the broker had made himself a quite indispensable part of the market mechanism. It was as fruitless, therefore, ran the argument, to determine the broker's commission as it was to license him. But there was, of course, a great deal more to it than the customary half per cent. By the so-called Statute of Frauds[45] no contract for the sale of any merchandise for the value of £10 or more was valid except the buyer accept part of the goods so sold, or give a deposit or a signed note; the brokers obviated these formalities through the exchange of 'bought and sold' notes. These were required by the broker's bond, which bound him,

Upon every contract, bargain, or agreement by him made, to declare and make known to such person or persons with whom such agreement is made, the name or names of his principal or principals, either buyer or seller, and shall keep a book or register intituled 'The Broker's Book', and therein truly and fairly enter all such contracts, bargains and agreements, and the day of the making thereof, together with the Christian and surname at full length of both buyer and seller, and the quantity and quality of the articles, sold or bought, and the price of the same, and the terms of credit agreed upon, and deliver a contract note to both buyer and seller, or either of them, upon being requested so to do, within

5. The London Commercial Sale Rooms – east side of Mincing Lane – from a drawing by G. Shepherd, published by Ackermann, 1815. *Radio Times Hulton Picture Library.*

A Perspective View of the CORN FACTORS EXCHANGE, *erected in Mark Lane 1751.*

6. The old Mark Lane Corn Exchange, erected in 1751. *John R. Freeman.*

7. The floor of the Baltic Exchange. *The Baltic Exchange.*

8. The auction chamber, Plantation House, venue of the tea and ivory sales. *The Times.*

twenty-four hours after such request respectively, containing
therein a true copy of such entry. . . .

Equally important in securing the broker's niche in the organization
of trade were the conditions of credit, for though the understood rule
was that the broker's authority to sell or buy was considered to expire
on account of price fluctuations unless acted upon on the day in
which given,[46] the allegiance of particular factors and merchants
to individual brokers was frequently assured by the advance of credit:
a contemporary account relates how three of the largest produce-
brokers 'maintain much of their business by the enormous advances
they make to merchants on their consignments'.[47] A witness giving
evidence to the Committee on Commercial Distress explained the
system very succinctly:

There are two kinds of bills drawn against Produce: the first is
the original Bill drawn abroad upon the Merchant who imports it.
In consequence of the Steamer the Bills which are drawn against
Produce frequently fall due before the Steamer arrives. The
Merchant, therefore, when it arrives, if he has not sufficient
Capital has to pledge that Produce with the Broker till he has
Time to sell that Produce. Then a new series of bill is immediately
drawn by the Merchant in Liverpool upon the Broker on the
security of that Produce lodged in the warehouse in Liverpool,
bonded or free. Then it is the business of the Banker to ascertain
from the Broker whether he has the Produce and to what extent
he has advanced upon it. It is his business to see that the Broker
has Property to protect himself if he make a loss.[48]

Almost a hundred years earlier, however, Campbell claimed that:
the word of some of these Brokers will pass upon 'Change for some
Hundreds of Thousands, though the Persons who deal with them
know them not to be worth as many Hundreds.[49]

6. Auction Sales

As we have already seen, many of the sales effected by the brokers
were conducted by auction, and in these only sworn brokers could
legally officiate. By the beginning of the nineteenth century, moreover,
the custom of the trade had become such that none but the brokers
bid for the articles to be sold. As Tate pointed out,

any other person certainly possesses the right of doing so, but from
the competition he would create, his interest would suffer a
material injury.

For this reason, in public sales brokers acted as principals (as they still
do), and a disclosure of the real purchasers and sellers was (and is)
seldom made, the brokers becoming completely responsible for the due
performance of the conditions of sale. These conditions were usually
circulated with the catalogues sent out by the selling brokers, but a

copy posted on the auctioneer's box was in fact sufficient in law to be binding. Conditions of sale varied somewhat for different produce, but those enforced by the East India Company provide a good if somewhat stringent example of their contents. Their burden was to declare the highest bidder to be the purchaser and to provide for the settlement of disputes by the selling broker, who could also request what now seems the quaint practice of a show of hands to resolve differences. The buyers were required to pay all duties on the goods except the auction tax which, where due, was paid by the sellers. Brokers were to declare their principals within three days after the sale, or else take responsibility as principals. Deposits were usually required a few days after the sale, but could be asked for immediately, defaulters being required, moreover, to pay any difference between the price originally bid and the price realized upon re-sale. In all cases where goods were exposed to public view, no allowances for alleged quality defects were payable (except when damage was discovered before payment fell due), nor were buyers allowed to relinquish any lots bought. The goods were, however, to remain at sellers' risk until prompt day (i.e. the date of payment), the buyer accepting responsibility for any damage and warehousing dues after that time.

For some goods, notably wool and sugar, samples drawn from the bulk were exhibited to the bidders at the time of sale. It had been established by legal precedent that the sample had to agree with the bulk, or allowances made in lieu, the acceptance of the samples by the successful bidder being considered sufficient part-delivery within the meaning of the statute of frauds even in the absence of a broker's memorandum. Various other court cases[50] determined, in the course of time, that declarations of the broker or auctioneer contrary to the printed conditions of sale were not admissible in evidence; that writing down the purchaser's name by the broker, auctioneer or his clerk, in the catalogue opposite the lot for which he had bid, bound both parties within the provisions of the statute of frauds. It was established in law that the bidder could always retract his bid before the hammer fell, because the assent of the seller was not signified until that took place: it was even upheld that the bidding could be retracted before the memorandum was made in the broker's book, but such behaviour would obviously incur the odium of the entire auction chamber, especially during periods when business happened to be brisk.

Many goods required weighing at the docks, and it became customary in such cases when their sale had been effected, for the broker to deliver to the buyer in exchange for deposit money, an instrument called a *weight-note*, which was negotiable upon endorsement until prompt-day, when it was exchanged, together with the remaining purchase money, for the dock-warrant authorizing its holder to receive the actual goods. Payments in the sugar market, for example,

were either made in cash on the Saturday following the expiration of
the day of prompt, or by bill at seventy days, at seller's option.

Apart from the difficulties resolved by case law, however, the
purchasers at the public sales of produce were far from being all
satisfied customers. According to some documents unearthed by the
Phoenix Assurance Company[51] fairly recently, one of the sugar
refiners' chief worries in the eighteenth century was the 'prejudicial
and injurious effect' of selling sugar by public sale. One hundred and
four of them are on record as agreeing not to purchase sugars at public
sales 'unless they be King's Sugars' (sugars held and sold in all probability, on behalf of the customs' authorities). Sugar sales by action,
however, were only part of the refiners' grievance, for they apparently
wished to be the first and sole buyers of any imported sugar. Their ire
was directed in particular towards the 'jobbing' of the commodity—
that is, to its purchase and resale. They agreed, in fact, not to have
any dealings with jobbed sugar in 1773, any signatory of the agreement
not abiding by its terms being deemed to be,

a person of very mean, base, and infamous character, and ought
to be despised, shunned, detested, and excluded from all bodies
and societies of men whatsoever.

Though this agreement was renewed more than once, its subsequent
history is one of an increasing number of defectors, and by 1780 only
forty-two members concurred in the ban.

It was an unmistakable sign of the times. A committee of dealers
and consumers of sugar already existed, from whose ranks the buyers
for re-sale probably sprang, while the coffee-houses were the haunt
of a large body of speculators in various commodities. We read, for
example, that Garraway's in particular, being the first to open in the
morning and the last to close at night, was distinguished by the
patronage of the 'late men' who operated after 'Change hours—'high
'Change' being between 3.30 and 4.30 in the afternoon, during which
most merchants put in an appearance there. The bulk of the speculation, however, appears to have been of a relatively unsophisticated
kind. Thomas Tooke, a close market observer, considered that even
the speculation which took place in certain spices in 1825—consisting
simply of successive purchases on a rising market without intermediate
deliveries—was a 'very rare occurrence in the market for produce'.
Speculation seems to have been predominantly concerned with bargains for actual forward delivery, made either on the basis of samples,
or else of a fairly commonly recognized standard with allowances for
quality variations upon delivery.

The seller's motive in selling 'in transit', 'to arrive' or even 'for
shipment' (i.e. before the vessel had loaded the specified cargo) was,
of course, to secure himself against the possibility of a subsequent fall
in price. As long as the importer continued to do this, the market in

future deliveries remained a market in actual produce, concerned with commodities which really had a physical existence somewhere. The eighteenth-century bear speculator in Amsterdam on the other hand, selling produce which he did not possess in the hope of gain (or to offset the risk of loss on his actual shipments through a fall in price), must have been doing so by means of contracts for fictitious goods. He was, in other words, selling promises to deliver in the future, produce which he did not at the time possess, hoping at the maturity of the contract either to buy back his promise at a lower price, or else, should delivery be demanded, to buy the produce for less than he originally sold the promise to deliver it.

The evolution which was required from dealings in dock warrants in present goods, or in contracts concerning shipments of goods known to be afloat or awaiting shipment, to transactions of a speculative nature in fictitious goods, was considerable—comparable in fact with the more familiar progression from the circulation of an intrinsically valuable currency, to a fractional reserve banking system. The creation of credit in this country was achieved after the system had first passed through an intermediate stage in which the circulation of actual specie was partially replaced by the public's acceptance of receipts in place of the gold or silver which they represented, and from there, the next stage of uttering receipts for which no specie existed, followed naturally.

By the middle of the nineteenth century produce markets in the United Kingdom had only succeeded, on any scale, in reaching the equivalent of the intermediate stage in the process. This was represented by the general warrant in Scotch pig-iron which evolved in Glasgow and Middlesbrough at that time as a convenient means of dealing with warehoused iron billets. It was new in departing from the 'cloakroom ticket' type of warrant, which provided a claim to specific produce, for the pig-iron warrant, in the interest of warehousing efficiency, provided a claim only to a stated quantity of pig-iron of the stated grade (divided by numbers, as for example, 'Scotch No. 1' etc.). The prerequisite of this development was obviously an accurate system of grading, which made the actual billets received a matter of indifference to the iron-masters. According to the Master of the Rolls in 1877,

> The form (of iron warrant) was invented about 1846 and the practice grew general about 1866, and, I think, from that time till now we must consider it, on the evidence, as an established custom, that any man who gives this warrant understands that it shall pass from hand to hand for value by indorsement and that the indorsee is to have the goods free from any vendor's claim for purchase money.[52]

Clearly, it was the desire of the ironmasters to maintain their furnaces in blast in spite of fluctuations in demand which led to the grading and warehousing of iron; but despite a 'wild rage for an adventure in the various descriptions of the staple' in 1845, following the second railway boom, no break-through to a contract in 'fictitious' iron for future delivery occurred. This was probably due to the fact that after the speculative bout of 1845, price changes in pig iron were more notable for their rhythmic fluctuations in conformity with the trade cycle than for major short-term fluctuations. In any case these developments were overtaken by the changes in trading methods which were occurring in connection with the storage of grain, and the disturbances occasioned by the American Civil War in cotton and some other produce markets. Before we examine these, however, we must first trace the growth of organized markets in goods which were domestically produced and marketed, to see, among other things, to what extent these became more sophisticated and speculative with the growth of trade.

Chapter Three

EARLY DOMESTIC PRODUCE MARKETS

1. *The Corn Markets*

In medieval times some manors, such as that at Southwark, being favourably situated for marketing, had corn surpluses from elsewhere sent to them regularly for sale. There had been a corn market on Cornhill, according to Stow, 'time out of mind there holden', in addition to the one at Leadenhall. Gracechurch and Newgate were centres for the sale of corn brought overland, while Queenhithe and Billingsgate were markets for shipments by water. Transactions in corn, in common with dealings in other goods, were governed by town ordinances supervised by city magistrates. The usual statutory regulations against forestalling, regrating and engrossing pertained to corn, which could only be sold on designated markets. The only approved method of sale for the owner or urban dealer was, in fact, for him to sell directly from open sacks of grain on these regular corn markets. The logical corollary of this, clearly, was that corn brokers were considered unnecessary.[1] There are, however, records of a Cornmongers' 'misterie' as early as 1328, for the corn producer was already finding it inconvenient to attend all the markets personally, while the cornmonger's capital was becoming an important factor in the trade even at this early date.

The greatest influence in the development of a sophisticated metropolitan corn market in London was the early phenomenal growth of numbers in the capital due to the canalization of over four-fifths of all English foreign trade through the port, and its growth in importance as the seat of government. The increase in the population of the capital from some 50,000 in 1500 to nearly 250,000 a century later gave rise to an enormous growth in the demand for food grains, during a century in which the enclosure of land as sheep runs was proceeding apace under the influence of the burgeoning cloth industry. The increase in population resulted in the development of recurrent scarcities during the Tudor century and later. Permits became necessary for the export of corn, and in 1534, it was virtually prohibited (25 Henry VIII c.2). The 'Statute of Regrators' carefully circumscribed the range of the cornmonger's activities in 1552, though the function of this dealer (who was variously known as a lader, kidder, carrier or cornman) was, not unnaturally, regarded with favour. After 1552, his purchases were only legal provided that he had been licensed by three justices of the peace. Even so, an upper limit of ten quarters was imposed upon his stocks of corn, in order to counter any tendency to speculate for a rise in prices; and forestalling the market continued to be strictly prohibited.

Under Elizabeth, this 'policy of provision' was destined to become even more comprehensive, for in addition to the prohibition upon export (unless the price was very low), and the establishment of 'The Commissioner for Restraint of Grain' to 'enquire as to the forestalling, regrating, and engrossing of the same', from 1565 all manner of local officials were mobilized to report monthly to the Privy Council on the state of the grain supply:[2] they were charged with maintaining supplies to the corn markets, and keeping the price of grain at a reasonable level.[3] Notwithstanding these arrangements, the centre-piece of Tudor paternalism during this period of dearth was the granary system, which grew from Henry VIII's 'prest and loone' organization of voluntary contributions of money from the various misteries and crafts for the provisioning of the city. As early as 1514, it was decreed that,

A Garner for wheat shall be made at the Briggehous . . . as hastily as it convenently may be don.

Other granaries were subsequently established in the City at Leadenhall, Queenhithe, Winchester House, the Halls of the Companies and at Bridewell. The system did not reach its full flower until after 1578, however, when a committee of aldermen, having found that the city provisions had 'bene troublesome to my L. Maior and his worshipfull bretheren the aldermen', proposed that 'prevision be made by the XII Companies'. After the turn of the century the granary provisions slowly lapsed, only to be revived again in 1630 to make good the dearth of that year and the next. Subsequently, with more adequate harvests and improvements in the organization of the metropolitan corn supply, the system fell into disuse once more, and by 1688, although orders were issued to continue the organization, these were totally disregarded.

One of the chief purposes of the Tudor granary system was to achieve through official intervention in the market what the authorities did not trust the private market operator to do—that is, to store corn when its price was low, in order to have a supply for the poor when prices rose, or, more generally, to ensure an adequate supply of corn for the city instead of relying upon the development of market middlemen to do this. In spite of official intervention, however, the growth of the capital during the sixteenth and seventeenth centuries ultimately resulted in the complete transformation of the market by the end of that period. At the beginning of the sixteenth century a supply of corn from 'some few shires neare adioyninge' ordinarily sufficed to feed the citizens of the capital. The subsequent rapid growth in their numbers was reflected in a tremendous increase in the river-trade from Berkshire and Oxfordshire, which transformed Queenhithe to a meal and grain market handling the overflow from Billingsgate. By the seventeenth century, north-east Kent, Norfolk, Essex and Sussex were being converted into granaries for London, while, in times of dearth, both the north-east and the south-west coasts made considerable contributions and a thriving coastal traffic built up. By this time, therefore, the London corn market with its considerable water-borne supply had come to possess many of the essential characteristics of a trade in imported produce. Nor was this confined to corn, for there were, too, growing shipments of dairy produce, but this, in striking contrast to the corn trade, was dominated by a handful of London dealers.[4]

The most important suppliers of the London market by the early seventeenth century were the country dealers, though their position was far from secure, for the London factors or dealers who served the rich London bakers and brewers had had permission from the Privy Council from as early as 1597, to buy 'out of the markets', while their superior knowledge of the prices prevailing in London enabled them almost always to outbid their local rivals with confidence. In this way the market for corn over the entire country became more perfect, so that local buyers everywhere had to pay the London price less the cost of transport to the metropolitan market to prevent the corn from being transported to the capital for sale. These trends were consolidated after the Restoration, for in addition to the 1663 Act, which permitted the engrossing of grain, subsequent legislation starting with the Act of 1670, allowed its export whatever the price on the home market.[5] The Acts of 1673 and 1689 went even further and provided bounties for exports of corn.[6]

This series of Acts, which transformed the corn trade in the Restoration period, was the result of the rise of the Tory free traders in Parliament, led by Sir Dudley North. The 1663 Act (15 Charles II c.7), permitting the engrossing of corn at low prices, was, too, the measure which Adam Smith praised so lavishly a century later in his *Wealth of Nations*[7] as the source of 'all the freedom which the trade of the inland corn dealer has ever yet enjoyed'. It is interesting, however, that not all the free traders of the time were wholly converted to the acceptance of corn middlemen, for even Sir William Petty, one of the leaders of the movement, referred to this class as 'being onely a kind of Gamesters that play with one another for the labours of the poor'[8], while the anonymous author of the *Essay against Forestallers* was clearly anxious not to appear to equivocate when he described the corn dealers in 1718 as a 'confederacy of Blood Suckers', and the 'vermin of the Body Politick'.[9]

Between about 1660 and 1760, a century of corn export, the ascendance of commercial pressures which began in the Restoration Parliament, resulted in the promotion of domestic interests in the corn trade and the elimination of the alien corn merchant. As early as the first year of Charles II's reign, as has already been observed, it was enacted (by 12 Charles II c.4) that the duty paid by foreigners should be twice that levied on native merchants, thus indicating that no long-term future was intended for Dutch carriers to the English market—an attitude confirmed later by the discriminatory provisions of the export bounties granted in 1673 and 1689. In the domestic trade the new freedom to engross, legalized in Charles II's reign, was followed by the growth of sales by sample, which had been forbidden by ordinance in London as early as the fifteenth century. For the buyer there were obvious advantages in the system because it reduced the need to purchase several small lots, probably at a higher price, while for the farmer who could only manage to transport a load or two to market it reduced the need to bargain with several small buyers when there were large buyers about. Defoe paints a clear picture of the mode of operation of the provincial corn markets of the day in the following terms:

The farmer that has perhaps twenty loads of wheat in his barn rubs out only a few handfuls of it with his hand, and puts it into a little money bag, and with this sample, as 'tis called, in his pocket away he goes to market. When he comes there, he stands with his little bag in his hand at the particular place where such business is done, and there the factors or buyers come also. The factor looks on the sample, asks his price, bids, and then buys—and that not a sack or a load but the whole quantity; and away they go together to the next inn to adjust the bargain. . . . And 'tis odds but the factor deals with him ever after by coming to his house, and so the farmer troubles the market no more. . . . Though on a market day there are very few waggons with corn to be seen in the market, yet the street or market place, nay the towns and inns, are thronged with farmers and samples on one hand, and with mealmen, London bakers, millers, and corn factors and other buyers on the other; the rest of the week you see the waggons and carts continually coming all night and all day, laden with corn of all sorts to be delivered on board the hoys (barges), where the hoymen stand ready to receive it, and generally to pay for it also; and thus a prodigious corn trade is managed in the market, and little or nothing to be seen of it.[10]

Such sales by sample, which were fully established by the early eighteenth century, were chiefly responsible therefore for the decline of local public markets, and the consequent ascendancy of the wholesaler and the centralization of the corn trade in metropolitan centres.

Not all the grain destined for London or overseas was bought in the provinces by factors for onward transmission to merchants, millers or shipping factors however. The Kentish Hoymen (i.e. barge owners), for example, came themselves to Bear Key in Thames Street, where the corn market had become centralized early in the eighteenth century owing to its proximity to the river, and sold the corn committed to their care, at approximately fortnightly intervals.[11] They thus combined the functions of ship-master, super-cargo, and factor, on the market at Bear Key, and afterwards on Mark Lane Corn Exchange. Their privileges in this respect dated from the Great Plague when, notwithstanding the danger, they continued to ship corn to the city. The more important metropolitan corn factor, though, owed his origin to the practice of the Essex farmers after about 1700, who

were accustomed to assemble at an inn in Whitechapel, and, having often small parcels of grain left on hand, they were unwilling to attend the next market day to sell them. The waiter, who was an intelligent man, offering to find customers for them, was the origin of the present system of factorage.[12]

The corn factors appear at first to have been mealmen[13] also, an occupation which was declining in importance as the millers and bakers took over their functions. As corn selling agents, however, the factors flourished, meeting at Jack's coffee house near Bear Key to do business. Ultimately they obviated the need for the Norfolk, Essex, and other nearby farmers to come to market at all, for most of these consigned the corn henceforward to the factors for sale. Eventually, owing to the discomforts which attended transactions in the open air at Bear Key, five factors covenanted on 11 March 1746 to 'erect a convenient place for the said cornfactors to meet and transact their business'. These, together with thirty others, determined that:

They will not afterwards at any time meet or use or frequent Bear Key or any other publick place to sell their corn in But shall and will from time to time and at all times Afterwards meet at and Use and frequent the said place so to be Erected and Built and sell their corn therein.[14]

By 12 May 1749 the number of factors was as many as fifty.

From the evidence of manuscript sources, moreover, it seems reasonable to suppose that the new market began to function sometime in 1747. Later, in 1801, it was observed that

strictly speaking, there is no regulated public Corn Market at this Day, existing in the City of London; the Corn Trade therein being wholly carried on at the Corn Exchange in Mark Lane, which was erected in a confined space, and on a limited scale, . . . and is consequently private property: That this property is divided into about 80 shares, most of which are held by Factors or Dealers in Corn, the Estate being managed by a Committee of Trustees, chosen by the Proprietors.[15]

Inside the Mark Lane Corn Exchange were seventy-two stands for the display of samples, rented by the Committee of Trustees to an approximately equal number of corn factors and dealers, together with the eight leased to Kentish hoymen. In practice, therefore, though the Exchange was nominally open to everyone, without the possession of a stand 'it appears wholly impracticable for any one to carry on the Trade of a factor or dealer in corn to any material extent', even though there were 'instances of persons attending the market at times who bring with them their samples in their pockets'.[16] For this reason, the House of Commons Committee of 1801 considered that in some instances large sums had probably been given in order to obtain this accommodation. In fact, by 1800 the Mark Lane Exchange was practically in the hands of some fourteen shareholding factors. These individuals, according to the evidence of William Rustin, paymaster of the Fellowship of Porters,

being corn factors, take care whenever any person applies to them for a stand, to prevent his obtaining one, if the said person is likely to employ himself as a Factor. . . . If the market was sufficiently large to allow all persons who choose to have stands to have them, on paying rent for them, I am of opinion that competition in the sales would take place in a greater degree than at present, and consequently the public be benefited.[17]

The evidence seems also to have pointed pretty conclusively to the manipulation of the market by the factors and dealers, since they were, to quote the House of Commons Committee on High Prices once more, 'at liberty either to expose all their samples at the same time on their stands, or, as few of them as they think fit'. It must be remembered, however, that the consequence of this practice might well have been to steady the flow of corn offered on the market, and therefore its price.

The corn factor at Mark Lane normally sold the corn consigned to him by farmers, provincial corn merchants, maltsters and millers, on a commission basis, 'in their own names, and on a *del credere* commission, standing as a sort of middleman between the principal in the country, and the buyer in London'.[18] The normal procedure in the domestic trade was for the factor to obtain the best possible price for his client, but advices from importing merchants of consignments from abroad were usually accompanied by instructions to sell at specified prices.[19] Though some witnesses before the House of Commons Committee of 1801 were careful to stress the need to keep the functions of factor and dealer completely separate, the evidence showed very strongly that 'in some instances factors import largely, and even deal in British corn to a great extent on their own account'. The factors themselves naturally argued that this practice, which had become common by the end of the eighteenth century, was beneficial to the public, but the House of Commons found in favour of those who felt that these factors-cum-dealers could easily use their superior knowledge to profit

unduly at the consumer's expense, and therefore recommended that
these agents should be placed 'on the footing of other Brokers in other
Trades carried on within the City of London'. No remedy was apparently found for the situation, for it appeared from evidence taken by a
Select Committee more than ten years later that, though corn factors
were required to swear that they would not deal on their own account
or act as merchants,

> there being one qualified Factor in the firm, they may feel the law
> does not preclude the others from being merchants.[20]

In brief, then, the corn factors sold wheat to the millers (either direct
or through buying factors) and, in times of export, to shipping factors,
while the flour from the country tended to be sold by flour factors to
town bakers at Queenhithe—which had long been transformed from
the chief landing place for upper Thames Valley corn to a flour and
meal market. Barley and malt were sold for provincial merchants by
the Mark Lane Corn factors to maltsters, distillers, and brewers, while
the oats were customarily sold by the corn factors to dealers, who by
long usage were called 'jobbers'. These dealers were a prominent
fraternity on the corn market, for even during the period of corn export
from this country in the eighteenth century, oats were being imported
in considerable quantities, especially from Ireland. This development
was undoubtedly associated with the phenomenal growth of the
capital and, at the end of the century, with the need to feed the large
number of horses kept by the wartime armies.

It is not directly apparent from the *Seventh Report* of the House of
Commons Committee whether these jobbers of oats and beans were
the same men as another small but important group of speculating
jobbers—Clapham's 'pure market dealers'—in which the Committee
was very interested. Clapham thought this unlikely,[21] but in view of
the long market experience of these dealers in oats, and the fact that
speculation in other markets seems to have been connected with distant,
and therefore uncertain, sources of supply, this conclusion must be
treated with some reserve, the more so because it was very largely
in oats that speculation was taking place. What we do know—from
the evidence of William Rustin to the House of Commons Select
Committee on the High Price of Provisions—is that notwithstanding
the distaste felt for these jobbers by the more conservative dealers,
about twenty of them had stands on the Corn Exchange and that there
were perhaps forty persons on the market who practised jobbing.
Whereas Rustin thought them useful 'in some degree, though they
certainly advance the price to the public', there were many more who
affected to despise them. R. Snell, a dealer in oats, for example, says,

> I mean by jobbers, people who stand between the consumers of
> this metropolis and the factors, those who buy up the oats and
> before the arrival of the fair Buyer or Consumer, place them in

the Hands of the Factor to sell again the same day or the same market . . . There is a term at Market when we ask for a sample of Oats, wishing to know whether they are on board ship or in Granary; and why we ask is, we suppose all oats in Granary to belong to those jobbers and all people who know the true character of jobbers will not buy of them.

Snell goes on to assert that he has no doubt that the factors and the jobbers have an 'understanding', and that 'by selling and reselling the same article the Factor gets a commission of 1s. 6d. when if it was sold to the consumer in the first instance, he would only get 9d'. This piece of intelligence obviously provides a good straightforward reason for the controlling factors' favourable treatment of the jobbers.

Though Snell's evidence indicates that the jobbers actually bought and stored grain, one of the interesting features of the corn market at this period was that these speculators had already learnt how to buy and resell without either actually handling the produce or paying for it. This was possible because it was the custom of the Corn Market to

engraft on parol a credit of one month for wheat, and two months for all other grain.

The London factor thus became a kind of banker to a great many of the farmers, who drew from him as they required money.[22] At the same time, of course, the custom enabled the factors to extend credit to the jobbers to speculate for a rise in price. Such practices did abate for some time following an adverse decision in the case of the King v. Rusby in 1800 when buying to sell again was pronounced to be an offence, notwithstanding the Act of 1772[23] which had repealed the ancient statutes against forestalling, regrating, and engrossing. Nor were these short-term speculations the end of the alleged iniquities of the jobbers, for there is also fairly conclusive evidence of attempts by members of this market group to maintain an artificially high price for corn by keeping the port of London closed to imports and thus foiling the intention of the Acts of 1663 and 1685.[24] The purpose of this legislation was to allow the import of corn whenever prices reached certain levels, but some of the more cunning jobbers managed, it appears, to frustrate this intention by flooding the market in April and October with the type of oats by which the Justices of the Peace biannually judged the price level.[25] Another device they found to be very effective in the markets of the day, which, it must be remembered, lacked up-to-date intelligence on crops and shipping, was to spread rumours at these crucial periods that great quantities of corn were shortly due, which had the effect of temporarily depressing prices, thus keeping the ports closed. John Lord Sheffield, for example, states boldly that,

Everybody knows the arts that are used, and the frauds that are committed respecting the corn trade; and that dealers, by selling and re-selling to each other large quantities of corn in a fallacious manner, have hither-to opened and shut the ports of a district for importation or exportation as best suited their purposes.[26]

On the other hand, a Committee reporting to the Lord Mayor of London in 1789[27] was

... unanimously of opinion that there does not appear to them sufficient ground to believe that improper practices have been used to procure an undue return of the price of wheat.

The House of Lords Committee of 1800[28] too, concluded that,

As far as has appeared to your Committee . . . they have not been able to trace, in any One Instance, any Thing more, than such suspicious and vague Reports as usually prevail in times of scarcity, and they are of Opinion, that what have been represented as deep schemes and fraudulent Practices to raise the Market, have been only the common and usual Proceedings of Dealers in all Articles of Commerce, where there is a great Demand, and Where great Capitals and great Activity are employed.

The Committee even assert that they

. . . are confident the fullest and most ample Protection ought to be afforded to all Dealers in Corn by the Legislature and by the Magistrates, . . . because Persons engaged in this Branch of Trade are highly useful, and even necessary for the due and regular Supply of the Markets, and may, therefore, be considered as rendering an important Service to the people at large.

From this distance the balanced perspective of the Committee's comments can only be admired for, while confessing that they 'do not take it upon them to determine that no Abuses have been in any Instance committed by Individuals', they go to the heart of the problem in recognizing that the dealers, including those who played the market for gain, also performed an economic function in ensuring supplies. They, at least, seemed to appreciate that, though on a short term view it appeared that the jobbers could not lose on a market which was rising almost continuously, in more normal times the activities of this fraternity could help to steady supplies and, therefore, prices. The House of Lords Committee would probably have appreciated Saville's remark, made to the Committee of the other House a year or so later, when he asserted that,

in time of plenty speculators tend to keep the market more on a level, whereas in times of scarcity they have it in their power to influence the market too much, to the disadvantage of the public.

This brief pronouncement would undoubtedly command considerable approbation in subsequent ages from those appreciative of the fact that in normal times speculation tends to make the market more perfect, enabling it to adjust both more quickly and with less violent fluctuations to changes in demand and supply, than would occur in the absence of the anticipation of market changes by these professional operators.

Though the jobbers of this period often succeeded in speculating for short periods without any outlay of capital, their longer-term ventures of course required the 'great Capitals' which the House of Lords Committee referred to. In view of the growth of the metropolitan corn market, and the development of an export trade after the middle of the seventeenth century, it is not surprising that the eighteenth century saw the rise to prominence of important corn merchants, who, like the Coutts family of Edinburgh and London, frequently became bankers into the bargain, for

> . . . to carry on every branch of the Corn and Flour Trades, a much larger sum of money is required than may commonly be imagined, but will easily be believed when it is remembered that the whole is paid for in present money, and though some part may be returned in a month, yet the whole, by those who have any considerable Trade, is not returned more than three or four times in a year; and he that cannot in plentiful markets lay in a Stock, but is obliged to buy in Proportion to his Sales in short Markets, will find his Trade turn out to little Account.[29]

At this period, of course, the jobbers were all bulls, buying to resell at a profit on a rising market: the day of the more sophisticated bear speculator lay in the future, to be born of the conditions which called for the storage of grain in the huge elevators of the North American prairies.

Already, however, the sale of corn had travelled a good distance along the road to being a highly organized world market. The development of sales by sample, as we have seen, had separated the location of the market in the product from the product itself, and so had facilitated the bulk-buying of grain by agents for central, wholesale markets. It was evidently an important stage also in the progress towards the grading of produce so accurately that it could be sold upon description without even the necessity for a sample. In the meantime, the intervention of the corn factor in local collecting markets had also introduced a degree of specialization which had become necessary with the growth of trade. In spite of the abuses of the system, the farmers of Essex, Norfolk, Kent and elsewhere, like the cloth manufacturers, evidently benefited from being relieved of the necessity of attending the market, for it allowed them considerably more time in which to produce. Finally, though the seemingly nefarious activities of the dealers often appeared to be a profitable way of 'playing with one another for the labours of the poor', as Sir William Petty would have us believe, yet in normal times, when their speculative gains were less certain, they obviously performed a useful economic function. As professional dealers they tended to come into the market as buyers when prices were falling in the belief, based upon their experience, that they would be able to resell at a profit, especially when scarcity prevailed in the pre-harvest month. The net effect of their activities would therefore usually be to steady prices and to ensure supplies. Unfortunately perhaps, the Committees of 1800 and 1801, which have given us such a clear picture of the operation of the Corn Market at this date, were born of abnormal conditions when the jobbers, and the factors, too, could hardly fail to make money and were seen as war profiteers.

2. *The Wool Trade*
By the first decade of the fourteenth century England was selling overseas some 32,000 sacks of wool a year. At the time this represented some 90 per cent of total exports, but the situation was changing rapidly in favour of cloth shipments. These had grown from some 5,000 pieces to 37,000 during the fourteenth century, while over the same period, wool sales had declined to 19,000 sacks. This trend continued throughout the fifteenth and sixteenth centuries, and by 1550, raw wool comprised only some eight per cent of total exports, while sales of woollen cloth accounted for nearly all the remainder— an exact reversal, almost, of the proportions of two centuries earlier.

With the decline in the export of wool, the substantial English woolman, having enjoyed a period of prosperity in the fifteenth century, was tending to diminish in importance. Some of them were transferring to the cloth industry, or else were growing wool which they 'exchanged' for cloth, and by this means gained control over its manufacture and sale. Until the second half of the sixteenth century, however, many of the wealthier clothiers, who would probably have been the customers of these substantial middlemen, found it quite convenient to obtain supplies locally, or else at one of the great wool fairs. Many of these clothiers had sufficient capital to make their whole year's provision beforehand.[30] Moreover, some clothiers resold part of their wool purchases to other manufacturers, and by so doing, earned themselves the title of 'brogging clothiers'.

The ubiquitous 'wool brogger' of the sixteenth century was by no means always to be distinguished clearly from the jobber or merchant. All on occasion bought clips directly from the grower, but the brogger, though he bought the wool, did so on behalf of exporters, manufacturers, or the larger merchants and jobbers. The last named were dealers who bought wool for re-sale to the manufacturer. They were, therefore, capitalists whose function was to enable the growers to turn their clips into money without delay, for the jobber stored wool and thus helped to steady the price. Moreover, by interposing themselves between the producer and the manufacturer, both the jobber and the brogger widened the market for wool, in addition to enabling the manufacturers who took advantage of their services to concentrate upon their specialist function of producing cloth. Though the larger manufacturers often did without the services of the broggers and jobbers in the earlier period of the growth of the cloth industry, as we have seen, this fraternity was indispensable to the smaller manufacturer. The poorer clothiers were, indeed, very frequently unable to afford to buy raw wool at all, but were constrained to shorten the process of manufacture by purchasing yarn instead. For this reason, wool dealers often became yarn makers as well. The impecunious clothiers were frequently in debt to the brogger or the jobber, the credit supplied by these intermediaries thus constituting a vital link between the farmer and the manufacturer.

As wool exporters the Merchants of the Staple shared with the rich clothiers both an ambition to bring down wool prices in England and a resentment of the broggers, with whom they were in competition for control over the domestic supply. The hostility of the larger clothiers towards the broggers reflected, too, their ambitions at the time to ruin their lesser competitors. Successful pressures, resulting in the anti-middleman legislation of 1552 (5 & 6 Edward VI c.7), gave the Staplers and manufacturers alone the freedom to purchase wool. Broggers were required to obtain licences, while alien merchants were forbidden to purchase wool at all between sheep-shearing and the Feast of the Purification (i.e. 2 February). Despite these attempts to check the brogger, he was indispensable to the growing cloth industry and so continued to flourish. As their fortunes ebbed some Staplers turned their attention to the export of cloth and joined the Merchant Adventurers, while others succumbed to the pull exerted by the needs of the internal market and used their capital to become a species of wool brogger—an entirely illegal activity, since the 1552 Act enjoined them to export all the wool which they bought. With the embargo upon the export of wool in 1614, the Staplers lost their nominal excuse for handling the commodity and were therefore virtually forced to petition the Privy Council in 1615. In this well-known document, the annexe to which has been reprinted by Unwin,[31] the Staplers admitted the transfer of their major interests to domestic dealing, and argued its justification, emphasizing the indispensable role of the middleman. Following this, the Staplers were granted the monopoly of middlemen functions for some years. It was an unpopular move, for they, 'being in number a fewe, combine together and buy onelie at their owne rates and make one purse'. When Parliament assembled after an interval of seven years in 1621, therefore, the Staplers paid for their unpopularity and were made scapegoats for the depressed state of the cloth trade. The Company's patent was confiscated,[32] and, in 1624,

the 1552 Act was repealed,[33] thus ending some seventy years' close
regulation of the wool trade.

Because Leadenhall was the embarkation point for much of the wool
bound for continental staples during the Middle Ages, it naturally
became the market where the Staplers sold and warehoused much of
their produce. The rooms in the Hall were rented by the Merchants
of the Staple from the City of London, and sub-let to members for
storage. Private houses were also sometimes hired, though by the end
of the seventeenth century there were many wool warehouses in
Southwark and Bermondsey. Most often, this wool was sold by direct
personal arrangement, usually in the market, at the dealer's house or
in the warehouse itself.[34] In the seventeenth century the ordering of
wool by letter became increasingly common: this was before the days
of the despatch of samples by post, for, though samples were sometimes
used at this date when both buyer and seller were present, sales by
description dominated.

Even by the end of the seventeenth century transactions by post had
not really succeeded in making any marked difference in the volume
of transactions in wool concluded on public markets and, in some
wool-growing and manufacturing areas, special markets for its sale as
well as that of yarn were still common. Cirencester, the great point
of distribution for the west country, was said by Defoe, for example,
to be handling some 5,000 packs of wool a year,[35] and, even as early as
1567, this centre was already importing some 125 cwt of Spanish
wool annually. Stourbridge fair, though in decline, was still enormously
important: it was here that the broggers brought a considerable proportion of the best Leicestershire wool, though some also found its
way to London via Yorkshire, Westmorland and Cumberland, after
having been spun into yarn. Fell wool from slaughtered sheep came
chiefly from the carcass butchers at Smithfield, and so appeared mainly
on the London markets. Some of this went to make white cloths and
blankets at Witney, but a great deal also flowed into the wool-growing
areas of Norfolk and Suffolk—the seat of the French and Flemish
immigrants—after demand had outstripped local supply. This area
also imported wool from Ireland, though much produce from this
source flowed to Manchester, which also drew supplies from as far
afield as the Mediterranean lands through the port of London.[36] The
main supply of Irish wool, however, went to feed the rapidly growing
manufacture of bayes and serges in south-west England. Throughout
the seventeenth century every effort was made to ensure that Irish
wool was transported only to England, the original intention being to
extend the British prohibition upon its export. Ultimately, in 1698, a
'most infamous' statute for the 'Incouragement of the Woollen Manufacturers in the Kingdom of England' was passed, forbidding the export
of Irish woollen textiles to anywhere but England and Wales—where

they were, in any case, subjected to an almost prohibitive duty.[37]

In spite of the belief cherished in England that its wool was indispensable to continental manufacturers, the latter got along quite nicely in fact by using Spanish wool instead, though the prohibition upon wool export from Britain continued in force down to 1825. There had even been a trickle of Spanish wool into England from as early as the twelfth century, and a regular import from the early sixteenth century, when it was highly esteemed for making felt hats. It was not, however, until the depression of the 1620s that some English clothiers started to experiment with Spanish wool in the production of cloth. Its superior texture made it immediately popular, its main centre of manufacture developing between Frome and Bradford-upon-Avon. There are sixteenth century records of patent grants for the import of Spanish wool, but at a later date much of the wool from this source came to be handled by the factors of Blackwell Hall—one of the most interesting and notable of the markets of the times.

According to Stow,[38] Blackwell Hall dated from the Norman Conquest, though its connection with the wool and woollen trade started later, during the reign of Richard II, when it became the property of the city. It then came under the control of the Drapers' Company, who were entitled to appoint its Keeper from 1405, and to warehouse cloths there. In 1516, by an Act of Common Council, it was appointed the exclusive market for woollens, and in 1588, the structure was re-built, to be destroyed, along with so many other famous buildings, in the Great Fire of 1666. It was replaced in 1672 and stood until 1820 when it was discontinued. The regulation of Blackwell Hall, as well as of the other cloth markets, was very strict indeed, being born, as Westerfield reminds us,[39] of the medieval theory of town policy which manifested itself in laws and customs to check engrossers, forestallers, and regraters. The commonest device by which the authorities sought to thwart the middleman was the prohibition to buy anywhere but on the market, which was held at certain specified times: thus in Halifax, for example, at the ringing of the bell at 10 o'clock each Saturday morning, the merchant buyers were admitted into 'Manufacturers' Hall' for a market which lasted two hours. Similar constraints operated at Blackwell Hall, which opened on Thursday, Friday and Saturday of each week from 8-11 a.m. and 2-4 p.m. This provided the opportunity for clothiers to travel from all over the country to London after the Sabbath—an important consideration at a time when almost all cloth exports, and a considerable volume of the home trade, were sold through London. For most of the sixteenth century especially, almost all overseas sales were effected in the Antwerp entrepôt, for which the port of embarkation was London, while the practice of interchanging different varieties of cloth among the different regions of Britain was also done by way of the capital, and this tended to centralize the organization of the trade.

The Blackwell Hall factor owed his origin to the practice of the non-resident clothiers storing their unsold cloth at the Hall for sale at a later date. By about the beginning of the seventeenth century this led the clothiers to seek agents from among the members of the Cloth-workers' Company at the Hall, to sell their cloth on commission, the factor who thus emerged from this situation being given official recognition by an Act of Common Council of 1678. This Act also revised the government of the Hall, and from this date, the supervision of the market was undertaken by a hallkeeper, the clerks and the master porters. These officials were, however, subject to the direction of the president, the treasurer and governors of Christ's Hospital. A register was kept of the factors, the owners, and the buyers and sellers of the cloths, and a monthly report was submitted by the officers to the Hospital, concerning the conduct of the factors: a Hospital board of six was also appointed to enquire into any offences committed by these middlemen.[40]

The Blackwell Hall factor thus interposed himself between the selling clothier and the buying draper or merchant at the Hall in exactly the same way as the corn factor was able to do after about 1700 on the metropolitan corn market and, having cut off the manufacturer from direct contact with his customer, very quickly found himself in a position to control the clothing trade. From the second half of the seventeenth century, moreover, this dominance was facilitated by the development of better road and postal communications, which made the transmission of commercial papers and money much safer. The practice thus arose of settlement by 'bank post bill' rather than in person, while an ever-mounting stream of patterns and samples also flowed through the postal system. This, though it enabled the clothier to concentrate upon manufacture, divorced him to an even greater extent from his market.

The greatest hold which the factor exercised over the trade, however, consisted in the advance of credit to the clothiers—a practice which started even when the factors were still nominally clothworkers. The necessity for these considerable credit operations in the cloth trade derived ultimately from foreign commerce, for though the merchants who purchased their cloth at Blackwell Hall paid for it by drawing drafts upon their foreign correspondents, the bills of lading had to be available to the overseas purchaser before these drafts could be accepted. As long as almost all cloth sales were effected in the Antwerp mart, of course, the finance of trade did not constitute a major problem, but when, after the 1551-52 crisis in the export trade, merchants began to ply their business further afield, the channels of settlement necessarily became longer and more complex. The usual arrangement between factor and merchant thus grew to a six-month credit period, but even after this lapse of time payment was frequently not forthcoming. The clothier, therefore, besides being compelled when short of capital to buy his wool on credit from the brogger, was also driven in many cases to ask his factor for payment before this was officially due.[41] These problems gave rise to considerable unrest among the clothiers, the real ground of which it is argued[42] was the feeling of subservience to the factors, who not only found a market for the cloth and furnished the credit, but also sometimes even supplied the wool.

This last activity burgeoned with the increasing prosperity of the factors. They were especially active in marketing Spanish wool, though they also handled some supplies from Ireland and the Mediterranean. It was argued by the discontented clothiers that the factors' initial monopoly of Spanish wool, as far as the smaller manufacturers were concerned (the larger ones tended to buy direct from merchant importers), reduced the small-scale clothier to paying factorage upon what was essentially his own money. Agitation led to legislation[43] though this proved no remedy for the clothiers. The act required the factor to obtain from the buyer within twelve days, a note of the sum due, which was to be passed to the clothier. It was not long, however, before the factors had tricked the clothiers into submission once more by promising the most needy of their number the speedy sale of their goods in return for foregoing the right to a note of credit. Once the position had been breached, all the smaller clothiers had ultimately to capitulate.

In spite of this exploitation of their power, there is no gainsaying the usefulness of the factors during this period in the cloth trade: as middlemen for Spanish wool, for example, their position was actually defended by the small manufacturers, when pressure by the large clothiers led to the introduction of a bill in Parliament in 1692 which would have prevented these factors from trading in Spanish wool on their own account. Such protestations, though, did not prevent other petitions (for example in 1698) from being laid before Parliament, complaining that the factors were guilty of engrossing wool and retailing it at excessive rates. In this, as in other similar cases, Parliament declined to act: the sentiment which most fittingly expressed their attitude was that 'the Proprietor or Grower of Wool be not restrained from selling his wool to any Chapman he shall think fit to deal with'.[44] Parliament was thus clearly converted by the eighteenth century to a belief in non-intervention—nor is it difficult to see why it was generally felt that the natural growth of middlemen in the wool and cloth market, in spite of abuses, best served the interests of the country. The factors performed an indispensable service in linking buyers and sellers, and this much more efficiently, furthermore, than the vastly uneconomic presence of the clothiers themselves in the expanding markets of the day. Even apart from the saving of time and effort implied in middleman selling, however, the wider connections of the factor improved the market by increasing the number of potential buyers and sellers. Despite sharp practice, too, the credit system was beneficial in enabling settlements to be effected notwithstanding the considerable lapse of time between the shearing of the sheep and the ultimate sale of the finished clothing to the wearer.

3. London's Coal

In the history of the marketing of domestic produce one of the most interesting stories is that of coal, mined by the Newcastle 'Vend' for sale in London and disposed of near Billingsgate market. The industry grew to prominence in the seventeenth century with the use of coal for space heating and brick making, after centuries of prejudice against its use in the chimney-less houses of the day. At this period the coal-owners were obliged to sell their produce to the magistrates of New-castle, a constraint upon their actions which developed from the medieval practice of requiring any foreign merchant to be 'hosted' to a freeman. In this coal-producing area the hosts had taken advantage of this contact to supply the non-freemen with coals, so that a Host-men's Company, which attracted coal-owners to its ranks, soon flourished. It was therefore able to assume the exclusive privilege of supplying coal without much opposition, being aided in this mono-polistic manoeuvre by the ancient custom of 'foreign bought and foreign sold'—that is, the rule whereby goods brought by a foreigner could be sold only to a freeman of the town. This ensured that one of the parties to every contract for purchase or sale was a freeman, while a statute of 1530 decreed that all traffic within the tidal limits of the Tyne was to load and unload at Newcastle. Henry VIII's customs collections were thus facilitated, and, as a fortuitous side-effect, so too was the Hostmen's control of the market and the consequent restrictions of the amounts which they chose to sell, for all the coal had to be canal-ized to Newcastle, and there sold, according to the usage of 'foreign bought and foreign sold', to the freemen of the city. Coal-owners outside the franchise had thus to employ members of the Hostmen's Company as middlemen to sell to foreign customers, and the monopoly was complete. In 1637, moreover, Charles I struck his bargain with the Hostmen that, in return for an extra shilling a chaldron,[45] they were to have the right not only to regulate the production of coal but also to sell it in common.[46] The immediate upshot was a boycott both by the London coal merchants and by the shipowners, as the result of which the agreement was rescinded in the following year, and the shippers incorporated as a Society of Coal Merchants.[47]

Until the Restoration Ipswich was the dwelling place of most of the ship-masters who plied between Newcastle and London, for it was here that most of the 'colliers' were constructed. It was to these mariner-merchants that the magistrates of Newcastle sold much of the coal outright, but during the seventeenth century a most remarkable change occurred in this section of the trade, for by the end of this period the Hostmen had been completely ousted from the organization of sales. The fundamental reason for the change lay in the growth of the industry for, according to Sir William Petty's testimony,[48] London's imports quadrupled between 1636 and 1676 to 80,000 tons, owing to the rise in population and the replacement of wood as a fuel by coal. The first breach in the position was opened by the appointment in 1604 of eight men as factors and book-keepers to deal with the loading of the ships. They remained servants during the first half of the century, being variously described as fitters, agents, and factors, whose task it was to arrange cargoes for distant buyers, and to effect the delivery of the coal on board ship. In the meantime, internal divisions occurred among the Hostmen, as some of them took to 'colouring' unfreemen's coal, while their ranks were diluted by the practice, due probably to the increase in trade, of taking apprentices. These, of course, ultimately became Hostmen themselves in spite of an absence of coal-owning interests, and, in the end, the Hostmen were ousted, with the fitters becoming dominant. By the second half of the eighteenth century, the Newcastle fitter normally operated as a *del credere* factor, guaranteeing a price to the coal-owner, and furnishing, after 1711, the certificate required by the legislation of that year.[49] This gave details of the date of loading, the name of the ship and shipmaster, the quantity of coal loaded, the colliery from which it came, and the price of each variety of coal—all in an attempt to prevent combinations, frauds, discrimination, and other undesirable practices. One such may be culled, for example, from Anderson, who notes that 'many of the fitters, having become men of such opulence as to engage deeply in shipping, were too apt to give such ships as they were concerned in an unfair preference'.[50]

Meanwhile at the London end of the trade, the 'hags', 'cats' and 'fly-boats' were unloaded by watermen and lightermen. The former enjoyed a monopoly until the Act of 1730,[51] while the latter frequently combined with the coal dealers of London in according precedence in return for secret commissions. The lightermen of this period in fact formed an exception to a market organization which was remarkably differentiated, in tending to act as factors, a practice forbidden by the Statute of 1730.[52] The commission agents who did actually predominate, of course, were the 'crimps', originally the term for unloaders of vessels, who were afterwards called 'coal undertakers' or 'heavers'. The crimps in their guise of commission agents actually stemmed from the wharfingers and watermen, whose advantages were due to the Act of 1730, which permitted ship-masters a free choice in employing as factors any persons who were not lightermen:

. . . several lightermen . . . have become crimps or factors to

the Masters of coal ships at the same time they are buyers of
coals on their own account. . . . No lighterman or other buyer
of coals for sale . . . shall act as a Crimp, Agent, or Factor for
any Master or Owner of any Ship . . . importing coals into the
Port of London. . . .

The duties of the crimp are very clearly stated by Anderson; for
example acting as a broker or factor to whom the ship's loading was
regularly consigned, selling the cargo, giving security, paying the
duties at the Custom House, collecting the amount of sales from the
buyers, and settling with the owners.[53] If, as has been suggested,[54] one
of the chief motives behind the 1730 Act was to acknowledge the
crimp's role as factor in order to protect the London Buyer, it did not
succeed for, in addition to selling coal unduly cheaply to wholesalers
with whom in reality they were often partners, crimps continued to
commit other frauds, including that of becoming ship-owners, a role in
which they succumbed to the temptation of selling their own cargoes
to the detriment of those of their principals. It was, however, against
the lightermen that an anonymous writer of 1743 still railed, for having
described the way in which these middlemen had taken over from
the old woodmongers with the growth of trade he goes on to say
that:

> when a fleet of ships was expected in, fifteen of the most consider-
> able of these upstart-engrossers used to hold a Cabal, in which
> having first settled the Market-place to their own minds, every
> one staked a moidore, by way of gage, that he would not make a
> breach in the combination, by giving more for his Coals than the
> Standard here agreed upon.[55]

The sea-coal from Newcastle was bought and sold in 'a place in Lower
Thames Street, called Room Land, adjoining to Billingsgate . . . very
early in the morning'.[56] For a hundred years or so Room Land was
simply a piece of open ground, so that 'when the Parties wishing to
treat for a Cargo were met', it was the custom for them

> to retire to some adjacent Tavern to conclude the Bargain, by
> which Mode of transacting Business great Inconvenience and
> much Delay and Loss of Time, was felt by all Parties, when it
> was at length determined to erect the present Building called the
> Coal Exchange. . . .[57]

Accordingly, in 1769, a property was acquired by thirty-five factors
and merchants on the eastern side of Billingsgate Dock on the north
side of Thames Street, the ownership of which was divided into
sixty-four shares held by trustees: though no record now exists, business
must have been conducted in the new building shortly afterwards.
It was some years, however, before the lower portion of the building was
enclosed to enable buyers and sellers to get together, and a daily
subscription of 6d., or an annual one of £3 18s. od., was imposed to

discourage the entry to the building of 'dirty and disorderly people'. Masters of Vessels (according to evidence before a Select Committee of 1800)[58] were, however, allowed to enter without payment in consequence of the due 'of One Farthing made by the Coal Factors on Account of the Ship Owner'. The enclosure did not go unopposed, for we hear that:

> Since this Exclusion of the Public, by inducing and enforcing the Sale of Coals to this interior Room, several unsuccessful Struggles have, at a great Expense, been made by Individuals to resist these oppressions, by defending Actions of Trespass, brought by the Proprietors of this Building, against such Persons as entered the Room without submitting to an Annual Payment of £3 18s. od. each, so that in Fact there is not at this Day any open Market for the Public to resort for the Purchase of Coals. . . .[59]

In fact, the coal crimps sold at a month's credit on the Exchange to merchants known as 'first buyers'; these were wholesalers who had emerged by process of natural selection from among the dealers, and who, in turn, distributed the produce in broken bulk to their lesser brethren, known as dealers, or more quaintly as 'small coal men', 'loaders-on-account', or 'second-buyers'. Of these second merchants or buyers the most important were the 'accounters' who unloaded direct from the colliers in order to carry on their trade up-river in their own craft.

In the meantime the coal itself had to be unloaded, a process which, especially in its seventeenth-century strait-jacket of tradition, was fantastically complex, for though the merchant often owned barges and wharfs, the former could only be navigated by freemen of the Waterer's Company. The process of unloading into barges was one for the 'coal whippers' (also called 'undertakers' or 'heavers'), supervised by the 'water-meters' who, in addition to weighing the coal, also saw that the multifarious Crown, City and other dues were paid over. Finally, the singularly useless 'land-meters' supervised its transference to three-bushel sacks which, according to the Act of 1730, were the only legal measure for this purpose.

In spite of this seemingly meticulous treatment of the coal itself, abuses appear to have abounded in the market, both in and out of the Exchange.[60] The coal-owners, for example, developed the custom of paying three or four guineas 'dispatch money' to the coal buyers (organized from 1770 into a Society of Coal-Buyers) to ensure the quick turn round of the vessel, while the accusations of combination levelled against the buyers were many. After the conclusion of an enquiry in 1788, moreover, an act was passed[61] which noted that the Coal Buyers had been in the habit of holding private meetings at the Exchange,

> professing to make Regulations for the Purpose of carrying on the

Trade in Coals, which Regulations may have a Tendency to prevent the Said Trade from being free and open . . . any Number of Persons united in Covenants or Partnerships, or in any way whatsoever, consisting of more than Five Persons, for the purchasing of Coals for Sale, or for making Regulations with respect to the Manner of carrying on the said Trade in Coals, shall be deemed and adjudged to be an unlawful Combination to advance the Price of Coals. . . .

Finally, in 1800, the select committee of the House of Commons declared:

The Monopoly created by the Factors dealing only with the Coal Buyers, and the Exclusion of the Masters and Ship-Owners from an interference in the actual Sale, which precludes a sufficient competition therein: the Exclusion also of all but the Seventy-five Dealers before mentioned from purchasing without paying a Commission, which must be repaid by the Consumers who derive their Supply through subordinate channels, are Subjects worthy of the Attention of the House; and Your Committee cannot hesitate in recommending some Measure for making the Sale of Coals perfectly free and open, either by authorizing the Purchase of the Coal Exchange, and future Regulation of the Market by the Lord Mayor and Aldermen of London, or otherwise, as a Measure which promises important Advantages to the Metropolis.

This was accomplished by 43 George III c.134, the Corporation market being opened in 1805, while in 1807 an attempt was made (by 47 George III c.68) to codify the practices of the trade and to embrace in one statute the mass of legislation on coal passed since 1688.

This ancient structure, which must have appeared fruitlessly complicated, even in the early nineteenth century, was destined to be eroded by changes in the economic environment, in response to which the trade was greatly simplified through the elimination of many of the intermediaries between the original coal-owner and the ultimate consumer. One of these changes was the growth of considerable waterside manufacturing establishments, among which the new gas undertakings buying direct from merchants were prominent.

In the subsequent evolution of the coal trade there was another legal landmark in 1831, which stemmed directly from the findings of two select committees—one from each house of Parliament. The 1807 Act was repealed, and the entire medieval structure of metage and meters abolished, all Customs duties payable on the coastal traffic having been repealed by a separate Act. The Coal Exchange was continued as an open market under the City authorities, but the Act brought to a close the factor's duty as a recorder of, and witness to, bargains. The use of these coal agents had been made optional ever since the market had been declared public in 1803, but the 1730 **Act**, which gave the factor's transactions statutory recognition when he was used, had continued in being until repealed in 1831.

By the 1840s, the North-East Coast Committee of the Vend had ceased to regulate output and the trade became intensely competitive, for several other would-be sources of supply had been waiting in the wings for years for their chance to compete. As an example of this, we find one writer commenting in 1824:

> although it appears to me that the Almighty has been more bountiful to the Welsh coal mines than those of other places . . . I cannot help observing that all Government contracts have been advertised to be let to the highest bidder but are granted solely to Newcastle and Sunderland and none to Wales. . . .[62]

But the stranglehold of the Vend was not destined to last for ever. As far as one other major coalfield, whose story typifies the development of competition, was concerned, entry into the London market was achieved in 1830. The first traceable order for Welsh steam coal appeared in Insole's day book—

> Samuel Welsford, Independent Coal Factor, London, orders of 'Wain Wilt' coal to be delivered within 3 months. . .[63]

The predominance of the Newcastle Vend area in the London market was still overwhelming in 1834, as the following figures illustrate:

from the Vend area	2,190,695 tons
from Scotland	40,955 tons
from Wales	35,420 tons
from Yorkshire	27,394 tons

For all that, the trends were unmistakeably against the anachronistic monopoly of the north-east. Writing in 1840, Insole remarks:

> . . . the great superiority of the intermediate or steam packet coal of South Wales is now well ascertained . . . our Wain Wilt or large engine coal, now sold at 8s. per ton, being preferred by London brewers and steamers in preference to any other.

At the same date an Association was formed in London for the encouragement and protection of the Welsh steam coal trade. By 1843 shipments of coal from South Wales to London had about doubled their 1839 levels but, with the opening of the Taff Vale Railway, there were dramatic increases, paralleled by the development of other major sources of supply in the British Isles, as the Newcastle Vend crumbled before the onslaught of a transport revolution and the clamant needs of the market. The demand for South Wales steam coal was especially great, for its superiority in raising steam had been decisively demonstrated to their Lordships the Commissioners of the Admiralty by Sir Henry Delabèche and Dr Lyon Playfair.[64]

By 1850 the total quantity of rail-borne coal which appeared on the

London market had risen to 1½ million tons a year, but it rose spectacularly thereafter to reach a figure of 7½ million tons by 1886, compared with sea-borne coal which fluctuated between 3½ million tons in 1850 down to 2½ million in 1873 and then back to 4 million by 1886. Like the sea coal, almost all the rail-borne produce was consigned for sale in the 1850s to the London Coal Exchange, which since 1849 had been housed in a fine new building, remarkable for having preceded the Crystal Palace by two years in the art of using prefabricated iron components. Dowling claims[65] that as late as 1929 as many as five or six hundred merchants, colliery agents, and factors sometimes dealt there, especially on Mondays, in spite of the existence of provincial exchanges (of which those at Cardiff and Hull were most important for the export trade). The direct marketing of coal was very much on the increase even by the 1870s. Purchasers who owned their own railway wagons bought direct and loaded at the pithead, thus short circuiting the Exchange, though much rail-borne coal was also bought by smaller dealers in order to supply consumers—with as little as 14 lbs at times.

The Coal Exchange was damaged during the second world war, but in 1949 an attempt was made to resuscitate the market on the occasion of the centenary of its re-erection. This failed—understandably, in the light of the considerable fillip given to direct sales by the discontinuity caused by the war and the nationalization of the industry. The Exchange was ultimately demolished for road widening in 1962, in spite of those who wished to preserve it as an excellent example of early Victorian public building. So ended the story of a coal market which in the eighteenth century was remarkable for the rigidity of its complex organizational structure, to say nothing of the monopolistic elements which it contained. Coal, from the outset, was apparently sold upon description or inspection only, while the comparative steadiness of the supply and price rendered any thought of futures facilities otiose. This regularity did not always characterize the trade, however, for it was only after about 1760 that the ship-masters were prepared to put their vessels at hazard in the North Sea in winter-time, the period of peak demand. It was inevitable, therefore, that middlemen should have arisen at an early date in the coal trade if only to iron out these differences in the timing of peak demand and supply, and as inevitable, too, that coal buyers should have attempted to combine under the conditions of the late eighteenth century, when their numbers, like those of the Committee of the Vend, were comparatively few.

4. *The Meat Trade*

In the animal and animal product trades the problem of supplying the city of London was overcome for many centuries by bringing in the meat on the hoof as livestock. The marketing centre was Smithfield,

known as a general market as far back as the twelfth century, and estab-
lised on its present site by Royal Charter in 1638. Cattle were brought
from all over the island by drovers, and it is clear from the statutes of
1552 and 1670, together with further Acts in 1692, 1699 and 1706,
that these people were generally both drovers (i.e. drivers to market)
and dealers in cattle.[66] The 1697 Act (to Restrain the Number and
ill-Practice of Brokers and Stock Jobbers) exempted persons buying
and selling cattle, like their confrères in the coal and corn trade, from
the necessity for being licensed as dealers. They had, however, long
been required to possess a licence as drovers, under the terms of Edward
VI's 'Statute of Regrators' in 1552, which entitled them to purchase
cattle at:

> free Liberty, and Pleasure, and to sell the same again at a reason-
> able Price, in common Fairs and Markets distant from the Place
> or Places where he shall buy the same, forty Miles at least.[67]

More than a hundred years later, in 1670, it was decreed[68] that no
drovers were to be licensed within eighty miles of London, each
drover being required to enter a bond, in an attempt to remedy abuses
in Smithfield market itself. By this time, though, the general relaxation
of regulations governing the conduct of commerce, which we have
previously noted, was also affecting this trade, causing the system of
licensing to fall into decay. During the late seventeenth and early
eighteenth centuries Welsh drovers, it appears, financed their purchases
by borrowing from the receivers of taxes at agreed rates of interest.
Later, private banks were established in country towns which took
over this function.[69]

By the eighteenth century, however, the drover as a middleman
was rapidly losing ground to both the grazier and the jobber. The
graziers were sometimes accused[70] of controlling the market by purchasing cattle which farmers proposed to have driven to London, and
withholding or augmenting supplies at Smithfield as they saw fit, a
process rendered possible by their small numbers. It seems more
certain, though, that by mid-eighteenth century the jobbers had very
largely attained mastery over both the drovers and graziers and so
controlled the livestock market. This they managed to achieve by
purchasing cattle and sheep en route for Smithfield and thus forestalling the market, bargains of this sort being

> frequently struck by the Jobbers and Forestallers at the Town's-
> end, or perhaps within a Stone's cast of the Market.[71]

Like the buying factor in the provincial corn markets, the jobber was
better informed about London prices than the local farmer or merchant, and so tended to be successful almost always in his attempts to
purchase, a process which ultimately led to the farmer's and grazier's
dependence upon him. It appears, in fact, that estimates of the proportion of cattle and sheep 'jobbed' before arrival at Smithfield vary

between three-quarters and nine-tenths, many of the animals having changed hands some four or five times on the road.[72]

At this time, too, regrating was added to the ancient iniquity of forestalling, for cattle bought at one side of Smithfield were often driven to the other side and sold there at a higher price, or else driven out of the market and kept for another day.[73] The jobbers were able to do this because of their ownership of pasture in the neighbourhood of the markets upon which they operated. From these pastures they could influence market supplies at short notice, a power which was apparently used on occasion to flood the market in order to buy up farmers' and graziers' stock cheaply. Such behaviour must have been highly inconvenient and embarrassing to individual sellers, and no doubt reprehensible from a moral point of view. In the long run, however, the jobbers were powerless to influence the underlying trends of the market, but they were, on the other hand, socially useful in augmenting supplies in the same way as the coal wholesalers, when prices were high, in markets in which stock was scarce.

By the first quarter of the eighteenth century Smithfield supplied about half of London's meat supplies, specializing in the larger and smaller animals, while calves and suckling pigs found their best market at Newgate and Leadenhall.[74] Nearly a century later, it appears that about 2,500 beasts and from 21 to 22,000 sheep upon average were sold at Smithfield on Mondays.[75] There was also a market on Fridays, while a hay market operated there on Tuesdays, Thursdays, and Saturdays.[76] Moreover, Southall Market, established in the early nineteenth century, became very popular.[77] Most of the other half of the capital's meat supply was provided both by farmers who slaughtered their animals outside the metropolis and brought in the carcasses, and by the carcass butchers, who bought up stock in the towns, the surrounding countryside, and at the fairs. At Smithfield itself, the animals were sold by commission factors known as salesmen, the stock having been consigned to them by farmers, graziers or jobbers, and taken over by the salesman's drovers at the 'resting places' on the outskirts of the City, of which Islington and Mile End were the most notable.[78] The salesmen sold for, or to, the jobbers for the most part, and finally to the carcass butchers, while these wholesale butchers and meat dealers of London sold in turn to the cutting, or retail, butchers.

Thus, in the case of Smithfield market there emerged patterns which had some essential features in common with the organization of Blackwell Hall and the London coal trade, the salesmen being the equivalent of the selling factors in the woollen cloth market, or the crimps on the Coal Exchange. In all cases the basic reason for their presence was that the market had grown too large for direct sales between producer and consumer to be possible any longer. In the meat trade, however, the salesman was not the dominant figure which the factor grew to be at Blackwell Hall even though on occasion the salesmen performed all the jobbers' functions, sometimes owning considerable areas of pasture to enable them to regulate market supplies, for they purchased on their own account as well as acting as agents.[79] Thus, on Smithfield market, purchasing for re-sale was practised by the jobbers, who used the salesmen for the purpose, and by the salesmen themselves who used their expertise to deal on their own account. It is thus clear, when these early produce markets are examined, that the jobber by no means always appears on the market itself as a buyer and seller, as a study of the Stock Exchange alone would lead us to suppose. The jobber was essentially distinguished by his dealing function, on or off the market. Moreover, as the example of the Smithfield salesman shows, the agent (variously called a factor, commission man, or salesman) frequently branched out into dealing on his own account: the Blackwell Hall factor used his earnings to become a dealer in imported wool, a process repeated, in the case of imported corn especially, by the Mark Lane corn factor. In the London coal trade, one of the chief objects of the Act of 1730 was to acknowledge the role of the crimps as factors, in order to protect the London Buyers, but as we have seen, it did not succeed, for the crimps frequently sold produce more cheaply to wholesalers with whom they were in league, in addition to being involved in other fraudulent operations. In brief, the crimps often became 'undercover' dealers.

Part of the reason for the Smithfield salesman's failure to measure up to his opposite number in corn and wool probably lay in the absence of a credit system at Smithfield. The salesman's function as selling agent for the breeder and grazier clearly represented a considerable economy for the latter. The best evidence of this lies in the Act of 1673,[80] repealing the legislation of 1670[81] passed to 'prevent frauds in buying and selling of Cattle at Smithfield'. The reason given for the repeal was stated to be that the 1670 prohibition upon the purchase of cattle (except pigs and calves), by jobbers, salesmen, or other brokers or factors within eighty miles of London, was:

> very prejudicial to the sale of cattle of this Realm, and a great Inconvenience and Discouragement to those that feed the said Cattle in their Respective Counties, who by reason thereof are forced to make Journies up in their own Persons to London, or to send others purposely for that Imployment, which commonly taketh up and wasteth all . . . of the Profit or Gain.

In spite of the re-enactment under William III of the 1670 legislation (except insofar as it concerned salesmen), however, this legislation was completely unavailing by the first half of the eighteenth century.[82]

Smithfield Market itself was altered and renovated in 1852, while the Newgate Market for dead meat closed in 1861. A new live cattle market was established at one of the most heavily-used 'resting-places', at Copenhagen Fields, Islington (i.e. Caledonian Road), where the Metropolitan Cattle Market had originally opened in 1833, to be followed by a Foreign Cattle Market at Deptford in 1872. These innovations must have been a tremendous relief to the local populace in the Smithfield area, not to mention the tradesmen for whom similes concerning bulls in china-shops held far more reality during the customary Monday congestions, than for present-day schoolboys studying figures of speech. The growth in the livestock trade, however, succeeded only in inflating the existing organizational arrangements at the new markets. It increased the volume of business which flowed in the direction of the commission salesmen, who by the second half of the century numbered many foreigners in their ranks, selling for continental jobbers and graziers. They sold to carcass butchers as before, who, together with the licensed slaughterers, had moved their premises to the new locations. Some carcass butchers retained shops in Smithfield, or else were content to sell through the specialist commission meat salesmen there. The latter were also used by the slaughterers of meat in the provinces, for the amount of dead meat coming from this source grew rapidly. With the advent of the railways long-distance cattle droving had, of course, died out, and with it, too, most of the killing of cattle on the premises by retail butchers.

The new Smithfield Market took in the London Central Meat Market, the London Central Poultry and Provision Market, and the London Central General Market:[83] it thus added a poultry and provision section, an inland fish section and, with the closure of the old Farringdon Market centre in 1892, a fruit, flower and vegetable section. Nowadays the Farringdon Market is best described as a retail Market associated with Smithfield. The hay market, too, continued to function at Smithfield until a few years before 1914. At the present time, the Corporation of London Central Markets (Smithfield Market's official title) under the surveillance of London Corporation is one of the largest markets for dead meat, poultry and provisions, in the world. Its importance in this respect grew greatly after 1876 when American, and, after 1881, New Zealand imports came flooding in with the introduction of successful refrigeration in ships.

Smithfield is at present essentially a wholesale market for both domestic and imported meat, foreign produce being imported direct by wholesalers. The meat is kept in cold-stores either underneath the market or else on the market fringe. In addition to cold stores and warehouses (some of which are leased by their owners) the market area also contains offices, banks, salerooms for meat equipment, and a bacon factory.

Sales of meat at Smithfield at present amount to between 400,000 and 500,000 tons per annum. The importance of this market can be gauged from the fact that this represents some 10 per cent of the United Kingdom meat trade, while the proportion of foreign meat handled by Smithfield wholesalers is as much as $15\frac{1}{2}$ per cent: for beef and veal imports alone, the figure, at 38 per cent, is even higher. There has, however, been some decline in the volume of market turnover: the proportion of the total U.K. meat trade which was channelled through Smithfield in 1955 was 13 per cent, while the foreign meat handled there was as much as one-fifth of total U.K. imports. Over this period the supply of poultry has increased significantly to meet a demand which seems set to increase as living standards rise. To an increasing extent, poultry is being supplied in frozen form to the public, a fact of direct significance to Smithfield market which tends to get by-passed in the distribution of this form of the produce. This trend has been accompanied by changes in production methods for poultry, which, however dubious their other merits may be, tend at least to produce a standardized product. The significance of this has already been grasped in the U.S.A. where a futures market now exists in frozen eviscerated poultry. Such changes in the pattern of consumption and marketing are reinforced by other factors, such as that of vertical integration in the trade. There has also been a growth of long-term contracts, nowhere better exemplified than by the arrangements of the Fatstock Marketing Corporation which now operates long-term contracts between bacon-pig producers on the one hand and bacon curers on the other.

A further prospective development, likely to be of major significance to Smithfield eventually, is the proposal contained in a White Paper on meat and livestock marketing in 1965.[84] This proposes a Meat and Livestock Commission, one of whose functions would be 'to bring together producer and producer groups wanting to enter into contracts with buyers wanting to place such contracts'. This would clearly result in the by-passing of wholesale markets. Finally, insofar as proposed British membership of the EEC is concerned, should this increase the worthwhileness of beef production to British farmers, increased output would tend to reduce rather than increase the amount of this produce channelled through Smithfield as the major import market. The conclusion to which these influences inevitably point is the likelihood of a further decline in the importance of Smithfield market. It is, however, unlikely to be of catastrophic proportions, so that this wholesale meat market is likely to continue to be an extremely large one for the foreseeable future.

5. *The Billingsgate Fish Market*

Billingsgate was the most important London market for fish long before 1699, when it was made a 'free and open Market for all Sorts of Fish' (10 and 11 William III), an enactment perpetuated by 10 and 11 George III c.24. Because fish becomes inedible so rapidly the middleman, as we would expect, made an early appearance in the fish market but was equally quickly regulated in medieval times, being prohibited from forestalling, while prices were fixed by assize. Almost everywhere middlemen were prevented from going aboard vessels and buying up their cargoes but, in 1552, the Statute of Regrators permitted 'all the King's Subjects' living within one mile of the sea, to buy fish (not forestalling the same) for resale 'at reasonable Prices'. The 1699 legislation, however, attempted to prohibit the prevailing practice among wholesalers (who were becoming more commonly known as fishmongers by this time) of operating in the same way as the jobbers or wholesalers on the other markets we have already examined—that is, of acting in collusion to engross supplies, buying up large quantities which they afterwards divided for resale. Campbell's definition of this class of dealer is noteworthy:

> The Fishmonger is likewise a Tradesman calculated for the Great and Wealthy. His Profits are without any Bounds, and bear no Proportion to his Outlayings. His knowledge consists in finding out the cheapest Market, and selling at the greatest Price. This and the Properties of the Goods he deals in may be learned in less than seven years without any notable Genious.[85]

The fishmongers frequently forestalled the market by buying up entire cargoes at Gravesend, storing them in wellboats, and supplying the market with lesser quantities. Unsold fish were thrown back in the river. In 1749, the monopoly power of the wholesalers at the Billingsgate market was challenged by the introduction of a rival market at Westminster, but so tight was the Billingsgate fishmongers' control over supplies that they ultimately forced the closure of the new market. An Act of the same year compelled masters of ships carrying hauls of fish to report their times of arrival, and the quantity of fish carried, to the Clerk of the Coast Office:

> it was made illegal to store fish in wellboats, or to connive to prevent it from reaching the market, the time allowed for its disposal being eight days.

(It must be remembered, too, that a considerable supply of fish came into Billingsgate market from the Thames itself in the eighteenth century, 400 fishermen, and as many assistants, being employed in this activity, between Deptford and London Bridge, according to the evidence submitted before a Parliamentary Committee in 1810. This industry disappeared after 1828 due to pollution from gas and other works.) The legislation governing the sale of fish cannot have been very effective; William Horsley, for example, remarked in 1753, in connection with the establishment of a herring fishery, that

> there seems to want encouragement for the bringing of fresh fish

to the London Market, which is, at present, a monopoly, and the fish scarce and dear.[86]

Meanwhile complaints appeared, too, in other reports of the day, especially the *Gentlemen's Magazine*.[87]

The fish was sold at Billingsgate either by the wholesale fishmongers themselves, or else by a 'salesman' or factor who operated on a commission basis. It was, therefore, very similar in operation to the Smithfield market in this respect. By the end of the eighteenth century the system was for the market to operate on a wholesale basis upon opening in the morning, dealers having first priority. When the salesmen's stocks were exhausted, they gave way, by about eight or nine o'clock, to the retailers, so that Billingsgate then became a retail fish market. The present main building, overlooked by the famous Monument to commemorate the Great Fire, dates from 1877—a further building was taken over in 1888 for the sale of dry fish—so that the area now looks nothing like the cluster of wooden sheds which once housed this market, vying in filth and squalor with Smithfield. The cutter owners of the early nineteenth century, who had brought in the fish by water, were eventually replaced by companies of fish carriers. These operators owned steam boats which collected the catch from trawler fleets while still at sea. With the development of the railways, moreover, Billingsgate became a marketing centre for fish landed at provincial ports. It was a business which was destined to develop to an enormous extent, for even by the third quarter of the nineteenth century it had grown to double the turnover of the fish brought by water. This fish was consigned for sale to the commission salesmen but, unlike the fish brought by water, it was generally sold by private treaty. Today, nearly all the fish sold at Billingsgate is discharged at provincial ports and sent to London by road or rail.

These developments have taken the number of stands from which sales are effected to the neighbourhood of 200. In the interest of speed a further class of middleman has developed, known as a 'bummaree', whose function it is to buy from wholesale merchants on the market, in order to sell to small retail fishmongers or fish friers. The necessity arises from the fact that the 'trunks' of fish, jammed with ice, contain fish of various sizes and sorts, many of which may not be required by the retailer, who in any case might not want a trunk full. The bummaree acts, therefore, as a sorter and re-seller, but his purchase of the fish in order to do so makes him also a risk-bearer in a market notoriously susceptible to price fluctuations.

The market is nowadays one in which the bulk of the fish arrives by road at a very early hour. The vehicles themselves are then used in effect as temporary market stores, for only some 10 per cent of the fish enters the market proper, which is thus a 'sampling' market. Even so, storage and 'chill' space under the market according to the Lockyear

Report[88] amounts to 114,000 cubic feet. Additional facilities at Monument and Blackfriars are also used by market tenants to accommodate some of the 67,411 tons of fish which now pass through the market in a year. This 1966 figure represents a dramatic fall from the 118,803 tons handled about a decade earlier in 1955. Some of this fall is accounted for by the growth of filleting at the ports where the fish is landed. However, if, as has been suggested, the figures are adjusted for this by increasing the tonnage figures by one-third, the decline is still a substantial one, giving on this basis a fall in the proportion of wet fish landed in the United Kingdom which passes through Billingsgate from 14.3 per cent in 1955 to 8.9 per cent in 1966.

This distinct drop in the throughput of the Billingsgate market is partly accounted for in terms of the fall in the annual consumption of fresh, frozen and cured fish per head of the population which has accompanied the rise in meat, fruit, and vegetable consumption. There are also discernible trends within the fish trade itself which redound adversely upon the turnover at Billingsgate. Thus, since 1955, the proportion of white fish quick-frozen for marketing in the U.K. has risen from one-twelfth to one-fifth, while for herrings the proportion has grown from one-thirtieth or so to about a quarter. The character of the fish trade is thus changing very rapidly at present as technological developments threaten to by-pass traditional markets to an ever-increasing extent. At the retail end the specialist fishmonger faces growing competition from other food retailers who now find it possible to stock fish in frozen food cabinets alongside frozen meat, poultry, fruit and vegetable packages. The implication of this is that retailers find it convenient to purchase all these products from the one source: processing has now become as important as, and often more important than, the type of produce being handled, in determining the channels of distribution. The growth of quick-freezing has also transformed for commercial purposes that prime characteristic of the fish trade—that is, perishability—and in so doing has reduced price instability. The outlook for the Billingsgate fish market, therefore, as well as for the Smithfield market, appears to be one of declining turnover in the foreseeable future: its importance as an outlet for 'marginal' supplies, and so therefore its price-setting role for other markets, is probably on the wane.

Chapter Four

THE LIVERPOOL COTTON MARKET TO 1914

THE invasion of the British market by Indian calicoes led to such an outcry from domestic trade interests that Parliament felt constrained to pass the well-known Acts of 1700 and 1721 prohibiting their use. In so doing, it laid the foundation for the development of home-produced 'fustians'; that is, cloths made of a mixture of cotton and linen. Nevertheless, it was not until after Arkwright's water frame became a commercial success in the 1770s that a modern cotton textile industry was really born.

1. *The Early Cotton Trade*

The growth of the industry from that time was accompanied by considerable switches in sources of raw material supply. Early cotton imports came from the Levant, while linen yarn originated in Scotland, Ireland and Northern Germany. The raw cotton entered for the most part through the port of London, to be trundled up to Lancashire over the derisory network of ruts and tracks which served as a road system at the time. Before the long era of American cotton dominance set in, the role of chief supplier, after the first decade of the eighteenth century, passed from the Levant to the West Indies, and most of the remainder came from Guyana:[1] 1781 saw the first shipments of Brazilian cotton arrive in England. A small quantity of seed, destined to be the source of all Sea Island cotton, was sent from the Bahamas to the United States in 1785, a year when imports of American cotton into this country amounted to only fourteen bags.[2] By 1802 imports of American cotton exceeded those from the West Indies for the first time, and in 1815 rather more than half the raw cotton supply of 101 million lbs derived from that source. During the 1820s imports of American cotton comprised some two-thirds of a rapidly mounting total. This proportion grew to some three-quarters during the 1830s and continued so until the 'Golgotha years' of 1862-5. By 1860, raw cotton imports were worth some £35.8 million, of which about 80 per cent came from America.

Until the 1790s London remained the most important port for cotton imports, tending to specialize in South American, Levantine, East Indian and, during the Napoleonic Wars, some Brazilian produce. Glasgow, Whitehaven, Lancaster and Bristol were also significant ports of entry, but Liverpool's rate of growth was far and away the most rapid. It never in fact lost its position as the leading port for the import of cotton after 1795; by 1802 it was the port of entry for about 48 per cent of U.K. cotton imports, whereas by 1823 this proportion was 87 per cent, and over 90 per cent by 1833.[3]

Down to the last decade of the eighteenth century West Indian cotton appears to have been imported entirely by general merchants as part of mixed cargoes which included sugar, coffee, rum, ginger, pimento, mahogany and logwood; the fruits of the twelve-month long triangular trade in which the purchase price for some of the produce was obtained from the sale of slaves. Mediterranean cotton by contrast was consigned almost exclusively to those specializing in the commodity.[4] With the development of American cotton, there grew a considerable organization for its assembly, finance and transport. It was bought in the first place by agents from the collecting markets either at 'gin' (where the seed was removed and the produce initially baled), or else at 'compress' points (at which the cotton was sorted into grades, compressed to a density of some 30 lbs per cubic foot, and marked). Cotton was sold at 'gin' either for cash or else by means of chits redeemable at local banks. When the cotton was forwarded to the 'compress' point, the local banker received a bill of lading to this point in exchange for the credit tickets which he had collected. He was paid by means of a draft made out by the buyer, drawn upon his principals. The purchasers were either merchants who in turn consigned the produce to Liverpool importing merchants or factors, or else they were agents for large Manchester merchants.

By 1847, according to A. H. Wylie's evidence to the Select Committee on Commercial Distress, the 'great bulk' of cotton was imported at that time either on account of the merchant in Liverpool or of the merchant or planter in America, this last being 'the smaller interest'. Most of the Liverpool merchants were connected with corresponding houses in America, and as Wylie explained:

> If for instance my house in New Orleans purchased cotton there for shipment to me in Liverpool, they would have to pay cash for it to the planter or to his agent, and we of course would be out of funds until either the cotton was sold or we obtained funds by some other means . . .[5]

With the growth of cotton imports direct selling by importing merchants gave way to a system of sale by selling brokers. Already by the end of the eighteenth century at least six specialist cotton brokers (such as Nicholas Waterhouse) had emerged, through whom importers (such as Rathbone, Hughes and Duncan) sold their produce. With this development, the general brokers who had interested themselves in cotton began to be driven to the periphery of the trade. It has been argued that the emergence of specialist selling brokers was due to the need for intermediaries with general experience, knowledge of

progressively specialized marketing conditions, administrative efficiency and capital.[6] Certainly, any agent expediting the sale of an
expensive cargo at a remunerative price would often more than earn
his commission from an importer lacking detailed knowledge and
contacts with the trade. It would seem, however, that the ability to
provide finance was probably a key factor in ensuring, for the selling
broker, his niche in the trade. Thus A. H. Wylie continued his evidence
to the Select Committee on Commercial Distress by explaining that
the exporting house at New Orleans customarily drew up a bill upon
the importing house at sixty days sight (i.e. for two months credit),
but that:

> If that credit be placed against the duration of the voyage, it is
> generally absorbed, so that the cotton is paid for by the time it
> arrives in Liverpool, or is placed upon the market.

Should the time for which the importer held the cotton be prolonged,
the broker generally intervened with an advance. Thus, when asked
who in general accepted the accommodation bills of the cotton trade,
R. Gardner, in his evidence before the same Select Committee, replied:

> Produce brokers; a person buys cotton, and places it in the hands
> of a broker, and draws upon that broker, and gets the bills dis-
> counted.[7]

In some cases, brokers even provided advances against future consignments, and in this way secured for themselves the exclusive right to the
handling of their debtor's produce.

During the early decades of the nineteenth century the main purchasers of the cotton from the selling brokers were the Manchester
dealers. They were stockholders who kept their supplies relatively
near the mills until required by the spinners. The latter had almost all
established themselves in the relatively inaccessible Manchester
hinterland and were preoccupied with the task of running their mills.
Moreover, these manufacturers were for the most part small-scale
operators who found it uneconomic to buy cotton in the large lots sold
by the brokers even when their capital proved adequate, which was
infrequent. The spinner's dependence upon the dealer was, therefore,
very often deepened by the credit facilities granted by the latter, for
most spinners were expanding rapidly, and hard pressed for capital.
Thus, in this relationship (as in the relationship of the importer with
the selling broker), it was the provision of capital which was the most
important factor in ensuring for the Manchester dealer his place in
the trade. With the increase in the size of the mills, and the growth in
the financial strength of their owners, therefore, the spinners tended to
look beyond the Manchester dealers to the Liverpool importers for
cheaper supplies.[8] The movement gathered strength after about 1810,
and was further buttressed by the opening of the Liverpool-Manchester
railway which made the Liverpool market much more accessible to the

mills. Despite this, the spinners still found it inconvenient to inspect and buy cotton personally from the selling brokers at Liverpool. However, not many were in a sufficiently large way of business to retain their own agents for this purpose, so they commissioned brokers to attend to the buying.

With the high rate of growth achieved by the cotton industry after the end of the French wars, the buying brokers grew both in number and strength, despite the considerable resistance to these changes put up by the Manchester dealers. In the event, almost all the elements in the situation turned against the latter. Not the least of their problems was that they had to compete against Liverpool prices when supplying the spinners, at a time when prices were falling: American fair Upland bowed cotton was 30d. per lb in 1814 and only 6½d. by 1827. Forced on the whole to buy dear and sell cheap, therefore, most of the dealers ultimately succumbed, and many of them became buying brokers for the Strutts, the Arkwrights, the Horrockses and the many others for whom they had once acted as dealers and financiers. Thus, when asked in 1833 who his principal buyers were, John Ewart of Ewart, Myers and Co. answered:

Spinners, a good deal now . . . the class of men intermediate between the merchant and the spinner are less numerous than they were ten years ago.[9]

This evolution encouraged many Manchester merchants to follow the brokers in establishing branch offices at Liverpool.

During the early years of the cotton trade much of the cotton was sold by auction, as befitted a commodity which was graded only in a rudimentary way and which was not infrequently packed fraudulently as well. Though expert inspection was therefore an essential preliminary to purchase, spinners entrusted this task to buying brokers, though they sometimes attended the sales in person. Moreover, though the importers themselves sometimes acted as auctioneers, especially during the early days of the trade, with the expansion of business they tended, as we have seen, increasingly to employ expert brokers for this purpose. The latter were paid a commission of one per cent for their services, while dealers and spinners generally paid ½d. to 1d. per lb to their brokers.

George's Coffee House in Castle Street (Liverpool) was the most favoured venue for the cotton auctions, which were usually held on Fridays after most private treaty sales were over for the week.[10] After the old Exchange went up in flames in 1795, a new one was built, but the merchants nevertheless continued to transact their business in the open air at the 'Rialto' at the top end of Castle Street. Here they constituted an enormous nuisance to others until they were eventually persuaded to take shelter in the New Exchange in 1808.

Though so useful at one time as a method of disposing of cotton, sale by auction was soon destined to die out in the trade. Its demise was a natural consequence of the growing import of American cotton, which consisted at the time almost entirely of short-staple Upland cotton remarkable for its even-running quality, and graded by American planters and exporters almost from the inception of the trade. According to Ellison,[11] it was a Robert Gill who first proposed the sale of these cottons by sample. The buying brokers objected to this innovation, reasoning that because samples could be sent direct to principals, buying agents would no longer be required to inspect the bulk in order to assess its value. In the event spinners still found the brokers useful adjuncts to their expanding enterprises, though the former's increased bargaining power resulted in a reduction in the brokerage to one-half per cent.

2. The Emergence of Futures Trading

With the cessation of public sales the raw cotton trade progressed significantly towards a more modern guise: with the founding of the Cotton Brokers' Association it took another considerable stride. The establishment of the Association stemmed from the need for an improved system of market intelligence as cotton imports grew in importance. A monthly *Prices Current* had existed from as early as 1787, and by the turn of the century statistics from the Custom House and from traders were being systematically collected and published annually by a group of prominent Liverpool brokers.[12] In 1832 a weekly circular letter began to appear which provided figures for imports, sales and stocks, and prices current for all overseas produce except bread grains and provisions. Meanwhile, a rota of brokers had begun to collect cotton statistics on a weekly basis, meeting briefly on Friday mornings in the sale-room of the firm whose turn it was to collect and announce the information. It was from this arrangement that the Cotton Brokers' Association emerged in 1841, with an initial membership of ninety firms, bent upon improving the dissemination of information and developing a common code of conduct. As such it was one of the earliest of the trade associations to be established on a formal basis. As with other associations, both in the U.K. and elsewhere, it proved a useful and enduring organization, besides being the parent body for the growth of more complex arrangements, notably the organization of futures trading.

It was, however, the great acceleration in the transmission of information which occurred during the 1840s and 1850s which was destined to have the most profound effect upon the cotton market. From being a novelty in 1840, Samuel Cunard's steam packets eventually developed into a regular service which took a mere nine days to cross the Atlantic compared with the six to eight weeks required by the cotton-laden sailing ships to make the safety of Mersey Sound. Crop reports, and samples, from which the sale of the bulk could be effected, moved

faster from that time forward than the produce itself. A market in
cotton 'to arrive' therefore developed as merchants hastened to divest
themselves of the risk of falling prices while the produce was still
afloat. The dealers and manufacturers to whom they sold bought 'to
arrive' to ensure a supply for the future at the going price rather than
at a higher one. In the early 1850s, however, selling 'to arrive' was
much more common in the New York than in the Liverpool market,
due to the fact that the former centre already enjoyed telegraphic
communication with New Orleans. A significant rise in transactions
'to arrive' first occurred in Liverpool in 1857 with the completion of a
partial cable to India just before the mutiny. Due to the prospect of a
short American cotton crop, appreciable shipments of East Indian
cotton were then bought afloat, though their arrival coincided with the
major financial crisis of the autumn of 1857, which made it impossible
for many merchants to take delivery and prices slumped.[13] With their
fingers thus burnt, most speculators resumed the previous state of
quiescence which the remarkable stability of cotton prices over two
decades had engendered.

After the outbreak of the American Civil War cotton prices began
to rise. With the confirmation of the capture of New Orleans by the
Yankee naval squadrons in May 1862 speculation rose to new high
levels. In July 1864 prices reached the stupendous figure of 31½d. a lb,
while the average over the whole year was as much as 27½d. Despite
the activities of the Cotton Supply Association, which had been founded
in Manchester in 1857 to reduce dependence on American supplies,[14]
Lancashire's dependence upon this supply source was by this time
overwhelmingly great. Thus, in 1860, 1,116 million lbs out of a
total of 1,391 million lbs came from America, but by 1863 the proportion was only one per cent of a much lower total import—a mere
6 million lbs out of a total of only 670 million lbs.

With the onset of this cotton famine, sales of specific cargoes 'to
arrive' at Liverpool became inadequate to supply the market. To meet
the growing demand from speculators and traders, therefore, cotton
contracts began to be concluded for much later periods than hitherto.
A contemporary account relates that during the last months of 1863
parcels of cotton were bought to arrive during the first six months of
1864.[15] The rash of speculation in cotton 'yet to be shipped' mounted
until the autumn, when the arrival of many shipments and a 9 per cent
Bank rate combined to subdue the market.

In August 1866 the trans-Atlantic cable was successfully laid and
virtually instantaneous communication between the world's foremost
commercial centre and one of its most important sources of food and
raw material supply became a reality. As a result, within twenty years
sales 'to arrive' had become the rule, and the sale of consignment
cotton had died out completely. 'Firm offers of cotton were cabled

from the other side, either by branch houses or agents of Liverpool firms or by independent sellers'.[16] With the disappearance of the consignment trade in cotton, the consignee factors also naturally tended to disappear from the scene, leaving only the merchant importers. Moreover, as an ever-increasing number of spinners took advantage of the cable to buy from origin themselves, the buying broker also tended to diminish in importance, though Ellison tells us that the large importing merchants continued to engage brokers for the benefit of their specialized knowledge. For a period also, there emerged a figure called the broker-merchant, who both imported and sold cotton. Thus, though the brokers did not disappear from the trade, we are told[17] that scarcely any of the raw cotton paid a double brokerage after the use of the cable became extensive. The chain of intermediaries was therefore shortened, and costs correspondingly reduced.

The speculation which accompanied the Civil War galvanized the Cotton Brokers' Association in 1863 into establishing a committee—their first—charged with the task of drawing up a set of rules for the conduct of the market. The customs of the trade were accordingly formalized, and some attempt was made to deal with the new 'arrivals' contracts. It was not, however, until 1869 that the Association issued regulations governing contracts 'to arrive'. The version of the 'Constitution, Laws, and Usages' then issued, provided for the proper delivery of the cotton; for procedure in case of loss or damage; payment for arbitration; and for appeal.[18] In the meantime, as the result of the cable, a considerable turnover in business 'for shipment', or future delivery, had emerged by 1867. This market, which may be regarded as the postwar successor to the wartime cotton 'yet to be shipped', existed alongside the trade in cotton arrivals, the latter being transacted for delivery for near months on the basis of an agreed quality. The 1871 amended version of 'The Constitution, Laws and Usages of the Liverpool Cotton Brokers' Association' makes it clear that two distinct types of contract existed in the market. The first of these was the familiar sort used for trading in specific cotton shipments, while the other was a general contract dealing with cotton for shipment in one of two named months.

Dealings in the general contract thus constituted the genesis of the cotton futures market, which greatly facilitated 'hedging' operations for traders. Although selling 'to arrive' rendered the importer immune from a subsequent decrease in the price of the commodity and protected the dealer or manufacturer from price increases after purchase, transactions in this market were attended by several difficulties. The early dealings on the arrivals market always concluded in the delivery of the produce. Protection against price fluctuations was thus a cumbersome process with financial interests confined, for the most part, to unsophisticated 'bull' speculation; that is, the purchase of produce on falling markets in the expectation of subsequent increases in price. Because of the need to take delivery of the produce and hold it in stock, even this primitive bull speculation was restrained. There were thus considerable incentives, ultimately decisive, in the direction of making offsetting sales or purchases in the arrivals market before the maturity of the contracts already made there, in lieu of tendering or taking delivery of physical cotton.

Despite the resolution of this difficulty, operations on the arrivals market remained less than completely satisfactory. Because contracts in this market were for specific cotton shipments, transactions were necessarily concluded in a variety of grades and for many different delivery dates. Thus, it was not always possible for the importer to find a buyer who required precisely the grade of cotton which he had to sell at the time when it would become available. Similarly, the cotton merchant or spinner could not always find a seller able to supply him with his exact requirements. Clearly, while traders could contemplate the conclusion of transactions in grades of cotton other than those precisely required when the purpose of their operations on the market was for hedging against price risks, the fact that they dealt in contracts for specific cotton meant that they might not succeed in selling or buying that particular cotton (i.e. of a particular grade and delivery time) when they wished to liquidate their cover. The solution evidently lay in the development of separate markets; one in rights to the physical produce, and the other a market in rights also, but expressed in a general contract promising the delivery of cotton of a particular grade within a certain period (one of two named months). The important innovation contained in the general contract was, therefore, the fact that it did not represent any specific parcel of cotton; in this sense, the contract represented fictitious cotton, and the market in these contracts for the future delivery of cotton was a market in promises. The main object of the development of the contract was to serve as the basis of a market in prices, to which the wartime contract in cotton 'yet to be shipped' had pointed the way. Furthermore, the introduction of the general contract enabled financial interests to play a greater part in the market by opening the way to 'bear' speculation; that is, the sale during a period of falling prices, of promises to deliver cotton at a future date, when the speculator anticipated that prices would be lower. The avenue to 'bear' speculation was thus opened by the introduction of the general contract, because these contracts could be simply drawn up without being backed by physical produce. (This is why sellers of contracts on futures markets are often referred to as 'short sellers'; that is, because they are engaged in promises to deliver produce which they do not possess.) The general contract also facilitated a more sophisticated form of bull speculation; that is, the purchase of general contracts on the futures market (in the hope of a rise in price), and their subsequent resale, without having to take delivery of the produce at any stage. As was the case with the arrivals market which preceded the futures market, the purchase and sale of the right to the future delivery of produce presupposed the widespread acceptance of a system of grading which put the quality of the promise beyond dispute.

It is claimed that it was a Liverpool trader named John Rew who actually conceived the notion of selling, on general contract terms, the same quantity of the commodity for delivery on a more distant date, as he simultaneously bought by cable in America.[19] By selling cotton 'short' (i.e. cotton which he did not possess), for future delivery on the Liverpool arrivals market, Rew perceived that he could protect himself to some extent against a fall in cotton prices before his purchases had been sold to the spinners. Thus, should the price of the cotton fall while in the possession of the merchant, he made a loss upon its re-sale: on the futures market, by contrast, given a parallel price fall, his offsetting sales would result in a corresponding gain when he bought back 'futures' contracts more cheaply than he had sold them on that market. The system which developed was that, once the hedging merchant had sold his cotton, he disposed of his liability to deliver cotton on the futures market simply by buying back for the same future arrival date the amount of the produce he had previously sold on that market. Were the price to rise on these markets while the merchant was in possession of cotton stocks he would obviously make a wind-fall gain upon the sale of the actual produce: on the other hand his transactions on the futures market would result in a corresponding loss. By hedging, therefore, the merchant was precluded from making unexpected profits, but the process offered him the important advantage of protecting his trading profit from losses due to price fluctuations. The traders' transactions may be set out in their simplest terms as follows, on the assumption that, during the lapse of three months, the price of cotton falls on both the actuals and the futures market from 1s. to 9d. per lb.

	Actuals Market.	Buys 100 bales (of 480 lbs) @ 1s. per lb	£2,400
Month 1.	*Futures* Market.	Sells 100 bales @ 1s. per lb	£2,400
Month 4.	*Actuals*.	Sells 100 bales @ 9d. per lb =	£1,800
	Futures.	Buys 100 bales @ 9d. per lb =	£1,800
Loss on transaction in physical market		=	£600
Gain on transaction in futures market		=	£600

A fuller discussion of the operation of futures markets is contained in the Appendix.[20] As for the birth of futures trading on the Liverpool cotton market, which was the earliest example of modern futures trading in the U.K., suffice it to say that the market operated without any great difficulty despite the fact that almost all the demand came from importers wishing to cover forward purchases of actual cotton. The accommodation of the importers was ensured by the considerable speculative interest which the market attracted. Thus whereas almost all traders came onto the futures market initially to sell promises of cotton for future delivery (in order to offset purchases of actual ship-ments of produce), there were usually sufficient speculative interests on the other side of the market to take up these contracts, and to sell contracts subsequently when traders wished to buy futures in order to dispose of their cover.[21]

The appearance of a general contract side by side with the familiar sort used for trading in specific cotton shipments helps to clarify the fact that the futures contract was, and is, essentially a forward com-modity contract, the parties to which undertake to deliver, or to take delivery of, a commodity for which the contract gives the grade, the quantity, the place and the time of delivery. It is only the fact that the cotton futures market (in common with other later markets) was developed as a means of providing cover which gave rise to the practice of discharging the obligation to deliver or to take delivery by making a further contract, for the same quantity and delivery date, but in the opposite direction.[22] When obligations were discharged in this way, it was obviously possible to expedite settlements by offsetting debits against credits, in order to enable firms to settle by the payment or receipt of 'differences' (i.e. net debits or credits). Thus, in the above simplified example, were a firm to be concerned only in the future sales and purchases noted, there would be a 'difference' due to it of £2,400 less £1,800, i.e. £600. What the cotton market required by the early 1870s, therefore, was an organization which would, in effect, short-circuit the transactions and obviate, in terms of the example, the need for the payment of the entire £2,400 to the firm concerned, and its subsequent repayment of £1,800 to other market traders.

During the early days of the futures market, settlements were effected bilaterally in cash. With the growth of business, the need for some less cumbersome method became manifest and a system of clearing was eventually devised and perfected by Joseph B. Morgan in 1876.[23] The settlements at the Cotton Market Clearing House were at first effected daily, the procedure being for a member of the Association to receive the cash balances due from firms which owed money after they had closed out their futures contracts. Thus armed, the Association official concerned was then in a position to pay out to all members to whom payments were due as the result of their operations in the futures market. Two years later in 1878 a settlement institution called the Cotton Brokers' Bank Ltd., staffed by members of the Liverpool branch of the Bank of England, was opened. This institution operated in the same way as a bankers' clearing house except that, after each member's debits were offset against his credits, vouchers were issued to creditors instead of cash. These were passed through members' accounts as though they were cash, while debtors were able to discharge their debts by cheque should they not have a credit balance at the Cotton Bank upon which to draw.

As the title of the Cotton Brokers' Bank implied, the clearing arrangements were operated exclusively for the brokers, so that merchant importers and dealers had to transact business on the cotton futures market through these intermediaries (who charged a commission of one per cent) whereas they had previously dealt freely on their own account in the future arrivals market. The merchants' reaction to this situation was to set up a rival organization in 1881, known as the Liverpool Cotton Exchange. The rivalry between these two bodies ended amicably during the following year when a new institution embracing both brokers and merchants was established called The Liverpool Cotton Association Limited, with an authorized capital of 600 shares of £100. Member firms were admitted to this organization by election, together with the payment of an entrance fee and the purchase of a share both in the Association and the Liverpool Cotton Bank Ltd. Moreover, member firms were required to be private unlimited partnerships of ascertained financial standing, though such firms were also qualified for all privileges of membership of the Association provided that one of the partners was a member. A class of associate membership was created, to which anyone over twenty-one years old operating as a principal in the cotton trade was eligible for election. Members of other cotton exchanges were also admitted, as a means of expediting business transactions. The rules of the Association also governed the charges payable to members acting as brokers. On contracts for future delivery members and associate members were required to pay one-quarter per cent compared with the one-half per cent payable by non-members.

Until 1884, as C. W. Smith pointed out to the Royal Commission of 1894,[24] neither 'differences' resulting from the changing values of future arrival contracts nor brokerage upon them were payable until their maturity. This evident imperfection in the organization of the market allowed speculators to build up considerable positions, and to carry heavy liabilities, without being called to account for them, for periods of up to a twelve-month. Smith averred that, after some commercial failures in 1878 in which these shortcomings were very evident, he recommended the adoption of a new contract which compulsorily limited the time of settlement.[25] Moreover, as the result of the benefits demonstrated by a voluntary settlement Association from its inception at the end of 1882, the Cotton Association adopted the system in 1884, and thus tightened the rein still further on irresponsible speculation.

All contracts of the Association were made thereafter on 'Settlement Terms', which reckoned the trading week from Monday to Saturday, and for which the succeeding Thursday was 'Settlement Day'. Official market prices for the settlement, known as 'Settlement Prices', were determined at 11 a.m. on the Monday preceding 'Settlement Day', by committees appointed by the Association for the purpose. These prices were then used by members on the Wednesday (the day before 'Settlement Day') in rendering statements to one another of all contracts on 'settlement terms' made between them. The statement distinguished between those contracts still open at the close of business on the previous Saturday, and those which had been closed out since the previous settlement. The accounts enabled a calculation of debits and credits to be made on both open and closed-out contracts, according to whether the bargains had been struck at a higher or lower price than the settlement price, or, when the contracts had been current for a longer time than the previous trading week, according to whether the latest settlement price was higher or lower than the previous one.

Should a contract be actually held to maturity without being closed out the clearing house became responsible for the process by which the obligation was discharged. Declaration forms in duplicate were filled up by the 'first seller' of the cotton, stating the number of bales, grade, date of arrival, etc. One of these was retained by the clearing house, and the other, after being numbered, was passed on to the buyer. This 'docket' was transferable; it was passed on, with the addition of a signature, to another buyer who could 'sign over' the docket to a further buyer. The 'last buyer' (whose name appeared last on the list of signatories), upon taking the docket to the clearing house, received the duplicate stamped by the Cotton Bank. When the last buyer had satisfied himself as to the quality of the cotton shipment with which the first seller proposed to discharge his contract, the latter had then to state in writing to the Cotton Bank the amount due to him for the produce, adding or subtracting the amounts due to or from the other intermediate signatories on the docket, and surrendering the warehouse receipt to the Bank. When the last buyer paid the clearing agent, at first clearing, he received the warehouse receipt, and at the second clearing on the same day, the first seller and the intermediate parties received their money.[26]

3.　*The Growth of Rival Centres*

By 1882 American cotton production had grown to some 7 million bales. Other traded growths included Indian cotton, whose total crop amounted to about 2½ million bales, Chinese cotton (total crop 1½ million bales), Egyptian (166,000 bales) and those of Central and South America and the West Indies (300,000 bales). Turkish and

TABLE 4.1

UK RAW COTTON IMPORTS AND RE-EXPORTS

Declared Values at Current Prices and Quantities

Quantities in million lbs　Values in £million
5 year Averages

Years	Imports		Re-Exports	
	Quantity	Value	Quantity	Value
1815–19	130·4			
1820–24	153·6		12·2	
1825–29	225·8		21·4	
1830–34	294·2		16·5a	
1835–39	415·0			
1840–44	586·2		41·8	
1845–49	626·6		71·4	
1850–54	826·6		119·6	
1855–59	1029·0		145·6	
1860–64	947·0		249·8	
1865–69	1233·4		327·8	
1870–74	1524·2	53·6	270·4	8·4
1875–79	1428·8	38·3	194·0	4·6
1880–84	1715·0	44·6	239·4	5·5
1885–89	1720·2	40·1	250·0	5·1
1890–94	1753·6	38·1	219·0	4·5
1895–99	1798·2	32·1	219·8	4·0
1900–04	1831·0	44·7	251·4	6·1
1905–09	2169·6	58·9	283·6	7·8
1910–14	2204·8	69·8	269·0	9·5
1915–19	1977·8	120·1	203·3a	9·6a
1920–24	1526·6	126·5	151·4	13·3
1925–29	1715·6	87·2	114·8	7·1
1930–34	1319·2	35·3	58·2	2·0
1935–39	1518·4	40·4b	59·0	1·9b

a　No figures available 1834–39 incl. or 1918 for re-exports, therefore 4 year averages for 1830–34 & 1915–19.
b　No figures available for values for imports and re-exports for 1939, therefore 4 year averages for 1935–39.

Source: B. R. Mitchell and P. Deane, *Abstract of British Historical Statistics* (Cambridge, 1962).

Persian crops amounted at the time to some 120,000 bales. Some cotton was also grown in Africa and imported into the United Kingdom through London by consignment to general produce brokers. It was sold on the basis of samples drawn in London and forwarded to selling brokers at Liverpool. Among these 'outsiders' (as non-American growths came to be called), imports of the fine long-stapled Egyptian cotton had grown by 1890 to some quarter of a million bales. In view of the limited cover provided by the American futures contract against the frequently dissimilar price fluctuations of the Egyptian produce, it was decided during that year to institute a separate futures contract for this market. The contract was based upon fully good fair brown Egyptian cotton as the standard grade, and remained a most useful hedging medium for 'Affifi' cotton and related varieties for many years.

Meanwhile, it was essentially the success of the American futures contract which enabled Liverpool to continue its remarkable progress as the largest spot cotton market in the world. In the absence of the facilities provided by the futures market the stock-holding of growths other than those readily saleable American cottons would have proved a hazardous undertaking, open both to the risk of a fall in prices, and to the possibility of high carrying costs should stocks remain unsold for any length of time. Gradually, however, merchants realised that by selling American futures they could effectively hedge against price fluctuations in most other growths also. With the passage of time, moreover, the purposes which the futures market served became known to a wider range of traders. Dealers and manufacturers used the market increasingly—some wishing to hedge uncovered forward sales complemented the interests of others having opposite commitments. Their interests broadened the market, which as time went on, therefore, became less dominated by importing merchants on the one hand and financial interests on the other. Thus, due mainly to the facilities provided by the futures market, stocks of cotton (all growths) carried in Liverpool increased from 372,950 bales in 1878, to over 1.5 million only fourteen years later.[27] These large stocks established the primacy of the Liverpool market as the centre at which spinners both at home and on the continent made good any sudden deficiency or fulfilled demands for the less common varieties of the produce.

By the third quarter of the nineteenth century the number of spinners on the continent of Europe had increased considerably, and an increasing proportion of business in cotton as in many other commodities was transacted directly between foreign merchant and consumer. After describing the Suez Canal as an 'unmitigated nuisance' in encouraging these direct contracts, W. R. Price, a shipowner and underwriter at Lloyds, remarked to a Royal Commission in 1886[28] that:

I was in Liverpool last week and talking to one and another . . .; they were saying that one trade had entirely gone from them. That is, buying cotton on the Liverpool market to export to Russia, and to various continental ports, now it goes directly from the various producing places to the continent.

In fact, the British re-export trade in raw cotton had already attained its peak figure of 389 million lbs as early as 1866. By 1882 it had declined to some 265 million lbs, worth some £5.5 million a year. Though the re-export of cotton ranked next in value only to that of wool, it was actually a poor second, for the latter commodity brought in three times as much foreign exchange during the same period.

The enormous growth of cotton stocks led to a considerable demand for warehousing facilities, and so Liverpool acquired its ranks of tall, sombre storehouses extending from Old Hall Street down to the quayside, lining streets down which the wind blew the fluff from sampled bales. But the existing warehouses were not alone in having become inadequate, for while business in physical cotton—the'actuals' market—usually took place in brokers' and merchants' offices nearby, the futures market was still conducted in the open, on 'the flags' behind the Town Hall, until as recently as 1896. The many contemporary accounts of the scenes on 'the flags' all describe the large audiences present to listen to the outcry of bids and to see the high fashions usually in evidence. Behaviour was not uniformly gentlemanly, however, for in their anxiety to take up attractive bids and offers for sale, the brokers and merchants frequently charged across the flagstones with a ferocity which would not have disgraced a pack of Welsh rugby forwards. In his memoirs one former president of the Liverpool Chamber of Commerce recalls how, during hard weather, snowball fights of such seriousness sometimes developed that the police were often called to intervene.[29]

By the 1890s the advent of the telephone, and the stimulus to futures trading which it brought about, helped to effect the eventual capitulation of the hardy outdoor traders. Accommodation was first rented at Brown's Buildings (where the head office of Martin's Bank now stands), which overlooked their old site. With the volume of transactions continuing to mount, Brown's Buildings quickly proved inadequate and a site was acquired nearby in Old Hall Street for the erection of a new exchange. The main feature of the six-storey building on its acre site was the floor of the Exchange itself (called, as in most other exchanges in the country, 'the room'). The support of 74 granite columns enabled the architects to provide a chamber of 165 feet by 140 feet, flanked under the gallery with telephone cubicles and an exchange which connected them directly with every member firm. There were telegraph and cable offices, too, which included a direct line to the New York Cotton Exchange. Most of the remainder of the Exchange was taken up with the offices of cotton firms, all connected with the Exchange floor by means of 'ticker tape' machines to record the movement of futures prices as these were put up on the quotation board adjacent to the 'ring'. The formation of a ring is a device which most futures markets seem to have hit upon as the most efficient way to enable a large number of floor members to see one another. The trading ring, in the case of the Liverpool Cotton Exchange, consisted of a well let into the floor in four concentric steps and was sometimes known as 'the pit', following the name given at an early date to similar arrangements by the Chicago Board of Trade. The remainder of the 'room' was planned as a meeting place for members of the market. Off the balcony were the Association's commodious offices, a Board Room, the Clearing House, and the Cotton Brokers' Bank. On the top floor, lit with the same true north-eastern light as an artist's studio, were the Arbitration and Panel Rooms where the appropriate committees of the Association settled disputes as to quality by reference to standard samples.

By the time the new Liverpool Cotton Exchange was completed, however, some of the incoming cotton was being imported direct to Manchester along the ship canal opened in 1894, the same year as the Manchester Cotton Association was established. The Association was formed explicitly in order to 'develop a competitive spirit in the interests of the cotton spinners, and to encourage spinners to buy upon c.i.f. terms instead of buying spot ex-warehouse Liverpool.'[30] (It was asserted in 1921 by the Manchester Cotton Association that there was a saving of over £10 on 100 bales of American cotton delivered c.i.f. at Oldham via Manchester compared with 100 bales delivered via Liverpool.) Fortunately for both the Liverpool and Manchester Associations, cotton imports continued to increase for almost two decades after the formation of the latter, so that friendly relations eventually supervened. It took a considerable time, however, for the older Association to recognise Manchester cotton stocks as comprising legitimate tender against Liverpool futures contracts. Despite the offer by the Ship Canal Company at one time to transport cotton free for this purpose, and the greater general ease with which produce could be brought direct to Manchester and other nearby spinning centres, the canal failed to eliminate the Liverpool market. A half-century or so earlier, the Liverpool-Manchester Railway had played a large part in the reverse process, of virtually eliminating the Manchester market, but the canal did not succeed in turning the tables. During the vital years of the growth of the cotton textile industry the Liverpool market had entrenched itself with the aid of superior facilities for shipping, warehousing, and hedging cotton.

During the decades before the outbreak of war in 1914 the facilities afforded by the cotton futures market proved their worth convincingly to most traders. Thus, despite the antipathy of growers during the period of low prices in the mid-nineties, bankers were becoming ever more insistent that produce should be hedged before being used as collateral for loans. Subsequently, advances of as much as 90 per cent of its value were often made. The turnover of cotton futures contracts consequently continued to increase with the growth of imports. Nor was business confined to Lancashire interests. Telegraph, cable and telephone communications meant that every cotton trader was within five minutes buying and selling compass of the other important world markets at New York, New Orleans, Bombay and Alexandria. To an increasing extent, therefore, business tended to gravitate to the market which happened to be open at the time the trader wished to place his hedge. Consequently, with the passage of time, these cotton exchanges became true world markets, registering ever more sensitively world-wide changes in supply and demand pressures. When the Liverpool market opened, traders were in possession of the closing prices at Bombay, while the exchange at Alexandria closed at 1 p.m.; that is, at 11 a.m. G.M.T., one hour after trading started at Liverpool. It also achieved continuity at the other end of the day by remaining open for one hour after the American exchanges started business. The overlap in trading hours enabled considerable arbitrage dealing to take place before the Liverpool exchange closed at 4 p.m. In futures markets these operations (which are called 'spreading' operations on American exchanges) consist of buying futures in the market in which prices are relatively low, and selling futures in the other where the price is higher, each contract being closed out in the market in which it is made when the price difference has narrowed, as it inevitably does due to the arbitrage operations.[31]

4.   *The Development of Market Techniques*
With the growth in the turnover of futures trading, market techniques became increasingly refined. Arbitrage between markets, for example, was only rendered possible by the development of an efficient communications system, and was, therefore, preceded historically by transactions arising from changes in relative values of different delivery positions, particularly over periods bridging two cotton crops. Market operators learned, for instance, to buy July deliveries and sell October deliveries, particularly when the former represented a period of scarcity at the end of a poor season's harvest, and the new season's crop looked promising. In Liverpool this became known as 'straddling' the market[32] and gave rise in time to a good deal of business. A further characteristic of the market, which professional speculators were not long in taking advantage of, was the 'autumnal dip' in futures prices occasioned by heavy selling orders due to the movement of cotton to market. Prices usually declined but normally recovered later in the season as the spinners liquidated their hedges with the disposal of their yarn. Financial interests took to buying at the low prices prevailing on the futures market in the autumn, which became recognized as such a safe procedure that it was known as 'investment buying'.

The procedure followed by the spinner in hedging his unsold stocks was much the same as that of the importer: he sold futures equal to his stocks, which were subsequently bought in as the stocks were sold. Similarly, when the spinner had secured an order to deliver yarn at a specified date in the future, he soon found that by buying futures he insured himself against serious loss due to price increases in raw cotton, even though the cotton which constituted good delivery in fulfilment of the futures contract happened not to be of the grade actually required by him. This system of buying futures also freed his capital, for during the time for which his futures were open all the spinner needed to do was to pay in periodic differences owed to the

Cotton Bank. Cloth and cotton goods manufacturers also developed an active interest in the futures market, particularly when 'making for stock' during periods of slack trade (when they sold futures in order to protect themselves from a decline in the value of their stocks). Obviously, the degree of protection thus afforded to the manufacturers was limited not only by the imperfections of the hedge cover,[33] but also to the proportion of the cost of production represented by raw material costs. Ultimately, with the growth of the cotton market to maturity, the prices offered to cultivators came to depend upon the prices ruling in the futures market, and it became usual to transact business so many points 'on' or 'off' the futures delivery prices of the current period. Clearly, the officially determined and globally quoted prices, issued daily by the Associations which organized the futures markets, performed a major service in providing a sensitive mechanism for registering all changes in market opinion affecting supply and demand pressures. One of the indications of this sensitivity is given by the progressively small fractions of a penny used for futures dealing, a trend to which the low prices of the 1890s gave impetus.[34] After the fractions had reached 1/64d. it was decided to abandon these awkward sub-divisions in favour of the decimal system. This was subsequently used to record price changes of 1/100d. per lb, and on occasion, 1/200d. per lb, or what became known on the market as a 'half point'. The half point was a variation just sufficient to change the price of the minimum trading unit (100 bales of 480 lbs each) on the futures market by £1.

In spite of occasional difficulties and setbacks, of which Morris Ranger's attempts to 'corner' the market between 1879 and 1883 were among the most important,[35] the market continued to gather strength and breadth. As it did so, it evolved in some respects in ways comparable to that of the Stock Exchange. Thus, a system of 'privileges' or 'options' trading developed.[36] Furthermore, the increase in the turnover of futures contracts led to the emergence on the market of the jobber, whose function, like that of the jobber on the London Stock Exchange, was to receive and execute orders for the purchase and sale of futures contracts. The jobber never became completely specialized on the Cotton Exchange, however, and remained part broker as well. The situation held an implicit threat for spinners, arising from the possibility that brokers would abuse their double role by supplying cotton at a price favourable to themselves. In the event, the spinners were protected by an understanding that this agent would never appear as principal in a broking transaction, or as broker for the seller in the same transaction.

By the eve of the first world war the trade had learnt how to use the futures market to the greatest possible advantage by selling cotton 'on call' to the spinner. It was the latter's aim to order cotton for distant delivery dates without exposing himself to the risk of price fluctuations. It was the merchant's ambition, on the other hand, to supply the spinner with his requirements without himself being caught either short of cotton on a rising market when committed to supply, or holding stocks of cotton on a falling market. The method eventually evolved to achieve this was for the merchant to order shipments from his overseas suppliers for the appropriate delivery dates, and hedge his purchases. Then, as the spinner called for cotton deliveries, the merchant supplied them for a price based upon what he had to pay in the futures market to buy back his hedge. Since the spinner likewise based his selling price for yarn on the prices ruling in the futures market when he 'called' for the raw produce, this made both spinner and merchant independent of price changes, their selling prices being based, in each case, upon their purchase prices.

There thus remains little doubt of the utility of the cotton futures market during its hey-day. In the years immediately before the first world war average stocks of cotton held at Liverpool were well over a million bales. If we take the bale as being 480 lbs, and the average price of Middling American at the 1913 average of 7.01d. per lb, then the value of cotton in store at Liverpool may be estimated to be of the order of £15 million. A fall of, say, 2½d. per lb—a common enough occurrence—would therefore suffice to reduce its value by some £5 million. Computed on the basis of total annual imports of over 2,000 million lbs, relatively mild fluctuations of 2½d. per lb could clearly account for a change in the value of imports of £20 million or more. In the long run, therefore, the absence of a market on which traders could hedge their stocks and commitments would have required higher profit margins in the industry in order to absorb the greater uncertainties.

In the event, total imports reached their all-time record figure of 2,806 million lbs in 1912, and the subsequent history of the Liverpool cotton market is one of decline, both in terms of sheer size, and as a free market having incomparable facilities by which traders could protect themselves against fluctuations in prices.

Chapter Five

THE COTTON MARKET SINCE 1914

1. *Wartime Arrangements*

THE crisis in the cotton markets of Liverpool and the U.S.A. actually preceded the outbreak of the seemingly inevitable war, and futures markets on both sides of the Atlantic were closed on 31 July 1914. The problem of the contracts which were still open (and they were held by friend, foe and neutral in all parts of the world), were dealt with, for the Liverpool Cotton Association, by its Quotations Committee, which fixed periodical settlement prices for their liquidation. An adequate stock position soon led, meanwhile, to the re-opening of the spot cotton market. Prices in fact were declining, and the losses for stockholding merchants resulted in successful pressure for the re-opening of the Liverpool cotton futures market on 6 November 1914.[1] Prices continued to decline to the end of the year, when they stood between 4d. and 5d. for American cotton. After the passage of a further two years they had risen steadily to rather more than 1s. a lb but, with the intensification of submarine warfare, prices shot up to 19d. by June 1917, whereupon the President of the Board of Trade asked the Association to close the futures market. On 28 June 1917 the Board of Trade appointed a Cotton Control Board, but this, though nominally a government agency, was composed entirely of members of the cotton trade. The Board issued licences for the purchase of cotton in order to regulate the competition for supplies,[2] which ultimately became so scarce in the case of American cotton as to result in unemployment among mill operatives. The futures market was allowed to re-open following the establishment of the Cotton Control Board, though for some months its dealings remained under supervision.

With the introduction of emergency contracts for both American and Egyptian cotton in October 1917, the Liverpool cotton market's operations became once more almost indistinguishable from their pre-war course, except that prices at one time topped 26d. The end of the war saw a massive boom in the United Kingdom's overseas textile markets, particularly in the east, which had been starved of supplies owing to shipping difficulties. The enormous demand for the finished product, coupled with the need to replenish depleted stocks, especially of American cotton, of which stocks were at one time as low as one week's supply, gave rise to a tremendous import of almost 2,000 million lbs for both 1919 and 1920. On 17 February 1920 the Liverpool price for current month delivery of American cotton was as high as 29.19d. per lb.[3] The boom conditions were not destined to last, however, for Japanese and Indian manufacturers had also become interested in the markets for cheap textiles as the result of British preoccupation with the war. Consequently, after the Lancashire manufacturers had supplied the backlog of demand, they then found that they could not compete in price with the Asian producers. The upshot was the sadly familiar story of the irrevocable loss of markets in the low-income countries and the large-scale contraction which seemed almost incredible to those accustomed to the industry as it was before 1914.

2. *Contraction and Adaption*

The dwindling size of Britain's cotton trade is reflected in the reduction in the purchases of its raw material, the secular trend of which is indicated in the accompanying table (Table 5.1), though this fails to highlight the catastrophic fall in imports of American cotton between 1920 and 1921 from 1,417 million lbs to 815 million lbs.[4] Not only did total imports contract but the breakdown by source also shows some interesting changes: imports of cotton from the U.S.A., from which the cheaper textiles were largely made, had long been typically three-quarters or more of total imports. After 1921 the proportion of American cotton in a declining total fell to below two-thirds and, by the outbreak of the Second World War, almost down to one-third. As the average for the years 1948-52 shows, the figure was then a bare 30 per cent, from which it has subsequently recovered to a third with a relaxation of discrimination against goods from North America after the worst of the dollar shortage was over. Egyptian cotton is, of course, a much more expensive commodity than U.S. cotton, its long silky fibres being used to make finer textiles. The Sakellaridis variety had, moreover, been subjected to considerable development and, since the contraction of British textile sales was taking place at the cheap end of the market, purchases were not nearly so much affected by the shrinkage of the industry. (As the table indicates, there has been a diminution in imports of Egyptian cotton especially over the past thirty years or so, while imports from former British African territories have increased. The largest increases in imports have been from the foreign countries group, the chief of which are listed in Table 5.1). In fact Egyptian Sakellaridis cotton had been improved to such an extent by the first war period that traders found its price movements no longer compared with those of the established Egyptian futures contract for Affifi cotton. The cover provided by the latter thus became progressively less effective against fluctuations in the price of the former. Eventually, in 1917, Liverpool followed the lead of the market at Alexandria with the introduction of a new contract, based on Fully Good Fair Sakellaridis, a title which was soon

TABLE 5.1

IMPORTS OF COTTON INTO THE UNITED KINGDOM, 1910–1967

(five-year annual averages in million lbs) a

	1910–14	1934–38	% of total imports	1948–52	% of total imports	1958–62	% of total imports	1964–67	% of total imports
Total	2,202	1,390		895		562		460	
U.S.A.	1,637	572	41.2%	266	29.7%	202	35.9%	94	20.4%
Egypt	363	276	19.9%	158	17.6%	10	1.8%	14	3.0%
India, Pakistan and Burma	79	192	13.8%	47	5.3%	14	2.5% c	16	3.4%
The Sudan	2	71	5.1%	109	12.2%	76	13.5%	30	6.5%
Other former British Territories	17	32	2.3%	77	8.6%	59	10.5%	37	8.0%
Brazil		113	8.1%	101	11.3%	25	4.5%	30	6.5%
Peru		82	5.9%	46	5.1%	33	5.9%	22	4.7%
Iran		—		2	0.2%	32	5.8%	35	7.6%
Turkey	87			5	0.6%	23	4.1%	65	14.1%
Soviet Union		5	0.36%	—		14	2.4%	28	6.0%
Mexico b		2	0.14%	21	2.3%	20	3.5%	9	2.0%
Other Countries		45	3.2%	64	7.1%	53	9.6%	82	17.8%
Re-exports including unmanufactured cotton waste	269	62		5		11		11	

Items do not necessarily add to exact total due to rounding.
a. Source: Commissioners of H.M. Customs and Excise, The Annual Statement of the Trade of the United Kingdom and the Department of Trade and Industry, Overseas Trade Statistics of the United Kingdom.
b. Incomplete figures. U.S.A. figures include transhipped Mexican cotton 1963–67.
c. No imports from Egypt in 1958.
d. No figures for Burma for 1958, 1964 and 1965. No figures for India and Burma for 1966 and 1967.

abbreviated to 'Sakel'. (The quality clause in the contract included Sudan cotton grown from similar seed.)

The cotton trade certainly needed its futures markets during the post war period, especially the American section of the trade, which went through the greatest tribulation as Japan and India took over the role of predominant suppliers of cheap textiles to Asian countries. The spectacular decline in Liverpool's demand for American cotton after the 1920 boom, at one time, brought down the 1921 prices for March delivery below 7d. a lb. Ironically enough, prices were saved from declining even further by the resurgence of the cotton boll-weevil in huge numbers, which destroyed a large percentage of the American crop of that year. Thus, after the spectacular fall by 22½d. to under 7d. in the spring of 1921, delivery prices for American cotton rose again to more than 15½d. during the autumn. Under these circumstances, losses and failures provided the trade with bitter lessons in the usefulness of hedging purchases. In consequence, though imports of raw cotton continued to decline, the turnover of the futures market at Liverpool actually increased. To a considerable extent, however, these opposite changes in the volume of business in the two markets are explained by the fact that the success of Lancashire's overseas competitors led to an increase in their demand for the facilities of Liverpool's futures market. During this period, therefore, Liverpool became even more truly a world market than ever before, despite the reduced volume of trade which flowed through the physical market.

The increase in business led to a number of modifications. During the war, for example, the practice of quoting in terms of 'half points' (i.e. one two-hundredth part of a penny) was finally abandoned, and delivery periods were reduced for the first time to single months instead of the double month period which was a legacy of the first trading in arrivals in 1840. A further Egyptian contract in 'Uppers' (i.e. the Ashmouni varieties of cotton grown in Upper Egypt) was introduced in 1924, the contract for which, like that in 'Sakel' cotton, was 50 bales (36,000 lbs). The sale of Empire-grown cottons, too, was being fostered and a futures contract, called 'Empire and Miscellaneous', to provide price insurance for these, was eventually introduced in 1925. Being in close competition with the popular American contract, however, it never flourished, even after being modified in 1931. In 1931 also an East-Indian futures contract was introduced, based on superfine Oomra cotton, with Punjab-American, Broach, Cambodian, Surtee and Tinnevelly cotton also tenderable against this contract. The American contract had meanwhile been extended in 1929 to cover delivery periods of up to two years.

In all, therefore, the Liverpool Cotton Exchange was splendidly armed to meet a sea of new troubles in addition to the major contraction in demand of the previous decade, to which it had at least become accustomed, if not reconciled. Thus, when Britain left the gold standard in September 1931, the market was faced with the fact that fluctuations in the dollar-sterling exchange rate affected values of cotton as effectively as changes in the price of American futures; this presented opportunities for arbitrage trading, to which market operators quickly became accustomed. New techniques of 'straddling' were developed which resulted in increased business for the futures market,[5] so that traders using the market to hedge were assured at all times that discrepancies due to fluctuations in the foreign exchange market were under careful surveillance by professional operators.

The sterling crisis did not occur in a vacuum, however, for commodity prices had broken before the autumn of 1931. In August of that year the price of October futures of American cotton had touched its lowest level, namely 3.38d. The decline in prices was already under way in 1930, presaging the beginnings of substantial government interference with the process of marketing in the producing countries. In the U.S.A. the apparatus for doing so preceded the slump,[6] the object being to compensate the farmer for the increase in his cost of living occasioned by high tariffs. Ultimately the fall in demand and tumbling prices led to the formation of a stabilization corporation which withheld a considerable quantity of cotton from the market,[7] while the Federal Farm Relief Board organized a scheme for restricting the acreage to be planted. In 1933 a processing tax was imposed upon the U.S. cotton industry, the proceeds of which were used to induce cotton planters to reduce the acreage sown. The Agricultural Adjustment Act of 1933 introduced a more comprehensive restriction of the acreage which could be planted with cotton. During the following year, however, the Bankhead Cotton Control Act sought to support prices by means of a physical limitation upon crops, and thereby penalized attempts to increase productivity from given acreages.

In Egypt interference in the affairs of cotton producers started early. There had been intermittent attempts ever since 1921 to sustain prices, especially during the early part of the decade. These interventions were renewed at the end of the 1920s, so that by mid-1931 the Egyptian government held about one-half of the world's total carry-over. The technique consisted simply of taking tenders of cotton from the market at fixed prices. Clearly, the weakness of the scheme was that it created a one-way option for market traders, who could count confidently upon the expectation that, as soon as prices hardened sufficiently, the government would start to sell to the market from its enormous stocks. The effect was to create a ceiling above which the price for near-month deliveries in Alexandria did not rise, while prices for distant-month deliveries in both Alexandria and Liverpool continued to be determined by free market pressures. The Egyptian government attempted to unload their cotton stocks in various ways, of which the most notable were cheap bulk sales to European spinners. Other examples of more or less contemporary government deals involving cotton may also be culled: thus there was an Indo-Japanese agreement in 1934 by which raw cotton was bartered against textiles, and there were similar arrangements between the U.K. and both Egypt and India prior to the outbreak of war in 1939.[8] A deal was also concluded between the U.S. government and Britain for the exchange of about £10 million of rubber for cotton in 1939, just before war broke out.[9]

3. *Government Intervention 1939-54*

When the war did come, the Cotton Control was reconstituted, and, though the Liverpool futures market remained open until 31 March 1941, the Liverpool Cotton Association had forbidden members to accept business from outsiders.[10] After the closure of the futures market insurance against price risk for cotton spinners was provided by the Cotton Control's cover scheme. The Control negotiated bulk contracts for cotton whenever possible and re-sold to the spinners on description only, the trade dispensing with the niceties of selection owing to the danger of air attack upon the warehouses. Price and quality were in any case of secondary importance when quantitative considerations remained uppermost. A cover against price fluctuations thus became particularly important for spinners who were obliged by the wartime arrangements to carry larger stocks than they would otherwise have done. Under the cover scheme spinners returned weekly reports to the Control on the level of their stocks and sales commitments, and paid or received price differences according to whether they were long or short of raw cotton. The amount of such compensatory payments was determined and settled on the occasions when the Control adjusted prices—which it did for all cottons simultaneously, at weekly intervals. The scheme, moreover, operated on an 'all or nothing' basis in that the Control required participants to cover all or else none of their transactions under it, but the scheme's greatest defect undoubtedly lay in its excluding from eligibility everyone in the trade except the spinners. Both the Liverpool and Manchester Cotton Associations continued to serve the Cotton Control throughout the war, and under the so-called 'care and maintenance' scheme each participant received £500 a year in order to keep his business (or the business in which he was a partner) in being, ready for the resumption of normal trading after the war.

In the event, of course, normal trading was not resumed, for the raw cotton trade was nationalized by a Labour government convinced of the advantages of bulk-purchasing and united in its denigration of the private speculator. In 1948, therefore, instead of allowing the distribution of cotton to take place via the free market, the newly appointed Raw Cotton Commission assumed the role of sole importer and distributor in Great Britain, under the authority of the Cotton (Centralized Buying) Act of 1947.[11] The succeeding four-year monopoly period gave the cotton trade, and indeed the British public generally, an opportunity to judge the performance under peace-time conditions of this alternative to free marketing, though any judgement had to take into account the unsettled world conditions of the day, not the least of which was the so-called dollar shortage.

In spite of the government's predilection for bulk-purchasing, this means of supplying the spinner was already being abandoned by the Cotton Control, even before the Commission had come into being. Official buying offices were closed in many producing countries in favour of purchases in small individual lots from the Liverpool agents of foreign cotton shippers. Bulk purchases in fact remained only for Empire and Sudan cotton, which together represented some 20 per cent of total imports.[12] Before the beginning of 1948 American, Indian and Belgian cotton from the Congo was being bought from the commercial agents of overseas shippers, while during the Commission's first year it abandoned its branch office at Sao Paulo, and discontinued business with its Lima agent, in favour of purchases through shippers' agents in Liverpool. A buying office was maintained in Egypt for reasons which had at least as much to do with politics as with economics.[13] If the justification for a monopoly purchaser lay with the need to deal with bulk-sellers,[14] it was only ever true of a relatively small proportion of the Commission's purchases, and these dealings with official agencies continued to decline throughout the period of its existence. Moreover, as has been pointed out in a penetrating study,[15] even where the Commission did continue to deal with organized official selling agencies, such as the Nigerian Cotton Marketing Board, or the Sudan Gezeira Board and its predecessors, its buying practices evolved from fairly specific advance price-fixing to arrangements in which the price paid was closely linked to that prevailing in world markets. Clearly, the issue of whether free-market prices were in any sense representative of overall demand and supply conditions before the addition of U.K. demand is highly debatable.

Sampling facilities were strongly demanded by the spinners, a convenience, together with centralized storage, which had to be created by the Commission. It was November 1949 before this body was able to produce a contract by which purchases for deferred or forward delivery, either at fixed prices or 'on call', were forthcoming, while its facilities for the 'earmarking' (i.e. selection) of the actual cotton bought for forward delivery were bedevilled by the Commission's admission, as a public body, of the principle of parity of treatment for all-comers. The selection of actual cotton was, therefore, restricted whenever it appeared likely that the larger spinning combines would cream off stocks of scarce types of cotton. The upshot of this situation was that spinners' requirements were not met as exactly as they had been by the free market, nor was cotton on deferred delivery, and 'on call', as worthwhile as had been envisaged, because it was never automatically available. Finally, as we have seen, the parity of treatment principle closely circumscribed the selection of actual cotton by the spinners.[16]

In common with the boards of the industries nationalized at about the same period, the Raw Cotton Commission was committed to balance income and expenditure 'on an average of good years and bad'; it was further enjoined to implement a price policy which would assure spinners of long-term stability in the price of their materials. The result was a policy of infrequent price changes and a consequent failure to keep prices in line with those prevailing on other world markets, with an ensuing failure by manufacturers to maintain competitive prices for their products. The policy of long-term stabilization was therefore abandoned at an early date[17] by the replacement prices of the cottons concerned as quoted on the world's markets. Nothing could be clearer than the Commission's abrogation of the pre-war function of the Liverpool cotton market as a world market whose members' activities constituted a major influence upon price formation: the Commission was content to accept world prices as determined elsewhere. Even so, for several reasons its price structure failed to synchronize exactly with that prevailing on world markets. The Commission never tired, for example, of pointing out, in reply to spinners' complaints, that the relative import prices of different types of raw cotton did not reflect their relative merits from the manufacturers' point of view but were very much influenced by the relative demand for 'hard' and 'soft' currencies.[18] Inevitably, too, the Commission as a stockholder was an 'unhedged bull', and therefore driven to protect itself in its pricing policy from unpredictable demand and price changes. Under these circumstances the Commission could obviously gain as well as lose from world price changes, but it did not follow that its position would necessarily balance out in the long run. This would have required a horizontal price trend with regular fluctuations about this trend. The Commission's level of stocks, moreover, would have needed to have been constant, which was far from being the case. This body in fact lost heavily from a price fall in reserves of Egyptian cotton which it had built up at one time; on other occasions, stocks melted away when spinners expected the Commission to increase prices.[19]

Despite the spinners' ability to profit from being able to predict the Commission's intentions to raise prices from time to time, it was, nevertheless, a confusing and uncertain period for them. Exchange control restrictions had obliged the Commission to mix their purchases of American cotton with more non-dollar American-type growths, and at significantly higher prices than the spinners would have paid under

free-market conditions. Sales of these cottons were, therefore, undertaken by the Commission at intermediate administered prices which put
the Lancashire industry at a competitive disadvantage in foreign
markets, particularly in relation to the Japanese industry.

The Commission inherited from the Cotton Control the 'cover'
scheme whereby spinners were able to insure against price fluctuations,
but introduced a modified scheme at the end of 1949 in an attempt to
eliminate the defects of the former arrangements. Apart from facilities
for purchasing 'on call', spinners were required, in return for complete
cover against price changes, to maintain a balanced position (within
given limits) as between purchases of raw cotton and sales of yarn. The
scheme also covered the requirements of spinners who wished to spin
'for stock', by providing that the price of raw cotton sold for this
purpose could be deferred. There were also provisions for deferred
delivery to spinners, with cotton available at 'on call' terms when
required by manufacturers, by means of forward contracts. Processers
of cloth (called 'converters' by the trade) were also provided for, while
a further scheme catered for weavers and doublers. Three separate
schemes were introduced to cover the needs of vertically integrated
organizations, and a scheme was devised to protect spinners with
interests in export markets.

In many ways the Commission's cover scheme was an improvement,
as far as the trade was concerned, over the facilities provided by the
pre-war futures market. The price cover was complete, whereas, as
indicated earlier,[21] free-market operations usually left residual price
risks. On the other hand, the 'all or nothing' basis of participation,
upon which the Commission insisted throughout the period before
private imports were permitted, led to a loss of flexibility. Inside the
ambit of the scheme nobody was allowed to speculate except the
Commission itself, which meant that as stockholder for the entire
trade, it stood to gain or lose enormous sums as world values fluctuated.
In addition, its provisions to cover facilities necessarily involved it in
further speculation with the trade which it supplied. The taxpayer,
therefore, took over the role of private speculator in the cotton trade
during this period, at a cost of losses amounting to some £38 million.[22]
Even so, the taxpayer was not called upon to shoulder the entire
burden. When, as notably in 1951, the Commission carried over a
large stock 'into the discount',[23] it used its monopoly powers to force
spinners to purchase this cotton at prices higher than those prevailing
in world markets, instead of bearing the loss itself. While this saved the
taxpayers' money, the policy inevitably made inroads into the international competitive position of the industry, and the Japanese share
of world markets continued to mount.[24] Various mitigating circumstances may be quoted in defence of the Commission's performance, all
of which may be subsumed under the umbrella of 'unsettled world

conditions'. Nevertheless, cotton price trends over the period of the Commission's existence were strongly upward on the whole,[25] from which it may be argued either that its personnel were peculiarly inept, or that the drawbacks lay in the system. Since there is no reason to believe that the former proposition was true, the most reasonable conclusion is that this statutory monopoly could not by conscious manipulation fulfil the complex requirements of an industry demanding a wide variety of raw cottons of fluctuating price in ever changing proportions, with the same flexibility as the free market. As a result of the Report of the Cotton Import Committee in 1952[26] spinners were allowed the option of buying their cotton privately. The outcome—some 30 per cent was bought privately in the first year, and about 60 per cent in the second year—prompted the government to end the Raw Cotton Commission's life, instead of following the Cotton Import (Review) Committee's recommendation in 1953 that the system of 'contracting out' from purchases from the Commission by spinners be continued.

4. The Tribulations of the Reopened Market

On 18 May 1954 the Liverpool Cotton Exchange, a survivor of the wartime air bombardment, witnessed the official reopening of the market after an interval of fifteen years. No great difficulties stood in the way of reactivating the actuals market except for the absence of a spot stock of the wide variety of cottons for which Liverpool had been renowned before the war. This led to the development of direct importing from producer countries by many of the spinners as soon as they were able to opt out of buying from the Commission, a circumstance which in turn detracted from the need for merchants to create stocks of anything approaching their pre-war size. The trend was encouraged by the ability of shippers in many producing countries to class cotton shipments to an even-run standard, which before the war could seldom be obtained without reclassification in the United Kingdom.[27] Above all, however, the costs of handling cotton in and out of warehouses had increased enormously as compared with before the war. These tendencies have continued with the centralization of mill processing of cotton, as well as with the increased concentration on the sales side.[28] Even when spinners do buy on what is called 'spot terms ex-quay' rather than c.i.f., moreover, the tendency nowadays is to purchase a considerable proportion from foreign shippers rather than from local merchants, as the result of the finer prices which the former are able to quote.

The injury resulting from the loss of a large spot stock was, of course, felt most of all by the spinners themselves, who were inconvenienced by the lack of immediate supplies to fulfil marginal requirements, or unexpected orders. Nor did the shortcomings end there, for the efficient functioning of the newly re-opened futures market was, in practice, highly dependent upon trading on spot terms. Futures markets need to have an adequate turnover to ensure continuous trading in them during the periods for which they are open, to enable hedge contracts to be supplied and absorbed without a disproportionate distortion of prices; the markets, in brief, need to be broad and stable. These conditions will be met only if sufficient business is created by the activity of merchants, spinners and others, operating on the futures market through their brokers. The partial elimination of the local stockholding merchant by spinners in combination, buying direct from producing countries in very large quantities and hoping to offset losses against the gains resulting from price fluctuations, tended to detract, therefore, from the volume of active trading on the futures market. It was, however, by no means the only or even the main shadow which was cast over this attempt in the middle '50s to turn the clock back to 1939. The chief reason for the disappointing performance of the re-opened Liverpool futures market, as we shall see, lay in interventions in the trade by the governments of the major supplying countries.

The new Liverpool futures contract was, inevitably, a contract for American cotton. As Table 5.1 shows, U.S. cotton still accounted for about one-third of total raw cotton imports by weight, while many 'outside' growths, being of American type, could also be successfully hedged by using this contract. Certain changes were made in this contract compared with its predecessor: double month delivery periods (as had been allowed from the inception of the market in 1840 to 1917) were revived to allow traders, forced to make delivery against futures, ample time to do so, thus removing as far as possible the threat of corners and squeezes. (Trading in a two-month delivery contract ceased at the end of the first month.) The other change in the system was the reintroduction of daily settlements of the losses or gains upon open contracts in order to safeguard traders against the enhanced risk of default, due to the much higher values and the possibility of wider price fluctuations. Daily settlements had been discontinued since the formation of the Cotton Brokers' Bank Ltd in 1878, the pre-war settlements system being on a weekly basis. Furthermore, due to the need for a further infusion of capital into the market after such a long closure (not to mention higher prices and very high rates of taxation), it was decided for the first time to extend full trading membership of the Cotton Brokers' Association to private firms having limited liability.[29] As a result some wholly-owned subsidiaries of large textile combines joined the market, while some pre-war partnerships formed private companies.[30]

The new futures contract was on the basis of middling 15/16 inch, the trading unit to be, as formerly, 100 bales (of 480 lbs) and trading positions (i.e. prices to be quoted) for October/November, December/January, March/April and May/June. The opening months of the contract were quite promising, in spite of the narrowness of the market in having only one contract and of the existence of the much broader New York market. The new contract had, however, been devised with the possibility of arbitrage straddling operations in mind between the two markets,[31] a process which helped to activate interest. It was made possible, despite stringent exchange controls, by a scheme administered by the Bank of England which allowed a number of commodity markets to achieve international status once more after the war. The Bank, while issuing a directive against speculation and 'undesirable practices', announced its readiness to permit dealings by persons with a continuous interest in the import or marketing of cotton. Operators were, moreover, to be allowed to trade or arbitrate on markets outside the sterling area.[32] The Bank stood ready to consider applications for foreign currency from traders operating in foreign markets, and allowed non-residents of the United Kingdom to operate on the Liverpool market, the 'differences' payable to or from them as the result of trading to be paid in the appropriate currency, or to or from the appropriate non-resident sterling account.[33]

Trouble was, however, near at hand. The American government found itself with large and growing stocks of cotton by 1955 as the result of its persistence in its price support policy. The trade confidently expected the American Commodity Control Commission's stocks to be sold abroad cheaply by the government with the help of a subsidy. In this expectation, the price of futures in Liverpool for forward months exhibited a growing backwardation, as the result of which the Association strengthened the contract by removing from the list of tenderable cottons all staple qualities below 15/16 inch—that is, the ones which it was expected the U.S. government would subsidize—and raised the basis of the contract to one inch of 'fair character'. In the event, the American administration embarked upon its first special export programme to sell one million bales of short staple cotton for export, at well below domestic prices. Thanks to the revision of the contract, this programme had very little effect upon the Liverpool market, but it heralded a dual-price selling system and greatly increased uncertainty concerning America's next move. The backwardation in the Liverpool futures market thus continued. Under the circumstances, hedging stocks was expensive, for initial hedge sales were at low prices relative to the cost of closing out these sales with purchases nearer to the delivery date. Some of this expense could be avoided by using the New York market, on which backwardation was not very marked because few people expected that government subsidies for export would be extended to depress prices on the home market. However, this creation of a divergence between the U.S. domestic price and the export price for cotton made the New York market an extremely hazardous one in which to hedge their stocks as far as British traders were concerned. Under these circumstances their loss on actuals would not be balanced by gains from sales on the New York futures market. The initiation of the American two-price policy for cotton also vitiated the straddle operations, and so further reduced the Liverpool market's turnover by severing the close connection between prices on the New York and Liverpool futures markets. (Straddling the markets is a process, as has previously been observed, of profiting from price discrepancies by selling in the dearer and buying in the cheaper market. The demand and supply pressures thus generated tend to bring prices on the markets together again.) Uncertainty about possible American government policy changes, moreover, lessened speculative activity on the Liverpool market, further reducing turnover and leading to a weakness in prices as would-be sellers of hedges tried to place their contracts with an insufficient number of professional buyers prepared to take them.[34] Futures markets enable traders to safeguard themselves against adverse price fluctuations. However, whereas those with a training in the trade are able to bring their knowledge and experience to bear to evaluate the likelihood of futures changes in market demand and supply conditions, expertise in the trade does not prove a great help in weighing up the uncertainties arising from government interventions.

The American contract introduced in 1954 was meant to serve as a hedge medium, not only for American cotton itself but also for other American-type cottons which competed for the same market. However, with the inauguration of a two-price system, the American contract did not always work too well in this respect, for prices of comparable cottons in Liverpool frequently got out of line because some of them were prevented from finding their true competitive level. Evidently, a traditional type of futures contract, operated by taking a specific growth as the basis grade, and regulating the value of all other qualities tenderable on the contract, according to the spot quotations as published daily on the evidence of current trading, was of singularly little use in this situation, and a new contract was devised, referred to as the 'mixed' contract. A number of alternative growths were specified as tenderable, with the price of the contract at any one time reflecting the value of the cheapest of the basis cottons. Allowance was made for fixed premiums or discounts specified for each cotton, and was expressed as a percentage of the contract price, assessed in relation to their spinning values.[35] It was an ingenious solution to a difficult problem, which was, however, resolving itself by the time the new mixed contract was introduced in July 1956. The American government determined to sell its stocks, in the 1956-57 season and subsequently, at competitive world levels, so that for almost all of that time the effective basis of the mixed contract remained American cotton. For this reason, it has not been used nearly as much as the more traditional American contract, the backwardation upon which disappeared as the result of the American policy of selling at competitive world prices. In the judgement of a past president of the Liverpool Cotton Brokers' Association, the contract was never permitted to show its worth because it 'offended the traditionalism of Liverpool market operators and bred fear of the loss of the big American arbitrage business'.[36] Nevertheless, the mixed contract represented an admirable attempt to overcome a serious technical difficulty, and one which other markets may be very glad to copy under similar circumstances.

In the meantime negotiations had been making progress for the re-introduction of contracts in Egyptian-type cotton, despite the opposition of some exporters who were insisting upon arbitration upon such contracts in Alexandria rather than Liverpool.[37] A contract in Egyptian Karnak cotton was introduced in September 1955, and a further one in Sudan cotton was approved by the Liverpool Association in March 1956.[38] The introduction of the former contract coincided with the re-opening of the Alexandria futures market, the cotton exporters' association of Alexandria having won their battle to arbitrate upon any cottons which concerned them—an interesting reflection of the change in the balance of power hastened by the disruption of the wartime and post-war periods. This market was, therefore, later in re-opening after the war than those at both Bombay and Karachi. The cotton futures market at Bremen, founded originally in 1914 and having a pre-war turnover of between 400,000 and one million bales, re-opened in October 1956.

Egyptian cotton shipments to the United Kingdom ceased abruptly as the result of the Suez incident, and were not resumed until 1959, the Lancashire spinners concerned with these cottons having in the meantime subsisted upon longer-stapled cotton from the U.S.A.[39] The contracts in the longer stapled cottons from Egypt and the Sudan, had, in any case, failed to attract a great deal of attention from the market owing to government control and official market interventions. Since the Suez episode, of course, Egypt has sold a large proportion of its cotton crop to Communist countries under bilateral agreements, and to other interests at official prices. Thus, in 1962, imports of cotton into the United Kingdom from Egypt totalled a trifling amount— £2 million—whereas in 1938, when price levels were approximately one-third of those of 1962, the cotton cheque to Egypt from the U.K. was £7.3 million, out of a total raw cotton import of £28.4 million. The proportion of United Kingdom cotton which now comes from Egypt, as Table 5.1 indicates, is less than two per cent. Cotton from the Sudan, on the other hand, which contributes 10 per cent to the total, is sold at periodic auctions by the Gezira Cotton Board, though here again, prices have to be above reserve values, and some bulk sales are made. China, for example, is now a purchaser of cotton from

Africa, through official channels rather than through the market. Other governments, too, intervene in the marketing of their cotton: India, for example, imposes a system of maximum and minimum prices. Market prices of cotton produced by those countries supplying the Soviet Union are very profitable on the whole, as Russia frequently outbids other countries, which trade on multilateral terms, in the knowledge that she is able to recoup these outgoings simply by increasing the prices of exports to the supplying countries.

As the result of the American price support programme for cotton, the New Orleans Cotton Exchange finally closed its doors on 9 July 1964, after 93 years' trading. On the New York Cotton Exchange the turnover of contracts was reduced to a mere trickle due to government intervention, and business on the Liverpool futures market was eliminated.[40] In fact, the Liverpool Cotton Exchange let most of its building, including the former trading floor, to other interests. Finally, in 1968, the building was demolished.

Meanwhile, the U.S. Commodity Credit Corporation was experiencing some difficulty, for whereas the subsidy paid to exporters benefited overseas sales, it did nothing to protect the domestic market from the competition of man-made fibres and from a mounting influx of foreign textiles. Congress reacted in 1964 by introducing a system whereby the price to the consumer was reduced by paying the seller a fixed sum per lb of cotton upon its sale within a specified period. The payments were made in the form of certificates (hence the term 'payment-in-kind, i.e. P.I.K.) of entitlement to cotton from the C.C.C. stock. The scheme was successful in stimulating domestic consumption, but U.S. export markets continued to be eroded by foreign competitors. In fact, C.C.C. stocks had risen to the vast total of 11.5 million bales by 31 July 1965.[41] Congress eventually reacted to this situation by enacting a scheme which aimed to reduce loan support to 90 per cent of the world price. Financial assistance to farmers was made conditional upon a 12.5 per cent reduction in acreages and there were further incentives in the form of P.I.K.s to growers who reduced plantings by up to 35 per cent. These decisions had the effect of withdrawing the 'price umbrella' which had previously existed over the world market in cotton. The U.S. share of that market began to increase again and the relative decline of the proportion of the market which cotton shared with the rapidly-growing, man-made fibre supply was checked somewhat.

5.   The Revival of a Market in Prices

The aggressive U.S. price policy resulted in the virtual elimination of saleable cottons from the C.C.C. stockpile. Thus ended what had been virtually a world 'ceiling' price fixed by the price at which buyers could always get supplies from this stock. At the other end of the price range, the reduction by Congress of its loan support to 90 per cent of the world price adversely affected the previous 'floor' price. In brief, the changes reintroduced uncertainties by admitting the possibility of appreciable price fluctuations once more. The New York cotton futures market, having switched to a new basis of longer-stapled cotton (1$\frac{1}{16}$th inch), accordingly revived. By this time, too, the re-appearance of price risks made it desirable for British cotton traders to have access to hedging facilities. There were difficulties, however, not the least of which lay in bringing together all the different growths of American-type cotton from all over the world into one market quality. By this time the emphasis of consumption was very much upon American-type cotton rather than American cotton as such, for the share of the latter commodity in world trade had shrunk to some 20 per cent of world exports (Table 5.2). Moreover, the price of American cotton was very much influenced by domestic demand, and its fluctuations did not match the price movements for comparable cottons elsewhere. Thus, while the introduction of a cotton contract based, like the new New York contract on the now more popular 1$\frac{1}{16}$th inch instead of the 1 inch staple, would be a comparatively easy matter, there were numerous other difficulties.

Under these circumstances the desirable solution would appear to have been the introduction of a contract which would cover a wide spectrum of different countries' growths—such as those of Greece, Guatemala, Mexico, Russia, Syria, Tanzania, Turkey and Uganda, in addition to America. However, a highly complex system involving many premiums and discounts would tend to militate against the success of the new market, especially amongst financial interests—and speculative interest constitutes a vital element in the success of these ventures. For this reason, too, it was considered vital that the new

TABLE 5.2
EXPORTS OF COTTON FROM MAIN EXPORTING COUNTRIES, 1926–1967
Five-year annual averages in million lbs

	1926-30	1934-38	1948-52	1958-62	1964-67
India	} 1440	} 1340	115	118	90
Pakistan			442	157	301
Brazil	52	428	308	280	462
Egypt	697	827	712	670	697
Mexico	43	51	326	791	776
Peru	112	165	144	254	229
Sudan a	58	111	146	266	295
Syria		6	40	202	314
Turkey b	36	39	110	179	433
U.S.A.	4321	2835	2289	2852	2023
Soviet Union		33		781	1044
Other countries		588	470	1258	1732
Estimated World Total		6483	5101	7539	8396

a. Previously Anglo-Egyptian Sudan.
b. 4 year average 1926-30.
Figures have been rounded and therefore do not necessarily add to total.
Sources: Empire Marketing Board, Fibres.
          Commonwealth Economic Committee, Industrial Fibres.

TABLE 5.3
RETAINED IMPORTS OF RAW COTTON INTO THE MAIN IMPORTING
COUNTRIES, 1926–1967
Five-year annual averages in million lbs

	1926-30 a	1934-38	1948-52	1958-62	1964-67
Canada	129	141	194	171	213
Hong Kong				198	308
India	90	188	399	322	245
United Kingdom	1509	1329	890	552	449
Belgium	190	169	199	200	167
France	811	580	535	627	585
W. Germany				658	606
Germany	868	556	389		
E. Germany				227	204
Italy b	499	336	406	468	518
Japan	1458	1696	639	1413	1571
Poland	141	154		263	322
Soviet Union	258	90		360	355
Other countries		1080	836	2126	2835
World Total		6319	4489	7586	8377

a. Figures for 1926-30 are Gross Imports.
b. Figures for Italy for all years are Gross Imports.
Figures have been rounded and therefore do not necessarily add to total.

Sources: Empire Marketing Board, *Fibres.*
Commonwealth Economic Committee, *Industrial Fibres.*

market should be in London. To be successful, now that the era of
Liverpool's dominance in cotton was over, the contract's continued
existence would depend essentially upon attracting interest on an
international scale. To ensure this, therefore, it was considered necessary to site the market in close juxtaposition to the other major
commodity markets in London.

In the event a futures market was opened at the London Commodity
Exchange at Plantation House in Mincing Lane, London,[42] on 19 May
1969, having been brought into existence by the Liverpool Cotton
Association Ltd (based at 16, Cotton Exchange Buildings, Liverpool).
The company was registered as the Liverpool Cotton Futures Market
Ltd with a capital of £24,502 11s. od. in 51 'A' Ordinary 1s. shares
and 49 'B' Ordinary shares of £500. The contract was based upon
Strict Middling Universal Standard cotton of $1\frac{1}{16}$th inch staple
length, with trading units of 24,000 lbs (i.e. 50 bales). The Liverpool
Cotton Association thus sought to overcome the difficulties involved
in making comparative assessments of quality between different sorts
of cottons by accepting produce of any growth or origin, but denying
premiums to cotton of better than basis quality, and by excluding
inferior quality types by limiting tenders to lots previously certified as
acceptable by a special Liverpool committee. Liverpool classifications
could thus become important were the Cotton Market to flourish.
Contracts were registered and cleared by the London Produce Clearing House Ltd, to whom margins were payable.[43]

In order to capture a significant proportion of European business—

and it must be remembered that European sales of physical raw cotton are now of the order of 6 million bales compared with only ¾ million bales for the U.K.—the delivery points were nominated as approved warehouses in Belgium or Holland.[44] Moreover, after much consultation with the U.K. authorities, it was agreed that the basic currency to be used in the new market should be the U.S. dollar, on the grounds that it was the traditional currency used in the raw cotton trade. The market thus became the first U.K. market contract expressed in U.S. dollars (actually cents per lb net weight, with minimum fluctuations of one-hundredth of one per cent per lb). New exchange control regulations were accordingly issued by the Bank of England in order to safeguard against attempts by speculators to use this terminal market as a means of hedging against sterling. Under the terms of the new arrangements all existing participants in the cotton scheme were required to apply to the Board of Directors of the Liverpool Cotton Association for recommendation to the Bank to continue to be participants. Participants were expected to have a continuing interest in the import or marketing of cotton. Without such an interest, dealings by U.K. residents were confined to sterling transactions only. Speculative purchases by private individuals in the U.K. were thus forbidden by the regulations, so that the success of the market depended very largely upon overseas speculators.

As it happened, this was not forthcoming in sufficient measure to ensure the continued existence of the market, which suffered in addition from the fact that the standard quality of Strict Middling Universal Standard $1\frac{1}{16}$th inch meant that many of the growths traded fell short of being tenderable by a narrow margin. The quality limits also prejudiced opportunities for arbitrage with New York. The upshot was the introduction, on 1 April 1970, of a sterling cotton futures contract with a broadened quality range tenderable: though the same quality standard obtains in the new contract, it contains an allowance for cottons up to 0.75d. per lb cheaper to be tendered, at a discount to be fixed monthly. The new arrangements permitted under the title of the 'Liverpool Futures Standard' thus allow a seller to deliver, against a short position, cotton bales of a quality previously excluded. In brief, therefore, an easier supply position should normally obtain for tendering and this should be reflected in lower prices. It was hoped, too, that the new-found strength of sterling in 1970 would make a sterling contract more encouraging to European speculators. Finally, the opportunity was also taken, with the introduction of a new contract, to reduce the weight of the trading unit from 24,000 lbs to 22,050 lbs (10 metric tons), in line with the change to metrication in the U.K.

The three decades since the outbreak of World War II have thus been years of almost incredible changes in the cotton market. Liverpool has been largely shorn of the magnificent cotton stocks which it once boasted, and even the daily official spot quotations by the Liverpool Cotton Association have been discontinued since November 1967. As we have seen, the discontinuity occasioned by war led to widespread mergers in the spinning industry. This resulted in enterprises of sufficient financial strength to cut out the stock-holding merchant middleman—a change which had its parallel in the grain markets as the result of the amalgamation movement among the millers. Whereas it was the cotton merchants who formerly brought the cotton to Liverpool and selected it, financed its holding, hedged it on the market and thus enabled spinners to obtain their requirements without risk or finance, by today much of this is done by the spinning combines themselves. In the long interval between 1939 and the termination of the Raw Cotton Commission's monopoly in 1952, much merchant capital had in any case left the market—a circumstance which helped to induce the spinners to amalgamate and take this risk upon their own shoulders.

Meanwhile, the rise in labour costs, too, had become a serious factor widening the gap between the old method of buying cotton on 'ex warehouse' terms, either 'on the spot' or else for forward delivery. To an ever-increasing extent spinning combines purchase on c.i.f. terms direct from foreign shippers, and thereby have rendered the warehousing space, for more than three-quarters of a million bales, even more excessive than the decline in the industry alone would have made it. Since most cotton shipments pass through the port of Liverpool 'in transit', rather than for warehousing, however, it is not surprising that there is delay and congestion, in which the statutory maximum period of seventy-two hours allowed for goods on the quay is more honoured in the breach than in the observance.

The contrast of empty warehouses and congested quays remains, but, as we have seen, the return of price uncertainties to the trade due to policy changes on the part of the U.S. government has led to a revival of a cotton futures market. The fact that this is in London rather than Liverpool, with delivery points on the continent rather than in the U.K., is obviously indicative of a lost glory. The turn-over of the new markets depends very greatly upon continental interest, but it is, in any case, very unlikely to attain the importance of the Liverpool futures market in its hey-day. The amalgamation movement among spinners and the extensive by-passing of the market are enough to ensure this. Over the longer term, too, the growth of man-made fibres is likely to be an increasing influence in the raw cotton market, not least in the direction of price stability. The prices of man-made fibres tend to be fixed over relatively long periods of time by manufacturers' and substitution possibilities therefore tend, to an increasing degree, to impose limitations upon the extent to which the prices of natural fibres can increase without provoking a decline in their use. Competition from man-made fibres is now on the increase, so that world consumption of some $11\frac{1}{2}$ million metric tons of raw cotton is likely to level off. Polyesters are likely to be the main substitute materials, though a further threat is now posed by the introduction of high modulus rayons.

Chapter Six

THE ORGANIZATION OF THE GRAIN MARKETS TO 1914

1. *The Trade Early in the Nineteenth Century*

LARGELY as the result of the increase in its population, Britain ceased to export very much corn after the late 1760s. During the Napoleonic Wars a vast acreage was brought under cultivation and after 1795 there was

> . . . an almost constant importation from abroad, from the high prices the corn has fetched in England, which has made a sort of revolution in the ancient system of the trade.[1]

Meanwhile the export to the enemy of certain 'enumerated goods', including corn, was prohibited except when licensed.[2] When the war was over corn prices slumped, and the succeeding years were characterized by the difference of view between the manufacturers, who wanted cheap bread so as to enable them to keep wage levels down, and the landowners and farmers, who wanted protection in the interests of high rents and profits. In 1815 an act[3] was passed which prohibited the importation of wheat when the domestic price was 80s. a quarter or less, and permitted duty free entry only above that figure.

These changes had profound effects upon the organization of the corn trade. With the virtual cessation of export the foreign trade corn factor diminished in importance, being left only with the re-export trade. The British miller's interest, on the other hand, lay with the encouragement of domestic production so that after the war, the miller, who had been a powerful figure for some time, grew even stronger. He commissioned factors to purchase from provincial corn markets. Some of this produce he later re-sold unground through the agency of a Mark Lane corn factor, while he milled the remainder for sale to other merchants for re-dressing, or else to flour dealers. Flour, it appears, was hardly ever sold directly to the bakers by the millers,[4] since the market had already grown too large for this. There was, however, the further reason that the bakers were usually in debt to the flour dealers.[5] Having thus become subservient to their factors, bakers were accorded no voice at all in the weekly councils of the more important flour factors and millers. It was the custom of these latter members of the corn trade to assemble in one of the London coffee houses after the corn market every Monday to agree on the price for the best flour, which was 'generally supposed binding for the week'. This was 'very unlike the mode of conducting the corn market'.

As the result of complaints and some agitation by members of the trade[6] a 'New Exchange' was opened in 1828. This was a year after the partial rebuilding of the 'Old Exchange' at Mark Lane (officially known as 'The Corn Exchange of London') to which it was adjacent. Dealers, merchants, and bankers henceforward frequently became members of both exchanges, whose role in the distribution of foreign corn was described at the time as follows:

> What comes direct to London for sale is sold off stands in Mark Lane, on samples taken from the ship when it arrives, and it is dealt in small quantities. It is mostly landed at the docks in London, and goes away from the quays of those docks to the various millers on the Thames, and by railway also to all the home counties, which are within easy reach of London and for which London is the especial port.[7]

By comparison with Mark Lane, provincial corn exchanges were at first comparatively unspecialized, consisting simply of local general merchants importing on their own account for local re-sale. However, as the century wore on and grain imports grew in volume, they too tended to become more specialized.

Meanwhile, the effect of the rigid demarcation introduced in 1815 between prohibition, and free import when wheat rose above 80s. a quarter, was clearly to assist the tendencies observed by a Select Committee of 1821. 'It is obvious', they pointed out, 'that whilst the difference is so great between the Continental and the British price of corn . . ., every temptation exists to get in a large quantity of foreign corn, and then to shut the ports'.[8] Huskisson, who had been chairman of this committee, succeeded in introducing a sliding scale of corn duties in 1827, spoiled, as C. R. Fay remarks, by the Duke of Wellington a year later when he introduced a revised scale which aimed at the impossible combination of a greater measure of protection with a show of real concern for a hungry public.[9] The effect of a further sliding scale of duties introduced by Peel in 1842 was, however, completely over-shadowed by the tragic potato blight which finally won the day for the Anti-Corn Law League. The modification and ultimate withdrawal of the corn laws resulted in increases in the import of both flour and corn and, as Table 6.1 indicates, the increase in the dependence of the United Kingdom upon overseas supplies of the major cereals continued unabated. The table shows the enormous increase in quantities imported by 1914; more than tenfold in the case of wheat, wheat meal and flour. The growth of imports was even greater for barley, while for maize and oats the change between 1840 and 1914 was from virtual self-sufficiency to imports of 41.5 million cwt and 17.3 million cwt respectively—a very sizeable trade, but eclipsed by the enormous inflow of more than five million tons of wheat a year into British ports by the outbreak of World War I. This commerce in cereals was thus

TABLE 6.1
UNITED KINGDOM IMPORTS OF THE MAIN GRAINS AND EXPORTS
AND RE-EXPORTS OF WHEAT 1840–1914 (Five-year annual averages)
million cwt.

| | | IMPORTS | | | | EXPORTS AND RE-EXPORTS |
Years	Wheat	Wheat Meal and Flour	Barley	Oats	Maize	Wheat, Wheat Meal and Flour
1840–1844	7·9	1·1	1·5	0·7	0·09	0·2
1845–1849	9·9	3·1	2·8	2·9	7·0	0·5
1850–1854	16·4	4·3	2·8	3·0	6·4	0·4
1855–1859	16·0	3·1	4·4	4·1	6·2	0·6
1860–1864	28·8	5·6	6·3	5·6	10·4	0·7
1865–1869	29·8	4·2	7·5	8·4	11·8	0·3
1870–1874	39·6	5·1	10·3	11·3	18·9	2·4
1875–1879	52·0	7·6	11·9	12·6	33·7	1·1
1880–1884	57·6	13·3	13·3	13·2	29·1	1·4
1885–1889	56·1	16·0	16·4	15·2	31·1	1·0
1890–1894	65·5	18·8	20·5	14·8	34·8	1·0
1895–1899	69·3	20·5	21·3	16·1	51·9	1·2
1900–1904	81·1	19·8	23·6	17·8	48·6	1·2
1905–1909	95·4	12·7	20·1	15·0	43·5	2·0
1910–1914	104·5	10·5	20·3	17·3	41·5	2·6

Source: Mitchell, *Abstract of British Historical Statistics*

the trade which, more than any other, succeeded in transforming the
sea-routes of the world into the busy thoroughfares of today.

The famine which occurred in the 1840s naturally gave rise to very
considerable price fluctuations and much speculation. In fact, according
to the testimony of the Governor and Deputy Governor of the Bank
of England, the financial crisis of 1847 began with failures in the corn
trade.[10] This they attributed to the appearance of large shipments of
grain from Europe and America coupled with the prospect of an
abundant harvest, which brought the price precipitately down from
about 120s. to some 60s. a quarter. This analysis is almost certainly
sounder than Morier Evans' sour attribution of the failures to 'Government interference in the importation of corn'.[11] This was a reference
to the fact that Baring's had been secretly commissioned by the government to buy maize and corn meal to tide over the crisis. Hidy claims,[12]
however, that this operation was carried out without materially
disturbing produce prices.

2. *Sales 'to Arrive' on the Baltic*

At the time, most of the large-scale purchases of grain from abroad,
together with re-sales by professional market dealers, were effected in
the Baltic coffee house, which was still housed in the former Antwerp
Tavern. After the losses sustained by many of its members in the unre-
strained tallow speculations earlier in the century, business on the
Baltic had long been organized so as to restrict dealings to merchants
and brokers. The first committee, of which Thomas Tooke was a
member, met in 1823 and drew up a set of Rules and Regulations, one
of which limited the number of subscribers to 300. Until the growth
of corn imports after mid-century, the bulk of the business consisted

of transactions in tallow, hemp, flax and oilseeds. The trade in hemp was considerable but, unlike tallow, there was little speculation in this commodity. The Russians shipped hemp to United Kingdom ports between May and October and sold it through their London representatives on the Baltic. The latter dealt through brokers who at one time held fortnightly auctions.[13]

Before the emergence of United States supplies with the opening up of the mid-west, the international corn trade was dominated by European and Russian suppliers. For many years after the Napoleonic Wars prices in the Danzig market governed the international movement of wheat. In 1847 some two-fifths of British wheat imports passed through the London market, the largest single supply source being Russia which contributed about a third of the 1.1 million quarters entering the port. About half the shipments of oats to London also originated there. Much of this produce was handled by Greek and other foreign merchants. Thus, in the 1850s, when the Baltic was transferred to South Sea House and membership was allowed to grow to 400, more than 300 members were Greek. (These included Ralli, Rodocanachi, Schroeder, Arjectis, Petrochochinos and Vaglianos.) In the eighteenth century the forerunners of these Greeks had functioned mainly as local agents for British or French merchants, in the latter's Levant factories, but by the 1830s, they had taken over a considerable proportion of that trade themselves.[14] Eventually the Greek merchants set up their headquarters in London, controlling first the British trade to and from Constantinople, Smyrna and other parts of the Levant and, by mid-century, the traffic of large areas of the Mediterranean, the Black Sea, and the Near and Middle East.

Their methods of buying on their own account predisposed the Greeks towards the development of the 'cargo trade'; that is, of selling 'to arrive'. The system developed after the establishment of a reasonable postal service between the Black Sea grain ports and the United Kingdom. Constantinople, being en route between ports of origin and the Mediterranean, grew to importance as a centre of information, especially since much of the grain was trans-shipped there.[15] It was from Constantinople that Greek merchants forwarded samples to their London counterparts so as to enable the latter to sell the grain on the Baltic 'to arrive'. A rapid system of communication between ports of call, such as Cork and Falmouth, and London enabled the Greeks to sell 'to arrive' on the Baltic and to send instructions to the captains of vessels who put in at the ports of call 'for orders'. This enabled ships' masters to proceed direct to the unloading port, for sales of grain 'to arrive' were almost invariably sold with buyer's option as to the unloading port. The low capital and running costs of these compact sailing vessels (whose average cargoes ranged from 1000 to 3000 quarters) made the procedure a profitable one. Demurrage rates on such a handy-sized vessel during the 1840s, for example, might only amount to £4 a day, which was a small consideration compared with the advantage to be gained from being able to direct the vessel to a market. Merchants could afford to keep sailing ships waiting at ports of call when business was slack on the Baltic, whereas the relatively high cost of demurrage for steam ships at a later date made the system unprofitable. The system of sending instructions as to final destination to vessels putting in for orders at ports of call, however, naturally afforded a fillip to the provincial ports.[16]

While they tended to be excluded from the trade in Mediterranean grain by the ubiquitous Greeks, English merchants were much more in evidence in the development of corn imports from other parts of the world. This was especially true of the Swedish oats trade. This produce was sold on the Baltic through English agents, the Swedish houses channelling their sales into the hands of comparatively few factors, apparently in order to ensure adequate supplies of credit.[17] Advances were made against consignments when the cargo was shipped, in addition to which about half of the considerable capital required to build granaries in Sweden was loaned by the London importers. Despite the development of a remarkably good information service, however, the Swedish houses continued to fear that their London factors speculated with the produce and actually received a better price than they reported. The sale of cargoes prior to shipment therefore ultimately predominated.

A perusal of bills of entry at mid-century indicates that the import of oats into London was much greater than into any of the outports, a circumstance connected with the enormous number of horses required for the distribution of goods in the capital. At this time however, Liverpool was 'even more extensively engaged in the Corn Trade than London',[18] despite the fact that less than half a century earlier corn was still being sold there in the open air in front of the Town Hall. A corn exchange, said to be more commodious than its Mark Lane counterpart, was completed in 1808. Trade was on a modest scale until the Irish potato failures and the increasing requirements of the North of England provided an impetus to shipments of American maize. By the 1851 season imports into Liverpool were as much as 1.1 million sacks of flour, 500,000 quarters of maize, and 150,000 quarters of oats and barley.

By mid-century Hull, Bristol and Glasgow were all importing grain and flour in significant quantities as the espousal of free trade, the growth of population and its increasing urbanization made themselves felt. According to Porter's well-known estimate the implication of the figures was that the equivalent of about a quarter of the population was already living on foreign bread grains.[19] Their source, however, was still principally the old world rather than the new, as the accom-

TABLE 6.2
PRINCIPAL SOURCES OF UNITED KINGDOM IMPORTS OF WHEAT 1828–1914
(Five-year annual averages)
million cwt.

Years	Russia	Prussia	Germany	Canada	U.S.A.	Argentine	India	Australia
1828–1832	1·0	1·4		0·3	0·05			
1833–1837	0·03	0·5		0·1				
1838–1842	0·9	3·2		0·1	0·1			
1843–1847	1·1	2·2		0·2	0·5			
1848–1852	2·8	2·7		0·1	0·8			
1853–1857	2·6	3·0		0·3	2·9			
1858–1862	4·5		5·7	1·5	7·3			
1863–1867	8·1		6·4	0·9	4·5			
1868–1872	12·6		4·5	2·2	10·7			
1873–1877	9·0		3·7	3·3	21·4		2·5	1·4
1878–1882	6·7		3·0	3·4	34·5		4·4	2·7
1883–1887	8·0		1·8	2·5	25·6	0·3	10·2	3·0
1888–1892	16·2		1·7	2·1	21·4	2·2	10·4	2·2
1893–1897	16·4		0·8	3·3	30·0	7·7	4·6	2·0
1898–1902	4·5		0·7	6·6	37·8	9·3	6·0	3·8
1903–1904	21·8			7·8	12·6	19·6	21·8	7·0
1905–1909	15·2			12·7	18·1	23·2	14·3	8·5
1910–1914	13·7			21·1	22·4	14·0	18·6	12·6

Statistics for 1828–1839 were in quarters in original source.
They have been converted into cwts. using the ratio 1·81 bushels = 1 cwt.
This ratio represents the average of British experience from 1910–1939 and whilst it cannot
be exactly correct for most years the margin of error cannot be large.
From 1858 Prussian Figures included in Germany.

Source: Mitchell, *Abstract of British Historical Statistics.*

panying table (Table 6.2) indicates. After the American Civil War the
depreciation of the American dollar, together with the growth of steam
transport by land and sea, gave the Atlantic grain trade a tremendous
impetus. The transition from sail on other routes was much more
gradual;[20] thus wheat from California remained far too bulky to be
carried by steam-boat. It also proved uneconomical to transport wheat
via the Panama Canal, so the 'Down Easters' and their successors, the
British iron sailing vessels, made the haul round Cape Horn. On such
a long journey the temptation to overload was considerable and the
losses consequently high, until the Plimsoll line brought the mariners
some protection against this hazard.

3.   *The Growth of the Liverpool Market*
The Californian wheat trade depended entirely upon the Liverpool
market, a circumstance which made rural California and mercantile
San Francisco, as one writer remarked, almost a colonial appendage to
Victorian Britain.[21] Liverpool importing firms established correspondents or branches in San Francisco, the greatest of which was Balfour,
Guthrie and Co. Not only did this company possess its own docks and
wharfs, but it also acted as agent for insurance companies and opened
branches at Portland, Tacoma and Seattle. When the growth in grain
imports really became considerable, all the Liverpool firms seem to have
realized the advantages of establishing branch houses or exclusive
correspondents as the most obvious way of maintaining an assured flow

of imports. This trend, towards increasing specialization by function in particular commodities rather than in particular areas, contributed to the decline of Greek control over trade in the Mediterranean. These merchants were ousted from Odessa by the Jews and the Germans[22] while British corn merchants extended their influence very considerably and began to buy direct from native exporters in corn-surplus areas such as Russia. The history of the firm of Ross T. Smith and Co. provides an excellent example of these trends, for they eventually added to their interests in Trieste by opening branch houses in New York, Odessa, Rostoff, Karachi and Buenos Aires. Liverpool firms were most in evidence in the Western Hemisphere, for Russian grain was mostly a London trade. Not unnaturally, therefore, when the U.S.A. took over from Russia the role of chief wheat supplier to the U.K., from France as the main supplier of flour, and from Southern Europe as the principal provider of maize to the U.K., Liverpool increased its lead over the capital until it became the greatest grain and flour port not only in the country, but in Europe as well.

Other factors, too, conspired to consolidate Liverpool's lead. By the 1880s the big millers had built their mills at the major ports so that by this time both the size of the corn-carrying vessel and the location of the mills gave less choice in discharge than was common up to about the 1860s. Duke's warehouse was already available for the increase in Liverpool's grain trade in 1853, and later others were added between Mann Island and Canning Dock. Eventually, the old flour warehouses behind the Dock Road, from Lightbody Street to Cornhill and as far back as the Ropery, were used for grain as the trade in imported Irish flour declined.[23] The Liverpool Dock Board added huge warehouses on either side of the river in 1868, the only ones in Europe which could accommodate a ship of 3,000-5,000 tons alongside for discharge. Other innovations followed: an alliance of shipowners and merchants established the Liverpool Grain Storage and Transit Company which, in 1885, introduced the 'silo' system of storing grain in vertical piles rather than horizontally on floors.

An organization known as the Association of the Liverpool Corn Trade was formed in 1853, a year before the Corn Exchange was re-opened after being enlarged. The Exchange was managed by a Corn Exchange Company which rented both office and marketing accommodation to the Association until these organizations amalgamated in 1886. In the meantime the space provided for the Association by the Company had become inadequate so that they resorted to renting space in 'Atlantic Buildings' opposite the Exchange in Brunswick Street. Here they established the 'Atlantic Newsroom' which provided all the intelligence available on shipping movements, crop reports and kindred matters in precisely the way initiated in the coffee houses of an earlier era. The Association became responsible for the form of contract governing transactions in the corn trade, for the settlement of disputes by arbitration and for representing the interests of its members. In 1859 it also succeeded in imposing order upon the veritable chaos of weights and measures in being at the time through the official adoption of the 'cental' (a measure of 100 lbs weight replacing less accurate volume measures). The Association became incorporated when it amalgamated with the Corn Exchange Company in 1886, and in 1897 the title changed to The Liverpool Corn Trade Association Ltd. This coincided with the transfer of the Atlantic Newsroom from across the road to the Corn Exchange itself. Members were required to pay an entrance fee upon joining the Association, to which they were eligible for election provided they were principals in the corn trade or had full authority so to act. Incorporated companies were ineligible for membership, but were allowed to nominate representatives as trading members. Members were required to furnish security and to purchase a share interest in the Association. The other main source of revenue was the rental from the stands on the floor of the Exchange, though business was also transacted in brokers' offices, as well as by post. In addition to grain and flour, transactions were also concluded for feeding-stuffs and oil-cake, while forwarding agents and sack dealers also rented stands from the market's earliest days.

There is little doubt that of all the foreign grain centres with which Liverpool merchants and brokers dealt, the one from which they learnt most was Chicago, for it was from there that the use of futures trading in grain spread to New York and Liverpool. Clearly this mode of dealing also owed something to comparable practices in the cotton trade, while in England there was also a background of some fairly sophisticated gambling in pig-iron warrants, and in sugar, too, it appears.[24] In grain itself, short selling had many antecedents in Antwerp and Amsterdam in earlier centuries, as the account in Chapter Two indicates. Moreover, H. C. Emery cites Fuchs as his authority for saying that similar practices were known at the Berlin grain exchange by 1832.[25] The study of the growth of futures trading in cotton has already served to reveal that the *sine qua non* for such transactions consisted of a contract which was general rather than specific in its reference to the commodity concerned.

Interestingly, the immediate antecedents of Chicago grain futures appear to have developed along the same lines as the Scotch pig-iron warrant, though the market in the latter never developed into a fully-fledged futures market. The prairie farmers received general receipts from the elevator companies following the accurate grading of the produce and, like the Scotch pig-iron warrant and the earlier warehouse warrants of both the Dutch and English East India Companies, these receipts were transferable.[26] In the pre-railroad era, deliveries tended to be uncertain and a trade in produce 'to arrive' developed.

A market in elevator receipts also sprang up in Chicago as those who feared a price fall sold out to others who were expecting a rise. With all the conditions favourable for a further development, it was not long before speculators and traders dispensed with the restrictions inherent in transactions in forward contracts for actual produce, and exchanged contracts for 'arrivals' of grain which did not exist at the time of sale.[27] In brief, a futures market sprang into existence. The first formal organization of the Chicago market dates from 1848, though a further eight years elapsed before grades and standards were determined. After 1856 the endorsement of a warehouse receipt constituted good delivery. It is in fact very difficult to pinpoint the beginnings of modern futures trading in North America. One authority, for example, argues that instances of futures trading 'probably occurred in a small way as early as 1855' in Milwaukee,[28] whereas Baer and Woodruff[29] point out that the quotations which appeared in the Chicago press before the Civil War were for forward rather than for modern futures transactions. Furthermore, it was stated in evidence before the Congressional Committee on Agriculture in 1892 that the government contracts for pork during the Civil War were the beginning of futures trading. However, in a Congress Committee Report on Agriculture in 1947, the first futures contract was alleged to have been made in connection with 'solving a problem incidental to supplying oats to the U.S. Army about the time of the wars between the States'.

Be that as it may, the Civil War brought a tremendous upsurge of speculation, so that by 1865 not only did the dealers in the grain trade fill the boardrooms in Chicago to capacity but both the Chicago Stock Exchange and also the facilities of the local Masonic Temple were pressed into service. There were a great many attempts to manipulate the market and, following these, the first printed rules governing futures trading appeared in the Report of the Chicago Board of Trade for 1869.[30] The first public call in grain on the New York Produce Exchange was on 17 May 1877.[31]

The consignment system in the grain trade did not survive modern means of communication and, as we have already seen, both steam and electricity were used in order to expedite transactions as these became available. To an increasing extent with the international development of the grain trade the key figure in the conclusion of transactions was the broker. With the laying of the cables, British, American and other merchant houses, branches or agents cabled offers of produce available in primary markets such as Chicago to brokers in Liverpool or London: the latter, after finding customers for the produce at the prices quoted, were able to telegraph acceptances within twenty-four hours. Business also originated from the purchasing end for as that most instructive witness, William John Harris, explained in 1882:

It is my business to know a certain number of millers and dealers

in various ports of the kingdom who send orders to me to buy cargoes; and very often I send a telegraphic message to houses in
America, ordering a cargo for my client, and that client would get
it at exactly the price that it was bought at, simply with my
brokerage added; there being no other middleman at all. The
receiver in New York or Chicago to whom the grower of the
wheat may consign his produce for sale, may sell it through me
to my client with only that one charge upon it in the way of
profit.[32]

Harris had earlier explained to his questioner that his commission on
a cargo of wheat was one half per cent on the value. The margin
between market and market had also become ridiculously small with
the growth in the speed and efficiency of the merchant marine. The
triple expansion engine was being developed at the time that
Harris was giving his evidence, and the pay-load the grain vessels
were able to take was the subject of continual improvements, until
cargoes of 10,000 quarters were becoming common. Though he had
retired in the meantime, we have the evidence of the same inform-
ative witness, to a Royal Commission of 1886 that,

When I first began business, I think the cost of bringing wheat
from Dantzic, which used to be then the great wheat exporting
port, was at least 6s. or 7s. a quarter in bringing it to London;
and the cost from Odessa must have been 8s. or 9s. Today the cost
of bringing wheat from Dantzic will be perhaps 1s. 3d. and the
cost from Odessa perhaps 2s. or 2s. 6d., or sometimes as much as
3s.[33]

The costs of carriage continued to decrease long after the Royal Commission of 1886 had reported. The carriage on prairie wheat, from
Chicago to Liverpool, averaged 11s. a quarter between 1868 and
1879, whereas in 1886 it was 6s. 2½d. By 1892, the produce was being
carried for 4s. 3d., and in 1902 the price was down to 2s. 10½d. a
quarter.[34]

Thus the introduction of the telegraph, together with cheap and
speedy transport, combined to reduce merchants' and manufacturers'
need to carry stocks, though the growth of import was an influence
which tended to offset this. What is certain is that the rapid transmission of intelligence concerning prices and the state of supplies in
producing countries led to the integration of the world's central grain
markets. Henceforward, until they were disrupted by major interventions, these markets were effectively welded into one, while the
rapidity and cheapness of transport and communications implied a
tendency for price fluctuations to become narrower.[35]

Once he had sold the grain the overseas exporter was able to draw
a bill upon the purchaser, and his uncertainty was virtually at an end,
especially when the draft was endorsed by a reputable acceptance

house. The grain, however, had still to cross the seas to reach the
growing body of millers on this side of the water, who at this period
were tending to cluster at the chief ports of entry following the introduction of steam-powered mills and the substitution of imported grain
in place of the local produce previously milled. As purchasers of grain
from considerable distances, these substantial millers sought the
protection afforded by the development of futures trading at Liverpool
for, even with the improvements in transport, wheat stocks in the U.S.A.
still took from seven to ten days to reach Liverpool. Other supplies
took longer to arrive, for while grain from Russia was afloat for between
twenty and thirty days, supplies from India were a thirty day voyage
distant from London, and shipments from California were still a four
or five months journey away.[36]

4. *Futures Trading in Grain*
Because they were stock-holders of grain the millers and the importing houses were usually heavy sellers of futures. Moreover, the hazards
of falling prices were aggravated, especially for the former group, by
the increase in the consumption of baker's bread by the public. This
put a premium on certain types of produce, such as the white flour
made from Californian grain, and the hard winter and spring wheats
of the prairies (which absorbed more water, and so made a larger
loaf). Once it grew accustomed to the loaf made from a particular
blend of flour the public demanded a consistent product. It was a
problem which could only be met by storage somewhere along the
line between the grower and the baker for, as John Hubback has
pointed out, grains from different origins arrived at different times of
the year.[37] For those who owned grain still en route, or who stocked
flour until it was required, the short hedge proved a most useful means
by which to insure against a decline in values. Not all, however, were
so situated: like his counterpart in Minneapolis and elsewhere, the
English miller frequently found himself committed to supply flour, but
temporarily unable to purchase his exact requirements of grain.
Under these circumstances an increase in prices in the interim could
spell catastrophe for him, so the obvious solution to this risk was to
become a buyer of future arrivals contracts.

In spite of their vulnerability to price changes, many English
traders had always been chary of using the facilities in Chicago following upon tales of the abuse of that market by would-be manipulators.
The establishment of comparable facilities at Liverpool thus followed
as a natural consequence of the growth of imported grain there. The
records of the Liverpool Corn Trade Association show that the first
future delivery contract was drawn up and adopted in November 1883.
The exact form of the contract is not known, but during the early days
of the market, the quoted prices of futures were for 'No. 1 Californian',

'No. 1 Bombay', 'No. 1 Delhi', and 'Kurrachee Red' wheats. According to the official account of the Liverpool Corn Trade Association, the probability is that during the early years buyers and sellers of futures contracts agreed on the type of wheat to be delivered when delivery was called for,[38] but C. W. Smith declared quite unequivocally in 1894 that he had never seen delivery demanded or the seller give delivery on any option contract at all.[39]

The first contract of the type with which present market operators would feel familiar was the 'No. 1 Californian', agreed upon by the Liverpool Association in 1886. As we have already seen, Californian wheat was in great demand at this time, while its comparatively uniform quality made it a suitable vehicle for futures trading, which relied upon widely acknowledged grades to enable traders to deal in promises to deliver merely upon the description of the grade. This contract served the market very well for some years;[40] there was always a premium on the forward positions which enabled wheat to be carried in store and hedged with a good return on the capital invested. Large stocks were therefore kept in Liverpool warehouses—a fortunate practice for investors in warehouse accommodation. With the development of overside delivery of bulk grain by the Liverpool Grain Storage and Transit Company, the waterside millers realized that they too could reap the resulting economies. They therefore increased the practice of buying on a c.i.f. basis, taking delivery into their own barges direct from the ship, the only buyers of grain ex quay or ex store thereafter being those who failed to buy it overside. The demand for grain storage capacity to satisfy the spot market thus fell off, but the establishment of the futures contract in No. 1 Californian, the year after the No. 1 Granary was built at Alexandra Dock, meant that this capacity was used thereafter as a store for grades tenderable against futures contracts. The Liverpool futures contract, which came to be used extensively only after 1889,[41] according to some observers at least, helped to stabilize prices for both farmers and consumers. At an earlier period shipments of grain between exporting and importing countries were determined by the size of the harvests with little reference to price changes. By the end of the century, with the growth of elevator storage capacity (notably in the Atlantic ports) and the development of futures trading, surpluses could be carried over to a much greater degree when prices were low and reduced again when prices rose. By this means futures facilities helped to safeguard the stockholder and the 'short' seller against price fluctuations. The former could henceforward withhold supplies on poor markets while the latter lost the urgency to buy on rising markets, provided that he had bought futures. In relation to the size of their business, therefore, the miller, the importer and other traders did not in principle need to employ the 'great capitals' which an eighteenth-century writer had considered to be so highly necessary for prosperity in the corn trade.[42] Moreover, the trader's ability to hedge his purchases or short sales and so to take a cooler view of price fluctuations undoubtedly played its part in reducing the magnitude of price movements. Henceforward, buyers could afford to delay purchasing when prices hardened while sellers could, equally, withhold supplies from the market when prices were falling. The effect of these reactions to market price changes under normal circumstances would, therefore, be to convert what, in the absence of futures trading, would have been major swings in price to more frequent minor oscillations.

Despite these arguments some observers, such as C. W. Smith, held the view that the introduction of futures trading had spelt the ruin of the grain trade. During the early days of these market operations there were undeniable abuses, notoriously in the Chicago grain trade, where many sharp practices had developed following the uncertainties created by the Civil War. Regulations were drawn up by the Chicago Board of Trade as early as 1865 in an attempt to curb excesses, but many fraudulent practices continued. One of the commonest features of the time consisted of attempts to corner the market: following B. P. Hutchinson's corner of 1867,[43] a further seven attempts were reported on the Chicago market alone in 1868, and it was only after one of these had squeezed the president of the Board of Trade himself that the Board resolved that such actions were 'essentially improper and fraudulent'.[44] In spite of official condemnation, several other well-known attempts to achieve corners were made in subsequent years: that of Pardridge on the Chicago market in the season 1891-92 was notable, while that of the young Joseph Leiter in 1898 turned out to be one of the most spectacular ever attempted. The former's activities provided a good example of bear speculation, for his operations were concentrated on the short side of the market, selling wheat for future delivery in the belief that prices were about to fall. As it happened, Pardridge was right and the leading statistical authorities wrong; he thus profited as the result of playing his hunch rather than by manipulating the market. Had harvests not been abundant, his forward sales would have succeeded in depressing the price only temporarily, for any shortage of the actual produce would inevitably have driven the price up, leaving him to pay the penalty of having to cover at higher prices than those for which he had sold promises to deliver. The Pardridge episode depended for its success essentially upon the correctness of anticipations and in this it was closely similar to many other operations in both the grain and other trades. (Sulley's corner of 1903-04, which depended upon the assumption that the cotton crop was going to be a short one, provides a further famous example of this kind of speculation.) In earlier days, however, those who sought to make quick fortunes from price fluctuations were not above positive acts of deception. Thus it was widely suspected, after the Atlantic cable had been laid in 1866, that Chicago speculators were operating hand in glove with Liverpool brokers to reduce prices.[45] The bribing of cable operators to disclose information also proved a problem until coded messages were allowed and standards of conduct improved. However, the American farmers reserved their deepest resentment for the Chicago warehousemen. The latter apparently discovered that it was possible for them to issue fraudulent 'receipts' and afterwards to spread rumours that grain in their bins was spoiling. These 'hot corn' reports always lowered prices, as the more nervous disposed of their 'receipts', which the warehousemen then proceeded to buy back at bargain prices.[46] However, even these practices were not nearly as scandalous as the suggestion, proposed in secret by the Russian Government to the United States in November 1896,[47] that the two countries might collaborate to corner the world's surplus wheat in order to double its price. To their credit the Americans refused to have anything to do with this.

Though the 'corners' of the last four decades of the nineteenth century were the market excesses which attracted most attention, there were also many lesser manipulations which were typical of the abuses with which those who attempted to run the speculative markets of the day had to contend. 'Wash sales', for example, were a frequent feature of the times. They consisted of fictitious transactions made on the floor of the exchange at artificially high prices in order to delude others into the belief that some genuine reason must underlie this hardening of prices. Closely allied to this was the technique of 'matched orders', so called when speculators attempted to manipulate the market by giving orders to different brokers—some to sell, and others to buy— giving price limits in each instance. This activated the market and, when the operation was successful, the official market price settled at the level determined by the manipulator. Normally, the chances of success were greater, the greater the volume of transactions inspired by speculators, but even so there were considerable risks involved. Not the least of these was that the buying brokers, acting innocently and in good faith, sometimes bought from producers' agents (who then frequently appeared on the market with large supplies in response to the enhanced price) rather than from the selling brokers instructed by the speculator.

Nor did the commodity markets, in common with share markets, fail to provide their quotas of 'bucket-shop' speculators, though these were more common in the U.S.A. than here. The 'bucket shops' were mere gambling establishments where bets were placed, in effect, on the future course of prices of some commodity. Unlike transactions in the futures markets themselves, however, the consensus of bucket shop opinion could exercise no conceivable effect upon the actual price of the commodity; that is, the official price of the day published by the exchange concerned. Though they exerted no market influence as such, the operators of the bucket-shops were open to the temptation—to which many succumbed—of selling short in order to depress prices, for the run of their clients, it appears, were incorrigible optimists and almost always chose to wager upon a rise in prices.

Commodity prices have been the subject of considerable agitation from time to time, usually led by producers during periods of low prices, which has resulted in a substantial body of legislation in various parts of the world. This was usually directed against futures trading, and in the U.S.A., for example, it culminated with federal legislation in the form of the Capper-Tincher Act of 1921 affecting the grain trade. The Act imposed the very considerable tax of 20 cents a bushel upon privilege bargains concluded anywhere in the U.S.A., together with a similar tax on futures trading except for hedging transactions. However, it was the German legislation which went furthest by banning futures transactions entirely from the Berlin Exchange from the beginning of 1897. This had the effect of transferring the business of German traders to other continental markets such as Amsterdam, but the grain business came mainly to Liverpool.

Meanwhile, the market organizations themselves also acted to prevent abuses and to increase the security of transactions. The Liverpool Corn Trade Association established clearing-house facilities for futures trading in 1893, so that henceforward not only did all such contracts have to be registered with the Association, but initial deposits and subsequent margins became payable by each party to a transaction. The Association's clearing house also handled tenders of produce whenever sellers opted—as they always have a right to do on futures markets—to deliver actual produce in discharge of contract obligations.[48] In addition to the clearing house, the Association also operated a subsidiary called the Liverpool Grain Contract Insurance Company, the revenues of which were provided by an allocation of 1s. from the 3s. registration fee for futures contracts. By this means the organization was able to provide £100 cover against default by a partner to a contract. This, especially in view of the original deposit and daily margins payable according to the direction of price changes, sufficed to provide ample security for the Association's members.

In the meantime the increase in grain imports had given rise to considerable development in many other outports apart from Liverpool. Glasgow's Corn Exchange dates from 1841, and is the successor to the one which formerly stood on the same site. The Exchange was originally run by a Corn Exchange Company, as was the case in Liverpool, and a Glasgow Corn Trade Association was founded in 1855. The present limited company dates only from 1935. In Hull the Corn Trade Association was founded in 1888, the first meeting taking place in the offices of Keighley Maxted and Company. Bristol followed a year after Hull with its Corn Trade Association, which was eventually incorporated in 1920.

In London, the grain markets were served in all essential particulars by the same sort of arrangements which we have traced for Liverpool. A Corn Trade Association was formed in 1878 and incorporated as a company in 1886, but the existence of the Baltic Exchange meant that the Association had to remain a separate entity from the Exchange. London's first efforts to establish a futures contract in 1887 were a failure because the Association attempted to cover several standards of wheat, and no one contract flourished. Contemporary evidence, too, suggests a certain prejudice among many in the trade against such dealings; according to W. E. Baer, for example, it was 'considered somewhat "shady" to belong to the comparatively small clique in London who have adopted the American fashion of dealing in grain'.[49] The records of the Bristol branch of the Bank of England also provide clear evidence that the trading community there, too, were both baffled and repelled by the new-fangled 'gambling system of dealing in options'.[50]

A further interesting difference between Liverpool and London practices in the early days of futures markets was that the clearing-house facilities, which were always under the aegis of the Liverpool Corn Trade Association in Liverpool, were initially supplied in London by the London Produce Clearing House (established in 1888). The volume of futures business cleared by the London Produce Clearing House is shown on the accompanying table (Table 6.3). Eventually, the London Corn Trade Association took over the task of clearing futures contracts itself, under the aegis of the Council of the London Grain Futures Association Ltd. The London Grain Futures Association Ltd was established as a separate organization from the London Corn Trade Association, although all its members were also members of the latter organization. Arrangements safeguarding the financial interests of members engaged in futures transactions were made in London along the same lines as those at Liverpool.

Transactions in futures contracts on both the Baltic and the Liverpool Corn Exchange were limited to members of the Associations concerned. Whereas on the Liverpool market membership of the Association also implied membership of the Exchange (due to the amalgamation of the two entities), on the London market members of the Association had also to be members of the Baltic. There was no real difficulty about the last named provided that the prospective member could surmount the initial discouragement of a 50 guinea entrance fee and the prospect of an annual subscription of 20 guineas. In spite of this financial hurdle there were more than 3,000 members on roll by the outbreak of war in 1914. (It was little wonder, therefore, that the Baltic nurtured rugby, hockey, golf, lawn tennis, cricket and yachting clubs, to say nothing of the existence of a flourishing Welsh society.)

TABLE 6.3

FUTURES TRANSACTIONS IN WHEAT AND MAIZE
1889–1904

Year	Wheat	Transactions	Maize	
1889	55,000	Quarters	3,000	Quarters
1890	441,000	,,	260,000	,,
1891	49,000	,,	11,000	,,
1892	44,500	Tons		
1893	2,500	,,		
1894				
1895				
1896				
1897	4,627,200	Centals a	201,600	Centals b
1898	38,956,800	,,	4,915,200	,,
1899	42,576,000	,,	9,686,400	,,
1900	54,019,200	,,	17,947,200	,,
1901	47,035,200	,,	13,372,800	,,
1902	26,750,400	,,	3,859,200	,,
1903	13,363,200	,,	422,400	,,
1904	6,072,000	,,	11,000	Quarters

a. Centals since 11 October 1897.
b. Centals since 25 November 1897.
Source: Figures supplied by the London Produce Clearing House Ltd.

The limitation of acceptable transactions to members of the Associations concerned obviously implied that non-members had to conduct their business through those who were members. A significant proportion of the membership of the principal corn trade associations consisted, therefore, of brokers. As opposed to corresponding members on the London Stock Exchange, however, brokers on grain markets were of more than one variety. They could, in the first place, be engaged purely in broking activities (i.e. as agents) between shippers, on the one hand, and millers or grain merchants and speculators on the other. In this capacity the broker frequently acted as the connecting link between shippers and clients in the smaller grain ports and (in former years especially) on the continent. Brokerage charges varied according to the expenses involved in a particular transaction or with the degree of risk assumed: the broker often guaranteed the solvency of his principal and, therefore, received an extra *del credere* commission. The broker on the grain markets, however, was by no means always a pure broker. Frequently he was also a jobber or a speculator as well for, as on the cotton market, the differentiation of function never proceeded to the lengths which it did on the London Stock Exchange. In the latter the jobbers constitute the market in a particular security while on the grain exchanges the nature and origin of the produce resulted in the evolution of another different organization. The larger merchants or importers of grain customarily brought it into the ports in cargoes or large 'parcels', whereas the many small buyers who existed before the First World War required it in smaller lots. The merchant, therefore, performed this vital function of selling the grain to these smaller traders in 'split parcels', very often upon credit terms. These grain importers served, therefore, as stock holders, selling to their clients very frequently on 'ex-ship' terms; that is, terms reckoned to include all costs up to the point at which the grain had been worked out of the ship, payment being due one month after the arrival of the vessel. The alternative consisted of sales 'ex-store'; that is from the warehouse, the terms on the Baltic being a fortnight's free rent and one month's credit. Larger quantities, especially in Liverpool, were sold for cash upon receipt of transfer orders, delivery orders, or warehouse warrants.[51]

Evidently, therefore, the grain importing merchant relied basically upon his turnover for his livelihood, and sold his produce in much the same way as the stock jobber, whether prices were softening or hardening. For this purpose he ran a book, the balance of which would show him to be short or long of produce at any particular time.[52] This balance obviously expressed the merchant's view of the market, and the more progressive of them used the futures market in order to safeguard themselves. The corn broker, too, in his dual capacity as jobber frequently required a hedge for his position on the market, to say nothing of the miller and other lesser interests.

Futures transactions were handled by brokers other than the intermediaries who bought and sold actual produce for clients. According to C. W. Smith, in his evidence of 1894,[53] it was the crisis of 1878 and the establishment of the clearing-house systems which gave birth to the rule on the exchanges that brokers had to put their own names upon futures contracts, thus making themselves liable as their own principals, and ensuring under the settlement system that every contract was compulsorily 'strung out' (i.e. that it featured in the off-setting process in the clearing).

5.   Contracts, Standards and New Supply Sources

Of all the tasks undertaken by the Corn Trade Associations in Liverpool and London, none was more vital to the success of hedging facilities than that of ensuring the most appropriate terms for the futures contract itself. Since 1886 the No. 1 Californian had replaced all others on the Liverpool market, though a primitive form of futures on 'Shipment-and-Delivery' terms in Indian wheat continued for some time afterwards. By 1894 interest in the No. 1 Californian had fallen away due to the declining yields of the Californian wheat fields and the growth of large shipments of wheat from Argentina. These shipments were largely attributable to the reduction in transport costs and to a depreciating currency.

The growing shipments from the Argentine into Liverpool naturally led to a demand for a futures contract in River Plate wheat while, by the end of the century, the No. 1 Californian was widely felt to be too narrow in coverage to constitute a satisfactory medium either for hedging or speculation. At this time the Liverpool Association rules forbade the tender of wheat, which was more than one halfpenny a cental inferior to the standard, in fulfilment of the contract. Moreover, the standard of the grade was changed from time to time, and not infrequently there was insufficient tenderable wheat in store with which to trade when deliveries against futures were required. The dissatisfaction with the No. 1 Californian eventually led to the first graded wheat futures contract in 1903. This established four grades in descending order of value from Grade A at the contract price, each subsequent grade being at so many pence less to the buyer. The grades included U.S., Canadian, and Argentinian wheats, but no Indian or Russian. When, some years afterwards, he aired the problems faced by the grading committee, John Hubback, the vice-president of the Liverpool Association at the time, emphasized that this omission was due to the very dusty state in which Indian and Russian wheat arrived. Home-grown wheat, on the other hand, he considered to be too damp usually to be suitable for warehousing, and seldom obtainable except in comparatively small lots at one time.[54]

The 1903 contract was remarkable for its high quality basis, the contract price itself being reserved for the very finest grades (Grade A). Unfortunately it transgressed against one of the cardinal requirements of a good futures contract: that is, an adequate supply of the wheat of contract price. In practice, deliveries were mostly of lower grade wheats, and these in turn were often of borderline quality within their particular grades as the result of the establishment of a system of 'fixed differences' between grades, determined by a committee of the Association.[55] The result was a further revision of the contract in 1906 which lowered the basis grade to about the average of the wheats which had been delivered under the previous contract, while 'commercial differences' replaced the previous system of 'fixed differences'.

The new contract threw more responsibility upon the grading committee who became responsible for classifying all the wheat accepted for tender. This involved ascertaining that the weight of the produce fell within the limits of tolerance, that it was free from admixture, in good condition, and free from any defect which would render it unsuitable for milling in the usual way. All produce for grading was placed in a sealed container and presented to the Committee anonymously, though the interested parties had the right of appeal to an arbitration panel. The responsibility for organizing both grading and arbitration groups rested with the Corn Trade Associations at the ports of import. Even in London, however, no system of arbitration existed at mid-century, except for the South Russia and Danube trades.[56] Its further development was strongly resisted by shippers, who customarily received their money in exchange for documents and were in the advantageous position of having been paid by the time the buyer discovered any defects. Nevertheless, a committee of arbitrators was formed in 1870 consisting of both buyers and sellers. The *modus operandi* after 1886 was for the Arbitration Appeal Committee to appoint a panel of two arbitrators, one nominated by each party to the dispute, together with an umpire should one be needed. The decision was then made by majority vote, with the right of appeal to the committee itself. Similar arrangements were made by the Liverpool and other associations.

One very important task entrusted to the grading committee of the Liverpool Corn Trade Association was to certify that the wheat tendered against futures contracts was of 'Liverpool grade'. There was an overlap of function, therefore, when North American supplies began to arrive under the formula 'trading certificate of inspection to be final as to quality'. Unlike sales in which the quality was specified as being 'about as per sample', or else 'of fair average quality of the season's shipments at time and place of shipment' (often abbreviated to f.a.q.), the American trading certificate brooked no question. Since disputes concerning the grade of produce actually shipped naturally affected not only tenders against the small proportion of futures contracts which matured in actual deliveries, but also the entire market in physical supplies, the difficulty involved in the demand that American loading certificates be accepted without question became at one time a very serious matter indeed. As far as the U.K. grain markets were concerned, the other methods of specifying quality worked much more smoothly, not least because the stated grade was open to challenge. As implied in their descriptions, sales effected 'about as per sample' are useful when producers' grading systems are rudimentary, or when sellers wish to take advantage of superior qualities. Sales of this kind are effected by the dispatch of an advance sample, sealed after examination by the importer or broker and held for comparison with the shipment itself. Sometimes, too, comparison is made against an earlier standard sample held by the Association. Sales by such methods, unfortunately, do not facilitate rapid transactions, and in many cases they have been replaced by f.a.q. dealings. The standard is ascertained by means of samples, taken from the bulk, of all shipments of the particular grade made during the month in question. The mixture of these samples then constitutes the standard with which corn trade association arbitration panels can compare any parcel of produce in dispute.

The attitude of the Liverpool Corn Trade Association to the North American loading certificates passed through various stages from initial embarrassment to eventual irritation. This was particularly true in relation to the large shipments of maize which came via Montreal because these were often alleged to be short of the stated out-turn (i.e. weight upon discharge), and to be of inferior quality. Ultimately, however, and in spite of the notorious independence of many elevator companies, the complaints of important customers at Liverpool proved of some avail in some quarters. Partly as the result of strong representations made by the Liverpool Association to a Canadian Royal Commission appointed to report on inspections and delivered weights of grain, the Canada Grain Act of 1912 transferred grading and inspection to government officials, and it became thereafter very strict indeed.[57]

Reprehensible practices were not entirely confined to the Western Hemisphere, however, for American shippers complained bitterly that the grading committees in grain-importing countries were inevitably buyer-orientated. They alleged, furthermore, that many buyers made a practice of buying 'off grades' at a little lower price than the standard grades and, at the same time, declined to insure against deterioration on voyage. This question of the deterioration of produce while afloat has always been a matter of considerable importance in the grain trade for, even with insurance cover, part of any damage due to heating remains uncovered because of the impossibility of ascertaining whether the produce was shipped in good condition. For this reason importers persuaded many exporters (for example, in Argentina, Russia and the Danube basin) to guarantee its condition upon arrival. Because such a guarantee was first made in respect of shipments of rye from Russia, contracts which guarantee the condition of the grain upon arrival are known as 'rye terms' contracts. The buyers' demands were resisted by exporters in the U.S.A., Canada and Australia, whose contracts are, therefore, on what is known as 'tale quale' terms; that is, shipped in good condition but the buyer to accept the produce such as it is upon arrival.

In the meantime new centres of importance had emerged in the grain trade. With the partial resolution of its rust and other problems, the Canadian crop had grown enormously as cultivation was pushed westwards, and the Winnipeg Grain and Provision Exchange developed into a primary market of world importance by the beginning of the twentieth century, after having first opened its doors in 1887.[58] Its futures market eventually became much more important than those of the American exporting ports, such as New York, Baltimore and Tacoma. By this time these futures markets, together with those at Minneapolis, Duluth, St. Louis and Toledo, were becoming important on a national rather than on a world scale. Even in Chicago itself the decline in the relative importance of American grain supplies for Europe, combined with the designation of a relatively limited number of storehouses to which produce was exclusively deliverable in fulfilment of futures contracts, led to a diminution in its European business.

In 1897, with the introduction of a single contract based on Northern

Spring No. 1 wheat, and No. 1 Northern Manitoba as an alternative, the London Corn Trade Association was at last beginning to foster futures trading. Its flowering, however, was short-lived, for the rust epidemic of 1904-5 more or less killed off the market, which dried up for the lack of contract wheat.[59] Other futures markets nevertheless continued to flourish and, in 1908, with the help of John Hubback of Liverpool, a futures market was established at Buenos Aires, primarily to provide price insurance for large growers and exporters. However, as Hubback has pointed out, its function of price registration enabled all growers to benefit by being able to ascertain the state of the market, instead of having to rely upon itinerant agents for such information.[60]

Notwithstanding the existence of so many grain exchanges in the primary markets and ports of the Western Hemisphere, Liverpool was of considerable importance in the international grain trade during the decades before World War I. It had become, together with Minneapolis, the greatest milling centre in the world, its total import of wheat in 1913 being $5\frac{3}{4}$ million quarters out of a total for the U.K. of $24\frac{3}{4}$ million, while maize imports amounted to $2\frac{1}{2}$ million quarters out of a U.K. total of $11\frac{1}{2}$ million. By this time the role of principal exporter of maize and linseed had passed from both Russia and the United States to Argentina; and Liverpool firms enjoyed an unrivalled ascendancy in Buenos Aires and Rosario. Both maize and wheat were re-exported in quantity from Liverpool to Ireland, in addition to being sold direct by Liverpool firms in South America to Irish and continental customers. The futures market at Liverpool, moreover, became a much more effective instrument for hedging. For the trader anxious to shift price risks from his shoulders to those ready to bear them, therefore, Liverpool's facilities were probably second to none, despite the fact that the volume of speculation was always a good deal higher in Chicago.[61] On the Liverpool exchange, should a local merchant wish to make delivery, the futures contract provided him with a wide range of choice for doing so, with the use of premiums and discounts adjusted to the tender by the grading committee. The Liverpool market was, therefore, probably the most flexible in the world at this time, and though the relatively low volume of speculative transactions made the market vulnerable to any concentration of hedging or manipulation, it succeeded in avoiding such hazards remarkably well. Nevertheless, the Liverpool futures market had not grown to full maturity by the decade before the war in 1914, for the large grain importers were still too conventional to use hedging facilities automatically. Because they drew from six major supply sources, concerning which they were equipped with first class intelligence,[62] they sought to play the sellers against one another. They secured the best terms for the charter of ships and, as far as possible, avoided the carrying of stocks in storage. Many merchants consequently found themselves in a position to buy and sell for cash, relying upon their experience to outguess the market seven times out of twelve. 'It was traditional that the cheapest wheats in the world were secured by British merchants; and while these wheats were often sold to continental countries on price bulges, so much remained in the United Kingdom that they enjoyed the cheapest bread in the world.'[63]

This statement would appear to contradict the argument that grain (or any other produce) will only be exported when it is at 'export price parity', or what is sometimes known as an 'export basis'; that is, when the price at the importing port is sufficiently greater than the price in the primary market to cover the cost of the freight, handling, interest and insurance involved. While this is generally characteristic of all highly organized markets in primary produce, it is, nevertheless, also true that it is usually possible to purchase on central markets, such as Liverpool, parcels of produce at prices lower than the prices of the day in the countries of origin, adjusted to the c.i.f. basis. This was at one time closely investigated by the Royal Commission on Food Prices in 1925, but the reasons for it, though various, are clear enough. Thus a miller or grain merchant may have imported more than he finds he can sell, or a foreign exporter may find himself in the same position, and may, therefore, offer part of his produce at cut prices. Again, there are differences in the cost of delivery 'overside', as compared with delivery into storage, to be considered: 'parcels' of produce are often sold, too, when a speculator in the cash market tires of holding them. It must be remembered, also, that arbitrage dealing and forward selling can have repercussions in the cash market, and that sometimes the futures contract price may drop below the parity of c.i.f. cost, when hedging could make it possible for a merchant to sell parcels of grain at a lower spot price.

6. The Baltic Mercantile and Shipping Exchange Co. Ltd.

One further undoubted advantage enjoyed by British grain importers was the amalgamation of the Baltic Exchange and the London Shipping Exchange at the turn of the century. The latter had decided to purchase a site at about the same time that the Baltic Committee's lease of South Sea House from the Baltic Company expired. A syndicate from both Exchanges eventually purchased Jeffrey Square and some adjoining properties in St Mary Axe, and an Exchange (the present building) was erected and opened in 1903. Here imported grain changes hands side by side with the charter of vessels for whole or part cargoes. The market in shipping is unique and serves the largest c.i.f. grain market in Europe, for a considerable proportion of the wheat discharged at Liverpool and elsewhere might be purchased initially not on the Baltic itself these days, but as the result of transactions between traders who are members of the Baltic Exchange. The chartering operations mainly concern tramp ships[64] and the freight market on the Baltic is, of course, for all kinds of commodities in addition to grain, such as coal, iron ore, lumber, sugar, sulphur and many others besides. The business is very much an international one, for generally speaking, the ships of all nations are available for charter by merchants of their own or any other nation. This results in a market in which some thousands of deep-sea tramp ships are always available for employment from merchants and shippers all over the world. By this time the freight market has attracted some hundreds of people who are actively engaged in the business. Chartering agents represent charterers, that is, the merchants or others who charter ships. Other agents are known as owners' brokers, for these represent the shipowners. Many firms number both charterers and shipowners among their clients, though many of the principals on both sides of the market employ their own staff rather than broking firms.

In addition to this freight market, a small number of firms—probably under a dozen—are chiefly engaged in the purchase and sale of ships, though there are some twenty firms of chartering brokers who maintain a department for this activity. The success of this market depends upon the constant flow of information from all over the world so that upon enquiry it is possible to find out without more than a few minutes delay which ships—be they in New York or Singapore—are being offered for sale, or which shipowners are in the market for ships. Sales are by negotiation and conditions of sale vary in each case. Successful negotiations result in a Memorandum of Agreement which is different for each transaction and therefore unlike the printed forms of charter parties. It is estimated that probably some 50 per cent of the world sale and purchase business still passes through firms represented on the Baltic.

There is now a well established air-freight market on the Baltic. It is claimed that the original air charter party was signed in February 1928 to cover a two-way flight of cargo between Croydon and Cologne. However, it was not until twenty years later that an Air Freight Advisory Committee of the Baltic Exchange was set up, to be superseded in the following year, 1949, by the present Airbrokers Association. There are now some 100 aircraft operating companies from all parts of the world, both national and independent, represented on the Exchange. The documentary committee of the Association has produced standard forms of charter parties which have regularized operations in air freight and set the pattern for much of the world's air freight transactions. The market is made up of charterers' agents and owners' brokers, with many brokers acting in both capacities. In the early days of the air market, the main cargoes were perishable items such as fruit, flowers, fish and cheese. This trade continues, but air charter is now increasingly used for passenger transport. Shipping companies frequently use the market for the exchange of ships' crews; it is also used extensively these days to fly out machinery replacements, especially for ships and other aircraft, to eliminate expensive delays. Many commodities, such as New Zealand scoured wool, are now sold on the basis of a sample flown to London in advance of the bulk, while other commodities such as furs are frequently sent for auction by this mode of transport.

Shipping thus represents the major activity on the Baltic with, in recent years, the chartering of aircraft cargo space. Transactions in commodities are now comparatively insignificant, but, of those which remain, grain is by far the most important. Tallow sales, for example, are not what they were, even though William Price's name proudly survives. Transactions in oil and oilseeds are more important, for every kind of oil-producing seed, and the equivalent oil and oilcake, is dealt in by members. These include soya, sunflower, linseed, groundnuts, castor seed, cotton seed, palm kernels and copra. All the principal shippers, crushers and brokers are members of the Baltic, and there are three trade associations to which all members of these trades belong. They are the Incorporated Oil-Seed Association, the London Oil and Tallow Trades Association and the London Cattle Food Trade Association. These Associations issue contract forms, and have their own machinery for arbitration in cases of dispute.

The oil trade has changed considerably as producing countries have established their own crushing mills of recent years. Imports therefore tend to be of oil and cake these days, though the seed trade is still far from finished as yet. The importance of the oil and oilseeds trade resulted in the establishment of a futures market in these commodities on the Baltic before World War II. Ring trading was not re-established on the Baltic after the war, but more recently, in 1967, a London Vegetable Oil Terminal Market Association was established which has now opened markets on the London Commodity Exchange in Plantation House, Mincing Lane, in soya-bean oil, sunflower oil, and coconut oil. A fuller account of these markets is given in Chapter 15.

The Baltic Mercantile and Shipping Exchange, to give it its full title, has a most impressive Exchange floor of over 20,000 sq. feet, decorated in 'free Renaissance style' with marble columns and walls. The scene on the floor of the Exchange at the height of activity (which at present occurs during mid-morning and late afternoon) has the appearance of utter chaos as shipping space is married to whole or part cargoes. No attempt is made to use the marble pillars on the floor of the Exchange as sites for markets in cargo space for particular destinations, though the members of the trade know that particular chartering agents are associated with the various geographical sub-sections of the freight market, much in the same way as jobbers on the Stock Exchange are known to deal in various groups of securities.

Members of the air freight market tend to congregate down one side of the Exchange floor.

In the midst of the planned chaos of the Baltic Exchange floor stands a rostrum, from which a waiter is able to announce members' names for the transmission of messages. The Baltic is, of course, equipped with a large battery of telephones, and members are constantly called to them, as instructions come through from their offices or from their principal clients. In addition, the Exchange has the usual teleprinter facilities which bring news from the ends of the earth to members with negligible delay. At the far end of the floor of the Baltic stands the 'ring' around which the brokers now trade in grain futures (and of which some account will be given in the next chapter). The market is called over with the ringing of a bell at 1 o'clock, when the market prices are marked up on the adjoining blackboard. These are the prices which are then taken by the press, and telegraphed to all the world's important markets.

A similar futures ring existed in the former Liverpool Corn Exchange. The old building was destroyed in an air-raid in 1941 and has now been replaced by a multi-storey block. A new 'ring' appears in the present exchange surrounded by the usual amenities of telephone booths, notice-boards, and so on, even though there is no futures trading in wheat in Liverpool these days.

There never was a futures ring at the third of Britain's famous corn exchanges, the 'Pacific' in Hull, though the possibility of establishing one was seriously considered during the 1920s. This Exchange was opened in 1901 in response to the needs of the oil-seed trade as much as to those of the grain trade, for Hull had become by that time the largest oil-seed milling centre in the country. The premises house the offices of the Hull Corn Trade Association Ltd, and the membership includes shipping, legal, accounting and insurance interests. The atmosphere is considerably more informal than at the other exchanges, and a glimpse may even be caught of a sample or two of grain on occasion whereas, on the Baltic, the same sight would be as improbable as hearing anyone shout to try out the echo in the Reading Room at the British Museum.

Chapter Seven

THE GRAIN MARKETS SINCE 1914

1. *Wartime Control and its Aftermath*

WITH the declaration of war the Liverpool Corn Trade Association decided that futures trading would serve no useful purpose under conditions of such uncertain delivery, and discontinued the market on 5 August 1914. In spite of the hostilities, however, grain supply problems did not become serious for the United Kingdom until 1916, when the intensification of submarine warfare and the closure of the Dardanelles in March 1915 denied to this country the benefit of Russian and Rumanian cereals. It was not until October 1916 that the government took over the control of ocean freight and created the Royal Commission on Wheat Supplies, extended by April 1917 to cover all cereals and cereal products, pulses and their substitutes. The Royal Warrant required the Commission to enquire into the supply of this produce; to purchase, sell and control the delivery of wheat and flour, and generally to take such steps as were deemed desirable to maintain the supply. After November 1916, with the creation of the Allied Wheat Executive, the Wheat Commission co-operated with France and Italy in the deployment of the tonnage available for the purchase and transport of cereals. The Allied Wheat Executive made enormous purchases of grain and flour, most of it from North America.[1] Little wonder, therefore, that there was considerable talk in the U.S.A. towards the end of the war of producers and merchants being 'entirely at the mercy of the foreign combination'.[2] From 1 September 1917, however, the American Administration stabilized the price of wheat at 217 cents a bushel.

The Royal Commission on Wheat Supplies took over from the normal channels of the grain trade by establishing agencies in the main producing countries, such as the Wheat Export Co. Ltd in Canada. Erstwhile wheat importers were employed as distributing agents, the amounts directed through individual businesses being calculated according to their previous turnovers. Sales of wheat on a c.i.f. basis while still afloat continued to be made but the flour purchased by the Commission was landed and allocated to the distributors, who sold to flour factors dealing directly with bakers. Importers were banded together into 'Landed Grain Committees', which, together with a 'Contracts Branch' of the Commission, were responsible for assuring supplies and co-ordinating their distribution. Under the direction of the Commission, these firms ceased to carry stocks and concentrated upon the essential though subordinate role of superintending the passage of cereals from shipboard to the consumer.

After the war decontrol was achieved relatively rapidly. The Commission first switched its purchases away from its overseas agencies, buying directly instead from private importers. Flat rate selling prices for grains of different qualities were next abandoned and then, with the trade channelled more or less in its pre-war grooves, the Commission was able to abandon its control altogether. For wheat the process was spread over five four-weekly periods, during which the stocks held by the Commission were progressively reduced, and the trade took over increasing responsibility for supplies. Final decontrol was accomplished by August 1921. The Liverpool futures market had reopened in the April of that year, when the average monthly price for spot wheat was 18s. 1d. a cental. This compared with a representative pre-war price of 7s. 3d. a cental, and 15s. 1d. when the Royal Commission took over in 1916. In 1920 prices rose at one time to 24s. 7d. a cental; that is, to more than 80s. per imperial quarter, while barley at 89s. 5d. a quarter was even more expensive. The price of maize exhibited a similar pattern. In Liverpool the peak price for this produce was 19s. 7d. a cental, attained in 1918. It had fallen to 11s. 8d. by 1921, a figure still considerably above the pre-war price of between 4s. 9d. and 5s. 8d.

In spite of these vast price increases, the grain trade appeared in 1921 to be set fair for the resumption of a prosperous period of competitive freedom. The aftermath of war was not without its repercussions in the grain trade in the 1920s, however, while the 1930s were destined to witness greater interferences with the operation of grain, as well as of other markets, than had been the case since the repeal of the Corn Laws. This movement culminated in a second complete take-over of the trade with the coming of war again in 1939. The principal effect of the period of control from 1916 to 1921 was to give rise subsequently to pressures which detracted from the perfection of the competitive structure of the grain market by reducing the numbers of both buyers and sellers. On the demand side, the swollen wartime capacity intensified postwar competition among the millers, and there were many mergers. Fewer small men remained to patronize the importing merchant. Among the producers, the failure of peacetime conditions to sustain the high prices attained during the war led to widespread discontent. In Canada the break in prices was associated by the farmers with the reopening of the Winnipeg Grain Exchange,[3] and even though three successive Royal Commissions[4] vindicated the free market system between the wars, voluntary wheat pools with a Central Selling Agency were organized, beginning in Alberta in 1923. At one time the Agency handled rather more than half the Prairie crops and acquired membership of the Winnipeg Exchange, though its sales were almost all made on overseas markets, especially the United Kingdom, where the Agency had established selling organizations. In Australia, too, dissatisfaction led to the formation of voluntary pools on a cooperative basis, though in Queensland compulsory marketing through a state Wheat Board was adopted.[5]

2. *Inter-war Problems*

In spite of this tendency for the structure of the trade to change somewhat, central markets were not radically transformed by these innovations during the 1920s, which was, on the whole, a prosperous decade culminating with record crops in most areas. During this time, futures markets proved their worth to traders as an aid to carrying the large stocks resulting from the bumper harvests. In 1929 the estimated sales of futures at Liverpool were 86,390,000 quarters, while imports of wheat and flour into the port for the same year were of the order of 5 million quarters. A number of reasons account for this enormous apparent disparity. Merchants and millers in other U.K. ports, for example, usually used the futures facilities of the Liverpool Corn Trade Association, though on occasion those of Chicago or Winnipeg were also utilized. Account must also be taken of purely speculative activity, though this was anything from ten to twenty times as great on the Chicago market (upon which some 80 per cent of American futures business was transacted). Finally, it must be remembered that the Liverpool market attracted business from a variety of Commonwealth and foreign countries. In Australia, for example, much of the wheat continued to be exported by a small number of shippers, often British. Shipment was frequently 'for orders', the produce not having been sold beforehand. When the entire venture was not purely speculative, it was usually hedged on the Liverpool market. Similar circumstances prevailed in the Argentinian export trade and, when hedged, the shipments were protected either in the domestic markets, or else in Liverpool.[6] The unusually high imports into Liverpool in 1929 required additional warehousing space, and an agreement was reached between the Liverpool Corn Trade Association and the Manchester Ship Canal Company whereby merchants could tender grain from the latter's Manchester warehouses and silos. Manchester was by this time, of course, a considerable grain port, its imports being greater than those of Cardiff, Glasgow or Newcastle, as the accompanying table illustrates (Table 7.1).

In 1929 a futures market was re-introduced by the London Corn Trade Association. It was a contract in a 'strong' wheat (i.e. one with a high protein content: the alternative would have been a market in 'filler' wheats), the basis being No. 3 Manitoba, with No. 1 and No. 2 tenderable at fixed premiums, and No. 4 at a fixed discount. In contrast

TABLE 7.1

LEADING PORTS OF ENTRY OF THE FOUR PRINCIPAL GRAINS INTO
THE UNITED KINGDOM (maize, wheat, barley and oats in million cwt)
(Five-year annnal averages)

	1925–29	1958–62	1968
Liverpool	31·6	27·3	20·8
Manchester	10·9	13·1	15·1
London	38·5	31·4	30·8
Hull	23·7	17·8	17·5
Bristol	16·1	20·3	16·2
Cardiff	6·0	3·4	2·7
Glasgow	6·0	9·3	10·1
Newcastle	3·6	5·3	4·2
Total Imports	158·6	166·1	156·5

Source: Annual Statement of Trade

TABLE 7.2

VALUES OF CEREAL IMPORTS FOR 1938, 1962, 1965 and 1968

£ million

Un-milled Cereals	1938	1962	1965	1968
Wheat	38·6	104·0	114·5	112·9
Barley	6·9	8·8	7·2	1·4
Oats	0·5	1·4	0·5	0·04
Maize (all sorts)	17·7	92·0	76·8	88·0
Milled Cereals				
Wheat	4·0	13·7	9·1	3·3
Other a	1·3	0·5	1·0	0·7

a. Other Milled Cereals = Oat meal, barley products and maize meal and other milled
products of maize.

1938 & 1962   *Source: Annual Statement of Trade.*
1965 & 1968   *Source: Overseas Trade Accounts.*

with that of the Liverpool Association, whose futures contract was for
wheat 'ex-store', that is, present at a nearby approved granary, the
London market was in a c.i.f. contract. This form of contract, it will be
recalled, concerns commodities which need to be transported to their
ports of destination, a form of trading which by this time predominated
over transactions in produce already warehoused. The London
contract, therefore, is best regarded as a move in conformity with the
times, while the Liverpool contract continued to bear the imprint of
the history of the trade. The London market, however, remained a
small one, achieving a turnover of 20-25 loads a day.[7] The market was
thus about the same size as the futures market at Rotterdam, the only
other one of note in Europe at the time. The annual turnover of futures
contracts on the Liverpool market during the thirties fluctuated
between about 40 million and 80 million quarters compared with
about 1000 million quarters a year handled by the Chicago market,
so Chicago was obviously the focus of interest for the international
speculator.

The new decade opened with a catastrophic break in grain prices
as well as in the prices of most other primary produce. In January 1930
wheat futures positions for near months on the Liverpool market stood
at 9s. 6¾d. a cental: a twelvemonth later the price had declined to
4s. 2d., and grain was often used as ballast. The Federal Farm Board,

established by the U.S.A. in 1929, like many other institutions and
persons, regarded the break in prices as a very temporary affair and
decided to support the market, making a loss of $180 million in the
process.[8] The Canadian Wheat Pool, too, was led into low financial
waters as the result of withholding supplies from a market which
failed to recover. Ultimately, the Canadian government felt forced to
intervene and it created a Wheat Board, though farmers' deliveries to
this body were on a voluntary basis between 1935 and 1943, after
which the open market channel was closed entirely.[9]

The break in wheat prices resulted in considerable international
consultation, from which the International Wheat Agreement eventually emerged in 1933. The Agreement[10] was notable as one of the
first to encompass both exporting and importing interests. The latter
undertook to relax import restrictions in order to encourage consumption, to hold domestic production steady, and to lower tariffs on wheat
should its price, as measured on British markets, rise above certain
levels. The exporting countries for their part agreed to restrict exports
in the hope that prices would harden sufficiently to increase their
total receipts. The U.S.S.R., however, refused to be so limited, while
the Argentine exceeded its quota, thus illustrating in classic form the
difficulties attending attempts of this nature: to the extent that such
agreements fail to embrace all exporting countries they will be less
effective, while the more effective they are, the greater the temptation
for participants to violate their agreed quotas. By 1935 the Agreement
was a dead letter, for the steps taken by consuming countries to implement it were negligible and, though the U.S.A. did make some attempt
to limit acreages by the Agricultural Adjustment Act of 1933, the
principal check to production during the middle thirties turned out to
be a series of crop failures.

As the above account indicates, the Liverpool futures market
continued to fulfil valuable economic functions throughout the 1930s
even though other markets—notably the Winnipeg Grain Exchange—
were affected for long periods by the vicissitudes of the decade. In
Britain farmers were guaranteed a fixed price on a given quantity of
wheat, paid for by means of a levy on each sack of flour, whether
milled or imported. Moreover, under the Ottawa Trade Agreements
of 1931-2, the United Kingdom government created a preference
system (which still exists) by imposing tariffs upon foreign wheat, flour,
and other cereals and products. It was a period of considerable uncertainty and, not surprisingly, in 1934 the Liverpool futures market
enjoyed its busiest period for five years. The difficulty occasioned by the
tariff was overcome for the purposes of futures trading by the introduction of a 'duty paid' contract, to supplement the one known as 'old
terms'.

In the 1930s, too, complaints were often expressed against the

American system of exporting grain 'certificate final'. From 1932 the millers decided that they would no longer purchase it upon this basis, and the impasse was only resolved when the Liverpool merchants undertook to purchase on the American terms for re-sale to the millers on sample. It was clearly a buyers' market.

3. *Wartime Controls Again*

The outbreak of war in 1939 saw the grain trade rather more prepared than it had been in 1914. The futures markets did not re-open after the declaration of war on 3 September 1939, and the State took over the responsibility for purchases of grains, flour and feeding-stuffs. The Cereal Import Division of the Ministry of Food, created at the time, used the services of grain importers for its supply, the system being for the merchants to pass on offers to the Division every day as these were received from their overseas agencies and connections. Prices of all grain and grain products were frozen at their immediate pre-war levels, but the administrative and accounting difficulties of fixing so many prices led the Ministry to ask the millers for only one price, for wheat of all grades. Flour was also reduced to a national standard at a fixed price. The grain was distributed under the supervision of Port Area Grain Committees in each of the seven ports in which a Corn Trade Association already existed (i.e. Liverpool, London, Hull, Bristol, Leith, Glasgow and Belfast). The members of the Grain Committees were drawn from grain firms and took their orders from the Cereals Control Board, the Imported Cereals Division, the Animal Feeding Stuffs Division, and the Home-Grown Cereals Division of the Ministry of Food. Among the Western Allies as a whole, grain supplies came under the surveillance of the Combined Food Board.[11] The Grain Committees also supervised the rationing schemes subsequently introduced for animal feeding-stuffs. The scarcity was due to wartime transport problems, for the Argentinian government, on the other side of the submarine-infested Atlantic, was so embarrassed by grain surpluses that it even resorted to their use as fuel in place of scarce coal and oil.

The War of 1939-45 posed the additional major problem of aerial bombardment for the Area Grain Committees. Several grain elevators were gutted in this way and, in 1941, both the Liverpool Corn Exchange and the Mark Lane Corn Exchange succumbed to the marauders. Largely because of the decline in horse-drawn vehicles on the roads, the two exchanges at Mark Lane had been amalgamated in 1929 under the title of the London Corn Exchange, which became a 'closed floor' (i.e. closed to the general public) in 1933. The Exchange was re-opened in 1953 after twelve years during which the market was conducted in the 'subscription rooms' annexed to the Exchange. Because of the amalgamation of the Exchanges the floor is now a large 'L' shape and flooded with natural light from the glazed roof. Surrounding this is the large new office block which provides accommodation for the corn and agricultural merchants, the flour and oatmeal millers, the seed merchants, the fertilizer and feeding stuffs manufacturers, in addition to many others interested in transacting business on the floor of this famous Exchange. The two main market days at present are Mondays and Thursdays, when some eager dealers may be seen waiting for the doors to be opened by the senior beadle, who retains the habit as well as the name bestowed on him in earlier times. (The more observant will also notice that the concourse of pigeons which congregate nearby is also greater during market days.) Nowadays the floor of the Exchange has 188 stands arranged along the walls and between aisles on the floor area. In addition, a further 600 firms hold what is commonly known as a 'walking ticket' at a reduced rental: this, as its name implies, enables these traders to do business anywhere on the floor with any of some 2,000 people who are at present members of the Exchange.

Some of the stands will be seen to contain small neat bags of labelled samples, for grain, especially barley, wheat and oats, is invariably sold on the Exchange by this means. The observant visitor will also see many other products on show, including fertilizers, pulses and examples of the work of bag manufacturers. A surprising variety of seeds is sold (for example, sunflower seed for use as bird food) cheek by jowl with dealers selling agricultural machinery. Three of the big five commercial banks are represented, in addition to firms of merchant bankers, insurance brokers and British Railways. Some of the main interests down in Mark Lane these days, without doubt, are the compound millers of feeding-stuffs and the dealers in barley. Wheat flour milling has by the present day become concentrated into very few hands as the result of the continuation of trends which started, as we saw, in the twenties. But, in spite of their purchases of imported grains in large parcels and shiploads, large firms still appear on Mark Lane (which has become more important with the closure of many provincial corn markets) in order to purchase English wheat and other home-grown grains, as well as to buy smaller specialized lots. British agricultural policy, moreover, has ensured a rising animal population on British farms, as the result of which the sale of feeding-stuffs for cattle is an important interest on the Exchange. Maltsters, too, such as Guinness and Whitbread, are big buyers of home-grown barley on this market. Because of these trends the amalgamation movement among the millers has been paralleled, though less spectacularly, by a similar concentration of merchants who handle the considerably increased home-grown cereal harvests these days. Thus, though the big names among the manufacturers are to be seen on Mark Lane and at the main provincial corn exchanges, they no longer buy in small quantities from the farmer or the small merchant, but predominantly from large merchants. Sometimes these businesses are simply amalgamations of smaller enterprises, but, more frequently of late, banking and international shippers are involved.

The relationship between the Baltic and the London Corn Exchange continues to be a close one. Both, for example, are served by the arbitration and other facilities of the London Corn Trade Association, though the use of the formal contracts of the L.C.T.A. tends to be confined to transactions in parcels of imported produce. Less formal contracts are used for purchases of smaller quantities, especially of home-grown cereals, from farmers and merchants. The National Association of Corn and Agricultural Merchants, which exercises surveillance over these transactions, is at the time of writing engaged in trying to devise a contract which would be uniform for the entire country for lots which fall outside the scope of the L.C.T.A. contracts. Many members of the one Exchange are, in any case, members of the other, so that of the dozen or so telephone booths in the anteroom at Mark Lane, three are direct lines to and from St Mary Axe. The others are divided between those used for incoming calls and those used for outgoing calls. The other communicating device consists of the Exchange Telegraph 'ticker tape' machine which is installed in the corner of the comfortable members' lounge.

In Liverpool, after an initial dispersal to various parts of the City, the Port Area Grain Committee solved its wartime accommodation problem by purchasing Copley estate on the Wirral. The organization moved back again to Wellington Buildings in the Strand in 1946 where members of the grain trade continued to work for the Ministry of Food. The foundation stone of a new Corn Exchange was laid by Lord Woolton on 19 June 1953, and the resulting tower block, bearing no resemblance to its predecessor, was opened in 1955. Among its ten floors there is both a trading room and a coffee room: the ring is now made of chromium and plastic and is complete with foot-rail in the manner of saloon-bars. The market is used on Tuesdays and Fridays as a venue for spot sales by millers, merchants and the other agents mentioned in connection with the Mark Lane Exchange.

4. The Post-War Grain Markets[12]

Despite the recommendation by a Select Committee of the House of Commons (appointed to enquire into Ministry of Food estimates) in 1949 that the grain trade should be restored to private channels at the earliest opportunity, the trade was not decontrolled until 1953. The Ministry's stocks were transferred in two stages; millers were given 6½ weeks' supply in the first instance, after which the Ministry arranged for the release of a specified tonnage of wheat each month.[13] In the meantime the Ministry had arranged for the disposal of its stocks of coarse grains by early 1954. Accordingly, the Liverpool Corn Trade

Association announced that its markets for both spot grain and wheat futures would re-open on 1 December 1953, while the London Association decided to organize trading in barley and maize futures, to complement its newly re-opened physical markets in barley and maize, in January 1954.

Changes in the sources of supply of United Kingdom grain imports since 1938 are shown on Table 7.3 Clearly the import of high protein Canadian wheat now overshadows all other grain imports. The growth of Canadian wheat imports complemented the decline in the importance of Russian supplies, which also consisted very largely of strong wheats. In 1962 imports from the U.S.S.R. amounted to 6.9 million cwt but harvest failures subsequently converted the Soviet Union into a major importer of grain from the West.

By contrast with Canada, Australian supplies have fallen sharply since World War II, a change connected with the fall in the overall total of wheat imports into the United Kingdom. As the result of the encouragement of domestic production, home-grown wheat harvests now yield crops of over 80 million cwt, and it is because soft British wheat is a very good substitute for Australian produce that imports from the latter source have declined. Most of the American wheat now purchased consists of 'filler' wheats as opposed to high-protein wheats, while the amounts purchased depend upon the price policies espoused by the U.S. Commodity Credit Corporation (the C.C.C.). As Table 7.3 indicates wheat from the U.S.A. now features much less prominently in United Kingdom supplies than before the war, though a great deal more United States maize is purchased at present. Maize imports from Argentina have correspondingly declined as manufacturers now prefer the American produce. Clearly the other major change is the great decline in the weight of imported barley which has taken place since before World War II.

Producers are now very much more organized than they once were as a result of dissatisfaction with falling prices after the First World War and the depressed prices of the 1930s. Free market prices for wheat at present are appreciably influenced by the level of price support afforded by the C.C.C. to American produce for export. Canadian wheat sales have been very largely controlled by the Canadian Wheat Board since 1935, while Australian wheat is also sold for export through a central sales organization. Consequently, these Wheat Boards can set their prices fractionally below American prices to ensure a market for their grain. Individual producers and merchants in other parts of the world have to accept these prices as part of the market situation.

The other major change in the structure of the trade in cereals relates to the manufacturers. The capacity created by the First World War subsequently gave rise to severe competition among the millers.

TABLE 7.3

UNITED KINGDOM IMPORTS OF CEREALS, ETC., BY SOURCE, 1938, 1962 and 1968

Weight in million cwt

Un-milled Cereals

WHEAT	1938	1962	1968
Canada	28·8	39·0	29·6
Australia	31·0	11·0	6·9
Argentine	5·8	8·8	1·0
U.S.A.	15·8	6·9	3·1
Soviet Union	9·5	6·9	4·9
Netherlands	0·2	0·7	6·6
Other Countries	10·5	5·1	28·6
Total Weight	101·6	78·4	80·7
Total Value £m	38·6	104·0	112·9

OATS	1938	1962	1968
Australia	0·03	0·6	0·02
Canada	1·5	0·6	
Other Commonwealth Countries and the Irish Republic	0·03	0·01	0·02
Argentine Republic	0·03	0·006	
Other Countries	0·01	0·084	
Total Weight	1·6	1·3	0·04
Total Value £m	0·5	1·4	0·08

Milled Cereals

WHEAT a	1938	1962	1968
Canada	3·6	4·8	1·1
Australia	2·9	1·2	0·2
U.S.A.	0·4	0·9	0·01
Finland		0·3	
Argentine Republic	0·4		
Other Countries	0·4	0·5	0·19
Total Weight	7·7	7·7	1·5
Total Value £m	4·0	13·7	3·3

BARLEY	1938	1962	1968
Canada	5·5	3·6	1·3
Australia	1·8	2·8	0·01
Soviet Union	3·8	0·2	
Irish Republic	0·01	0·1	0·03
Iraq	3·1	0·07	
U.S.A.	2·7	0·1	
Other Countries	2·99	0·13	0·06
Total Weight	19·9	7·0	1·4
Total Value £m	6·9	8·8	2·0

MAIZE (ALL SORTS)	1938	1962	1968
U.S.A.	23·2	61·7	38·4
Republic of S. Africa & S.W. Africa Terr.	2·3	6·5	16·3
Netherlands	1·9	5·0	11·9
Canada	3·6	4·6	0·4
Argentine Republic	17·7	2·0	0·5
Yugoslavia	2·4		
Other Countries	6·5	11·4	7·0
Total Weight	57·6	91·2	74·5
Total Value £m	17·7	92·0	88·0

OTHER MILLED CEREALS b	1938	1962	1968
Total Weight	3·1	0·4	0·7
Total Value £m	1·3	0·5	0·8

a. The figures given for 1962 and 1968 include Semolina and Wheat Germ.

b. Other Milled Cereals – Oat meal, barley products and maize meal and other milled products of maize.

Sources: Figures for 1938 and 1962 calculated from *The Annual Statement of Trade*. Figures for 1965 and 1968 calculated from *Overseas Trade Accounts*.

This led to an amalgamation movement which has by this time resulted in the concentration of manufacturing into the hands of only four really large concerns (i.e. Spillers Ltd, Rank Hovis McDougall Ltd, Associated British Foods Ltd, and the Cooperative Wholesale Society Ltd). Moreover, by buying up baking establishments, these enterprises have sought to become vertically integrated in order to ensure outlets for their flour. These changes have resulted in several interesting modifications to the pre-existing channels of the trade. The large millers have sought to rationalize their organizations by concentrating milling capacity in the larger ports of entry and this, together with the reduction of imports due to increased domestic production, has led to changes in their relative importance as grain ports. These changes are summarized in Tables 7.1 and 7.2, page 153.

In general the manufacturers' policy has been to ring the British Isles with milling capacity at ports which, while not so few as to give rise to transport problems in the internal distribution of the flour, are not so numerous as to create difficulties for the import of relatively large shipments. Economies are possible by purchasing on a single port, or even a two-port, basis which would be lost if parcels of grain were required to be delivered at several milling centres. However, there are at present some problems which face the British grain trade in this connection. The Suez incident in 1956 created a boom followed by a slump in the demand for oil-tanker capacity, and as a result many of these large vessels were used to carry grain. However, British millers are very reluctant to accept ex-oil-tanker or ex-ore-ship grain as they are afraid of contamination and of the labour problems involved in discharging these cargoes. Furthermore, there is a marked reluctance to purchase in shipments of more than about 14,000 to 18,000 tons, except when prices are notably low, when some stocking-up takes place. However, deliveries to any one of the national manufacturers will seldom be a complete ship's cargo, but usually a parcel of some 5,000 tons. It is argued by the manufacturers that grains have to be blended so that the purchase of the huge quantities of one particular type of grain, which modern tankers are able to carry, does not represent the only shipment which has to be purchased in order to bake an acceptable loaf. Of greater significance is the fact that the major wheat terminals in the United Kingdom cannot accommodate the very large tankers now being built and, with existing facilities, even the smaller tankers take longer to unload than conventional vessels.

These factors provide some of the reasons why grain handling equipment at the U.K. ports cannot be compared with that at Rotterdam, Amsterdam and Antwerp. A further reason is that, as a rule, in the U.K. ports the facilities for handling grain are owned by individual millers for working ships at their own premises. This stands in contrast with the organization at continental ports which do a very large transshipment trade. Consequently, the major international grain shipping firms have undertaken large-scale investment there in huge transit silos and the new suction gear for fast unloading.

These international shipping firms play a vital role in distributing grain to U.K. manufacturers. Five of these firms have world-wide connections and operate on a near-global scale. They handle other commodities in addition to grain, and have interests in manufacturing, banking and insurance. None of these is British: Bunge has its head office in Argentina, Louis Dreyfus is a French firm, Tradax is American (and known there as Cargill), Wm. H. Pim Junior, at one time British-owned, is now a subsidiary of an American parent called the Continental Grain Company, while the European Grain Company is a Swiss firm known outside the U.K. as Garnac. These firms, together with a number of smaller ones, some of which are British, sell imported grain to millers, compounders and merchants at the ports. They are principals rather than agents, even though these days almost all the grain being unloaded at U.K. ports is sold before it arrives. These large importers own ships, though they do not reserve these for the transport of their own grain. They often own their own elevators, especially in the U.S.A. and in Argentina. The large shippers have offices in all the main importing countries and, as large-scale stockholders and transporters, are completely equipped to 'originate' produce and deliver it duly graded and cleared to the miller. Canadian grain purchases are made by the shipper or on an f.o.b. basis through his Canadian office, while he normally arranges for insurance, finance and freight in the United Kingdom. The process is much the same for purchases from the Australian Wheat Board except that some specially nominated shippers (John Darling and Overseas Farmers) act for the Wheat Board in U.K. and other markets.

Capital requirements for an international grain shipping company are evidently very high, especially since there is an almost inevitable need for such companies to' take a view of the market', that is, to back their judgement as to which way prices are likely to move. British millers usually buy two or three months or even further forward, if they consider that prices are favourable, and the shipper has to meet this situation. Should the shipper consider that prices will rise or continue to rise in the near future, he tends to add to his stocks. Conversely, he will keep them at a minimum compatible with supplying his customers should he consider that prices are weakening. Clearly the shipper's risks may be reduced by hedging on futures markets, and these traders make extensive use of the facilities afforded by the markets at Kansas City, Minneapolis, Chicago and elsewhere.

Prior to the enormous concentration among the manufacturers, the grain merchant was a major figure in the trade. He was, as we have already seen, served by the broker who acted as an intermediary between him and the shipper. This pattern still survives, though it has been much eroded by direct purchasing by the millers from the shippers and, more especially, by the tendency for the Canadian Wheat Board and other central selling agencies to sell direct to the large millers. Thus whereas the previous chain of distribution, which was predominantly from shipper via broker to merchant and then to manufacturer, meant that the shipper purchased a high proportion of his turnover before re-selling, this is not at present necessary to quite the same extent. Now that the shipper tends to take orders directly from manufacturers, it is possible for him to await these orders before he himself purchases the produce at origin. Insofar as the shipper does this he is clearly usurping the function of the broker, who often acts as principal in this way in the grain trade, that is, on what is known in the trade as a 'back-to-back' basis. Thus, though he acts as a principal by purchasing and re-selling, he never speculates by holding stocks but performs a function akin to that of a jobber (as well as of a broker) on the Stock Exchange.

These tendencies, together with the switch from spot to forward purchases, have reduced the number of brokers, especially the number of smaller men, in the grain trade. It is unlikely, however, that grain brokers will become an extinct species. Their position seems to have stabilized since even the very large manufacturers often find it convenient to use them if they wish to deal anonymously. The broker is an expert whose business it is to know how the market is moving from hour to hour, and his commission of $\frac{1}{4}$ per cent to $\frac{1}{2}$ per cent remains exceedingly low. Meanwhile, the development of an export trade in some grains also redounded to the broker's advantage.

We have already seen that the importing merchant, or 'port merchant' as he is sometimes called, used to be an important intermediary in the supply of grain to the miller. His activities were necessarily confined to the domestic trade during World War II, and his subsequent recovery has been much impaired by the increase in direct buying from shippers or government agencies. Though depleted in numbers, however, these merchants still play a role at the ports. Despite the fact that almost all the grain which arrives in the U.K. is already sold on arrival, shippers frequently make up a full shipload by adding a parcel of grain for sale to a port merchant. (In the trade this is described as shipping 'unsold balances' in order to avoid 'dead freight'.) The larger port merchants sell to the smaller manufacturers and also to the smaller 'country' merchants. In addition, the latter obtain supplies from the major manufacturers and sometimes direct from shippers though, understandably, the shipper is not normally anxious to make up a cargo of very small orders (some 250 tons appears to be the minimum transaction for direct buying). It is more usual for small-scale merchants to use brokers to procure their supplies rather than to negotiate directly with the big shippers. The employment of this expertise appears to suit the needs of the country merchant, one of whose prime concerns must be to avoid overhead costs out of keeping with the size of his business. Despite the essentially large-scale nature of their activities, however, some of the big shippers have been observed to be buying agricultural merchants' businesses. This is one of the ways in which the amalgamation of merchants, referred to earlier in connection with Mark Lane and the provincial corn exchanges, is being effected. This enables erstwhile small-scale enterprises to buy up supplies from other merchants for re-sale in larger lots.

5. *Price Insurance in the Grain Trade.*
It will be recalled that from 1883 to 1939, apart from a break occasioned by the First World War, the wheat trade in this country was mainly served by a futures market run by the Liverpool Corn Trade Association. After the Second World War the Liverpool futures market in wheat reopened on 1 December 1953 with what appeared to be the promising augury of a turnover of some 25 loads a day. However, though the market remained open until 31 March 1958, it failed to re-establish itself as a widely accepted means of price insurance. There were very good reasons for this.

Both the Canadian and Australian Wheat Boards, which, as Table

7.3 indicates, together account for a high proportion of our wheat imports, provide a degree of flexibility in their pricing policies. Every day these Boards publish an official price based on supply and demand pressures and the movement of prices in other markets. Moreover, should the purchaser so wish, he is able to buy from them on a 'price-to-be-fixed' basis. This deferred pricing system allows the buyer to purchase, for example, a parcel of wheat in October for January shipment at an unfixed price. The buyer then has the option at any time prior to the final fixing date (generally just before the arrival of the wheat in the U.K.) of nominating the date on which he wishes the price to be fixed, at the Wheat Board's official price of the day.[14] Because of this the hedging of Canadian and Australian wheat has become quite unnecessary for the buyer, who is able to purchase for forward shipment confident in the knowledge that when the produce arrives the cost to him will be very near its spot price. On the other hand, should the buyer feel that the price of his purchases is almost certain to be higher in three months time, it is possible for him to take a view of the market (i.e. to back his hunch as a speculator) by buying a forward shipment at a fixed price.

Unfortunately for traders, wheat from other sources cannot be bought by means of a deferred pricing arrangement. It might be argued that this is probably not of very great moment due to the possibility of hedging on the major American futures market. However, whereas the international shippers use these markets, they are not very useful for United Kingdom traders. These markets function well enough for domestic users inside the United States, but they are virtually unworkable for United Kingdom traders due to the element of export subsidy, in the c.i.f. price in the U.K., of U.S. produce. Sales for export from the U.S.A. are exempt from the standard prices which apply domestically, so that changes in export subsidies by the C.C.C. could affect the price c.i.f. U.K. very significantly while leaving the internal price in the U.S.A. unchanged. Because of this, British millers have adopted a philosophy in relation to these unhedgeable grain purchases of trying to buy as well as possible, and of offsetting losses against gains. The feeling amongst them is that they can contemplate this with greater equanimity because of their large size than could their smaller-scale counterparts in the past. Moreover, since movements in grain prices affect all millers about equally, it has become possible, with the concentration of the milling industry, for one of them to change the price of the product in the expectation that his rivals will follow suit. As the industry has become more vertically integrated, these manufacturers' end product has become the loaf rather than flour and this has made it easier for the smaller number of millers-cum-bakers to achieve tacit understandings. The Restrictive Practices

Court pronounced the bakers' price rings illegal in 1959 and declared that there should be more competition in baking.[15]

As for barley and maize, the London Corn Trade Association established futures contracts in these commodities in January 1954 while the Liverpool Association followed suit five years later. Initially only imported barleys were tenderable but, as the result of increasing domestic production, home-grown barley was introduced as an additional tenderable commodity in January 1961 in Liverpool and in June 1964 in London. The maize contract never really stimulated interest in the north and became moribund there. In London maize futures attracted more interest though the turnover was always smaller than that of imported barley. Thus, during the year ending 31 March 1964, contracts for maize amounted to 179,250 tons while for imported barley futures they totalled 529,500 tons. The contract in imported barley, superseded by its rival in home-grown barley, was withdrawn in July 1965 while the futures market in maize finally petered out in December 1967. A contract in home-grown wheat was introduced in July 1965 partly to cater for the increase in domestic production and partly to meet the difficulty of securing effective insurance against price fluctuations in the U.S.A. Thus at present cereals markets in the U.K. are served by futures contracts in home-grown barley and home-grown wheat, both of which are traded in London, but the Liverpool Association operates only the barley contract.

Should the positions taken by traders not be 'closed-out', naturally the seller of a futures contract must tender produce in settlement. For this purpose granaries ('tendering points') have been nominated by the Association. These belong to 'Approved Service Operators' chosen from dryer-operators authorized by the Ministry of Agriculture under the Cereals Deficiency Payments Scheme. A large number of official stores are used (almost 100 for the London market and 30 or so for Liverpool), the choice being at seller's option.

Both markets are small, as the accompanying table (Table 7.4) illustrates, but London now appears to be much the stronger centre with a larger turnover in the barley contract and the addition of the small but growing wheat contract. The London market is under the control of the Council of the London Grain Futures Association, the members of which are also members of the London Corn Trade Association. The Rules require an 'original margin' of £50 per contract unit of 125 tons (known as a 'load'). At 1.00 p.m. each trading day settlement prices are fixed for open positions, and any adverse movement of 5s. or more must be met by additional payments of differences to the clearing house by 11 a.m. on the following day. The clearing house, as previously explained, is thereby enabled to settle all closed contracts of intermediate traders in cash. In addition to the protection afforded by the payment of margins and differences, both Associations

TABLE 7.4

TOTAL TURNOVER OF HOME-GROWN CEREAL FUTURES CONTRACTS,
1963-4 to 1969-70

tons

	London barley	London wheat	Liverpool barley
1963-4	a	a	203,375
1964-5	236,500	a	121,500
1965-6	381,375	38,125	94,875
1966-7	321,625	66,500	55,525
1967-8	294,625	129,625	94,125
1968-9	507,500	206,625	15,000
1969-70	417,625	69,125	12,000

a. Market not operating.

Sources: London Corn Trade Association Ltd and Liverpool Corn Trade Association Ltd.

operate insurance funds, the antecedents of which have already been described. Both the beginning and end of the morning and afternoon sessions (11.30 a.m. to 1 p.m. and 2.45 p.m. to 4.15 p.m. respectively) are marked by the sounding of a bell in a corner of the floor of the Baltic reserved for ring trading. Business is transacted across the ring (a circular handrail) by open outcry, and the resulting prices are marked on the nearby board. The official closing price is determined by a panel of ring traders, the members of which take it in turn to act as chairman. A group of adjacent telephone booths, each marked with the name of a broker and equipped with a light to attract the ring trader's attention to answer calls, ensures instant contact between the market and the broker's clients.

As is usual on futures markets the number of ring traders is small, and they hold their position by virtue of their election by the Association concerned. Non-members must trade through members and pay according to a higher scale of commission than that which obtains for members. Users of the futures market are mainly shippers, followed by merchants, and a relatively small number of farmers. According to those who have been connected with these markets since their inception, the amount of speculative activity is very low; indeed, the danger is that there may be too little to maintain the markets in existence and to provide an adequate turnover to make broking activities worthwhile. With the turnover on these markets at no more than some 4 per cent of production in barley and wheat, the scope for improvement is obviously very great indeed. However, in the cereals trade, the concentration which has taken place among the manufacturers, together with the deferred pricing policies of the Wheat Boards, has served to discourage the major potential clients from using the market to any great extent. It has been suggested[16] that most merchants and farmers either lack the knowledge of the ways in which futures may be used, or else lack the capital for speculation if they pride themselves upon their expertise in taking a view of the market. Clearly farmers are at present partially protected from price fluctuations by the Government's guarantee arrangements and, for the rest, consider that futures trading is too obscure and complex, though futures prices are often used as a basis for forward contracts between merchants and farmers.

Meanwhile it appears unlikely that official intervention will make any significant changes in the system of cereal marketing in the United Kingdom, though it may exert a considerable influence upon the amount and disposition of imports. Normally there is no purchase of output by the government. Domestic producers sell for such prices as they can get on the market and the government pays them the difference between the average realized market price, calculated from statutory grain returns, and the standard price determined after the annual review undertaken each February—March. Producers of above average efficiency thus retain the benefit of a deficiency payment based upon average prices, while the spread of sales over the season is encouraged by means of a seasonal scale of standard prices. By orders laid before Parliament in June 1964, moreover, new import arrangements were introduced following British agreements with the main suppliers to observe minimum import prices for cereals, coupled with the limitation of price guarantees to 'standard quantities' of produce only. Agreements have subsequently been entered into with other suppliers, and in cases where no agreement to observe floor prices has been reached, the United Kingdom now imposes a levy. This has been done in order to stabilize prices and to limit the total of subsidy payments to farmers. The government has also introduced bonus payments to farmers who enter into forward contracts to sell their produce. It is hoped by this means to even out the distribution of crops over time and thus help to stabilize prices.

Commonwealth preference has evidently played a minor part in determining the relative importance of U.K. sources of overseas supply of recent years, as the table footnote indicates[17]. The International Wheat Agreements and their successor, the International Grain Arrangements, were so framed that the agreed purchases and sales would only operate at the prescribed price limits. In essence the treaties are multilateral contracts which provide for the purchase and sale of certain fixed quantities on the part of importing and exporting countries, should the minimum or maximum prices written into the contract happen to prevail. The major difference between the superseded International Wheat Agreements and the International Grain Arrangements which came into force in June 1968 is that the latter prescribe not just one basic price range for one 'reference' wheat but an entire schedule of minimum and maximum prices covering all the main wheats traded.[18] The Arrangements suffer from the defect that price differentials between the various types of wheat become artificially rigid whenever market prices reach their respective minima. The possibility that this might give rise to serious distortions in the normal patterns of trade was foreseen. Article 8 of the Wheat Trade Convention, therefore, provides machinery for review of and adjustments in the minimum price schedule by the Price Review Committee and, if necessary, the International Wheat Council itself. Virtually since its inception, however, the I.G.A. has suffered from such an abundance of wheat supply and sharp competition from non-member countries[19] that the prescribed minima have already been breached. Consultations have taken place within the framework of the Wheat Trade Convention, but so far there has been no effective solution to the problem of maintaining the price minima.

In the future, United Kingdom grain traders may witness both some changes in the framework within which the market operates and some shifts in supply sources. Major changes in the structure of the trade, however, are unlikely. Most of the big changes, notably the concentration of manufacturers and their vertical integration with the bakers, have now taken place. Port merchants have been greatly reduced in importance and various changes have resulted in a decline in the role of the broker. Because of the inducements provided by successive governments home cereal production has expanded very significantly, and market intermediaries have naturally become involved in its distribution and export. This change appears to have interested the international shippers, with their ramifications of banking, insurance and finance, who have bought up some country merchant interests in the recent past. The changes in futures trading in the U.K. have reflected the changes in the structure of the trade. The internationally important futures markets at Liverpool have now disappeared, and in their place have appeared the small-scale markets in home-grown barley and wheat contracts with London as the more important centre.

All these changes have had their repercussions on the corn markets. A large number of provincial corn exchanges have disappeared, and this has increased the importance of the London Corn Exchange at Mark Lane. Activity on the floors of both the Liverpool Corn Exchange and on the Baltic has been reduced, though this owes something to the improvement in communications as well as to direct buying. Most of the trade now takes place over the telephone or the telex, but this has only become possible because of the concentration among the manufacturers—there are now fewer people to contact on the telephone. When there were many more it was easier for them all to meet on the floor of the Exchange. Meanwhile, visits to the Exchange still provide a 'feel of the market' unobtainable on the telephone. There is the excitement engendered by the throng of people, especially on the Baltic, where the activity is now predominantly on the shipping side. And finally, of course, there are the friendships to be kept in good repair by means of personal visits.

Chapter Eight

THE ORGANIZATION OF THE MINCING LANE MARKETS

THE Pool of London has been an important berth for ships since medieval times and, as we saw in Chapter 2, traders tended to establish themselves for the purchase and sale of incoming cargoes on the acknowledged route to the Royal Exchange from the 'legal quays' of the upper pool. It was this which accounted for the importance of Mincing Lane and for the erection of the London Commercial Sale Rooms there in 1811. At this major venue for the disposal of imported commodities the sale by public auction of produce which was already 'on the spot' was the rule for many years. By today public sales are exceptional, and even 'spot' sales of commodities warehoused in London tend almost all to be by private treaty. Moreover, though an exchange of information still takes place on the market floor, many transactions are now concluded over the telephone, but most of the trading in the physical product, whether on or off the market, is done on a c.i.f. rather than on a 'spot' basis these days.[1] In fact the real successor to the auction chamber with its hectic atmosphere of bids and counter-bids is, clearly, the futures market, or, to give it its London name, the terminal market.[2] There are at present eight of these located in Plantation House, Mincing Lane.

1. *The Decline of Auction Sales*

One of the most immediate reasons for the decline of the auction may be seen from an examination of quayside and warehousing arrangements for imported produce, for charges naturally vary according to whether or not produce is to be taken across the quays for warehousing. For the sake of speed and economy, for example, purchasers may wish to take delivery directly onto barges from over the ship's side, or the produce may be required for trans-shipment by coaster to other ports. However, even though produce is actually landed on the quays, it by no means follows that it is intended for warehousing. In the case of the Port of London Authority, for example, the importer may ask for delivery to a conveyance on what is called 'Immediate Delivery' terms. This means that the importer is obliged to accept his goods from the transit sheds within seventy-two hours of their being ready for delivery. The special Quay Delivery Schedule charges are obviously lower for this service than for warehousing.

Economies of this kind obviously awaited developments in transport and communication which rendered it possible for traders to purchase goods in advance of requirements with a fair degree of certainty that delivery dates would be met. These requirements were fulfilled in due course, as we have already seen in the case of cotton and grain, by the cable links laid during the third quarter of the nineteenth century. These provided a means of placing orders to overseas shippers within minutes of their receipt by brokers, while the widespread adoption of steampower at about the same time meant that delivery dates could be quoted with a reasonable chance that they would be kept. The Suez Canal, moreover, besides cutting down delivery times for much Far Eastern produce also provided an impetus to the whole process, including, of course, the use of the steamship, for the canal was not suited to sailing vessels. The communications revolution has continued, notably with the telephone, the teleprinter and the telex machine, while, for tomorrow, international communications by satellite will buttress these changes.

In addition to a degree of certainty that delivery dates would be met, manufacturers also required some assurance as to quality before they could happily enter into advance commitments. Thus the presence of a transport and communications system which enabled traders to buy forward gave a considerable impetus to the accurate grading of produce in order to enable it to be bought and sold on description. Where standards of grading become sufficiently reliable, this obviates the need to inspect the bulk at a warehouse before purchase, or even to examine samples. Often 'type' samples suffice: these are used in many branches of commodity trade (e.g. rubber, rice) as a standard of reference for the grade of the produce concerned. In the rubber trade, for example, these permanent type samples, clipped together rather like tailors' pattern books, are kept for reference in cases of arbitration by the Rubber Trade Association of London. More recently, and especially since the Second World War, the dispatch of air-freight samples by overseas shippers has developed as a method of trading. The usual procedure is for part of this sample to be kept in case of subsequent dispute, while the other part is made available by the selling broker for inspection by possible buyers.

A further method, which has been developed and is at present widely used as an efficient method of sale of raw produce by private treaty, is the formula known as 'fair average quality', or most often by the initials f.a.q. The determination of this involves the sampling of the bulk after arrival for purposes of arbitration in cases of dispute. Thus, to take an important and clear example, the London Corn Trade's f.a.q. contracts lay down the conditions as follows:

A parcel of . . . fair average quality of the season's shipments at time and place of shipment, to be assessed upon the basis of, and by comparison with, the London Corn Trade Association's official F.A.Q. Standard of the month during which the Bill of Lading is dated . . . An average sample of the delivery shall be taken and sealed jointly at Port of Discharge by the Representatives of the Holders of the Bill of Lading or Shipper's Delivery Order, and shall be forwarded immediately to the Association for the purpose of establishing the F.A.Q. Standard.

The increase in the volume of trade and the intensification of competition were also influences leading to the decline of the system of consignment for auction. The growth of trade led to an increase in specialization and this encouraged many firms of brokers to establish associations for the particular produce in which they specialized: in this way organizations pertaining to tea, coffee, cocoa, hemp, skins, rubber, shellac and other commodities were brought into being. The General Produce Brokers' Association of London, for example, was established in 1876. Thus, whereas previously each firm made its own conditions of sale and held its own auctions, frequently in its own sale-room, the associations brought uniformity to the trades. Disputes concerning quality, compensation and other matters, which were becoming increasingly troublesome with the growth of trade, were dealt with in accordance with sets of Rules devised by these organizations. Standard forms of contract were drawn up, and periodically revised, while arbitration panels were brought into being for settling disputes by reference to defined standards.

Thus the coming of rapid transport and communications, the development of reliable grading, sampling, f.a.q. standards, intensified competition and fair arbitration machinery have all led to a decline in the use of the warehouse and the auction chamber as essential links in the chain of distribution. Even within living memory, commodity auctions in Mincing Lane sometimes attained a frequency of sixty a day, for, in addition to the better known 'colonial groceries' such as sugar, cocoa, tea, coffee and spices, there was a large trade in an incredibly wide variety of other produce, notably rubber, copra, jute, shellac and general produce—the last named category covering a host of items. Some of these, such as chinese rhubarb, indigo, tragacanth and palma rosa, are easily classified into categories, namely, drugs, dyes, gums and essential oils respectively, while others, such as asbestos, defy grouping. The general picture, however, is clear: for the reasons adumbrated, auctions of all manner of produce, ranging from important public sales such as those of coffee, to lesser events, such as the auctioning of tortoiseshell and mother-of-pearl, have now been discontinued. For the most part supplies are obtained via brokers or merchants these days and though some stocks may be carried, especially in a commodity such as coffee, the bulk of the trade is on a c.i.f. basis.

The decline of commodity auctions and the use of c.i.f. trading accelerated after World War I. There was a growth in the demand for raw materials by other industrializing countries with the decline in Britain's over-riding importance in world trade. Direct communications between producing countries and the newer centres of manufacture improved, as London ceased to be the market to which overseas purchasers automatically turned for supplies of raw materials and foodstuffs. However, the loss of business in many cases was more apparent than real, for the change which not infrequently took place was that the seemingly direct transactions between overseas producers and foreign manufacturers were actually arranged by London merchants. This 'third country' trade, which was frequently important, depended upon expertise and existing trade connections between U.K. traders and foreign shippers. Clearly, it was enabled to emerge because of the technological revolution in transport and communications referred to earlier. As far as the commodity markets were concerned, however, the decreasing need for shipping to 'break bulk' in London (and other U.K. ports), meant a diminished flow of produce through these markets. The growth of direct import, whether arranged by London merchants or not, therefore, was inevitably accompanied by a decline in the concourse of bidders at the London auctions and this naturally contributed to their demise.

The argument most widely used to justify public sales is that they are the most satisfactory way to dispose of produce which it is difficult to grade reliably. There is obviously a good deal of truth in this argument: one hears, for example, that even the teas of neighbouring tea estates can be of a different flavour, while the same estate will produce teas of varying quality from season to season, depending upon the vagaries of the weather. Despite these arguments tradition and inertia undoubtedly play a part in determining whether disposal is by public or private sale. The classic case in this respect in the United Kingdom of recent years is undoubtedly that of coffee, while that of the tea auctions in the United States is also interesting: the New York tea auctions were discontinued in 1903 and never subsequently resumed.[3] The coffee auctions were a notable feature of the trading scene in Mincing Lane before the War, but in spite of efforts by the Ministry of Food to revive them when the trade was being handed back to private traders, there was no longer sufficient interest. The trade had flown too long in Government controlled channels; the protracted discontinuity had stifled international interest, and some buyers had transferred their attentions elsewhere.

Among the commodities usually listed as 'General Produce', the only public sales which remain are those of ivory and bristles. Of these the ivory sales are now held in the auction room at Plantation House, which is on the seventh floor, and otherwise given over to the tea sales. The auctions are quarterly and continue to attract overseas buyers, but the volume of sales is much less than formerly: increasing amounts of this produce are now bought at origin rather than in London, but other influences have also reduced the importance of the auctions here. Prohibitions against killing animals for the sake of their tusks are now more strictly observed than formerly, but above all, of course, most traditional uses for ivory are being invaded by the ubiquitous plastic substitute.

Each quarterly sale of ivory lasts for a day and realizes between £8,000 and £10,000 usually. Gross imports are of the order of £35,000 a year nowadays, of which about one half is re-exported. Before being catalogued and displayed in the warehouse the produce, which apart from elephant tusks may also include mammoth, walrus, rhinoceros and hippopotamus tusks together with narwhal horns, is graded for sale. The classification is according to size (tusks normally weigh between 40 and 50 lbs, though a very large one may weigh over 200 lbs and have a length of over 10 feet); according to quality (for ivory is subject to disease); and according to the use for which the individual tusks may be suitable. These are still many, even though certain difficulties attend the use of some tusks for certain purposes. Billiard balls, for example, have to be of standard size, so that the hollow part of the tusks together with the scrivellos (the tips), are useless for this purpose. Scrivellos are, on the other hand, ideal for quality piano and organ manufacturers. Buyers will, therefore, obviously be after particular tusks as more suitable for their purpose than others; hence the continuation of the auctions for their disposal. However, for the reasons already mentioned, it is a declining trade, for plastics are sufficiently cheap to supplant even the cheaper natural substitutes for ivory in some cases; even the cult of grinding certain horns to powder for use as aphrodisiacs seems to be on the decline, though there are as yet no plastic substitutes.

Bristles, another item of general produce, are still auctioned approximately quarterly, but there now seems to be no fixed venue for these sales. Public sales of bristles have been held both at Winchester House and at Beaver Hall. Their import is typically of the order of £4 to £5 million per annum: here again, the growing popularity of synthetic substitutes such as nylon for use instead of animal bristle in toothbrushes, hair brushes and similar articles, does not augur well for the trade. Not all the bristles are auctioned these days: the Chinese now prefer to fix a price for their produce, though they have had to reduce their notions of what to ask of recent years because of the above-mentioned factors. The Chinese have, however, demonstrated that this product can be accurately graded and so sold upon description by private treaty rather than auctioned. Cheap labour is obviously a great help in this respect.

On the seventh floor of Plantation House, a little way from the offices of the Tea Brokers' Association of London, is the tea auction

room leased to this organization. In this chamber, with its neat amphitheatre of seats facing the auctioneer's rostrum, the internationally
famous public sales of tea are held on Monday, Tuesday and Wednesday of each week. The first and last days of the sales are reserved for
teas from Northern India, Africa, Indonesia, Japan, Formosa, Mauritius, Malaya, China, Iran and the Argentine, while on Tuesdays, tea
from Ceylon and Southern India is auctioned. Of a total annual
import in excess of 500 million lbs, about one half to three-fifths is sold
under the hammer at Mincing Lane (i.e. usually somewhere in the
neighbourhood of 3 million packages of 108 lbs each). Of the remainder,
some will have been bought at overseas auction centres, and the balance
either imported direct from estates owned by distributors, or purchased
privately by distributors under contracts made with producers or with
exporters overseas. Of total U.K. imports more than one half come
from Northern India, and about 10 per cent from Southern India:
a quarter originates from Ceylon, while remaining supply sources are
of lesser significance. A fuller description of the tea trade is given below,
in Chapter 9.

As far as the Port of London is concerned the change in trading
methods has meant an almost continuous decline in the demand for
warehousing facilities. The Annual Reports of the Authority also
refer[4] to the resulting inadequacy of the space and access for traffic
that leaves the docks shortly after ships are unloaded. It is not really
surprising that technological change has overtaken the adequacy of
the Dock provision, for the first impetus for the establishment of a
wet dock followed the Report of a Parliamentary Committee of Enquiry
of 1796; i.e. more than 150 years ago. The West India Docks which
resulted from this were opened by Pitt as early as 1802 and a system
of bonded warehouses was inaugurated a year later. The East India
Company, of course, already had theirs but a new wet dock, the East
India Docks, was completed for the Company in 1806. This was one
year after the opening of the London Docks with their vast warehouses,
intended primarily to house valuable imports such as wine, brandy
and tobacco. Some years later, in 1828, the nearby St. Katherine's
Docks were completed along with warehouses intended for the storage
of specialized cargoes such as indigo, tortoiseshell, marble and scent,
at a convenient distance from the Royal Exchange, the markets in
Mincing Lane and elsewhere in the City.

By today, more wet docks have been added. As the ships became
progressively larger, however, the disadvantages of London as a port
compared with many others in the U.K. (such as Southampton)
became manifest. The upper reaches of the Thames limited the size
of the ships able to navigate that far, while the state of the tide also
imposed constraints upon the times at which those wishing to do so
could berth or sail. As the vessels increased in size and capital value,

moreover, rapidity of turn-round became an ever more significant factor. These considerations consequently led to the excavation of docks at ever increasing distances from London Bridge, such as Tilbury Docks, 26 miles away.

It is thus a feature of the Port of London that a significant proportion of imported goods is discharged at the outlying docks of Tilbury and the immense Royal Docks group, the diminishing tonnage intended for warehousing being taken further up the river by barge. The East and West India Docks have, therefore, lost the trade for which they were built. This is also partly true of St. Katharine's Dock, the sale of which is at the time of writing being negotiated with the Greater London Council. The future of the London, Surrey, Commercial and East India Docks is also being reviewed. The next decade is thus likely to see great changes in the Port, especially now that the effects of the imaginative improvements in goods handling (palletization and containerization) are beginning to make their impact.

2. *The London Commercial Sale Rooms and Plantation House*
With the growth of imports in the nineteenth century, accommodation for the disposal of the 'colonial groceries' and the multitude of drugs, dyes, gums, waxes and general produce at the London Commercial Sale Rooms at Mincing Lane became inadequate, and several extensions were made. When further additions proved impossible the building was demolished and a larger building erected in its place in 1890. At the same time, the London Commercial Sale Rooms were incorporated as a public limited liability company with a capital consisting of 16,247 £10 shares and £120,000 of debentures. The total number of subscribers—and it was only subscriber members or their nominees who were admitted to the Subscription Room—numbered some 1,500 at the time. By tradition, particular areas of the Subscription Room, which took up virtually the entire ground floor area of the Sale Rooms, were given over to the sale of particular commodities. As opposed to the frequent auction sales, which were open to the public and held on the upper floors, transactions in the Subscription Room were by private treaty. As was also the case on the floor of the Baltic, no samples were allowed to be displayed in the Subscription Room, the quality of produce being determined by the permanent type samples available in the offices of the relevant trade association or else by means of the samples which could be inspected at the brokers' offices nearby. As is still usual in the City of London, transactions were initially concluded by word of mouth, the details being noted by clerks. When terminal markets were introduced for some Mincing Lane commodities towards the end of the nineteenth century, these were also accommodated at various points on the floor of the Subscription Room.

The Second World War ultimately brought dramatic changes to Mincing Lane markets by adding a further impetus to the course of their evolution, as well as forcing upon them an unforeseen change of habitat. In 1941 the London Commercial Sale Rooms were destroyed by enemy action, but its members were nevertheless able to continue to transact business near the same spot by taking space in Plantation House. This building, which spreads over most of the area bounded by Mincing Lane, Fenchurch Street, Rood Lane and Great Tower Street, was built almost opposite the Commercial Sale Rooms. In 1936, when these premises were completed, The London Rubber Exchange Ltd occupied part of the building, including the Exchange floor built for this commodity trade. Traders in rubber had held their market for some years at the Sale Rooms, but in 1923 had moved out to premises at 7 Mincing Lane. These were demolished during the early 1930s as part of the clearance scheme necessary for the erection of Plantation House. The 1930s, however, were on the whole a depressed period for the commodity trades, so that though (as its name implies) Plantation House was intended as a centre for the commodity trade, the lessors did not succeed in filling the building with commodity traders. As it turned out, therefore, when the Sale Rooms were gutted during the early part of the war, Plantation House was able to provide sufficient accommodation for all those trades made homeless by the bombing.

In 1945 there was an amalgamation of interests and what had been known as the Rubber Exchange on the ground floor of Plantation House became the London Commodity Exchange. In 1954, a new company, called The London Commodity Exchange Co. Ltd, was formed with a nominal capital of £45,000 divided into 300 shares of £150 each. It is this company which holds the lease of Plantation House, the lessors being the St. Regis Property Company. To some degree the 'special relationship' enjoyed by the rubber interests in the Exchange has been perpetuated in that the staff of the London Rubber Exchange continue to run The London Commodity Exchange organization, for which they are paid a fee.

As of January 1970 the number of sponsor members (i.e. those who hold a share in the London Commodity Exchange Co.) was 160. Sponsor membership is, however, purely nominal, carrying no privileges other than that of the right to representation, but individuals from sponsor firms are eligible for trading membership of the Exchange. Trading members may, in turn, appoint nominees who are eligible to trade on the floor of the Exchange. In January 1970 there were 258 trading members and 300 nominees. The operation of the Exchange is in the hands of a Board of Directors and a Floor Committee, but these bodies exercise no control over the methods or conditions of trading of the various markets which operate on the

London Commodity Exchange. These are governed solely by the trade associations concerned, the key figures of which are their secretaries.

Plantation House is a complicated place, extending over eight floors, the London Commodity Exchange being at ground-floor level. It is the largest market floor inside Plantation House, but a considerable proportion of its area is taken up by various terminal markets. At present the Coffee Terminal Market Association of London occupies one end of the trading floor, and the Rubber Trade Association of London occupies the other. It is also the location of the United Terminal Sugar Market. Some of the floor area has, however, been taken over since 5 July 1967 by the London Vegetable Oil Terminal Markets. A square 'ring' of chairs has been arranged across which trade takes place, as is usual, by means of open outcry. A similar ring in Fishmeal futures also took over the place formerly occupied by the defunct Shellac terminal market between 12 April 1967 and 25 June 1970. Moreover, the Wool Terminal Market has now given up the separate accommodation which it occupied on the ground floor of Plantation House between 1953 and 1970, and now shares a trading space in the Commodity Exchange with the Raw Cotton Futures Market. Transactions in rubber are concluded both by brokers on the floor of the Exchange and over the telephone.

In addition to housing the terminal markets the London Commodity Exchange provides the venue for both spot and forward trade in 'actuals' in a variety of commodities.[5] Rubber has already been mentioned. The other commodities dealt in are cocoa, coffee, copra, jute, shellac and sugar, though the value of transactions in some produce which are actually concluded on the floor of the Exchange tends to be very low. This is because much of the business is now transacted in the brokers' and merchants' offices in Plantation House, or else in the near vicinity. One such firm, with offices and agencies scattered around the world, occupies an entire floor of Plantation House in addition to further space on the ground floor. Other parts of the building are occupied by two large insurance firms who moved in during the depressed 1930s, but much of the remainder is taken up by commodity traders.

The Cocoa Terminal Market occupies a room which was once the waiting room for the London Commodity Exchange. Members complain of the lack of space, and of the inconveniently large number of pillars which obscure the view in a market for whom the motto, as in every terminal market, could well be 'see and be seen'.

In spite of such shortcomings (from which the whole of Plantation House suffers), the terminal markets operate at a high level of sophistication. Each market is organized by the terminal market association for that particular commodity. In the case of sugar, cocoa and the vegetable oils, a secretary acts on behalf of all three associations, while for coffee, wool, and the recently closed Fishmeal Terminal Market, the secretary is a senior member of the London Produce Clearing House Ltd. Each market association has a set of rules governing the conduct of these markets, which need to be detailed and cover every contingency. Admission to the exchange floor concerned is limited to members, and the codes all specify the number of brokers who shall be allowed to deal: floor members, in other words, are limited in number by the association concerned, and all traders or speculators who wish to buy or sell futures on the market do so via the floor members. In addition to floor members, the associations also have associate members who do not themselves deal on the terminal markets, but do so through their broker members. The advantage of associate membership, as in the case of the other exchanges already considered, lies in the reduced commission payable upon transactions, and a voice in the affairs of the association concerned.

Floor members belong to firms which may be of widely different character: some are specialized in the commodity concerned, or possibly in a few related commodities, and handle transactions for clients not only in the terminal markets but also in the physical produce, thus providing a complete service in that particular commodity. Still larger firms, in addition to their broking activities on behalf of customers in both the terminal and delivery markets, may also be merchants—that is stockholders taking their own title to commodities in a number of market centres. They may be floor members of several terminal market associations both here and abroad, and engage regularly in arbitrage activity. They may be floor members in the futures market for one commodity and associate members only in another. In the world's physical markets, a large part of their turnover may consist in having arranged for the export of produce from one foreign country to another and while they have hedged it for their clients on the London market, and insured it at Lloyds, or arranged for freight on the floor of the Baltic, the commodity itself will not have touched the shores of the United Kingdom. The full extent of such 'third country trade' is almost impossible to quantify;[6] it is, indeed, often very difficult to trace all the ramifications of such merchanting firms. Generally, there is an area pattern of commodities which serves to remind us that the ancestors of such enterprises are the Elizabethan and other chartered companies whose monopoly was almost always granted for a particular area rather than a particular commodity. Many have subsequently diversified, however, sometimes into interests as separate as sugar, mushrooms and hovercraft. Many such firms are famous names, such as C. Czarnikow Ltd, who are pre-eminent as sugar merchants and brokers; Gill and Duffus Ltd, with their world-wide interests in cocoa and (through their subsidiary Pacol Ltd) in coffee; and others, some of whom may be merchants only in one world centre and brokers in another.

Other firms are, by contrast, purely commission houses. Sometimes they may specialize in one commodity, but this pattern is not very common and is becoming less so. The offices of specialist firms tend to be small, whereas the really large houses spread across many markets and are truly international. An example of a British commission house active in most United Kingdom markets is G. W. Joynson & Co., a subsidiary of the Inchcape Group. The most famous international commission houses, which are a great deal larger, are Merrill Lynch, Pierce, Fenner & Smith Ltd, and Bache & Co. Ltd, who are, of course, also very important stockbrokers.

Nothing is truer than that on an active futures market time may mean money, and the amounts involved are often impressive. The communications systems of floor members are correspondingly sophisticated. Some maintain a private quarter-speed cable between themselves and important clients across the world, in addition to teleprinters, telex machines and direct telephone lines. By means of these, overseas clients as well as home customers are in virtually instantaneous touch with their brokers. Between the brokers' offices and the market floor, rapid communication is equally vital, and here again all the terminal markets have batteries of direct line telephones. The sugar terminal market has two-station closed circuit television, and in one market 'bleepers' carried in floor members' pockets as a signalling device have already been introduced.

As with all ring trading, there are certain specified times laid down during which trading may take place. Most markets are officially 'called over' once or twice a day—at the end of the morning and/or the afternoon trading, or even more frequently. The United Sugar Terminal Market, for example, is called at 10.40 a.m., 12.30 p.m., 3.30 p.m. and 4.50 p.m. (This is clearly why these markets are sometimes referred to as 'call' markets). The bargains are marked up on a prominently displayed board on all terminal markets so that the latest prices, with quantities, may be seen by newcomers. Various other details of futures trading, such as the price of puts, calls and double options, where relevant,[7] are also entered. After the end of the call, if it is an official one, the official price is established by the London Produce Clearing House. This is determined from the trade which has taken place during the call and will often be a mean of prices at which trade has taken place. The official price for each futures position having been established, the news is conveyed to other markets and to the outside world generally. (Reuters, Exchange Telegraph and some other agencies are members of all the exchanges in London and other important centres.)

3. *The London Produce Clearing House Ltd*

Clearly, the registration of an official price is an important outcome of terminal market operations for, in the process of speculating upon likely price movements and hedging, financial and trading interests focus all the demand and supply pressures which bear upon that commodity at that time. Official prices are particularly important for the purpose of clearing the contracts entered into, and in Mincing Lane it is the London Produce Clearing House Ltd which is responsible for this for all markets except that of rubber. The Clearing House is independent of the individual terminal market associations and is at present a wholly-owned subsidiary of United Dominions Trust Ltd. The origins of the London Produce Clearing House Ltd go back to 1888, when it was founded by immigrant German financiers; in fact, its present methods of operation are virtually identical with those laid down in the constitution of the German Exchanges. What is of even greater historical interest is that the London Produce Clearing House also operates in an identical manner with its Amsterdam equivalent, the Nederlandse Liquidatiekas N.V. These connections suggest that the London Produce Clearing House has inherited methods of operation which have been handed down from the seventeenth and eighteenth centuries when Amsterdam was the centre of the world's commodity trade.

The first futures markets served by the London Produce Clearing House were those in sugar and coffee. (It is easy to speculate that the connections between Hamburg and London must have been close in the sugar trade for, as the account in Chapter 10 indicates, the subsidized German sugar beet industry was burgeoning during this period and the Hamburg futures market was correspondingly active.) The Rules governing the conduct of the London terminal market in sugar were drawn up according to the German model by the London Produce Clearing House, and its features—including the separation of broker members from others and the notion of a secretary reporting to a board—turned out to be a blue-print to which all the succeeding Mincing Lane terminal market associations adhered. Subsequently, the London Produce Clearing House cleared terminal market transactions in wheat, maize, pepper, rubber, raw silk, silver, indigo and even in tea at the turn of the century.[8] The Clearing House survived the appearance of a rival house during its early years by amalgamating with it. The business remained entirely in German hands until the First World War and very largely so until the Second World War. In 1939 the London Produce Clearing House was clearing contracts in cocoa, pepper and shellac.

After the period of enforced inactivity occasioned by the war and its aftermath, the London Produce Clearing House had seemingly reached the end of the road, with many shareholders demanding its liquidation. Inflation, inadequate reserves, and inappropriate exchange rates led to the prolongation of exchange controls, and the aim of husbanding supplies of scarce currencies appeared to be incompatible with the re-opening of the major markets.

The course adopted by the directors of the London Produce Clearing House at the end of the war was to look for a buyer of the equity, and this it found in the shape of the United Dominions Trust Ltd. The latter in turn secured the services of Antony Gibbs and Sons to buy the shares, to call meetings and generally to re-establish the business. In fact the U.D.T. made the participation of Anthony Gibbs and Sons as secretaries of the London Produce Clearing House one of the conditions of purchase, and they were later appointed managers. When the reorganization had been accomplished, the rules for terminal market trading were revised, and all the record books reconstituted as futures trading was allowed once more.

From time to time during the postwar years the London Produce clearing house has gone beyond its traditional function of serving as a clearing house for existing markets, by actively seeking the establishment of futures trading in particular commodities which it considered to be suitable. A terminal market in copra, for example, came very near success during the early 1950s, but failed to be established mainly because of lack of interest on the part of Unilever Ltd. On the other hand a Wool Terminal Market was successfully brought into being in 1953, and a coffee terminal market in 1958. (The short-lived Fishmeal Terminal Market was also due to the efforts of the London Produce clearing house.) More recently, too, the Liverpool Raw Cotton Association also appointed the London Produce Clearing House Ltd as secretaries of its London committee. Thus the secretaries of these markets are members of the London Produce Clearing House Ltd which has a separate secretarial department to look after the interests of these organizations. By contrast with this arrangement the terminal markets in sugar, cocoa and the vegetable oils are serviced by the secretary of Commodity Services Ltd, an organization which is entirely separate from the London Produce Clearing House and financed by its member associations according to turnover. It was felt in some quarters that the complete separation of the secretarial and clearing functions would avoid the possibility, however remote, of any conflict of interest

The London Produce Clearing House Ltd has its own capital and reserves with which to back its guarantees and needs to know, in addition, that its members are individuals or enterprises of substance. The Clearing House requires initial deposits from both parties to a contract and subsequent margins from the buyer or seller of the futures contract according to the direction of the price fluctuation. Their extent is, of course, calculated from the official prices established every day on the call markets. The frequent payment of margins is rendered much easier by the practice of accepting letters of guarantee obtained from approved London banks on behalf of members. U.K. Government securities with a 'good margin' of safety are also accepted.

The normal progress of a transaction on one of the Mincing Lane call markets, therefore, is that it starts life as an entry in the books of market traders on the floor of one of the terminal markets. Particulars are then notified to the Clearing House in the form of confirmed Daily Dealing Statements signed by the floor members of the terminal market concerned. Frequently, however, clients of floor members will themselves be members of the Clearing House, in which case the transaction may be registered directly in the client's name upon receipt of the client's signed confirmation of the transaction by the Clearing House. Statements of the previous day's business must be in the hands of the Clearing House not later than 11 a.m. on the working day following the sale and purchase to be cleared.

Stripped of its complexity the clearing itself works as follows. Should any party surrender to the Clearing House two certificates of guarantee, in one of which he is named as the buyer and in the other as a seller for the same commodity for the same month of delivery, this 'middle party' then ceases to be under any liability to receive or to deliver the commodity. Having thus closed out his position, his seller and buyer are deemed to contract with each other to deliver and receive the commodity. In principle, therefore, the contract is fulfilled by these parties at the market price of the day as determined by the Clearing House, and any difference between such price and the contract prices is settled between the Clearing House and each of the contracting parties.

The Clearing House in effect registers the contract only when it has received a deposit, or has ascertained that it already has the appropriate cover. The amounts of such deposits are fixed from time to time by the London Produce Clearing House and published. (At the time of writing, for example, the purchase and sale of one contract unit of sugar must be accompanied by a deposit of £100 each from both the buying and selling brokers.) This deposit remains with the Clearing House until the contract against which it stands is closed or fulfilled, and must remain independent of any margins due. In practice, however, deposits are actually required only on the imbalance of each member's position, as shown in the following example:

In this example, because there are more sold contracts, deposits will be due from the member on the imbalance on the selling side, that is, for 15 lots.

Delivery Month	Contract Units Sold	Contract Units Bought	Uncovered Position	Deposits Charged
July	10	5	5 sales	5
Sept.	75	70	5 sales	5
Nov.	32	42	10 purchases	
Jan.	125	125	0	
March	175	170	5 sales	5
	417	412		15

Deposits for the spot months (i.e. for trade in delivery month contracts) are considered separately from all the other months, since these contracts may at any time be under tender. Deposits are charged on the uncovered spot position.

For example:

Delivery Month	Contract Units Sold	Contract Units Bought	Uncovered Position	Deposits Charged
May	5	8	3 purchases	3

The overall total of deposits due in the above two examples is, therefore, 18 lots. After registering contracts the Clearing House sends to each contracting party a 'certificate of guarantee' and it henceforward becomes responsible for the fulfilment of these contracts.

When the book value of any contract shows a depreciation in terms of official quotations, the Clearing House calls for the payment of a margin from the client concerned, where its value is not provided by the security deposited with the Clearing House. Should the additional margin or security not be forthcoming, the Clearing House reserves the right to close the member's account by buying in, or selling out, against the defaulting interest. Similarly, margins may be used under certain circumstances to offset debits elsewhere when prices have changed in the member's favour. The price of each contract is compared with the official quotation at the final evening call and a new margin figure is calculated every night.

In the calculation of margins, contracts for the spot month are considered first and separately from all the other delivery months. If the member's position shows an overall loss, then margins are required from him. If his position shows a profit, this figure cannot be allowed against any other debit margins on the remote months, since spot month contracts may at any time be under tender. Following the consideration of the spot month by the Clearing House, margins are then calculated on all the open contracts for the remote months (as forward futures contracts are sometimes called). The margin figures for each month are totalled to produce a net balance, which then becomes the member's remote month's liability for that day. Should the final figure be a credit margin, it may be used to the benefit of the member if (a) he has a debit margin on his option contracts,[9] or (b) he has an open position showing a debit margin on another futures market cleared by the London Produce Clearing House Ltd. In both these instances the Clearing House will allow his credit margin and debit margin to be offset.

The taker of an option contract is not charged any deposits, but a member who grants an option contract is charged deposits on every open contract at the ruling rate for that commodity. The taker can only have a credit margin since it is assumed that the option will be abandoned if the position shows a loss. Conversely the granter can only have a debit margin. Option margins are calculated in the same way as for contracts by comparing the basis price with the current evening call price. The resulting margin figure for each member will then be offset against his margins on remote months of non-option contracts for that commodity.

As has been remarked, the Clearing House will allow a member to offset the value of credit margins on one market against debit margins on another. This system does not, however, apply to spot month contracts, on which margins are calculated separately (because spot month contracts may at any time be under tender). The facility does not apply to the calculation of deposits. An example of the way in which the Clearing House may combine deposits and margin calculations across more than one market in accordance with the system outlined above, is given below:

	Combined Deposits £	Spot Margins £	Remote Margins Debit £	Remote Margins Credit £
Market 1	100	100 Dr.	1,000	–
Market 1 Options				200
Market 2	200	100 Cr.	200	–
Market 3	100	100 Dr.		2,000
Market 4		200 Dr.	500	–
Market 4 Options	200		250	–
Market 5	400	100 Dr.	250	–
				–
	£1,000	£500 Dr.	£2,200 Dr.	£2,200 Cr.

The total cover required for deposits and margins is therefore:

Deposits	£1,000
Spot month margins	£500
Remote-month margins	nil
TOTAL	£1,500

Until the end of 1959 the procedures of the London Produce Clearing House Ltd were carried out manually and comprised the following basic operations.

1. As commodity brokers bought and sold commodity lots on the markets, the transactions were recorded on market sheets showing the name of the buyer and seller, the delivery month of the

commodity and the price. Similar details were recorded in their
market books by members.

2. From these market books members of the market prepared
   contracts in their own offices and copies of these contracts were
   submitted to the Clearing House.

3. The Clearing House married the bought and sold parts of each
   contract and checked that the contents of the two documents
   agreed with each other.

4. The particulars of each contract were entered in monthly
   registers and in records of clients' positions.

5. Each day members' deposits and margins had to be calculated
   in order to ensure that their deposits still represented adequate
   cover despite any unfavourable price fluctuations during the day.

6. Certificates of guarantee and settlement statements were prepared. The preparation of the former necessitated their being
   checked against the monthly registers and the records of clients'
   positions in order to ensure their accuracy.

These procedures necessitated a great deal of copying of particulars of
a deal from one document to another, with all the attendant risk of
error and loss of time. Consequently, following a survey by the management consultancy division of Price Waterhouse and Co., the Clearing
House decided in 1960 to install punched card procedures to carry out
the clerical and accounting work associated with the registration and
processing of contracts. The Clearing House also adopted the consultants' suggested changes in the approach to the system for recording
deals. Instead of requiring members to prepare contracts for submission
to the Clearing House where they had to be checked and married, a
daily dealing statement was prepared for members from the punched
cards and this statement was accepted by members as official evidence
of their transactions.

The new system had considerable advantages over the old. The
original bought and sold slip became the single source document for
each deal since all data punched was based on this document. The risk
of errors arising from copying to contract documents was avoided.
Individual members of the Clearing House were saved the task of
preparing a contract for each deal, thus saving a considerable amount
of clerical work in members' offices. (Previously, members had had to
rush back from the markets to their own offices to have contracts typed
out in triplicate from details contained in their market notebooks.
These contracts had then to be sent to the Clearing House for registration and checking with the counterpart contracts prepared by the
other parties to the deals concerned.) In the Clearing House itself it
was no longer necessary to marry the separate bought and sold records
of a deal manually since the daily bought and sold totals were now
checked electronically by a 'zero balancing routine' (i.e. a check to

ensure that the number and value of 'bought' contracts is equal to the number and value of 'sold' contracts). Guarantee certificates issued to members were also prepared mechanically from the same source data. Moreover, a rapid updating of members' positions and the subsequent calculation of the exact amount of margins and deposits required from every member each morning became possible.

Following the installation of the punched card system the turnover of the markets increased very considerably; over the decade of the 1960s the sugar and cocoa terminal markets have expanded some twenty times, and though there has been some decline in turnover on the wool terminal market, the three vegetable oil markets have added to the amount of business done. The value of a contract unit obviously varies with market prices, but is often of the order of £2,000, and in one day the value of contracts cleared may range from £5 million to £20 million. The rapid increase in turnover led to an early change from punched card to computer methods in 1963 and subsequently, in 1965, from a card computer to one backed by magnetic-tape storage. This has enabled the 500,000 or so updatings of contracts required each night (i.e. to re-establish for the following day each member's open position and margins), to be accomplished with relative ease. As a result, the London Produce Clearing House Ltd is now able to offer daily computer services to brokers and dealers on the commodity exchanges (including the London Metal Exchange). Daily margin reports, settlement accounts, open position reports etc. would by this time have become quite impossible to render but for the services of a computer. With its aid, however, the Clearing House has been able to look further afield; thus, since November 1969 the London Produce Clearing House Ltd has been clearing and guaranteeing contracts for the Sydney Greasy Wool Futures Exchange Ltd, for which purpose data transmission facilities have been added to the system.

4. *The Role of the Bank of England*

As has already been suggested, inflation, inadequate reserves and an inappropriate exchange rate led to the prolongation of exchange controls after the war. The need to husband scarce foreign currencies appeared for some time to be incompatible with the re-opening of major markets. In some cases the obvious difficulty was that, left to themselves, many traders would have purchased a significant proportion of their supplies from 'hard currency' areas. However, even where this was not a problem, the purchase of produce imported from other parts of the world with 'soft' inconvertible currencies could be highly unsatisfactory when the authorities already held more than sufficient supplies of these currencies to satisfy traders' demands. There were also dangers of allowing too free a rein to traders for fear of encouraging the re-sale for dollars of commodities bought in the U.K. This could be done profitably should the sterling used for the purchase happen to have been bought cheaply on unofficial markets, though much re-selling of this sort was undertaken by foreign traders without the benefit of purchases at a discount; the premium which the dollars from the sale of produce often commanded after the war in unofficial markets provided sufficient incentive for the conclusion of such transactions.[10]

For many of the commodities dealt with at Plantation House (notably coffee, copra, cocoa, rubber and sugar), the Bank of England produced schemes similar to the ones introduced in the grain and cotton trades, by means of which it was possible to resume private trade in the produce concerned in a manner compatible with the operation of the exchange control regulations. The effect of the arrangement was similar to that introduced governing the conduct of the financial agents, which the Bank allowed in 1951 to engage in exchange arbitrage; that is, the Bank granted permission to these traders to conduct business with foreigners without prior consent for each separate transaction. The schemes were operated in consultation with the trade associations concerned, which were required to approve each member firm entering the schemes and to guarantee their compliance with the arrangements. The system thus represented the delegation of responsibility by the Bank to the market associations for ensuring that the several hundred firms involved kept within the limits of the facilities allowed. Initially, a record of all payments and receipts for imports and exports was required from each firm, to be rendered in the form of monthly returns to the Bank for scrutiny. These accounts could be checked by the Bank against the figures of transactions under the schemes which were recorded for each participant by its banker, from whom similar returns were also required in respect of each participating client. For this purpose each trader had to open a separate account with his banker which recorded the flow of transactions relevant to the schemes. These requirements were subsequently relaxed, especially following the convertibility of externally-held sterling, and in 1960 separate banking accounts and monthly returns ceased to be required.

Not all commodities needed to be subject to such close supervision. The sterling-area countries constituted a group of nations among whom sterling was freely transferable and, in spite of its being inconvertible, acceptable without limit. Thus for commodities such as oil, oilseeds, tea and wool, which were supplied to the U.K. from within these scheduled territories, no such intricate arrangements were used.[11]

Naturally the inauguration, supervision and modification of these schemes brought the Bank and the executive committees of the commodity trade associations closer together when the markets re-opened. Regular consultations were held which developed from the discussion of matters relating to exchange control regulations affecting the markets.

Periodic discussions are still held between representatives of all the commodity trade associations and the Bank on commodity agreement problems, price and sales forecasts, sources of supply and other matters of interest.

At the end of 1967, however, many traders on the physical markets were provoked into outspoken criticism of the Bank to an extent which indicated that the understanding between it and commodity traders had become somewhat less than ideal. The controversy arose because many countries did not devalue along with sterling in November 1967. This left dealers on the London markets committed to purchasing commodities, especially from Nigeria and East Africa, facing serious losses, since many deals were denominated in the currencies of the countries of origin of the produce. The Bank of England eventually offered a low-cost five year loan of £5 million to help such traders over what seemed likely to be a loss of up to £30 million, but this was criticized as a grossly inadequate gesture. The argument used to justify its attitude by the Commodity Committee representing the six associations primarily affected was, that despite repeated requests over the previous few years, they were not allowed currency hedging facilities by the Bank of England. In its defence the Bank pointed out that the traders wanted to cover forward in dollars, whereas official policy decreed that dealers were only allowed facilities to cover forward in the currency of their contracts. It was out of the question, therefore, so the Bank's argument ran, to allow dealers to hedge a sterling commitment in dollars: these traders should have insisted that they would deal only in United Kingdom (as opposed to Nigerian etc.) sterling. In retrospect, it seems that the liaison between these institutions must have left a great deal to be desired: the Bank could well have warned the commodity markets of the risks involved in concluding purchases denominated in uncovered African currencies. As it is, the Bank has since appeared to be encouraging the establishment of forward markets in sterling area currencies—a belated recognition of the diminishing importance of the U.K. market in the world economy and the consequent dethronement of sterling.

Chapter Nine

THE TEA TRADE

1. *The End of the East India Company Monopoly*

WHEN on 25 September 1661 Samuel Pepys 'sent for a cup of tea (a Chinese drink) of which I had never drank before', the beverage was already the subject of taxation if made and sold in coffee houses.[1] Tea was then still very much an expensive form of indulgence for Europeans, whose sole source of supply was the Dutch East India Company. By 1670 its English counterpart had begun to import small quantities of Javan tea and by 1680 the Hon. Company had opened up a direct trade in the commodity with China.

The East India Company's auction sales have been described in Chapter 2, but it was not until 1784 that the Commutation Act[2] made statutory the holding of four public sales of tea every year. The Act decreed, moreover, that sufficient quantities of the produce were to be offered to meet the demand, whatever that might mean. The tea had to be sold to the highest bidder without reserve, provided that an advance of one penny per lb was bid above the price at which the produce was put up for sale. This 'upset price' was not to

> exceed the prime cost thereof, with the freight and charges of importation, together with lawful interest from the time of arrival of such teas in Great Britain, and the common premium of insurance, as a compensation for the sea-risk incurred thereon.

This requirement, like the government's earlier threat in 1744 to allow non-Company imports of tea should prices fail to bear comparison with those obtaining in other European centres, does not appear to have been taken very seriously. Perhaps it was felt by John Company that, since it had imposed an *ad valorem* duty, the government was also fundamentally interested in maintaining high tea prices. Thus in spite of the publication of its accounts, intended by the Commutation Act as a check on the level of the company's 'upset' prices at the auctions, many contemporary observers fulminated against the prices obtained by the East India Company at its public sales, especially as compared with those obtained at New York and Hamburg. J. R. McCulloch was a notable example of one such critic.[3]

The scandalized McCulloch and others of a like mind had to wait for almost another decade before the expiry of the Hon. John Company's charter. When the opportunity did eventually come for the private merchant to participate in the China tea trade the occasion

189

TABLE 9.1A

OFFICIAL VALUES OF TEA IMPORTS AND RE-EXPORTS, 1706–1855

Ten-year annual averages   £ thousand

Years	Imports	Re-exports
1706–15 a	73·3	
1716–25	92·0	
1726–35	99·9	
1736–45	132·5	
1746–55	355·7	
1756–65	495·7	
1766–75	781·6	
1776–85	574·1	
1786–95	1965·6	
1796–1805	2406·9	
1806–15 a	2254·1	684·7
1816–25	2898·4	103·7
1826–35	3381·0	80·7
1836–45	4248·4	613·9
1846–55	6397·5	891·6

a. No figures available for 1813 or 1712, therefore 9 year average.

Sources: Schumpeter, *English Overseas Trade Statistics* (to 1808), Mitchell, *Abstract of British Historical Statistics* (to 1855).

England and Wales	1706–1791
Great Britain	1792–1829
United Kingdom	1826–1855

TABLE 9.1B

VALUES AT CURRENT PRICES OF TEA IMPORTS AND RE-EXPORTS OF THE UNITED KINGDOM, 1854–1968

(1854–70 computed values)   £ million

Five-year annual average figures

Years	Imports	Re-Exports
1854–58	5·2	0·58
1859–63	7·9	1·26
1864–68	10·6	2·50
1869–73	11·3	2·74
1874–78	12·7	2·50
1879–83	11·3	2·48
1884–88	10·5	2·08
1889–93	10·1	1·62
1894–98	10·3	1·44
1899–1903	9·8	1·66
1904–08	10·0	1·96
1909–13	12·6	2·48
1914–18	19·0	2·30
1919–23	28·5	3·26
1924–28	38·8	7·56
1929–33	30·3	5·86
1934–38	28·1	4·50
1941–45	31·68	1·00
1946–50	51·90	2·46
1951–55	98·32	6·50
1956–60	120·94	8·74
1961–65 a	112·32	10·02
1966–68	105·8	12·01

a. From 1965 figures include maté.

Sources: *Annual Statement of Trade.*
Overseas Trade Accounts.
Mitchell, *Abstract of British Historical Statistics.*

TABLE 9.2

LONDON FUTURES TRANSACTIONS IN TEA, 1889–1900

	China Tea (half chests)	Indian Tea (chests)	Ceylon Tea (chests)	Tea (half chests)
1889				572,000
1890	830,000	5,600 a		
1891	797,500	112,800		
1892	134,000	213,600		
1893	223,500	169,000		
1894	86,000	217,400		
1895	80,500	132,800		
1896	39,000	180,000	4,400 b	
1897	22,500	46,000	400	
1898		2,000		
1899		7,600		
1900		6,400		

a. Since 15 November 1890.
b. Since 20 April 1896.
Source: Figures supplied by the London Produce Clearing House Ltd.

seems to have aroused considerable emotion, as this produce, which had previously all passed through the Company's London warehouses, began to arrive at many of the outports. In March 1834, for example, the *Glasgow Herald*[4] records that when the *Camden* came to anchor off the steam-boat quay at Greenock bearing the first fruits of free trade with China 'the crew assembled on the quarter deck and gave three cheers, which were immediately responded by the people assembled on the quay'. The *Camden* was, in fact, one of three vessels consigned from Canton in 1834 by the mercantile house of Jardine, Matheson and Co. The other ships were the *Georgina* and the *Princess Charlotte*, despatched to Liverpool and London respectively as an experiment to ascertain whether London or the outports afforded the best market for tea.[5] In the event, the London sales proved most advantageous and it was there that the firm ultimately flourished. Liverpool, however, remained a significant sales centre until 1870 as northern merchanting firms such as Rathbones continued to sell tea and other produce there.[6]

The opening up of the tea trade to private merchants was inevitably accompanied by a considerable growth of British mercantile houses such as Jardine, Matheson and Co., Harrisons and Crosfield, and Rathbone Bros and Co. The first named company, having been founded in 1782 by John Cox, a dealer in English 'sing-songs', was forced by the East India Company to leave Canton but the firm was later able to return by resuming business as a 'Prussian' company. This was but one of several devices by which Canton was penetrated by private merchants. In addition to tea, it also typically handled a flourishing trade in silks and rice: Singapore became an important entrepôt for the former commodity after about 1825. (The most important markets for silk in the United Kingdom were Manchester and London.) Harrisons and Crosfield also provide an example of a firm of East India merchants whose ramifications eventually grew to world-wide proportions. In addition to supplying the Liverpool and London markets, they built up a large re-export business in tea in the course of the nineteenth century. By the 1890s this trade extended from Odessa to Morocco, Spain, Portugal and South America. They had agents in Marseilles, Hamburg and New York, in addition to which they also traded in South Africa and Canada.[7]

Merchant firms such as these were characteristic of the way in which the primary producing regions of the Far East were linked with the more advanced industrial and commercial world centres. Their activities did not stop short at merchanting, moreover, for they also had considerable business connections as agents, insurers, bankers, bill brokers and shippers. The tea which they consigned to the United Kingdom might either be produce which they were merchanting (i.e. which they had bought and were re-selling) or else handling as commission agents, sometimes for Chinese houses. After about mid-century a more complex arrangement seems to have been on the increase, characterized as 'joint-account' trading. This was essentially a profit-sharing arrangement between merchants and commission houses to allow the spreading of risks.[8]

The first public sale of tea after the cessation of the East India Company's monopoly was concluded at the Commercial Sale Rooms, Mincing Lane, on 19 August 1834. A short while later tea auctions were also being conducted at Garraway's Coffee-house. The sales were organized by the Committee of East India Merchants, but the produce itself was entrusted for sale to resident selling brokers in Liverpool and London. The establishment of free private trade in tea in the United Kingdom was attended by a number of initial difficulties, and some early practices even resulted in the seizure of the tea by the customs.[9] The absurd method of taxing tea by the volume of the beverage offered for sale in the coffee-houses had long since (i.e. after 1689) given way to the more orthodox system of levying duty on the dry leaf. Pitt had reduced the tariff in 1784 to check the widespread smuggling of tea into the country from Holland, and in 1833 'An Act to provide for the Collection of Management of Duties on Tea' superseded earlier *ad valorem* rates. Congou teas then became liable to a tariff of 2s. 2d. per lb while Boheas attracted a 1s. 6d. duty: the remaining expensive teas (i.e. Souchong, Hyson, Gunpowder, and Flowery Pekoe) were taxed at 3s. Not surprisingly, therefore, many Congou teas were discharged at British ports masquerading as Boheas, and were duly seized by the customs authorites. There were, too, many incidents such as that which took place at the sale of 9 October 1834, when '24 chests, called Bohea, were at the unanimous opinion of the trade withdrawn, not being tea'. Finally, during the early days of the open trade, the selling brokers, in London especially, seem to have been very much in the ascendant; merchants frequently complained in their correspondence that their produce was being treated incompetently, and even dishonestly, by this fraternity. Ultimately, however, the worst difficulties appear to have been resolved. The tea duty eventually became a 'poll tax on a very low scale' with the movement towards tariff-free trade and the loss of the British public's heart to this peculiar beverage. Eventually, too, many of the Eastern houses established their own expert agents or branch houses at the auction centres. With the growth of the tea trade under these conditions of closer supervision, the selling brokers ultimately became the supplicants for business. Thus the convenience of auction sales as a means of disposing of the produce had impressed itself on traders in spite of early shortcomings. Consequently, as the century progressed direct shipments and private trading in tea declined in favour of sales through an organized market.

Perhaps the best glimpse we have of the benefit of the freeing of the trade from the grip of the East India Company is *The Economist's* statement that within twelve years of the expiry of the East India Company's charter the cost price of tea had been reduced by some 30 per cent.[10] Notwithstanding John Company's monopoly, prices had, however, been falling since the end of the Napoleonic Wars: the average duty free price of tea between 1814 and 1820 was 3s. 6d. a lb, but by 1825-30 it was down to 2s. 8d. The further decline in cost price referred to by *The Economist* was by no means uneventful, for the atmosphere at the early tea auctions was frequently tense and speculative, as many contemporary accounts testify.[11] However, the most hectic episode in the history of the tea market without doubt was that of the so-called 'opium war' with China. D. Morier Evans,[12] for instance, relates that:

The tea speculation which suddenly sprang up at the time of the great war with China, about the year 1840-41, was another of these mercantile phrenzies which, commencing on a legitimate basis, was afterwards stimulated by enlarged transactions, till prices were carried on to an undue height, leaving many of the operators penniless, and others deeply embarrassed . . . Company's Congous—the brand of East India Company's import— were soon made the consols of the tea market . . . the quotation in the space of ten or twelve months was run up from 11d. to 3s. 6d. per lb; and in the meanwhile, on the arrival of every China mail, variations ranging from 3d. to 6d. and even 9d. per lb ensued in the course of twenty-four hours. Mincing Lane was never so crowded . . . Business was transacted there in the morning. Later in the day, it was continued on 'Change. There was a regular closing price for Congou consols; and if any special news arrived, fresh operations were continued with vigour at Garraway's, Tom's, or any of the neighbouring coffee-houses.

2. *Indian Tea and the Growth of the Trade*
At the time China tea was virtually alone in the market, hence the

excitement occasioned by the hostilities. Early attempts to introduce
the native Chinese tea plant into India had failed, but an indigenous
bush was ultimately discovered in Assam which led to the rapid
development of its cultivation. The first sample of Indian tea was sent
to London in 1836. By 1854 Indian tea exports were a quarter of a
million lbs, and by 1866 had increased a further tenfold despite the
fact that Chinese tea exports were at the time also at their all-time high
level. Ultimately, however, as the accompanying table indicates,
Chinese tea was superseded and in time totally eclipsed by Indian
teas (Table 9.3). The distance over which the commodity had to be
carried was, of course, greater, and so were the inherent difficulties,
such as the language, faced by the China houses. Western merchants'
contacts were solely with Chinese middlemen rather than with producers, and the former were often unreliable, bankruptcies being
frequent. There were considerable foreign exchange problems, feuds
between western merchants, and hostilities between the British and
the Chinese.[13]

The Indian tea companies formed to purchase estates on which to
grow tea almost all bore new unfamiliar names. The first of them was
established in 1839, after which they burgeoned. The system which
came into being was one in which agency houses acted for the smaller
tea companies, who could by this means economize on management.
As the Imperial Economic Committee pointed out:

These 'agents' are more properly described as merchant bankers.
In many cases the present tea producing companies were established on the initiative of these agents, who had financed the
original planters, and they were not only represented on the
Boards but in reality control the companies of which they are
economically the servants.[14]

As we have already seen, the third quarter of the nineteenth century
ushered in considerable improvements in communications; steamships
became more common-place, the Suez Canal was opened, and Britain
was in telegraphic communication with India by 1865, and with
China by 1871. The opening of the Canal route between Britain and
India coincided with the enormous growth in the popularity of teas
grown in the latter country. Thus in marked contrast with exports of
Indian cotton, for which the Cape route by sailing vessel remained
cheaper for many years, exports of Indian tea showed an astonishing
increase after the opening of the Suez Canal. In 1870 exports were
some 11 million lbs, but by 1893-94 they had increased to 120 million
lbs. Clearly such figures in themselves tell us nothing one way or
another about the direct influence of the canal in promoting Indian
tea exports. What is clear, however, is its effect upon the timing of the
new season's arrivals on the London market for whereas tea imports
into the United Kingdom during the month of July 1870 were only

TABLE 9.3

EXPORTS OF TEA FROM MAIN PRODUCING COUNTRIES, 1896–1968

million lbs

Country	1896-7	1913-14	1927-28	1934-38b	1954-58b	1964-68b
India	150	292	371	336	456	446
Pakistan					15	2
Ceylon	110	197	227	220	370	465
Indonesia				149	78	71
Japan				39	26	6
Taiwan (Formosa)				22	25	41
Kenya				7	16	47
Uganda					6	19
Tanganyika (Tanzania)				0·2	4	13
Nyasaland a				8	19	33
Mozambique				0·7	13	27
Others				3	16	69
China (Mainland Post-war II)	240	192	116	90	76	71
Total				875	1120	1310

a. From 1954 Federation of Rhodesia and Nyasaland, from 1964 Malawi.
Figures have been rounded and therefore do not necessarily add to total.
Sources: F. W. F. Staveacre, *Tea and Tea Dealing* (London, 1929);
F.A.O. Commodity Bulletin Series 30 – *Tea Trends and Prospects*,
International Tea Committee, *Annual Bulletin of Statistics*.
b. Five-year annual averages

711,000 lbs, for the same month two years later they had risen to 23 million lbs.[15]

For commodities of relatively high value in relation to their bulk, such as fermented black tea, the cutting of the canal could not fail to have dramatic consequences. The sailing vessels of the day took the best part of a year to make the journey from India to the United Kingdom, and their arrival could not be predicted within a month or two. It was therefore imperative for the trade to have large stocks readily available, and it was this fact which gave rise to the highly developed warehousing system at Britain's ports, encouraged by rapidly growing industries and explosive population growth. Apart from their importance, moreover, British ports were also the logical locations for breaking bulk and the re-sale of imports from the Far East. Britain's re-export trade in tea accordingly flourished.

With the introduction of steamers which could make the journey to India via Suez in one month and virtually instantaneous telegraphic communications the situation was transformed. Both British and continental traders now found it possible to order direct and to take direct delivery of many goods. Indian exports, especially to Germany, France, Holland and Belgium, increased very considerably. Thus, as Fairlie points out,[16] whereas in 1870 the value of exports to the United Kingdom was some $70 million and to the remainder of Europe only $13 million, by 1893-4 Indian exports to the U.K. had increased some 40 per cent to $93 million while exports to the rest of Europe had grown sixfold, to $85 million. Over the same period the proportion of Indian exports to continental Europe which was trans-shipped in the U.K. declined from 83 to 53 per cent. This is the chief cause of the failure of U.K. tea re-exports to grow at the same rate as the tea trade: in 1872, for example, tea re-exports realized £3.3 million, a figure which was virtually unchanged at the outbreak of war in 1914, though during most of the intervening period annual values were lower.

The Suez Canal, the steamship and the telegraph, by dramatically shortening the duration of the journey from the Far East and enabling business to be transacted without delay, also had inevitable repercussions upon the United Kingdom's system of warehouse distribution. These store-houses were not required to nearly the same extent as formerly. Such changes as we have already seen in the case of grain and cotton were potent influences in transforming the trade, though in the tea market the influence of buying 'to arrive' was less strong owing to the difficulty of grading the produce. However, the general reduction of risk and the need for considerable capital implied by these changes brought many new merchants into the Eastern trade. Often their capital was inadequate, but many succeeded by means of commercial loans and the facilities provided by the banks. They were thereby enabled to undercut the existing 'merchant princes', and some of the older houses consequently went out of business, along with dealers in six months bills of exchange, since these were no longer required. As far as the tea trade was concerned, the effect of these changes was to bring in more plentiful tea supplies and prices accordingly fell—a feature of the times which also contributed to the declining value of the re-export trade.

In all the produce trades the effect of the spectacular improvement in communications was to unify the world's markets, so that, taking transport costs and fiscal barriers into account, it was no longer possible for prices to depart appreciably in one centre from their levels at others without giving rise to equalizing movements of produce. The strength of the pressures exerted by the British market varied for different commodities, though in almost all cases it was very considerable throughout the nineteenth century. This was especially true for tea, and though China remained the largest producer because of its huge domestic market, a mounting acreage of tea was planted in India to serve the United Kingdom market. The production of tea in Ceylon, for example, was undertaken only in the 1870s after the failure of coffee crops and in response to the pull of the British market. By 1896, exports were in excess of 110 million lbs compared with China's 240 million lbs of black and green tea (but excluding 78.6 million lbs of brick, tablet and dust teas) and Indian exports of 150.4 million lbs. In 1900, Ceylon's exports had already overtaken those of Chinese black and green tea, and the gap continued to widen.

These changes occurred to the accompaniment of rising British consumption, which had grown from some $1\frac{1}{4}$ to $1\frac{1}{2}$ lbs per head during the last year of the East India Company's monopoly, to some 6 lbs per head of a much greater population by the end of the century. As is indicated by the accompanying table (Table 9.4), annual average consumption for the United Kingdom for the year immediately prior to the outbreak of war in 1914 was 293 million lbs compared with imports of 157.7 million lbs into Russia, the then next largest consumer, and 98.9 million lbs into the U.S.A. However, whereas U.K. consumption shows a rising trend after World War I, imports into the U.S.S.R. dwindled sharply, while those of the U.S.A. show no discernible pattern. From the table showing imports of tea into the U.K. and U.S.A. by source it is clear that in 1913 the United Kingdom remained the overwhelmingly important market for Indian and Ceylon teas—the two major black tea exporters—while the American market was more important for the smaller Chinese and Japanese exports (Table 9.5). These were the facts, in conjunction with the regular public sales held in Mincing Lane (tea auctions having been discontinued in the U.S.A. since 1903), which accounted for the unchallenged position of London as the world's premier tea market at this time.

TABLE 9.4

NET IMPORTS OF TEA BY MAJOR IMPORTING COUNTRIES, 1909–1968
million lbs

Country	1909–13	1925	1934–38c	1951–55c	1964–68c
United Kingdom	293	402	427	499	509
Ireland		23	23	24	25
Netherlands	11	16	23	18	20
United States	99	100	83	101	138
Canada	38	36	39	44	44
South America			11	10	17
U.S.S.R.	158	23	41	23 a	50 b
Iran			15	14	15
Iraq			6	26	40
United Arab Republic – Egypt	2	10	16	38	57
Morocco	7	12	17	29	26
Union of South Africa	5	10	14	25	38
Australia	35	49	46	58	64
New Zealand	8	11	11	15	17
Rest of World			77	102	247
World Total			849	1026	1307

a. 1955 only.
b. 4 year average.
Sources International Tea Committee, *Annual Bulletin of Statistics*,
        Edward Ewing Pratt, *International Trade in Staple Commodities* (New York, 1928),
        C.E.C., *Plantation Crops*.
    c. Five-year annual averages

3. Market Interventions 1914-1955

Between 1914 and 1917 tea prices in London approximately doubled. More of this beverage was called upon to sustain the British army, stocks fell and transport costs increased. Ultimately, in 1918, the blending of teas was standardized into a single 'National Control Tea', and sold at a fixed price. Supplies were handled by the Ministry of Food, which contracted for proportions of the Indian and Sinhalese crops. As was the case for grain, cotton and other foodstuffs, 1917 saw a shortage of shipping so that stocks became depleted in the United Kingdom while they piled up in the producing countries.[17]

The cessation of hostilities led to the release of shipping, and so to an enormous growth of stocks in the United Kingdom as the accompanying table shows:

1913	..	138.0 million lbs	
1915	..	151.9	,, ,,
1917	..	37.4	,, ,,
1919	..	154.0	,, ,,
1920	..	214.0	,, ,,

The high prices obtained during the war, moreover, had encouraged the planting of additional acreages, together with the habit of plucking coarser leaves from the plants to increase yields. In consequence, the market weakened markedly in 1920 as the British government returned the trade to private hands and sold off its stocks.

The upshot was an agreement by producers' associations to reduce the 1920 crop to 90 per cent of average annual production for 1915-19. By the end of 1921 the difficulty was over as the result of 'finer plucking, low prices, unfavourable weather, shortage of labour and the high exchange value of the rupee'.[18] A renewed weakness in the market in 1925 led to a limitation of offerings at the London auctions by the India and Ceylon tea associations. It was the weather, however, which eventually induced a sharp climb in prices (1s. 6d. per lb between September and December), but, notwithstanding this, an official Board of Trade enquiry into tea prices led to a criticism of the policy of limiting offerings,[19] though like the Monopolies' Commission Report of 1956 it considered such practices permissible when done simply to even out the seasonal flow of supplies.

Tea prices started to fall well ahead of the great depression at the end of the 1920s and by 1929 tea stocks in London represented over six months supply. The decline was strong enough for the tea producers' associations of India, Ceylon and the East Indies to agree to reduce output by 57.5 million lbs below that of 1929 for 1930 only. The conclusion of the International Tea Committee on the scheme was that though it failed in its ostensible object it probably prevented a large increase in exports.[20] The arrangement is chiefly notable for the elegance with which the reductions were worked out, producers of cheaper varieties of tea being asked to make greater reductions than the growers of the more expensive kinds.

TABLE 9.5

IMPORTS OF TEA INTO THE U.K. AND THE U.S.A.
million lb

From	To U.K. 1913	1958	1966	1968
India	204	326	216	250
Ceylon	111	161	156	168
China	16	9	4	7
Java	10			
Japan		1	0·2	0·2
Pakistan		10	5	
Indonesia		16	6	14
Mozambique		11	19	23
Taiwan (Formosa)		0·5	2	1·5
Tanganyika		4	11	12
Uganda		4	6	10
Kenya		11	41	45
Malawi a		18	19	19
Others		16·5	31·6	46·3
Total		588	515	596

From	To U.S.A. 1913	1958	1966	1968
India	4	30	20	24
Ceylon	14	39	54	50
China	24	0·5		
Java	0·1			
Japan	44	3	3	4
Pakistan				
Indonesia		15	18	20
Mozambique		0·5	2·5	3
Taiwan (Formosa)		6	8	7
Tanganyika				
Uganda		4	14	20
Kenya				
Malawi				
Others		5	14·5	28
Total		103	133	156

Figures have been rounded and therefore do not necessarily add to total.
a. From 1955-64, Federation of Rhodesia and Nyasaland.

Sources: F. W. F. Staveacre, *Tea and Tea Dealing* (London, 1929).
International Tea Committee, *Annual Bulletin of Statistics.*

By 1932 stocks had once more reached record levels, while prices declined to their lowest points. The average price of tea then reached 9½d. a lb, almost half the average of 18.4d. for the years 1926-28. Tea, of course, will not keep indefinitely and so the large stocks increased pressures to sell despite lower prices. It was out of this situation that an International Tea Agreement was born which was destined to run, albeit in attenuated form, until 1945, and again from 1950 to 1955.

The 1933 Agreement was signed by producers' associations which accounted for almost all world exporters of black tea—the form of the produce which accounted for more than three-quarters of world tea exports. The Agreement was backed by the governments of the producing countries concerned and given statutory effect: its main features consisted in the regulation of exports (this time without distinction as to quality) and the prohibition of new planting except in special circumstances. Export quotas were fixed by the International Tea Committee, representing the tea growers, to which delegates from the governments of India and the Dutch East Indies were appointed. Interestingly, quotas were made transferable as an aid to flexibility and efficiency.

Prices did not fluctuate appreciably during the period of the first Agreement (i.e. 1933-4 to 1937-8) after which the threat of war began to push them upwards from their level of about 14d. per lb. The Agreement was on the whole fairly successful partly because the Committee did not restrict quotas unduly in order to drive up prices; a narrowing of export quotas for 1935-37 to 82½ per cent of basic quotas was the most severe restraint attempted. The success of the Agreement also owed something to the fact that the important non-signatory nations were China, Japan and Formosa, almost all of whose output was green tea. Japan did, however, try to take advantage of the Agreement's export restrictions by installing machinery for making black tea, so that by the end of the decade, Japanese exports of this produce were of the order of 7-8 million lbs a year. The export restriction scheme was assisted by the fact that, unlike much other produce, tea deteriorates in quality with long storage. Crop variations, too, can be overcome to a considerable extent by coarser or finer plucking of the tea plants, while demand is relatively insensitive to price and income changes. Finally, there were favourable factors on the administrative side: tea production in signatory members' countries had long been a plantation industry by the 1930s, and thus was more amenable to control than if individual growers had been bringing produce for sale to local markets. At a higher level, as J. W. F. Rowe points out,[21] the number of countries exporting black tea in quantity was, in reality, very small: India, Ceylon and the Netherlands East Indies—which in the 1930s meant that agreement need be reached only between Britain and Holland.

Though it remained in existence after the outbreak of war in 1939, the International Tea Exports Regulation Agreement ceased to have any practical effect after the Japanese invasion of the Netherlands East Indies in 1942. Meanwhile, the British Ministry of Food had taken control of all British bonded stocks of tea and arranged for future supplies by means of contracts with India and Ceylon. These were concluded initially on the basis of average 1936-38 f.o.b. prices in those countries plus allowances for increased costs—that is, the so-called 'dearness allowance'. At a later date British East African teas were contracted for in the same way.

Following the entry of the Americans into the war, the United Nations Combined Food Board appointed the Ministry of Food as 'managing agent' for all purchases of tea for the United Nations. Allocations to individual countries were made in accordance with the recommendations of the Tea Committee of the Combined Food Board.[22] British control over supplies was intended to cater both for Allied and neutral countries, the Ministry of Food guaranteeing, in effect, a market for all the exportable surpluses of the exporting countries. This arrangement was intended to scotch the free market which had arisen in Calcutta and Colombo in teas sold there surplus to the amounts contracted for by the Ministry of Food. Auction sales did, however, continue in Calcutta in order to dispose of the teas intended for India's domestic market, and by early 1943 the price of common tea on this market had risen some 500 per cent over its level at the outbreak of war. In Britain both wholesale and retail prices continued to be controlled during and for some years after the war by the Ministry of Food. It also organized internal distribution and re-exports to Eire. Other former overseas buyers at the London auctions received supplies direct from purchasing countries during this period.

There were undoubted advantages for the British government— indeed for the Allies as a whole—in the bulk purchase of teas during the war. Economies were gained in the use of shipping, the allocation of the produce was rendered easier and some control over prices could be maintained. The wisdom of the post-war Labour government's decision to continue the bulk-buying of tea, as of other raw materials was, however, much more questionable. Contracts were negotiated on a cost basis, which in any case varied from plantation to plantation: much ill-will was engendered, particularly between the British and the Sinhalese governments, by the former's obduracy in standing out in 1948 for a contract price which was 2d. a lb below the price of the re-opened Colombo auctions. The British argument was that in view of the amounts which were being removed from open markets by their bulk-buying at the time, the Colombo auction prices could not be considered to reflect supply-demand pressures very accurately. In the meantime, of course, the London auctions remained closed and many overseas buyers, especially from the United States, were 'more or less forced to deal directly with producing countries'.[23] The only concession to the maintenance of the erstwhile flourishing re-export trade was the official permission given to private merchants from August 1947 to import tea for blending and re-export. In the meantime, because stocks were still low, the rationing of the British consumer continued, while bulk-purchasing exerted its bias in favour of quantity at the expense of quality. However, perhaps the worst aspect of the entire arrangement was the annual bickering which took place—sometimes in an atmosphere of considerable asperity—between government representatives. Matters commonly settled in the market-place without political overtones were, by the bulk-purchase of tea, given considerable political significance, and that at a particularly delicate juncture in Britain's relations with the Indian sub-continent. Thus in 1947, because of dissatisfaction with the price offered by the British negotiations, both the Indian and Sinhalese governments decreed that all teas from within their territories should be sold at the auctions in Calcutta and Colombo. Though this step was later abandoned as impractical, it was a clear indication that the continuation of bulk-purchasing policies would constitute an open invitation to producer countries to succeed to the Mincing Lane Auction's former rôle as the world tea market par excellence, and this in spite of Britain's habitual consumption of half the world's exports of tea.

The signing of the bulk purchase agreements of May 1950 was coupled with the announcement that the government intended to discontinue this mode of purchase: its loss of faith in this method of trading was accompanied a few months later, in July, by an actual reduction in the tea ration—virtually at the same time as Australia discontinued rationing altogether. In the event, the Mincing Lane auctions re-opened on 16 April 1951, with an offering of 11,514 packages only.[24]

The wartime 'second period' of the International Tea Agreement, due to expire in 1943, was extended to March 1948. This was followed by an Interim Producers' Agreement for two years, signed by India, Pakistan, Ceylon and Indonesia. Despite the absence of a 'burdensome surplus' (which would have justified the establishment of an International Commodity Control Agreement under the auspices of the United Nations), the Interim Producers' Agreement was followed in 1950 by a further International Tea Agreement scheduled to run for five years. The arrangements leaned very heavily upon the Agreement's 1933 predecessor in allocating export quotas and limiting the further extension of tea plantations. The need for the agreement was not at all apparent, for the principal need of the times appeared to be to meet existing world demand. Consequently, the Agreement was not renewed in 1955.

Subsequently there have been some interesting changes, not the least of which has been the emergence of the independent régimes of former British East Africa which have increased their tea production since before the war, though their exports are still much less than those of India and Ceylon, as the table of exports indicates (Table 9.3). Inspired possibly by the gains in the export field made by Ceylon since 1938, these and other countries do not seem prepared to enter into any restrictive agreements at the moment. This was the decision of a tea producers' conference convened at Nuwara Eliya in May 1965, despite the weakening of tea prices during the 1960s: the average price of the Mincing Lane auctions for 1959 for example, was 4s. 4.7d. per lb, but for 1965 it was down to 4s. 0.86d.

Tea prices would undoubtedly have weakened further but for the reversal of exporting trends by two major suppliers. Recent Indonesian exports have never approached the 89 million lbs exported in 1954. Chinese exports have declined similarly after having reached a post-war peak of 108 million lbs. They are currently in the region of 60 million lbs only, with future developments uncertain. In most other countries the yield of tea per acre has improved enormously, and this, too, would have contributed to a weakening of prices but for the fact that it has been offset by rising domestic consumption in the growing countries. Whereas in the inter-war period, for example, Ceylon exported 99 per cent of its production, the proportion is currently more than 10 per cent lower, while tea consumption has risen by nearly 50 per cent in both India and Pakistan over the past decade.[25] This trend compares with some tendency for consumption per head to decline in the U.K. Consumption was 9.9 lbs per head for 1958 but by 1966 only some 9 lbs. This is still phenomenally high by comparison with most other consuming countries, the next highest being Eire at 8.3 lbs.

4. *The Mincing Lane Auctions*
The London sales are organized by eight firms of selling brokers acting in concert under the title of the Tea Brokers' Association of London.[26] For the selling brokers auctions are the end product of a lengthy process which sometimes starts with the receipt of samples of tea from overseas clients for report and valuation while its manufacture is still proceeding. When the tea ultimately arrives in the U.K. for auction, it still comes via the agency companies who frequently manage the estates, and arrange the manufacture, shipment and sale of the teas. Agency companies are now of two categories: those registered in the United Kingdom and others registered overseas. They are, therefore, commonly referred to as 'sterling' and 'non-sterling' companies (or 'rupee' companies in the case of those registered in India, Pakistan and Ceylon). According to the Report of the Monopolies Commission,[27] almost one half of the total amount of tea imported into the U.K. in 1954 was forwarded by sterling companies in Northern India and Ceylon; of the remainder, a large proportion was consigned by rupee companies in these same areas. These organizations are banded together into various associations: the sterling companies in Northern and Southern India, Pakistan (which of recent years no

longer permits its tea to be sold at the London auctions), Ceylon and Indonesia, each have an association with London offices. The tea selling organizations of the countries of former British East Africa also have their London representatives. Moreover, on the purchasing side there is a Tea Buying Brokers' Association, and all these organizations are represented in a joint organization called the Tea Trade Committee. Since its formation in January 1953 this body has been the forum at which matters of interest to the trade as a whole have been thrashed out.

Before the tea is auctioned in this country it is taken after arrival at the docks to a bonded warehouse where each package is marked with an identification of the vessel in which it was shipped, together with the date. After being weighed[28] in the presence of a customs officer the packages are opened or sometimes a small hole is bored with a boring iron in order to obtain a sample. This is done in the presence of the selling broker's representative in order that he might compare these samples for similarity of leaf, size, colour and smell, before deciding whether to bulk the consignment for repacking and sale as 'London bulked'.[29]

Despite the difficulty of grading tea so that it can be sold on description it is fairly readily classified into two broad groups: these are the 'broken' and 'leaf' grades. Of these, the former makes a darker brew and is more highly prized these days, though leaf grades are still widely consumed in many European countries. In the Near East the smaller-sized broken grades known as 'fannings' are preferred, while in India domestic consumption is largely of the grade known as 'dust'.[30] Thus the main difficulty in grading tea lies in doing so according to quality rather than leaf size. In these matters the agent, or importing merchant, relies upon the judgement of his selling broker. However, should the buyer consider after purchase that the bulk is not fully equal to the sample upon which he has relied, he may appeal and the issue goes to an arbitration panel. This normally consists of two members of the London-based associations already mentioned (one to be chosen by each disputant). The arbitrators themselves, should they fail to agree, may appoint their own umpire to settle the issue.

The weighing and sampling over, the selling brokers then proceed to make up their catalogues for sale. In addition to the 'conditions of sale'—most of which have been inherited, as was seen in Chapter 2, from the early days of the trade—this document will indicate the date and time of the sale, the names of the selling brokers, the present location of the tea (e.g. at Orient wharf or Butler's wharf), the merchants or other agents for whom the produce is being sold (e.g. the Dooars Tea Co. Ltd), and the garden from which the tea was harvested (e.g. the Indong Estate). Each 'break' or 'lot' of tea, which is usually between thirty and forty chests, is numbered in the catalogue, the number depending upon the selling broker's luck in drawing lots for position at the auction. In addition, opposite each lot number there appears a description of a grade of tea (e.g. Orange Fannings or Pekoe Dust), and the weight in lbs of the 'break'. Underneath this in brackets is given the weight of six chests, because the weight notes from the warehouses are normally made up in sixes.

The people who buy tea in quantity are the tea dealers and packers who blend different types of tea: a small number of firms dominate the mass market by this time, especially Brooke Bond Ltd, J. Lyons & Co. Ltd, Typhco Tea Ltd, and the English and Scottish Joint Cooperative Wholesale Society Ltd. The buyers first taste the tea on offer, though plain tea is often bought 'on the nose', that is by smell and appearance. Quality teas, used for blending with plain teas, will, however, generally be cup-tested. The usual classification by quality consists of separating 'quality tea', 'medium tea', and 'plain tea' (sometimes called 'common tea'). Judgements are made according to cup quality only, so that each of the grades by size of leaf can fall into any of these quality divisions. The tea is tested in cups of the beverage poured off from the infused leaves, with or without milk added to the taste of the taster. The taster operates by re-arranging the cups in order of preference and, after the dry leaf has also been examined, the taster values the tea. Sometimes teas recently sold are used as a guide in fixing a ceiling valuation upon the produce (which is then noted in code on the buyer's catalogue). The total number of teas to be valued at any one time may exceed a thousand, for the total number of varieties is in the region of 2,000. This is a task which evidently calls for specialization among the tasters and partially explains the sale of different sorts of tea on different days.

When the auction starts one firm of brokers may have marked in its catalogue three or more orders for the same lot of tea all at the same price. Competitive bidding has therefore started before the actual auction, and this saves unnecessary time in eliminating preliminary bidding. This is a considerable advantage where speed is essential in order that all the lots may be put up for sale. The work done in catalogue preparation and sampling ensures that no time needs to be spent by the auctioneers in describing the produce: the buying brokers start the bidding quickly, and when they finish there is an abrupt tap of the hammer to signify a sale, and bidding for the next lot is opened.

Though the sales are public, in practice brokers do all the bidding, but representatives from the packers and dealers on whose behalf they buy are almost always in attendance. Usually maximum bids have previously been agreed between buyers and brokers, but changes in the state of market demand cannot be accurately forecast. The consequent signalling between these parties is often ingenious and almost always puzzling, as it is meant to be, for buyers are not anxious that their competitors should know for how many or which breaks they are bidding. This, in addition to his expertise, is the reason why a buying broker is employed. When a break has been sold, the auctioneer announces the name of the broking firm, or of the individual broker, deemed to have bought a particular lot rather than the name of the buyers for whom the brokers are acting. The name of the principal for whom a broker has successfully bid must be declared in writing within twenty-four hours for the approval of the selling brokers, otherwise the buying brokers are themselves held responsible for payment. The degree of trust and confidence is such, however, that brokers very frequently omit this procedure in the case of clients of standing.

It is a distinctive feature of the auctions that the selling brokers sometimes bid for buyers, or in the language of the tea trade, buyers sometimes give their orders to 'chair', which is the name given to the 'market men' who stand in the box on either side of the auctioneer. It is a strange sight to the uninitiated to hear brokers responsible for the conduct of the sale themselves joining in the bidding, which advances the price almost invariably by increments of $\frac{1}{4}$d. per lb. Nor is it easy for the visitor to follow the bidding once the auctioneer has initiated the sale of a particular lot by suggesting a price at which the bidding may start. The rapidity of the proceedings may be gauged from the fact that as many as 200 'breaks' may be sold in an hour, and though such a 'lot' may vary from 6 to 120 chests (each being one grade of tea from one invoice and from one particular estate), the average 'break' is between 30 and 40 chests of about 110 lbs each. Buyers on a fairly small scale are evidently precluded from buying any one tea in such quantities, but they are able to circumvent this difficulty by means of the custom of requesting a share in part of the break being auctioned. A cry very frequently heard in the sale room is 'Can I have part?' A 'part' in this connection is a minimum of six chests, the weight of which, it will be recalled, is contained on the warehouse weight notes and printed on the catalogue. The system thus serves as a means by which buyers may share in the greatest number of varieties of tea at one time. Sometimes, of course, large buyers may want as much as possible of a particular grade or quality, in which case the buying broker currently bidding on their behalf will refuse, or explain his position where he already has several buyers requiring the particular tea for sale. Precluded from sharing, the would-be sharer will then either let that particular 'break' go, or else advance the bidding for it.

Thus in spite of the rapidity of the bidding, the expertise of the auctioneers (who are usually senior members of the firms of selling brokers), and the short lunch break (1.30 to 2.15 p.m.), the auctions often go on until as late as 6 p.m. This happens, moreover, despite the existence of a joint organization of the producers' and selling brokers' associations called the Regulation of Sales Joint Sub-Committee, a body of evident *prima facie* concern to the Monopolies Commission. The Sub-Committee's existence arises from the prevalence of two diffi-culties: the seasonal nature of tea supplies (the bulk of which arrives during seven or eight months in the year), and the physical limit to the amount of tea which can be handled weekly at the London auctions.[31] It was urged upon the Commission that if all the North Indian tea (the largest single source of supply) were to be offered for sale during the seven months or so of its production season, the financial burden of stock holding would probably cause buyers to refrain from bidding eventually, so that some spreading of sales would then be forced on producers. The argument of the trade was that it is far better for this to be organized in an orderly way through the Regulation of Sales Joint Sub-Committee. For the Commission, this arrangement clearly held implications of possible deliberate collusive manipulation of supply in order to secure the best prices. The Commission's conclusion, however, was that:

> though no doubt in its absence there might be more marked fluctuations in the auction prices, the regulation of sales has in practice relatively little effect on the general level of prices but that in so far as it has any effect it is to secure some levelling out over the year. There was certainly no evidence that the average level of prices over a period was altered by these arrangements. On the contrary, the evidence was that buyers calculated the price they were prepared to offer for tea by reference to the total supplies estimated to be available or coming forward in the world market generally and that a change in the quantity offered in an individual London sale has little if any effect. If prices in London did become high in relation to those ruling in overseas auctions the immediate result would be that buyers would tend to transfer their purchasing to other auctions . . . There was some evidence also that the present system benefits the smaller buyer, who may not in any case find buying abroad a practical alternative. Only the largest buyers could afford to buy forward heavily even in times of low prices and it would, therefore, be in the interest of the smaller buyer that fluctuations in price, already serious enough, should be reduced as far as possible.[32]

These considerations led the Commission to conclude that the regula-tion of sales scheme does not operate against the public interest. This body also declared that there was nothing contrary to the public interest in the uniform conditions of sale which apply to all the tea auctioned in Mincing Lane.[33] They were, however, also interested in the long uniform period of credit of ninety days normally allowed. This is unusually long, but it is claimed that this, too, helps the small buyer. A discount at the rate of 5 per cent per annum for payment prior to prompt day encourages these traders to buy a forward supply of tea which they can take up as they require it. Financial considerations therefore appear to tie them effectively to the London auction in preference to those held at overseas centres.

Though the Monopolies Commission found in favour of the auctions, a number of criticisms have been levelled at the system over the years. The regulation of sales is obviously a very delicate matter. An official Report pointed out more than forty years ago that:

> The system is open to abuse, and we consider that the auction which took place in the spring of 1925 by the producers' associations is a definite instance of such abuse.[34]

Complaints against the power of the brokers have been numerous. As we have seen, despite the large turnover of business, the number both of selling and buying brokers is small, and their influence as valuers of the produce, it is argued, could be very great in determining relative prices. It is claimed, moreover, that to the extent that 'market men' function as intermediaries who keep both buyers and sellers informed of one another's views as to prices, this influence is reinforced.[35] The Imperial Economic Committee also considered it to be its duty to report the following:

> Although the auctions are public, and normally anyone is entitled to bid, it has been stated to us that if a bidder, not a recognized buying broker, were to enter the market, or, if any of the big distributors were to instruct his buyer to bid at the market, not through the intermediary of a buying broker, the buying brokers would 'run' the price with the object of securing that all sales of tea should pass through their own hands.[36]

The weekly turnover of the London tea auctions is in the region of £1.5 million and occasionally £2 million, representing an average sale of some eight million lbs a week. The sales cover the requirements of the re-export trade and those of the home market, though some sales are conducted by private treaty also. In 1968, for example, total tea imports amounted to 595.6 million lbs, the value of which was some £112.4 million. Of this total 44.6 million lbs was re-exported, and realized £13.8 million. There is in addition some 'third-country' trade; that is business done for shipment from countries of origin direct to other destinations. For this trade the London broker usually buys through his correspondents in Calcutta or other overseas markets, the price being determined, in the absence of advance samples, on general indications of the variety of tea, or on 'garden marks'.

How then are we to assess the future prospects of the Mincing Lane tea market? In its pre-war reports the then Imperial Economic Committee customarily prefaced its section on 'Tea in the United Kingdom' with this proud assertion:

> London is the centre of the tea trade of the world. More than half of the tea shipped from exporting countries is consumed in the

TABLE 9.6
RE-EXPORTS OF TEA FROM THE UNITED KINGDOM
thousand lbs

Country to which consigned	1938	1958	1966	1968
Eire	18,273	3	26	87
Channel Islands	2,052	2,410	—	
Canada	4,069	4,273	6,928	8,451
Soviet Union	8,550	0	2	1
Sweden	588	1,430	2,685	3,231
Denmark (including Faroe Islands)	954	859	1,180	1,333
Poland	2,396	113	16	22
Germany	8,018	2,617	1,903	2,255
Netherlands	2,063	5,261	2,005	2,442
Belgium	395	423	555	994
Switzerland	539	407	689	936
Egypt	256	64	4	3
United States of America	13,146	5,245	10,075	7,721
Argentine Republic	1,221	19	6	25
Norway		453	831	885
France		741	2,025	2,052
Republic of South Africa		2,020	3,522	2,861
Finland		257	593	587
Italy		286	753	766
Total other Countries	3,576	5,158	8,061	10,038
TOTAL	66,093	32,039	41,859	44,690

Sources: Figures for 1938 taken from the *Annual Statement of Trade*, Vol. II,
Figures for 1958 and 1966 taken from International Tea Committee *Annual Bulletin of Statistics 1967*,
Figures for 1938 have been rounded and therefore do not necessarily add to total.

TABLE 9.7

AUCTION SALES OF TEA

Quantities sold at London and European auctions and at auctions in producing countries

million lbs

Country	1934-38e	1951	1952	1958	1959	1960	1961	1962	1963	1964	1965	1966	1967	1968
London	403·4	108·5	288·0	321·9	354·9	297·6	339·2	360·7	367·0	361·1	357·9	340·0	286·5	331·2
Amsterdam a	26·7	14·4	11·2	1·8										
Antwerp b					0·5 d	3·2	2·5	1·4	0·9	0·4	0·7	0·1		
Hamburg c						0·8	4·2	3·1	3·3	2·8	0·9			
Calcutta	122·8	276·0	286·1	329·0	331·2	299·5	342·9	331·7	320·9	361·4	337·2	353·0	344·9	376·0
Cochin		20·2	25·2	54·7	59·0	72·4	75·5	86·6	95·8	89·7	107·1	119·0	116·8	128·6
Chittagong		16·3	18·5	31·8	55·5	40·7	55·6	47·6	52·9	59·8	57·2	60·6	63·1	59·7
Colombo	102·7	214·6	237·9	285·2	309·7	333·7	355·5	356·5	369·6	346·6	367·7	358·9	365·9	369·1
Nairobi				4·6	8·6	10·3	12·2	16·1	16·4	18·8	17·2	22·9	17·9	24·3

a. Auctions were resumed on 27 January 1949, but were again suspended after 10 July 1958.

b and c. Auctions began in Antwerp on 17 September 1959, and Hamburg on 20 October 1960, but no sales have been held after 24 November 1966 and 25 February 1965 respectively.

d. At Antwerp the following quantities were offered for sale but were sold privately afterwards –
1959 – 0·6; 1960 – 6·3; 1961 – 5·5; 1962 – 4·9; 1963 – 5·3; 1964 – 3·9; 1965 – 2·5; 1966 – 1·8.

Sources: The International Tea Committee: *Annual Bulletin of Statistics*,
F.A.O. Commodity Bulletin Series 30 *Tea – Trends and Prospects*, and
The Tea-Brokers Association of London.

e. Five-year annual average.

United Kingdom and if re-exports are taken into account, three out of every five pounds of tea entering world trade pass through United Kingdom Ports.

This claim is no longer made. The re-export of tea from the U.K., which reached a peak of 95 million lbs in 1929 and averaged 70 million lbs during the late 1930s, is now of the order of 40 million lbs. The accompanying table of re-exports by destination shows the dramatic changes which have taken place during the last thirty years (Table 9.6).

Sales in countries of origin, too, are currently of much greater importance than before the war. The story of these changes is summarized in Table 9.7 from which we can see clearly the basis of the pre-war claim that London was the centre of the world's tea trade. The present picture shows how London has declined both in terms of the quantity sold under the hammer at Mincing Lane, and relatively to other market centres. Both the Calcutta and Colombo auctions now have a larger turnover than London, while sales centres in other producing countries have burgeoned since the war. The upshot is that whereas before the war the public auctions in Mincing Lane accounted for some two-thirds of all teas sold by auction, the present proportion is between one-quarter and one-third.

The development of central markets for this produce in countries of origin took place, therefore, very much later than it did for some other commodities, such as wool: in fact the transfer of the sale of a significant proportion of tea to the producing countries had to await the disruptions occasioned by the war, and the subsequent dissolution of the British Empire. In Britain, meanwhile, higher prices, taxes and storage costs, together with tighter credit conditions, made London far less attractive as the pre-eminent world market for tea than it was before the war. With independence, too, the Indian government's Tea Board imposed export quotas, and attempted to restrict the re-export of its teas by foreign merchants. During the first half of the 1950s a policy of reducing the amounts of tea allowed for sale at the London auctions was implemented by both India and Ceylon.[37] This was discontinued in 1961. Export taxes were also imposed, at rates which varied from time to time, by the Indian government, while both Ceylon and Pakistan imposed export taxes upon tea, plus export cesses.[38]

To a considerable extent these trends are the natural consequence of the emancipation of Asian and African territories formerly under the British flag, whose rulers are now concerned to secure the organization of their own commerce. Such countries have been encouraged in this desire by the remarkable growth of their figures of domestic consumption, while for the United Kingdom the increasing popularity of coffee and other beverages has given rise to some decrease in the consumption

of tea. For many other consuming countries the upshot of these changes
has been to make the advantages of buying tea in London rather less
obvious than they used to be. Additional auction centres were established after the war both at Antwerp and Hamburg, but, as the
accompanying table indicates, they have recently been discontinued.
Meanwhile, the Amsterdam tea auctions of Java and other teas were
resuscitated after the war and, though the public sales were discontinued
in 1958 at the time of the troubles with Indonesia, the re-export trade
has continued to grow at a rate which must give pause to members of
the United Kingdom tea trade. The Dutch re-export trade is now some
31 million lbs per annum, or nearly 60 per cent of its total imports,
compared with 11 million lbs before the war.[39] Britain is still the
destination of almost half the world's exports of tea, and the variety of
teas offered in Mincing Lane is far greater than it is in any of the other
auction centres. Sources of supply, moreover, are getting more diverse,
expecially with the increases in Central and East African production,
so that export prohibitions or quotas by any one country may well
become less crucial in the future. Most African teas continue to be sold
in London though there is a significant growth of auction at Nairobi,
where £24 million was sold in 1968 as compared with £5 million in
1958 (Table 9.7). Nevertheless, the massive size of the domestic U.K.
market will suffice to ensure for Mincing Lane a highly important niche
in the tea trade for the foreseeable future. Moreover, despite the
dissatisfaction expressed from time to time with auction sales as the
method of distribution, it seems unlikely that this will be strong enough
to overturn the present system.

Chapter Ten

THE U.K. SUGAR MARKET

1. *The Early West Indies Trade and the Growth of European Sugar Beet*

AT a time when imports were mostly luxuries or semi-luxuries, the West Indies were of considerable importance in British overseas trade. This area was the main source of coffee, cacao, spices, ginger, indigo, pimento, precious woods, sugar and sugar by-products. Of all these commodities sugar was easily the most important in the early nineteenth century, imports during the 1820s being not far short of a quarter of a million long tons. Prices fluctuated as supplies varied due to weather conditions, but Thomas Tooke's opinion was that £20 per ton was probably a representative one for the period.[1] The retail price of sugar was seldom if ever less than 6d. per lb but, notwithstanding this, domestic consumption was some 20 lbs per head a year. The re-export trade was of the order of 40,000 tons per annum, and the remainder was shipped to Ireland.

Ragatz[2] describes how during this period the crops grown on estates in the West Indies were hauled to the nearest legal port of clearance to be loaded on board a waiting merchantman for delivery to English factors. Upon arrival at a U.K. port they were claimed by the consignee who met customs duties, freight charges, primage, wharfage, lighterage, warehouse rental, insurance, cooperage, the expense of weighing, plus the 'trade rate'. This last named item was an assessment upon the value of the shipment, the proceeds of which were used to advance the common interests of West Indian merchants, for the famous 'West India interest' had long been a powerful lobby in British politics by this time.

Samples of the malodorous muscovado sugar—produce in the early stages of refinement—were drawn from the bulk and submitted to prospective purchasers.[3] Brokers were customarily engaged to do the actual selling, having secured a niche in this trade, as in others, through their access to finance. It was the factor, however, who decided how much of the consignment to sell and the time of selling, as we have already remarked in Chapter 2. Proceeds from the sale of sugars were credited to the planter as the produce was sold but, because of the shipment of a wide variety of articles by the factor to the West Indian consignor, the latter's account was frequently very much overdrawn. Transactions both ways were rewarded by commission, the traditional scale of which was 6 per cent on advances, plus 2½ per cent on sugar

214

sold, and ½ per cent for brokerage. The commission for obtaining estate supplies was usually 5 per cent.

Some sugar was, of course, shipped to the United Kingdom as part of the triangle of trade which started with the export of manufactures from Liverpool, London and Bristol to Africa in exchange for slaves. By the beginning of the nineteenth century Liverpool accounted for far and away the highest number of vessels cleared for Africa from these U.K. ports. In spite of this, the sale of West Indian produce was centred chiefly upon London, due in all probability to the efforts exerted by the exclusive companies, such as the Sugar Refiners' Company, which were established in the capital.[4] However, important subsidiary sales centres existed not only at Bristol and Liverpool, but also in Glasgow, Leith, Lancaster and (after 1788) in Cork and Dublin. According to Hutcheson, the Sugar Exchange at Greenock, which was contiguous to the railway station, was opened in 1857. 'Each refiner had his own sample room, where every morning within an hour the production of all refiners was exposed for sale.' A Clyde Crushed Sugar Dealers' Association followed in 1866, the chief objects of which were the publication of a daily report, the settlement of disputes and the arrangement of satisfactory systems of sampling, weighing and forwarding the produce.[5]

When sugar and other tropical produce was imported on the final leg of the triangular trade between the U.K., Africa and the West Indies, these commodities were frequently bought outright from the proceeds of the sale of slaves. On occasion, however, merchant traders succumbed to the temptation of using the cash from the disposal of the slaves to buy the cheaper sugar grown in the neighbouring French-owned islands. When traders bought French sugar it had to be fraudulently sworn to have originated from a British possession since it was, as is well known, official policy to close English markets to tropical produce from all competing non-British sources—the planters' *quid pro quo* for the various acts restricting their freedom to trade with foreign countries.[6]

With the passage of time the emphasis of the trade changed decisively away from the system whereby merchants sent out manufactures and bore the risks upon the sale of the return cargoes. Gradually the trade evolved into a more modern pattern in which U.K. merchants became simply the factors for the West Indian planters—or at least such of them as remained after the rise of the European sugar beet industry.

The possibility of extracting sugar from beetroot was first demonstrated by the German chemist Marggraff as early as 1747, but this was not widely explored until the British blockade of Napoleon's Europe fostered its use. After the peace of 1815 little was heard of beet sugar until the second quarter of the century, when some European farmers discovered that it was more profitable than cereal production. As the century progressed British West Indian growers found it increasingly difficult to compete with European beet farmers. Moreover, the emancipation of their slaves in 1833 deprived planters in the British possessions of cheap labour some fifteen years in advance of emancipation on the French-owned islands, and exposed them for an even longer period to the most daunting competition from slave-grown sugar in Cuba and Brazil. Finally, by mid-century, the preferential duties which had afforded some measure of protection to British producers in the U.K. market were first reduced and finally equalized. The free trade lobby triumphed completely in 1874, when all sugars from whatever source were admitted to the United Kingdom free of all duties.[7]

Meanwhile, European beet production was growing apace to meet a rapidly increasing demand. Beet production was given a further impetus by bounties, freight subsidies and cartel agreements, thus aiding growers to switch from grain production rendered unprofitable by the vast increase in cheap supplies from North America and elsewhere. The upshot was that by 1869-70 almost a third of the total world sugar production of 2.6 million tons was beet, and by the end of the century the proportion had grown to some two-thirds. This was reflected in the changing proportion in British imports. These in 1860 (apart from a trifling 13,000 tons) consisted entirely of cane sugar; by 1900, refined beet-sugar imports had increased to 962,000 tons, while raw sugar imports had grown only from 435,000 to 662,000 long tons.

The result of the Brussels Convention of 1902 was to abolish the direct bounties paid, especially by Germany and France, upon the export of sugar. The European industry was very firmly established by this time, however, and continued to hold the major share of the British market. Moreover, exports of beet sugar were mostly refined, so that domestic refiners in the U.K. survived only by increasing their efficiency to a sufficient extent to enable them to prevent their absolute volume of sales from falling in a market which had increased enormously in total size. By the eve of World War I half of total British imports consisted of continental refined beet sugar, chiefly from Germany and Austria-Hungary. When raw beet-sugar imports are added to this, Britain's dependence upon continental supplies was for some three-quarters of total consumption, as the accompanying table of U.K. Sugar Imports by source indicates (Table 10.1). When war came sugar supplies from Europe declined catastrophically and in August 1915 the government appointed a Royal Commission on Sugar Supplies with power to buy and sell, and to regulate the supply.[8] Imports were maintained at near pre-war levels for two years through purchases from Java and Mauritius. With subsequent shipping shortages, however, rationing was imposed in 1917 which proved to be the fore-runner of the rationing of many other foods.

The postwar boom in sugar was a spectacular one and Cuban sugar

TABLE 10.1

U.K. SUGAR IMPORTS BY SOURCE, 1911–1968

thousand metric tons raw value (Five-year annual averages)

	1911–1913	1922–1924	1936–1938	1950–1952	1955–1957	1964–1968
Belgium ⎱ East	83·6	45·2	1·7	19·8	2·8	2·1 c
Germany ⎰ West	767·2	13·8	3·9	0·5	0·4	1·3
Hungary	302·3 a	2·9	—	—	—	—
Netherlands	213·2	115·9	6·9	—	2·3	14·0
U.S.S.R.	78·8	—	—	—	—	—
Dominican Republic	26·8 b	60·2	217·9	423·2	362·5	14·8
Cuba	106·6	457·1	604·7	776·0	317·0	70·2
Brazil	10·7	75·3	17·8	—	72·6	53·8
West Indies	32·6	53·0	216·4	334·7	516·5	162·6
Jamaica	—	—	—	—	—	57·5
Trinidad & Tobago	39·6	23·2	182·3	11·8	—	116·5
Republic of South Africa	—	98·8	101·1	11·3	142·8	56·2
Peru	40·8	1·0	83·5	14·2	46·8	11·7
Fiji	16·0	22·7	—	—	51·9	145·4
India	—	31·7	70·0	—	0·3	57·5
British Guiana	136·6	167·4	69·5	95·4	148·9	114·0 d
Indonesia	—	14·9	—	—	—	8·2
Australia	0·4	0·4	366·5	182·6	394·6	340·6
Mauritius	42·5	183·0	277·6	228·3	442·6	430·7
Others	94·3	457·7	123·4	77·6	19·1	487·3
Total	1992·0	1823·8	2343·3	2175·4	2521·1	2143·4

a. Austria/Hungary.   b. Including Haiti.   c. Belgium/Luxembourg.   d. Guyana.

Sources: F.A.O., *The World Sugar Economy in Figures, 1880–1959*; International Sugar Organization, *Sugar Year Book*, 1961, 1966 and 1968.

at one time touched 10d. a lb f.o.b. before plummeting to 2d. within six months. This violent swing in prices was symptomatic of the fluctuations which were destined to occur in the fortunes of various producing countries after that date. In Britain, for example, the high wartime tariff was continued and made discriminatory in 1919 with the introduction of Imperial Preference. The failure of sugar prices to fall immediately after the war led to pressures for the official encouragement of home production, but this was not forthcoming until sugar prices had fallen catastrophically with the recovery of world production. The excise duty of 19s. 5½d. per cent on home-grown sugar was then dropped so that the preference over foreign sugars enjoyed by the home producer shot up from 5s. 2⅔d. to 24s. 8d., compared with an Imperial Preference of 4s. 3⅓d. This, however, did not last very long, for in 1925 the government passed the Sugar Industry (Subsidy) Act which provided instead for direct Exchequer assistance on a decreasing scale for ten years. It was hoped by the end of that period that the industry would be competitive with imported supplies. The policy of favouring commonwealth sugar at the expense of foreign sugar was continued and, in 1928, imports of refined sugar were, in the interests of domestic refiners, taxed at a penal rate.

The upshot of the disruptions caused by the war and the introduction of discriminatory tariffs and subsidies was to transform British supply sources for sugar. Imports of beet sugar from the continent were whittled down from their dominant position in 1913 to a mere 8 per cent of the total by 1930. By this time domestic beet-sugar production had expanded to about half a million tons. The British West Indies felt the benefit of imperial preference by the 1930s, but, despite this advantage, Cuba continued to occupy a dominating position in British sugar imports until after the middle of the century. These and other changes are summarized in Table 10.1. Meanwhile the taxation of refined-sugar imports at a higher rate transformed the character of the imports. Whereas in 1914 one-half of total sugar imports consisted of the refined product, after 1928 all incoming foreign supplies were of raw sugar, and British refiners found themselves able to export white sugar at a profit. This major switch from refined to raw sugar imports is brought out in the accompanying table of World Sugar Imports by countries (Table 10.2). This also shows how the changes in British policy affected the relative importance of the United Kingdom market in relation to other important importing countries. At the turn of the century Britain was by a considerable margin the world's largest market for exported sugar. In the years immediately prior to World War I Britain and the U.S.A. imported almost identical amounts of some 1,820,763 tons per annum. By 1925-29, however, U.S. imports had become more than twice as great as those of the U.K. (which had, in the meantime, remained approximately constant) in spite of the establishment of a domestic beet industry in the former country dating from 1890.

Major changes were also wrought in other countries by protection. India, for example, was at one time a considerable importer, at first from Europe and subsequently from Java, until supplies from the latter were cut off by duties in 1930. By 1940 India had become a sugar exporting country. Japan, too, had made itself self-sufficient by the end of the 1920s. The major producers accordingly suffered: Cuban exports, for example, which had doubled between 1914 and 1925, were cut back once more to pre-war levels, a reversal of fortune which contributed directly to the revolution of 1933.[9] Exports from Java, the world's lowest-cost source of sugar, declined by almost 60 per cent between 1929 and 1934 as they were squeezed out from one market after another by protection. European sugar-beet suffered similarly, and a considerable amount of dumping resulted. Britain was far from being alone in aggravating the distortions created by nationalistic policies in discriminating severely against imports of refined sugar, and instances abounded of refined sugar actually selling for less than raw produce on the topsy-turvy world markets of the day.

If producers outside preference zones suffered, domestic producers and favoured overseas suppliers gained correspondingly. As far as Britain was concerned the switch in supplies from the outbreak of war in 1914 to 1937 was very impressive. By the latter date some 60 per cent of U.K. supplies were Empire-grown compared with only 4 per cent in 1913. Perusal of the table of U.K. imports by source provides an insight into the particular countries which gained or lost in this market. The benefit to Australia was particularly marked, followed, as already intimated, by those to the West Indies and Mauritius.

2. *The Restriction of Sales and the Commonwealth Sugar Agreement*

The difficulties experienced by many of the exporting countries as the result of the policies described above led to attempts to restrict sales. The first collective attempt to do so resulted in the 'Chadbourne Agreement' signed in Brussels on 9 May 1931. The signatories were countries which exported sugar without the benefit of preference duties —the so-called 'free market' exporters—except Brazil and the Dominican Republic, which agreed instead to drastic output reductions. The effect of the Agreement, however, was only to reduce the share of world sugar supplies contributed by the 'Chadbourne' countries from 45 per cent in 1929-30 to 25 per cent by 1933-34, as protected production expanded in response to this attempt to restrict world supplies. There were nevertheless some more fruitful attempts to stabilize the situation by the mid-1930s: in the U.S.A. the Jones-Costigan Act of 9 May 1934 introduced a quota system for both domestic and overseas producers which partially restored Cuba as a major

TABLE 10.2

WORLD SUGAR IMPORTS BY COUNTRIES, 1896–1968

thousand metric tons (Five-year annual averages)

		1896-1900	1909-1913	1925-1929	1935-1939	1950-1954	1955-1959	1960-1964	1965-1968
U.S.A.	*	1458·0	1841·0	3788·1	2359·3	3065·5	4009·3	4068·4	4185·5
	**	49·0	1·8	110·7	362·3	329·3			
U.K.	*	714·7	936·9	1493·9	3194·1	2378·6	2530·9	2274·9	2240·5
	**	855·3	906·1	448·6	38·4	34·1	39·4	120·8	49·7
Japan	*a	150·3	301·7	581·1	323·9	690·4	1147·0	1331·0	1597·8
	**	70·2	9·4	320·3	725·0	76·6			
Canada	*	124·5	239·7	458·3	439·7	541·1	650·9	712·6	841·7
	**		12·5	15·5	3·1	9·1			
France	*	108·1	152·6	383·4	345·9	310·3	189·0	142·6	158·2
	**		16·3	34·6	20·9	16·7			
Germany	*c	0·5	0·6	28·6	1·4	209·3	289·1	181·1	297·1
	**	0·7	2·5	55·5	10·6	196·2 b			
Netherlands	*	52·7	66·8	259·0	112·1	264·9	239·9	189·2	152·2
	**	14·9	8·3	29·1	37·3	12·5			
U.S.S.R.	*		—	—	—	280·0 e	548·8	2165·6	955·0
	**		0·2 d	54·4	0·2	—			
Morocco (ex-French)	*	—	0·1 f	103·2	60·0	154·5	349·0	384·1	320·7
	**	—	566·4	—	113·7	90·9			
Morocco (ex-Spanish)	*	—	—	0·1	31·7 g	10·5			
	**	—	0·4	—					

    * Raw sugar.   ** Refined sugar.

a. Including non-centrifugal sugar   *b.* Including imports from East Germany
c. West Germany from 1950   *d.* 1 year only
Based on export statistics of exporting countries and excluding trade with Czechoslovakia
e. 1 year only
f. 1 year only   *g.* 2 year average

Sources: F.A.O., *The World Sugar Economy in Figures 1880-1959,*
    International Sugar Organization, *Sugar Year Book,* 1961, 1966 and 1968

supplier. In the U.K. a Committee of Inquiry was appointed in the same year to help the government to decide whether to continue with state aid now that the ten year period allowed by the Sugar Industry (Subsidy) Act of 1925 was drawing to a close. In the meantime sugar prices had fallen, and it appeared extremely unlikely that the domestic industry could continue in being without some sort of assistance. The Committee was, however, unable to agree, and two members, including the Chairman, protested that:

We are unable to find positive justification for the expenditure of a sum of several millions per annum on an industry which has no reasonable prospects of ever becoming self-supporting, and on the production of a crop which, without that assistance, would at present prices be practically valueless.[10]

This Report led to the passage of the Sugar Industry (Reorganization) Act of 1936 which specified an upper limit of the equivalent of 560,000 tons of refined sugar for subsidization. A licence system governing the imports of sugar from dependent territories was also introduced to restrict their expansion. The 1936 Act provided, too, for the appointment of an independent Sugar Commission and the amalgamation of existing factory companies into a single corporation—the British Sugar Corporation. It has been averred that there was also a strong feeling at the time in the U.K. that London's entrepôt trade in sugar would be very adversely affected should colonial preferential imports continue to increase at the expense of foreign imports.[11] At all events it was felt on many sides that something should be done to alleviate world overproduction, and some countries, such as South Africa and Australia, tried unilaterally to limit the acreage devoted to sugar cultivation. Sentiments of this kind resulted ultimately in formal arrangements for international co-operation and the International Sugar Agreement was signed in 1937. Signatory countries included importers as well as exporters, but both Canada and Japan, though declaring themselves to be sympathetic, remained non-members. The Agreement buttressed the limitation imposed upon domestic beet production by the U.K.; specified export quotas for protected overseas suppliers (at about their existing levels); and threw the remainder of the British market open to 'free market' exporters.[12]

Within a year of the signing of the 1937 Agreement the threat of war dominated all else and a modest amount of stockpiling began. When hostilities did start U.K. sugar supplies in common with supplies of most other important commodities were controlled by the Ministry of Food: the Sugar Division took over the task of purchasing, mostly on a fixed-price basis by bulk-purchase contracts, and of allocating these supplies for refining and consumption. Sugar brokers became agents handling shipments on behalf of the Ministry, and continued to receive brokerage from foreign exporters, except for refined sugars when it was paid by the Ministry of Food. The internal distribution of sugar was effected by means of 'documents of entitlement' issued to buyers and all intermediaries (dealers, wholesalers, retailers and sugar users) by the Ministry of Food. Sales by sugar refiners to these traders were at fixed prices. The mechanism of distribution was all handled by traders who had previously been leading figures in the business, and so the top management of firms, such as Tate and Lyle and Czarnikow, now appeared under new hats as Area Sugar Officers or in other supervisory rôles.

The sugar supply problem which confronted the British government in 1939 was in many ways far easier than it had been in 1914 when more than three-quarters of the total import came from Europe, much of it from enemy territory. At the outbreak of World War II by contrast, more than two-thirds of British consumption was supplied from domestic, dominion and colonial sources. The breakdown of imported supplies by major countries of origin may be seen in the table of U.K. Sugar Imports by source. Despite a basically easier situation as far as countries of origin were concerned, however, the problems faced by the Ministry of Food were often frustrating. As R. J. Hammond has pointed out,[13] when the Ministry could get the sugar there were no ships to be had; when it could once again get the ships sugar was chronically scarce all over the world. Finally, when both ships and sugar were more plentiful, the dollars with which to buy the produce were scarce.

The 'dollar shortage' after the end of the war provided the basis for the British government's postwar policy of continuing its commitments to purchase from Commonwealth sugar producers. This ultimately led to the Commonwealth Sugar Agreement of 1951, which secured for the dominions and colonies a share of the U.K. market of some $1\frac{1}{2}$ million long tons a year under an annually negotiated price (hence the description of this arrangement as the 'negotiated-price quota'). In addition, the United Kingdom guaranteed a further market for 800,000 tons which would be sold at world market prices and be subject to duty at the preferred rate in force for Commonwealth supplies.[14] Moreover, in order to provide growers with an assured market for sufficient time ahead to ensure an adequate return upon capital investments involved in turning over to sugar production, the Agreement was to run until 1959, with provision for annual renewals which would ensure a commitment by the U.K. for a minimum period, at all times, of eight years ahead. In fact, it was calculated that after taking U.K. domestic production of some $\frac{3}{4}$ million long tons raw value equivalent into account, only about $\frac{1}{4}$ million tons would be required from the free market. The possibility that requirements from free market suppliers would ever exceed this was obviated by a further United Kingdom commitment to increase quotas of 'negotiated-price' sugars proportionately for any excess in domestic consumption above 2,550,000 long tons.

Unlike other bulk-purchase agreements negotiated by the British government, the guaranteed price under the C.S.A. was to be a uniform one for all Commonwealth producers, fixed at a level which would ensure a 'reasonably remunerative price to efficient producers'. Annual price adjustments were to be based upon cost changes in producing countries as a group, and it was planned that the negotiated price would agree closely with internal U.K. sugar prices. The sole importer at the time of the Agreement was the Ministry of Food, which resold imported raw sugars to refiners at prices intended to equalize the cost of Commonwealth and foreign produce. It was these prices which in turn determined the price of domestic beet sugar.

The Commonwealth Sugar Agreement led to a vast increase in the sterling price of 'free-market' sugar, and even before the Korean boom Cuban sugar, c.i.f. the U.K., was more than 500 per cent above its 1938 figure. The price changes were rather less for Commonwealth sugar, but they were nevertheless considerable; in Australia, for example, the U.K. market became a much more attractive one in which to sell than the domestic market, whereas in the 1930s Australian sugar was dumped abroad at well below domestic prices. As far as the U.K. itself was concerned, a high 'free-market' sugar price at least had the considerable attraction, for negotiators under the C.S.A., of reducing the annual bargaining pressures for a high price for the 'negotiated-price quota' sugars, for the return on the remaining third of the Commonwealth countries' quotas depends upon the level of the 'free-market' price. Meanwhile the restoration of the U.K. re-export trade, and with it the hope of re-establishing London as a pre-eminent world market centre for sugar, hinged upon a world price which allowed U.K. merchants sufficient margin to refine and re-export this produce at a profit.

Because sugar was a 'dollar good'[15] the British government was very cautious in returning the trade to private hands: to have allowed non-residents the freedom to purchase unlimited amounts of sugar in the conditions of the time would have led to the use of inconvertible currencies for large-scale purchases, with the aim of economizing on dollars or of earning more upon the re-sale of the produce at highly competitive prices. In October 1952, however, U.K. refiners were allowed to purchase raw sugar on private account provided that it was re-exported to specified non-sterling areas,[16] but exports of sugar to certain sterling countries remained in Ministry hands until the beginning of 1954. In July of that year members of the sugar trade association were granted permission for the purchase with sterling of raw sugar originating in the dollar area. By the Sugar Act of 1956 the government established a Sugar Board as the means by which to continue operating the Commonwealth Sugar Agreement while itself continuing the import of sugar. This body became responsible for the purchase of 'negotiated-price' sugars, which it resold in countries of origin at the current commercial price to refiners and other traders, who then made their own arrangements to ship the produce to the United Kingdom.[17] Thus, should world prices be below the negotiated price, the Sugar Board would incur a deficit on its sales of Commonwealth sugar. Similarly, the British Sugar Corporation was permitted to incur a deficit in respect of any excess cost of home-produced sugar, the B.S.C. being required by the Act to purchase sugar beet from domestic producers at prices determined by the annual agricultural price reviews. B.S.C. deficits were to be made good by the Sugar Board, while surpluses were also payable by the B.S.C. to the Sugar Board when they occurred.

The 1956 Act decreed that the Sugar Board's own books were to be balanced from the proceeds of a surcharge to be levied on all sugar and sugar-containing goods upon entry into the United Kingdom. (Molasses were excluded in 1962.) In the event of world sugar prices becoming higher than the negotiated prices under the Commonwealth Sugar Agreement, the 1956 Act prescribed that any trading surplus then earned by the Sugar Board was to be distributed by making payments in respect of sugar and sugar-containing goods liable to sugar duty. The surcharge was collected on behalf of the Board by the Commissioners of Customs and Excise at the same point as customs and excise duties were collected: it was repaid where drawback of sugar duty was paid upon re-export. To avoid frequent changes in the rates of surcharge or distribution payments the Board was authorized to borrow up to £25 million. Despite this, however, in the twelve months ended May 1964, for example, the rate of distribution payment had to be altered fourteen times in order to counteract changes in market prices.[18]

The levy of a surcharge, or the distribution of payments by the Sugar Board, was thus a device for averaging the prices of sugars brought in at world prices on the one hand, and of 'negotiated-price' and domestic sugars on the other. By these arrangements the government succeeded in withdrawing from the trade without disrupting the guaranteed market for Commonwealth sugars, and paved the way for the re-opening of London's sugar terminal market.

3. *The Post-War International Sugar Agreements*
There were many difficulties to be overcome before the postwar International Sugar Agreement was signed. The Commonwealth Sugar Agreement constituted one major stumbling block inasmuch as sales quotas in the U.K. market guaranteed to members were some 50 per cent higher than those established under the 1937 Agreement. More-

over, a special committee of the International Sugar Council (which had been kept in being by annual signatures to protocols of the 1937 Agreement), declared a new agreement to be unnecessary in 1949 because no possibility of a surplus existed. However, the decline in sugar prices from their Korean war peak of 8 cents per lb f.a.s. Cuba to some 3 cents by 1953 expedited negotiations which led to an Agreement by the latter year, when the Commonwealth countries agreed to sign provided that their export quotas were at least as great as those negotiated under the Commonwealth Sugar Agreement of 1951.[19] Similar safeguards were written into the Agreement to protect other preferred suppliers (notably Hawaii, Puerto Rico, the Philippines and Cuba) which enjoyed privileges in the U.S. market.

The postwar International Sugar Agreement thus succeeded in safeguarding the position of preferred suppliers to such an extent that only some 45 per cent of the trade remained for 'free-market' suppliers. This situation has continued in essence to the present time. In 1966, for example, the net raw value equivalent of sugar entering world trade totalled 17.3 million tons. Thus the total quantity of 'free-market' sugars entering international trade is of the order of 8 million tons compared with total world production of some 63 million tons (excluding a further 8 million tons of non-centrifugal[20] sugars produced mainly in Asia for local consumption). The free market is therefore essentially a market for residual suppliers and as such liable to considerable price fluctuations. Foreseeing this, the signatories of the 1953 Agreement paid considerable attention to the problem of securing sugar supplies at equitable and stable prices. Prices were to be contained within a range of between 3.25 cents and 4.35 cents f.a.s. Cuba, the criterion being the spot price as quoted on the New York Exchange. Should the price fall below the 'floor' for fifteen consecutive days, the Sugar Council was empowered to reduce export quotas, and conversely, subject to certain limitations. The Agreement's signatories also sought to regulate production so as to limit carry-over stocks to 20 per cent of annual agreed outputs, and to hold minimum stocks of 10 per cent. In contrast with the 1937 Agreement, the postwar arrangement was that exporters' and importers' voting power was equal, even though the number of importing members was much greater than in the earlier Agreement when importers had the majority of voting rights.

The 1953 Agreement was obviously modelled upon its 1937 prototype in most respects, except for the greater attention paid to the aim of price stability. Despite this, the arrangement did not provide for any restriction upon importers' domestic sugar production, though imports from non-members were more firmly limited (to a ceiling figure of actual imports from those countries in any of the years 1951, 1952, 1953). Until the Suez crisis of 1956 the course of the Agreement was uneventful, after which the price broke through the I.S.A. ceiling to reach 6 cents a lb, whereupon all restrictions imposed under the scheme were removed. This gave rise to a considerable increase in production by 1958, the year in which the I.S.A. was reviewed and renewed in virtually unchanged form apart from the adherence of Brazil and Peru as new members. Prices then began to decline as the result of increased production and the failure of postwar demand to continue growing. Export quotas were accordingly reduced to their minimum permissible levels under the Agreement, but, despite this, the price of sugar declined to rather less than 2 cents a lb f.a.s. Cuba by the end of 1961.

The members of the International Sugar Agreement met in Geneva during the autumn of 1961 in order to revise the 1958 quota arrangements but were unable to reach agreement because Cuba insisted that its contracts of 4.9 million tons with the countries of the Communist bloc be added to its basic I.S.A. quota of 2.4 million tons. The refusal of the other signatories to countenance this spelt the end of the regulation of 'free-market' supplies. Subsequently, prices at first fell in response to heavy crops but they soon rose due to disturbed conditions following the American ban on imports of Cuban sugar and the heavy purchases of Cuban supplies by Russia and China. The dramatic increase in sugar prices which occurred during the spring of 1963 was the market's reaction to the realization that 'free-market' supplies were likely to be about a million tons less than 'free-market' requirements for that season. Buyers consequently hurried to build up stocks and a speculative boom was set in motion. By May 1963 prices reached nearly 12 cents a lb, or, in terms of the then recently amended form of quotation on the London market (previously expressed in shillings per cwt), some £105 a ton for spot and near supplies. By the end of August prices had returned to under £50 a ton but rose again to over £100 a ton following reports of hurricane damage. The subsequent history of sugar prices and the failure to regulate the trade is a classic illustration of the difficulties for which trade in primary produce is notorious.

The high prices of 1963-64 soon led to expanded acreages under sugar crops, as the result of which 1965 was a year of record harvests: 1966 crops were almost as great. There was no comparable increase in demand, so stocks accumulated and prices declined (Figure 10.1). Already by January 1966 the price was down to £24 5s. od. a ton, but worse was to follow, for a year later, in January 1967, the price was down to £12 10s. od. As has been pointed out,[21] for countries depending to a large extent upon exports to the 'free-market', this price was lower in real terms than the average price during the depression years of the 1930s.

Meanwhile, most of the crops grown in Commonwealth countries are protected from having to be sold at such fantastically low prices by the Commonwealth Sugar Agreement. In 1966-68 'negotiated-price'

FIGURE 10.1
RAW SUGAR MONTHLY PRICES
London Daily Price raw sugar 96° c.i.f. London

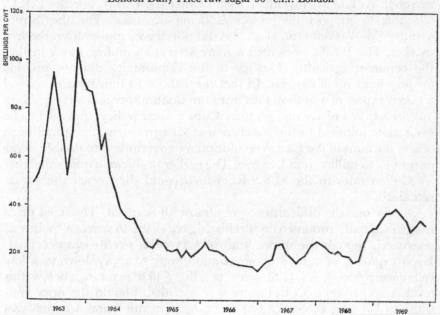

Source: compiled from C.E.C., *Plantation Crops,* No. 11, 1967 and No. 13, 1970.

quotas were fixed at £43 10s. od. In addition to this a supplementary two-part payment to less developed exporters was also arranged (to consist of a basic increment of £1 10s. od. and an additional increment ranging from nil to £2 10s. od. in inverse relationship to the world price).

Towards the end of the 1960s the British government was faced with the problems involved in extending the Commonwealth Sugar Agreement without damaging hopes of joining the European Economic Community. Talks were initiated in London with representatives of signatory countries in November 1968 which resulted in the continuation of the agreement with certain new provisos. One of these was that if Britain were to gain entry to the E.E.C. it could not be committed to continuing contractual obligations under the agreement after 1974. Assurances were given, however, that Britain would attempt to fulfil its obligations even though it did not prove possible to extend the formal agreement after 1974.

Meanwhile, the attempts to resuscitate the International Sugar Agreement ultimately proved successful, and a new Agreement came into being on 1 January 1969. The arrangements, scheduled to run for five years, were accepted by seventy countries, though in some cases negotiations ran into severe difficulties. Japan and Australia, for example, did not find the original proposals made by Raoul Prebisch for a fixed price range acceptable, while the Soviet delegates rejected an export quota of 1.05 million tons (equivalent to their actual export in 1967). As late as November 1968 neither the U.S.A. nor the E.E.C. felt able to support the proposals being discussed. For the former country this was not crucial since it did not draw supplies from the free market. The E.E.C. presented a more serious stumbling block in that the common agricultural policy of the Community did not provide for any limit upon exports. In fact the E.E.C. Commission envisaged a target export of a million tons from the Community and were holding out for a quota of 1.2 million tons. Cuba's sugar policy appeared to be even more inimical to the conclusion of an agreement, for it had been one of the aims of the Castro revolutionary government to double sugar output to 10 million tons by 1970. The earlier problem of quota dodging by Cuban sales to the U.S.S.R., which could then resell the sugar, remained.

One by one the difficulties were almost all resolved. The fixed price range originally proposed by Prebisch gave place to a set of 'points of reference', though the upper limit of 5.25 cents per lb was accepted. Export quotas, as agreed by negotiation, were to apply down to a low reference price of 3.5 U.S. cents per lb (£36.6 per ton). Below this level, a 10 per cent cut in quotas was specified. Should the price continue to fall to 3.25 cents (£34 per ton) then the Sugar Council was empowered to call for a quota reduction of a further 5 per cent. The new Agreement was thus designed to stabilize the free market price of sugar at about 4 U.S. cents a lb, with obligations on the controlling Council to adjust export quotas at points between 3.25 and 5.25 cents. The price range established is thus a generous one, equivalent to nearly half the mid-point price. In agreeing to allow fluctuations within this relatively wide range, the new Agreement will not be the major hindrance to the operation of markets which marred the International Coffee Agreement. (The price range established in the latter was only one-eleventh of the mid-range price of Colombian coffee, and about one-eighth for Robusta grades.) A 'hardship fund' of 150,000 tons additional to export quotas, which the Sugar Council could permit a developing member country to export in excess of its quota, was also a feature of the Agreement which in most other respects repeated the provisions of the 1953 Agreement.

Japan and Australia, which had found it impossible to accept the original fixed price ranges, were satisfied by the variable export quotas, while the Soviet Union accepted a quota of 1.1 million tons, thereby sealing off part of the problem of the re-export of Cuban sugar. However, Cuba, being in need of foreign exchange, decided that the best policy was one of co-operation and agreed to accept a limit of 250,000 tons on its exports to Czechoslovakia, Poland and Hungary. It also accepted export limitations upon its shipments to non-members, China and East Germany. The European Economic Community, however, remained a non-signatory to the Agreement and thus a major potential source of disruption, especially in the event of the enlargement of that community.

Thus the growth of protection in order to foster domestic European beet supplies, and of preferred sources for imports, has resulted in a situation in which fluctuations in domestic harvests of importing countries have been reflected entirely in variations in demand from the free market. Moreover, when war has threatened, importers have been understandably anxious to build up stocks from the free market at the same time as the suppliers have also wished to build up stocks. Over the past half century or so, therefore, the result of governmental intervention in the sugar trade has been to make the free market narrower, and to confine the effect of shifting demand and supply schedules to this relatively small sector of world production and consumption—demand and supply schedules which are, moreover, notoriously inelastic.

4. *Futures in Sugar*

The sugar trade was thus one in which traders were able to benefit from hedging the risk of price changes. It was found at an early date to be a fairly easy task to grade the sugar by means of chemical tests. It is also easily stored in temperate climates, and normally available from a number of sources—a most desirable attribute for a commodity in which futures markets have been organized, for traders are thereby safeguarded from the manipulation of prices through 'corners' and 'squeezes'. In fact the early development of the European beet sugar industry led to the establishment of the world's first sugar exchange at Hamburg in 1880. It was closed during World War I, re-opened in 1925, closed again in World War II, and re-opened in August 1954. The London market in sugar futures was opened in 1888 with a contract unit of 400 tons raw beet sugar f.o.b. Hamburg, as was appropriate to the heavy dependence of the United Kingdom upon supplies from this port at that time (Table 10.1). After closure during World War I the London market re-opened in September 1921, but when it did so, transactions were for 50 ton units of white sugar ex-bonded warehouse, London. The virtual cessation of refined sugar imports with the change in the tariff structure in 1929 was accompanied by the introduction of a raw sugar terminal market contract. This (as amended in 1930) was for cane sugar delivery c.i.f. London or Liverpool, with seller's option to deliver beet sugar f.o.b. at named continental ports, and cane or beet ex-store London or Liverpool. Thus, equipped with a more appropriate contract for current trading conditions in the United Kingdom, the market lost interest in the older white sugar contract which was finally withdrawn in 1931.

The establishment of an organized market in sugar futures occurred later in the U.S.A. than in Europe, though the trade was evidently highly speculative, with much forward buying and selling.[22] Dealing began on the New York Coffee Exchange in 1914, stimulated by the earlier wartime closure of the London and Hamburg Exchanges. Transactions in sugar futures quickly became important, and this was reflected in the amendment of the title of the American Exchange in 1916 to the New York Coffee and Sugar Exchange. When the U.S.A. entered the war in 1917 this Exchange also closed, and re-opened in February 1920 when it became the world's most important sugar exchange. On the eve of the outbreak of World War II the New York Exchange was trading in two sugar contracts: the No. 3, introduced in 1934, served the requirements of the domestic market, while the No. 4, commonly known as the 'world contract', met the needs of international trade. This important contract was introduced in 1936 due to the divergent trends of the domestic and the world markets which resulted from the quota protection which the U.S.A. administration had introduced by that time. The No. 4 contract was re-introduced after the closure of the New York Exchange during the Second World War, but, being effectively an f.a.s. Cuba contract, its usefulness ultimately came to an end in 1960.[23]

The United Sugar Terminal Market Association of London re-opened for trading on 2 January 1957, after the government had finally withdrawn from the scene. The revival of facilities for hedging and speculation thus completes the institutional picture as far as the U.K. sugar trade is concerned. As we have seen, the period since 1914 has witnessed a considerable shrinkage in the relative importance of the free market with a consequent development of price instability. However, the trader in sugar needs protection against price fluctuations equally for his purchases of domestic and Commonwealth sugar as for 'free-market' sugar. This is because the Sugar Board resells negotiated-price sugars at the current commercial price to refiners and other traders. These transactions are effected while the sugar is still in countries of origin, and purchasers then have to make their own arrangements to ship it to the U.K. A surcharge is levied upon all sugar and goods containing sugar upon entry into the United Kingdom. As far as home produce is concerned, it will be recalled that the British Sugar Corporation is required to purchase sugar beet from domestic producers at prices determined by the annual agricultural prices review. The refined produce, however, must obviously be sold at prices which conform to the prices at which other sugar is sold. Thus, whether the buyer purchases 'free-market' or Commonwealth sugar, its price to him may fluctuate and so occasion losses. Hence the need for the re-establishment of the London terminal market.

The contract introduced by the United Sugar Terminal Market

Association was very similar to its pre-war counterpart, despite the seventeen-year interval; it was for non-preferential raw cane sugar of 96 degrees polarization,[24] in bags, delivered c.i.f. London or Liverpool at seller's option, in contract quantities of 50 tons, payable in sterling. The seller was also given the option of delivering in bulk, delivering preferential duty sugar or delivery ex-store, at the appropriate adjustments in price. The sugar had to be eligible for importation into the U.K., in compliance with the International Sugar Agreement.

The terms of the contract resulted in some confusion during its early days. When quota restrictions imposed under the International Sugar Agreement were removed in 1957 Brazilian sugar became legitimate tender under the terms of the contract, but was ineligible for import into the U.K. when I.S.A. quotas were later re-imposed. The situation was met by amending the contract to embrace produce from I.S.A. signatories only. Even in its amended form, however, the No. 1 contract frequently created difficulties for refiners bound by contract to receive supplies from traders who had been forced in turn to accept tenders of non-Commonwealth sugar in contravention of international agreements. The situation often resulted in distortions of the structure of sugar prices on the market for futures nearing maturity. A No. 2 (Preferential) contract accordingly replaced the earlier one. The No. 2 excluded from tender all sugars other than those entering the U.K. from members of the Commonwealth Sugar Agreement. The terms of the contract were c.i.f. London or Liverpool, no ex-store delivery being allowed.

The United Terminal Sugar Market is 'called over' at 10.40 a.m., 12.30 p.m. and 4.45 p.m., but business is also concluded between calls and may also be concluded after the Exchange is closed. Trading is by open outcry: sellers shout their offers and buyers their bids in the ring and nominate the month of delivery. Quantities may be named but must, of course, be for a minimum of one contract unit of 50 tons. If a buyer or a seller is asked 'how many?' it implies that the enquirer is prepared to trade five contracts or more. All transactions are recorded and registered, as previously explained, with the Clearing House. The prices at the end of a 'call' record the official quotations and business done and so publicly establish the price levels for sugar, at that particular time, for various delivery months in the future.

It is the closing call which is taken as the basis for the daily payment of margins through the Clearing House, but there is also a Price Committee, appointed by the United Sugar Terminal Market Association, whose function it is to establish the London Daily Price (abbreviated to L.D.P. in press reports) at 11 a.m., after the market's first call of the day. Before World War II Czarnikow's published spot price for sugar was generally accepted as authoritative by the trade, so that the market Price Committee is a postwar innovation, whose prices were first published in April 1956. The L.D.P. is expressed in pounds and decimals of a pound sterling per ton c.i.f. the United Kingdom, and represents the value of prompt delivery raw sugar at the time it is determined. All sugars, cane or beet, which originate from a member country of the International Sugar Agreement are taken into consideration irrespective of whether they are traded in the U.K. or not. For this reason and because the L.D.P. can be based on business reported, on offers, or on the tone of the market, it need not always coincide exactly with the price of the prompt month on the terminal market.

The London Daily Price is widely used. The Sugar Board uses it as the basis for its sales policy: refiners and the British Sugar Corporation use it as their raw material costing for refined-sugar quotations. Internationally the L.D.P., together with the estimate of the spot price published by the New York Coffee and Sugar Exchange, is used by the International Sugar Council as the measurement for the market level for quota variations. The International Sugar Council Daily Price is actually arrived at by calculating the arithmetic average of the L.D.P. and the New York No. 8 contract Spot Price for that day, after conversion of these prices to U.S. cents per pound f.a.s. Cuban port basis or, if the difference between the two f.a.s. prices is more than six points, by adding three points to the lower of these two prices. (See, for example, the Council's *Sugar Yearbook* for 1966, p. 355.) Finally, in the trade itself, these official spot prices are very important for transactions in the world's physical markets. Contracts are often concluded on the basis of an 'average price over a period', or else on 'price on day of arrival' terms, and it is the prices which emanate from the London and New York Exchanges which are used.

The regulations of the United Sugar Terminal Market Association of London limit its full members (i.e. brokers allowed to deal on the floor of the Exchange) to a maximum of sixty-three. In fact the membership has always been well below the limit specified. It is only these members or their market representatives who are allowed to deal free of commission on the market floor. Associate, Affiliated and Overseas Affiliated members number some 150 at the present time. The rate of commission charged to non-members is $\frac{1}{2}$ per cent (for what is termed an 'in and out' transaction – i.e. for entering the market as a buyer or seller, and ultimately 'closing out' the contract(s) by means of an offsetting transaction). Trading is in contracts for up to twelve months ahead, with dealing possible in contracts pertaining to a particular month up to the last week of that month. Delivery may be made against a futures contract on any day in the month in which the contract expires, though normally less than one per cent of registered contracts are settled by this means.

The accompanying tables (Tables 10.3, A, B, and C), kindly extracted

TABLE 10.3A

LONDON SUGAR TERMINAL CONTRACTS, 1888–1915
(contract unit 500 bags)

White Beet Contract 88

Year	Transactions	
1888	403,500 bags	
1889	5,386,000 ,,	
1890	5,170,500 ,,	3,100 tons Crystals
1891	4,410,500 ,,	600 ,, ,,
1892	4,382,500 ,,	
1893	8,288,500 ,,	
1894	4,452,000 ,,	3,000 bags Granulated
1895	8,622,500 ,,	
1896	10,658,000 ,,	
1897	5,790,000 ,,	
1898	6,340,000 ,,	
1899	8,079,000 ,,	
1900	9,629,000 ,,	
1901	7,282,000 ,,	
1902	9,559,000 ,,	
1903	6,759,500 ,,	
1904	15,392,000 ,,	
1905	14,058,000 ,,	
1906	13,461,500 ,,	
1907	18,341,000 ,,	464,600 bags Granulated
1908	24,666,500 ,,	43,450 ,, ,,
1909	24,793,500 ,,	57,410 ,, ,,
1910	31,333,000 ,,	61,210 ,, ,,
1911	37,945,000 ,,	49,750 ,, ,,
1912	33,533,500 ,,	6,300 ,, ,,
1913	25,086,000 ,,	20,465 ,, ,,
1914	12,268,000 ,,	6,110 ,, ,,
1915	9,500 ,,	

1912   12,600 tons Raw Cane

Source: Figures supplied by the London Produce Clearing House Ltd.

TABLE 10.3B

LONDON SUGAR TERMINAL CONTRACTS, 1921–1939
Transactions

Year	White Sugar Contracts a	Raw Sugar
1921	61,050 tons	
1922	437,500 ,,	
1923	1,479,350 ,,	
1924	1,447,450 ,,	
1925	1,858,150 ,,	
1926	2,596,900 ,,	
1927	2,807,600 ,,	
1928	1,558,650 ,,	213,600 tons
1929	303,650 ,,	2,127,100 ,,
1930	37,850 ,,	2,036,250 ,,
1931	300 ,,	1,806,900 ,,
1932		2,165,550 ,,
1933		2,605,300 ,,
1934		2,301,400 ,,
1935		1,770,600 ,,
1936		1,965,450 ,,
1937		3,930,000 ,,
1938		2,690,700 ,,
1939		1,221,300 ,,

a. Contract unit 50 tons.

Source: Figures supplied by the London Produce Clearing House Ltd.

TABLE 10.3C

a

LONDON FUTURES TRANSACTIONS IN SUGAR, 1959–1970

(Contract unit 50 tons)

Year	Transactions in tons
1959*b*	166,400
1960	1,119,150
1961	2,256,000
1962	3,967,000
1963	15,121,000
1964	13,092,900
1965	10,132,700
1966	8,602,300
1967	23,850,000
1968	19,800,000
1969	28,750,000
1970	26,543,500

a. Sugar No. 2 Contract. Business in the No. 1 Contract, which ran from 3 January 1957 to 31 August 1960, amounted to 1,905,400 tons. Of the total business transacted in sugar, 1,071,550 tons were in options.

b. From 2 October 1959.

Source: Figures supplied by the London Produce Clearing House Ltd

TABLE 10.4

AVERAGE WEEKLY NET OPEN INTERESTS ON SUGAR FUTURES EXCHANGES, 1947–1969

long tons

Years	London	U.S. (World)	U.S. (Domestic)
1947			106,000
1948		40,000	161,000
1949		63,000	166,000
1950		72,000	162,000
1951		86,000	151,000
1952		111,000	264,000
1953		181,000	231,000
1954		223,000	233,000
1955		128,000	140,000
1956		95,000	116,000
1957		354,000	117,000
1958		335,000	82,000
1959	66,000	383,000	179,000
1960	116,000	277,000	
1961	221,000	49,000	98,000
1962	343,000	141,000	91,000
1963	1,159,000	398,000	42,000
1964	1,109,000	288,000	112,000
1965	839,000	448,000	177,000
1966	756,000	775,000	174,000
1967	1,259,000	1,080,000	53,000
1968	1,267,000	1,320,000	50,000
1969	1,437,000	1,029,000	52,000

Source: Calculations to 1960 from R. H. Snape, 'Protection and Stabilization in the World Sugar Industry', Table 19. Figures 1961–69 (inclusive) supplied by C. Czarnikow Ltd.

from their files by the London Produce Clearing House Limited, indicate the magnitude of the London Sugar Terminal market since its inception in 1888. The New York Exchange was larger than its London counterpart during the inter-war period, while the Hamburg Exchange had failed to regain its former importance following the disruptions of World War I. The volume of business on the New York Exchange during the late 1920s was in fact greater than that of any subsequent year down to 1957 – even the Korean war failed to provide very much excitement on the market it would appear – but it must be remembered that at the time much of the international trade in sugar was still in official hands. Close currency regulation, too, made it difficult for non-American speculators to operate. Table 10.4 provides an indication of the relative size of the U.S. and the London markets since World War II, as given by the average weekly net open interests.

The Suez action in 1956, together with the disquiet felt at the sight of Russian tanks in the streets of Budapest, led to some speculative fever, though this was at a time when the London market was still preparing to open. When it did open, it remained the minor market until 1960, because many U.K. interests continued to trade in the No. 4 'world' contract on the New York Exchange, especially in view of the confusion occasioned by the London No. 1 contract to which reference has already been made. However, when the U.S.-Cuban difficulties began in 1960 a dramatic change in the relative importance of these markets took place. The American No. 4 contract was abandoned because it was essentially a Cuban contract. At the same time the London Sugar Terminal Market Association succeeded in resolving its difficulties with the introduction of the No. 2 (preferential) contract. This became extremely popular and, as the table of open interests indicates (Table 10.4), the London market easily surpassed its New York rival in 1961. The U.S. market failed to regain its former importance through the first half of the 1960s due to the unsatisfactory nature (notably its vagueness as to delivery terms) of the No. 8 contract. The No. 6 contract serving the domestic market was suspended in January 1961 and replaced by the No. 7, while in November 1966 yet another change was made with the introduction of the No. 10. In spite of this, there has been a decline in the use of domestic contracts in the U.S. in the recent past which appears to have been connected with the careful operation of the U.S. Sugar Act. This limits the extent of daily fluctuations in the price of futures, which makes traders chary of going to the expense of opening terminal market positions. In any case, market quotations are only for two or three positions for the domestic contract, which provides cover for up to six months ahead only. Understandably, therefore, the panic rise and fall of sugar prices did little to stimulate business in the U.S. domestic contract, but the figures also indicate that in 1963-64 it was the London rather than the New York market which witnessed the real excitement.

With the growth of the London market of recent years, arbitrage operations between London and New York have also grown in importance. It will be recalled that this technique of 'spreading', as it is sometimes termed, consists at its simplest in buying in the market where the price is low and at the same time selling for forward delivery on another market on which the price is relatively high. However, whereas on physical markets the trader transports the produce which he has bought from the one market to the other, all that the dealer needs to do on the terminal markets is to close out each contract on the market where it was made. The profitability of the transaction depends upon the fact that the actions of arbitrageurs will tend to bring the markets into line without much delay. Clearly, where arbitrage transactions are international, dealers must take into account the complication of exchange rate fluctuations. The Articles of Agreement of the International Monetary Fund decree that such fluctuations should normally be kept within one per cent on either side of declared parities by means of official intervention. Usually, therefore, the degree to which exchange rates themselves stimulate arbitrage activity is limited, but when a country changes the par value of its currency, this must obviously constitute a major disturbance for the terminal markets. This was certainly true for the sugar trade, where November 1967 saw a ferment of activity, especially on the United Terminal Sugar Market of London. There was a great deal of hedging against sterling devaluation on this and other futures markets, the transactions consisting of buying London and selling New York positions. The pure speculators, however, were content to buy on the London market, gambling on the probability of a devaluation of the pound and a consequent increase in sterling quotations for positions on the terminal market.

The world's consumption of sugar continues to increase rapidly: the International Sugar Council estimate that the growth per head has been from 31.5 lbs (raw value) for 1955 to 41.2 lbs for 1966. U.K. consumption figures have not reflected this increase, though the consumption figure of 116.4 lbs per head continues to be well above the world figure. This consumption led to the import of 2,180,000 tons (raw value equivalent) for 1966 of which 298,000 tons were exported in refined form. U.K. domestic production for 1966 was 921,000 tons (raw value). The re-export trade brought in £316,000 in foreign exchange. An import bill of between £90 and £100 million a year (Table 10.5) obviously represents a considerable trade, though as far as the commodity markets are concerned transactions in the physical product have by this time ceased to take place on the market floor. Little if any 'actuals' business is now concluded on the London Commodity Exchange at Plantation House, though brokers' offices contained cupboards and counters for the display of samples not many years ago. All this has now disappeared with the spread of c.i.f. sales arranged over the telephone and telex. There has been a certain amount of backward integration by refiners, some of whom now own plantations. However, the efficiency and world-wide contacts of the

TABLE 10.5

VALUES OF THE UNITED KINGDOM RAW SUGAR IMPORTS AND RE-EXPORTS 1938, 1958, 1962 and 1968

£ thousand

Unrefined Beet and Cane Sugar

IMPORTS

From:	1938	1958	1962	1968
Mauritius	3,601	14,908	11,483	23,910
Australia	3,518	12,245	11,520	17,397
Fiji	955	3,363	2,742	7,130
Barbados			2,944	6,908
Jamaica			5,250	11,120
Trinidad	1,733	19,137	3,329	6,610
Antigua: St Christopher Nevis & Anguilla: Monserrat	527	7,801	1,040	1,517
British Guiana	199	344	3,982	7,208
Other Commonwealth Countries	3,264	16,308	574	6,328
Cuba		1,370	2,914	279
Brazil	775			289
Java	1,401	11,263		
St Domingo b	348	1,472		
Peru	1,976	6,197	4,643	809
Republic of South Africa a	96		2,591	1,004
Poland	480		914	1,795
Other Foreign Countries				
Total	**18,873**	**94,408**	**53,926**	**92,304**
Refined Sugar	315	1,154	2,742	1,580
RE-EXPORTS (Sugar, sugar preparations and honey)	31	175	226	353

(Barbados, Jamaica, Trinidad, Antigua: St Christopher, Nevis & Anguilla: Monserrat are bracketed together as British W. India Islands.)

a. Previously the Union of South Africa and South West Africa Territory.
b. Dominican Republic.
Source: The Annual Statement of Trade and Overseas Trade Accounts.

large sugar brokers have enabled them to remain the principal channels of distribution of sugar.

These sugar brokers also deal with a significant volume of 'third country trade' (such as the sale of Australian sugar to Asian countries). The sugar trade's own privately commissioned surveys for the years 1956, 1957, 1958 and (in conjunction with the Bank of England) 1963, revealed yearly net earnings of £0.6 million from these transactions. This figure, however, excludes terminal market transactions and commissions on U.K. imports and exports. When members of the sugar trade were asked by the Committee on Invisible Exports for an estimate of the gross profit earned in trade from non-residents; gross commissions paid to them by non-residents; and total differences received from or paid to non-residents in respect of terminal market contracts, the returns aggregated £3.7 million.[25]

The sugar trade centred on London is thus obviously an important activity, and, given the volatile nature of sugar prices, the re-opening of a terminal market in the city was obviously desirable not only for markets, dealers and refiners, but also for traders concerned with the internal distribution and use of sugar in manufactures of various sorts. The growth of the United Terminal Sugar Market has for these reasons been carefully nurtured by the trade since it re-opened in 1957. The large refiners have been especially interested, and have frequently come into the market in order to accommodate short hedgers. By their activities in the early years of its post-war existence they enabled the market to absorb appreciable sales of futures contracts without its having a disproportionate effect upon prices. The characteristic pattern of the terminal market in London in fact appears to be one in which as much as one-third or more of the long interests are often those of Tate and Lyle Ltd, while most of the remaining futures contracts on offer are bought by manufacturers based on Britain, Western Europe, the U.S.A. and the Far East. On the other side of the market, the sellers are mainly European and American traders, continental producers and United Kingdom dealers, who stand between the refiners and wholesalers. The remaining buying and selling interests, which comprise roughly a quarter of the market turnover, consist of hedging by broker members of the Association acting for themselves.

The largest firms of brokers on the United Terminal Sugar Market are normally responsible for a high proportion of market turnover. Such firms are not only full members of the terminal market but also highly important agents and suppliers of the physical product all over the world. As such they are stockholders of sugar, and sometimes they find themselves committed to supplying more produce than they possess. They therefore need to hedge their own positions with great frequency and in considerable amounts. Moreover, since they aim to provide their clients with a complete service in this commodity, a substantial part of the remainder of the terminal market broking activities is on behalf of these customers. Market turnover of futures contracts obviously depends upon expectations as to the probability of major price changes in the foreseeable future. Thus, though the volume of the sugar trade might change but little over a given period, transactions in futures markets may fluctuate violently, for in quiet times traders may take a view of the market and not go to the expense of opening a position on the terminal market. This provides us with the main explanation for the changes in market turnover and the variations in the average net open interests we have observed. By either of these criteria, however, the United Terminal Sugar Market of London is now very much larger than it was during its early years and, though the New York Exchange has now regained its former stature, the London market seems set fair to continue and to flourish in the future.

Chapter Eleven

THE COFFEE MARKET

1. *The Genesis of the Coffee Trade*

THE coffee tree is thought to have originated in the Kaffa district of
Abyssinia. Somewhere about the year 1500 it became an established
drink in Arabia where it was called 'kahwah' (pronounced 'cahveh'
by the Turks), a name derived from its original use as a stimulant.
It was to this quality that the English public's attention was primarily
drawn in the earliest known advertisement for coffee – a hand-
bill produced in 1652. This claimed that coffee 'quickens the spirits,
and makes the heart lightsome . . . is good against sore eyes . . .
excellent to prevent and cure the dropsy, gout, and scurvy . . .'

Coffee cultivation started in Batavia in 1690, and in 1712 the first
shipment reached Amsterdam from Java. The Dutch remained the
chief sellers of coffee throughout the eighteenth century but by the
end of that period the French auctions had become the most important.
These were originally held at Bordeaux, but were ultimately superseded
by those of Le Havre due to the latter's close proximity to the Paris
market.

After the Napoleonic Wars England gained a dominant position in
the coffee trade and world prices from that time were virtually determined by the London auctions. During the period after the French
Wars gross imports fluctuated between 17,000 and 23,000 tons a year,
of which a high proportion – in some years considerably more than
one half – was re-exported (Table 11.1). The Report of the Select
Committee on Import Duties summarizes the bewildering variety and
variation in the duties on coffee during the first half of the nineteenth
century.[1] One of the chief features of the early part of the period was
the imperial discrimination in favour of the West Indies at the expense
of the East Indies, while coffee from origins outside the British Empire
was taxed even more heavily. In 1825 all duties were cut by 50 per
cent, and the intra-imperial preference disappeared in 1827. Further
reductions followed in later years; in 1851 duties were consolidated at
3d. per lb for coffee from all origins and in 1872 the duty was further
reduced to 1½d.

As a result of these tariff cuts, consumption increased very considerably. In 1831 British demand was some 195,000 cwt, or 1.549 lbs per
head, according to Porter.[2] By 1900 it had grown only to 260,000 cwt,
but by today it is 1,794,422 cwt.

240

London became an important centre for the trade during the early nineteenth century because many producers banked in London. Of even greater significance was the availability of capital seeking investment which meant that stocks could always be disposed of: even though there might not be many direct buyers at any given time, many London firms would bid for the coffee in order to reship it to continental markets. In this sense London was a reservoir for this as for so much other produce at the time. Banking services, moreover, were more sophisticated and flexible than at other major centres; it was easier in London than in any other major market centre for shippers to obtain immediate ready cash by borrowing against commodity shipments.

In the London Commodity Sale Rooms coffee was sold in 'piles'. Prices were quoted in shillings per cwt and as many as 7,000 bags (each bag containing 132¼ lbs) were sometimes sold in the course of an auction. Planters or trading companies consigned the produce to importing merchants, but the public sales, as with other commodities, were arranged by selling brokers. Except for Brazilian produce, coffee was 'bulked' (i.e. mixed) in the warehouses, and often husked also. The coffee was inspected by buyers at the warehouses and the auction sales were normally held at 1.30 p.m. on Tuesdays and Thursdays throughout the year, with the addition of Wednesdays and Fridays between January and July.

2. *The Restriction of Supplies and Wartime Control*

At the turn of the century most of the world's coffee came from Brazil. Perhaps because of the expansion in demand, methods of production were not notably efficient. During the early years of the new century a coffee glut embarrassed producers and, in 1906, the three coffee states of Minas Geraes, Rio de Janeiro and Sao Paulo, decided upon a 'valorisation plan'. However, the federal government failed to guarantee a loan of £15 million and so the first two states withdrew, leaving Sao Paulo to proceed on its own. An amount of some £18 million was secured from London and New York banking houses and an attempt was made with this fund to purchase coffee in order to withhold supplies from world markets to improve the price. Sao Paulo normally produced almost two-thirds of the Brazilian crop and exported coffee to the virtual exclusion of every other commodity. Nevertheless it was clear early in 1908 that the plan had failed. Prices were prevented from rising by the large stocks which had been pushed into the market in anticipation of the operation of the scheme. A loan from the Federal Government became necessary to rescue Sao Paulo from bankruptcy. Some experience was gained, however, and the scheme did help to introduce greater efficiency into coffee cultivation due to government preference for better grade coffee in making its purchases.

Apart from some attempt at control towards the end of World War I,

TABLE 11.1

VALUES OF U.K. COFFEE IMPORTS AND RE-EXPORTS 1700–1938 a
Ten-year annual averages
£ thousand

Years	Imports	Re-exports
1700–09 b	39·4	
1710–19 b	64·1	
1720–29	83·1	
1730–39	81·7	
1740–49	74·4	
1750–59	140·0	
1760–69	296·0	
1770–79	348·5	
1780–89	226·5	
1790–99	1547·5	
1800–09	3520·9	
1810–19 b	3950·8	3950·9
1820–29	2790·9	2036·6
1830–39	2415·7	968·7
1840–49	3222·7	991·5
1850–56	3584·4	1459·1
1854–63	2300·0	1200·0
1864–73	4900·0	3800·0
1874–83	6400·0	4900·0
1884–93	3800·0	2700·0
1894–1903	3300·0	1900·0
1904–13	2500·0	1700·0
1914–23	3500·0	1900·0
1924–33	4100·0	1800·0
1934–38	1700·0	300·0

1700–1856	Official Values.
1854–1870	Computed Values.
1871–1938	Declared Values.

a. England and Wales   1700–1791
    Great Britain   1792–1829
    United Kingdom   1826–1938

b. No figures available for 1705, 1712 and 1813, therefore a 9-year average.

Source: Mitchell, *Abstract of British Historical Statistics.*

the next major scheme was introduced in Brazil in 1923 – again by Sao Paulo. Essentially the plan provided for the storage of a proportion of the crop when harvests were good in order to achieve a stable and acceptable price level. Prices did rise during the period in which the scheme operated. Rowe, however, argues that this was due to an actual shortfall of supply in the face of rising demand.[3] However that might be, the scheme appeared to be working until the end of 1928. Then, in 1929, the Sao Paulo government failed to obtain finance for the bumper crop of that year, having extended itself by holding a proportion of the large 1927 harvest. Consequently, on 11 October 1929, the Sao Paulo Coffee Defence Institute's broker failed to intervene in the market and prices collapsed. The protagonists of the scheme argue that it could have continued to function satisfactorily but for the peculiarly difficult financial conditions of the time. On the other hand we know that further bumper crops were a feature of the early 1930s, which makes it

TABLE 11.2

WORLD COFFEE EXPORTS 1929–1968

thousand long tons (Five-year annual averages)

Country	1929–33	1934–38	1946–50	1951–55	1956–60	1961–65	1968
Costa Rica	22·2	22·8	18·2	22·6	37·1 a	51·8	66·8
El Salvador	49·8	53·3	62·0	65·4	76·6	95·0	115·6
Guatemala	42·8	27·4	51·9	54·9	75·4	84·8	87·7
Haiti b	30·3	46·4	24·9	25·7	25·4	23·7	17·2
Mexico	29·3	35·9	38·0	64·6	78·5	83·9	93·4
Brazil	883·6	861·0	968·9	854·9	924·3	960·1	1090·0
Colombia	183·7	227·3	312·6	331·6	327·0 a	35·9	389·0
Venezuela	49·4	47·0	29·0	29·5	28·4	20·8	9·5
Uganda	3·5	10·4	29·2	45·7	85·9	134·7	149·6
Tanganyika c	10·7	14·3	12·1	17·4	21·4	27·4	48·5
Kenya	12·2	15·6	9·8	14·1	25·5 a	35·8	37·0
Indonesia	78·3	83·9	4·1	27·1	42·7	72·4	73·6
French West Africa d	0·9	7·8	50·8	74·6	127·5	170·6	211·1
Angola	10·6	16·4	44·9	56·6	80·7	139·6	185·7
Others	88·0	132·0	154·6	222·3	335·0	420·2	554·1
World Total e	1495·4	1601·3	1811·0	1907·0	2291·3	2679·8	3128·8

a. 1956–59
b. Haiti years ending 30 September from 1961.
c. From 1961 Tanzania.
d. Ivory Coast from 1961.
e. Total for 1961–1968 inclusive = Total from Principal Exporting Countries.
Figures have been rounded and do not necessarily add to total.
Sources: F.A.O. Commodity Bulletin Series 33, *The World Coffee Economy*, 1961, and Commonwealth Economic Committee, *Plantation Crops*, No. 11 1967, and No. 13, 1970.

doubtful whether prices could have been prevented from softening very appreciably.

As it was, the federal government of Brazil decided that the solution to the problem was to burn its surplus coffee, an act now immortalized in economics textbooks all over the world. New plantings were prohibited and a heavy tax imposed upon exports to defray the costs of the 57-60 million bags of produce destroyed up to 1937.

War broke out in 1939 without any sort of contingency plan for the control of coffee, cocoa, fruit, vegetables and other minor foodstuffs.[4] In the event, however, the U.K. imported more coffee than before the war, probably because of the shortage of tea. Consumption continued at a high level in the U.K. (Table 11.3 shows that between 1936-8 and 1950-2 coffee imports doubled.) Buoyant world demand generally resulted in a clearing of stocks held by producer countries, as the result of which the wartime Inter-American Coffee Agreement established by the U.S.A. was suspended in 1948.

The ceiling previously imposed upon coffee prices by the American administration had already been removed. This paved the way for the reopening of the New York Coffee and Sugar Exchange during the same year. Its reopening thus reactivated a market in coffee which had first emerged in 1882 as a result of the threat posed by the excess supplies stockpiled in New York at the time. Transactions on the New York Coffee and Sugar Exchange are conducted by open outcry around a ring on the floor of the Exchange. The contracts were, until 1968, based on Santos coffee B ('type no. 4 strictly soft in the cup, fair to good roast, solid bean'), and C ('sweet in the cup'). There was also a contract in East African Robusta coffee.

The reopening of the New York Exchange was followed by that of the Bolsa at Santos. Trading on the former Exchange was briefly suspended during the last two days of January 1951 due to the price freeze imposed by the U.S. Government owing to the enormous interest in coffee (and other commodities) generated by the Korean War. However, trading was resumed on 1 February, and the authorities subsequently clarified the situation by announcing their price ceilings for both coffee and cocoa.[5]

By August 1952 the British government were considering how they might best withdraw from the coffee trade, in spite of their considerable stocks. Accordingly, an open general licence was granted to importers of coffee from the Commonwealth (except for Canada which was in the dollar area) and importers from Brazil and other non-dollar area countries were given a block licence. In the hope of fostering re-exports no restrictions were placed upon this trade. Moreover, the Ministry of Food sought to re-establish the pre-war system of selling coffee by public sale by itself holding an auction on 9 January 1953.[6] However, the discontinuity occasioned by the war proved fatal to the auction system,

TABLE 11.3
UNITED KINGDOM COFFEE IMPORTS BY ORIGIN, 1913–1968
thousand long tons (annual averages)

Country of Origin	1913	1930–2	1936–8	1950–2	1955–7	1958	1968
Costa Rica	9.6	13.8	8.0	—	0.2	0.7	0.7
Kenya		16.4	7.5	3.9	14.5	12.8	8.5
Tanganyika (now Tanzania)		—	—	9.2	2.8	3.4	2.1
Uganda		1.8		6.9	8.5	11.1	33.7
Brazil	12.9		0.2	12.4	5.4	5.2	7.0
British West Africa—Sierra Leone							3.0
Ghana					2.3	2.4	2.6
Nigeria							1.0
Colombia	4.6	1.2	0.2	0.2	0.3	1.2	2.0
Others	15.2	5.3	4.2	9.1	7.0	6.6	29.6
Total	42.3	38.5	20.1	41.6	40.8	43.4	90.2

Figures for 1930–57   Coffee not kiln dried, roasted or ground.
         1958–68   Coffee whether or not roasted or freed of caffeine: coffee substitutes containing coffee.
Figures have been rounded and therefore do not necessarily add to total.
Sources: F.A.O. Commodity Bulletin Series 33, The World Coffee Economy, 1961, and the Annual Statement of Trade.

which never revived when the trade finally returned to private hands.[7]
The character of the trade, too, had changed considerably. Though
coffee from the dollar area was not allowed in until towards the end
of 1954 – and even then on limited licence – a different major source
of supply had established itself by that time. As the table of U.K.
Coffee Imports by Origin (Table 11.3) shows, the supply of mild
Robusta coffee from East Africa (Uganda, Tanzania and Kenya) was
considerably greater by the mid-fifties than it had been during the
mid-thirties. Coffee cultivation having been encouraged within former
British East Africa, mainly with the help of British capital, it is hardly
surprising that London should become an important market for this
produce. This, together with a tendency for British domestic consumption of coffee to increase, made London a rather more important
central market than previously. Moreover, as Table 11.4 shows, the
re-export trade was far from being entirely lost – in 1958 it was not
far short of one-third of its pre-war volume at that time.

The high prices of the early 1950s were accompanied by heavy
planting, which in turn brought forth heavy crops after 1955. Prices
accordingly began to fall and a pressing demand thus arose among
traders and colonial interests for the establishment in London of a
market to provide price insurance. This was seen as obviating the need
to use the New York market, or the smaller Le Havre and Amsterdam
markets which had already re-opened. A Coffee Trade Association had
in fact been established as early as 1888 in London – the same year
as its Le Havre counterpart – in order to trade in coffee futures
(Table 11.5 and Table 11.6). The basis of the contract then introduced
was No. 5 Santos type. Transactions were settled through the London
Produce Clearing House, the Board of Directors of which appointed a
Coffee Type Committee annually whose purpose was to revise the
official coffee 'types' and the scale of premiums and discounts allowable
for tenders of various grades of the produce in settlement of contracts.

3. *The Post-War London Coffee Terminal Market*

The Coffee Terminal Market Association of London re-opened on
1 July 1958, almost four years after the Le Havre Coffee Terminal
Market, which re-opened on 17 November 1954, some three years after
the Amsterdam and Rotterdam markets, and two years after the
Hamburg market. The initial entrance fee for floor membership of the
London market was fixed at £500, with a limitation of membership to
forty, the Formation Committee reserving the right to increase this
maximum at their discretion. Entrance fees for Home or Overseas
Associate Membership were fixed at £100. The contract unit is for
five long tons of Uganda unwashed, native-grown Robusta coffee for
the delivery months of January, March, May, July, September and
November; that is, for 'positions' of up to a year ahead. Quotations

TABLE 11.4

RE-EXPORTS OF COFFEE FROM THE U.K. TO MAIN DESTINATIONS, 1938, 1958 and 1968

Quantities – long tons   Values – £

To	1938		1958		1968	
	Quantity	Value	Quantity	Value	Quantity	Value
New Zealand	—	—	9·6	4,752	—	—
Canada	757·2	43,127	134·2 a	47,986	113·4	41,481
Eire	274·8	21,072	—	—	—	—
Sweden	316·8	17,908	—	—	—	—
Poland	518·2	35,711	—	—	—	—
Germany	524·2	34,088	439·2 b	187,046	—	—
Netherlands	1350·6	73,983	85·6	26,006	—	—
Belgium	722·4	43,042	—	—	—	—
U.S.A.	484·8	28,732	522·4	187,720	88·3	30,991
France	94·5	4,113	761·8	274,840	—	—
Denmark	35·8	1,737	196·7	72,183	—	—
Norway	56·8	3,011	226·7	78,060	—	—
Others	981·9	61,334	—	—	309·3	109,221
TOTAL	6118·0	367,858	2376·2	878,593	511·0	181,693

a. Irish Republic.
b. Western Germany.
1938 and 1958   Not kiln dried, roasted or ground.
1968   Coffee whether or not roasted or freed of caffeine, coffee substitutes containing coffee.
Figures have been rounded and therefore do not necessarily add to total.
Source: Annual Statement of Trade.

TABLE 11.5

LONDON FUTURES TRANSACTIONS IN COFFEE, 1888–1928

Year	Transactions (in thousand bags)			Year	Transactions (in thousand bags)
	Santos	Rio	Brazilian		Santos
1888	—	1986·5	1002	1909	2150·8
1889	—	1141·5	3852	1910	2623·3
1890	210·5 a	1087·5		1911	4026·3
1891	266·5	1058·5		1912	3100·3
1892	88·0	743·0		1913	3180·8
1893	4·5	433·0		1914	1604·8
1894	—	113·5		1915	267·8
1895	—	1·0		1916	715·8
1896	498·5 b			1917	505·5
1897	1536·3			1918	33·8
1898	1578·5			1919	129·0
1899	3061·5			1920	105·0
1900	4159·8			1921	174·8
1901	3557·3			1922	118·3
1902	3906·8			1923	15·3
1903	5943·4			1924	4·3
1904	7941·0			1925	18·0
1905	3858·5			1926	34·3
1906	3079·0			1927	6·0
1907	2387·0			1928	—
1908	1760·0				

a. From 2 June 1890.
b. From 20 April 1896.

Source: Figures supplied by the London Produce Clearing House Ltd.

TABLE 11.6

LONDON FUTURES TRANSACTIONS IN COFFEE, 1958–1970

(contract unit 5 tons)

Year	Transactions (in tons)
1958 a	53,935
1959	127,165
1960	115,180
1961	39,985
1962	26,650
1963	79,195
1964	315,555
1965	448,465
1966	324,180
1967	190,000
1968	190,000
1969	240,000
1970	375,685

a. From 2 July 1958.

Source: Figures supplied by the London Produce Clearing House Ltd.

are on a hundredweight basis (112 lbs) in shillings. Fluctuations are recorded in units of 6d., representing £2 10s. od. on each contract unit. All prices quoted are 'in warehouse London, Liverpool or Bristol'. The Rules and Regulations of the Association permit the tender of a limited number of qualities below the official standard, as well as

Robusta coffee from most other countries, at differential prices fixed periodically by the Association. The market opens with an official call, and further calls are made at 2.45 p.m. and when the market closes. Business is carried on between official calls by open outcry, and the newcomer onto the floor is able to tell at a glance from the board on the wall what has been happening on the market. Contracts are guaranteed and cleared by the London Produce Clearing House Ltd, to whom an original deposit of £100 per contract is payable, in addition to the Clearing House fee of £1 per contract. When about 25 per cent of the original deposit has been depleted by price movements, variation margins are called to make good the deficit. The current Coffee Terminal Market Association of London minimum commission for the purchase and sale (i.e. a 'round turn') is £8 per futures contract if the price is below 150s. 6d. per cwt and £10 when the price is below 300s. 6d. and above 150s.

Although by this time the London market may be said to have the only successful Robusta coffee contract in the world, the opening of the terminal market in London paved the way for a good deal of arbitrage business between the two main centres of London and New York. The London market turnover increased from a low point of 26,650 tons for the year ending May 1962, to a peak of 448,465 tons for the year ending May 1965. This still represents the peak of the market, though business continues to flourish. The turnover for the year ending May 1970 was 375,685 tons.

The London market thus continues to function normally despite the agreements which have been arrived at to control the marketing of coffee. Falling prices after the mid-fifties led to an Agreement among the Latin American countries by which a proportion of the 1958 crop was withheld from world markets. France and Portugal introduced export quotas on green coffee from their African colonies in 1959, while Britain and Belgium also undertook to restrict exports from their African colonies. Britain did not join this International Coffee Study Group as a full member until 1960, when its inclusion increased the proportion of the world's green coffee covered by the Agreement to 70 per cent.

Prices, however, continued to fall during the early 1960s owing to heavy planting in 1954 prompted by the short crop and soaring prices of that year. Each season's crop was considerably greater than the exports. Thus, for 1962 the exportable supply was some 60 million bags but demand was only for some 44 million, so that prices would have fallen a good deal further but for stockpiling. As it was, by 1962 prices had fallen by some two-thirds of those prevailing in the mid-fifties. The situation led to the negotiation of a more comprehensive five year agreement by the Coffee Study Group. It was the period of the 'Alliance for Progress' following the Cuban crisis which found the

Americans in a particularly positive mood to try to help stabilize the economies of the Latin American countries. A pact was adopted in 1962, and in 1963 the International Coffee Organization was formed to operate the Agreement.

4. *The International Coffee Agreement*

It is estimated that about one-third of the world's coffee crops are produced on very small farms of less than ten hectares[8] which makes it extremely difficult to control production. The Coffee Agreement was, therefore, based on export quotas, determined annually for each country for the first three years. In addition to this basic quota an actual quota was calculated for each member country in the light of world demand. This was expressed as a percentage of the basic quota. The aim of the Agreement was to prevent coffee prices from falling below the levels prevailing in 1962. The political flavour of the Agreement as a counter to the Cuban situation was universally acknowledged,[9] for the prognostications of the Food and Agriculture Organization were gloomy. They argued that even though coffee beans were used for oil, animal feed and fertilizer, world import requirements would only amount to 80 per cent of total production for 1965. It is against these conditions of coffee glut that the declining fortunes of the New York Coffee and Sugar Exchange must be viewed. With the prices of Santos 4 S and Colombian Manizales coffees (the basis grades for futures trading) virtually stabilized, the market became inactive and has remained so.

The price ranges permitted for the four categories of the coffee recognized by the Agreement (i.e. Colombian milds, Other milds, Unwashed arabicas and Robustas) became 4 cents for 1966-67 and have remained so to the present (1969). A price range of 4 cents a lb to permit fluctuations from 43.50 to 47.50 cents is extremely narrow; in fact some one-eleventh of the mid-price for Colombian milds in 1966-67. For the same period the permitted range for Robustas was 30.50 to 34.50 or one-eighth of the mid-price range. The permitted price range for Colombian milds was 38.75 – 42.75 for 1967-68, giving a possible fluctuation of one-tenth of the mid-price range.[10] The narrowness of the range provides the explanation for the virtual collapse of the New York market and the appreciable decline in the turnover of the London market, as Table 11.6 indicates. It was the realization that artificially supported prices did not represent a long-term solution to the problem of low coffee prices which led to new discussions. In August 1965 the International Coffee Organization considered a scheme for the participation of the World Bank in the provision of finance to enable countries to limit production and to shift resources out of coffee cultivation. The talks resulted in an agreement signed in November 1965 by the World Bank, the F.A.O., and the International

Coffee Organization. A coffee study of 12-18 months was proposed to discover the best means of setting production limits in order to try to equate world supply with demand at a reasonable price level.

Unexpectedly, coffee was in short supply by the end of 1965 and quota increases were made. Despite this, there was a good deal of smuggling of extra-quota coffee in the Caribbean and it was estimated that about one million bags evaded the Agreement during the 1965-66 season. This so-called 'tourist coffee' had a depressing effect upon the market, and even though certificates of origin were required regardless of where coffee originated, there was a feeling that there was a great deal of 'tourist coffee' still in transit to world markets, some of it being sold in the guise of parts of the domestic crop of non-member countries. Moreover, the prices of Robusta coffees were seen to have maintained greater firmness in the face of the quota increases than the prices for the American coffees. This led to a demand for an increase in quotas from the Ivory Coast countries, which, with a fixed global quota, could only be met under the terms of the Agreement by a cut-back in the quotas of Brazil and other Western Hemisphere countries. There was a good deal of acrimony and a welter of accusations that stocks were being manipulated and under-the-counter deals being concluded. The disputes culminated in a London conference in August 1966 to try to solve these problems.

What emerged was an attempt to run the Agreement with a greater regard for market pressures. A system of flexible export quotas was established which allowed exporters to exceed normal quotas for two reasons: firstly, should acute economic problems arise and secondly, should the price of any of the four basic varieties of coffee move outside a predetermined range for fifteen consecutive market days. For prices in excess of the recognized ceiling price, quotas could be relaxed on a pro rata basis by $2\frac{1}{2}$ per cent, and conversely for prices below recognized floor levels. It was hoped in this way to prevent serious hardships and to take into account unforeseen changes in the market situation. Moreover, in order to try to establish a fund to encourage some movement out of coffee cultivation, a proportion of increases in exports above quota were required to be set aside for this purpose.

The International Coffee Organization decided in principle in August 1967 to renew the Agreement, which was due to expire in September 1968. Despite this resolution, the Coffee Council was left to solve a number of basic problems. Among these, the issue of curtailing production and creating a 'diversification fund' to assist cultivators to move out of coffee could be considered as long term aims, but the distribution of quotas posed immediate problems. In the meantime, too, a further source of disagreement had arisen between Brazil and the U.S.A. concerning the dumping of processed ('instant') coffee in the latter country. However, a five year extension to the International

Coffee Agreement was finally decided upon on 19 February 1968. Adjustments were made to quotas, which totalled 55 million bags, and the new Agreement allowed importing countries to take action against the dumping of processed coffee after the case had been judged by an independent body. Funds were established to aid coffee-dependent countries to diversify their economies while quota-free exports were agreed upon as a means of developing new markets. Finally, as a longer term aim, it was decided to set production ceilings to be implemented by the 1971-72 season. This last step would appear to be in the long-term interest of the coffee growers. The burning of Brazilian coffee during the 1930s achieved a wide notoriety. What is less well known is that as recently as 1960 world supply was 116 million bags, of which only 55 million were taken off the market. More than a year's supply was thus left in store. In fact, the situation since World War II has been that production increases have threatened a glut more often than not.

As is apparent from the tables the United Kingdom's interest in coffee is not nearly as great as it is in tea. The United States is far and away the largest consumer (Table 11.7) and takes some 45.4 per cent of world green coffee imports. West Germany takes 9 per cent, France 7.3 per cent, Italy 4.5 per cent, Sweden 3.2 per cent, the Netherlands 3 per cent and Britain 2.7 per cent. Furthermore, as may be seen from the table of U.K. re-exports (Table 11.4), this trade is no longer very significant. Nevertheless, London has a flourishing coffee trade. With the failure to revive the coffee auctions the trade in the physical product is now a matter of transactions on the telephone, with a good deal of direct buying between manufacturers and shippers' agents on a c.i.f. basis. Merchants still handle smaller parcels, however, and some broking business remains.

Meanwhile, the narrowness of the permitted spread of coffee prices has had repercussions upon the turnover of business at the London coffee terminal market. Though a high proportion still finds the hedging facilities useful, the market has become less active since the signing of the International Coffee Agreement. At present, the London Coffee Terminal Market Association has thirty-five floor members and ninety associate members. Of the latter fifty-five are overseas members and thirty-five are home members. But though turnover has declined somewhat on the London market of recent years, 1970 proved to be one of the busiest in its history, as Table 11.6 indicates. This is largely accounted for by the virtual failure of the New York market. As has already been explained, the effect of the Agreement on the higher-priced Colombian coffee (the basis of the New York contract) has been to impose tighter restrictions upon price fluctuations from the mid-point price. There are, however, other reasons which help to explain the moribund state of coffee futures in New York. There never was a very

TABLE 11.7

IMPORTS OF RAW COFFEE INTO PRINCIPAL IMPORTING COUNTRIES, 1930–1968

thousand long tons (annual averages)

	1930–32	1936–38	1946–50	1951–55	1956–60	1961–65	1968
Canada	13.9	17.8	36.1	44.0	54.0	72.5	82.3
United Kingdom	38.5	20.1	42.8	36.4	47.7	67.1	90.3
U.S.A. a	723.1	808.7	1192.0	1161.2	1269.6	1355.4	1498.6
France	183.7	177.8	89.9	163.2	186.5	210.8	241.6
Germany	144.7	174.1	20.8 b				
West Germany				78.5	164.3	239.4	295.6
East Germany				3.7	16.3	32.0	35.4
Italy	42.7	34.7	35.5	63.5	82.4	112.8	149.6
Belgium	52.4	50.9	75.9	49.2	56.6 c	60.1	62.1
Netherlands	45.7	42.3	25.4	33.9	54.9	73.5	100.4
Sweden	44.5	48.1	39.2	47.6	63.1	84.9	104.5

a U.S.A. Customs area, i.e. Alaska, Puerto Rico and Hawaii.
b Germany from 1948 Federal Republic of Germany.
   from 1956 East and West Germany.
   No figures for 1946 and 1947, therefore 1946–50 = 3 year average.
c Netherlands 1951–60 General Imports.
Sources: Commonwealth Economic Committee, *Plantation Crops*, 1938, 1948, 1952, 1967, and 1970.

strong market in 'second hand' Brazilian coffee in New York, and this detracted from the strength of demand for hedging facilities on that market. In addition, there is also the considerable history of intervention by Brazil in its coffee trade with the object of stabilizing the price.

Thus, though the Agreement has led to a fall in turnover on the London market the strong growth in the demand for Robusta coffee (the basis of the London contract) used in soluble coffee preparations has helped to sustain activity. Consequently, when the New York contract ceased to attract very much interest, American traders turned increasingly to the Plantation House market to hedge their stocks and commitments. The London coffee terminal market is, therefore, very much an international market these days, for it is also very well placed to attract European business. One consequence of this situation is that the London Robusta contract is now very responsive in price to influences which affect the demand and supply, not only of mild coffees but of all the world's grades.

Meanwhile, in the U.S.A., the authorities of the New York Coffee and Sugar Exchange tried to resuscitate coffee futures there by introducing a new 'U' (for Universal) contract in Robusta and/or Arabica coffee at the end of 1968. At the time of writing, however, it would appear that this contract has not found favour and turnover remains negligible.

Chapter Twelve

THE COCOA MARKET

1. *The Development of the Trade*

IN all probability the cocoa plant originated in the Amazon and Orinoco basins of South America. Certainly when the Spaniards landed in Mexico cocoa seemed to have been in existence there for centuries. It was very highly prized, as may be gathered from the belief (widespread in that part of the world at least) that Quatzalcault, a Mayan Indian saint, brought the original seeds from paradise. On the other hand the conquering Spaniards were acutely disappointed when they found that Montezuma's treasure troves were filled with huge mounds of cocoa beans. As was to be expected, English pirates were also highly contemptuous of this produce and regularly threw it over the side whenever they conquered a Spanish ship with any on board.

It was only with the introduction of sugar that the popularity of cocoa increased. Then its use spread from Spain into Italy, Germany and France. Maria Theresa is said to have popularized it in the court of France when she married Louis XIV in 1660. Its popularity spread from France to England, though it was at first regarded there with some suspicion as an inflamer of the passions. Pepys, however, said nothing about this when he recorded in his diary in 1664: 'To a coffee house to drink jocolatte, very good.' This was some seven years after the first chocolate house was opened in London in 1657, when cocoa cost ten to fifteen shillings a pound.

Venezuela was the most important producer of cocoa until 1820, after which it was overtaken by Ecuador. Trinidad was also an important producer. Indeed, most of the islands of the Caribbean and the northern areas of South America were already cultivating the cocoa plant by the end of the seventeenth century. However, many received a considerable set-back during the second decade of the eighteenth century, when a 'blast' (probably a blight) completely devastated the crop. As a result cocoa production was abandoned by many growers; in Jamaica, for example, cocoa production was only re-started during the latter half of the nineteenth century. The major expansion in cocoa cultivation in Brazil took place at about the same time. In West Africa developments stemmed from early cultivation by the Spanish, the Dutch and the Portuguese in the Gulf of Guinea. By today African cocoa production accounts for almost three-quarters of world supply

255

and, whereas cocoa was typically grown on large estates up to the 1920s, most of the crop is now harvested on small farms.

It was in 1828 that Van Houten discovered a method of preparing cocoa powder by removing most of the cocoa butter. This made for a much lighter drink and its popularity grew quite rapidly, especially after the mid-century. Consumption in the U.K. was some 500,000 lbs when Van Houten's refinement appeared. By 1858 it was 2,860,034 lbs; rather more than $10\frac{1}{2}$ million lbs in 1880; and in excess of $44\frac{1}{2}$ million lbs by the end of the century.[1] Messrs Cadbury Brothers entered the trade in 1866, and Fry and Sons two years later.

World production in 1900 was some 100,000 tons, of which some four-fifths were still grown in the Western Hemisphere. Total world production grew between four and five fold between 1900 and 1919 and increased by a further 30 per cent during the inter-war period. World cocoa production is currently some 1,173,000 long tons, and was as high as 1,470,000 long tons for the 1964-5 season. The accompanying table (Table 12.1) shows the proportion of exports from each source, from which it is apparent that Ghana, Nigeria and Brazil are now the major exporters.

British imports of raw cocoa amounted to some 35,000 long tons in 1913. By the eve of World War II they had grown to more than 131,000 tons. Currently (1968) the figure is of the order of 76,000 tons. This fall owes something to the decline of the re-export trade (from 6,778 long tons for 1913 to 4,557 long tons for 1968), but it is mostly due to the increase in the price of cocoa, since the demand for chocolate, and for cocoa as a beverage, is very elastic.

As may be seen from Table 12.2, the United States is easily the greatest importer of cocoa. West Germany takes about half as much as the U.S.A. The Netherlands come next in order of importance, with the U.S.S.R. and the United Kingdom about equal fourth.

Over the years there have been some interesting changes in supply sources. Thus, in 1913 the British West Indies rivalled British West Africa as a supply source, whereas today only some 2 per cent comes from the former countries, and 64 per cent now originates in former British West African territories. Before the First World War, too, Ecuador and Ceylon were important suppliers from whom we now receive no cocoa supplies at all.

When consumption was centred mainly on royal courts, ships were dispatched to the Americas for cocoa and other produce. With the growth in the popularity of cocoa, however, it was bought by freelance shippers who then searched for a market. With further increases in the volume of trade, buyers for export in countries of origin began to purchase from small growers, to hold stocks and sell at the best obtainable prices to shippers. John Holt and Co., Franc, Rusell and Miller

TABLE 12.1
EXPORTS OF RAW COCOA FROM PRINCIPAL PRODUCING COUNTRIES
thousand tons

	1957-61 (annual average)	1962	1963	1964	1965	1966	1967	1968	% of world exports
Ghana	279	421	405	382	494	392	330	330	(32.3%)
Nigeria a	138	195	175	197	303	190	244	203	19.8%)
Sierra Leone	3	5	3	3	3	4	4	7	0.7%)
Brazil	106	54	68	74	91	111	113	75	7.3%)
Ecuador	29	31	35	26	39	32	44	64	6.3%)
Dominican Republic	20	18	23	26	22	26	24	25	2.4%)
Venezuela	13	11	12	12	12	12	12	12	1.2%)
Mexico	4	12	18	3	9	8	6	6	0.6%)
Costa Rica	9	12	9	9	7	8	6	6	0.6%)
Ivory Coast	67	99	98	122	124	122	104	120	11.7%)
São Tomé e Principe	9	10	9	9	9	10	11	11	1.1%)
Cameroun	55	65	75	57	76	70	64	65	6.4%)
Trinidad	8	6	7	4	5	5	5	6	0.6%)
Other Countries	51	88	75	82	81	88	85	93	9.1%)
Total	791	1027	1012	1006	1275	1078	1052	1023	

a. Shipments of cocoa from West Cameroun are included with Nigerian trade figures until September 1960, and are since included with Cameroun.
Source: Commonwealth Secretariat, Plantation Crops, No. 13, 1970.

(bought by Lever Brothers) were among the most notable of the early shippers (around 1900). Most of these companies were swallowed up by the East Africa Trading Co. which bought cocoa from the exporters and sold it in Liverpool. In 1914 the largest shipper was the United Africa Co., which had amalgamated with the Niger Co. (i.e. Levers). At this time, too, Jurgens amalgamated with Lever Brothers, to become Unilever, whose cocoa trading enterprise was the United Africa Co. During the early 1920s, moreover, the larger chocolate manufacturers (Cadbury Brothers, Fry and Sons and Rowntree and Co.) moved into what is now Ghana and Nigeria, and established their own buying organizations.

Up to 1939 cocoas from origins other than Africa and Brazil were sold on the basis of a sample. These were held by some six firms of brokers who were in daily contact with dealers and agents. These traders were specialists whose business it was to supply the seventy-five or so manufacturers with their exact requirements from among the three or four recognized grades of cocoa. In the case of African cocoas, by contrast, the quality was nearly constant and sales were made upon description. For these cocoas, therefore – in addition to Brazilian produce – trading on a c.i.f. basis was already well established before World War II. Its constant quality and mild flavour ensures a steady demand for African cocoa, which is easily blended with other flavouring. The important attributes of cocoa which are specified in contracts on c.i.f. terms are that the produce should be sound, well fermented and free from infestation and mould. By today the former practice of sales by sample has entirely disappeared and all transactions are concluded upon the basis of a description. The same channels, nevertheless, exist in the market for actuals. The general picture is one in which statutory boards, shippers or growers, sell to manufacturers via brokers and dealers, though large manufacturers carry on some direct trade with the producer boards.

The U.K. market in the physical commodity is now a 'telephone' market. There are direct lines between manufacturers and their suppliers, both dealers and brokers. The large dealers maintain direct lines to the principal countries of origin, while contact with continental suppliers is virtually instantaneous by means of telex and teleprinter. The number of direct lines from manufacturer to broker is, however, fewer than in the past, for the larger manufacturers, especially, are tending to by-pass the broker in favour of the dealer; thus, whereas about ten years ago there were about ten firms of brokers active in the cocoa trade, their number has now been reduced to four or five. Some of these firms have switched from broking to dealing, and some amalgamations have also taken place. There are now some ten active dealers, of whom three or four are mainly market operators supplying marginal requirements and using specialist knowledge to purchase parcels at very favourable prices for resale at higher prices. The remaining merchants are straightforward suppliers to manufacturers.

TABLE 12.2

IMPORTS OF RAW COCOA INTO THE PRINCIPAL IMPORTING COUNTRIES (thousand tons)

	(annual average) 1957-61	1962	1963	1964	1965	1966	1967	1968
United Kingdom	91	113	114	77	81	106	87	76
Canada	14	16	15	18	23	16	17	18
Australia	11	8	12	14	13	12	17	11
United States	251	286	282	267	354	319	283	228
West Germany	106	135	132	141	164	146	136	135
Netherlands	90	102	99	105	117	115	108	111
France	56	68	64	59	63	63	49	43
Italy	27	36	39	37	41	40	44	40
Belgium	12	15	13	16	17	16	17	16
Spain	20	21	15	27	25	19		1
Switzerland	12	13	12	17	15	14	13	15
Austria	10	10	10	11	13	10	11	13
Japan	8	23	30	32	25	37	32	35
Soviet Union	30	48	53	65	07	58	80	107
Czechoslovakia	12	12	13	13	14	19	15	13
East Germany	10	14	14	14	15	18	16	16a
Poland	8	11	12	14	17	12	20	22a

a. Provisional.
Source: The Commonwealth Secretariat, *Plantation Crops*, No. 13, 1970.

TABLE 12.3A

LONDON COCOA TERMINAL CONTRACT TURNOVER, 1928–1939

Year	Futures Transactions (in tons)
1928	28,320
1929	66,120
1930	20,370
1931	7,030
1932	18,000
1933	21,950
1934	235,110
1935	102,470
1936	229,520
1937	352,250
1938	226,160
1939	80,280

Source: Figures supplied by the London Produce Clearing House Ltd.

2. *Terminal Market Transactions*

The establishment of futures trading in cocoa owed its origin essentially to the growth in the volume of world trade in a commodity which was in seasonal supply. Most cocoa crops are harvested from October to the end of January so that warehouse stocks grew with the growth of production. Traders thus felt an increasing need to hedge their stocks and commitments. The boom which followed World War I resulted in a considerable amount of buying and re-selling of cocoa and many

TABLE 12.3B
LONDON FUTURES TRANSACTIONS IN COCOA, 1951–1970
(Contract unit 5 tons)

Year	Transactions in tons
1951	52,265
1952	121,850
1953	146,420
1954	284,795
1955	191,225
1956	211,920
1957	222,290
1958	365,110
1959	292,850
1960	257,890
1961	420,410
1962	459,395
1963	901,550
1964	712,210
1965	1,243,680
1966	1,946,155
1967	2,085,000
1968	3,540,000
1969	4,970,000
1970	5,646,260

Source: Figures supplied by the London Produce Clearing House Ltd.

merchants, as well as speculators, suffered losses. Because of this a demand arose for a market in prices which would enable traders to hedge, and the New York market opened in 1925.

The Cocoa Association of London was formed in 1926, and a terminal market was opened two years later in 1928. The trading ring was established in a corner of the floor of the Rubber Exchange (originally at 7 Mincing Lane). Futures trading continued until the outbreak of the Second World War, when the Ministry of Food purchased U.K. cocoa supplies, organized internal distribution, and controlled the price from 1 October 1940 to 1 November 1950. The trade was returned to private hands again soon after the war, in 1948, since sources of supply lay entirely within the sterling area. The London Cocoa Terminal Market was reopened in 1951 on the basis of a contract unit of five long tons of Ghana Fair Fermented, ex store London, Liverpool, Hull, Avonmouth, Amsterdam or Hamburg. Sellers have the option to deliver other growths at a premium or discount. The maximum number of broker members – broker membership is personal – permitted by the rules and regulations of the London Cocoa Terminal Market Association is eighteen, and that of home members is thirty-six. These two classes of members, who constitute the voting membership, are permitted to deal free of commission on the market floor but, in contrast with the brokers, the home members may not transact business for one another. Associate and overseas members number nearly two hundred. Such members are not permitted by the rules to deal directly with one another but have to pass all contracts through a broker or home member. Rates of commission vary according to class of membership and, as in other markets, the 'round turn' (i.e. purchase and sale)

involves only a single brokerage. For non-members the commission is
£4 per contract unit when the contract price is 200s. or under, £5
when 300s. or under, and £6 over 300s. This brokerage is reduced
by 50 per cent for all types of membership. The tender of cocoa in
fulfilment of a contract, however, involves a double commission. All
voting members bind themselves to register, with the London Produce
Clearing House, all contracts made between themselves on the conditions of the Association. Registration fees are payable to the L.P.C.H.
by the principals to the transactions. The affairs of the London Cocoa
Terminal Market Association are run by a committee of management
representative of manufacturers, brokers and merchants. In order to
maintain a balance, the rules and regulations specify that two members of the committee shall be representatives of the manufacturers
with a further eight representing the brokers and the merchants.
Neither the brokers nor the merchants are permitted to be represented
by more than five committee members.

The terminal market, which is separately housed in what was at
one time the waiting room of the London Commodity Exchange, is
open from 10 a.m. until 5 p.m. Trading is by open outcry, but there
are official calls, with a central price caller, upon opening at 3.30 p.m.,
and before closure at 4.50 p.m. If the price fluctuates by £20 per ton
or more, the rules specify that trading must be suspended for thirty
minutes, after which trading is resumed with a special call. This is in
direct contrast to the rather chaotic conditions of the New York
market, where any fluctuation in price of £9 in the ton or more, stops
the market for the day. In London the Call Chairman records all
business transacted at the call on a Daily Sheet, which must be accessible to all floor members of the market. Sellers are required to record
on the Daily Sheet all business done between calls. It is from this
market sheet that the London Produce Clearing House extracts the
business of each broker and home member. Separate accounts of his
previous day's transactions are then rendered to each such member
before noon on the following day. He is required to testify to the
correctness of this Daily Dealing Statement by signature and this
(coupled with the counterpart acknowledgement of the opposite party
in each transaction) constitutes a binding contract for the sale and
purchase of cocoa on the terms quoted.

The accompanying table (Table 12.4) gives the comparative
turnover of each of the world's cocoa futures markets. From this it may
be seen that the London market was still small compared with its New
York counterpart a decade after it opened in 1951. From 1963 onwards,
however, the tonnage traded jumped to an extent which made the
London market comparable in size with that of New York. Thus, as
may be seen from the table, by 1969 there was very little to choose
between the volume of turnover in the two centres, with both markets

TABLE 12.4

QUANTITY OF COCOA DEALT WITH ON THE LONDON, NEW YORK, AMSTERDAM AND PARIS FUTURES MARKETS, 1958–1970

Year	LONDON Total (long tons)	NEW YORK Total (long tons)	AMSTERDAM Total (long tons)	PARIS Total (long tons)
1958	364,970	1,693,232	25,973	
1959	292,290	1,272,442	35,131	
1960	258,540	946,728	40,278	
1961	422,045	1,710,362	23,896	
1962	456,890	1,548,496	25,382	
1963	907,965	2,761,045	21,395	
1964	706,715	1,553,879	29,437	
1965	1,244,915	2,977,768	34,865	172,927
1966	1,951,765	6,824,879	33,478	193,870
1967	2,086,605	5,455,406	45,327	214,580
1968	3,546,245	5,320,112	25,412	313,438
1969	4,969,435	5,452,942	14,885	703,482
1970	5,618,190	4,200,014		

Source: Calculated from Gill & Duffus, Cocoa Market Reports.

very active and considerably larger than their Amsterdam and Paris counterparts, though the two latter markets handle a considerable volume of physical trade. The London-New York axis is the accepted world market and is effectively integrated by the lively arbitrage between the two centres. No figures exist for trade in physical markets, but it is evident from Table 12.4 that the physical markets on the continent must be considerably greater than the size of their terminal markets seem to suggest. In fact continental manufacturers and merchants use the London futures market a good deal and still purchase some physical cocoa from London merchants. There is, too, an element of 'third country trade' which is hedged on the London market. Market members are of the opinion that the physical trade in London has also increased considerably of recent years. Certainly the number of direct deals with marketing boards appears to have been on the decrease over the past decade. For much of the time the marketing boards ask a price at or above that of the open market, thus discouraging such transactions, which are in any case usually limited to the very large manufacturers because the boards will only sell large shipments.

A further factor in the growth of terminal market activity has clearly been that of price fluctuations.[2] During the 1950s the outstanding features of the cocoa market consisted of the bull markets of 1953-54 and 1957-58. The former was unique in being caused by an unprecedentedly rapid rise in U.K. confectionery consumption following the end of rationing. From rather less than 6 oz per head a week for 1952 confectionery consumption (including non-chocolate confections) jumped to 9½ oz a week for 1953. As a result, U.K. grindings of beans increased some 19 per cent for the latter year, while the price of spot Accra cocoa in London reached a peak of 560s. 0d. in June 1954.

The bull market of 1957-58 occurred against a background of record world cocoa absorption by March 1957, with prices at their lowest since 1949. After the African producers had marketed most of their crops for the season the Brazilian government declared that they would sell their produce abroad at a minimum price which was some 4 cents a lb over the then ruling price. This had the effect of withdrawing Brazilian cocoa completely from the world market. Because produce from this source was normally the principal supply for shipment during the summer months, the world market was thrown into confusion, and the price of cocoa rose by June to some 8 per cent above March levels. As luck would have it, there followed a succession of forecasts of short crops from Ghana and Nigeria, so the price continued to climb until it passed the officially announced floor at which the Brazilians were prepared to sell their Temporao crop. This large-scale gamble thus turned out to be brilliantly successful.

Cocoa became a bear market from 1958 to 1962 as surpluses developed. Prices fell to low levels during 1962, the average for the

year being 170s. per cwt (spot price Ghana, London). By mid-1964
prices were at one time down to 93s., while the average price for 1965
(140s. 7d.) was the lowest since 1947. However, the 1960s ended with
fears of cocoa shortages and rising prices once more. Speculation became
very active and forced up prices to even higher levels, with some effect
upon consumption.

The tribulations of the producers arising from these price fluctuations
have not unnaturally led them to attempt from time to time to intervene
in cocoa marketing.[3] With falling prices in the early 1960s the producers
manifested considerable interest in a scheme to stabilize prices, though
consumer countries were notably unenthusiastic. Manufacturers
seemed on the whole against a price stabilization scheme, but at the
same time they felt that they could not continue to try to offer support
to a sagging market by stockpiling to an unlimited extent[4]. It was a
very unsettled period for the cocoa trade, with the complete withdrawal
of Russia from the market at one stage, and what proved an unsuccessful
attempt by Ghana and Nigeria to withdraw from the London market.
A producers' alliance was established between these two West African
countries, but the attempt to move the sale of Ghanaian produce to
Accra did not appear to occasion much hardship in London, while the
London dealers for Nigerian cocoa still carried on most of their business
as usual despite the resiting of their selling agency to Lagos.

In 1963 there was an international conference of producer and
consumer countries in Geneva. However, talks broke down in the
November with a major disagreement over the level at which a floor
price should be set. Prices continued to fall, as the result of which there
were indications that Ghana would be prepared to accept a lower
floor price than it was previously inclined to do. Preliminary talks
between representatives of Ghana and the U.S.A. during the summer of
1967 established in principle that an agreement should consist of
quotas for producers, and that a buffer stock should be set up, to be
financed from a levy on all cocoa sales. Prices of £160 and £232 per ton
were advanced as reasonable floor and ceiling levels at which the
manager of the buffer stock would buy or sell respectively. It was not
envisaged that daily market intervention would be necessary as it was
with tin. Almost all the trade in cocoa is for forward delivery, so that
if, for example, a surplus should appear to be developing, the buffer
stock manager would simply need to take up contracts.

To say the very least, the British and American cocoa traders were
not at all pleased with the proposals.[5] During the negotiations it was
found impossible to agree on some fifteen items but one of the main
issues arose from the Brazilian delegation's drive to abolish preferential
tariffs. United Kingdom interests felt that the terms would result
in a considerable loss of trade and invisible earnings for London.
Fears were also expressed concerning the likely level of administrative

costs and the encouragement of substitutes, and so the negotiations broke down once more in December 1967.[6]

In consequence, the price of cocoa remains governed by the pressure of market forces, modified to some extent by the policies espoused by the marketing boards and agencies. As we have already seen, the consequent price fluctuations have rendered resort to a futures market very necessary for traders. This state of affairs seems likely to continue.[7] Moreover, should an agreement eventually materialize, it is likely to be fairly closely comparable with the coffee agreement, by which price movements are somewhat moderated but by no means eliminated. Should this be so, the London Cocoa Terminal Market is likely to continue to flourish. The character of the physical trade, meanwhile, is unlikely to change greatly from its present pattern. Perhaps the most interesting statistic is the growth in grindings of raw cocoa in producing countries from 16,000 long tons in 1930 to 280,000 for 1968. The latter figure represents rather more than 20 per cent of world production for the latter year. The other interesting development is the emergence of the U.S.S.R. as a major consumer of cocoa. Thus the Gill and Duffus market report for June 1969 points out that Russia has displaced the U.S.A. as the main buyer of Brazilian cocoa. Over the past decade cocoa grindings in Eastern Europe have almost doubled. In 1968 combined Soviet and East European grindings were estimated to have been 178,000 long tons.

Chapter Thirteen

THE RUBBER MARKET

1. *The Growth of the London Market*

THE growth of the rubber trade was a spectacular accompaniment to the development of road transport in the modern world. The use of rubber on wheels first became popular during the great cycling craze which overtook Britain during the last decades of the nineteenth century and which still accounted for one quarter of total rubber utilization in 1907. World production was then less than 70,000 long tons. However, the stimulus to rubber production provided by the bicycle was destined to be but a prelude to the growth of the industry in the wake of world motor-vehicle manufacture, so that world natural rubber production for 1968 reached the enormous total of 2.5 million tons. The history of rubber trading epitomizes most of the difficulties associated with trading in a natural raw material: rubber is notorious for the amplitude of the fluctuations in its price and for the difficulties associated with the time lag between new plantings and resulting increases in production. Of recent years, moreover, the industry has had to accommodate itself to the emergence of a close synthetic substitute, with a world production which has actually been greater than that of natural rubber since 1962 (Table 13.1). For 1968 synthetic rubber production was 3.6 million tons; that is, more than one million tons or some 44 per cent greater than that of natural rubber. With the growth of the industry to major proportions rubber rapidly became a plantation product – and that on the other side of the world from the natural home of the Para rubber tree in the Amazon Basin. Finally, the years since the First World War have been witness to considerable changes in the marketing of rubber. Major markets have now grown in countries of origin and final consumption, with a consequent weakening of the once all-important central market in London.

Rubber is made from the coagulated milky juice called latex which is obtained from incisions in the bark of *Hevea braziliensis* and some other rubber tree varieties. Europeans first discovered this substance when French expeditions were made to Brazil and Peru in 1735. The natives of the area apparently used latex to weatherproof their garments, but it was about 1820 when a Mr. Mackintosh discovered a successful waterproofing process – in Manchester, appropriately enough. However, the greatest advance came when Charles Goodyear of America and Thomas Hancock of London independently hit upon a method of

TABLE 13.1
WORLD RUBBER PRODUCTION, 1955–1968
thousand long tons

Year	Natural												Synthetic			
	Ceylon	India	Vietnam	Indonesia	W. Malaysia	Sarawak	Thailand	Africa	Brazil	Other Latin American	Cambodia	World Total	Canada	W. Germany	U.S.	World Total
1956	95·4	23·4	69·1	686·7	626·0	40·7	134·6	113·5	23·7	6·0	31·6	1893	120·7	10·7	1080	1211
1957	98·2	23·8	68·6	684·5	635·9	41·0	134·0	116·3	24·0	6·0	31·2	1903	132·1	11·6	1118	1263
1958	100·2	24·3	70·5	685·2	660·9	38·9	138·4	123·3	20·3	6·0	33·1	1940	135·0	22·7	1055	1243
1959	91·7	23·4	74·2	693·5	695·5	43·4	171·3	141·8	21·1	7·0	33·9	2040	100·7	48·1	1380	1633
1960	97·3	24·8	75·4	610·5	706·0	49·7	168·2	147·0	22·7	7·0	36·5	1985	159·7	79·8	1436	1880
1961	96·0	26·6	77·9	671·4	734·6	47·3	183·2	142·0	22·4	7·0	39·3	2093	164·5	85·6	1404	1975
1962	102·4	30·9	74·0	670·8	749·4	43·4	192·3	150·8	21·3	7·0	40·9	2120	168·3	88·2	1574	2240
1963	103·1	36·6	70·7	573·1	786·7	43·6	186·8	151·8	20·2	7·0	40·1	2068	178·7	106·5	1608	2438
1964	109·8	43·5	73·3	638·4	824·1	42·9	218·2	158·8	27·9	7·0	45·1	2235	197·5	135·7	1765	2803
1965	116·4	48·6	60·0	705·7	870·4	40·0	213·1	157·0	28·8	7·0	48·1	2343	203·0	161·4	1814	3013
1966	128·9	52·4	48·1	704·4	925·3	33·5	203·9	174·0	24·0	7·0	50·5	2398	199·7	182·0	1970	3330
1967	140·9	61·5	40·0	750·0	933·2	27·8	210·9	161·3	20·8	7·0	52·8	2453	197·1	180·0	1912	3415
1968 a	143·4	63·0	28·3	750·0	1042·0	25·0	212·0	170·0	20·0	7·0	50·5	2500	193·7	185·0	2000	3600

a. Preliminary.

Source: Commodity Research Bureau, Commodity Year Book (New York, 1969).

vulcanizing rubber in 1839 and 1840 respectively.[1] Rubber was then used for a wide variety of purposes: the name itself comes from its main early use as an eraser, but india-rubber, as it was often called, was also used to make balls, waterproof shoes and garments, as well as for some of the multifarious purposes which plastics now serve. In 1888 Dunlop processed his pneumatic tyre and in doing so ushered in the world-wide large-scale use of this remarkable new material.

During the early period of its industrial use supplies consisted of 'wild' rubber from a number of trees, such as *Funturnia elastica* and *Ficus elastica*, which were part of the natural vegetation of Peru, Bolivia and other South American countries. The most important tree was, however, the *Hevea braziliensis*, with Brazil the main country of origin. Methods of collection were crude and uneconomic while the supply was uncertain. With the growth in demand, therefore, there was a strong incentive to organize rubber production on a more systematic basis. Several attempts were made to cultivate the Hevea but these proved unsuccessful until 1876. In that year the Kew Gardens Authorities commissioned a Mr. Henry Wickham to obtain a further consignment of seeds. The story of the birth of a major plantation industry is interesting:

It happened that by good luck a large steamer of the Inman line – the first to visit the Amazon – was without freight for the voyage home just at the right season for the transfer of the seed. Mr. Wickham seized the opportunity, chartered the vessel and with a body of Indians as carriers, explored the forests and obtained 70,000 seeds and, although fearing a prohibition of the Brazilian authorities, the ship managed to get away without hindrance or delay. Fortune still favoured him, for fine weather obtained throughout the voyage; and it was, therefore, possible for the hatches to remain open; a condition favouring the preservation of the seeds.

Even with all these advantageous circumstances only 4 per cent of the seeds were productive, but these were sufficient to obtain a number of plants at Kew. From Kew, in due course, plants were transferred to Ceylon and Malaysia, and from these sources the plantations have developed which have given the British Empire the lead in world production.[2]

The rapid increase in the establishment of plantations dates from 1910 when demand from the motor industry started to soar. The average price of rubber for that year jumped to 8s. 9d. per lb, and many companies were formed, in London especially, to buy up estates in the Far East. The companies then sent out managers to develop their properties. Other companies, controlled by merchant firms in London, were established in the East. By 1922, 94 per cent of the world's rubber was produced on plantations in the Far East, 70 per cent of them were inside the British Empire, 25 per cent were located in the Dutch East Indies, and 5 per cent in French Indo-China and elsewhere. Less than one-third of the plantations were native-owned at that time, and many of these were financed from British sources. To a very considerable degree, therefore, the control of rubber as a raw material was in British hands. This caused some concern to Americans, for although U.S. consumption amounted to some three-quarters of the world total, American companies held only about 3 per cent of the total acreage.[3]

'Wild' rubber collected in the South American forests was usually coagulated by smoking the latex on sticks until large round balls, called 'negro-heads', were produced. On the plantations coagulation is brought about by the addition of acetic acid, after which the coagulum is passed through a species of wringer grooved to give it a ribbed surface. The sheets are then smoked and the resulting product is called Ribbed-Smoked-Sheet, a term very well known in the trade. The rubber, especially that produced on European-owned estates, was disposed of through firms based on centres such as Singapore, Kuala Lumpur and Penang. These firms acted as accountants, secretaries and agents to the plantations, in much the same way as they did for the tea planters. Frequently they exercised a very close control over these plantations and provided the channel through which the planters procured their supplies. It was a system which tended to stifle the enterprise of local managers but which worked admirably for plantations owned by London companies who felt reassured when they were able to secure this close supervision.

The agents sold the rubber for the planters either on the local Eastern markets or else in London and Liverpool. These two cities had gained an early importance in this trade due to the ease with which credit, shipping and insurance facilities could be provided. When rubber became a plantation crop located largely inside the British Empire the pre-eminence of these world rubber-distribution centres was consolidated. This was especially so since overseas purchasers found standards of reliability of weighing and grading to be beyond reproach.

Until the First World War much of the rubber sold in the United Kingdom was disposed of by auction. London had almost complete control of imports of eastern rubber, while by 1875 Liverpool was the principal port for western rubber. However, as an historian of the rise of the rubber industry avers, it would be wrong to assume that Liverpool's influence over internal distribution was in proportion to its imports, for it seems that much of the rubber landed at Liverpool found its way to the London market.[4] At the former centre the rubber was auctioned either in brokers' offices or at the Public Sale Rooms at the Exchange Building, while in London the auctions were held at the Commercial Sale Rooms in Mincing Lane. The trade organizations at both centres consisted of manufacturers' buyers and agents, dealers,

brokers and representatives of British plantation companies – though a
Rubber Growers' Association was formed in 1907 to promote the interests of the planters and to encourage technological advances in
production. The auctions were very active before 1914. They were held
fortnightly and grew so large that in the first few months of 1914 each
series lasted for four or five days. From its inception, in 1913, the Rubber
Trade Association of London regulated the public sales there which
were made upon the basis either of a sample obtainable from traders'
offices or else of inspection of the bulk.

Before the First World War auctions of wild rubber were also held
at other European centres. Antwerp was the centre for Belgian Congo
grades; Bordeaux was the market for French Equatorial Africa grades;
Hamburg served as a market centre for German Africa produce; while
Lisbon became the central market for rubber from the Portuguese
colonies. At Amsterdam, Antwerp and Bordeaux, however, the
auctions were conducted in an entirely different way from those of
London and other centres: buyers sent in sealed bids to the selling
brokers to be opened on the day of the sale. These 'inscription sales'
resulted in high bids, but, understandably, were not popular, especially
with large manufacturers.

The public sales of rubber predominated until the increasing volume
of standard grades of plantation rubber of more uniform quality
eventually eliminated the need for them. In the United Kingdom the
quiet trading conditions which followed the outbreak of World War I
provided the occasion for the discontinuance of auctions. Thereafter
sales could be made at any time, with rubber being examined and
sampled in warehouses and brokers' salerooms. Forward sales, too,
grew in importance and were made upon description as the major
manufacturers increasingly adopted the practice of planning for their
needs up to a year ahead. The London market was not really organized
until 1921, when the Rubber Trade Association drew up contract
forms for both spot and c.i.f. trading, having defined criteria for
recognized grades of rubber.[5] Standard samples of these grades made
up of pieces of ribbed smoked sheet and other varieties, in the manner
of a tailor's pattern book, are now kept by the Association. The General
Regulations of the Association also provided for two essential committees within its organization, namely the Standard Qualities Committee and the Committee to appoint arbitrators.

The Qualities Committee is appointed by the Committee of the
Association

> to examine all samples of Plantation Rubber sold under any of
> the standard descriptions . . . submitted to such Committee by
> Importer or Dealing Members . . . on their own behalf or by
> Brother Members . . . for the purpose of certifying before
> tendering whether such samples conform to the recognized Market

Standards . . . unless a certificate is given that the sample is of the description specified, the parcel shall not be tenderable.

The arbitration machinery is something of which the Association is justifiably proud, for it quickly built up a considerable world reputation for unimpeachable standards of impartiality. Disputants apply to the secretary of the Association for the appointment of arbitrators, following which the chairman appoints two (one only to be a dealer), and an umpire, who has to be a broker. The names have to be approved in writing by one (formerly three) member of the Committee. Should the arbitrators fail to agree, they refer the dispute to the umpire. Appeals are accepted if made within five working days, upon receipt of which the Chairman appoints a tribunal consisting of the Chairman (or one of two Vice-chairmen) and six persons chosen by the Chairman (or his representative), of whom at least one is drawn from each of the following classes of members; selling agents and importers, brokers, and dealers.

2. *Market Structure and Organization*

The structure of the market as given by the official publication of the Association[6] includes the above categories of members, together with the producer members. The last-named are known as 'PA' (producer associate) members. They are of minor importance on the rubber market itself and have their own organization, the Rubber Growers Association. To qualify for membership of the Rubber Trade Association (R.T.A.), however, they have to be British registered companies in order to ensure that they are within the reach of British jurisdiction. For the same reason British registration is also necessary for selling agents and importers who wish to become members. These are designated by the Association as Class 'A' members. The brokers, all of whom have offices in and around Plantation House, are categorized as Class 'B' members, while dealers are grouped as Class 'C' members. The Regulations of the Rubber Trade Association are notably more restrictive than those governing other Mincing Lane markets. Thus, broker members are only permitted to accept rubber for re-sale from consumers or agents on the Association's approved list. Similarly, brokers are permitted only to purchase rubber for members of class P.A., class 'A', class 'C' and non-member producers or their agents. The class 'B' members are only permitted to purchase on behalf of non-Association members when buying salvage or unclaimed rubber. However, the most restrictive clause is that which specifies that one principal to every contract shall be a member of class 'C', except when selling or purchasing estate rubber first hand for producers or their agents domiciled in the U.K. The Association is thus committed to a policy of forcing brokers (with certain exceptions) to transact business with the dealers rather than with the manufacturers. In return, the dealers undertake not to purchase rubber from or sell rubber to producers or their agents (whether members or not) except through broker members of the Association. By this means, therefore, the R.T.A. sought from the outset to preserve the structure of the trade and to prevent any of its member intermediaries from being by-passed. In defence of this system it has been claimed that:

> The London Market . . . is a necessary buffer between producer and consumer and it is a well known fact that when producers want to sell, consumers are not buyers and when consumers want to buy producers are not sellers.[7]

The Regulations require every member of the Association in classes 'A', 'B' and 'C' to acquire and hold as his qualification for membership one fully-paid ordinary share of £50 par value in the Exchange Company. (As was explained in Chapter 8 the Rubber Exchange Co. Ltd provides the financial structure of the London rubber trade.)

The year 1921 was also the date of the establishment of the Rubber Settlement House, an organization whose purpose was to effect the registration and settlement of the forward contracts of members. During the early years of the trade, especially, the risks attaching to transactions in rubber were considerable. Thus the use of samples or inspection of the bulk was not a sufficient counter to fraudulent packing or variability in the quality of the rubber, which could only be truly ascertained during manufacture. Most of the rubber dealers before the First World War were concerned solely with the actual delivery of the commodity but, when their order-books got fuller, their need for some form of price insurance became correspondingly greater. The need for protection was further enhanced during the early days of the trade by the existence of syndicates of speculators who hoped for success by buying up supplies, especially since a large proportion originated from but one region of South America. In fact, lack of capital and the emergence of African and Asian producer countries eventually foiled these ambitions.

By the 1890s the buying and selling of futures, chiefly by non-manufacturing interests, had become an accepted practice. Futures had been available to traders, it seems, since the last quarter of the nineteenth century, having grown, as was true of so many other markets, from trading in forward contracts.[8] From 1921 futures dealing acquired a location and a name in the form of the London Rubber Exchange in the London Commercial Sale Rooms. The Rubber Settlement House was set up by the R.T.A. 'to facilitate the fulfilment of contracts and to secure the continuity of contracts for the sale and purchase of identical rubber'. Membership of the Settlement House was open only to members of the Association itself. Dealing in rubber futures was covered by the usual provisions of a registration fee, and initial deposits payable upon the exchange of contracts. Then, according to the Rules issued by the London Rubber Exchange Co. Ltd (the financial authority), on each alternate Tuesday, 'the sub-committee shall fix the current market prices of rubber for future delivery. . . . These prices shall regulate the fortnightly or special settlements'. This method of settlement every other Tuesday was adopted as a means of safeguarding traders from incurring very considerable losses due to price fluctuations over a longer period, though the Rules provided a further safeguard to traders by requiring each member to deposit £100 as security for the payment of his fees. This deposit must, moreover, be increased when the total amount of fees payable exceeds £100. The Rubber Settlement House performs the tasks customarily undertaken by a clearing-house; that is, of determining how much the dealers have to pay or receive as the result of transactions during the preceding fortnight. This net figure is calculated from the differences in the prices at which the transactions are concluded. The Settlement House is assisted in these calculations by statements rendered to it by brokers, who list the prices and quantities relating to the business which their clients transacted with them during the fortnight.

Contract units are for five tons and positions are bought and sold for up to three years ahead. A seller of a futures contract may, as on other futures markets, decide to honour his obligation by tendering the physical commodity rather than by 'closing out' his promise to deliver with the purchase of a further contract. In this event, the Rules specify (at present) that such tenders must conform to the conditions of the R.T.A. Delivery contract No. 6. This is for rubber of a quality, price and month of delivery to be written in on the contract form according to the bargain struck, to be ready for delivery in warehouses in London and/or Liverpool at seller's option. Since 1957 the Rules have contained an addition which allows a special sub-committee, when required, to fix a discount at which the seller is permitted to deliver rubber of an agreed quality lower than that stipulated in the contract.

Thus far, then, rubber sold on 'Settlement House terms' conforms well enough in broad outline to the methods of futures trading adopted at other terminal markets – except that it is now the only one in Mincing Lane which does not employ the London Produce Clearing House Ltd as its agent. However, the rubber market does differ in one important respect from the other markets in that transactions are not by open outcry. Business may be concluded both on and off the floor of the Exchange. There are no 'calls', and consequently brokers and dealers do not have comprehensive and continuous information concerning the state of the market. It cannot, therefore, claim to be such a perfect market as the other terminal markets in the vicinity. The Association has been criticized from time to time for this, together with the secrecy with which it has, in consequence, managed to shroud the fluctuations in the turnover of the market. There has been no effective defence against this criticism, though representatives[9] claim that the way in which the Rubber Settlement House is conducted keeps undesirable speculation to a minimum, and that it is a better means of negotiating the quantities to be transacted than the hurly-burly of open outcries.

The total absence of figures for transactions on the London rubber market makes it difficult to provide any account of the growth of this centre. By the close of the last century the Liverpool market had become distinctly subordinate to that of London, even though it was a signifi-cant world centre for the distribution of Para and Peruvian rubber. Due to the expansion of trade, therefore, the London rubber market moved out from the London Commercial Sale Rooms to 7 Mincing Lane, almost opposite, in 1923. According to an account written in 1929 these premises were 'neither large nor imposing' and that 'it is expected larger premises will soon be taken over, more fitted to the dignity and necessities of this important industry'.[10]

In fact the modest premises at No. 7 were demolished some years later to make way for the much more imposing Plantation House into which the London Rubber Exchange Co. Ltd moved in 1936. But the tide was already on the turn for the London Rubber Trade Association. Between 1850 and 1900, the export of crude rubber from the U.K. increased from about 50 tons to 14,700 tons. As Table 13.2 indicates, this had grown to 45,000 tons by the outbreak of World War I. For the following forty years this figure remained virtually static, apart from the wartime hiatus, despite a more than seventeen-fold growth in world production from 108,000 tons to 1,893,000 tons (1956). Over the same period Britain's domestic usage of natural rubber had grown more than five-fold, from some 25,000 tons to 233,000 tons. Then, as is indicated in the same table, there was a sharp rise in the re-export trade during the 1950s, reflecting the currency and other difficulties of the period. By today, however, the re-export trade has almost completely disappeared (Tables 13.2 and 13.3).

The reasons for this are not hard to find for, though in the early days Britain had most of the controlling elements which ensured its central position in the trade, established markets nevertheless existed at an early date in other manufacturing countries. Their growth was, therefore, assured with the expansion of their financial and transport facilities and as the discontinuity of war and relative decline as an industrial power affected Britain. Thus it was inevitable that the London market should lose much of its trans-shipment trade to the U.S.A. when the industrial power of the latter was such that it absorbed some three-quarters of world supply (Table 13.4). Clearly, this change was linked with the growth of major markets in countries of origin. By this time, the market at Singapore, if not those of Penang,

TABLE 13.2

UNITED KINGDOM TRADE IN NATURAL AND SYNTHETIC RUBBER, 1913–1968
thousand tons (Annual averages)

Natural rubber	1913	1919–22	1930–34	1935–39	1940–44	1945–49	1950–54	1955–59	1960–64	1965–66	1968
Imports from:											
British Borneo								7.0	6.0	4.0	3.7
Ceylon a	0.2	1.1	11.4	10.0	0.6	2.8	6.6	13.8			
Malaysia b	6.7	15.3	99.4	88.4	20.0	28.2	18.4	126.4	146.0	108.5	69.5
Singapore	25.0	51.4			66.2	142.6	228.6	78.0			61.2
India	0.9	4.3	3.2	4.4	3.2	8.0	11.4	19.8	21.8	24.5	17.7
Nigeria c	0.4	0.2		0.8	5.4						
Cameroun									3.4	5.5	4.9
Indonesia d	1.5	10.7	22.4	20.2	9.4	3.2	18.8	22.2	8.8	18.5	20.5
Thailand								2.0	16.4	14.5	8.9
South Vietnam								2.2	10.4	7.0	3.8
Brazil	16.2	5.7	2.0	1.0							
Others	19.4	1.7	3.2	5.6	8.4	5.0	6.2	5.6	9.4	7.5	9.5
Total Gross Imports	70.3	90.4	141.6	130.4	113.2	189.8	290.0	277.0	222.2	190.0	199.7
Re-exports	45.0	49.9	45.8	48.0	5.4	45.6	56.8	81.6	66.0	7.5	8.9
Net Imports	25.3	40.5	95.8	82.4	107.8	144.2	233.2	195.4	156.2	182.5	190.8

Synthetic rubber	1951–55	1955–59	1960–64	1965–66	1968
Imports from:					
Canada	5.0	22.1	23.3	19.3	25.1
U.S.A.	6.0	21.5	19.3	9.8	10.1
Netherlands			5.7	16.8	22.0
France		0.1	2.0	7.2	9.4
Others		0.5	1.8	4.5	7.4
Total Gross Imports	11.0	44.3	52.0	57.6	74.0
Exports (incl. re-exports)		1.6	29.3	54.6	69.8
Net Imports	11.0	42.6	22.7	3.0	4.2

a. 1913–22 Ceylon and Dependencies.
b. 1913–22 Straits Settlements and Dependencies (incl. Labuan) and Federated Malay States. Later British Malaya.
c. Including British Camerouns.
d. Previously Netherlands East Indies.
In 1936 there was an excess of re-exports over imports, i.e. Gross Imports 62, Re-exports 69.
Figures have been rounded and therefore do not necessarily add to total.
Sources: Commonwealth Economic Committee (Commonwealth Secretariat), Plantation Crops and the Annual Statement of Trade.

TABLE 13.3

RE-EXPORTS OF RAW RUBBER FROM THE UNITED KINGDOM,
1938, 1952 and 1968

thousand tons

	1938	1952	1968
Irish Republic	2	3	2
Soviet Union	14	88	
Germany	8		
West Germany		3	0·02
U.S.A.	3	31	0·02
Belgium	2	1	
Spain	3	1	
Rumania			4·2
Others	4	9	1·56
Total	36	136	7·8

Source: Annual Statement of Trade.

Kuala Lumpur and Colombo, sells a greater quantity than that of
London. Rubber from the estates is shipped by commission merchants –
often Chinese firms – to these markets where it is bought by large
American, Asian and European firms, who were able to establish
themselves there when the availablity of capital ceased to be a near-
London monopoly. Many originally represented rubber interests in the
London and New York markets and subsequently broadened their
interests. Other remain general import-export merchants. Some,
however, act as agents for manufacturers and ship direct to them, while
the very large manufacturers have developed their own buying
organizations in the Eastern markets.

3. *Restriction Schemes*
By 1920 the release of wartime stockpiles led to very low prices and
a voluntary cut of 25 per cent in output for one year by the Rubber
Growers Association. The scheme failed due to lack of cooperation,
especially on the part of the Chinese. Some two years later a Colonial
Office committee under the chairmanship of Sir James Stevenson
recommended a sliding scale of export taxes graduated according to the
percentage of rubber exported, in stated quarterly periods, compared
with a base period (the twelve months ending 31 October 1920). This
plan became the Stevenson Restriction Scheme, which was put into
effect on exports from Ceylon, the Malay States, and the Straits Settlements. The fundamental principle underlying the scheme was the
introduction of a penal rate of duty on exports in excess of agreed
quantities. Export quantities permitted at the minimum rate of duty
were to be determined by the London price of standard quality ribbed-
smoked-sheet, and expressed as a percentage of the productive capacities of each estate and holding assessed for the purpose. A pivotal
London market price, deemed to be fair to both producers and con-

TABLE 13.4

DISTRIBUTION OF EXPORTS OF RUBBER FROM PRINCIPAL EXPORTING COUNTRIES, 1938, 1949, 1958 and 1968

thousand tons

From:	*Malaya*				*Ceylon*				*Indonesia*			
	1938	1949	1958	1968	1938	1949	1958	1968	1938	1949	1958 c	1968
United Kingdom	99·2	164·4	191	126	10·4	16·4	17	4	28·5	8·1	99	78
Canada	22·7	32·4	26	42	1·6	4·4	4	3	—	—	—	b
Australia	8·8	22·7	30	36	1·5	0·3	b	—	—	—	—	b
South Africa	2·7	18·9	18	b	—	0·1	b	—	—	—	—	—
Hong Kong	1·6	23·3	2	—	—	—	—	—	104·9	115·6	140	192
U.S.A.	214·7	265·3	135	262	24·3	38·7	10	10	—	—	—	—
Argentina	5·4	10·6	26	21	1·1	0·3	—	—	—	—	—	—
France	69·4	57·4	52	69	3·2	2·4	1	1	10·3	3·8	1	7
Germany a	22·7	56·7	80	78	4·0	8·0	15	9	21·7	12·0	31	99
Italy	26·7	33·5	50	61	2·4	5·2	3	5	5·8	4·3	3	5
Netherlands	2·0	36·3	17	18	0·1	2·3	1	1	19·5	106·0	1	8
Belgium	3·5	10·7	8	7	0·7	1·8	b	—	—	—	—	4
Soviet Union	—	63·4	68	239	—	—	4	8	—	—	5	42
Japan	33·8	25·9	111	130	—	0·5	8	5	9·0	16·8	17	81
China	1·4	7·0	64	129	—	1·3	23	82	—	—	79	b
Poland	—	—	39	37	—	—	—	5	—	—	—	19
Malaya	—	—	—	—	—	—	—	—	78·7	147·0	176	—
Others	12·3	70·7	163	307	1·9	6·2	7	14	22·6	8·5	14	88
Total	526·9	899·2	1080	1562	51·2	87·9	93	147	301·0	422·1	566	623

a. From 1958 West Germany.   b. Included, if any, in Others.   c. Recorded shipments only.

Sources: Commonwealth Economic Committee, *Plantation Crops*, 1952 and 1960,
Commonwealth Secretariat, *Plantation Crops*, 1967 and 1970.

sumers, was initially fixed at 1s. 3d. per lb. For the first quarter during which the scheme was in operation (November 1922 to January 1923) the percentage of standard production allowable for export was fixed at 60 per cent, on which the duty was the ½d. per lb minimum rate. The scheme provided that should the London market price rise to between 1s. 3d. and 1s. 6d. per lb the standard production allowable for export at the minimum rate of duty was to increase by 5 per cent. When the price exceeded 1s. 6d. per lb permitted, exports at the minimum duty rate could be increased by 10 per cent. Between the pivotal price of 1s. 3d. and 1s. per lb the scheme provided for a 5 per cent reduction in exports permitted at the minimum duty rate, should the quota be at 65 per cent or over. No reduction in exports below 60 per cent of quota standards was envisaged unless prices of 1s. a lb or lower had obtained over the previous three months. The scheme also provided for an automatic drop of standard quotas to 55 per cent, regardless of existing export quota levels, should the price of rubber average less than 1s. per lb over the preceding quarter.

Initially the scheme appeared to be working well, but the rigidity of the pivotal price system became manifest during the third year of restriction. During the first quarter of the third year the average price worked out at 1s. 5.998d. and so quotas were only increased by 5 per cent despite the running down of stocks and rising world demand. This undue restriction of supply in the face of an expansion of demand led to a rapid increase in prices to 4s. 8d. a lb as the fourth year of the scheme opened. At this point the export quota was raised to its maximum of 100 per cent, whereupon prices fell by 50 per cent. In an attempt to prevent a recurrence of such violent price fluctuations, the pivotal price was increased to 1s. 9d. and from 1 November 1926, new adjustment arrangements were introduced. These ranged from a 100 per cent export quota, when the average price was more than 3s. for the preceding quarter, to 60 per cent when the average price was less than 1s. 3d. a lb. Despite this greater degree of elasticity the price failed to recover and throughout the fifth year of restriction permitted export quota proportions at the minimum rate of duty remained at 60 per cent. Thus the basic defect of a rigid pivotal price, especially in conjunction with inflexible price limits, based the whole trade upon short-term considerations and proved fatal to the aims of the scheme.[11]

Despite a weakening of prices for some years after the end of 1929, hesitation over the difficulties of controlling rubber output in the East Indies was responsible for the lack of any further attempt to regulate the market until mid-1934. As before, the scheme aimed to reduce stocks and to guarantee a 'fair and equitable price level'. Exports were to be regulated by the prohibition of new planting and by the allocation of export quotas to member countries (except for French Indo-China). These were to be reviewed periodically by the International Rubber

Regulations Committee. Stockholding was also restricted by the new scheme.[12]

In common with attempts to regulate other commodity trades at the time, the scheme enabled high-cost producers to remain in business. Prices increased steadily from the inception of the scheme until 1936 and then, with a rapid upsurge of demand, the price reached 1s. 2d. a lb by early 1937. Belatedly, quotas were liberally increased and this resulted in a fall in prices to 7d., whereupon restrictions were rapidly tightened once more.[13] When war broke out in 1939 Britain and France elected to remain within the jurisdiction of the International Rubber Restriction Committee in order to prevent a slump in prices. However, by 1941 supplies were tight and purchases were centralized in both the U.K. and the U.S.A., and allocation schemes were ultimately adopted.[14] The wartime scarcity of rubber also led to the remarkable development of the synthetic rubber industry in the U.S.A. during this period. Following the Japanese invasion of South-East Asia rubber output from Ceylon and Africa was increased but, because of the rise in prices, the Allies agreed that the total supply of rubber from British, French and Portuguese territories should be bought for re-allocation by the Ministry of Supply.

The rapid recovery of rubber supplies after the war led to early moves to restore the trade to private channels. From 24 October 1946 members of the London Rubber Trade Association were allowed to enter into contracts for the purchase or sale of physical rubber for delivery or shipment within the sterling area. On 1 January 1947 arbitrage facilities were granted to dealers on markets outside the sterling area. Naturally, it was the committee of the Rubber Trade Association which represented the traders during the close and regular consultations with the Bank of England, which were necessary to accommodate private international trade in rubber within the framework of the stringent exchange-control regulations of the day.

4. Synthetic Rubber and Other Developments

Prices were buoyant after the war due to stockpiling by major consuming countries. However, the passing of the Shafer Bill (the 'Rubber Producing Facilities Disposal Act' of 1953) denoted the arrival of the synthetic rubber industry: in the interest of national security this Act stipulated that there should be provision for a minimum annual domestic consumption of 222,000 tons of the synthetic product and a total capacity of 665,000 tons to be maintained for emergencies. The sensitivity of the rubber market during the early post-war years was well exemplified by events during 1950. By June the price was at the very high level of 2s. 3d. per lb, with U.S. consumption at a considerable height, despite the fact that the price of the synthetic substitute was considerably below the price of natural rubber. With an official announcement by the American administration that it was considering the possibility of extending synthetic capacity, the bulls began to unload, and the price of natural rubber fell back to 1s. 10d. In November 1950, however, the Korean boom drove the price up to 5s. 10d. and in so doing ushered in a period of rapid expansion of synthetic rubber. Substitution was inevitable due to the greater stability in the supply and price of the latter product compared with the extreme sensitivity of natural-rubber prices. The high prices which obtained for rubber, moreover, also retarded the extensive planting of high-yielding trees by enabling existing trees to show a reasonable profit.

During the early 1950s the rubber stockpiling programme of the American General Services Administration occasioned considerable anxiety in the trade, despite the fact that, outwardly at least, the market appeared to be reasonably stable. The reason for this was that this stability depended essentially upon the U.S. programme, which could close at any time. In the meantime the Americans were playing the market by selling spot to depress prices and buying forward to advantage.[15] The re-entry of Russia into the market considerably benefited producers. Russian and Chinese buying aided the stability of the market, especially when the U.S. and U.K. governments became net sellers from rubber stockpiles during the early 1960s (Table 13.5). Here again, however, these purchases suffered from the same short-comings as those for Western stockpiles; that is, that they might, without warning, come to an end, or even reverse.

In the meantime, by the end of the 1950s, the U.S. government had sold most of their synthetic rubber capacity to private manufacturers. Many of the large tyre manufacturers in that country were turning over to the synthetic produce and, once changed, it was not conceivable that they would revert to the natural raw material unless it carried a large and prolonged discount over synthetic rubber. As the table of total production indicates, there has been a very considerable rise in the production of synthetic rubber during the 1960s, with the U.S.A. accounting for almost all of it at the beginning of the period. In Britain Dunlop Ltd announced in 1954 that they were launching into this field. (A synthetic plant was planned at Fawley in 1956, but did not start production until 1964.)[16]

An even more dangerous threat to natural rubber was posed by the arrival on the market, in the early 1960s, of the new polydiene synthetics. These new blends fully match the qualities of natural rubber. However, as Table 13.1 shows, though world total synthetic rubber production is now greater than natural-rubber output, the latter has nevertheless continued to grow, albeit slowly. The competition has eventually resulted in some changes in the industry. An appreciable acreage is now planted with high-yielding trees and rubber is now being graded much more rigorously. This is an attempt to prevent manu-

TABLE 13.5
EXPORTS OF SYNTHETIC RUBBER, 1952–1968
thousand tons

From	1952	1953	1954	1955	1956	1957	1958	1959	1960	1961	1962	1963	1964	1965	1966	1967	1968
U.S.A.	22·1	22·7	30·1	93·7	149·4	203·5	193·9	290·5	342·0	297·0	303·9	283·4	321·3	282·6	308·5	300·2	290·6
Canada a	43·3	45·4	59·6	68·0	80·0	93·4	99·2	75·8	108·2	117·0	112·5	117·8	136·1	128·6	129·5	114·4	134·0
United Kingdom						0·2	0·8	6·8	20·1	2·8	27·9	34·7	43·4	51·0	58·3	54·8	69·8
Fed. Rep. Germany	0·3		0·9	1·0	1·6	2·6	4·9	11·8	21·1	18·3	24·5	39·0	43·9	53·2	59·2	60·4	77·0
Italy							0·6	24·3	36·4	45·2	40·7	51·5	53·7	60·0	42·3	45·8	25·0
France									2·3	6·2	23·5	41·3	57·5	73·4	80·6	94·8	120·0
Netherlands								1·0	6·5	9·7	39·7	61·3	78·3	100·0	109·8	118·5	137·0
Japan									0·5	22·3	6·2	8·2	15·4	30·8	49·2	57·5	84·0
Brazil										5·4	1·4		5·0	6·9	10·8	6·0	1·0
Belgium b													15·0	20·0	20·0	20·0	25·0
South Africa														1·0	2·0	2·3	3·0

a. Canada, since January 1966 exports have been estimated.
b. Belgium, figures estimated.
Source: Rubber Statistical Bulletin, Vol. 21, No. 7, April 1967, and Vol. 18, No. 4, January 1964. Published by the Secretariat of the International Rubber Study Group. Commonwealth Secretariat, Plantation Crops, No. 13, 1970.

facturers from being tempted by the more uniform quality of the synthetic product. The price of the latter is also more stable and, because of this, it may be expected to exert some stabilizing influence upon the price of natural rubber. Certainly, as the example, previously cited, of its price behaviour in the U.S.A. in 1950 has indicated, the threat of synthetics does influence the market. In any assessment to date, however, account must be taken of the very disturbed conditions which have prevailed for the natural product, stockpile purchases and sales by the major powers, the troubles in Malaya, and the former Indonesian policy of 'confrontation'.

Perhaps the most authoritative independent survey of the future prospects of the natural-rubber industry which has been carried out is that of the World Bank Rubber Enquiry Group.[17] This group pointed out that the allocation of new land for rubber cultivation would be the most effective way of providing fresh capital for the industry. It would permit the growers to plant high-quality trees while still obtaining income from their old trees. The Bank's Report suggested that the prospects for world consumption justified new planting as well as re-planting, especially since much of the empty land was only suitable for rubber cultivation.[18] The report continues by stating that cost data from a representative cross-section of rubber estates indicate that the production of high-yielding rubber on well-managed estates could continue to compete effectively with synthetic rubber, even if the prices of the latter were to fall well below present levels. They conclude by remarking that small-holdings of high-yielding rubber cultivated mainly on a family or a crop-sharing basis would be even less vulnerable to lower synthetic-rubber prices.[19] This is an optimistic picture which appears, apart from all else, to neglect the strategic attractions for industrial countries of being independent of natural-rubber supplies. After all, German U-boat batteries were among the first uses for synthetic rubber.

In the meantime Britain's growing import (and export) of synthetic rubber is not on the same scale as its trade in the natural product, as Table 13.2 indicates: neither is the price of natural rubber sufficiently steady, as the accompanying graph shows (Figure 13.1), for the market to be ready to dispense with facilities for hedging. The London market, therefore, continues to operate and is believed to have an annual volume of transactions of the order of 134,000 tons. This is a great deal larger than the New York futures market, which has now fallen into a moribund state due to the overwhelming competition from synthetics. (It will be seen from Table 13.1 that the U.S.A. alone produces 2 million tons of synthetic rubber out of a total world production of 3.5 million tons.)

On the London market transactions in spot rubber and for rubber on 'Settlement House Terms' continue to be made both on and off the

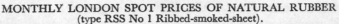

FIGURE 13.1

MONTHLY LONDON SPOT PRICES OF NATURAL RUBBER
(type RSS No 1 Ribbed-smoked-sheet).

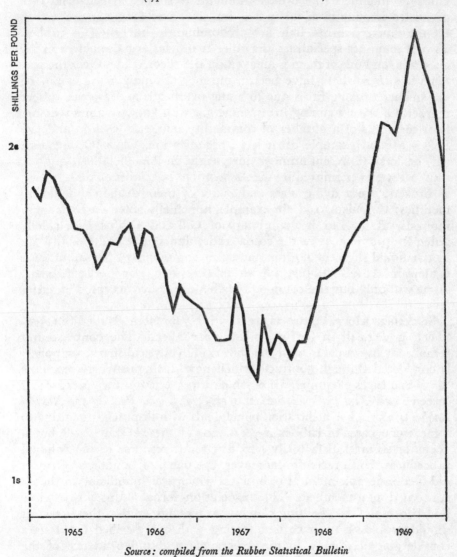

Source: compiled from the Rubber Statistical Bulletin

floor of the London Commodity Exchange at Plantation House.
Physical market turnover is very much affected by direct purchases
from the Eastern markets on the part of larger manufacturers. Meanwhile, the business which is concluded in London has to flow through
the channels of intermediaries prescribed by the Rubber Trade
Association of London. There are at present some eighteen class 'A'

members (i.e. selling agents and importers) out of a maximum number of thirty-five permitted by the General Regulations of the R.T.A. Class 'B' members (the brokers) amount to some fourteen firms of a permitted maximum of thirty-five, but far fewer than this are active. Of the fourteen firms, four are predominantly interested in rubber. Two of them are specialists; the other two firms are also active in the tea trade, and one of them is an agent in the cocoa trade. Over the past ten years or so there have been a number of amalgamations among the smaller broking firms due to rising overheads and a weak rubber market. Of the remaining firms, some are well known names who are floor members of a number of commodity markets. Joynson and Co. Ltd is a good example of such an organization. Class 'C' members (the dealers) at present number thirty-eight on the official list, out of a total of seventy permitted by the Association. Specialist dealers, as well as brokers, are a dying class and many of them deal in other commodities: Czarnikow Ltd, for example, are chiefly noted for their sugar interests, Pacol Ltd is a subsidiary of Gill and Duffus Ltd, chiefly noted for prominence in the cocoa trade, and Bunge and Co. Ltd are international shippers of grain and other commodities. Not all of these dealers, moreover, will take a 'position' (i.e. go long or short of rubber). Some will only buy the commodity when they have accepted an order for it.

Settlement House contracts are invariably for No. 1 Ribbed-Smoked-Sheet, now dealt in for up to one year ahead. The contract unit remains at five tons, though the spot trade (physical market supplies) is conducted through contracts which now distinguish between some thirty-one types of rubber, all of which are defined in the Association's 'green book' (*International Standards of Quality and Packing for Natural Rubber Grades*). The arbitration panel deals with disputes amounting to some 1,000 cases of rubber a year and, of these disputes, all but a dozen or so are satisfactorily settled without recourse to the tribunal procedures. Until recently, moreover, the panel of London arbitrators did a considerable amount of business which was 'unofficial' in that it concerned non-members. The Association forbade this for a while but, because of the resulting clamour, it was agreed that these services should be placed on a regular footing with a prescribed fee. It is a considerable testimony to the experience and independence of the London arbitration machinery that this demand, which is often from traders from the continent and even further afield, should continue to be so strong. Meanwhile the Eastern markets are now more important distributors of rubber than the London market, and large manufacturers stand in less need of hedging facilities than formerly because of their ability to pass on cost increases. Both these features have contributed to a weakening of the London market which has, as we have seen, become very largely of domestic rather than of international importance of recent years. It is, however, still a large market and seems likely to retain some importance due to the size of domestic demand and to the world significance of its free-market prices.

Chapter Fourteen

JUTE, SHELLAC AND GENERAL PRODUCE

1. *Jute and Allied Fibres*

When the East India Company first imported jute into this country from Bengal in 1796, it was almost certainly the bast (i.e. the inner bark) from either white or tossa jute (i.e. *corchorus capsularis* and *corchorus olitorius* respectively). It remains to this day a peasant rather than a plantation crop. The plant grows to a height of some nine feet in about four months, after which the harvested stalks are steeped in water until the gum which binds the fibre to the stem under the epidermis decomposes – a process known as retting. The fibre is then separated from the pith by hand, washed, and dried. The result is a fibre characterized by a total lack of moisture, which the Dundee flax spinners first found impossible to spin with their existing machinery. By 1832, however, the spinners had learnt to combine another product of this fishing port – whale oil – with more suitable machinery, and this resulted in a satisfactory yarn. Despite this, when jute was first used in quantity by these manufacturers owing to the failure of the flax crop in 1835, they still complained bitterly of the weakness of this fibre, its unsatisfactory colour, and its total lack of moisture.[1]

In spite of this inauspicious start, jute spinning was destined to flourish in and around Dundee. A fillip to the use of the fibre was administered in 1838, when the Dutch government specified bags made of jute instead of flax for moving their East India coffee crops. A further impetus was provided by the Crimean War when raw flax supplies from Russia failed, and again by the American Civil War when cotton supplies were severely curtailed. Imports mounted rapidly from 14,000 tons in 1850 to a peak figure of 351,000 tons in 1913. The re-export trade was also at its height at this time, accounting for the movement of some 130,000 tons of the produce. By 1968 imports had fallen back to 115,000 tons (Table 14.1). The re-export trade has become virtually a thing of the past, though 'third country trade' is still arranged by London brokers. The produce, moreover, is not now confined to white or tossa jute, for by today many close substitutes, though mostly of a somewhat inferior nature, have appeared. The most important of these are kenaf (variously known as mesta, Siam jute, Ambari hemp, stockroos, etc.), roselle, and urena fibre (also known as Congo jute or paka).

According to a contemporary account, by the 1860s orders were

286

TABLE 14.1

UNITED KINGDOM IMPORTS AND RE-EXPORTS OF FIBRES, QUANTITIES AND VALUES, 1913–1968

Quantity: thousand tons   Value: £ thousand

IMPORTS	1913		1928		1938		1958		1968	
	Quantity	Value	Quantity	Value	Quantity	Value	Quantity	Value	Quantity	Value
Hemp and Hemp Tow and Sisal	146·3	4350·2	94·0	3480·9	87·1	2020·7	95·1	7689·3	63·4	4841·5
Jute	350·8	9246·6	204·9	6293·5	195·5	3729·7	132·3	12418·5	115·1	14202·7
Kapok			0·9	85·5	1·7	89·1	0·6	85·7	0·9	89·7 a
Coir Fibre			4·9	69·7	9·3	77·4	25·1	925·6	21·2	982·7

RE-EXPORTS	1913		1928		1938		1958		1968	
	Quantity	Value	Quantity	Value	Quantity	Value	Quantity	Value	Quantity	Value
Hemp and Hemp Tow and Sisal	52·5	1526·0	19·4	679·2	4·6	110·7	1·2	95·4	0·002	0·089
Jute	129·8	3475·3	10·4	329·2	35·3	678·4	0·4	31·6	2·5	314·7
Kapok			0·1	7·6	0·02	1·3	0·004	0·6		
Coir Fibre			0·3	5·9	0·4	4·0	0·07	3·0	0·028	2·3

a. 1968 includes Milkweed.
Source: Annual Statement of Trade.

sometimes sent out to Calcutta by merchants or spinners, but the bulk
of the jute was bought on ship's account in order to complete a cargo,
or to put a vessel into proper sailing trim – entire cargoes of this
produce were rarely sent because it was too light in relation to its bulk.[2]
In both Liverpool and London, parcels of jute were at that time
occasionally sold 'to arrive', in which case they were transferred direct
to the buyer if the purchase price had been paid. The bulk of the
import however was warehoused, and though parcels were frequently
sold privately by the selling brokers, most of it was sold at the public
sales which took place almost every week. In common with many
other commodities the London venue for the sale of jute was at Mincing
Lane, and Warden tells us that

> The auction sales are conducted with great regularity and
> rapidity, on certain rules which are understood between the
> selling and buying brokers, the whole business being done by
> them. Any merchant may buy, but the deposit must be then and
> there paid down, and as the selling broker charges him a buying
> commission or brokerage, the merchant has no saving by not
> employing a broker to purchase for him. The whole business is
> therefore transacted by the brokers, and as they are appointed
> by the Corporation of the City and their number limited, the
> trade is a very profitable one when they get into a good con-
> nection.[3]

It must indeed have been, as was the case for many another trade at
the time, especially since the buying and selling brokers each charged
a commission of one-half per cent, and when the one broker acted in
both capacities, as he often did, he was able to claim both commissions.
The terms were, it appears, more favourable in Liverpool than in the
capital, for no charge was made in the former for brokerage upon the
jute bought either at auction or by private sale. The tare allowed at
Liverpool (5 lbs per bale) was also more favourable than in London
(1 lb per bale) but, despite these advantages, it was London which
finally emerged as the principal centre for the purchase of jute. This
was probably due in some measure to the convenience of London as
the port for trans-shipment to Dundee, but a further major factor must
undoubtedly have been the superior financial facilities of the metropolitan centre: in Liverpool the terms of sale were cash, whereas in
London they were 'three months prompt' (i.e. allowing a credit of
three months), subject to the payment of a 15 per cent deposit.

Nor was the payment of brokerage the only expense borne by the
jute spinner, for he usually bought his produce through an agent
resident in London or Liverpool. As in other trades already examined,
it was the agent's task upon receiving an order from the spinner to
examine the parcels on sale and, having made his selection, to buy
either from the selling broker privately or else through the medium of

another broker at the public sales. For this these agents charged a commission of one per cent, with a further fourpence a bale in Liverpool, and five shillings a ton in London. Like the Lancashire cotton spinners, however, the Dundee jute spinners occasionally complained of the dual function performed by these agents, who sometimes turned merchant and bought on their own account when they considered prices to be low. 'This', remarks Warden, 'they are enabled to do in London without much capital, through the instrumentality of the system of prompts; but the practice is disliked by the trade in Dundee, as it induces speculation, and frequently raises the price unnecessarily to the consumer.'

Today jute is no longer sold by auction in Mincing Lane, though the floor of the London Commodity Exchange and adjoining brokers' offices are still the venue for the exchange of information and often for settling prices. The London Jute Association, established in 1875, is a body representing the principal jute merchants and brokers located in London, who deal with Dundee spinners – mostly through Dundee jute merchants – and also extensively with spinners on the continent of Europe. Members of the London Jute Association, who number twenty-seven at the present time, thus clearly have close connections with the Jute Importers' Association, also an old-established body, representing the interests of importers of jute in Dundee and district. The latter Association, which altogether has some fifty-six firms on its roll, fulfils two functions.[4] The first of these consists of acting as a clearing house for problems arising between spinners who use raw jute and merchants or brokers who supply it to the spinners; and, secondly, that of acting as an organization for representing the common interests of those two bodies versus Pakistan or other raw jute supplying countries. Spot transactions in jute from warehoused stocks are still far from unknown, but most of the business is now c.i.f. trade. The contract forms, and arrangements for the prompt arbitration of disputes, constitute the main raison d'être of the London Jute Association. Trade on the L.J.A. contract is world-wide. The Association itself is a very active one and its committee meets about once weekly to consider questions which have arisen in the course of trade.

As is the case with many other commodities, markets have sprung up in countries of origin, to which the jute finds its way through a chain of dealers from the grower. One of the less fortunate results of the partition of the Indian sub-continent in 1947 was that whereas it left most of the growing areas of jute in Pakistan, the jute mills were almost all located in India. The Indian government has thus decreed for many years that all domestically grown jute must be utilized by domestic manufacturers. There is an important Jute Exchange in Calcutta called The East India Jute and Hessian Exchange. This, following the recommendation of the Parliamentary Jute Enquiry

Commission of 1954, re-established a futures market in jute goods on 5 April 1958. In Pakistan there is an important raw jute market in Narayanganj. Much of the produce is, however, still exported; in fact, jute exports provide Pakistan with over 50 per cent of its foreign exchange, and they represent some three-quarters of the world trade in the raw produce. Consequently, though Thailand is an important producer of roselle, Pakistan's output virtually determines the world price.

Of recent years Pakistan has tried by means of a Jute Board and a Jute Trading Corporation to set up minimum prices for this crop, and has generally attempted to maintain a stable market for the commodity.[5] Recently, too, efforts have been made on a wider basis to achieve some degree of stability: under the auspices of the U.N. Food and Agriculture Organization, a consultative committee on jute, kenaf and allied fibres has been at work. This committee, which includes delegates from Belgium, France, Western Germany, Ghana, India, Italy, Pakistan, Poland, Portugal, Thailand and the U.K., has been concerned to establish indicative export prices for each crop year, though without stating how the minimum prices indicated as suitable are to be enforced.

The seven restrictive agreements against which the Restrictive Practices Court gave judgement in 1963 were concerned with jute goods rather than the raw produce,[6] but they were indicative of an inability to compete against cheap imports which was the chief cause of the depressed condition of the industry at Dundee before the Second World War. In fact, jute is one of the industrial fibres which has so far been least affected by the introduction of synthetic substitutes but, even so, the severe Indian competition has meant that the use of Dundee-woven jute for packaging purposes is now a relatively small trade. A predominant proportion of jute yarns and cloths manufactured in the U.K. is now sold to other U.K. manufacturers who require a tough low-cost textile material as a component part of their own goods. Among the greatest users of the material nowadays are the floor-covering manufacturers, who use jute for both woven and tufted carpets. Jute material is also used in the building, furnishing, cable and other industries. World production of jute manufactures, which showed a generally rising trend until 1966-7, has subsequently declined. Though it is not possible to predict the future prospects of the Dundee industry and, therefore, the U.K. raw jute market from this, it is at least indicative that the demand for jute packaging material made in the U.K. has been declining for some time. In fact, United Kingdom output has been declining since 1964; in some years, moreover, by a considerable percentage. Further indications for the future may be seen in the rising output from the mills of Pakistan, Brazil, and a number of other countries in Asia, Africa and Latin America.

As is well known, today jute has been joined on the markets of the world by other fibres, some of which are loosely called hemps. The true hemp (*Cannabis Sativa*) yields a soft fibre from the inner bark just as jute does. In tropical latitudes this plant also produces a resinous juice from which hashish or marijuana is obtained. (This produce was once sold in Mincing Lane a great deal more freely than at present, now that a Dangerous Drugs licence – and considerable supervision – is necessary.) Other so-called hemps are grown for the fibres derived from their leaf tissues. Of these, sisal (*agave sisalana*), cultivated mainly in East Africa, Angola and Brazil, is by far the most important. Other very close substitutes for sisal are grown in the Philippines (abaca or Manila), Mexico and Cuba (henequen). Still others are known as Mauritius hemp, New Zealand hemp, and Maguey.

Trade in sisal and substitutes in London is carried on by direct negotiation between merchants and shippers' or growers' agents here or abroad. The London merchants re-sell to spinners. The London Sisal Association arranges the contract and the terms on which trade is transacted. The same method of trading applies to abaca, for which the Manila Hemp Association arranges the conditions and terms of contract.

Sisal and its substitutes have been affected to a far greater extent than has jute by the introduction of synthetics, but this is illustrative of the kind of fate which might befall jute industries should prices remain at a high level. The impact of such substitutes as nylon and terylene has not always been direct; for example, these synthetics by taking a large share of the market formerly supplied by Manila hemp have so reduced its price that it has now become competitive with sisal. Moreover, 1966 saw the launching of polypropylene at the same price as sisal. It thus becomes a strong competitor with the natural material for securing grain and hay harvests. Like sisal, and unlike many substitutes, polypropylene does not harm animals when eaten with hay.

Such changes have given rise to an unprecedented crisis in hard fibres markets, posing a considerable threat to the economic development of countries for which these commodities are important foreign exchange earners. Starting in 1967, meetings have been held under the auspices of the F.A.O. which have produced informal agreements among sisal producers to control exports and prices. Experiments are being promoted into new uses for the sisal and similar plants – it has been found for example that cellulose pulp from the whole plant can be used for paper-making – and the Tanzania Sisal Corporation has announced schemes for cutting production costs. It remains very doubtful, however, whether the winning back of lost markets is compatible with rising living standards in countries which are heavily dependent upon fibre crops.

2. *Shellac*

Lac is the resinous matter exuded by the insect *laccifer lacca* onto the twigs of certain host trees for which conditions in the Central Provinces of India and Northern Thailand are ideal. The lac-covered twigs are harvested and the resinous matter is melted off. This has remained a small-scale activity in which conditions are essentially primitive; in the melting-off process, for example, charcoal from the collectors' fires becomes the main source of impurity and affects the grade into which each maund (about 82 lbs) is sorted.

Like jute and other produce, shellac has been sold in Mincing Lane for many a year and in its day has vied as a medium for speculation with pepper. These activities were encouraged by the very considerable price fluctuations to which the commodity was at one time subject; thus the price reached 820s. a hundredweight at one period in 1920, but by the outbreak of war in 1939 it was as low as 40s. Some protection against such uncertainties was available at one time on futures contracts organized entirely by the trade itself, i.e. by the London Shellac Trade Association.[7] However, speculation in this commodity, together with pepper and tin, was the subject of unfavourable comment in the House of Commons on 7 March 1935,[8] and the remedy, according to one member, was more frequent settlements.

In the event, a properly regulated futures market did not appear until more than twenty years later with the formation of the London Shellac Terminal Market Association under whose auspices trading commenced on 23 June 1956, some eighteen months after the Indian government had banned futures trading in shellac.[9] In the meantime, business proceeded on the old contract until the October delivery, and it was only the new contract, starting with the December position, which was cleared and guaranteed by the London Produce Clearing House Ltd. Membership of the Terminal Market Association consisted of two classes; that is, brokers, and privileged members. Official calls, held in one corner of the floor of the London Commodity Exchange, were agreed for 11.30 a.m., 3 p.m. and 4.30 p.m. from Monday to Friday. The original contract was extant until the end of 1959 and business amounted to 71,650 bags. The contract unit on the terminal market was for 50 bags, equal to 72 cwt 21 lbs, the basis grade on this contract being pure T.N. London Standard. For purposes of arbitration both on the actuals market and on terminal contracts which conclude with the tender of the actual commodity, the London Shellac Trade Association has standard samples, by reference to which colour and general appearance may be checked. A series of tests is also carried out to determine the degree of insoluble matter. The sample used for this purpose is drawn from the bulk at the warehouse by an accredited wharfinger and sent under seal to the selling broker. When shellac is quoted the degree of insoluble matter finds its place in the description;

for example, Pure T.N. London Standard (formerly used for 78 r.p.m. gramophone records) is quoted 2.5 per cent. This implies that the basis of the grade allows on average that amount of insoluble matter. The By-Laws of the London Shellac Association prescribe that, in the case of arbitration, the maximum amount of insoluble matter permitted for this grade shall be 3.5 per cent. Similarly, Standard 1 is basis 1.5 per cent, with a permitted maximum of 2.5 per cent.

In fact, the London contract basis grade was changed to Standard 1 (a higher grade than pure T.N.) from February 1959 to the end of 1965, but the total turnover amounted to only 8,400 bags. The terminal market was actually moribund for a considerable period before 1966 and monotonously returned 'nil' against 'business done' in the daily press reports. The reason for this was that the Indian government decided to intervene in the market from 1958 to control the export price. An Indian Lac Exporters Association was formed, official warehouses opened, and the important Futka market at Calcutta encouraged. From time to time this Association, which has established 'Calcutta Standards' for the produce, issues schedules of minimum and maximum prices. Because of this, stocks of shellac held by merchants in the U.K. and elsewhere have dwindled, for there is little incentive for the trade to hold produce when prices are fixed. The demand for a hedging medium thus ceased, and speculative interest fell away.

When stocks start to pile up in the Calcutta warehouses because the official schedule of prices seems on the high side to London and other importers, this creates difficulties for Indian export interests. Furthermore, it does not seem that fixed export prices do very much to relieve the lot of the poor Indian cultivators who prepare the produce for sale at local collecting markets. No fixed prices are operative at this stage and the cultivator is frequently faced with heart-breaking offers from local dealers and little bargaining strength with which to negotiate for a better settlement. The situation is well summed up by a statement in one of the periodic Market Reviews published by some brokers in the trade;

This has been another disappointing year. With the exception of a lowering of 10s. to 12s. per cwt in the price of Seedlac from origin, the Minimum Export Selling Prices have remained unchanged. Imports of Lac and Seedlac into the U.K. to date have averaged around the same quantities as last year, reflecting an even demand, but, unfortunately, showing no increase in consumption. With the continuation of Controlled Selling Prices in Calcutta, resulting in a non-fluctuating market, it is obvious that there is little of interest to report. Internal prices in Calcutta are still well below the Minimum Export Selling Prices, and it would appear that the Producer up country is not obtaining any benefit from this situation. Forward trading on the Terminal Market has been stultified by the control of Calcutta prices, and no transactions have been recorded.[10]

Shellac has suffered severely from the invasion of its traditional markets by synthetics. Thus, shellac gramophone records have been superseded by microgroove 'long playing' plastic records, while the top hat (which owes its shine to a shellac varnish) is not perhaps such a conspicuous item of apparel as once it was. The use of shellac varnish for securing the lids of cardboard packing cases has also been hit to some extent by the use of newer forms of packaging by steel bands or self-adhesive tape and polythene. On the other hand, some new uses have been promoted. Pressurized hair sprays containing shellac are at present quite popular, while a highly refined type of bleached shellac is now used for 'self-polishing' floor waxes. Shellac is also used in the manufacture of playing cards, lipstick, car varnish, and leather finishing. On balance, however, the use to which shellac is put is declining, and this, together with the greater use of c.i.f. trade encouraged by fixed prices, has resulted in a decrease in stocks held in public warehouses in this country from a one-time average figure of 300,000 packages (each containing two maunds, i.e. about 164 lbs), to some 10,000. It seems unlikely that shellac will ever again approach its former importance as a raw material. It has been described as a forerunner of plastics, and, as such, the likelihood is that ultimately even its remaining uses will be overtaken by plastics. Clearly, this process is likely to be accelerated by high fixed prices.

3. General Produce

Though many of the brokers who joined together to found the General Produce Brokers' Association subsequently formed associations which specialized in the organization of trade in particular major commodities such as tea, coffee, cocoa, shellac and others, a bewilderingly large variety of produce is still described as 'general produce'. Of course, many brokers remained members of more than one organization, and this was especially the case when the less important commodities started to boast associations of their own. Thus, many traders, besides being members of the General Produce Brokers' Association, are also members of the Bristle Trade Section of that Association, the Mica Trade Association, the Almond Trade Association, the Association of Indian Carpet Importers, and others. Some commodities have terms which from the broker's point of view are very different from certain others; thus, for example, it is usual for both the buyer and the seller to pay a brokerage – in the comparatively specialized mica trade as much as $2\frac{1}{2}$ per cent and 2 per cent respectively – but on the Incorporated Oilseed Association's contract the buyer pays no brokerage.

The mode of sale of bristles, like that of ivory, has already been dealt with in Chapter 8 above in connection with our description of the auction sales in Mincing Lane, and need not detain us further. Bristles from China, Argentina, Formosa, India, Korea, Persia, the U.S.S.R. and Yugoslavia are, however, usually handled by the same brokers who handle hair of various kinds. The descriptions of this species of produce range from dressed horse-tail hair, cattle-tail hair and goat hair (from Argentina, Australia, Canada, China and the U.K. itself), through 'raw' versions of these tails, to human hair, and even pig hair. Dressed tails are used in brush manufacturing; the non-dressed descriptions are used in upholstery; the pig hair is used in textile manufacture, while the human hair is used for wigs. The accompanying table (Table 14.2) of general, and what for convenience may be termed 'allied', produce, is incomplete. It does, however, include imports of hair of various sorts. Only the values exist for the period before World War I: the figures show a fall from some £1.7 million to just under £1 million between 1874 and 1913. The weight of hair imported fell considerably between 1938 and 1968, though its value has increased from just under £600,000 in 1938 to as much as £2,314,200 by 1958. In 1968 the value of imports was £720,500. In terms of weight, the re-export trade has been declining steeply ever since 1913 so that it is almost negligible by today, though its money value is almost twice what it was in 1938. The bristle trade, with imports of over £4½ million, of which about half is re-exported, is thus the larger trade (Table 14.3). Moreover, if past trends as shown by the table are anything to go by, it seems likely to remain so, though synthetic and other substitutes pose a decided threat to both trades.

The Mincing Lane brokers are actually concerned not only with Indian carpets but with oriental carpets generally. To a considerable extent this trade is still a spot trade of consignments which may be viewed before purchase. Oriental carpets are stored along with much other exotic produce and sold on the contract of the General Produce Brokers' Association at the famous Cutler Street bonded warehouses: the collection of goods includes raw silk, essential oils, cigars, wine, drugs and many other commodities. The carpets may be viewed against a background of white-washed walls and late eighteenth century iron pillars, which merchants in effect use as a showroom. In addition to those made in India, carpets and rugs can be seen from a wide variety of countries – there is usually a stock of more than 100,000 items worth over £20 million – such as Pakistan, Persia, the Caucasus, Asia Minor, Central Asia and China. Before the First World War the trade in oriental carpets was largely in the hands of the traders of Constantinople, but the disruption occasioned by the war (in which the Turks were on the 'wrong' side as far as the Allies were concerned) provided London traders with their opportunity, which they exploited with the aid of London's facilities for marketing. The trade is still

TABLE 14.2

UNITED KINGDOM IMPORTS OF SELECTED GENERAL PRODUCE 1874–1968

Quantity: thousand cwt   Value: £ thousand

	1874		1913		1938		1958		1968	
	Quantity	Value	Quantity	Value	Quantity	Value	Quantity	Value	Quantity	Value
Tapioca and Sago			1421·6	732·9	686·1	374·7	140·7	345·7	97·5 c	268·4
Essential Oils	4·9	254·7	23·1	591·0	41·9	1265·6	54·6	5227·0	77·8	8593·1
Drugs (raw and simply prepared)		995·7		1984·6	159·0	704·0	106·3	2584·6	105·6	2886·2
Spices	296·4	1132·4	243·4	687·3	165·7	338·5	194·1	2429·8	165·7	2848·4
Gums and Resins	1304·0	1566·1	2376·0	2899·8	1956·0	1926·6	1878·0	8162·1	1590·0	9274·8
Waxes	26·2	134·7	89·0	386·8	100·8	519·5	48·7	1246·2	36·6	892·2
Nuts (in shell and shelled)		771·7	868·4	1782·0	1408·2	3031·6	1423·4	13807·5	1204·1	17440·8
Bristles	23·8	420·5	42·7	798·7	36·8	1200·2	33·6	3014·7	27·3	4565·4
Hair		1734·6		989·8	171·2	595·3	81·6	2314·2	32·6	720·5
Agar Agar							5·9	311·5	8·1	688·4
Balata (including Gutta Percha)	30·0 a	299·5	111·2 a	1370·7	23·3	148·0	15·5	384·3	6·8	150·9
Eggs (not in shell)				151·3	966·6	3383·8	473·0	5445·0	216·2	2091·7
Feathers	24·1	730·6	64·6	3689·0		361·5	18·6	380·0	36·1	594·0
Gall Nuts	24·3	46·6	13·5	32·5	8·0	19·4	13·7	243·3	10·3	161·5
Gelatine, Glue and Size			258·3	524·9	165·6	647·3	88·2	762·1	100·9	1044·2
Honey			31·8	50·7	102·5	189·2	140·8	739·5	290·9	2045·7
Ivory			10·2	489·7	2·2	77·2	0·5	45·1		
Tortoiseshell and Coral								28·6	255·3	200·8
Rattan Cane				113·6		106·0		585·8 b	118·1	108·1 b
Asbestos			232·0	151·0	1076·2	1137·5	2196·9	9575·2	644·6	1548·9
Maté Tea					0·8	44·7	0·4	3·0	0·5	4·1
Menthol							1·2	248·4	2·8	485·8
Mica			45·0	162·2	75·6	558·2	102·7	1676·7	254·9	1617·1
Mercury	26·8	841·2	30·4	338·5	30·1	508·3	13·1	1441·6	12·4	4049·6
Fibre	5605·8	5944·3	9942·0	13596·8	5872·0	5916·9	5062·0	21119·9	4012·0	20116·6

a. Gutta Percha only.   b. Including Tsinglee Garden Canes.   c. Including Tapioca and Sago substitutes.

Source: Annual Statement of Trade.

TABLE 14.3

UNITED KINGDOM RE-EXPORTS OF SELECTED GENERAL PRODUCE, 1874–1968

Quantity: thousand cwt   Value: £ thousand

	1874		1913		1938		1958		1968	
	Quantity	Value	Quantity	Value	Quantity	Value	Quantity	Value	Quantity	Value
Tapioca and Sago	1·9	77·2	94·6	74·3	12·0	9·9	0·6	2·8	0·06 c	0·4 c
Essential Oils		276·1	6·3	144·1	6·0	219·7	6·3	794·2	10·2	1260·2
Drugs (raw and simply prepared)	234·2	860·7	119·6	805·0	24·2	297·3	8·1	224·0	5·7	153·4
Spices	163·7	746·3	344·1	340·4	41·5	99·3	23·5	446·1	24·4	368·4
Gums and Resin	19·7	99·7	16·1	1076·9	142·9	325·4	40·4	449·4	31·7	526·5
Waxes		133·2	136·3	104·8	8·1	48·3	3·7	110·7	3·1	60·3
Nuts (in shell and shelled)	0·7	15·5	21·1	345·4	71·2	174·5	55·6	717·6	32·0	521·2
Bristles		45·8		418·6	13·3	396·8	15·0	1685·0	10·9	2330·6
Hair				161·8	5·8	26·4	4·2	290·5	0·9	34·6
Agar Agar							0·2	16·1	0·2	30·1
Balata (including Gutta Percha)	2·5 a	17·9 a	8·9 a	111·7	2·6	22·2	1·0	27·2	0·9	95·6
Eggs (not in shell)			21·9	88·4	50·2	154·2	15·1	150·4	0·9	17·5
Feathers	1·5	175·3	4·6	254·6		30·2	0·1	16·5	0·5	29·4
Gall Nuts	16·1	39·0	18·7	11·3	0·6	1·7	0·04	0·7	0·003	0·08
Gelatine, Glue and Size			1·4	30·7	4·1	12·8	1·1	14·4	0·8	10·8
Honey			7·1	3·3	3·1	9·1	2·7	22·8	5·8	54·3
Ivory				414·4	1·7	59·6	0·2	15·4	0·5	14·2
Tortoiseshell and Coral								1·9		
Rattan Cane			13·8	13·9	11·3	20·3	1·6	3·7 b	0·2	3·1 b
Asbestos							0·006	10·6	0·5	1·4
Maté Tea							0·2	0·1	0·02	0·2
Menthol					0·07	4·6		51·5	0·5	95·7
Mica			25·3	163·6	21·4	265·5	8·2	336·0	92·6	559·0
Mercury	21·6	652·1	18·0	192·9	10·5	215·1	3·5	397·9	2·4	781·0
Fibre	840·5	809·2	3646·0	5001·3	806·4	794·4	33·5	130·6	50·6	317·1

a. Gutta Percha only.   b. Including Tsinglee Garden Canes.   c. Including Tapioca and Sago substitutes.

Source: Annual Statement of Trade.

competitive, and business is sometimes dull in London because traders find better conditions for selling their commodities on North American and Australian markets. Certainly as far as Indian carpets are concerned, the dependence upon the U.K. market is not nearly as great as it once used to be. For 1966, the import of these carpets was £11½ million, of which as much as £6.6 million was re-exported.

4. Drugs

The General Produce Brokers' Association of London have a duplicated list, the title of which runs as follows: '*List of Commodities Handled by Members (Not Exhaustive)*'. If there is a hint of despair in the description, it should not deceive us into the belief that the list is valueless, for it is in fact extremely useful. Its contents are sub-divided into main categories, viz. bristles and hair, drugs, essential oils, gums, spices, waxes, and other articles. Though still quite a long list, the number of items shown under the heading drugs is not nearly as long as it was a hundred years ago, when the reliance placed upon vegetable drugs was much greater. Table 14.4 shows that the value of imports (as far as can be ascertained from the Annual Statement of Trade), was some £427,000 for 1874. The value of such of these raw drugs as remain in use has risen very considerably by this time to almost £3 million, but the quantity changes since 1938 indicate that the volume of trade is a declining one. The re-export trade, too, is but a third of its pre-war weight. The Association's list of drugs reveals omissions in plenty; opium, marijuana and cantharides for example are not accorded a mention, though the list of drugs actually given is still formidably long. In addition to readily recognizable items such as rhubarb (a well-known drug), ipecacuanha and senna, there are a number of more obscure items such as dragon's blood (used mainly these days for colouring medicinal preparations), papain (made from the juice of the tropical paupau fruit as a treatment for indigestion and the preparation of tough meat), cactus juice and many more. The herbalist's art is, however, a dying trade, so that the overwhelming likelihood is that the import of such drugs will continue to decline in amount.

5. Essential Oils

The essential oils, widely used for flavouring foodstuffs, perfumery and pharmacy, constitute quite an important group of commodities the import of which was worth £9.7 million in 1966 (Tables 14.5 and 14.6) and the re-export trade more than £1 million. This produce ranges from the very familiar oils, such as aniseed, camphor and eucalyptus, to others such as orange oil, ginger grass and palma rosa from India. Essential oils are prepared sometimes from the bark of trees (as in the case of cinnamon), sometimes from the roots, sometimes from the leaves and fruits, or even from the dried flower buds of certain trees (e.g. the

TABLE 14:4

UNITED KINGDOM IMPORTS AND RE-EXPORTS OF DRUGS (RAW AND SIMPLY PREPARED), 1920–1968

Quantity: thousand cwt Value: £ thousand

IMPORTS	1920		1928		1938		1958		1968	
	Quantity	Value	Quantity	Value	Quantity	Value	Quantity	Value	Quantity	Value
Ipecacuanha	1·1	85·4	0·6	39·5	0·9	29·6	1·2	353·8	1·4	105·2
Other Roots	47·3	262·4	24·0	85·9	36·6	85·9	20·2	125·0	16·3	184·3
Cinchona Bark	22·4	166·0	21·0	95·5	16·3	116·1	13·1	81·0	15·3	236·5
Nux Vomica	28·1	82·3	12·6	14·5						
Aloes	10·9	30·0	7·5	15·0						
Ergot of Rye	0·6	58·2	1·6	22·2						
Opium	3·8	408·5					3·3	835·4	3·9	965·7
Senna	18·0	87·5	17·4	57·7	10·4	23·1	6·6	51·7		
Others	147·5	977·7	84·4	523·6	94·8	449·3	62·0	1137·8	45·9	652·7
Total	279·8	2158·0	169·1	854·0	159·0	704·0	106·3	2584·6	82·8	2144·4

RE-EXPORTS	1920		1928		1938		1958		1968	
	Quantity	Value	Quantity	Value	Quantity	Value	Quantity	Value	Quantity	Value
Cinchona Bark	5·0	66·4	4·5	25·6	2·0	21·2	0·3	2·6	0·05	0·9
Ipecacuanha	0·3	30·1	0·1	6·0	0·2	8·7	0·3	92·7	0·3	23·4
Other Roots	10·4	132·7	3·7	18·2	3·6	20·1	1·1	17·8	1·3	57·5
Opium	0·8	112·7					0·02	5·8		0·02
Senna	14·3	65·9	11·4	32·2	2·4	5·4	1·7	12·6		
Nux Vomica	4·8	14·8	0·5	0·4						
Aloes	5·7	25·2	4·8	10·2						
Ergot of Rye	0·06	5·4	0·3	4·1						
Others	56·3	454·6	16·5	156·3	16·0	242·0	4·8	118·9	4·0	71·7
Total	97·7	907·8	41·8	252·9	24·2	297·3	8·2	250·5	5·7	153·4

Source: Annual Statement of Trade.

TABLE 14.5

UNITED KINGDOM IMPORTS OF ESSENTIAL OILS, QUANTITIES AND VALUES, 1913–1968

Quantity: thousand lbs   Value: £ thousand

IMPORTS	1913		1928		1938		1958		1968	
	Quantity	Value	Quantity	Value	Quantity	Value	Quantity	Value	Quantity	Value
Aniseed							144·2	58·0	51·9	248·0
Bergamot							65·3	272·8	35·6	32·7
Bois de rose							297·3	264·0	999·5	215·4
Citronella							939·0	198·7	515·6	303·1
Clove							145·3	51·5		
Eucalyptus							220·7	33·5	53·0	236·9
Geranium							74·3	393·4	81·0	162·1
Lavender							79·6	156·1		
Lemon							381·2	628·7	719·4	1418·0
Lemongrass							583·1	193·0	279·6	194·1
Lime							130·0	272·9	132·1	400·3
Orange							637·5	296·0	1096·2	377·3
Peppermint							735·8	836·5	1046·7	1702·8
Petitgrain							76·9	70·1		
Sandalwood							49·4	162·8	42·0	200·7
Spike Lavender							245·2	182·1	134·9	138·5
Other							1305·8	1156·4	3524·2	2963·2
Total	2584·0	591·0	4422·9	1218·9	4691·3	1265·6	6110·6	5226·5	8711·7	8593·1

Source: Annual Statement of Trade.

TABLE 14.6

UNITED KINGDOM RE-EXPORTS OF ESSENTIAL OILS, QUANTITIES AND VALUES, 1913–1968

Quantity: thousand lbs   Value: £ thousand

RE-EXPORTS	1913		1928		1938		1958		1968	
	Quantity	Value	Quantity	Value	Quantity	Value	Quantity	Value	Quantity	Value
Aniseed							20·6	10·8	11·3	56·6
Bergamot							11·1	45·9	7·5	7·8
Bois de rose							62·2	64·5	163·5	41·7
Citronella							38·7	9·7	56·0	41·3
Clove							41·1	19·3		
Eucalyptus							17·5	4·2	1·4	6·4
Geranium							6·3	30·4	4·4	6·3
Lavender							27·3	41·6		
Lemon							53·2	96·5	163·0	359·3
Lemongrass							24·9	9·3	44·5	44·9
Lime							14·8	41·1	16·1	49·5
Orange							136·0	81·3	200·3	146·3
Peppermint							87·9	127·9	148·6	161·6
Sandalwood							12·7	42·8	4·6	21·4
Spike Lavender							14·6	11·1		
Petitgrain							7·4	8·4	3·8	4·7
Other							124·2	137·8	314·3	312·4
Total	703·7	144·1	785·1	307·8	675·6	219·7	700·5	782·6	1139·3	1260·2

Source: Annual Statement of Trade.

cloves of Zanzibar). Essential oils vary enormously in price; attar of roses, for example, usually fetches about £500 a kilogramme, while the common eucalyptus normally realizes only 5s. or so a lb. The usual method of sale these days is for the buyer to obtain a delivered price from an importer, together with a sample should this be required. Where the oils are of high value in relation to their bulk, they are delivered by air.

The trade in essential oils is a thriving one, the import values for which have grown steadily (Table 14.5). Moreover, as Table 14.6 shows, it is one of the comparatively few commodities in which the re-export trade is growing, not only in money terms but also in terms of weight. Artificial flavouring is, of course, an innovation which has been with us for some time but, despite this, it is likely that public preference, aided in some cases by legislation, will be a considerable protection to the trade in the future.

6. *Gums*

The complete list of gums is still a very long one, and their import was worth some £3.7 million in 1968. They were at one time classified either as resins (such as copal, mastic, etc.) or as aromatics (e.g. galbanium, olibanium, myrrh, scammony). Nowadays the gums tend to be categorized according to whether they are soluble, soluble in spirits, insoluble, or emulsifiers. Gums have a fascinating range of uses; one of the aromatics lit for demonstration will momentarily provide an unmistakeable whiff of the East even in the prosaic setting of a produce broker's office. Other gums are so pure that they sparkle in the light as they are emptied from sample packets onto the broker's counter. These gums are used in confectionery and pharmaceutically, while others such as gum tragacanth are widely used as emulsifiers (for holding oils and water in a mixture such as 'mayonnaise', or for keeping cheese moist). Spirit-soluble and heat-melting gums are used for making varnish and as an ingredient in paints; the cheaper varieties are used in linoleums and esterified gums. With the advent of synthetics some of the gums used for paint and linoleum are tending to be superseded – Congo gum copal, and gum karaya are particularly affected. Natural gums will doubtless continue to be used, especially in the quality foods for which demand continues to rise in the United Kingdom and other western countries along with living standards. The outlook for these commodities would therefore appear to be reasonable, though import values have been declining somewhat of recent years (Table 14.7).

7. *Spices*

It is somewhat difficult in the twentieth century to appreciate the importance which attached to spices in the medieval world. Their real

TABLE 14.7

UNITED KINGDOM IMPORTS OF GUMS AND RESINS, 1913–1968

Quantity: thousand tons   Value: £ thousand

IMPORTS	1913		1928		1938		1958		1968	
	Quantity	Value	Quantity	Value	Quantity	Value	Quantity	Value	Quantity	Value
Arabic	} 6·7	} 229·8	5·3	434·0	6·4	216·7	11·2	1347·9	8·7	1761·8
Tragacanth			1·9	154·4	1·5	67·9	0·5	407·4	0·4	480·8
Kauri	7·3	602·9								
Rosin	87·9	1120·7	70·-	1333·6	66·0	811·0	72·8	4759·3	63·9	5612·6
Copal	—	—	9·-	397·4	10·6	270·1	3·5	418·5	1·2	141·0
Shellac, seedlac and sticklac	5·4	418·4	8·4	1742·6	6·3	272·8	4·2	864·6	3·6	739·8
Others	11·5	528·1	2·0	145·5	6·6	120·7	1·8	364·3	1·7	538·9
Total	118·8	2899·8	97·2	4207·4	97·8	1926·6	93·9	8162·1	79·5	9274·8

Source: Annual Statement of Trade

function at the time was to act as a preservative, and on occasion to lend interest to foods which lacked flavour – or possibly possessed too much of the wrong kind. Meat was very scarce during the winter months in medieval times, and what there was of it was the result of curing by salting or smoking. This process was not in general possible with offal, and the solution in this case was to spice it in salami-type mixtures, the art of charcuterie being well developed. Thus, although the market in spices is now quite a small one in the U.K. – total imports were worth rather less than £3 million for 1968 – it is one of the very oldest, the Guild of Pepperers having been established early in the twelfth century. It was spice, it will be recalled, which provided the main inspiration for the search which began in the fifteenth century for the North-West Passage to Cathay (China) and the Spice Islands. It was this produce more than any other which subsequently gave rise to the clashes between the Dutch, Portuguese and English merchants in the East when these lands of promise had been found by merchants unwilling to share their preserves.

Among the spices, pepper and ginger are the most popular, as the accompanying table shows (Table 14.8). However, best 'Calicut' ginger is now so expensive (about 300s. per cwt) that it is marketed almost entirely in the United States, while United Kingdom supplies come mainly from Africa (at an average price in the region of 100s. per cwt). Price movements, which are often related to political changes, notably the virtual absence of China as a source of supply for many years after the war, have brought about considerable changes in the pattern of trading. Many peppers (e.g. 'Mintok') are no longer offered for sale, while other spices, like best Calicut ginger, have become prohibitively expensive; Pimento, known as Jamaican pepper, for example, has increased in price from about 2d. a lb before the war to around 2s. a lb at the present time. Most pepper supplies are now of the black or white variety from Sarawak and Indonesia.

In addition to pepper and ginger, Mincing Lane brokers handle a large variety of other spices; for example, cardamoms (for curry and liqueurs), cinnamon, cloves, mace, and nutmeg. It is the last named, apparently, over which the spice 'garblers' of the Port of London authority have to take the greatest care when sorting out sound from defective produce before grading for quality. (The term 'garbler' of spices is, of course, an ancient and honorific title, appointments to these posts being one of the duties – nominally at least – of the Lord Mayor and Aldermen of the City, as prescribed by the Act of 1708 'for the well-garbling of spices').

Spices are sold in lots of one to five tons, generally on a c.i.f. basis these days, though spot sales are by no means rare; in 1964, for example, London stocks of pepper alone were in the neighbourhood of 600 tons. Because spices keep almost indefinitely, stocks are actually very

TABLE 14.8

UNITED KINGDOM IMPORTS AND RE-EXPORTS OF SPICES, 1913—1968

Quantities: thousand cwt Value: £ thousand

	1913		1928		1938		1958		1968	
IMPORTS	Quantity	Value	Quantity	Value	Quantity	Value	Quantity	Value	Quantity	Value
Pepper	117.6	361.2	109.8	962.2	68.6	125.4	66.0	821.0	58.8	878.2
Ginger	39.3	72.8	21.8	83.1	38.1	71.1	36.7	287.6	30.4	216.7
Cinnamon	7.2	21.9	4.4	22.9	5.4	17.9	11.9	71.3	14.2	159.0
Cloves a			39.0	121.0			0.6	202.3	0.4	108.6
Vanilla									11.1	329.6
Nutmeg, mace and cardamoms	79.3	231.4			3.3	28.0				
Mace							5.1	251.2		
Nutmeg							73.9	796.4		
Others			35.0	189.4	50.3	96.3			109.5	1156.4
Total	243.4	687.3	210.1	1378.5	165.7	338.5	194.1	2429.8	224.4	2848.5
RE-EXPORTS	Quantity	Value	Quantity	Value	Quantity	Value	Quantity	Value	Quantity	Value
Pepper	51.2	148.4	147.5	1195.0	27.4	55.0	2.9	36.5	1.6	30.5
Cinnamon	2.8	13.0	1.1	12.5			7.5	60.8	3.7	62.4
Ginger	13.3	23.8	10.3	30.3	3.4	7.6	2.5	17.6	13.4	127.3
Nutmeg							2.8	168.4	0.9	71.0
Nutmeg, mace and cardamoms			13.7	66.5	3.0	10.5				
Vanilla							0.1	18.5	0.02	4.6
Cloves a										
Others	52.3	155.2	15.0	76.2	7.8	26.3	7.7	144.4	4.8	72.6
Total	119.6	340.4	187.6	1380.5	41.5	99.3	23.5	446.1	24.4	368.4

a. Included in others from 1913.

Source: Annual Statement of Trade.

significant in a trade which has been notorious for speculation and the amplitude of price fluctuations. The way in which stocks play their part in speculative activity is illustrated by the fact that whereas London stocks of pepper (which normally comprise some 80 per cent of U.K. spice stocks) are often of the order of the above figure of 600 tons or even more, they were only 46 tons in November 1949 immediately after the devaluation of sterling. On the London market since the Second World War few commodities have experienced greater price instability.[11] During the 1930s there was a notorious attempt to establish a corner in pepper by a group of speculators in this country, but the attempt failed because of the enormous yield of the pepper harvest, and because they had made an inadequate estimate of the stocks of black pepper available to counter the corner. As a result, a properly constituted futures market, run by the London Produce Clearing House Ltd, was inaugurated in 1937 and continued until the outbreak of war. Business, however, was not very great; turnover was 145 tons for 1937, 120 tons for 1938, and 80 tons for the eight months of 1939 during which the market was open (Table 14.9). The terminal market was never revived after the War.

A futures market in pepper contracts exists in Amsterdam, but the most active centre of speculative activity these days is usually Singapore, where the so-called 'merchant princes' sometimes form syndicates which are notorious for the way in which they attempt to manipulate the market. Singapore is the only really large market for spices in its part of the world, and it attracts much of the output of surrounding areas, especially since Singapore merchants very frequently finance the growers. Thus, re-exports of pepper from the Singapore market were as much as 548,000 cwts per annum for 1955-9. The situation, however, is changing quite rapidly; re-exports from that market are declining – the figure was down to 371,000 cwt per annum for 1965-6, while Hong-Kong figures, though much smaller, have been growing significantly (from 3,800 cwt per annum to 22,100 over the same period). Sarawak also started its own finance and warehousing scheme in the 1960s, but Brazil has meanwhile entered the world spice market on a much larger scale. Since 1955-9, that country's exports of pepper have increased from a per annum rate of 14,700 cwt, and were 135,700 cwt for 1965-6.

United Kingdom trade in pepper has shown a declining trend since 1930-4, when its imports, at an average figure of 166,400 cwt, were second only to those of the United States (300,400 cwt). By today U.K. imports are not only considerably less than those of the U.S.A. (381,700 cwt), Singapore (295,900 cwt), and the Soviet Union (129,700 cwt), but also those of West Germany (99,700 cwt), and France (62,800 cwt). As far as spices as a whole are concerned, viewed in the perspective of rather more than half a century, import quantities fell steadily from 1913 to 1958, since when they have shown greater stability. This pattern is closely connected with the re-export trade, which has fallen from some 120,000 cwt in 1913, to about a tenth of that amount at present, as Table 14.8 illustrates. Since the U.K. has now virtually lost its former importance as a re-export centre for spices, its recent pattern of stability seems like to continue.

TABLE 14.9
LONDON FUTURES TRANSACTIONS IN PEPPER, 1911–1939

Year	Transactions (in tons)	
1911	12,290	
1912	13,120	
1913	12,440	
1914	5,130	
	Transactions (in tons)	
	White Pepper	Black Pepper
1937	50	95
1938	85	35
1939	90	50

Source: Figures supplied by the London Produce Clearing House Ltd.

8. Waxes

The only other classifiable group of goods among the list of general produce are the waxes. These are mainly used for polishes and in the paper-making trade, but some varieties are also utilized in confectionery manufacture. The fist-sized lumps of produce which roll obediently from the broker's sample packets stimulate the mind to the contemplation of the number of bees which must contribute to the fulfilment of a ten-ton order for wax. Transactions of this magnitude are frequently concluded in Mincing Lane in the course of a working day as though it was so much coal – and handled, in common with the host of other commodities subsumed under the title of general produce, for a brokerage ranging between $\frac{1}{2}$ and $1\frac{1}{2}$ per cent. The trade is not a large one. Beeswax comes mainly from Tanzania, and the U.K. import bill is of the order of £250,000 per annum. Carnuba and Ouricury waxes (mainly from Brazil) and Montan wax (from East Germany) make up most of the remainder of the import, and add a further £500,000 or so to the U.K. import bill.

9. Other Produce

At this point in the General Produce Brokers' List of Commodities Handled by Members (Not Exhaustive) we reach the miscellaneous category headed 'Other Articles'. This section is interesting not only for the items it includes but also for those which it excludes. It has been possible to trace many of the items given in the List, in the Annual Statement of Trade: Table 14.2 provides some idea of the variety of produce involved – the fact that it is incomplete must be accepted, as unavoidable, just as the omissions in the Association's own list.

TABLE 14.10

LONDON FUTURES TRANSACTIONS IN INDIGO, 1900–1905

Year	Transactions (in chests)
1900	3,380
1901	10,300
1902	7,080
1903	2,050
1904	970
1905	100

Source: Figures supplied by the London Produce Clearing House Ltd.

TABLE 14.11

LONDON FUTURES TRANSACTIONS IN SILK, 1889–1898

Year	Transactions (in bales)
1889	2,660
1890	3,760
1891	2,460
1892	1,160
1893	1,140
1894	440
1895	5,580
1896	4,840
1897	820
1898	140

Source: Figures supplied by the London Produce Clearing House Ltd.

Some of the omissions from the official list are nevertheless surprising. There is, for example, no mention of dyes, despite the fact that
the speculation in cochineal and indigo in Mincing Lane was once
notorious – but then, vegetable dyes are not much in evidence these days
(Table 14.10) Most of the other offerings are omitted from the lists for the
same reason; that is, because the trade in them has become so minute
with the passage of time that they no longer qualify for mention. Nevertheless, Mincing Lane is still the place to enquire about green snail-
shells, or to shop for the castorum of beaver or civet to serve as a base
for making perfume.

Perhaps one of the most interesting of the trades which has now
dwindled to insignificant proportions is that of ostrich feathers. As is
well known, the fashion trade dictated the widespread use of these,
together with osprey feathers and those of birds of paradise, just prior
to the first World War. However, although Paris was the centre of
the fashion trade, London was the acknowledged world market in
feathers, and at its height in 1913 an auction series for this produce
might last for as long as three days. They were held every three months
in Mincing Lane, and as much as £1 million of these feathers would
sometimes change hands during the course of a single day.

One very arresting feature of the trade in these feathers was that the
buyers were frequently Tripolitanian Arabs. These usually very large.

often short-sighted, and completely illiterate people first became involved in the periphery of the Paris fashion trade because of their expert knowledge of the feathers concerned. When ostrich feathers first became high fashion the birds were caught wild in North Africa, though ultimately the depletion in their number was such that later supplies were provided from specialist farms in southern parts of Africa. However, though they no longer had any feathers to sell, the Tripolitanian Arabs still had their expertise, and this they proceeded to exploit. They attended the London auctions and bought for re-sale to Paris. During the evenings after the auctions, they paid cash for the feathers, usually by proffering huge wallets stuffed with 100 franc notes to the Mincing Lane brokers concerned, who were expected to help themselves. Alternatively, they handed over cheque books for the brokers to fill in a cheque, and to this they then attached a thumbprint.

Usually, these improbable middlemen stayed in the same hotel, adjacent to the station where they caught the boat-train for Paris. Though the sales themselves often did not finish until after 6 p.m., the brokers' offices in Mincing Lane always stayed open to complete the documentation of the transactions affecting the Arabs. When complete, the documents were taken round to the hotel concerned and, with authorized delivery orders made out to the Cutler Street warehouse, the cases of ostrich feathers were soon on their way – often by gig – to the station, to arrive in Paris on the day following their purchase at auction in Mincing Lane.

Chapter Fifteen

THE VEGETABLE OIL, OIL-SEED AND OIL-CAKE MARKET

1. *The Origin of the Trade*

THE earliest references to oil-milling in England occur in 1377, in the parish of Gainsborough,[1] though the cultivation of oil-seeds is certainly of much greater antiquity than this; the earliest notices of hemp growing in Russia for example go back to the fifth century B.C.[2] In England, rape seed was for centuries an important agricultural crop, especially on the farmsteads of East Anglia where the soil and drainage conditions are most suitable for its cultivation. We know that rape seed was being exported, mostly to Amsterdam and Rotterdam, between about 1590 and 1650. It was used in the manufacture of cloth, for which purpose it ousted the more expensive olive oil. Rape seed was also widely used as a fuel for lamps, and the residual oil-cake as cattle-food, but with the coming of gas lighting the need for this produce gradually declined.

The modern revival in the use of edible oils started with the discovery of hydrogenation, which enabled the margarine industry established in the Netherlands during the 1870s, to switch from the use of animal to vegetable oils, which were very much cheaper. Vegetable oils are used for a variety of other products in addition to margarine, and though some interchangeability is possible, these different uses provide the basis for the classification of the many oils which come onto the market. The 'edible' oils – sometimes referred to as the 'soft' oils – consist of groundnut, soya bean, cotton seed, rape seed, sunflower, sesame, and olive oils. The 'edible-industrial' group – sometimes known as the 'hard oils' – comprise the palm, palm kernel and coconut oils, used both for certain varieties of margarine and some other foods; for soap manufacture, synthetic detergents and certain other chemical preparations. Finally, there is the 'industrial' group, which consists of the drying and technical oils used as drying agents and for lubrication. These are mainly linseed, tung and castor oils. (The last named group is now also used on a considerable scale in making certain types of nylon.)

The world's principal suppliers of vegetable oils are the U.S.A., the Philippines, and Nigeria: these three countries together account for about one half of world exports, with the U.S.A. predominant. Exports from the U.S.S.R. vie with those of Nigeria, while Canadian, Malaysian, Argentinian, Chinese and Indonesian supplies are also significant. Nowadays, a quarter of the world's exports of vegetable oils consists of soya beans and soya oil, of which the U.S.A. supplies over 90 per cent. Next in importance come copra and coconut oil, with the Philippines as predominant supplier. The third in order of importance is groundnut oil, with West Africa as the principal supplier. Sunflower seed and oil together now account for about one-eighth of world trade in vegetable oils, and the bulk of this comes from the Soviet Union.

Some three-fifths of the vegetable oil which enters international trade goes to the countries of Western Europe, and of these the United Kingdom is one of the largest importers. Mainly as the result of an increase in the demand for margarine and soap on the part of Britain's rapidly growing population, large oilseed-crushing plants were established at the principal ports of the U.K., especially during the last quarter of the nineteenth century and in the period immediately preceding the First World War, to cope with the expanding impact of this produce from tropical and sub-tropical areas. This was the era of Sir William Lever's expeditions to prospect likely districts in the Belgian Congo, and the resulting concession of 750,000 acres to be turned over to palm-oil production under the direction of a Company formed for the purpose: La Societé Anonyme des Huileries du Congo Belge, with head offices in Brussels.

In the United Kingdom, the market for vegetable oils was of course the floor of the Baltic. Despite the fact that there had at one time been an export of rape seed, hemp products from Russia were a long established import into the U.K. along with other 'Baltic goods' such as tallow, flax and corn. With the growth of import from tropical and sub-tropical areas, therefore, a venue for the sale of this produce was already in existence. In fact, because of the practice of adulterating oil, which was common in the nineteenth century, oil-crushing manufacturers had organized an Association as early as 1863, the main object of which was to establish a standard upon which linseed should be bought. The Linseed Association initially established a maximum of 4 per cent impurities; subsequently, the Association provided standards for admixture, fixed charges and fees, in connection with which they introduced standard contracts for the trade. In 1881 the Association became the Incorporated Oil Seed Association, and in 1903 opened membership to overseas interests: there were 190 of these by 1914.

The formation of an Oilseed Brokers' Association, however, had to await the exigencies of war. The Government suggested in 1917 that such an Association might be the most expeditious way of dealing with the trade. At the present time there are three Associations which are responsible for overseeing trade in oilseeds, viz. the Incorporated Oil Seed Association, the Seed, Oil, Cake and General Produce Association of Liverpool, and the London Copra Association. In addition, the oil and oil-cake trade is transacted on the contracts of two further Associations, the London Oil and Tallow Trades Association and the London Cattle Food Trade Association.

In spite of a substantial absolute growth, Britain lost her place to Germany as the principal European importer during the decades immediately before the First World War. Thus, the German imports of oil-seeds increased in quantity from nearly 600,000 metric tons in 1895, to nearly $1\frac{1}{2}$ million by 1912 (representing an increase in value from £5¼ to £23½ million), while over the same period the British industry imported annual amounts which increased from 900,000 tons to $1\frac{1}{2}$ million tons. This growth represented an increase in value from £6 million to £16 million only, because the U.K. customarily bought the less valuable sorts of oil seeds. It would appear that German policy at this time was to impose a heavy duty[3] upon imports of oils and fats, while admitting oil-seeds and oil-seed cakes free of duty. Moreover, the Indian Trade Enquiry[4] were able to point to numerous other advantages enjoyed by Germany. These included the factor of more modern machinery, the greater readiness of the German banks to extend long term credit facilities and the cheaper port facilities at Hamburg. It was this last fact, together with the port's convenient location for the Russian market, which provided the main reason for the declining British share in the transit and re-export trade in oil-seeds[5] as compared with Germany during this period before War I – though other influences such as the *surtaxe d'entrepôt* levied by France on non-European products imported from European countries must also have been significant.

Subsequently, conditions of trading have changed for all these European countries, especially during the years following World War II. Many of the oilseed producing countries, particularly India and Argentina, have established their own crushing mills and so export only the oil and cake. Despite this, however, considerable quantities of oilseeds are still dealt with by members of the various Associations. This applies particularly to linseed and soya beans shipped from Canada and the U.S.A. to the U.K. and to European countries. Significant quantities of groundnuts, too, are supplied by East African countries, Zambia, South Africa, Nigeria and Gambia. Castor seed is shipped from East Africa, Brazil and elsewhere, while cotton seed is still exported from the Sudan, Aden and Nigeria. The annual value of imports of all oilseeds and vegetable oils into the U.K. is nowadays of the order of £75 – £80 million, though the weight of the import is much less than in 1912, being at present rather less than half a million tons (Table 15.1 and Table 15.2). This is broadly of the same order as the imports into France, but less than those of West Germany, which still maintains its lead with an import of about one million tons a year.

UNITED KINGDOM IMPORTS OF VEGETABLE OILS AND FATS, WAXES, GUMS AND RESINS, 1913–1968

TABLE 15.1

Quantity: thousand tons   Value: £ thousand

	1913		1928		1938		1958		1968	
	Quantity	Value	Quantity	Value	Quantity	Value	Quantity	Value	Quantity	Value
VEGETABLE OILS										
Soya Bean	17.7	590.0	24.7	810.8	3.2	55.8	7.1	734.7	14.6	1227.6
Cotton Seed			7.5	264.0	5.7	104.4	2.0	207.1	11.5	1108.8
Ground Nut			15.8	716.8	2.8	61.8	27.7	2914.0	124.7	13068.8
Olive	9.1	515.4	9.4	711.1	9.2	495.5	2.1	496.7	3.1	935.6
Rape Seed	7.6	222.6	1.9	77.0	0.1	4.3	0.7	66.5	10.7 c	716.8
Linseed	11.9	310.7	22.5	687.0	18.8	392.0	65.1	6416.3	38.3	3754.2
Palm a	81.0	2468.8	52.1	1796.5	131.5	1902.3	182.3	14853.0	107.0	7709.1
Coconut (copra)	58.5	2558.7	63.3	2593.7	38.3	676.6	32.4	3395.4	46.9	7064.6
Palm Kernel			0.9	36.9	1.9	57.9	1.0	192.6	22.9	3129.6
Castor	1.4	41.9	3.4	147.5	3.4	97.2	14.6	1626.7	21.0	3300.0
Tung					7.6	448.1	10.9	1129.6	4.9	476.1
Others	20.4	767.8	20.9	1030.2	6.0	184.8	4.6	800.6	70.5	5646.9
Total	207.5	7575.9	222.4	8871.5	228.5	4480.5	350.4	32833.3	476.1	48138.1
FATTY ACIDS										
Soap Stock	2.6	41.5	1.7	37.4	2.6	37.9	1.5	146.9	2.2	198.9
Stearine	4.1	167.4	2.4	111.5	3.2	58.5	1.1	108.9	1.6	147.4
Oleine					1.1	23.6			9.2	775.4
Tall Oil Fatty Acids							9.8	730.5		
Other					0.5	10.6			2.5	417.5
Total	6.7	208.9	4.1	148.9	7.4	130.6	12.4	986.3	15.6	1539.2
Other Acid Oils										
WAXES										
Ozokerit or Earth Wax					0.1	12.0	1.0	453.3	0.7	520.4
Beeswax			1.1	67.8	1.6	151.3	1.3	721.3		
Carnauba, Candelilla and Ouricury			1.1	164.4	2.6	310.8				
Spermaceti (crude, pressed or refined)			1.4	175.2	0.8	45.3	0.2	71.6	0.007	1.0
Others			0.5	33.2					1.1 d	370.8
Total	4.5 b	356.8	4.1	440.6	5.0	519.5	2.4	1246.2	1.8	892.2

a. Includes Palm Kernel Oil for 1913   b. Not shown separately for 1913.
c. Includes Colza and Mustard Oil   d. Including Carnauba, Candelilla and Ouricury.

Source: Annual Statement of Trade.

TABLE 15.2

UNITED KINGDOM IMPORTS AND RE-EXPORTS OF OIL SEEDS, OIL NUTS AND OIL KERNELS, 1913–1968

Quantity: thousand tons   Value: £ thousand

IMPORTS	1913		1928		1938		1958		1968	
	Quantity	Value	Quantity	Value	Quantity	Value	Quantity	Value	Quantity	Value
Ground Nuts										
In shell	a		70·8	1154·7	8·2	69·9	5·8	535·5	3·4	390·0
Not in Shell	a		50·4	1048·4	318·2	3516·7	206·4	13155·1	114·4	8584·1
Copra	30·9	896·7	61·9	1647·9	113·7	1352·7	92·1	6237·9	47·4	4705·2
Palm Nuts and Kernels			164·3 b	3259·5	133·5 b	1329·4	273·2 b	14184·3	50·9	3640·7
Soya Beans	76·5	635·7	191·6	2202·6	98·6	765·3	127·9	4422·7	236·9	10854·5
Flax or Linseed	654·8	7195·4	348·4	5495·7	276·4	3583·5	121·0	6085·1	60·4	3553·3
Cotton Seed	615·3	4648·6	574·5	5620·4	620·5	3432·0	102·6	2715·8	20·5	695·6
Castor Oil Seed	60·3	710·6	36·9	634·4	31·8	317·4	13·9	719·1	18·6	1427·7
Rape Seed	53·1	531·7	36·9	659·2	21·2	234·0	4·4	195·3	79·3	3354·4
Others	75·5	1269·6	19·9	332·2	7·5	78·8	15·3	1570·2	34·8	4112·9
Total	1566·4	15888·4	1555·6	22055·0	1629·5	14679·7	962·5	49821·0	668·0	41385·8
RE-EXPORTS										
Ground Nuts										
In shell			0·5	10·7	0·05	0·6	0·2	18·7	0·6	84·0
Not in shell			1·1	23·4	0·02	0·2	0·3	29·3	1·8	189·2
Flax or Linseed	5·8	69·7	1·2	22·9					0·001	0·5
Rape Seed	0·3	3·8	0·2	5·9						
Cotton Seed	0·1	1·6	0·09	2·4						
Soya Beans	0·8	6·8	22·0	1·1						
Copra	16·7	481·5	0·1	584·2	0·8	3·8	0·05	1·1		0·2
Palm Kernels				2·7						
Castor Oil Seed	12·8	154·1	1·5	35·8	0·03	0·7	0·2	18·8	0·008	1·5
Others	11·3	190·2								
Total	47·9	907·8	26·8	689·1	0·9	5·3	0·7	67·9	2·5	275·3

a. Included in others for 1913.   b. Palm Kernels only.

Figures have been rounded and therefore do not necessarily add to total.

Source: *Annual Statement of Trade.*

2. *Market Interventions*

By today, markets in oils, seeds and cakes are subject to considerable intervention of various kinds. Thus, the U.S.A., alone responsible for about one-quarter of world trade in these commodities, supports prices, usually by loans granted through the agency of the Commodity Credit Corporation. The consequent expansion in production has of recent years resulted in surplus stocks of the important soya crop which have had to be bought by the C.C.C. Moreover, there has arisen an imbalance between the demand for soya meal and soya oil which has been met under Public Law 480. This permits the sale of surplus commodities on concessionary terms. Under the authority of P.L. 480, soya oil (and cotton seed oil) has been disposed of with the help of long-term credits, and given away as emergency relief to foreign countries hit by famine.

Argentina also declares support prices annually and since 1966 has announced a legal minimum price below which trade is forbidden. In the European Economic Community, the Commission has declared common support prices for rape seed and sunflower seed since July 1967. Moreover, the Community's oils and fats regulation allows compensatory levies to be made on imports of this produce at subsidized prices. A levy was in fact imposed in 1967 upon imports of sunflower oil from the U.S.S.R. and some other Eastern European countries.

In other countries, price supports are operated through statutory marketing boards, the managers of which purchase the harvests of growers at fixed prices. The produce is then sold by the boards on world markets at world prices. Because of this, the prices at which the boards purchase from the producers are adjusted periodically, though in certain cases, notably those of E.E.C. purchases from Niger and Senegal, production payments are made from the importing to the exporting countries when prices fall below established reference prices. [6]

Notwithstanding these official interventions in the marketing of vegetable oils, price fluctuations are a feature of the trade. Many edible oils and oilseed prices reached peak figures in 1965, to be followed by falling prices in 1966 and subsequently. In the case of olive oil, some attempt has been made to regulate international competition by means of the International Olive Oil Agreement of 1963, subsequently extended under a new protocol to the end of 1973. However, the international agreement does not regulate prices or stocks but attempts, largely through consultation, to control this rather unusual international market. (Production and trade are almost exclusively 'latin' – Italy is the largest producer, and also imports the greater part of the 200,000 tons which enter international trade, mostly from Spain, the world's second largest producer.)

3. Futures Trading

In certain countries, traders are able to avail themselves of the facilities afforded by futures markets. Thus, the Bombay Oilseeds and Oil Exchange Ltd re-opened after a lapse of thirteen years in June 1956 with the introduction of a contract in groundnuts; futures trading in linseed oil, linseed expellers and meal, opened in Buenos Aires in January 1958.[7] In the U.S.A., the growing interest in soya bean cultivation after the first World War led to the introduction of futures contracts in soya beans, soya bean meal, and soya bean oil in Chicago; there is also a subsidiary market on the New York Produce Exchange in soya beans and soya oil.

Soya bean meal futures are also traded on the Memphis Board of Trade. Other North American futures contracts include cotton seed oil on the New York Produce Exchange and the Chicago Board of Trade (though activity on the latter is now limited). A cotton seed meal contract is traded on the Memphis Board of Trade. Flaxseed futures are traded on the Minneapolis Grain Exchange, and also on the Winnipeg Grain Exchange: the latter also has a rape seed futures market.

On the continent of Europe a terminal market in copra exists in Amsterdam, while in Rotterdam a futures contract in linseed oil is traded.

In the United Kingdom, a futures contract in linseed oil was traded on the floor of the Baltic Exchange before the Second World War, but war-time control, when all dealing in edible and technical oils came under the control of the Ministry of Food, brought this to an end. Private imports of oil-seeds and vegetable oils were resumed only in June 1954, and it was a further thirteen years before a terminal market became a reality. Then, on 5 July 1967 a new association, the London Oil Terminal Market Association, introduced trading in soya bean oil futures – not, on this occasion, on the Baltic, but the floor of the London Commodity Exchange in Plantation House. The chief reason for this shift of venue is to be found in the presence of so many other terminal markets in Mincing Lane, and their comparative absence on the Baltic, apart from the new markets in home-grown barley and wheat. Moreover, with the growth of c.i.f. trade, transactions in oils and related products have tended (as in the case of grain) to be concluded to an increasing extent in traders' offices rather than on the floor of the Baltic. With the growth in importance of the larger broking firms skilled in the trading techniques of futures markets, it was also logical to locate the new oil terminal markets near to those of other commodities. This enables floor traders to be switched from one market to another according to the relative activity of the markets and the association officials to be in touch quickly and easily with a number of trading floors. (The first secretary of the London Oil Terminal Market

Association was also the secretary of the United Sugar Terminal Market Association, and of the Cocoa Terminal Market Association.) Finally, the excellent specialist facilities provided by the London Produce Clearing House Ltd are on hand in Plantation House to guarantee and clear the contracts. These advantages have proved sufficiently attractive not only to determine the location of the London Vegetable Oil Terminal Market Association, but also the fledgling Liverpool Cotton Futures Market.

On a more general level, the formation of the London Oil Terminal Market Association probably owes a great deal to the growing importance of oilseeds, oils and fats: thus 1967 saw a record world output (37.5 million tons) for the tenth consecutive year, the annual average rate of growth of production for the ten year period ended in 1966 having been 2.8 per cent.[8] A further factor consists in the difficulty for U.K. traders of operating in American futures markets due to government price support programmes. It is also undeniable that considerable disquiet must have been felt in U.K. trading circles following the American 'salad-oil scandal' of 1963. In that year, the Tino de Angelis empire based upon the Allied Crude Vegetable Oil Refining Corporation collapsed when it was discovered that the receipts for soya bean and other oils held by customers of the company could not be honoured, despite the fact that these warrants were supposed to represent actual oil stored at the huge tank farm at Bayonne in New Jersey. The smash was not unconnected with the Russian grain shortage during 1963, which led to negotiations for the sale of wheat from North America. This in turn inspired bullish tendencies among speculators in a variety of primary products, and the de Angelis corporation was among the heaviest speculative buyers. Unfortunately for all concerned, the New York Produce Exchange did not require processors, exporters, and other trade interests buying or selling futures as an offset to stocks or commitments, to put up any initial deposits upon these transactions. The de Angelis corporation took advantage of this ability to speculate without putting up any cash, but when prices started to fall, their brokers demanded margins amounting to some $19 million. When the Allied Crude Vegetable Oil Refinery Corporation were unable to produce this money, it heralded the beginning of the end for them. The losses due to their collapse were stated to be in excess of $100 million, and embarrassed firms on both sides of the Atlantic. In addition to causing the liquidation of one Wall Street brokerage house and the disappearance of another, the well-known Baltic Exchange firm of Faure and Fairclough were left holding several dubious receipts for considerable amounts. The upshot of this was the formation of a new company, Faure Fairclough, the shell of the old company being left to deal with commitments arising from the Allied bankruptcy. In addition to Faure and Fairclough, no less than seven London merchant banks found themselves, to borrow the words of one journalist, 'tossing in the wake'.

However that might be, on 5 July 1967 the London Oil Terminal Market Association introduced trading in contracts in soya bean oil futures on the London Commodity Exchange. The London contract was the first step in a strategy for the establishment of a number of contracts to afford cover against the possibly divergent price fluctuations in soft and hard oils. In fact, the original scheme was to introduce a coconut oil contract as the forerunner, but this planned order of events foundered due to difficulties in establishing the quality specifications for this market. Coconut oil is, in any case, a difficult commodity to tender: it solidifies when cool, so that whenever stocks have to be drawn upon, the entire tank has to be heated however small the quantity required. These problems were eventually solved by keeping relatively low stocks in each tank, and by nominating one day a week for deliveries. The next contract which actually appeared was for sunflower seed oil on the 16 May 1968, and it was not until 1 July 1969 that the coconut oil contract appeared. (All the oil contracts are for units of 20 long tons with the delivery point ex-tank Rotterdam.) The Association had decided to proceed with the third of this trio of contracts despite the rather disappointing turnover in the soya and sun oil contracts, especially in view of the opportunities for 'straddling' the market thus presented.

In addition to these three contracts a terminal market in fishmeal – in many respects a competing commodity with soya bean and other forms of animal feed and fertilizer – was opened, this time directly under the aegis of the London Produce Clearing House Ltd, on the 12 April 1967. Its inauguration was preceded by the commencement of trading in a similar contract just over a month earlier on the New York Produce Exchange.

The demand for fishmeal has increased enormously since the Second World War after it was found that the small anchovies discovered off the coasts of Chile and Peru constituted an ideal protein-rich additive to poultry-feed in the rapidly growing broiler industry. The apparent need for a terminal market was given by the considerable price fluctuations in the commodity, the price of which was tending to range between £20 and £80 per ton. After the opening of the futures market, however, the Peruvian government decided to establish machinery to try to stabilize the price. The export of fishmeal was made subject to licence from January 1967, and export marketing placed in the hands of a consortium and three syndicates. Largely as a result of this, and the failure to attract major German interests, the London Fishmeal Terminal Market closed on 25 June 1970, having been moribund for a considerable period. Meanwhile the three markets associated with the London Vegetable Oil Terminal Market Association remain open, though after an initial spurt, the turnover of each contract has declined. The great obstacle which the Vegetable Oil terminal markets have not overcome is the lack of interest shown by the very largest users of these oils, that is Unilever Ltd, H. J. Heinz Co. Ltd, and Procter and Gamble Ltd. As has already been noted in connection with other commodities, the very large size of individual enterprises militates against the success of futures markets. However, London's terminal market in sugar flourishes despite this. The answer may lie in part in very slim profit margins in the sugar trade, which makes manufacturers keener to protect them. From the speculators' point of view, the existence of very satisfactory contracts in other markets more active than those in vegetable oils (notably sugar and cocoa) has also resulted in a relative lack of interest.

Chapter Sixteen

MARKETING DOMINION WOOL

1. Early European Supplies

WHEN the nineteenth century opened, total imports of raw wool into the United Kingdom were less than 10 million lbs a year, compared with a domestic clip of 90 million lbs. The prohibition of the export of wool, which doubtless served to limit the need for imports to some extent, remained until 1825, though a clandestine trade existed, the order of which is indicated by the fact that wool exports for 1827 amounted to some 280,000 lbs.

Before the end of the century total imports had grown to nearly 700 million lbs while domestic production had increased by only 50 million lbs. This hundred year period was, moreover, witness to more than one quite dramatic switch in supply sources, as the accompanying table indicates (Table 16.1). The first of these was within Western Europe, for, whereas virtually all raw wool imports had come in duty free from Spain during the Napoleonic Wars, the return of peace and the reduction of duty upon Silesian and Saxon wool were accompanied by the growth to favour of this much improved produce. By 1828, the date of the famous Report of the Select Committee of the House of Lords on the British Wool Trade, as much as two-thirds of the total import originated in Silesia and Saxony. Despite the retention of a 1d. per lb duty, the German produce competed very successfully with South Down wool, the price of which had consequently declined between 1804 and 1827, from 24d. to 9d. per lb, compared with a fall of only 2½d. from 14d. to 11½d. in the price of long wool over the same period.[1]

John Ireland, a Blackwell Hall factor, explained to their lordships[2] that the imported wool from Germany was first collected from the small farmsteads by Jewish dealers and then sold to larger merchants who graded the fleeces before sending them to Hamburg, and thence to the United Kingdom for sale. There, according to Ireland's evidence, the produce was handled by some half a dozen houses of German origin, which sold both in London and Leeds. According to James Macarthur's testimony in a letter to his brother William in Australia, the finer German and Spanish wools were sold at the time by sample and by private contract at one month's credit, though this was sometimes extended to six months.[3] English woolstaplers languished, and little thought that within a generation imports of German wool were destined

320

to fall to less than 10 million lbs, of a total import of over 74 million lbs.

The reason for this decline lay not in any defect of quality: it was due essentially to industrialization and the accompanying growth of population in Western Europe, which served to make food production more profitable than sheep rearing. The switch in supply sources was also facilitated by the appearance of Australian wool on the British market. Antipodean wool was not an immediate success and it was some years before the major dealers were convinced that the Australian commodity had a significant future. Prominent buyers such as Benjamin Gott shook their heads over the inadequacy of Australian supplies and the great distance over which they had to be carried, though Henry Hughes, a factor at Blackwell Hall, asserted in 1827 that he could already bring wool from Sydney or Hobart Town more cheaply than from Vienna or Leipzig.[4] The Australian producers had also to disprove the suspicion among the manufacturers that 'there was a degree of harshness about the wool which rendered it fitter for Yorkshire than for the West of England'.[5]

TABLE 16.1

UNITED KINGDOM RAW WOOL IMPORTS, 1810–1850

million lbs

Year	Australasia	Germany	Spain	Total
1810		0·8	5·9	10·8
1820	0·09	5·2	3·5	9·7
1830	1·9	26·7	1·6	32·3
1840	9·7	21·8	1·2	49·4
1850	39·0	9·1	0·4	74·3

Source: A. Barnard, *The Australian Wool Market, 1840-1900* (Melbourne, 1958).

2. *Early Antipodean Supplies*

The Antipodean supplies initially consigned to London for sale were very meagre. They first appeared in the metropolis in 1807: three years later, New Holland and Van Diemen's Land are reported as having provided only 167 lbs of a total import of more than 10 million lbs. In the same year, the Cape of Good Hope supplied 29,717 lbs.[6] The wool, as was most other colonial produce at the time, was auctioned shortly after arrival in one of the London coffee houses, of which Garraway's was the most important for this commodity. In the case of domestic wool, manufacturers either purchased supplies at the fairs, or else used the services of wool-staplers. These agents were not qualified to judge the merit of colonial wool, however, so the manufacturers had at first to undertake this task themselves. London thus became, because of its port and marketing facilities, the obvious place where the produce could most conveniently change hands, though many consigning agents offered facilities to both London and Liverpool during the 1840s and 1850s.[7] Eventually, this practice died out, as too did the brief attempt to establish rival auction sale facilities for colonial wool at Bristol and Leeds.

In the producing colonies, whereas the sheep farmers of substance, such as the Macarthurs of Camden, the Rileys and some others, consigned their own produce, the numerous small growers sold their clips in the colonies to merchants and speculative purchasers who then undertook the risk of shipping the produce to London for resale at a higher price. Speculation, however, was not the only motive for the purchase of wool and its re-sale in the United Kingdom for, as Barnard points out,[8] the desire to acquire foreign exchange was a significant feature in a country where the foreign exchange market was still in a very rudimentary state. During these early days of wool export the houses which handled the commodity were general merchants. In addition to exporting other produce, they imported a variety of goods required by the pastoralists: the Dalgety organization and Elder, Smith and Co. were prominent examples of this type of business. The system worked very well during the 1830s, when the capital required for essential supplies was available only from the quick sale of produce to merchants who had access to ready money. During this period transactions were often extremely informal, and the produce frequently changed hands at the roadside leading to Sydney, when the wool was still packed high on the bullock drays making the annual journey. Otherwise, the clips were sold by auction in Sydney or Melbourne.

A great change in the mode in which British manufacturers received their wool occurred during the 1840s and 1850s, when the world's wool market became decisively centred in London. The transformation in the situation lay in the improved access to the English capital market obtained by the growers and the enforced acquiescence of the merchants in this new situation. It is an argument which compels us to reappraise the commonly accepted romantic notion of the multiplication of small growers (i.e. the 'emancipists'): there seems rather to have been a vast increase in the number of large-scale farmers. These were relatively wealthy immigrants, often in formal partnership with 'sleeping' British investors, or else having substantial friends and business acquaintances in England. In either case they were able to draw bills on London houses and discount them in Australia, a process which enabled these settlers to obtain, with an ease unknown to most of their predecessors, both short-term finance after shearing and longer-term capital for development.

The change in the situation compelled the Australian merchants to adopt a dual role for, in addition to being purchasers of wool, they became to an increasing extent consignment agents for the onward transmission of growers' wool to London. These consignment services came to be provided by such firms as Gilchrist and Alexander in the Sydney area; Dalgety, Borrowdaile and Co., and Richard Goldsbrough in the Port Philip District; and Kemp and Co. in Van Diemen's Land. Apart from the merchant houses, the main consignment agents were the banks, especially from the end of the 1860s, following the lead publicly given by the Colonial Bank of Australasia.

3. London Channels of the Trade and the Rise of Sales at Origin

The English consignees were financiers, whose complementary function was to act as agents for the wool owner. This they did both for the colonial growers and merchants, though their preference was to receive the wool consigned at growers' risk, for this gave them control over receipts from the sale of the produce. Specialized importing agencies thus developed in England which were closely connected with the antipodean exporting agencies. The New Zealand Loan and Mercantile Agency is a good example of the way in which British capital became involved in Australasian production and sales. At the same time, many merchant houses in the producing countries (e.g. the Dalgety organization and Elder, Smith and Co.) established branch offices in London. The London agents supervised the unloading and warehousing of the produce at the docks, and then arranged with selling brokers for its sale at the auctions. With the growth of import, some wool dealers and buying brokers entered the trade on a large scale, one of the bext examples of these being F. Huth and Co., who proceeded within a short space of time to build up a large continental business. The re-export trade grew to formidable proportions, as Table 16.2 indicates, since it was much cheaper for continental manufacturers to buy from London than from origin, and London was in any case the entrepôt at which clippers broke bulk and was thus the natural sales point.

By the 1870s the number of London wool selling brokers had risen to fourteen. After commissioning one of these firms (such as W. P. Hughes and Co. or Willans, Overbury and Co.), the London agents of the overseas consignor usually handed over the shipping documents, leaving the brokers to value the bales from samples drawn by official warehouse keepers. This formed the basis of the brokers' judgment of the reserve price should the consignor have stipulated that there should be one.[9] The buyers inspected the wool at the warehouses shortly before the sale and marked the catalogues supplied by the selling brokers with the selection they wished to bid for. The prospective buyers were manufacturers, or their broker representatives, and merchants.

If we are to believe John MacArthur[10] the sales at Garraway's coffee house afforded 'many opportunities for combination which it is

TABLE 16.2

UNITED KINGDOM RAW WOOL EXPORTS AND RE-EXPORTS BY DESTINATION, 1860—1967

million lbs

Year	France	Belgium	Germany	U.S.A.	Holland	Total Re-Exports	Total Exports
1860	15·7	7·9	1·3	n.a.	—	30·6	11·3
1870	50·4	18·6	10·9	4·6	—	92·5	9·1
1880	113·3	43·2	41·9	30·7	—	237·3	17·2
1890	90·3	62·7	83·2	67·2	32·1	340·5	19·5
1900	52·7	26·8	53·0	47·9	9·8	195·3	24·9
1910	94·5	72·0	92·5	62·5		335·2	37·0
1922	128·2	98·9	105·4	75·6		449·0	61·3
1930	112·5	45·0	98·2	14·1		288·2	32·7
1939	93·5	45·2	10·7	9·6		197·1	29·0
1950	26·4	23·1	15·8	12·6		114·3	45·5
1960	16·2	3·5	9·8	1·7		48·0	54·8
1967	1·7	4·9	4·2 a	7·4		15·2	38·7

Re-exports do not include treated imports for 1930–50.

a. Western Germany.

Sources: Barnard, *The Australian Wool Market 1840–1900*,
Commonwealth Economic Committee, *World Trade in Wool and Wool Textiles*,
Overseas Trade Accounts,
and the *Annual Statement of Trade*.

difficult to counteract'. The system of the time, the same writer informs us, was, as a rule, to separate the finest bales, and sell one fine lot, near the commencement 'to excite the spirit of competition as early as possible'. Other witnesses affirm that the wool auctions were sometimes very exciting indeed, whether held at Garraways or at the Hall of Commerce at which the sales were held prior to the erection of the Coleman Street Wool Exchange, which was opened in 1875. A description of a sale[11] some time later runs as follows:

> The sale takes place in one large room in the Wool Exchange on Coleman Street. Selling begins at 4 o'clock. The room is constructed similar to an amphitheatre. The moment the first lot is called out (the densely packed audience) burst forth in one wild chorus of yells and howls. The next number (is sounded) and immediately a dozen or more excited bidders leap to their feet and so on. Excitement on the Stock Exchange is tame compared with it. An Australian said: 'We call our wool sales in Sydney the dog fight, but this is the world's menagerie turned loose'.

Although the total weight of wool imports into the United Kingdom continued to grow after the end of the nineteenth century, the sale of Southern Hemisphere wool in Coleman Street reached its absolute zenith in 1895 when about a million and a half bales were sold there: it was very much a peak year for imports from these sources. By this date, however, the period of centralization of wool sales in London had really passed its peak, as auctions in producing countries ceased to be mere collecting markets for onward transmission to London and started to become central markets of world significance in their own right.

There were a number of features which accounted for this relative eclipse of the Coleman Street auction sales. Of these, the most fundamental was the development of efficient and reliable selling institutions in producing countries, and here two figures stand out in Australian history as the architects of this change. Richard Goldsbrough and Thomas Mort were wool auctioneers who determined at the end of the 1850s to compete with the consignment trade, building upon the local auction sales which had been established by Lyons and Stubbs in Sydney, and by Hind and Bakewells in Melbourne during the 1840s. Other broking firms were established, and auctions organized: the main Melbourne and Geelong houses came into being in the 'fifties and early 'sixties, while those of Sydney date from the late 'sixties and 'seventies. In Adelaide Elder, Smith and Co. established their broking business in 1878.[12] Others followed later: Hobart and Albany, for example, also established auctions before the end of the century. In each town the significant evolution was from public sale by individual firms in different buildings to cooperation by a number of brokers in mounting auctions collectively at one centre – a growth in other words, of an organized market for the convenience of (or sometimes as in Sydney in 1863, at the insistence of) the buying public.

These colonial institutions could obviously not have flourished without clients who wished to sell their wool locally rather than in London. These came from the growing number of small sheep farmers for whom the fixed costs of marketing in London were particularly onerous. As the century neared its end, however, the colonial selling brokers also succeeded in attracting the clips of the larger growers. These were obtained by canvassing and through the offer of substantial advantages in terms of selling costs, for the colonial brokers not only sold the wool but also performed the tasks usually entrusted to importing agents on the London market. The saving of this commission (of between one and two per cent), together with cheaper warehousing charges, could amount to a gain of as much as 0.355d. a lb on wool fetching 12d. a lb in London, and 8d. a lb in the colonies. To this must be added transport costs and the loss of interest involved on the long journey.

Major success in attracting business to the colonial sales, however, hinged upon the possibility of providing the growers with long-term finance. This the colonial brokers achieved by promoting local banks, such as the Australasian Agency and Banking Corporation Ltd (associated with Goldsbrough), with offices in London or other major British cities. This enabled them to accept deposits, and sell debentures; in brief, to tap the resources of the London capital market. Various other examples may be cited, such as the Union Mortgage Agency Co. Ltd, and the various Dalgety partnerships, which amalgamated to form one limited liability company in 1884.[13] The other change which took place at the same period was the migration to the colonies of agencies having their head offices in England. With reliable selling institutions, based initially upon the patronage of the small grower, once established, colonial auctions were enabled to expand to present a challenge to the London auctions by the beginning of the fourth quarter of the nineteenth century, as finance ceased to limit the facilities offered by local public sales. However, the large farmers would not have been induced to forsake the London auctions but for the pecuniary attraction of local sales. It is also widely argued that the price differential between the London and the colonial markets narrowed considerably and so eliminated the advantage of consigning to London. Certainly, during the years in which prices fell markedly (1869-70, 1871-2, and 1879-80), there was a significant rise in colonial selling. When prices recovered after 1894-5, moreover, there was an equally marked fall in local sales. It appears justifiable to conclude from the evidence that price trends after 1870 did play some part in shifting sales from London.

As far as the buyers were concerned, wool could almost invariably be bought more cheaply in the colonies than in London, even after taking transport and other costs into account. In addition to the fact that the colonial markets remained speculative ones through the 'seventies and 'eighties, there were also some savings to be effected on transport. For example, English manufacturers had the possibility of directing shipments nearer to the centres of manufacture than the port of London, while for continental traders after 1880 it became possible to ship produce direct from Australia to the continent. The chartering of ships also became more common, with attendant savings in transport costs. Meanwhile, on the other side of the Atlantic, the nature of the tariff upon wool imports made it more advantageous to import wool in the grease rather than scoured. This was more abundantly and cheaply available in the Antipodes than in London, so that the latter centre steadily lost American business after about 1867.

In the absence of powerful offsetting advantages, such trends were the inevitable accompaniment of the growth of foreign manufacturing centres. Thus, by 1880, the consumption of domestic and foreign wool in France alone was 403 million lbs compared with 355 million lbs for the U.K. That of the U.S.A. was 357 million lbs, while German consumption was 181 million lbs. Competition was intensified, particularly for British manufacturers, who saw their markets sadly eroded by French all-wool worsteds. Profit margins shrank and thus provided enterprising suppliers with their opportunity to introduce cost-saving innovations in the pattern of distribution. A new class of continental wool merchant emerged to supply the rapidly-growing continental industries. They bought to an increasing extent at the colonial auctions and re-sold by private treaty to manufacturers. Increasingly, too, wool was brought to Europe to be auctioned at centres other than London. Antwerp, growing once more as an important entrepôt,[14] was already the major European sales point for South African wool by 1860, and by the mid-seventies auction sales of Cape wool were also being held in Berlin. By 1880 public sales were being held at Roubaix-Tourcoing to serve the textile industry of Northern France, and some time later the list of auction centres included Le Havre, Bordeaux, Hamburg, Bremen, Forst and Leipzig.

For a considerable period the overall growth in the demand for wool masked the eclipse of London as the pre-eminent world market: indeed, the peak year of the London auction sales was not reached until 1895, when the quantity offered for sale was 1,688,000 bales. The number of bales offered for sale in the whole of Australia and New Zealand in the same year amounted to less than one million bales. Nevertheless, by 1922 the Sydney auctions alone had overtaken those of London. The trend has subsequently continued (apart from the boom years both before and after World War I and some increase due to speculative purchases before World War II). United Kingdom raw wool imports, as Table 16.3 shows, declined from 1,111 million lbs in 1922 to 517.9 million lbs in 1969. The total import bill is now of the order of £100 million a year. The figures for the London wool auctions are more difficult to ascertain, but are at present in the region of 150,000 bales, or rather less than one-tenth of the volume sold at Coleman Street in 1895. Meanwhile in Australia the number of bales, auctioned annually at a dozen market centres, is in the region of five million. A further 1.3 million bales are auctioned in New Zealand: altogether, more than 90 per cent of the clip in Australia, New Zealand and South Africa is now sold, either by public sale or private treaty, in the countries of origin.

The figures for re-exports in the table of U.K. Raw Wool Exports and Re-exports (Table 16.2) shows that the re-export trade continued to grow strongly in volume right up to the 1890s, the largest customer almost always being France. There was a considerable temporary revival during the post-World War I boom, after which the figures have continued to fall away. The decline since 1950 has been quite dramatic, from 114.3 million lbs to 15.2 million lbs. It would appear that the trade is now irretrievably lost.

TABLE 16.3

UNITED KINGDOM RAW WOOL IMPORTS, 1860–1969

million lbs

Years	Value £ m	Total Imports	Australia	New Zealand	British South Africa	South America
1860	11·2 a	148·4	59·2		16·6	9·0
1870	16·2 a	263·3	175·1		32·8	12·7
1880	27·2	463·5	300·6		51·4	10·3
1890	27·9	633·0	323·1	95·6	87·2	11·2
1900	22·7	559·0	250·1	136·2	32·2	35·6
1910	35·4	803·3	314·5	189·7	104·3	69·6
1922	59·9	1111·5	457·9	304·7	146·9	103·7
1930	43·5	786·5	257·0	174·7	158·2	126·5
1939	41·6 b	904·2	355·1	223·8	84·4	141·0
1950	186·2	708·5	383·6	180·1	60·5	13·2
1960	134·4	645·5	265·2	161·0	49·7	90·0
1966	110·0	521·6	139·6	135·9	40·6	107·7
1969	99·2	517·9	147·0	148·5	38·2	125·8

a. Computed values up to 1870 inclusive.
b. 1938 value.

Sources: Mitchell, *Abstract of British Historical Statistics*, The *Annual Statement of Trade* and the *Overseas Trade Accounts*.

The counterpart to this trend appears in the table of the Proportion of Exports of Raw Wool to Main Importing Countries from Main Exporting countries (Table 16.4): for the first period (1928-34), the U.K. is shown as the largest buyer of Australian, Argentinian, New Zealand and South African wool, and second only to Germany for Uruguayan wool. After the war, the table shows some interesting

TABLE 16.4

PROPORTION OF EXPORTS OF RAW WOOL TO MAIN IMPORTING COUNTRIES FROM MAIN EXPORTING COUNTRIES (Annual averages)

From:	U.K.	France	Germany	Japan	Belgium	Italy	U.S.A.	Others
			Proportion imported by:					
1928/29-1933/34								
*Australia	31·0	17·0	13·0	18·3	11·1	6·1	1·6	1·9
**Argentina	26·7	18·4	18·1	—	13·2	9·0	9·2	5·4
***New Zealand	73·3	8·3	4·6	3·1	2·7	0·9	1·8	5·3
****South Africa	33·0	25·8	19·3	—	10·3	7·5	0·9	3·2
**Uruguay	21·5	15·3	24·7	0·9 a	10·0	12·8	7·0	7·9
1956/7-1961/2								
*Australia	21·1	13·1	5·9	24·0	8·2	10·1	3·3	14·3
**Argentina	16·7	10·6	6·1	8·1	5·0	7·8	27·8	18·0
*New Zealand	34·5	17·9	6·7	4·6	6·2	5·5	12·8	11·9
*South Africa	21·1	18·5	15·7 b	5·8	4·5	11·3	12·6	10·6
**Uruguay	23·6	6·1	9·0	1·3	2·4	5·3	13·0	38·9
1965/66-1967/68								
*Australia	10·9	8·4	6·6	33·9	6·6	10·1	5·8	17·8
**Argentina	18·6	6·8	5·4	9·7	5·0	10·0	19·4	25·1
*New Zealand	22·3	14·7	6·0	9·2	6·4	5·7	15·2	20·4
*South Africa	16·1	17·6	14·1	16·1	3·9	14·1	12·2	5·9
**Uruguay	42·2	2·0	5·9	2·9	2·0	2·0	18·6	24·5

a. Figures not available for 1928/29.
b. East and West Germany to 1958, West Germany from 1959.
*Season July to June.
**Season 1 October to 30 September.
***Calendar Years.

Sources: Imperial Economic Committee, *Wool Production and Trade 1928/1934*, (London, 1935) and the Commonwealth Secretariat. (Commonwealth Economic Committee), *Industrial Fibres*.

changes: Japan has long since become the most important buyer of
Australian wool, purchasing twice as much as the U.K. of recent years.
On the other hand, the U.K. is now the most important buyer of
Uruguayan wool by a considerable margin, the Germans having
effected a considerable shift in favour of South African produce.

4. *The London Sales*

Though the quantities of wool offered for sale at the London Wool
Exchange no longer match those at Sydney and some other centres,
the London sales nevertheless still attract an international clientele.
The domestic industry in the U.K. is a large one, and the variety of
produce used is reflected in the wide selection of qualities usually to be
found on offer. London remains a convenient centre for some smaller
manufacturers, both in Britain and on the continent, who are precluded
by their lack of size from having an organization which enables them
to purchase the raw material half way around the world. The larger
domestic and some continental manufacturers, too, continue to rely
upon the London sales series for their marginal spot supplies, either at
one remove through stockholders, or else directly.

The six firms of wool-selling brokers who handle the wool sales had
amalgamated into one organization when the government intervened
in the trade during World War II. The wool which they handle is
frequently 'second-hand' wool, which has already changed hands in
an auction chamber or by private treaty in its country of origin. It is
consigned by the merchant owner, by a bank, by a grower, or else by
organizations such as Dalgety's, to the selling brokers in London.
(In addition to selling about one-quarter of the total number of bales
auctioned in Australia and New Zealand, Dalgety's provide advances
against stock and crops, an activity which it has extended of recent
years through amalgamation in 1961 with the New Zealand Loan and
Mercantile Agency Co. Ltd. In addition to wool, Dalgety's act as
agents for grain, sisal, coffee, tea, sheepskins, meat, dairy products,
tallow, copra and minerals. They operate as shippers of produce,
wharf and bonded-store owners, in addition to being travel and insurance agents.) When the wool comes into the hands of the London Wool
Selling Brokers Ltd the bales are warehoused, and a proportion of them
are placed on the display floors: the display of the entire offering is
now precluded by the high labour costs involved. Samples are taken
from 'blows' cut in the 'gunny' (i.e. holes cut in the sacking) and placed
on trays or baskets at the Port of London Authority or other warehouses
(such as those of Reber, Cook and Garnham) set aside for the storage
of this produce. The selling brokers value the wool for the sellers and
prepare catalogues for distribution to prospective buyers. These are
manufacturers, merchants and buying brokers. Most frequently it is the
buying brokers who do the actual bidding at the auctions, even though

their principals may also be present. Buying brokers are experts in the commodity, as well as in auction-room bidding. They may receive an order, for example, to purchase '100 bales 46-50 good topmaking, limit 60d. "clean price"' (i.e. washed and combed). The broker is expected as a matter of course to be able to estimate to within a one-per-cent margin of error, from inspection of wool in the grease, what the clean scoured yield will be. For his expertise in selection and bidding, the broker is paid a commission of from one to two per cent. In other cases, the wool for which the broker bids in the auction chamber will have been chosen by his principal. Catalogues are marked and, when the appointed hour arrives, would-be purchasers assemble at the auction chamber, which since the early 1960s has been one of twin chambers formerly used by the London Fruit Exchange, Spitalfields. (With the restriction of imports of fruit, during the war and after, and when exchange rate changes virtually priced North American apples out of British markets, one auction room became surplus to the Fruit Exchange's requirements).

Entry to the auction chamber from second-floor level reveals a large amphitheatre of solid oak pews, occupied by the buying brokers, merchants and manufacturers, perusing their catalogues and attending to the bidding. Separate catalogues are issued for each series, of which there are seven or eight during the course of a year, each lasting for about one week. The pages of these catalogues, reading across, provide, firstly, abbreviated descriptions of the wool, followed by identification letters and symbols; finally comes the number of bales of the particular lot, together with a star should the bales number three or less. In order to expedite the sales 'starred lots' continue, as in the Coleman Street Exchange, to be auctioned separately.

The proceedings are conducted by auctioneers, who change every hour. An initial figure is suggested from the rostrum, and bidding proceeds by increments of a farthing a lb when the bids are under 75d. per lb. Thereafter they change by ½d. Bids are difficult for the uninitiated to follow, for the tens and units are omitted in the interest of speed. When the tap of the auctioneer's hammer signifies a sale, a member of the firm of selling brokers on the rostrum makes a note of the price, which is afterwards checked with the buying broker. Should a lot be withdrawn through failure to reach the reserve price sometimes stipulated, the selling brokers are obliged, for a period of an hour after the sale, to inform the highest bidder, before selling the withdrawn lot to anyone else. Details of the withdrawn lot, including the highest price bid, are otherwise displayed on a notice-board on the elevated 'promenade' at the back of the auction chamber, so that anyone who wishes to bargain for it may approach the brokers with an offer.

Nowadays, wools offered at auction are not confined to those already in warehouses in the U.K. Scoured New Zealand wool is at present also sold c.i.f. by means of 10 lb samples flown in for inspection. Of this quantity, 3 lbs are retained by the London Wool Selling Brokers Ltd, as a sealed sample for purposes of arbitration in case of dispute, while the remainder is available for inspection by prospective buyers on the show floor of a warehouse. Some private treaty sales have always taken place alongside the public sales in the main market centres: in fact, the public sale of wool was discontinued many years ago in the U.S.A., while in the South African centres of Port Elizabeth, East London and Cape Town, a significant proportion of growers' wool is sold by private treaty. As far as London is concerned, most Italian wool is now sold by private treaty through the London Wool Selling Brokers, the usual practice being for the overseas merchant to specify the price required.

5. *Wartime Control*
During both world wars the peacetime method of distributing wool was discontinued. In addition to instituting the compulsory purchase of the domestic clip at a fixed price, the British government negotiated for the purchase of Dominion wool from the central selling agencies set up in those countries. During World War I the auction of wool was suspended from 1916, the produce being categorized instead into 848 different types. The wool surplus to Australian and New Zealand requirements was sold to Britain at a price 55 per cent greater than that prevailing at the outbreak of war.

The scheme was a success in the sense that it ensured the continuity of supplies to manufacturers, to whom they were sold at a fixed price. After the end of the war the British-Australian Wool Realization Agency Ltd (B.A.W.R.A.) was established, as the result of negotiations between the Australian Central Wool Committee and the British Director of Raw Materials, in order to control the liquidation of stocks and help stabilize prices. With accumulated stocks standing at more than $5\frac{1}{2}$ million bales, prices would have slumped disastrously without some such body as BAWRA. On more than one occasion during the 1920s, moreover, when prices weakened significantly, many of the growers expressed considerable regret at the passing of a central organization which had so effectively controlled the supply offered for sale on the market.

Upon the outbreak of war in 1939 the British government contracted to purchase the entire Australian and New Zealand wool clip, and undertook to do this also for the first postwar year. An average price (of 13.4375d. Australian per lb greasy) was agreed upon, and revised upward by 15 per cent in 1942. In the producing countries the organization of sales was, as during the previous war, in the hands of Central Wool Committees which supervised the appraisement of the wool.

As Munz points out, the personnel involved (i.e. wool selling-brokers, wool buyers and the shipping houses) was identical with the peacetime personnel.[15] On this occasion a Table of Limits was prepared, which classified the Australian clip into some 1,500 types and sub-types. An estimated yield for each type of wool was worked out and related to the average price payable by the British government for the entire clip, so as to determine the price of each category of wool. Inside the U.K. normal channels of distribution were suspended but, as the war approached its final stages, the chief officials of the control, in consultation with representatives of the industry, evolved a scheme for the re-instatement of wool merchants and top makers. The Control sold wool at fixed prices to wool merchants and top makers, and they in turn sold wool or tops to spinners and manufacturers, also at fixed prices which allowed a profit margin.[16]

At the end of the war the trade was presented with much the same problem of the liquidation of accumulated stocks (equivalent to about two years' clips), as in 1919. On this occasion, however, the solution adopted was the establishment of a private company, registered as U.K. Dominion Wool Disposals Ltd (Joint Organization).[17] The J.O. was established to hold, buy and sell wool after hostilities ceased, when the trade was gradually allowed to buy more wool: the Wool Control came virtually to an end as early as 30 September 1946. The Joint Organization was authorized to draw up schedules of reserve prices at which it would itself buy wool, and to stimulate demand by any appropriate means. The J.O. thus had wider powers than the BAWRA, its post-World War I predecessor.

The London Wool Conference of 1945, at which it was agreed to set up the Joint Organization, affirmed that wool auctions should be resumed as soon as practicable, and public sales were in fact held at Liverpool as well as in London, the last one being on 27 October 1950. The J.O. started with a stock of 10.4 million bales, valued at £170 million, which it was thought at the time might take twelve or more years to dispose of. In fact it was all sold before the end of 1951, after which the J.O. went into liquidation. Before it did so, however, the International Wool Study Group had canvassed support for a permanent successor to the J.O., which would operate reserve prices and, if necessary, buy in the wool. A scheme for a joint fund of £66 million to finance a buffer stock was eventually drawn up, but it was rejected by Australia; New Zealand, however, started one of its own in the 1951-2 season.

6. *Futures Trading*

The 1951-2 season was, of course, a year after the outbreak of the Korean conflict, with its accompanying spectacular rise in most primary product prices. Wool prices rocketed by 40 per cent at the opening of the season in September 1950, and rose still further after the Americans entered the market to buy for the stockpile. Prices plumetted when they later withdrew. It was these 'boom-bust' conditions which served to revive talks, in British wool circles, of the possibility of establishing price risk insurance for the trade. There had been a wool top terminal market at Antwerp from as early as 1884. Subsequently, futures markets in wool were established at Roubaix and New York, the latter being run by the Wool Associates of the New York Cotton Exchange. When wool prices were disturbed by the Korean war, some wool firms managed to wring permission from the exchange control authorities to use the Roubaix, and even the Antwerp and New York markets in order to hedge their trading risks. None of the markets was in the sterling area, and of the three the two last named involved the use of 'hard' currencies. However, such action was only attempted by a few of the most persistent, the obstacles presented by exchange-rate calculations and the different standards used as the basis of contracts being a sufficient deterrent to prevent others from applying to do so. Market conditions in these foreign centres also differed a good deal from those in the U.K., and the New York and Roubaix futures contracts proved especially unsatisfactory hedging media for British trade interests for this reason.

A number of top makers eventually approached the Board of Trade to ask for assistance to enable them to use the New York market, and this led the Board to remit the question of whether a futures market should be set up in the U.K. to the Wool Textile Delegation. This body's sub-committee reported adversely, and there was considerable controversy in the trade: those opposed to the notion tended to reiterate the conclusion, widely held in Bradford when similar proposals were made in the 1930s, that the existing system of forward contracting in wool-tops provided sufficient price insurance. Despite this opposition, Antony Gibbs and Sons proposed to the Board of the London Produce Clearing House that the possibility of establishing a terminal market in the U.K. should be examined. After some hesitation about whether Bradford or London should be the venue for the market, it was decided to go ahead. Arrangements were concluded with the Bank of England for the establishment of a 'wool scheme' to enable traders to obtain foreign currencies in order to engage in arbitrage operations with overseas futures markets and, on 29 April 1953, the London Wool Terminal Market, on the ground floor of Plantation House[18] was opened for trade (Table 16.5).

Provision was made in the Association for two types of member: floor members and associate members, the latter being divided into a home and overseas membership. (Home associate members number sixty, of whom twenty are wool-clearing members of the London Produce Clearing House Ltd. The overseas associate members number

TABLE 16.5
LONDON FUTURES TRANSACTIONS IN WOOL, 1953–1970 a
(Contract unit 5,000 lbs)

thousand lbs

Year	Transactions
1953 b	34,695
1954	95,045
1955	73,100
1956	108,755
1957	184,780
1958	202,885
1959	281,850
1960	269,540
1961	265,780
1962	149,090
1963	238,235
1964	233,550
1965	162,970
1966	121,700
1967	140,000
1968	95,000
1969	40,000
1970	26,590

a. The Crossbred Wool Tops Contract, which was current from 2 November 1956 to the 23 January 1961, turned over 16,475,000 lbs of business. The Greasy Wool Contract, current from 30 April 1963 to 31 December 1964, registered a turnover of 7,686,000 lbs. Trading in a Dry Combed Top Contract commenced on 2 December 1968. Trading in the Oil-combed Top Contract ceased on 23 March 1970.

b. From 30 April 1953.

Source: Figures supplied by the London Produce Clearing House Ltd.

some seventy-three of whom seventeen are, at the time of writing, wool-clearing members of the L.P.C.H. Ltd.) The initial entrance fee was fixed at £650, with annual subscriptions of £105 for all members. As on the other terminal markets, all business has to be transacted through floor members. The minimum commission per contract unit for purchase or sale is: home and associate members £5, non-members £10. Should the contract be fulfilled by tender of produce, additional commissions of like amount are payable by both seller and buyer.

Floor members include international commission houses such as Bache and Co. (London) Ltd and Merrill Lynch, Pierce, Fenner and Smith (Brokers and Dealers) Ltd – two American-owned companies – and G. W. Joynson and Co. Ltd, a London firm. Other floor members are U.K. registered branches of enterprises whose parent firms are foreign merchants – thus Diversalon Ltd is French owned, while Wm. Houghton and Co. (Futures) Ltd is a subsidiary of an Australian shipping firm: Kreglinger and Masural (Futures) Ltd is the subsidiary of a Belgian banking house, while Lohmann and Co. Ltd is an offshoot from an Amsterdam company. Other firms, such as R. G. Bailey and Co. (Futures) Ltd and Schwartze Buchanan and Co., are essentially extensions of merchant interests, while the top-makers and manufacturers are represented on the list of floor members by Richard Fawcett and Sons Ltd, Hirsch, Son and Rhodes (Futures) Ltd, and Nichols and Co. (Woolbrokers) Ltd.

The London Wool Terminal Market Association initially provided its market with a contract in Bradford 64's B Top (the Merino wooltop contract), which was the basis contract in use in the American, Belgian and the French markets at the time. The adoption of a 64's, therefore, provided the opportunity for arbitrage. The unit of trading was 5,000 lbs with a weight tolerance of 200 lbs over or under. It was a basis contract; that is, the Association's rules were framed to permit the tendering of tops of between Bradford 70's and 60's quality with an appropriate premium or discount in price. These differentials are fixed at the beginning of each month by the Association's management committee by reference to relative values prevailing on the actuals market. The contract could be traded in for eighteen months ahead, ten 'positions' being normally quoted in addition to the current month.

The London Wool Terminal Market opens with a call at 11.15 a.m. and open trade is carried on around the ring until 1 p.m. The market opens for business again at 2.15 p.m. and is finally called over at 4.55 p.m. However, the official call is the opening call at 11.15 a.m. Closing prices, for clearing purposes, are decided by a Floor Committee. Deposits of £100 per contract are required by the London Produce Clearing House Ltd, in addition to subsequent margins. Quotations are in pence per lb, the minimum fluctuation being 0.1d.

The terminal market got off to quite a good start and, within a short time, the contract turnover at Antwerp and New York was overtaken. By 1956 annual turnover was more than 100 million lbs and, at the end of that year, a Crossbred contract was introduced. This Bradford 50's Carded Top contract was also a basis contract, with tenders allowed from Bradford 50's super, down to 46's quality, with appropriate discounts.

Some years later new ground was broken in Australia with the establishment in Sydney of a Greasy Wool futures market on 11 May 1960. It was this development, together with the tendency of the London wool-top market to become rather more idle, which resulted in a decision to discontinue the Crossbred contract on 23 January 1961. It was felt in some quarters that the London tops contracts had become too exclusively 'Bradford' and lacked sufficient international appeal. This certainly tended to be true during periods of heavy deliveries in that manufacturing centre – and it will be recalled that, when the formation of a terminal market was under discussion, Bradford was very actively canvassed as its most natural locale. Ultimately, however, the proximity of financial and clearing house facilities, together with London's tradition as the centre of the market for Dominion wool, prevailed. The upshot is that the secretary of the London Wool

TABLE 16.6

COMPARATIVE TURNOVER OF THE WORLD'S FUTURES MARKETS IN WOOL

(In contract units of 5,000 lbs)

1 April–31 March	London	New York	Sydney	Antwerp	Roubaix
1963/64	50,946	31,796	102,389	6,174	10,434
1964/65	42,195	29,051	119,844	8,191	14,131
1965/66	29,970	40,929	68,133	6,330	10,310
1966/67	22,885	28,432	63,414	6,963	9,527
1967/68	29,629	16,486	72,762	9,011	7,104
1968/69	16,093	8,658	43,053	6,330	6,022
1969/70	6,037	5,250	40,523	2,401	5,144
1970/71	5,165	3,297	69,372	2,619 a	5,040

a. 1 April - 31 December, 1970

Source: Compiled from figures supplied by the London Produce Clearing House Ltd, the Secretary of the Sydney Greasy Wool Futures Exchange Ltd, the Commercial Attaché of the Belgian Embassy and the Commodities Editor of the Financial Times.

Terminal Market has to spend a fair proportion of his time in Bradford consulting with local trade interests there.

Meanwhile, the Sydney Greasy Wool futures market continued to flourish, and a similar contract, described as 64's Good Topmaking Australian Merino Fleece, was established on the London market on 30 August 1963. It only remained extant, however, until 31 December 1964, during which time 1,281 contracts of 6,000 lbs each were turned over. Despite the fact that the turnover of the merino contract had been declining, the London greasy wool contract foundered for lack of support. Some traders (particularly in Bradford) held the view that the basis of the contract should have been 'delivered Bradford' rather than London, while others felt that the deliverable range of wools was not sufficiently wide to allow the market to flourish. Arbitrage operations with the important Sydney market also proved difficult owing to the lack of overlap in the times for which the two markets were open – Australian prices were thus being made while U.K. traders were all asleep. When reasons are sought for the failure of a particular contract, moreover, it must be borne in mind that it is often difficult to establish a new contract when a reasonably satisfactory one already exists. The tendency is either for the new contract to fail to catch on, or else for it to kill the existing one: the financial interests necessary for the maintenance of a broad continuous market will see no reason for switching their allegiance to a new contract when they find the existing one perfectly satisfactory. Traders, too, will have no incentive to try to make a new market when the price fluctuations of the basis grade are broadly in line with the fluctuations of the grade or type of produce in which they are interested.

The accompanying table of turnover figures for the world's wool terminal markets (Table 16.6) indicates that, after 1963, the volume of business declined in all of them, though the small Antwerp and Roubaix markets have not suffered to the same degree as the others. The greatest decline has occurred in the Sydney and London markets, as the result of which the annual turnover on the latter is now of the same order as that of New York. Despite the loss of about half of its 1963-4 turnover, the world's largest wool futures market is now at Sydney. (As was observed in Chapter 8, since November 1969 this market has been served by the London Produce Clearing House Ltd.)

Thus far no mention has been made of the Japanese markets, for the very good reason that they are virtually of domestic interest only. No written rule exists which prohibits overseas operators, but even should they wish to trade, the Japanese monetary authorities impose such tight exchange controls that it is virtually impossible to do so. However, it is interesting to note that textile exchanges were established as early as 1950 in Osaka, and in 1951 in Nagoya and Tokyo. The Tokyo Textile Commodities Exchange ran a market in knitting yarn from October 1953, but this was eventually wound up five years later in favour of a worsted contract. Meanwhile, futures transactions were for worsted yarns from the outset at both the other exchanges. Market organization in Japan is closely similar to that elsewhere, the deals being concluded by floor members, who are restricted in number. Settlement is, however, on a cash basis, there being no clearing houses attached to the markets. The contract units are for lots of 300 kilogrammes and the average monthly turnover (January–August 1971) is, Nagoya 63,000 lots, Tokyo 83,000 lots and Osaka 38,000 lots. This average monthly range of between 25 million and 55 million lbs turnover, compares with an average monthly figure of some 29 million lbs for Sydney, the largest of the non-Japanese markets. On the same basis of calculation, both London and Roubaix come out at some 2 million lbs with New York and Antwerp at approximately 1.4 million lbs. Thus, even though the Japanese markets have no international significance, they are obviously considerable in size, and a well-developed feature of the domestic wool industry.

The Japanese textile exchanges also run futures contracts in cotton yarn and, interestingly, in rayon filament. There are as yet no markets in greasy wools or in wool tops, though it is understood that they are under active consideration. With a successful greasy wool futures market operating in Sydney, it would be surprising were Australia's best customer for wool not to establish one or more of these markets when Japanese exchange control regulations permit.

Activity in the world's wool futures markets has been adversely affected for some years now by the steady decline in wool prices. There has been no violent fluctuation in price and so hedging and speculative activity has been discouraged. On the London market it was widely believed during 1968 that the nature of the contract, that is, in oil-combed wool tops, detracted from the usefulness of the market, for most continental and British top makers had by that time made the change from oil to dry-combing. Accordingly, a new contract in Dry-Combed Wool Tops was introduced on 2 December 1968, and the old contract ceased on 23 March 1970. The new contract is the first of its kind in the world. The advocates of the new contract argued that, since oil combing is now largely confined to Bradford, London futures trading was tending to serve only a local market. (The settlement of contracts by tender to continental manufacturers was out of the question because Bradford oil-combed tops are quite unsuitable for most European textile machinery.) The new contract unit is, as before, one of 5,000 lbs, but the delivery is based on Rotterdam warehouses in the hope of capturing continental business. Despite these efforts, however, turnover has continued to decline on both the London and other markets. Meanwhile, auction prices have declined to such low levels that both New Zealand and South Africa have virtually had to abandon their systems of reserve prices; producers have been forced to stockpile so much wool that it became too expensive to maintain. The Wool Commission in both these countries has now determined to operate through a deficiency payments system, and to intervene in the markets to purchase wool where possible to try to sustain prices. However, the prices which both commissions are prepared to pay will be flexible, and adjusted in accordance with market fluctuations. With prices at a twenty-year low level, no other policy appears possible. In introducing a new statutory authority to market its wool clip, which is to start operating in mid-1971 under the title of the Australian Wool Commission, the Commonwealth Government did not feel able to do anything other than to follow the examples of New Zealand and South Africa by announcing that its Commission, too, would pursue a flexible reserve price policy.

7. *Wool versus synthetics*

Most of the weakness in the wool markets – and indirectly therefore the inactivity of associated terminal markets – is explained by the growing importance of synthetic materials on world markets. Synthetic fibres are produced and sold by a comparatively small number of large-scale manufacturers, sometimes with the benefit of unexpired patent rights. The prices of these man-made fibres are, therefore, fixed in effect by these manufacturers and though they may be changed from time to time, they are free from short-term fluctuations. Because many of these fibres are regarded as close substitutes for wool the demand for the latter is clearly affected by its price relationship with synthetics. This situation results in a tendency to stabilize, and to weaken, the price of raw wool. Thus the future prospects for both the London sales of Dominion wool and the London Wool Terminal Market are obviously bound up a good deal with the outlook for the British wool textile industry. This is in turn influenced greatly by the development both of man-made fibres and of strong competition from foreign textile industries.

The decline in the volume of British wool imports is apparent from inspection of Table 16.3. Even more spectacular is the fact that Japan currently takes more than one-third of the Australian clip, compared with a little more than ten per cent for each of the two next largest customers, Italy and Britain. (The last named is tending just recently to fall to third place.) In fact, Japan now consumes more than ten per cent of the world's raw wool exports and this figure is expected to increase rapidly in the foreseeable future. Furthermore Japan, largely as a result of the subsidization of its wool-processing industry, is increasingly scouring Australian wool for European customers, formerly an important British interest. Considerably more scouring is also undertaken in Australia nowadays, encouraged by rising freight and insurance rates.

Freight charges from distant countries of origin also constitute an encumbrance to the wool industry in its fight against man-made fibres, the output of which is currently expanding at about six times the rate of increase of wool production. Over the past few years substantial reductions have been announced in the prices of artificial fibres (bri-nylon carpet fibre, for example, was 82d. a lb in 1964, but three years later its price was down to 54d. per lb). In their staple form the major man-made fibres are now cheaper than merino wool,[19] while the enormous growth in the capacity of the man-made fibres industry, economies of scale, and the abandonment of gentlemen's agreements among the large producers, hold out the promise of still lower prices for the future. The substantial fluctuations characteristic of wool prices in the past have also been detrimental to the continued use of wool as a raw material. Each time wool prices rise manufacturers tend to substitute one or other of the three types of synthetic fibre; that is, polyamide (nylon), polyesters (terylene) or acrylics (courtelle, orlon and acrilan). When wool prices decline, on the other hand, little or no substitution of wool in place of man-made fibres takes place. There is no guarantee that the low price will be maintained, since wool prices, unlike those of artificial fibres, immediately reflect upward fluctuations in demand.

A further set of reasons for the rapid advance of man-made fibre output lies in the fact that most of the technical advances are taking place in that field rather than in the processing of the natural fibre.

Machine knitting, for example, has grown rapidly lately at the expense of weaving, and the knitting process is able to absorb a greater proportion of synthetic yarn than weaving. Again, the production of tufted carpeting is expanding enormously, at the expense of some woven carpet production, and wool accounts for only 2 per cent of the pile of tufted carpets compared with 63 per cent for woven carpeting.[20] Further innovations include the introduction of a 'high twist' or 'compressive crimp' to man-made fibre carpeting, the effect of which is to make it handle more like wool, while a texturing process known as 'bulking' has increased the moisture absorbency of artificial yarn.

By contrast with this history of development, major technical advances in wool processing are harder to find. The Belgians have invented a machine for scouring wool by solvent. A machine has also been developed to determine the precise yield of greasy wool,[21] which will undoubtedly enable buyers to bid with greater confidence at auctions and will foster the growth of wool sales on a guaranteed-yield basis. Such developments may tell in the end against the auction system altogether. The continuing growth in the importance of man-made fibres, too, may well exert pressures in the same direction ultimately. It seems reasonable to suppose that wool prices will come to be dominated increasingly by the prices of artificial fibres, whether or not wool succeeds in establishing an acknowledged differential for itself over the synthetic product. The influence of an increasingly important man-made fibres industry will, therefore, be in the direction of wool price stability, thus encouraging private treaty sales. From the producers' point of view, too, greater price stability would appear to be in their interest, especially since, as the Australian Bureau of Agricultural Economics has recently confirmed, U.K. demand (and by implication world demand) for wool is becoming more responsive to price changes than hitherto. The overwhelming likelihood, therefore, is of a further decline in the weight of wool offered in the London auctions in the foreseeable future. The analysis also points to a similar continuing decline in the demand for the facilities offered by the London Wool Terminal Market.

Chapter Seventeen

THE LONDON METAL EXCHANGE

1. *Early U.K. Metal Markets*

In pre-industrial Britain the use of non-ferrous metals was quite limited. Copper was used for kitchen-ware, brass-ware and coinage, though in wartime the need to cast additional cannons, other arms and 'copper-bottomed' naval vessels, always gave rise to a considerable increase in demand. The pattern was much the same for lead, the peacetime use of which was confined to the manufacture of pipes and sheets for roofing. In time of war, however, demand was augmented by the need for lead-shot. Tin was mainly used for pewter-ware, while zinc was not much in demand apart from the amount required to make small quantities of brass. Because of these relatively limited requirements, the export of non-ferrous metals from domestically-mined ores persisted well into the nineteenth century. This was handled by merchant stockholders who, when Britain became an importer of these metals, turned their attention to the re-export trade.

The Worshipful Company of Pewterers and the Haberdashers exercised almost complete control over the distribution of tin from medieval times until about 1660.[1] Ultimately, however, Cornish businessmen and the associated tin smelters succeeded in ousting the London financiers and, by the early nineteenth century, the system of distribution was by consignment of block tin from Cornish smelters to agents in London, Birmingham and Bristol. Export was either through merchants and agents to Europe, or else further afield via the East India Company. Meanwhile, tin from the East was virtually excluded from Britain by a 60 per cent *ad valorem* duty. Even so, the Warehousing Act of 1823, which permitted the import and subsequent re-export of tin and copper without payment of duty, gave rise to a flourishing re-export trade of Straits and Australian tin to the continent.[2] The higher tin content of this ore from overseas led to the reduction of duties in 1838 and 1842 and so to the growth of import. Subsequently, with the rise of the canning industry, United Kingdom consumption grew from some 6,600 tons of tin metal in 1860 to 13,800 tons in 1875. The rapid increase in the import and re-export of block tin after mid-century is shown in Table 17.1. In fact, by the 1870s London merchants were finding a market in the U.K. or elsewhere for more than one-half of all foreign tin produced.

They had become the clearing house not only for Cornish tin but

TABLE 17.1

UNITED KINGDOM IMPORTS AND RE-EXPORTS OF TIN, COPPER AND LEAD, 1845–1938 (10 year annual averages)

thousand tons

YEARS	TIN			COPPER			LEAD		
	Imports		Re-exports	Imports		Re-exports	Imports		Re-exports
	Ore	Blocks etc	Blocks etc	Ore a	Unwrought and part wrought	Unwrought and part wrought	Ore	Pig and Sheet Lead	Pig and Sheet Lead
1845–54		1·7	0·6	48·5	2·9	0·9	b	9·7	3·2
1855–64		3·2	0·7	93·1	11·4	4·1	0·7	19·6	b
1965–74		6·6	1·6	99·0	32·1	16·0	12·3	53·7	b
1875–84		19·6	8·9	140·6	38·5	14·0	16·5	94·4	4·1
1885–94	2·3	29·1	16·1	200·9	42·5	13·7	19·4	147·0	12·0
1895–04	8·4	33·3	20·1	176·2	67·6	14·5	31·6	201·2	13·7
1905–14	25·9	43·9	31·1	155·8	101·9	18·7	16·9	215·5	13·6
1915–24	39·4	24·1	13·7	43·5	129·1	8·2	6·6	190·9	11·5
1925–34	61·6	11·7	6·1	38·6	172·5	5·8	2·6	290·5	15·7
1935–38	50·9	15·1	7·8	15·5	352·8	73·8	0·3	365·4	27·2

Southern Ireland treated as foreign from 1 April 1923.

Copper a   Includes regulus and precipitate.
           Postwar figures for copper ore are negligible.

Lead b.   Negligible

Tin and Copper   1845–54 year ended 5 January following. From 1855, calendar years.

Source: Mitchell, *Abstract of British Historical Statistics*.

for the output of the Straits and Australia; users in Germany, France and the United States depended upon them for most of their requirements. Only Amsterdam, where the produce of the Dutch islands of Banca and Billiton continued to be sold at bi-monthly auctions, rivalled London as a market.[3]

From 1725 sales of Cornish copper ore were held in Redruth at frequent intervals. 'Parcels' of ore from each mine, previously sampled by the smelters' agents, were bid for by means of 'tickets' on which each smelter wrote his offer before sealing it and handing it in to the sellers.[4] While the smelters were a small, closely-knit group, the sellers' organization (known as the 'mines adventurers') appeared to have no provision for withholding ore during periods of glut.[5] By the nineteenth century this method of sale had, nevertheless, spread to Swansea, where the smelting firms emulated the behaviour of their eighteenth century predecessors at Redruth by colluding to secure ores at low prices.[6] Copper ore began to be imported during the 1830s to augment the domestic supply and, by mid-century nearly all the world's copper ore was being shipped to Swansea for smelting. Braithwaite Poole's figures for 1849 show that of the British ores some 13,000 tons were purchased at the Swansea and Cornwall ticketings compared with only 500 tons purchased by private contract. Of the foreign ores, 8,000 tons were purchased at the Swansea ticketings compared with only 1,000 tons bought by private treaty.

By the 1860s, however, the structure of the copper trade was beginning to change. Provoked by the exercise of monopoly power by the Swansea smelters (who colluded both to buy ore at low prices and to sell copper bars at high prices) the Chilean producers determined to establish their own smelting facilities. As a result, domestic smelting did not grow as strongly as the expansion of the electrical and other industries using copper would have warranted. As Table 17.1 shows, copper ore smelting in the United Kingdom suffered a major reverse with the outbreak of World War I, from which it never recovered. On the other hand, the table indicates a rapid rise in the import of refined, or matte, and blister copper[7] since the beginning of the century. Meanwhile, the ore owners had pressed successfully for the abandonment of the ticketing system[8] and, by the 1890s, private treaty sales had resulted in 'keener competition and in the corresponding forcing down of prices to a level less remunerative, sometimes painfully unremunerative, to the copper smelters'.[9] By the 1870s an appreciable proportion of the world's output was being channelled through London merchants, and, with the opening of the London Metal Exchange, London's lead became decisive.

The export of lead from the British Isles has as long a history as that of tin. There were lead merchants in the York area from the thirteenth century. During the seventeenth century Chesterfield became the most important lead market in the United Kingdom. Lead was brought there by pack horse and taken by river to Hull which was, along with London and Bristol, one of the leading exporting ports. There were many local lead markets in the United Kingdom (of which Aberystwyth was one example) until direct purchases by merchants from the mines brought about a decline in their activities. Lead was still being exported during the 1860s, but by the 1880s imports of pig and sheet lead from Spain, Belgium and Germany were of the order of 100,000 tons, while imports of lead ore had also reached some 16,000 tons, as Table 17.1 indicates. Imports were in fact some three times the size of domestic production at this time, and were destined to double again by the eve of World War I as electricity absorbed an ever mounting tonnage of both copper and lead.

Until comparatively recently the most important markets for zinc – often called spelter – were on the continent, in Breslau and Hamburg. The London market was small and, as will be observed at greater length below, failed to attain any significance until the twentieth century was well advanced.

When London gained a pre-eminent position in the non-ferrous metal trade, the merchants, who were attracted by the growth in demand, came from a variety of backgrounds. There were erstwhile agents of Swansea smelters, ex-wharfingers and merchant bankers. Practices in the trade varied, but usually the metal was purchased from the shipper or the producer. As in so many other trades, the financing of the metal in transit was effected by the acceptance and discount of bills of exchange. 'Third country trade' was also financed in this way, while merchants financed their warehouse stocks by using warehouse warrants as collateral for bank loans. The merchants frequently dealt with intermediaries less substantial than themselves. Many of these were brokers who had been employees of Swansea smelting firms, or of tinplate and lead manufacturers. After 1860, as London established an international lead as a world centre in the metal trade, these brokers were joined by others from continental firms.

For some years these intermediaries transacted business in the south-east corner of the Royal Exchange at 4 o'clock in the afternoon, though the acknowledged centre for trade intelligence and the discussion of business was the Jerusalem Coffee House in Cowper Court. At its inception, and for some time afterwards, the metal market consisted of transactions in warehouse warrants, with attached certificates of assay of weight and quality, for the handing over of warehouse receipts was regarded as the equivalent of the delivery of the metals themselves. This was true at least for tin and copper. Lead and zinc were not normally warehoused and transactions in these metals were therefore concluded by transfer of bills of lading or of delivery orders for shipments waiting in port. As with so many other markets which

we have examined, therefore, business was enabled to be conducted in
the City at some distance from the physical commodity. In brief, the
metal market developed as a market in rights for, with quality guaranteed by independent assay, it became a matter of indifference whether
the actual metal happened to be in Swansea, Birmingham or London
at the time of sale.

2. *Imports and the Growth of Futures Trading*

The growth of import increased uncertainty in the non-ferrous metal
trade and tended to make prices more volatile. Compared with the
market in pig-iron warrants (to which reference has already been made)
a market in prices of non-ferrous metals was destined to greater
development, and this for sound economic reasons. As previously
mentioned, in order to keep their furnaces functioning during periods
of slack trade, the Scottish ironmasters produced for stock and used the
ingots as the collateral against which they borrowed money. A Scottish
Pig-Iron Association was established as early as 1845, and by 1850
there were officially recognized storekeepers and issuers of warrants
from central stores. Warrant markets flourished in Glasgow, Middlesbrough, Liverpool and London for some sixty years following this
development, but a fully-fledged futures market never emerged at
any of these centres despite considerable speculation from time to time.
Bear speculation was a feature of these markets during unsettled
periods. The reason usually adduced for the failure of these markets
to develop further is that there was little recourse to the market for
hedging, since price and output changes occurred rhythmically with
the trade cycle rather than unpredictably with the uncertainties of
the seasons.[10]

By contrast with pig-iron, transactions in the non-ferrous metals by
the second half of the century were increasingly for imported metals.
Accordingly, the first step in the direction of modern futures trading was
the development of 'arrivals' markets. These flourished as merchants
used the cable to receive advance information of metal shipments
which they were able to sell to manufacturers 'to arrive' and thus
divest themselves of the risk of falling prices while the metal was afloat.
However, the arrivals markets in non-ferrous metals, like those in other
commodities, suffered from essential defects as a protection against
adverse price changes. The shipments in which transactions take place
are of various grades and of times and places of delivery. Because of
this it is not always possible for merchants to sell particular consignments 'to arrive', nor is it always possible for manufacturers to purchase
their exact requirements for forward delivery.

These shortcomings led to further changes in market organization
during the 1870s when a standardized contract evolved for copper and
tin for which futures trading emerged. Contracts in copper were

standardized on 25 tons and those for tin on units of 5 tons, while three months became the standard delivery time for contracts in metals sold other than 'on the spot'. Meanwhile, from the limitations imposed by refining processes, standard grades emerged, and the location of industry determined delivery points. Negotiations in both spot and forward metal transactions were thus enabled to concentrate upon price alone – an essential prerequisite for the development of a futures market.

3. The Metal Exchange and its Early Contracts

In 1869 metal trading was introduced into the comparatively new Lombard Exchange and Newsroom (built on the present site of the Crédit Lyonnais). 'The Lombard' soon proved inadequate and so, when a large first floor room became vacant at 4 Lombard Court, its hire was negotiated by the London Metal Exchange Company formed for the purpose. Trading began at Lombard Court in 1877 and before 1890 membership had grown to more than 300. It was a membership which included provincial ironmasters, tinplaters, brass founders, zinc galvanizers, copper smelters and white-lead manufacturers, and though they sometimes transacted business through London dealers they attended Lombard Court in order to exchange information or to make contacts, exactly as their predecessors had done on a smaller scale at the Jerusalem Coffee House.

As the membership continued to grow, the Lombard Court premises proved inadequate and in 1881 a new company was formed to build new accommodation. The Metal Market and Exchange Company was floated with an authorized capital of £10,000, of which £5,000 was paid up. However, this amount, together with the existing assets of the former Board, proved insufficient and the new building, at Whittington Avenue, was financed privately and leased to the Exchange Company. The new premises were occupied on 18 September 1882 and the market has remained there ever since. The Board of Directors of the Exchange Company (elected from among the shareholders and familiarly known as the 'House of Lords') undertook responsibility for the premises, the facilities and matters pertaining to membership and finance, while a Committee of Subscribers – fifteen members elected annually – undertook responsibility for the conduct of business. The latter committee introduced separate times for copper, tin and pig-iron transactions, all of which were traded on the same 'ring' system which, having originated in the form of 'the pit' at Chicago, was becoming a widely accepted means of conducting business in futures contracts. Lead and zinc transactions were concluded on a separate ring until the 1920s.

The severe limitations imposed upon the times at which official trading in each metal could take place gave rise to a considerable volume of 'unofficial' transactions outside these times. Attempts were made to eliminate this trade, but the Subscription Committee eventually had to recognize it and a time was allocated for it after the close of official business. It continues to be called 'kerb' trading, though it now takes place around the ring. The ring was originally a chalk circle, but in 1886 this was displaced by benches. This arrangement for seating members naturally limited the numbers of those able to deal at any one time. In 1895 the right to deal was restricted to London members and authorized dealers. This restriction, together with a substantial increase in entrance fees, resulted in a major decline in members from 367 in 1883 to 163 in 1905, despite a considerable growth in the turnover of the Exchange. Further, it was determined in 1903 that ring dealers should lodge securities with the Exchange of an amount of £3,000, a figure which the Board had the authority to increase at its discretion. An additional proof of substance was required a few years later when ring traders were required to pay a fee of 500 guineas for ring membership. This policy of requiring substantial guarantees of financial standing is one to which the Exchange has since adhered. The London Metal Exchange (L.M.E.) thus differs from many Exchanges in the means by which it seeks to protect its members: most trade associations, as we have now seen, attempted to solve the problem of ensuring against default by requiring initial deposits and subsequent margins, together with the establishment of insurance funds, whereas the L.M.E. relies upon the coverage provided by the securities deposited by the dealers.

The Exchange devised its present system for clearing contracts in 1909. Each member renders a daily return listing the warrants he owes or which are due to him from other members on the 'prompt' date, together with a list of his transactions with the market as a whole. The secretary then calculates from whom and to whom delivery of warrants is to be made. The buying and selling price differences are settled privately by the members concerned.

From its early days the Exchange served both as a delivery market and as a market for hedging and speculation, and the attempts by the L.M.E. to provide contracts which would prove satisfactory to traders requiring physical metal, and to others entering the market to hedge stocks or commitments, has been one of the central features of its history. Broadly-based contracts tend to encourage sales in the physical market by providing a variety of grades and of delivery points. Likewise, a broadly-based contract encourages its use as a medium for hedging or speculation because the price changes experienced would then be representative of price fluctuations occurring for particular grades of the metal concerned. However, whereas both these considerations favour a broadly-based contract they expose the purchaser to the danger that metal quite unsuited to his needs may be delivered in fulfilment of contract. It is not surprising, therefore, that owing to this failure to separate the physical markets from the futures markets, contracts devised by the Exchange have been subject to very frequent change. Thus the first copper contracts issued in 1883 proved too narrowly based when imports from Chile, Spain and Portugal declined in favour of U.S. copper. However, the contract was adjusted only after Secretan, the French metal manufacturer, attempted to corner the market in Chile Bars (the basis of the L.M.E. contract) in order to squeeze those who had sold forward metal on the London contract. Unfortunately, the contract in Good Merchantable Brands introduced in 1888 was, by contrast, so broadly based as to be almost useless to manufacturers and it penalized producers of high-grade metal. (The former could not use the rough copper deliverable, while the latter received no premium for tendering metal purer than the 96 per cent basis grade.) Consequently, following the introduction of an alternative contract in Refined Copper in 1898, a single contract appeared in 1904 which was destined to remain without major revision until the outbreak of World War II. This Standard Copper Contract was for a basis grade of between 99 and 99.3 per cent purity, with Electrolytic Copper deliverable at a premium and Rough Copper (down to 94 per cent) at a discount. The contract was an admirable medium for hedging and speculation but, because it permitted delivery of copper of much lower grade than many manufacturers could use, it tended to bias the Exchange market in copper much more in the direction of a futures, in preference to a delivery market than the founding fathers of the L.M.E. would probably have considered desirable. Thus, despite the addition of Birmingham and Newcastle to London, Liverpool, Birkenhead and Swansea as points of 'good delivery' under the contract, its breadth resulted in the by-passing of the Exchange as a physical market for many copper transactions. The use of 'fixed' rather than 'commercial' differences[11] to determine the premiums and discounts payable when deliveries of metal were other than the basis grade provided further difficulties: contracts tended to be fulfilled by the tender of metal of low purity whenever the actual differential between its price and that of the basis grade was greater than the 'fixed' difference declared by the Exchange.

Similar difficulties faced the tin market. The contract for Good Merchantable Quality which replaced several earlier ones in 1891 was joined in 1897 by a further contract for Mixed Tin. This added Banca and Billiton tin to the Straits and Australian metals which were in effect the only ones tenderable under the earlier contract. The breadth of this later contract led to its almost exclusive use for hedging while the Good Merchantable Quality contract was used for physical transactions. In 1912 a Standard Tin contract was introduced in an attempt to end the several successful corners which had resulted from the

combination of low stocks and distant supply sources. This contract
created two classes of tin, Class A at the contract price and Class B
at a rebate of £7 per ton. The former was for Straits or Australian tin
and Refined tin of not less than 99.75 per cent purity. Class B was
created for Common tin assaying a minimum percentage of 99.
Inevitably, the Standard Tin contract was used almost exclusively as
a hedging medium, so that in the following year a c.i.f. contract was
introduced for the sale of physical tin, the grade of which was to be
specified by the buyer.

The markets in lead and zinc on the London Metal Exchange were
markets in physical metal until 1903. There were several reasons for
this, which included the wide range of quality in the case of zinc, the
fact that neither lead nor zinc was a warehoused commodity, and the
high handling costs in relation to bulk. Because quality differences are
not of great significance in the lead trade, it proved possible to introduce
a contract in Good Soft Pig Lead in 1903 without specifying a basis
quality, delivery of which (since lead was not kept in store) was
deemed to have been effected by the release of bills of lading or of
delivery orders. For the same reason the contract did not carry a prompt
date. (The seller was allowed fifteen days after the period specified
in which to deliver.) The contract resulted in many disputes during its
early years, thus occasioning an increase in activity for the Subscription
Committee's arbitration machinery. However, having realized that
little improvement was possible, the members of the lead trade eventually settled down and accepted the shortcomings of their contract,
which has subsequently remained in existence in virtually unchanged
form.

It was 1915 before a broadly similar contract to that for lead was
introduced for virgin spelter. However, whereas London was the
sole delivery port for the former, the zinc contract also specified
ex-quay (or ex-warehouse) delivery at Liverpool, and free on rail
Swansea.

The market in pig-iron warrants flourished for a long period on
the London Metal Exchange. Contemporary reports in 1890 are of a
collapse of the Glasgow market with a steep fall in prices and some
failures following considerable speculation.[12] Nevertheless, it was in
that year that dealings in pig-iron warrants were revived on the London
Metal Exchange. The contract was for Good Merchantable Pig-Iron
of 500 ton units of Scotch, Haematite or Cleveland pig-iron in storehouses in Glasgow, Cumberland, Furness or Teesside. Further grades
and delivery points were subsequently added. The market was active
until 1916, but it never really revived after the war, due to the declining
quantities of pig-iron stored as production methods became increasingly
integrated. However, the promoters of an Iron and Steel Exchange
did open such an Exchange in 1919 at Cannon Street Hotel, and for

some years rented the Metal Exchange Rooms every Tuesday afternoon.[13]

By 1890 the U.S.A. had overtaken the U.K. as the world's largest consumer of copper but, despite this, the U.S.A. remained self-sufficient in that metal. By the turn of the century German consumption of copper and lead also had overtaken that of the U.K. with the phenomenal growth of its electrical industry. French demand for copper was also increasing very rapidly and the increase in imports which this necessitated for both French and German traders led to an increasing tendency towards direct purchases from countries of origin rather than through London. Similar trends were becoming manifest in the lead and zinc trades, so that, of the world's non-ferrous metal trade, only in tin was London the undisputed delivery market by the eve of World War II. In part this was because tin production and smelting processes were almost all within British-controlled territories at the time. However, the success of the London tin market also owed more than a little to the fact that, as compared with copper especially, quality variations in tin were not so crucial as to prevent the market from functioning successfully both as a delivery market and as a market for hedging and speculation. Thus, whereas the tin market continued to operate in this comprehensive way, the other major non-ferrous metal market – that in copper – became predominantly a hedging and speculative market. The market in physical copper on the L.M.E. in fact became increasingly used by domestic and foreign merchants for clearing excess stocks. Indeed, for all the non-ferrous metals, London had become very much a reservoir to which traders turned in the confident expectation that it would absorb excess supplies or provide marginal requirements. In this respect, therefore, it was a centre which closely resembled the other great U.K. staple markets, of which the Liverpool cotton market in its heyday is probably the best example. Because there were always buyers on the London Metal Exchange willing to absorb consigned metal in times of surplus and to warehouse it until prices hardened once more, prices were prevented from plummetting as much as they otherwise would have done. Conversely, the reduction of these stocks by the London merchants during periods of scarcity prevented prices from rocketing as high as they otherwise would have done.

A metal exchange was opened in New York during the 1890s, but it lasted only a few years because American traders continued to hedge and speculate on the London market. A metal exchange was established in Hamburg in 1910, and markets in copper were opened in Le Havre and Berlin in 1911. The turnover in copper contracts on the Hamburg exchange grew to approximately half that of London by 1913 (274,160 tons compared with 523,900 tons), while Berlin succeeded in turning over 110,040 tons during the last full peacetime year. The Hamburg turnover for the tin contract, however, was only 7,895 tons for 1913 compared with 134,600 tons on the London market. A considerable proportion of the continental turnover consisted of arbitrage activity with London and so did not represent a net loss of business for the L.M.E. Had not the war intervened, the Hamburg copper market would doubtless have presented a serious challenge to London as the world's premier copper market. As it was, the London daily closing prices for copper, tin, lead and zinc determined the prices for the conclusion of transactions all over the world, and that not only for refined metals, but also for ores, residues, semi-manufactured, manufactured metals and scrap. The L.M.E. was able to continue to act as the register of prices, despite the progressively smaller proportion of world trade which passed through the Exchange, because it faithfully reflected the marginal changes in demand and supply and survived the phenomenal growth of the American copper industry which had remained purely domestic.

4. *The Markets from* 1914 *to* 1939

When war seemed inevitable the London Metal Exchange was closed on 31 July 1914 but with the continuation of unofficial private trading, it was reopened on 18 November. The government ultimately intervened with Orders in Council on 1 March 1916 prohibiting further speculative dealings in copper, lead, zinc and iron. Private trading for delivery in copper, lead and zinc was discontinued in December 1916 when the Directorate of Materials in the Ministry of Munitions undertook the bulk purchase of these metals. Supplies to U.K. manufacturers were rationed by a licensing system and maximum prices were fixed for lead and zinc. When the U.S. government fixed the American copper price in September 1917 this in effect put a ceiling on the price of U.K. copper also. Tin was not brought under complete government control until April 1918.

The war resulted in much disruption and change in supply sources. Australian and Spanish copper output declined while Chilean and Canadian mining enterprises benefited. The U.S.A. was still self sufficient in copper at the end of the war despite accounting for over half of entire world consumption. Indeed, American producers supplied 80 per cent of world imports as well. In the tin trade the greatest change wrought by the war was that it encouraged U.S. merchants and manufacturers to purchase direct from the Straits rather than through London. Moreover, when shipping difficulties made themselves felt, a trade developed in nearby Bolivian ores, which had previously been smelted in the U.K., but this proved relatively short-lived. The loss of German zinc smelting capacity together with the destruction of many Belgian and French enterprises during the war resulted in the doubling of the American smelting industry and some growth in British capacity.

Changes in the lead trade followed much the same pattern; there were notable changes in the industry as widespread German control over production was replaced by national organizations. In the U.K. the British Metal Corporation was established at the end of the war to implement the government's guarantee to purchase Australia's zinc ores for ten years and to develop metal production throughout the Empire.

(a). *Copper*

As were so many other markets, the metal trade was greatly affected by disturbed economic conditions during the inter-war period. These led to interventions in the market processes. In the copper trade, for example, a significant decrease in demand coupled with increases in supply led to the formation of the Copper Export Association of U.S. and Chilean producers as early as December 1918. This achieved a reduction in American output for some years. By December 1920 the governments of Malaya and the Dutch East Indies introduced a species of tin buffer-stock scheme with the establishment of the 'Bandoeng Pool'. During 1921 purchases of tin for the Pool prevented increased supplies from exerting their full impact upon the market.

During the latter half of the 1920s the metal trades were prosperous, and the Bandoeng Pool was wound up. By 1924, too, the Copper Export Association declined in significance and became merely foreign agents for the Anaconda Group.[14] However, in 1926 the American copper companies, together with those of the Katanga, Rio Tinto and the German companies (together comprising about 95 per cent of world production) formed the Copper Exporters Inc. The objects of this cartel were to attempt to fix prices and to encourage direct sales from producers to manufacturers, thereby by-passing the London and other metal exchanges and eliminating all the middlemen associated with these organizations. European consumers were dealt with by a central agency established in Brussels. This permitted deliveries of copper only for immediate use in order to eliminate stockholding merchants, so that during the two years between 1926 and 1928, U.K. stocks were reduced from over 50,000 tons to some 5,000 tons, and this was mainly Rough copper.[15] Turnover on the L.M.E. declined steeply and control over copper prices passed unequivocally to the American-dominated cartel. When the boom sent prices zooming to £114 per ton for Electro-copper some members of the cartel broke rank and unloaded supplies onto the market. However, the price was pegged by the Copper Exporters Inc. at £84, but by this time the boom was over and so the trade witnessed the inevitable concomitant of this situation, that is, the intervention of non-members to take advantage of the artificially high price. The fixed price for Electro-copper eventually weakened to £66,[16] but the continued decline in demand, together with the supplies of non-members resulted in loss of control by the cartel. It was a period of growth for Rhodesian copper producers who captured an appreciable slice of the American producers' markets, thereby increasing their output from 5,000 tons to 75,000 tons between 1929 and 1932. In the meantime U.S. production had fallen to about one-quarter of its 1929 level.

The failure of the Copper Exporters Inc. led to a substantial revival of business in the copper contract on the London Metal Exchange. The merchants had survived the threat to their existence while the reversion to purchases through the Exchange was a considerable relief, especially to smaller manufacturers, who were accustomed to the benefit of three months credit from merchant stockholders. Fundamentally, the Copper Exporters Inc. succumbed to the impossibility of effecting a substantial decrease in output from its members, but a mere decrease in output would not have been enough to have saved the situation: the curtailment required was of high-cost production, which would have enabled the cartel to have competed with low-cost non-member output. However, this is precisely the discipline which the free market imposes, so that in reproducing free-market conditions, most of the value of the cartel from the producers' point of view would have disappeared.

Following the depression the American administration imposed a duty of 4 cents a lb on copper imports and thereby virtually closed that market to outside suppliers. American refining capacity for blister and matte copper suffered, and within the British Empire links were strengthened between U.K. traders and Rhodesian and Canadian producers; purchasers from France and Belgium bought an increasing proportion of their supplies from Katanga, while German producers satisfied their requirements from Katanga, Rhodesia, Turkey and Yugoslavia.

The failure of copper prices to recover with returning prosperity during the early 1930s – due largely to the expansion of low-cost capacity and to American exports from enormous stocks – resulted in the conclusion of an International Agreement in 1935. South African and South American producers signed the agreement in its entirety; American and Canadian producers offered cooperation. It was agreed to cut back output to 75 per cent of capacity from mid-1935 and a ceiling of 100,000 tons a year was imposed upon U.S. exports. Difficulties occurred after some eighteen months, however, when a commodity boom sent the price of Standard Copper (which had fallen to £25 12s. 6d. in October 1934) up to £75 5s. od. It was decided to increase quotas, but this was so late in being implemented that it only exacerbated falling prices when the recession came. The cartel thus provided one more example of the inability of the controllers to predict accurately and to adjust quotas in time. The organization did not survive the outbreak of war in 1939.

(b) *Tin*

The years 1926-7 were notable for an investment boom in tin which led a few years later to surplus capacity, greatly increased by the depression at the turn of the decade. A Tin Producers' Association was formed in 1929 which exhorted its members to restrict output. This proved ineffective and by the end of 1930 the price of tin had declined to £112 a ton. The first International Tin Restriction scheme was organized in 1931.[17] It was an organization instituted by the governments of producing countries, with the exception of China and the Belgian Congo. Output quotas were allocated through a Committee – the International Tin Committee – which, in 1932, restricted output to as little as one-third of standard tonnages. By the end of the following year the results of restriction began to show, as prices revived to £230 per ton. In 1934 a 'buffer pool' of tin was established in order to try to stabilize the price at this level. Hedging tin transactions on the London Metal Exchange became practically a thing of the past as quotas continued to be held at low levels and merchants' stocks were depleted. Thus would-be short sellers were deterred from selling by the fear of a squeeze, and a backwardation (i.e. a spot price higher than the forward price) persisted.

The Third International Tin Agreement was signed in 1936 and, with increasing demand, the price of tin reached £311 when the buffer stocks were exhausted. With recession in 1938 the price fell to under £200 and a second buffer pool was established. On this occasion the buffer stock manager was charged with the task of confining price fluctuations within a floor of £200 and a ceiling of £230. Tin control ceased to be operative with the outbreak of war, but it had in the meantime seriously weakened the dominance of the London Metal Exchange as the world's central tin market, for, with restriction, the London market had become narrow and volatile, reflecting only marginal demand pressures for restricted supplies.

(c) *Zinc*

The new low-cost supply sources which resulted from the difficulties occasioned by wartime conditions subsequently gave rise to considerable competition for European producers of lead and zinc. A European zinc producers' cartel was formed in 1928, but it lapsed a year later because of the narrowness of its membership and the continuing weakness of demand. By 1931 the London price of virgin spelter was down to £9 13s. 9d. per ton and all producers outside the U.S.A. were sufficiently concerned to get together to establish the International Zinc Cartel. After output had been cut to some 55 per cent of registered capacities, prices began to recover. However, the unity of the world market was disrupted by the departure of the U.K. from the international gold standard and the imposition, a year or so later, of a 10 per cent duty upon foreign zinc imported into the U.K. Germany retaliated with a subsidy, and low-cost producers in the cartel also violated their quota limitations. After being suspended in 1933, the cartel was renewed and, with economic recovery, quotas were enlarged. However, the protection afforded to particular producers in certain markets led to a decline of interest and the cartel came to an end in 1934.

(d) *Lead*

The increase in the output of lead during the 1920s ultimately gave rise to an appreciable weakening of prices. By 1930 the London price of the metal was £14 12s. 6d. a ton. Producers were sufficiently concerned to establish the Lead Producers' Reporting Association. However, the disruptions occasioned by the departure of sterling from the gold standard and the duties imposed in 1932 upset the arrangements, which were terminated in 1932. With economic recovery, the price of lead improved to £36 7s. 6d. in 1937 and fell subsequently with recession, except for a brief period in 1938 with the formation of a Lead Producers' Association once more.

As the foregoing account of the non-ferrous metals trade in the inter-war period has shown, the disturbed conditions of the time exercised a profound influence upon the volume and conditions of trade on the London Metal Exchange. The unsuitable nature of the copper and tin contracts for transactions in physical metal emphasized the role of the L.M.E. as a hedging and speculating market, though some attempts continued to be made to modify the contracts to enable the Exchange to function more satisfactorily as a delivery market. Much thought, and some action, was devoted to the problems associated with the system of 'fixed differences' for metals other than the basis grade. In the lead trade there was opposition to the addition of Liverpool to London as an official delivery point, with the result that the increasing amount of lead which was shipped to ports other than London was not sold on L.M.E. contracts. The import duties imposed in 1932 had a particularly deleterious effect upon ring trading in lead and zinc. Empire metal, which came into the U.K. free of duty, was forced up in price upon resale and tended to disappear from the ring. Contracts in foreign metal were endorsed 'duty for buyer's account' and so reduced the amounts sold through the ring because buyers wished to avoid paying the duty if possible. However, there was an appreciable revival in the use of the Exchange for lead and zinc trading after 1935 with the change to specific rates of duty and the amendment of the L.M.E. contracts: from this date the seller was permitted to deliver either Empire metal at the quoted price plus the appropriate rate of duty, or foreign metal at the quoted price, with duty for buyer's account.[18]

Despite this success story, many trends during the inter-war period operated to the detriment of the London Metal Exchange: for example, concentration in mining and smelting tended to result in the founding of marketing agencies. Merchants were sometimes induced to work for these in return for a commission but sometimes the agencies did without these traders altogether. When this happened, intermediaries played no role in marketing and agencies such as the Copper Export Association and the British Metal Corporation sold directly to manufacturers.

These changes inevitably affected turnover on the L.M.E. The Exchange flourished between 1924 and 1929 with an increase in its use for hedging and speculating and, as the accompanying table (Table 17.2) illustrates, both the lead and zinc contracts enjoyed a period of prosperity. Furthermore, though an increasing proportion of American business in tin failed to pass through the Exchange after the First World War, much of the business was still transacted by London dealers, who hedged the shipments on the Exchange. The depression reduced turnover figures, but the market was assisted to some extent by the use made of it on the part of producers wishing to rid themselves of growing stocks. Aided by the advent of cheap money the merchants were able to fulfil their traditional role as reservoirs and official warehouse stocks mounted. Turnover in copper contracts was appreciably reduced between 1928 and 1930 owing to the activities of Copper Exporters Inc., while the International Tin Agreement cut turnover from 1933. Lead and zinc turnover was very much reduced, as Table 17.2 indicates, between 1932 and 1935 when the *ad valorem*

TABLE 17.2

TURNOVER ON THE LONDON METAL EXCHANGE, 1911–1938

tons

	Copper	Tin	Lead	Zinc
Average 1911–13	474,000	138,400		
1924	368,225	208,525	278,450	218,125
1925	398,950	184,050	298,200	255,200
1926	330,525	192,275	287,100	238,225
1927	328,200	165,425	319,050	216,850
1928	163,425	152,000	226,200	143,550
1929	246,000	138,425	217,100	159,525
1930	167,075	123,000	138,700	126,925
1931	227,100	152,750	141,850	162,500
1932	209,900	136,340	133,550	138,800
1933	226,625	97,305	162,600	128,500
1934	256,200	73,600	114,850	92,225
1935*	597,250	68,075	259,200	127,325
1936*	457,225	78,340	335,100	248,250
1937*	711,375	99,945	482,000	594,700
1938*	475,400	91,065	387,300	296,475

* Figures for these years include the afternoon sessions.

Source: The Secretary, The London Metal Exchange.

duty was in operation. With the rearmament drive the Exchange was the scene of increasing activity once more between 1935 and 1937.

Organizational changes in the London Metal Exchange included the introduction of a rule which required all members to become shareholders of the Metal Market and Exchange Company. This met the criticism that the Board merely represented a small group of shareholders. In 1928 the chairman of the Subscribers' Committee was elected to the Board, and the innovation of having members on both bodies was subsequently continued in the interest of good communications. After World War I, moreover, limited liability companies were allowed to become ring traders, though they were required to deposit securities (or provide a banker's guarantee) for £20,000. No further one-man firms were admitted after 1928, and in 1932 the Board arrogated to itself the power to examine the accounts of any member firm about which it felt at all dubious. At this time, too, the Board encouraged ring traders to require periodic margins from their clients.

5. *World War II and its Aftermath*

When war broke out in 1939 stocks of metal were taken over and their distribution for manufacture and export was organized by the Non-Ferrous Metals Control.[19] This body suspended dealings in copper, lead and zinc and within a week of the outbreak of war the Ministry of Supply announced maximum prices for these metals. Private trade in tin was allowed to continue, though a ceiling price (£230 a ton) was fixed, and export became subject to licence. The near-normal tin trade came to an end with Japan's entry into the war, after which all metals were purchased by the Ministry of Supply for official distribution. Because of the relatively easy supply situation in all the non-ferrous metals except tin, as the war approached its end, the bulk-purchasing commitments which had been entered into with the Dominions were concluded and licences (except for lead) were issued freely.[20] More general scarcity returned with the growth of industrial demand – by 1948 U.S. copper consumption was double the pre-war record consumption of 1937 – and the government continued to control the trade in the interests of the balance of payments position. Thus the L.M.E. was destined to remain closed and its foreign clientele kept away for some time after the war. It was a difficult situation and one which with its economic philosophy, the government of the day elected to tackle by means of controls.

Despite continuing restrictions, and largely because of the enormous growth of American demand, prices increased rapidly after the war. With its commitment to bulk purchasing the Ministry of Supply was unable to take advantage of relatively small supplies of non-ferrous metals, as private traders were accustomed to do, but of even greater importance was the Ministry's lack of flexibility for, whereas private traders in any commodity customarily vary the amounts which they buy and sell according to their view of the prevailing market situation, the Ministry tended to pay prices determined at the margin by American purchasers.[21] In brief, the system was beset by most of the difficulties which also attended the operations of the Raw Cotton Commission[22] so that, on the whole, British consumers probably paid higher prices for their supplies than their overseas competitors. In addition, they were denied the facility of hedging against unpredictable price fluctuations.

Eventually, in 1949, complaints from the trade evoked a response when the government announced a scheme for selling the metals at the daily prices established in New York. Henceforward, too, manufacturers were enabled to purchase forward upon payment of an insurance premium against a rise in prices. No comparable facility for hedging against a fall in prices was made available. However, as has already been observed from an examination of the Raw Cotton Commission, the chief stockholder was the Ministry of Supply and as such it was an 'unhedged bull' acting on the taxpayer's behalf – for it was the latter, naturally, who had to foot the bill when falling prices made for heavy trading losses. Despite the disintegration of world markets in non-ferrous metals[23] and the need for more adequate hedging facilities the government felt unable to allow a free market to reopen, because it would need to be so severely circumscribed in order to prevent a net loss of dollars – and at the time some two-fifths of British copper supplies originated in the dollar area, together with nearly half the virgin zinc and about a quarter of the lead.[24] Sales of these 'dollar goods' through the L.M.E. to overseas buyers would thus have been tantamount to providing a means of convertibility via commodities for, though it is true that the exchange control authorities could to some extent counter this, contemporary experience suggests that after some time evasions become inevitable.[25]

Few of the above difficulties applied to tin, which was a sterling area commodity. Consequently, from 15 November 1949, the London Metal Exchange was re-opened and its members were permitted to export both English refined and Straits tin from the U.K. Tin was thus one of the earliest markets to re-open after the war (the fur auctions were first, followed by coffee and rubber) and, as for these others, special arrangements were made between the tin trade and the Bank of England in order to enable the Bank to maintain oversight. The Committee of the Exchange provided the supervision for the Bank: a list of approved firms was drawn up to whom licences for foreign transactions were then issued. Their dollar earnings were reported and sales to the continent were permitted on the understanding that these would not be resold to the dollar area. Finally, under this

Bank of England scheme, each approved firm was required to report its purchases, sales and stocks to the Bank each month.

The inadequacy of available supplies of tin gave rise to a backwardation when dealing first started, but this had disappeared by the time the Korean war affected the market. This event had a cataclysmic effect upon prices in the tin trade, which shot up from some £600 a ton in early 1950 to a peak of £1,615 on 14 February 1951. During that month the American government decided not to continue purchasing for their stockpile until prices had subsided, whereupon the price fell to near normal levels within six months. It was a difficult time for London traders, for the Korean episode revived the practice of 'commodity |shunting' which did not disappear completely until 1955 when the sterling exchange rate was supported in all markets.[26] It was only after this date that London dealers succeeded in staging some revival in the traditional 'third country' trade in tin direct from the Straits to the U.S.A.

At the height of the Korean conflict, despite some attempt to allocate supplies of copper, lead and zinc through the International Materials Conference, Ministry quotations soared to £190 per ton for zinc and £180 for lead, though these were much lower prices than obtained in unofficial markets, which at one time reached some £500 for copper, £400 for zinc, and £200 for lead. When prices started to fall once more British manufacturers found that the Ministry of Materials was unable to supply them as cheaply as their foreign competitors were being supplied. Moreover, members of the trade were still unable to obtain protection against falling prices and felt this disadvantage keenly at the time. Accordingly, the government was pressed to restore the trade in copper, lead and zinc to private channels. By this time there was a Conservative government in office, the worst of the Korean crisis was over, and the European Payments Union was operating a reasonably successful system of multilateral settlements, payable partly in gold or dollars. (E.P.U. operations thus provided a greater incentive than had existed hitherto to purchase metals from the dollar area for subsequent resale.)

The trade in lead was returned to private hands on 1 October 1952, the Ministry of Materials having arranged for the gradual disposal of its stocks.[27] As for tin, arrangements were made for Bank of England surveillance of the activities of approved firms and of their foreign currency expenditures. The Committee of the Exchange acted as the body for liaison with the Bank.

Encouraged by the ability of private traders to market tin and lead at lower prices than those prevailing immediately before the restoration of trade to private hands (the price of lead fell some £50 within three weeks to £80 a ton) the government relinquished its control over the zinc trade on 1 January 1953: private dealings on the London Metal

Exchange were scheduled to start on the following day.[28] In this trade, too, the price fell steeply by almost £50 to £63 10s. od. a ton within some four months.

Aluminium was restored to private hands from 1 July 1953 (there were no L.M.E. transactions in this metal) and on 5 August 1953 the copper trade followed suit. Arrangements, similar to those for tin, lead and zinc, were made for a government broker (C. Tennant Sons & Co. Ltd) to handle Ministry sales of copper on the L.M.E.; the intention was that the government broker would be a seller only when the needs of the market could not be met from other sources.[29] The price of copper also fell – by some £20 a ton – within a short time of the trade being freed, though for all the metals there was an awkward period for users of the Exchange during which the price of forward metal was lower than that of spot supplies. The persistence of this backwardation militated against hedging operations for short hedgers (whose transactions will result in an undercompensation in these circumstances[30]), but transactions in physical metal for forward delivery were not encouraged, despite the seeming cheapness of three months metal in relation to spot prices. This was because buyers appear on the whole to have taken the view that markets would weaken and that the whole level of prices, spot as well as forward, would fall. This bearish sentiment in turn reinforced the tendency toward the persistence of a backwardation.[31]

6. *The Exchange Re-opened*

The accompanying table of the turnover on the London Metal Exchange since World War II (Table 17.3) indicates that, for some years after the trade was restored to private hands, business was on a comparatively small scale. The backwardation discussed above partly explains this, but there were also other factors to be taken into account.

(a) *Copper*

Whereas before World War II the U.S.A. was self-sufficient in lead and zinc, and the world's chief exporter of copper, that country became a substantial importer of these metals after the war – some of them for the strategic stockpile. This expansion in demand, coupled with Europe's greater need, reduced the flow of metals into London (customary before 1939) formerly purchased by London merchants through the L.M.E. The continuing dollar shortage and the consequent restrictions upon the convertibility of sterling also played their part in attracting surplus supplies of non-ferrous metals to New York rather than to London. Nor must the discontinuity of the long closure of the Exchange be overlooked, for the producers had become well satisfied with the system of long-term contracts with the Ministry of Supply (after-

TABLE 17.3
LONDON METAL EXCHANGE ANNUAL TURNOVERS, 1950–1970
long tons

	Copper	Tin	Lead	Zinc	Silver (troy ozs.)
1950		48,380			
1951		40,470			
1952		30,375			
1953		27,120	235,300	217,050	
1954	253,400	29,550	159,100	194,825	
1955	346,500	39,760	163,025	212,825	
1956	395,175	47,910	209,825	222,300	
1957	467,250	60,595	201,375	301,075	
1958	634,625	64,850	274,575	336,100	
1959	772,250	42,965	398,275	334,750	
1960	767,025	40,990	388,875	299,800	
1961	796,275	98,170	428,950	373,725	
1962	509,750	80,840	350,900	346,175	
1963	187,350	75,325	447,025	396,350	
1964	725,600	82,465	569,750	518,675	
1965	886,950	95,690	579,025	352,725	
1966	1,282,975	87,695	438,775	303,475	
1967	1,805,525	86,415	454,500	222,725	
1968	2,099,450	122,675	555,775	271,975	214,190,000
1969	2,298,800	120,585	688,850	385,450	379,830,000
1970	2,384,777	135,688	633,817	264,978	330,620,000

Source: The London Metal Exchange.

wards the Ministry of Materials) which had provided a secure outlet
at generous prices. Some of these producers sought to re-establish a
similar system of trade with manufacturers during this time. Thus, in
1955, the Rhodesian Selection Trust group, which had previously
made use of running contracts at prices based on those of the L.M.E.,
decided to change their methods of selling. Thereafter they decided to
sell to selected customers at fixed prices which they adjusted
periodically.[32] (The other major Commonwealth group, the Rhodesian
Anglo-American group, reaffirmed its confidence in selling at prices
linked to those of the London Metal Exchange.) Outside the Commonwealth some large American producers and the Union Minière du
Haute Katanga followed suit. In the tin trade, similarly, direct dealing
at prices not subject to day to day fluctuations was also much more
prevalent than before the war, especially between Straits producers
and American manufacturers. The result of this situation was that the
re-opening of the Metal Exchange did not by any means automatically
re-establish London as the centre of the non-ferrous metals trade,
especially for copper. The market was narrow; hedging transactions
were discouraged by the persistence of backwardation; and the
direct dealing between some producers with selected users at fixed
prices made the L.M.E. market very volatile. Under these circumstances the copper market especially did not operate reliably – or at
all, for some years – as a market which faithfully registered changes in
overall world demand and supply pressures.

In fact the mid-1950s were remarkable for the violent fluctuations
which took place in copper prices because of the time lag involved in

making adjustments. Bearish sentiment caused consumers to reduce purchases early in 1954 and some producers cut back production: the U.S. government bought 90,000 tons of seemingly surplus Chilean copper for the stockpile in order to support the market. Then, with commercial stocks reduced to a minimum, labour difficulties in many copper fields in Chile, Rhodesia and the U.S.A. between mid-1954 and the end of 1955 caused a loss of some six per cent of the world's refined production, just as economic activity was beginning to boom both in the U.S.A. and Europe. The price of copper shot up to the region of £430 a ton on the L.M.E. though U.S. producers continued to sell both their domestic and Chilean copper at prices well below this level. In the meantime the pressure of demand also forced the Rhodesian Selection Trust group to raise its fixed price of £280 a ton to £325 on 2 August 1955 and to £360 on 5 September. In 1956, on the other hand, there were no significant strikes and production levels were extremely high. By this time consumption had declined because of the high price and the U.S. automobile industry was in recession. By mid-year the L.M.E. price collapsed even more rapidly than it had risen.[33]

Despite these vicissitudes the London copper market continued to function; indeed there was a widening of its clientèle as, for example, the Japanese copper consuming industries were permitted by the Japanese government to hedge on the L.M.E. in January 1957.[34] Then, in October 1957, after nearly two and a half years, the dual-price structure for Rhodesian copper ended when the Rhodesian Selection Trust group announced it would revert to a London Metal Exchange basis of pricing.[35] It would in any case have been quite impossible for it to have maintained its policy of trying to sell at a fixed price, pegged at a level which appeared low some months before, for by this time the price of L.M.E. cash copper was less than £200 a ton. Producers' dissatisfaction continued, however, for they felt that price instability would tend to drive ever more users to substitute aluminium, steel and plastics for copper.

Eventually in 1961 the Rhodesian producers were sufficiently encouraged by the stability of copper prices to revert to the system of selling copper to their long-standing customers at the fixed price of £234 a ton for cash copper. Having been given a lead, other large producers such as Anaconda, Anglo-American, Kennecott, Noranda, Roan Selection Trust and the Union Minière followed suit. The major producers had initiated a policy of voluntary production cuts since 1960 – of the order of 10 per cent, amounting to a quarter of a million tons a year – but these companies found it daunting to absorb the tonnages, coming in from the continent for sale on the L.M.E., in order to support their fixed price. The situation was that, with the price almost completely fixed on the London Exchange, on the continent, where consumers found themselves overbought on their long-term contracts, copper prices began to weaken. Consequently, continental interests began to sell on the L.M.E. and shipped copper to the U.K. in fulfilment of these transactions. During some periods, moreover, this flow of copper coincided with shipments of fire-refined copper in the opposite direction (en route to continental electrolytic refineries) which the producers had bought on the L.M.E. in order to prevent prices from weakening. The situation was a difficult one for the producers and gave rise to further voluntary cuts in production.

In 1963 Rotterdam was added to the L.M.E. warehousing area for copper and three separate contracts for wirebars, cathodes and fire-refined copper were introduced in July to replace the single standard copper contract. The change led to a further difficult situation for the producers while both old and new contracts were operative for they then had to absorb, not only the wirebars which came on to the Exchange, but also cathodes and fire-refined copper, which sellers were eager to sell because the fixed discount from the standard price did not adequately reflect market pressures. With economic recovery copper prices hardened and by early 1964 the producers' fixed price of £234 quite suddenly seemed cheap. Consumers hastened to take advantage of this, but most producers, other than the Zambian group, unfortunately for them, had already disposed cheaply of the stocks which they had bought to maintain prices in 1963. By June 1964 the L.M.E. cash wirebar price was £51 above the producers' price and rose to a peak of £530 10s. 0d. on 6 November.

In September 1964 producers' fixed prices were already beginning to look rather less secure as some American and Chilean producers increased their prices to £280 a ton. In 1965 producers' prices remained unrealistically low despite the price increases. The effect of this upon demand, coupled with a big strike in Chile and fears that Zambian supplies might be endangered by a unilateral declaration of independence in Rhodesia, was to send prices on the L.M.E. still higher. Cash wirebars touched £551 5s. 0d. on 21 April and finally reached £569 10s. 0d. on 28 December. The producers' reaction to the increasing scarcity of copper was a further relaxation of the fixed price ceiling. The year 1965 opened with Zambian, Congolese and some other producers quoting £260 a ton and Chilean producers £280 a ton. American producers increased their prices from £272 to £288 at the beginning of May, and in October Chile raised its copper price to £304. Most other producers immediately followed suit and the North American producers fell into line when U.D.I. (the Unilateral Declaration of Independence) was finally announced by Rhodesia. The upward shift of producers' prices would have gone further but for the release of 200,000 tons from the U.S. stockpile within a week of the U.D.I. declaration.

Due mainly to strike action in the Chilean and Zambian mines, copper prices on the London Metal Exchange went even higher in 1966 than the 1965 peak, to reach £787 10s. 0d. on 5 April. The copper producers reacted to the continuing scarcity by pushing their 'fixed' price up from £304 to £336 a ton in January. Then, on 14 April 1966, the Chilean producers broke rank and declared an increase of £160 to £496 a ton, whereupon the Zambian producers reacted by announcing that they were reverting to pricing their copper on an L.M.E. basis. Other producers 'soon fell into ragged line'[36] so that the producer pricing of copper outside the U.S.A. was in effect abandoned by early May.

There can be little doubt that the very high copper prices recorded on the London Metal Exchange in 1964 and 1965 were the concomitant of the artificially low producers' prices established during those years; that is, the L.M.E. copper prices were established in a narrow volatile market and were, therefore, unrepresentative of true demand and supply pressures. A number of distortions were created by this situation, not the least of which was the inequality to which this disintegration of the world copper market gave rise for manufacturers. On average during this period most of the large copper fabricators obtained some 70 per cent of their needs at producer prices and the remainder at L.M.E. prices. There were, however, major discrepancies between countries. British consumers with their Zambian connection obtained a very high proportion of their supplies at pegged prices while, at the other extreme, Austrian manufacturers got hardly any. The Germans obtained some 40 per cent of their supplies from producers. Thus the profitability of copper production for the manufacturers depended very much upon the extent to which they could obtain supplies from producers as opposed to the market, rather than upon their efficiency. Copper and copper alloy semi-manufactures came to be sold during this period on a weighted average basis of the producer and L.M.E. prices. For this reason their prices appeared to be low and so, in a buoyant world economy, users of copper and copper alloy semi-manufactures, and of components and finished goods substantially composed of copper, tried to increase their stocks. This in turn tended to exacerbate the disintegration of the copper market by forcing L.M.E. prices up even further. Except in the U.S.A., therefore, where the pegging process continued, the effect of the producers' reversion to L.M.E. pricing was to unify the market once more, and in so doing to bring about a subsidence in the free-market price. The average price for cash wirebars on the London Metal Exchange for 1967 was £416.9, compared with £553.7 a year earlier. Subsequently, prices in 1967-8 soared to more than £800, but this was due entirely to changes in demand and supply affecting the whole market.

The table showing the post-war turnover for copper on the London

Metal Exchange may broadly be interpreted in terms of the foregoing analysis. During both 1953 and 1954 turnover was adversely affected by a persistent backwardation, while the boom of 1955 did not increase L.M.E. turnover very spectacularly because of the attempt by certain producers to peg their copper prices, thus distorting London prices. Between 1958 and 1961 turnover increased steadily as the Rhodesian Selection Trust reverted to L.M.E. pricing. There followed two years in which turnover decreased sharply as all the major producers reverted to fixed prices in more depressed market conditions: the turnover for 1963 was only a quarter of its 1961 level. There followed a period of hardening prices and a scramble for supplies. Moreover, there had been a change in the Exchange's copper contract: the standard contract was withdrawn in mid-1963 and replaced by the three separate contracts for wirebars, cathodes and fire-refined. This improved the Exchange as a delivery market, for copper buyers of wirebars on the L.M.E. could henceforth depend on getting wirebars and not risk being saddled with other forms of copper. The inability of manufacturers to obtain all their supplies at bargain prices from producers led to an increase in the use of the Exchange in 1964 and 1965 to hedge supplies at fluctuating free-market prices and then, when producers outside the U.S. reverted to L.M.E. pricing once more, turnover rose steeply. In 1967 it was about ten times as great as its 1963 level. (The main market in copper on the Exchange is for wirebars: on 1 November 1965 a further trading category of high conductivity fire-refined wirebars was introduced. The wirebar contract itself has also been changed to electrolytic only, following complaints by producers of the higher-quality electrolytic wirebars that the cheaper-grade wirebars were tending to depress the price of their product.)

(b) *Tin*

The early history of the re-opened market in tin on the London Metal Exchange was greatly influenced by the actions of the U.S. Reconstruction Finance Corporation and its successors which were often a major factor in maintaining prices by absorbing tin for the American stockpile. A further major factor in the tin market after 1956 was the International Tin Agreement originally drawn up by the U.N. International Tin Study Group. The new Agreement was accepted in 1953 and came into force in 1956. The main difference between the post-war Agreement and its pre-war predecessor lies in the participation of consumers in addition to producer members. The 1956 Agreement provided for equal representation of producers and consumers with equal voting rights. The main instrument of control continues to be a buffer stock reinforced by export restrictions, though there is a more detailed breakdown of price ranges within which the buffer stock

manager has to activate his stock either of money, or else of tin. Producer members provide about 90 per cent of non-communist world
output of tin in concentrates, but tin consumers are not so well
represented. Because of the failure of the U.S.A. and West Germany to
join, less than 50 per cent of primary tin metal is bought by consumer members.

As has recently been emphasised, a major advantage of the inclusion
of consumer members in the International Tin Agreement is that it
enables the International Tin Council to exercise some control over the
disposal of non-commercial, strategic stockpiles of tin metal.[37] Thus the
International Tin Council (I.T.C.) has sold tin from stockpiles at the
request of both the United Kingdom and Italian governments without
disrupting the market. The American stockpile is, however, much
larger, and the continued failure of that country to sign the post-war
Tin Agreements has meant that control over its strategic stockpile has
remained solely with the American government. Therefore, since the
London Metal Exchange re-opened after the war, the American disposal programme has been a major factor in determining the price of
tin, and the continuing changes in this programme have often
hampered the I.T.C. in its attempts to deal with price fluctuations.

Despite the Agreements, there have been to date three occasions on
which the buffer stock manager has failed to prevent the price of tin
from moving outside the prescribed range. In 1958 the price declined
below the floor of £730 in spite of reductions in the exports of member
countries, and dealings were temporarily suspended on the L.M.E. By
the following year the buffer stock manager was selling tin and, when
his stocks were threatened with exhaustion, the second International
Tin Agreement of 1961 was revised upwards (as Table 17.4 indicates)
in January 1962 and again in January 1963. Prices continued to rise
and, despite efforts by the U.S. General Services Administration to
put sales from its stockpile on a regular weekly footing and to augment
the amounts sold, the price of tin finally shot through the ceiling in
April 1963 when Russia entered the market to cover against a possible
short-fall in supplies from Indonesia. The price persisted at a high level
and on 28 October cash tin reached the buffer stock's 'must sell' limit
of £965, whereupon the Council had to announce on the Exchange
that the buffer stock had no more tin. In November a delegation from
the International Tin Council met representatives of the U.S. government in Washington and, according to the Council's communiqué,
'The I.T.C. delegation was informed that the U.S. government is
preparing a long-term tin disposal programme and that in the preparation of this programme the impact of disposals on the long-term future
of the world tin industry and the views expressed by this delegation
would be taken into account'. However, by the end of 1963 the price
had topped £1,000 and was more than £1,700 a ton by the end of

October 1964, following reduced releases from the U.S. stockpile owing to the fighting in Vietnam. The Tin Council had little else to do but revise the floor and ceiling prices upwards once more. This was done in November 1964, when the floor price became £1,000 and the ceiling price £1,200 a ton.

When the five year period of the second post-war International Tin Agreement came to an end a Third Agreement was negotiated to commence in July 1966. Floor and ceiling prices were again raised, to £1,100 and £1,400 a ton. The regulations governing the buffer stock manager's conduct were changed so that henceforward he was obliged to buy tin at £1,100 and had the choice of buying between £1,100 and £1,200. Henceforward he was obliged to sell tin at £1,400 and had discretion as to whether to sell between £1,300 and £1,400. The 'target' price in the new Agreement appeared, therefore, to be £1,200 and, when a delegation from the I.T.C. met representatives of the U.S. government in the autumn of 1966, there emerged an implicit understanding that the General Services Administration (G.S.A.) would act to support this price level.

TABLE 17.4
THE TIN BUFFER STOCK PRICE RANGE
£ sterling per long ton

	Floor	Middle Range	Ceiling	Price Range
1956 Agreement				
Initial	640	720–800	800	160
Revised: March 1957	730	780–830	880	150
1961 Agreement				
Initial	730	780–830	880	150
Revised: January 1962	790	850–910	965	175
January 1963	850	900–950	1000	150
November 1964	1000	1050–1150	1200	200
1966 Agreement				
Initial	1000	1050–1150	1200	200
Revised: July 1966	1100	1200–1300	1400	300
November 1967	1283	1400–1516	1633	350
January 1968	1280	1400–1515	1630	350
		£ sterling per metric ton		
1969 Price range expressed in metric rather than long tons. (Previous levels still in force.)	1260	1380–1490	1605	345

Source: British Metal Corporation, Review of Non-Ferrous Metals.

The price of tin was in fact held close to £1,200 until the devaluation of sterling in November 1967 when the Tin Council immediately acted under Article XII of the Agreement to adjust the price ranges established. Sterling was devalued by one-seventh and the new prices were adjusted by one-sixth and shortly afterwards rounded to a £1,280 floor and a £1,630 ceiling. The range, which was initially £160, thus became widened to £350. However, much of the tin held as a hedge against devaluation was subsequently sold off, so that, before the end of 1967, the buffer stock manager was buying in tin on a weakening market. He continued to buy heavily until August 1968 in order to keep tin as close as possible to the new target price of £1,400, but the market proved too weak to sustain a price of this order and the manager eventually stopped buying on 9 August. The price dipped below £1,300 but did not at the time reach the £1,280 at which the buffer stock manager would have been obliged to take in metal. Acting under the terms of the Agreement, the Tin Council introduced a curtailment of exports of between 3 and 4 per cent.

As the evidence from other markets serves to confirm, the declaration of output or export quotas because of falling prices is very difficult to time accurately, and so it was on this occasion. This small export restriction was progressively lightened after the first quarter of 1969 but with the market continuing to move ever higher, it was too little and too late. In March 1969 the buffer stock manager was authorized to operate within the middle sector (£1,400 and £1,515) and, when the price went above £1,400 in April, he started selling from a stockpile which at the time amounted to 11,290 tons.[38] The manager stopped selling in November when his buffer stock was reduced to some 5,000 tons. The price was still moving upwards and the Council, at its meeting in December 1969, decided that, instead of trying to hold the ceiling price of £1,630 should it be reached, it would hold its remaining tin in reserve. (The Council is allowed to do this by invoking Article XI, paragraph 6 of the Agreement.) The Council was then left facing a situation in which the price was in fact driven up to a December peak of £1,660, with speculative interests ready to snap up the remaining tin in the Council's stockpile should it be released.

It is patently obvious from the history of the tin market over the past two decades that the Council's buffer stock of 20,000 tons has been inadequate; a puny stock compared with that of the G.S.A. which, after many years during which releases were made, still stood at some 257,000 tons at the end of 1968. The declared stockpile aim of the U.S. government is 200,000 tons, leaving some 57,000 tons for future issue. Even so, a recent study suggests that, in conjunction with the export controls administered by the Council, that body could expect reasonable success from a stockpile of some 35,000 tons.[39] Obviously, too, a great deal hinges upon the width and the level of the range of prices within which it is decided to hold the market. Inevitably, when conditions are as disturbed as they have been since the war, by the threat of further conflicts, not to mention the problem of the American stockpile, periodic shifts of the range of prices within which the Council can reasonably expect to contain prices are to be expected.

These uncertainties have exercised their influence upon the London Metal Exchange tin market. The table of turnover for the post-war period indicates the variations in the intensity with which the uncertainty was felt by traders. It will be seen from the figures that, despite the existence of the International Tin Agreement, the London market still performs a useful function as a hedging medium, though it is also used to some extent as a delivery market.

(c) *Lead*

On the London Metal Exchange trading in lead restarted in October 1952 with the aid of government-owned lead. The fall from the opening price of £111 a ton to £80 a ton within three weeks was almost certainly due to a more insistent selling programme in a free market than under bulk purchase for, when there are no willing purchasers, the government does not seek to sell its stocks with the same vigour as private stockholders. Market activity was hampered by a backwardation, due to consumers' optimistic expectations, until the end of 1953.

As was true for tin, the American stockpile programme exerted a major influence upon world lead prices after the war, as indeed did the U.S. import quota, imposed in 1958. The London market fell to a low point of £70 a ton in December 1957 and failed to show much recovery owing to the world surplus. Various countries introduced voluntary curtailments of supplies and the United Nations set up a Lead and Zinc Conference in 1959. Prices were down to £61 17s. 6d. for spot lead by 29 December 1960 and declined to £57 12s. 6d. on 14 November 1961. The Lead and Zinc Study Group countries, under the auspices of the United Nations, agreed to further cuts in output. With the fall in prices, and more normal relationships between spot and forward quotations the rule rather than the exception, forward hedging sales on the L.M.E. became more worthwhile and, as the table of turnovers indicates, the lead contract gained in popularity.

Lead prices recovered in 1963 and rocketed during the second half of 1964 to reach £154 10s. od. cash. (In the Korean boom, 'free' market prices for marginal quantities touched £200 a ton.) This was the highest price since the 1955-56 boom, when the peak lead price was £126 10s. od. By contrast with the mid-1950s, however, when U.S. stockpile purchases played a decisive role in the market, the 1964 price was notable for the fact that the American authorities were selling lead. Despite these very high prices the end of U.S. import quotas did not come until 1965, leaving an import duty of $1\frac{1}{8}$ cents per lb (approximately £8 10s. od. a ton). Thus, the normality of price relationships between London and New York is ordinarily to be judged by this differential. Certainly, with a differential below £5 a ton, lead supplies would tend to be attracted to the U.S.A. American interests were of the opinion in 1966 that a differential of from 2.5 to 3 cents a lb between

American and London prices was the most that could be permitted if imports of metal were to be held within normal competitive bounds.[40] During the year the Committee of the London Metal Exchange approved the addition of Rotterdam to the delivery points for lead and zinc contracts, thus widening the effective area of London as a central world market for these metals.

(d) Zinc

When zinc trading was re-introduced in the London Metal Exchange in 1953, it was characterized during its early months by much the same conditions as for lead, that is, a backwardation in which the spot price was declining. This came to an end with growing world demand and American stockpiling in 1954. By 1957 the heavy U.S. stockpile purchases had had the effect of strengthening the attraction of the U.S. market for, as the British Metal Corporation Report for that year explained,

> The metals have been attracted to the pre-empting U.S. market and away from the residual London market, which largely explains the prevalent backwardations on the postwar London Metal Exchange.

In 1959 and 1960 zinc was a strong market due to an upsurge in European consumption. The International Lead and Zinc Study Group's restrictions upon supplies were lifted and U.S. stockpiling ceased. The peak price of £96 17s. 6d. was reached on 21 October 1959, but the market held firm until the end of November 1960. As it had been for lead, a contract modification was introduced to take effect in October 1960. This was a change in delivery terms from 'ex ship' to 'in warehouse', with a daily settlement. The change gave rise to an increase of some 20s. to 25s. a ton in price quotations. After a weakening of prices during 1961 and 1962, zinc prices recovered in 1963 to reach £148 10s. od. a ton on 24 July 1964, which was well over twice the low price of £63 touched in August 1962. The high price gave rise to considerable concern among producers who feared that it might induce manufacturers to substitute other materials (such as plastics and aluminium in dye casting and for other uses) in place of zinc. Accordingly, on 13 July 1964, when the spot price was still £139, the U.K. Imperial Smelting Corporation issued the following statement:

> In view of the negligible tonnage of zinc stocks remaining in London Metal Exchange warehouses, the principal producers supplying the U.K. and Continental markets consider that the price quoted on the London Metal Exchange has become unrealistic and most harmful to the long-term interests of the consumer industries and therefore also of producers. Imperial Smelting

Corporation have accordingly today decided to offer their customers zinc metal against all new sales and unpriced balances of existing contracts at a base price of £125 a ton. This price is effective today and will remain in force until further notice.

The zinc market on the Exchange was thus confronted with a situation similar to that on the copper market, for several other producers followed the I.S.C.'s lead and £125 became the effective base price, at least until the following month, when the L.M.E. price fell below the producers' price, whereupon the latter reduced theirs to £110. During 1965 London Metal Exchange zinc prices largely revolved round this level. For most of the time the price was the outcome of ordinary demand and supply pressures, but there were occasions when the producers intervened in the market to buy up warrants in order to maintain the price. It was a year in which the U.S. disposed of some 269,000 (short) tons of zinc from the stockpile, which was readily absorbed in the U.S. because of the tight supply position; this was sufficiently encouraging in fact to lead to the abolition by the U.S. government of its zinc import quotas. It was a change which could not but result in making movements in zinc prices in the U.K. and U.S. markets more responsive to each other.

In March 1966 the quotation for three months zinc fell below the producers' fixed price and acted as a signal to them to adjust their own selling price. Accordingly, on 22 March, Imperial Smelting Corporation announced a reduction in its price to £102, and the other producers followed suit within a few days. The continuing downward drift of the zinc price on the London market eventually led to a further cut in the producers' fixed price to £98 a ton on 20 June 1967. Following devaluation in the November this quotation was raised by $16\frac{2}{3}$ per cent to £114 6s. 8d. a ton. With prices on the L.M.E. mostly in the range £110 to £115 a ton during 1968, producers maintained the fixed price quotation of £114 6s. 8d. throughout the year. During 1969 the market strengthened to register a total price rise of some 14 per cent over the year. Despite this rising market the leading zinc producers outside the U.S.A. adhered to their basis selling price c.i.f. main European ports of £114 6s. 8d. a ton until 2 May 1969, when they increased the quotation to £121, and on 8 September they once more increased it to £130 a ton. Meanwhile, on the London Metal Exchange the zinc contract suffered a decline following its peak turnover of over half a million tons for 1964, the year when the producers' fixed price was introduced. At present, therefore, the producers' fixed price continues, but its success owes a great deal to the frequency of the change of its pegged price. In fact the system has been not so much one of fixed price, but an adjustable peg system which yields to market pressures by means of large discrete jumps instead of, as on free markets, by means of smooth continuous price changes.

(e) *Silver*

Towards the end of the nineteenth century a contract in silver eventually became possible on the London Metal Exchange when the major bullion firms in London agreed to become storage points and to issue warrants. In 1897 transactions in silver were admitted to the main ring of the Exchange and continued there until a diminution of interest set in, so that by 1911 Exchange business in silver was completely moribund (Table 17.5).

TABLE 17.5
LONDON FUTURES TRANSACTIONS IN SILVER, 1891–1914
oz

Year	Transactions
1891	2,450,000a
1892	1,310,000
1893	7,675,000
1894	20,860,516
1895	23,510,522
1896	9,115,450
1897	12,677,630
1898	1,857,800
1899	610,000
1900	440,000
1901	180,000
1902	150,000
1903	240,000
1904	240,000
1905	410,000
1906	50,000
1907	100,000
1908	110,000
1909	410,000
1910	200,000
1911	
1912	
1913	40,000
1914	80,000

a. Since 23 March 1891.
Source: Figures supplied by the London Produce Clearing House Ltd.

After World War II the London bullion firms sold silver at prices which were dictated by those of New York. Thus between 1955 and 1961 the New York price fluctuated between 89 and 92 cents an ounce, representing a London Bullion Market price of between 77d. and 80d. an ounce. This steady price was possible because the U.S. Treasury, despite growing deficits of silver production, met the shortfall of production at this price from its stocks. In 1962 the U.S. Treasury raised its selling price and, for the years 1964 to 1966, the London average price was near 112d. an ounce, corresponding with the fixed New York price of 129.3 cents per ounce. However, the world demand for silver continued to mount and on 18 May 1967 the American Treasury ceased to make silver available to foreign buyers at 129.3 cents. Following this, the U.S. Treasury announced in the July that silver at its official price would only be handed over in exchange for Silver Certificates. The General Services Administration henceforward offered two million ounces a week for sales from its surplus stocks. (On

1 January 1959 these were 1,900 million ounces, or about 6½ times
annual world consumption for that year.) This change thus heralded
the introduction of a free-market price for silver in New York which
registered a peak price of 217 cents an ounce on 27 November,
following the currency disturbances attendant upon sterling devaluation. The London Bullion Market's highest price of 224¾d. was reached
on 14 December 1967.

As an increasingly important industrial metal traded in a free
market, silver immediately attracted the attention of the members of
the London Metal Exchange. The L.M.E. eventually introduced a
Silver Contract for which the trading lot is 10,000 troy ounces of silver
of a minimum fineness of 99.9 per cent, with quotations in pence and
farthings an ounce. There are daily official price quotations for spot
silver and also for three and for seven months ahead. Trading on the
L.M.E. commenced in February 1968, not without misgivings, for
many thought that the prospects for two markets in London were
rather bleak. However, the turnover on the silver contract grew
throughout the year and was 21,419 lots (i.e. 214 million ounces) for the
year as a whole. By contrast with the turnover, the price of silver
declined from its peak of 264d. an ounce for 21 May 1968, to 161d. for
June 1969, a fall of nearly 40 per cent in just over a year, and against
the trend of the other L.M.E. metals, the prices of which were all rising
during these months.

The explanation for the price behaviour of silver lies in its considerable attraction as a medium for speculation. Thus if, as is widely
believed, the base metals have a demand which in the U.K. is about
four-fifths industrially based and one-fifth speculative, probably the
balance in the silver market is exactly the opposite. As *The Economist*
remarked, silver had become the speculative metal par excellence –
second best, admittedly, to gold, but without legal restrictions on buying
or holding.[41] Naturally, therefore, the demand for silver is very greatly
influenced by expectations of international currency changes and when
the world's foreign exchange markets settled down after the considerable upheavals of 1967-8, the price of silver declined to levels of some
180d.

Meanwhile, official American stocks declined from the massive
1,900 million ounces of 1959 to a mere 110 million ounces at the
beginning of 1970, representing rather less than 25 per cent of world
demand for one year. Estimated world consumption for 1968 was
425 million ounces while new mine production was 281 million ounces,
or some two-thirds of consumption. However, supplies from secondary
sources were sufficient not only to make good this shortfall but also
to increase the holdings of investors and speculators by almost 220
million ounces.[42] This roughly corresponded to the U.S. Treasury
supply sold during the year to industrial consumers, for minting and

in redemption of silver certificates. When these G.S.A. sales ceased towards the end of 1970, therefore, it was expected that the world demand for consumption – as opposed to speculation – should be in approximate balance with supply. In 1968, the remaining secondary sources of silver consisted of that illegally imported from India and Pakistan and largely marketed through the Trucial States (some 80 million ounces), and that recovered from demonetized coins (about 40 million ounces). For the future, therefore, much depends upon the possibilities of tapping these sources of secondary supply, which will almost certainly need prices considerably higher than those recently prevailing in order to induce a sufficient supply to satisfy demand once the U.S. Treasury has ceased to sell. The price of silver, now that it has been turned over to a free market seems, therefore, full of uncertainties, and consequently one for which the London Metal Exchange is an ideal medium.

Since it re-opened after World War II, the London Metal Exchange has encountered a great many difficulties, not the least of which were the shortfall of world production of copper and the absorption of lead and zinc by the United States. Towards the end of the 1950s, however, most abnormalities of this nature – apart from those connected with fluctuations in U.S. stockpiles – were over, and the L.M.E. resumed its traditional role as a clearing market for marginal supplies. Stocks in registered warehouses were built up once more to satisfactory levels and though the markets have experienced long periods of backwardation, this has now ceased to be the major difficulty which it once presented for would-be sellers of forward contracts. As will be evident from the foregoing account, the Exchange never was a market in which the predominant activity consisted of the sales of actual metal, even in the days when London was the world's central supply depot for non-ferrous metals. Increasingly, therefore, as the years have gone by during which the U.K. has become steadily less important as a market for non-ferrous metals relative to other countries, the L.M.E. has succeeded in retaining its importance by producing a ready free market for metals. Thus, when a surplus threatens, producers and manufacturers can always find buyers in London. Similarly, during periods of scarcity, when buyers cannot obtain all their supplies through more direct channels they are normally able to turn to the markets of the Exchange, to which supplies will usually be flowing, attracted by the rise in prices. By thus registering the continuously changing pressures of demand and supply at the margin – and the proportion of the world's trade which passes through the Exchange is certainly no more than five per cent, and often less – the London Metal Exchange has become the main acknowledged barometer for price determination. Except during periods when the market has become very unrepresentative due to major interventions by producers, therefore, many

European and other smelters purchase their ores and concentrates on the basis of London quotations. Moreover, a significant number of contracts for the sale of metals is made upon the same basis, with suitable premiums or discounts for delivery at some point other than London. By comparison, the New York Commodity Exchange has received only limited recognition from producers or consumers as far as price determination is concerned. This is true despite the fact that, until recently, the turnover in copper on the New York Exchange was about four times that of London. (They are at present more nearly of comparable size.) The New York markets in tin, lead and zinc are insignificant compared with those of London.[43]

The Exchange's success as a free market for marginal physical supplies has led, as has been observed, to the establishment of officially recognized warehouses at Rotterdam, Hamburg and Antwerp. These moves have extended the L.M.E.'s trading basis very considerably; for example, in mid-1965, out of total L.M.E. warehouse stocks of 7,881 tons of copper and 1,390 tons of tin, as much as 6,450 tons of copper and 920 tons of tin were held in five warehouses in Rotterdam and seven warehouses in Hamburg. In fact about 70 per cent of Exchange business now originates from overseas, and this provides some indication of its function as a market which, more than any other, acts as a unifying medium for demand and supply pressures on an international scale.[44] Also, with much of the stock in official warehouses at overseas centres, price fluctuations due to local difficulties tend to get ironed out. The Exchange is considering further overseas delivery points (including one in Budapest) which will tend to make artificial price fixing increasingly difficult, for competitive stocks attracted by artificially high prices would make such prices inoperative. Japanese traders, too, are considering setting up a centre near the Exchange through which to coordinate their world purchases. It is reported,[45] moreover, that their ultimate ambition is to stockpile copper which would be hedged on the L.M.E. as a means of ironing out smaller price fluctuations. This notion is consistent with ideas currently under discussion by the copper producers' organization (the C.I.P.E.C.). Having abandoned fixed prices, they are now considering running copper banks which lend to markets in shortage and borrow during temporary gluts. Such an organization, if established, would not, therefore, aim to eliminate the L.M.E.'s copper market, but would merely seek to smooth out short term fluctuations from the price trend.

The London Metal Exchange is peculiar in being used much more extensively as a delivery market than other futures markets are. Delivery on copper contracts, for example, is as high as 20 per cent of turnover, which is a great deal higher than the 5 per cent or less which is usual on most hedging and speculative markets. This fusion of price risks with trading risks on one market floor has posed considerable

TABLE 17.6

UNITED KINGDOM IMPORTS OF COPPER AND COPPER ALLOYS a, 1913–1968

Quantity: thousand tons   Value: £ thousand

IMPORTS FROM:	1913		1928		1938		1958		1968	
	Quantity	Value	Quantity	Value	Quantity	Value	Quantity	Value	Quantity	Value
Union of S. Africa and S.W. Africa Terr. Republic of South Africa			0·9	57·0	5·8	254·9	0·8	171·3		
Zambia (previously N. Rhodesia)									16·3	7902·8
Canada	6·9	568·7	0·1	5·9	89·8	3800·0	82·4	16515·0	168·8	84710·3
Germany W. Germany			0·7	45·0	113·6	5305·8	0·1	37·1	92·8	45913·4
E. Germany			3·6	323·0	3·4	232·9			11·9	6693·3
U.S.A.	55·4	3980·5	98·3	6741·5	37·1	1715·3	99·4	20466·2	0·7	397·9
Chile	6·9	477·4	49·6	3263·2	124·7	5336·1	80·5	15498·0	25·5	13692·7
Australia	21·9	1514·5	2·4	162·9					68·5	34026·9
Netherlands			0·3	31·7					2·6	1127·4
Rhodesia & Nyasaland							118·4	35361·9	2·8	1934·7
Others	28·8	2074·4	18·3	1331·9	4·4	273·1	10·1	2016·1	34·1	19427·5
Total	119·9	8615·4	174·2	11962·1	378·8	16918·1	461·6	90065·5	424·0	215826·9

UNITED KINGDOM RE-EXPORTS OF COPPER AND COPPER ALLOYS a, 1913–1968

Year	Quantity	Value
1913	19·5	1360·3
1928	6·6	430·0
1938	95·2	4289·2
1958	3·2	600·9
1968	3·1	1653·7

a. Includes wrought, unwrought, electrolytic, wire, plates, sheet etc.
Source: Annual Statement of Trade.

TABLE 17.7

UNITED KINGDOM IMPORTS OF TIN AND TIN ALLOYS a, 1913–1968

Quantity: thousand tons   Value: £ thousand

IMPORTS FROM:	1913		1928		1938		1958		1968	
	Quantity	Value	Quantity	Value	Quantity	Value	Quantity	Value	Quantity	Value
Straits Settlements and Dependencies (including Labuan) Federation of Malaya	40·1	8103·5	13·2	3043·5	4·9	913·9	3·6	2621·2		
Singapore							0·7	490·4		
Malaysia									1·0	1375·3
Australia	2·3	449·4	0·5	122·8	0·7	137·6	0·8	548·8		
Netherlands					2·1	366·0	6·5	4788·5		
Soviet Union									7·9	10556·3
Nigeria	3·3	699·2	3·0	735·8	4·1	753·4	1·6	1156·8	0·6	725·4
Others										
Total	45·7	9252·0	16·7	3902·1	11·8	2170·9	13·2	9605·6	9·5	12657·0

UNITED KINGDOM RE-EXPORTS OF TIN AND TIN ALLOYS a, 1913–1968

Year	Quantity	Value
1913	30·2	6147·2
1928	7·8	1820·1
1938	4·4	901·7
1958	1·1	838·5
1968	0·02	14·5

a. Includes wrought, unwrought, tubes, pipes etc.
Source: Annual Statement of Trade.

problems for the Exchange almost from its inception, for the history of the market has been one of almost continuous attention to the various contracts, since the basis contracts used for hedging and speculation are less than ideal as media for transactions in physical metal. When many grades can be tendered in fulfilment of a contract the manufacturer faces the risk of having to take delivery of metal which is unsuitable for his process. On the other hand, the high proportion of contracts which go to delivery tends to drive out the financial interests which are essential to the efficient functioning of a futures market. The Exchange is also limited in providing contracts only for deliveries of up to three months ahead (except for silver for which positions may be held for up to seven months). Despite these short-comings, the markets of the Exchange, except for zinc, which is still affected by producer pricing, are in a flourishing state, with a copper turnover of more than 100,000 tons a year, and a lead contract turning over more than half a million tons. The market is self-confident and the Committee of the Exchange have some further possible candidates, such as aluminium, for inclusion in the ring trading.

In the meantime, trading on the London Metal Exchange is conducted in much the same way as it always has been. The benches have now been replaced by rather more modern seating. Seats are numbered up to forty and the number of ring members is currently some thirty-two, while the total membership of the Exchange is at present some 150. These members transact business through the ring members who are now required to provide guarantees to the Exchange authorities of the order of £100,000. Understandably, therefore, these dealers are highly specialized in ring dealing. They diversify their brokerage activity by dealing in more than one metal, and some of the large firms are not only ring-dealing firms on the L.M.E. but have a number of subsidiary companies and departments specializing in different aspects of the metal industry, besides being members of other futures markets. Rudolf Wolf and Co., for example, are leading ring traders on the L.M.E., have subsidiary specialist organizations, and are also full members of the cocoa, sugar, coffee, vegetable oil and rubber terminal markets in Plantation House. This provides a further instance of a tendency which we have noted on other futures markets, for larger enterprises to be specialists in the activity of dealing on these highly technical markets.

The London Metal Exchange holds two sessions during the course of every day, one of which starts at midday, and the other at 3.40 p.m. In the first session each metal is traded separately in ring trading sessions which last for five minutes. The order of the markets is copper, silver, tin, lead, zinc. This, together with an interval, takes the time up to 12.35, after which further five minute markets are held in turn for copper wirebars, copper cathodes and fire-refined copper, tin, lead, zinc and silver. This takes the time to 1.05 p.m. and kerb trading then starts, in a haze of blue tobacco smoke, to finish at 1.25 p.m.

The second session starts at 3.40 p.m. with a combined market in lead and zinc for five minutes to be followed by copper, tin and silver. After a five minute interval at 4 p.m., further markets in lead, zinc, copper wirebars, copper cathodes and fire-refined copper, tin and silver are held. These are followed by kerb trading from 4.35 p.m. to 4.50 p.m. As on other such markets, transactions are still by open outcry. Principals of ring-dealing firms or their representatives shout bids and offers to one another across the ring. The transactions are checked at the end of each session by the clerks who stand on the fringe of the ring, and the contracts are sent out before noon on the following day.

The official prices are the closing prices of the second ring in the first session. These are agreed by the 'fixing committee' and announced by the secretary of the Exchange. Although dealings in the afternoon are identical with those of the morning session, they are not followed by an official announcement. The prices, known as 'settlements', are the official sellers' prices on the Exchange, and form the basis of the majority of long-term domestic and international transactions. The other terms peculiar to the L.M.E. are those of 'borrowing' and 'lending', known collectively as 'carries'. A buyer may carry forward a 'long' position by selling out on, or before, the prompt date and, at the same time, re-instate his long position for a forward date. This sale of a near date and simultaneous purchase of a date further forward is termed 'lending'. Conversely, a trader who has sold 'short' may carry his position forward by re-purchasing the appropriate delivery date and re-selling further ahead. This simultaneous purchase of a near date and sale of a forward date is termed 'borrowing'. The terms make sense, in the context of physical delivery, in that metal has been lent to the market in the one case and borrowed in the other.[46]

TABLE 17.8

UNITED KINGDOM IMPORTS AND RE-EXPORTS OF LEAD AND LEAD ALLOYS a

Quantity: thousand tons   Value: £ thousand

IMPORTS FROM:	1913 Quantity	1913 Value	1928 Quantity	1928 Value	1938 Quantity	1938 Value	1958 Quantity	1958 Value	1968 Quantity	1968 Value
S.W. Africa	77·6	1424·4	17·3	370·8			6·1	428·5	12·8	1290·2
Spain	24·2	443·3	47·9	1015·7	0·03	0·4			0·06	101·1
U.S.A.	10·4	182·8	8·7	182·7	41·5	643·2	0·5	36·9		
Mexico	72·2	1308·2	93·6	1973·8	187·8	2502·4	105·9	7770·4		
Australia			48·0	1027·5	107·7	1691·0	40·4	3003·0	144·4	21263·8
Canada			38·1	795·8					48·7	4946·8
British India	3·1	53·4			61·3	958·3				
Burma b					14·1	185·7				
Others	16·7	306·1	12·0	346·7			12·0	878·3	7·3	987·7
Total	204·1	3718·1	265·6	5713·0	412·4	6431·0	164·9	12117·0	213·5	28589·6
RE-EXPORTS:										
Total	13·6	247·0	18·8	403·8	25·1	399·6	2·3	163·7	1·6	155·9

a. Includes wrought, unwrought, plates, sheet, strip, tubes etc.
b. Prior to 1958 Burma included in British India.

Source: Annual Statement of Trade.

TABLE 17.9

UNITED KINGDOM IMPORTS OF ZINC (WROUGHT AND UNWROUGHT) AND ZINC ALLOYS, 1913–1968

Quantity: thousand tons Value: £ thousand

IMPORTS FROM:	1913		1928		1938		1958		1968	
	Quantity	Value	Quantity	Value	Quantity	Value	Quantity	Value	Quantity	Value
East Germany									0·3	33·6
Germany	71·4	1708·9	27·8	752·9	7·1	119·4				
West Germany							0·8	54·4	8·1	1040·7
Netherlands	14·4	349·8	4·2	116·8	4·2	65·4	10·7	779·4	1·1	126·9
Belgium	63·6	1568·2	68·8	1919·2	42·0	648·5	0·8	75·0	2·7	381·8
U.S.A.	4·7	118·9	22·0	602·7	1·3	41·7	73·4	5188·6	0·8	129·6
Canada	1·0	18·5	10·5	280·0	88·7	1290·6	6·3	446·6	96·8	11594·4
Australia	0·2	3·1	10·0	267·7	15·6	231·9			5·7	654·8
France	6·3	158·5	1·7	47·3						
Soviet Union							15·9	1061·4		
Poland a			3·7	101·9	2·3	45·4	8·5	560·1		
Others	2·3	54·2	10·5	279·5	12·3	181·5	19·0	1318·3	54·9	6275·0
Total	163·8	3980·1	159·0	4368·1	173·5	2624·3	135·4	9483·7	170·4	20236·8
RE-EXPORTS:										
Total	2·4	60·7	5·0	93·2	2·7	51·9	1·1	76·3	0·7	81·6

a. Poland 1928 and 1938 includes Dantzig.
Source: Annual Statement of Trade.

Chapter Eighteen

THE HUDSON'S BAY FUR AUCTIONS

1. *Early Fur Trading*

DURING the early history of mankind fur was a necessity, and it is more than probable that the Greek legend of Jason and the Golden Fleece may have had its origin in some unusually perilous and fortunate trading voyage to the Euxine.[1] Given the proclivity of the human race to create distinctions of class whenever the opportunity presents, it is not perhaps surprising that by Greek and Roman times, if not earlier, the variety of furs was already being used to distinguish social rank. By medieval times the use of furs in Europe had become a luxury and the designation of certain furs to distinguish the nobility and high officers of Church and state had become well established. Sumptuary laws forbade the use to commoners of certain furs, such as ermine, except as headgear.[2]

Until the seventeenth century Northern Europe and Russia were the principal sources of the world's supply of fur. The Baltic ports were the great collecting points for the trade and for centuries most of the international commerce was handled by the Hanseatic merchants. In Britain, London became the centre of the fur trade and the Skinners' Company was one of the largest livery companies in the metropolis. This organization dates from 1327, and was thus earlier even than the Leipzig furriers' guild which was founded in 1423. During the reign of Elizabeth I Russia was still the origin of most imported furs and the Muscovy Company was granted the English monopoly of trade for this area.

When Europeans turned their attention to the exploitation of animals in the New World English adventurers concentrated upon the New England area during the first half of the seventeenth century. Later, English supplies were greatly augmented from the conquered territories of New Netherlands and the Hudson-Mohawk route to the Great Lakes. Further north, the French were in possession following Jaques Cartier's penetration of the St. Lawrence as far as the Lachine rapids and the establishment of Montreal as the terminus of fur supplies from the West. Thus, though the London fur market had been strengthened by supplies from those parts of the New World dominated by the English, the French market with its access to Canadian supplies was obviously a main competitor. However, the real impetus to English domination in the Canadian fur trade did not come until the arrival of

Groseilliers and Radisson in London[3] after they had failed to interest the king and his ministers at the French Court. It was they who conceived the notion of setting up trading posts on the shore of Hudson's Bay in order to avoid the taxes incurred by the use of the French-controlled St. Lawrence. Radisson was not without experience, having spent his life in Canada, and was the first European to explore the upper reaches of the Mississippi and the Missouri rivers. Charles II was impressed, and the result was the famous expedition of 1668 in the *Eaglet* and the *Nonsuch*. The latter vessel completed the voyage and returned laden with furs. A royal charter was granted on 2 May 1670 to 'The Governor and Company of Adventurers of England trading into Hudson Bay'. The new company thus calmly assumed monopoly trading rights over half a continent and proceeded to organize its own army and navy and to exercise full plenary powers within its territories.

Asian furs were channelled to European centres through more than one route. The role of the Hanseatic League in selling furs from north-west Russia has already been remarked upon. These pelts were brought to the centres of population via the Baltic Sea, whereas furs from north-east Russia were brought south to the Black Sea and the Caspian Sea. The Russian penetration of Siberia brought still more furs. Alaska, too, became a rewarding territory for the trappers, though costs proved high in this area and led to centralized political and commercial control – the latter through the Russian American Fur Company.[4]

The Hudson's Bay Company started inauspiciously in conditions of glut and the furs were disposed of privately in very small lots, or else were shipped to Amsterdam, Leipzig, Paris and Vienna for sale. Buyers from the Continent were attracted by the abundant supplies and soon appeared in strength. The Company had therefore to find a saleroom, and in December 1671 a notice was posted outside Garraway's Coffee House in Exchange Alley, announcing that '3,000 weight of Beaver Skins, comprised in thirty lotts, will be offered for sale',[5] and within a few years pelts sold on the London market were being exported directly to Russia.[6] In fact during the eighteenth century on average some 70 per cent of imported furs were re-exported, the principal markets in order of importance being Germany, Holland, Flanders and Russia. The demand from the two latter countries was of negligible importance until Holland declined as a distribution centre for French furs after the English conquest of Canada. Despite the prominence afforded to the fur trade in English colonial history, however, its importance must not be over-rated, for as one writer has emphasized,

> . . . fur, both in its raw and manufactured state, played a most insignificant role, not only in the total English economy, but even in the total colonial economy. During the period surveyed imports

of fur accounted for less than half of one per cent of the total value of English imports; exports of raw fur, both domestic and foreign, account for less than one quarter of one per cent of the total value of English exports.[7]

Not surprisingly, in view of the many commodities auctioned there, Garraway's Coffee House soon became inadequate for the Hudson's Bay fur auctions, and for two hundred years public sales were held in a saleroom in Fenchurch Street. For the first century of its existence the Hudson's Bay Company's chief problem was French rivalry but, despite this, the Company prospered. By 1690 the original capital of £10,500 had been raised to £31,500, and to £94,500 in 1720. However, after the end of the Seven Years' War, when Canada became a British possession, a rival company, the North-West Fur Company of Montreal offered considerable competition. In contrast with the Hudson's Bay Company, moreover, it espoused a policy of selling furs in centres other than London, and in this way built up a very considerable connection. Following heavy losses an amalgamation was carried through in 1821 and the fortunes of the new united Hudson's Bay Company began to revive – though the introduction of silk hats in 1839 proved something of a set-back.

In response to the recommendation of a Select Committee appointed in 1857, the Hudson's Bay Company agreed 'to surrender to Her Majesty all the rights of government, property, etc., in Rupert's Land, and also all similar rights in any other part of British North America not comprised in Rupert's Land, Canada, or British Columbia.'[8] The Canadian government paid compensation, and made considerable stretches of fertile country available to the Company upon completion of the arrangements in 1872.

TABLE 18.1
VALUES AT CURRENT PRICES OF U.K. IMPORTS AND RE-EXPORTS OF HIDES, SKINS AND FURS, 1854–1938 (ten-year annual averages)
£ million

Years	Imports	Re-exports
1854–63	3·6	1·3
1864–73	5·0	1·7
1874–83	6·2	2·2
1884–93	6·5	3·1
1894–1903	7·3	4·3
1904–13	11·0	6·4
1914–23	19·3	7·6
1924–33	18·6	11·5
1934–38	18·5	9·2

1854–70 Computed Value. 1871–1938 Declared Value.
No figures available for 1854, therefore 9 year average.
Source: Mitchell, *Abstract of British Historical Statistics*.

In London, meanwhile, sales continued to increase (Table 18.1), and the accommodation at Fenchurch Street was beginning to prove inadequate. As a result the old silk warehouse of the East India

Company in Wine Street was leased and fur sales were held there from 1865 until 1928. On 28 January in the latter year the venue for the Hudson's Bay auctions became the present building, that is, Beaver House, Great Trinity Lane, on Garlick Hill, in the City. By this time, moreover, the fur sales had ceased to be the exclusive preserve of the Hudson's Bay Company but were vested in the Committee of the London Public Fur Sales. Currently the auctions are arranged by the Secretary but are held under the auspices of the Hudson's Bay Fur Sales Ltd. The London Fur Traders' Association has established arbitration machinery for dealing with disputes. A Fur Exchange was also opened on 22 February 1933 in the Strathcona room at Beaver House.[9] However, owing to the structure of the trade, the term Exchange does not imply – as it frequently though not invariably does – a centre for the conduct of sales by description. In fact, the room is merely a convenient meeting place for members of the fur trade.

In some ways the subdued murmur of the present day auctions of 'ranched' furs is a far cry from the hectic sales of hunted and trapped furs which were held at Garraway's and Fenchurch Street almost three centuries ago, and yet in other ways the system has remained surprisingly similar. Clearly, the most obvious similarity lies in the fact that furs are still sold by auction, for, like high quality tea and greasy wool, furs for the most part have to be seen in order to be properly evaluated for size, colour, quality and nap. However, great strides have been made with sorting skins – in Copenhagen, for example, the process is completely automatic – as the result of which sales of some classes of fur are sometimes made upon the basis of samples. Furthermore, it is not unknown for some forward trading to take place in some furs for which demand is greatest. Communist China sells all its furs upon description. This country is an increasingly important source of supply (Table 18.2), and large quantities of weasels, kolinskies, goatskin, ponies and lambskins are offered each year under contract to foreign buyers. State agencies in China sort, size, sex and grade the skins, generally very accurately, before sale by specification. This enables contracts to be concluded in London, though the most important buyers have China agents, while in France Rothschild's disposes of the furs received in barter exchange for French exports to China.

2. Fur Production

By today only some 10 per cent by value of the world's furs are from wild animals; these come mainly from Russia, which supplies sables, martens, ermine, fox, squirrels, muskrats, marmots and fitch. Other principal sources of wild furs are the U.S.A., which supplies muskrat, wild mink, opossum and racoon, and Canada, from which come the skins of beaver, wild mink, squirrel, muskrat, foxes, seals and some other animals. Unlike ranched furs, almost all of which are sold by

TABLE 18.2

U.K. IMPORTS OF UNDRESSED FUR SKINS IN 1968 SHOWING THE MAIN COUNTRIES OF ORIGIN

Number of skins: thousand   Value: £ thousand

IMPORTS

From:	Rabbit		Mink		Lamb a		Other	
	Number	Value	Number	Value	Number	Value	Number	Value
Afghanistan					1471·3	4006·0	154·4	288·0
Argentine Republic			132·3	636·0			3163·9	1910·3
Canada			59·4	211·8			1612·9	1066·2
China			493·1	2538·9	159·5	60·9	14·8	69·9
Denmark			209·7	879·9			116·0	139·2
Finland			27·1	115·0			483·8	151·0
France	3437·7	456·1	56·8	207·8				
Japan			235·8	1219·3				
Netherlands			150·4	836·3			422·3	93·1
Norway							27·4	58·2
Pakistan					686·2	496·1	24·9	49·9
Republic of South Africa					477·6	1339·3	10·6	40·2
South-West Africa					4146·6	11523·6	33·5	71·0
Soviet Union			728·7	2625·7	280·0	675·3	2616·6	1368·2
Sweden			116·5	577·7	13·6	35·7	132·5	144·4
U.S.A.	477·2	54·5	183·4	973·4	85·6	195·4	2782·6	2666·4
West Germany			54·6	316·2	40·3	69·5	286·5	238·1
Others	874·2	95·3	290·9	1321·0	128·5	201·6	1023·2	2821·8
Total	4789·1	605·9	2738·7	12458·9	7439·2	18603·4	12905·9	11145·9

a. Including Persian Lamb, Astrakan, Caracul, Broadtail and similar skins.

Source: Annual Statement of Trade.

auction, much of the wild fur changes hands privately, often direct from the trapper or his agent to the consumer. This holds true particularly for what the trade calls 'spotted goods' (e.g. ocelot), and for American muskrats which are numerically very important. It is thought that nearly 1½ million China weasels are sold each year and almost 400,000 Chinese kolinskies. In 1965 the U.S.A. produced some 450,000 wild mink, compared with 125,000 for Canada and 75,000 for Russia. The rest of the world produced 10,000 of the skins. The catch of wild fox is of the order of 300,000 annually. Wild squirrel production in Russia varies between 3 and 5 million and during 1965 over a million marmots were offered at the Leningrad, Leipzig and London auctions. It should be noted, however, that wild goods sold by auction may be withdrawn and put on offer again a number of times should the reserve price not be reached. Each time this happens the figure is recorded so that double counting takes place. Moreover, goods not sold in Leningrad are often shipped to London for sale.

Following over-trapping, successful schemes for protecting particular animals have been launched. Thus, an upper limit to the annual catch of Alaska seal has been set, while other animals, such as Russian sables, have been moved to other areas. Before World War I the number of chinchillas was seriously reduced and the governments of Peru, Argentina, Bolivia and Chile prohibited the export of pelts until numbers had recovered. More recently, overtrapping led to a serious depletion in the number of beaver. However, the Canadian government has now set up reserves, with Indians in charge, as the result of which a very satisfactory resurgence of numbers has taken place.

There has been a massive increase in ranched furs to keep pace with the rise in demand and to compensate for the loss of wild furs due to over-trapping. Despite early abuses and many failures fur farming has now become a substantial industry. A very rough estimate of world mink production would be some £120 million a year, of which more than £100 million consists of ranched furs. (Some indication of its importance is given by the establishment of chairs of mink genetics at some American universities.) The rapidity of growth may be gauged from the increase in farmed mink in Canada. The number sold in 1919 was 47, while in the 1965-66 season it was 1¾ million. In Europe the Swedish figures provide a similar indication: at the first Swedish auction of ranched mink in 1935 700 skins were sold, whereas the figure for 1965-66 was 1.7 million. Altogether, world production for 1965-66 was almost 22 million pelts, the chief producers being the U.S.A. (8.3 million), U.S.S.R. (2.8 million), and Denmark (2.4 million). With the failure of mink prices to keep pace with costs during the first half of the 1960s a number of smaller farmers sold out, and the trend in mink farming appears to be firmly in the direction of large mink ranches producing 1,000 pelts and upwards per annum. Some farms, such as the Keppo Oy farm group in Finland, and the Dalchosuze Mink Farm in Perthshire, are very large indeed.

Persian lambs are now ranched almost exclusively in South-West Africa, the U.S.S.R. and Afghanistan. Total annual production is of the order of 10 million 'Persians', worth more than £20 million. France alone farms 6 million rabbits a year, while blue fox production from all sources amounts to about 300,000 a year. Chinchillas are also farmed for furs.

3. *The London Auctions*

The world's chief distribution centres are at Leningrad, New York, London and Copenhagen. To the auction houses at these centres come the pelts to be sorted for size, colour and nap, before being put into lots for inspection prior to an auction sale. In London the Hudson's Bay Company, which also has auction houses in New York and Montreal, dominates the proceedings, even though furs are now a minor part of the total activities of this organization. In May 1968 the Company's sales were £163.4 million plus fur consignment sales of £34.9 million: its primary function is that of retailer in the Northern parts of the American continent, though at each of its stores it is prepared to buy furs from trappers for cash. The Company also has mining and oil interests. (In fact more than 90 per cent of its profits are earned in Canada). Recently, however, there has been some further expansion of the Company's fur interests, particularly in securing almost exclusive rights to the sale of Afghan Persian lambskins. London is the world's main centre for the disposal of 'Persians', especially those from South West Africa, which account for about half of total world production. The lambskins from S.W. Africa are sold without reserve prices, but this is not true of the Russian and Afghan state-owned selling organizations which are prepared to withdraw lots which may subsequently be sold privately or else offered at the next auction series. Most of the Russian lambskins are offered for sale at the Leningrad auctions, whereas almost all the Afghan pelts come to London and New York for disposal. Small quantities are also sold at Leipzig. The Hudson's Bay also receives most of the Polish mink production – of some 275,000 skins – which is sold outside Poland. Mink shippers from most of the Western European countries and Japan also consign mink pelts for sale to the Company though London has lost its supremacy for the sale of mink. It now handles about 2½ million pelts a year, which is about half the amount sold in Copenhagen. The bulk of the Polish blue fox skins is sold by the Company, and finally, it also sells a range of wild furs from North America.

Two other auction houses channel their consignments to the Hudson's Bay Company sales on Garlick Hill. Anning, Chadwick and Kiver

Ltd, and Eastwood and Holt Ltd have their premises between Beaver Hall and the river, on Upper Thames Street, only a matter of yards away. Eastwood and Holt is owned by Thorrers of Germany. It specializes in the sale of S.W. African Persian lambskins of which it sells the greatest number (1.85 million skins in 1966). It has connections with the largest S.W. African cooperative, while the Hudson's Bay Company is linked with the second largest. Together, these two houses alone offered almost all the 4.2 million S.W. African 'Persians' on the London market in 1966, compared with a total of 2.79 million for all Persian lambskins offered in Leningrad in the same year. In addition to the African 'Persians', the Hudson's Bay Company alone disposed of more than two million Afghan 'Persians' in 1966, though some of these were sold in their New York auctions.

Annings' traditional connections have been with the Russian trade. Unfortunately for this Company the U.S.S.R. has staged a considerable revival of the Leningrad auctions, so that though some shipments of muskrat, squirrel, marmot and other skins were still received, profit levels were at one time adversely affected. The firm did, however, sell some mink from other origins and S.W. African 'Persian' lambskins. Anning, Chadwick and Kiver, which was a public company whose shares were quoted on the London Stock Exchange, eventually became the subject of a successful take-over bid some years ago, and is now owned by the Woodhall Trust. The membership of the Committee of the London Public Fur Sales is completed by Goad, Rigg and Co. who specialize in rabbit skins. Another firm, Flak, Chandler and Co. Ltd, auctions consignments of tanned East Indian goat and sheepskins every seven or eight weeks at the London Leather Wharves. They are now the sole selling brokers of tanned skins in the United Kingdom since Dyster, Nalder and Co., for many years by far the biggest brokers in tanned skins, decided to go out of business in 1959. Domestically-cured hide is auctioned at frequent intervals at a number of centres in the United Kingdom. Public sales are held weekly, alternatively in London, Birmingham and Bristol and Manchester, Glasgow and Leeds.

The auction houses sell pelts in return for a commission, most of which is paid by the shipper and which varies according to the skin handled. The consignors of furs range, as we have already seen, from state owned selling organizations, to private cooperative ranches, merchants, and sometimes banks. S.W. African Persian skins are unusual in that the commission on their sale is 3 per cent of realized value from buyers in addition to 3 per cent from sellers. Commission rates for Afghan lambskins are 5 per cent from seller and one per cent from buyer, while for general furs, including mink, they are 6 per cent from seller and one per cent from buyer. In return for this commission the auction houses not only grade and lot the furs, but also provide insurance and warehousing for up to six months. However, the relations between the auction houses and the farmers do not end there, for the most important service which the sellers provide is finance. The auction houses lend money on the basis of the year's production to mink, 'Persian' and other farmers to help them to finance the rearing of the animals. Every year, moreover, the selling brokers send out experts to advise farmers on quality control, market trends and other matters. (The Hudson's Bay Company, for example, now has advisers in countries as diverse as Afghanistan and Poland.) Clearly, these experts also use these visits to solicit business, while many auction houses in North America employ travellers specifically for this purpose.

The Hudson's Bay Company has large inspection rooms for the 'showings' of furs prior to the auctions, and vaults in which unsold or uncollected furs are kept. Catalogues are drawn up and sent to likely buyers at least five days before each series of sales, which are held in February, May, July and in September or October. The catalogues are large, and each series usually lasts for about two weeks, for the range of furs on offer is normally very wide. In addition to these general sales, other public sales of particular furs are held when fresh skins arrive in the warehouses. The main sales of mink are held in December and January and those of Persian lambskins about six times a year. Sales of rabbit skins are held at monthly intervals from October to July.

Beaver Hall, where the London auctions are held, is a broad amphitheatre fitted with an impressive mahogany rostrum and seating of green leather upholstery topped with brass. The proceedings take place under the eye of a magnificent moose's head, which gazes across to the auctioneer representatives of the selling brokers, who have drawn lots for their position in the order of sale – except that 'Bay' furs are by tradition sold first, starting with beaver. One of the features of the fur auctions is the system of 'strong lots' whereby the successful bidder is entitled to purchase remaining skins in the same series of lots of the same quality at the same price. Another buyer can only get into the string by bidding up, or if the original bidder decides that he has bought enough lots. Excitement normally mounts at this point. In order to expedite the process of sale, other auctioneers sit on the rostrum to take up bids from the floor which are then relayed to the auctioneer. Mink furs are sold at a rate of some 150-175 lots per hour: the number of skins in a lot varies widely, but about fifty is now a very frequent figure. The auction room has an electric indicator upon which prices are displayed. These are also relayed downstairs to the Strathcona Room.

Traditionally the chief purchasers of furs at the public sales are the fur merchants from whom the coat manufacturers or trimmers then purchase their requirements. The merchants are an international fraternity and at the London auctions there are hundreds of overseas buyers. However, the recent growth of overseas fur auctions and the lotting of furs in small quantities (e.g. mink in fifties, and 'Persians' in two hundreds) has encouraged the manufacturers to purchase at the sales. They may bid themselves, or else employ dealers to do so for a commission of some 3 per cent. Many of the wealthier dealers have encouraged this trend by granting credit to the small scale manufacturers. As yet this weakening of the fur merchant's position is not universal for many skins, notably 'spotted goods', are only sold in large expensive parcels which few manufacturers can afford. Increasingly, therefore, the financial aspect of the fur merchants' business is being emphasized, for it is only by breaking down expensive lots or providing credit in competition with the dealers, that the fur merchant is able to maintain his connections. Not a little of London's continuing importance as a world fur auction centre, therefore, derives from the ability of its merchants to give credit, not only to the coat makers and trimmers who honeycomb the vicinity of Garlick Hill, but also to overseas buyers. Similar considerations affect the auction houses. As has been mentioned, these brokers frequently finance the rearing of animals on an annual basis. Moreover, within forty-eight hours of the end of an auction, accounts will have been rendered to suppliers, and cheques paid over. Meanwhile the auction companies have to wait for prompt day for the buyers to settle their accounts. For S.W. African 'Persians' prompt day is fourteen days after sale, and thirty days after the first day of sale for other furs. Bridging this financial gap requires the ability to command resources running into millions of pounds. Some notion of the order of magnitude involved is given by the annual import bill, which for 1968 was £42.8 million.

4. *Auctions at Origin*

One of the results of the decisive shift in the emphasis of fur production from wild to ranched animals has been the emergence of many countries (such as those of Scandinavia), which had previously been of negligible importance, to prominence in the trade. This, coupled with the enormous growth in demand, has led to the development of major auctions in countries of origin. It is a development which has had its counterpart, as has already been observed, in many other commodities for which London initially served as the world's central market. As was true for many other commodities, moreover, the shipping and other difficulties associated with the U boat blockade of World War I provided a considerable impetus to the establishment, or else the development, of major markets outside the United Kingdom. The American and Canadian fur auctions owe their genesis to these wartime problems of the fur trade, and by today the growth of sales in producing countries poses relatively minor transport problems for would-be buyers, who are able to fly to these primary markets quickly and easily to purchase their requirements.

Despite these radical changes, the London auctions continue to be important and cosmopolitan, even though they are certainly smaller than the New York and Leningrad sales. The furs in the New York auctions are sold mainly to domestic merchants and manufacturers, whereas the British domestic market is comparatively unimportant except for muskrat and Canadian squirrel. The small size of the domestic market is clearly indicated by the high proportion of imports which is re-exported (Table 18.3). As far as mink, the world's most important fur, is concerned, of some 21 million skins produced in 1966, the U.S.A. bought 11 million and Germany between 5½ and 6 million, so that the purchases of all other countries amounted to no more than some five million pelts. Germans are heavy purchasers of mink at Copenhagen and of Leningrad 'Persians', while about half of Russian mink output, surprisingly enough, is consumed internally. One of the consequences of this is that there are times when, with a weakening of demand, London's vulnerability as a centre for the auction of mink tends to come to the surface. Thus American and certain other countries' support for the London series falls off when the supply position eases. London's weakness during such periods is also exacerbated by the auction houses' practice of withdrawing lots.

TABLE 18.3
UNITED KINGDOM IMPORTS AND RE-EXPORTS OF UNDRESSED HIDES,
SKINS AND FURS, 1938, 1952 and 1968
Quantity: million cwt   Value: £ million

| | IMPORTS | | RE-EXPORTS |
	Value	Quantity	Value
Undressed Hides and Skins			
1938	6·7		1·4
1952	20·6	1·6	1·0
1968	19·7	1·5	0·3
Undressed Furs			
1938	11·5		8·2
1952	19·9	0·07	17·8
1968	42·8	0·08	36·3

Source: Annual Statement of Trade.

Prices can often vary by more than a third from those established during the previous season, and when this happens the auction houses tend to withdraw lots rather than sell at what they consider to be too low a price. Thus in the April 1967 series of auctions in London, only 35 per cent of the mink offered was sold and the remainder was withdrawn, while during the June series in the previous year, only 498 blue-fox pelts were sold out of a consignment of over 10,000.[10]

The financial facilities provided by the auction houses enable them to act in this way, but buyers are naturally reluctant to attend sales at which most of the goods might be withdrawn.

As has already been mentioned, London is the world's main centre for the sale of Persian lambskins, of which the Germans are heavy buyers (Table 18.4). The connections established between the London auction houses and the South West African and Afghanistan farming organizations appear to be very firmly cemented by financial assistance, buttressed by technical and marketing expertise. However, a disruption in the African connection could easily follow in the wake of political disputes, in which case the grandsons of the German settlers who originally started farming Karakal lambs in 1907 have a ready-made sales centre in Frankfurt if not in Leipzig. The latter was one of the world's foremost fur centres before World War II, and when the Nazi blight descended in the 1930s the London fur trade benefited considerably from the influx of Jewish refugees from that centre.

The Leningrad auctions, now the world's largest, were instituted by the Communist regime in the 1930s and, since the early 1950s, have become a major international event in the fur trade. Auction series are held three times a year and are notable for that very highly-prized fur, the sable, though other furs have now become much more important numerically. The U.S.S.R. fur industry, comprising hunting, farming and sales, is organized by the Sojuzpushnina, a state body needless to say. The atmosphere at the Leningrad sales is very 'western' and the bidding is in dollars. Their effect upon the London auctions is frequently very direct, especially upon Anning, Chadwick and Kiver Ltd. The following report typifies a recurring situation: 'Owing to the Leningrad sales, Annings did not participate in the London sales, but issued a catalogue, mainly of mink, for sale by private treaty.'[11]

The Leipzig fur auctions are also run by a state-owned auction house, which aims principally to re-establish its pre-war reputation by selling skins from non-Russian countries in the Communist bloc. At present these auctions are chiefly notable for Mongolian furs such as red fox, lynx, fitch, marmot, ponies and wolf. The West German auction centre is at Frankfurt.

During the latter half of the 1960s the Scandinavian countries became the world's largest producers of ranched mink. In 1969 total output was some 9½ million skins. The auction houses established in Norway, Sweden and Denmark are cooperatives owned by the farmers and, of these, that at Copenhagen has emerged as the largest centre. Its lead has been consolidated by securing connections with Finnish farmers, in addition to which it also handles the Royal Greenland Trade Department seal crop. The auction room is a recent building outside the city, where the process of sorting and selling is the admiration of visitors accustomed to traditional methods and more hum-drum

TABLE 18.4

U.K. RE-EXPORTS OF UNDRESSED FUR SKINS IN 1968

Number of fur skins: thousand Value: £ thousand

RE-EXPORTS TO:	Rabbit		Mink		Lamb a		Others	
	Number	Value	Number	Value	Number	Value	Number	Value
Canada			110·4	507·6	48·0	93·8	227·5	317·6
France			66·2	306·8	409·7	1293·0	293·3	461·4
Italy			404·9	2353·3	935·7	3440·0	363·7	1634·5
Japan							149·6	465·8
Switzerland and Liechtenstein			108·9	577·0	222·0	836·2	75·5	313·2
U.S.A.			469·8	2007·4	688·9	2039·6	483·2	1604·9
West Germany			735·9	3305·9	3513·3	9103·0	1256·4	2505·8
Others			171·6	869·2	514·8	1303·4	686·8	794·2
Total	285·5	23·1	2067·7	10109·2	6332·4	18109·0	3536·0	8097·4

a. Includes Persian Lamb, Astrakan, Caracul, Broadtail and similar skins.

Source: Annual Statement of Trade.

surroundings. Scandinavian mink is marketed and promoted under the brand name Saga. Skins are sorted into bundles matched according to colour, size, quality and sex regardless of the farms from which they originate. This, it is claimed, makes for such accuracy that a buyer could with confidence purchase from the catalogue description. Naturally, this system complicates the accounting enormously but the computer is able to cope with these problems without apparent difficulty. The modernity and the efficiency – not to mention the provision of meals without charge and free fashion shows – all contribute to attract bidders who almost always number more than 300; that is, as many as attend the auctions at Leningrad and London. Equally important is the fact that all the offerings are for sale and will not be withdrawn if prices happen to be low. The Paris fur auction is a very minor affair established to sell some of the French mink production, which is of the order of 200,000 skins a year.

In the U.S.A. there are four auction houses, of which the New York Fur Auction and the Minneapolis Fur Auction are owned by the same company: the other two houses are the Seattle Fur Auction and the Hudson's Bay Company in New York. If the Trappers' Association at North Bay is excluded, there are six auction houses in Canada. The Hudson's Bay Company and a subsidiary of the New York Fur Auction Company, the Canadian Fur Auction Company, both have houses in Montreal. There are two houses in Winnipeg, namely the Soudack and Dominion Auctions. The two others are the Edmonton Fur Auction and the West Canadian Raw Fur Auction in Vancouver.

The members of the Committee of the London Public Fur Sales thus face formidable competition, especially since there is no large domestic market to which they can look for support. Climatic factors contribute to the explanation for this, but only partly. Fur coats tend to be expensive and this, many wholesalers would claim, owes not a little to the extremely generous margin demanded by the retailers. To the outsider, too, many of the premises at which fur coats are manufactured appear to be rather seedy and mysterious. Some fashion experts point to what they regard as shortcomings of style, and the failure of furriers to modify their ideas to suit young people. Perhaps more important has been the swingeing purchase tax imposed by the government, which was stepped up to 55 per cent in 1968. The hope always expressed, when such tax changes are made in response to the need to try to abate inflationary pressure, is that they might induce firms to export more. Unfortunately the U.K.'s main competitors in dressed furs, 'shells' (i.e. partly made up garments) and finished goods have home-based markets which are large, and the domestic manufacturers which supply them have already been disciplined by competition to be efficient. Even so, the enormous growth of ranch fur production, especially mink, poses the problem for the trade as to whether the continuation of such trends will produce better returns, from lower prices, finer margins and greater turnover, than exist at present.

In the meantime, London's continued importance as one of the world's fur distribution centres must depend upon its expertise in tendering advice on quality control and other aspects of production, and in its skill in sorting, grading, and marketing – and indeed in buying, for many U.K. dealers attend overseas auctions to purchase on behalf of foreign clients. It is some reflection of a continuing advantage which London has to offer that the Hudson's Bay Company of New York regularly takes advantage of the skill and the comparatively low wages of its London house to send lower priced skins across the Atlantic to be sorted and returned to New York for auction. London's present importance for some members of the trade is also illustrated by a further peculiarity, that is the practice of returning S.W. African 'Persians' to South Africa for dressing and dyeing (because of the superiority of the South African process) after being sold in London. The 15 per cent surcharge imposed by the U.K. government put an end to this business just as, in the long run, difficult money conditions and high interest rates will tend to erode what has been one of London's most telling advantages as a fur trade centre.

Chapter Nineteen

THE LONDON DIAMOND MARKET

1. *Free Marketing*

HATTON GARDEN is the London headquarters of the diamond industry and the chosen centre of operations of De Beers' Central Sales Organization, through which over 80 per cent of the world's output of diamonds is sold.

The area has a romantic history, for it was first identified separately when Elizabeth I granted one of her favourites, Sir Christopher Hatton, a part of the grounds of Ely Place in which stood the town house of the Bishop of Ely. Subsequently the whole of Ely Place was given to Hatton, and in the middle of the seventeenth century Baron Hatton turned it into a residential district. John Evelyn recorded in his diary for 7 June 1659 that he went to 'see the foundations laying for a long streete and buildings in Hatton Garden'. As late as 1824 the area was still 'an esteemed situation for the gentry' whose forebears had, for the most part, been city merchants who had moved to The Garden after the Fire of London in 1666. However, with a decline in rentals during the second quarter of the nineteenth century, watchmakers and jewellers had begun to spill over from the Clerkenwell district to Hatton Garden. Ironically enough, these traders had flourished initially at Clerkenwell as the result of the patronage of the rich merchants who lived in the 'esteemed situation' of The Garden.

Hatton Garden thus became a centre for precious stones of all kinds. It was, and for that matter remains, a considerable centre for the sale of pearls which were channelled to London from all parts of the British Empire. However, the pearl trade was destined to be quite overshadowed by the growth of the diamond trade before the end of the nineteenth century.

In 1870, when Cecil Rhodes emigrated to South Africa for the benefit of his health, he remarked in a letter home that 'people out here do nothing but talk of diamonds'. Before the South African rush such diamonds as were available came chiefly from India, China and Malaya. (The Koh-i-noor, the Orloff, the Regent and the Hope diamonds came from Golconda, near Hyderabad.) The supply was augmented by the opening of the Brazilian mines in 1729, but these were not nearly so rich as those which the early prospectors hit upon in South Africa during the latter half of the nineteenth century and later. When Rhodes joined in the diamond rush Johannes Nicolas de

Beer, the farmer on whose land the richest finds were made, was already assured of a fortune. Kimberley, which was to become the world's largest excavated hole, was still a hill into whose yellow and blue earth thousands of prospectors were burrowing with equipment which usually consisted of nothing more elaborate than a bucket and spade. By 1888 Cecil Rhodes and his partner, Rudd, had gained control of the De Beers' mines and, under Rhodes' guidance, this Mining Company began to buy up all the undertakings in the area.

London was the obvious location for diamond selling during the last quarter of the nineteenth century, and it was for this purpose that the two famous Barnato brothers, Solly and Joel, settled in Hatton Garden in the early 1880s. At the time, the individual marketing enterprise of some thousands of diggers gave rise to very considerable price fluctuations. It is not altogether surprising, therefore, that even before the turn of the century a syndicate of merchants was formed which for some years bought up the output of the former Cape Colony mines. Eventually the syndicate foundered because of competition from new discoveries of alluvial deposits in other parts of the continent. Subsequent finds included deposits on the coast of South West Africa, the Congo, Angola and in what is now Ghana. However, the greatest threat to existing producers appeared with the unrestricted sale of stones from the rich mine at Lichtenburg in South Africa in 1927. Many producers were still in disarray in 1929 when the depression came and forced some of them to close down.

It is at this point that Sir Ernest Oppenheimer enters the story. He was originally a diamond dealer in Hatton Garden who went out to South Africa and eventually rose to become chairman of De Beers in 1929. He conceived the notion of establishing a marketing cooperative which, to succeed, required the support of other producers in the industry. Because of the depressed condition of the trade, Oppenheimer managed to secure the cooperation of the producers in West Africa, the Congo and Angola to create a Central Selling Organization for diamonds, which dates from 1930. Ernest Oppenheimer established the Diamond Corporation as a De Beers' subsidiary, which then negotiated with producers outside the De Beers group. In return for marketing all the diamonds produced by these other enterprises, the Diamond Corporation guaranteed to purchase an agreed quota of stones from each, regardless of the state of the market. Quotas were decided by the Diamond Producers' Association (the D.P.A.), which consisted of the main producers in the De Beers group in South and S.W. Africa, the South African Government (which owned digging enterprises in Namaqualand) and the Diamond Corporation itself. It was argued, and continues to be argued,[1] that the aim of the D.P.A. is not to restrict output, but to regulate the flow of diamonds to the market according to the strength of demand.

Until 1934 most of the diamonds purchased by the Diamond Corporation were put into stock until the depression had passed. In that year Oppenheimer launched the Diamond Trading Company (D.T.C.) as the selling agency in order to leave the Diamond Corporation free to concentrate on the task of regulating supplies and acting as the link between De Beers and outside organizations. Thus the Diamond Corporation sorts and values all outside stones while the Diamond Producers' Association does the same for all South African stones. The Diamond Trading Company sold both gem stones and industrial diamonds until the establishment of Industrial Distributors (Sales) Ltd. As its name implies, this third organization handles the industrial end of the market for which demand had grown enormously as the result of wartime development. The stones are channelled to Industrial Distributors (Sales) Ltd by Industrial Distributors (1946) Ltd, just as the Diamond Trading Company now has a feeder organization called the Diamond Purchasing and Trading Company. The quota arrangements for gem stones do not apply to industrial stones, the prices of which are fixed by agreement, but both the marketing firms are prepared to hold substantial stocks in order to maintain prices. The Central Selling Organization was very lucky in this respect after the war, for having accumulated substantial stocks both during and before the war, it was able to sell them at post-war prices and thus add substantially to its financial strength. Since the war, the C.S.O.'s prices have been raised several times and never lowered. Sometimes the increase in the quotation has been a uniform one, and at other times for particular qualities. Demand has continued to rise strongly, though on one or two occasions (1958 and 1962-62) the C.S.O. has had to stockpile in order to preserve diamond values.

The three companies which are concerned with marketing over 80 per cent of the world's diamonds – the Diamond Corporation, the Diamond Trading Co., and Industrial Distributors – are London based, and it is to this centre that the stones are sent. The world distribution of rough diamonds thus starts by their being sent to the Diamond Producers' Association (South African stones) or the Diamond Corporation ('outside' stones) for sorting and handling. At this stage the stones are still 'rough' diamonds and require sorting into one of the 2,500 established categories. Account is taken not only of size and shape but also of colour and quality. The basis for sorting is shape: they range from stones which are perfectly formed crystals with straight sharp edges to cleavages, which are stones split along the grain. The 'maccle' and the 'twinned crystal' have a distinctive line around the edge with a herringbone pattern, Finally, the gem known as 'the flat' is distinguished: this is a flat-shaped crystal. An important factor in determining the value of a stone is the weight, and to sort each consignment into rough categories the stones are put through a sieving process. Stones below one carat (142 carats weigh one ounce) are known as 'melee'. Nearly all rough diamonds have some impurity in them, and grading for impurity is one of the most skilled jobs in the world. The difficulty is to estimate precisely where the impurities lie in the stone and how much loss of weight will occur when it is cut and polished. A flawless example, apart from being 'clean' (that is, it has no flaws known as picqués) should have no colour and be completely cloudless. This allows the light to be reflected from its inner surfaces and broken, as in a prism, into a dazzling spectrum of colour.

Gem stones are next sold via the Diamond Purchasing and Trading Company to the Diamond Trading Company. Except for the stones required by the South African cutting industry all the gem diamonds are then sent to London where, under a system of monthly offerings (ten in the course of a year) known as 'sights', they are sold to West European, American, Israeli and other cutting and polishing firms, and to a small number of dealers.[2] The Diamond Trading Company was housed until recently in St. Andrew's House, Holborn Viaduct, but has now moved to premises at 2 Charterhouse Street, E.C.4. In each of the 'sights' the rough diamonds are re-sorted and re-weighed, and the choicest stones are valued by senior executives of De Beers. The D.T.C.'s list of cutters and dealers contains only some 220 names. The ability to purchase stones on the scale which is normal at the 'sights' – for a parcel may cost as much as £5 million – obviously requires considerable resources. The declared policy of the Central Selling Organization is to sell only to firms which are 'financially strong and have complete integrity'. Each buyer on the list is notified by his broker of the date of the next 'sight'. The number of buyers present at any one 'sight' ranges from twenty to fifty. Every sale is negotiated through a broker firm, of which there are rather more than a dozen in London, which transacts this business for a one per cent commission. The small number of dealers who are privileged to buy at the 'sights', however, may make from 5 to 20 per cent profit upon resale. Prices are fixed and, despite the astronomical sums paid for the individual parcels, the C.S.O. will very rarely split a parcel to allow a purchaser to buy only those gems which he would most like to secure. Were the parcels made up according to the clients' previously expressed wishes, this would not be very significant, but, in fact, though indications might be communicated to the C.S.O., the latter pack the parcels according to their view of the supply situation. Clearly they are also aware of their clients' requirements, for most buyers tend to specialize in certain qualities, reflecting the specialization of their own cutting centres. De Beers argue that were they to make up parcels precisely to their clients' requirements, this would tend to increase the shortage of some goods and cause accumulations of others. This is undoubtedly true, as is evident in other industries characterized by competitive pressures and difficult joint-supply problems. What happens in these cases is that for those categories of product, where the accumulation of stocks threatens, the price declines, whereas the prices of other goods threatened with scarcity move up. However, the C.S.O. was established with the object of preventing price fluctuations, and in this it has been successful because of its determined policy of adding to buffer stocks during periods of slack demand. Merchants thus have, in effect, only the choice of taking or leaving the parcel offered to them by the C.S.O., which does not countenance any haggling over price. Occasionally, when a purchaser disagrees strongly with the C.S.O's valuation, he may ask to see someone with the authority to change the price in order to state his case. Obviously, however, the frequent repetition of such action would hardly endear him to the management, and his inclusion on the list of those invited to the 'sights' is something which every dealer or manufacturer considers to be valuable.

Because of this policy, the C.S.O.'s prices are sometimes above, and at other times below, prices in secondary 'open' markets. In fact, demand for both gem and industrial diamonds has continued to grow strongly since World War II, so that the total value of C.S.O. sales has quadrupled since 1950 and is now £288 million (1969 figure) a year. De Beers no longer issues separate figures for its business in gems and stones used for industrial purposes, but it is thought that about 70 per cent of the value of the turnover is in gem diamonds. (Though gem diamonds are, of course, a very much smaller proportion – normally some 20 per cent – of the quantity produced.) The terms in the diamond trade are cash in advance.

The buyers who fly in for the 'sights' are mostly from Antwerp, Amsterdam, New York, Paris and Tel Aviv. The first named is the world's main diamond cutting centre, employing some 16,000 people. The Amsterdam trade, established in 1585 after the first diamonds arrived from India, suffered particularly from the wartime invasion by the Germans, especially since many cutters and polishers were Jewish. Some of these are now working in other diamond centres, but others have established an important cutting industry in Israel. Firms are small – mostly employing fewer than fifty people – and diamonds are marked for cutting by the head of the firm. Such decisions are crucial when more than half a rough stone must be cut away. One cut may take several days to make, and to achieve its brilliance, a diamond must be cut so as to have fifty-eight surfaces at predetermined angles to one another.

Such considerations help to explain why diamonds are so expensive, but they are only part of the explanation. Mining itself is clearly a costly operation for, on average, some 80 tons of rock must be processed in order to find between 5 and 35 carats of rough diamond. Next, through the Diamond Producers' Association, the South African government receives 5 per cent of their value before export. When the diamonds arrive in London they have cost De Beers some £12 per carat. The diamonds are then sold through the C.S.O. for between £15 and £800. The diamond cutters buy the diamonds for an average price of about £100 per carat. Fifty per cent or more of the weight is lost in the cutting process, but the cutting and polishing add to the value, so that when the diamond leaves the hands of the cutter it is worth, on average, some £250 per carat. The cutter sells to a manufacturing jeweller, sometimes through the intermediacy of a merchant, who must charge a margin. The manufacturing jeweller sets the stone in a ring and adds a 25 per cent margin, which takes the price per carat up to some £337 even in the absence of further dealers, who often intervene at this stage to sell to the retail jeweller for a further one per cent. Add to the £340 which the retailer pays, the U.K. government purchase tax of 55 per cent, that is, £187. The retailer, who may have to carry the ring in stock for a long time before selling it, may add a mark up of perhaps as much as 100 per cent. Even on the assumption that it is no more than 50 per cent, the piece of jewellery consisting of a one carat diamond in a plain £20 platinum setting will thus cost the customer some £700.

2. *Cutting Centres*

Because Antwerp is the world's main centre for cutting diamonds it has also become the main market for polished stones. Diamonds are not standardized goods and this, together with the fact that the market (unlike the one in rough diamonds) is competitive, means that each diamond must be separately priced. In Antwerp the transactions take place in the vicinity of the Pelitzanstraat with a degree of bargaining which varies according to whether or not the manufacturers are selling to established customers. The diamonds are sold on behalf of the cutters by brokers, who have to carry these wares on their persons to the offices of diamond merchants, or else to one of the four bourses which serve the trade. The buyers are experts who must be able to judge the value of a gem from subtle colour gradations, marginal differences in clarity, and the quality of the cut. When a potential buyer has made a firm offer for a stone, the diamond is put into an envelope, which is not opened until the transaction has either been concluded or else has fallen through. After the envelope has been weighed and registered the broker returns it to the seller who considers whether he is able to accept the offer which has been made. This code of conduct dictates that if the seller accepts the buyer's offer, then the latter must honour his bid by purchasing. The system is designed to protect the buyer, for the sealing of the envelope signifies that the seller cannot offer the diamond to anyone else in the meantime.

In Antwerp, as in other markets in polished gems, the broker is a key figure. It is to him that the dealer or manufacturer hands the stone so that he may find a seller. He is thus a trusted figure who will often be walking around to his market contacts with a fortune in his pocket. Contracts of sale are rarely drawn up, and a deal between the parties concerned is usually sealed with the Hebrew word 'mazalubracha' ('Good luck and be blessed'). These oral contracts are rarely questioned. In recent years, moreover, the growth of the diamond business has resulted in the granting of credit to the buyer. Here the knowledge of the broker in his dealing at market level is the judgement upon which the seller relies when considering an offer.

As has already been remarked, the London market in polished stones is situated in Hatton Garden, which houses a considerable number of unobtrusive dealers' and brokers' offices – often rather shabby, for expertise is all that matters – alongside the equally dingy premises of manufacturing jewellers. Until some years ago many of the transactions of the smaller dealers and brokers took place on the pavement or else in the cafes in and around Greville Street. Under these conditions the main defence possessed by this very cosmopolitan fraternity against inquisitive outsiders was to conclude their business in a variety of foreign languages ranging from Yiddish to Persian. Since 1962 the need for street and cafe trading has been eliminated by the establishment of a bourse at 32 Hatton Garden. Thus the London market in polished diamonds has now become a good deal more formal for it boasts a secretary, a porter to bar the door to strangers and even a library. In the interests of security no list of members is made available (except to Scotland Yard) and there are always plain clothes police on duty in the vicinity. Across the road, the London Diamond Club at 87 Hatton Garden has been in existence since 1941, when it was founded by refugees from Holland and Belgium. Many diamond traders are members of both bourse and club, though at the latter most of the members are concerned with rough or industrial diamonds. The amounts of diamonds retained in the U.K. and the quantities re-exported cannot be determined because figures for the trade in diamonds are not published. The import figures include both rough and cut stones, industrial diamonds, diamond dust powder and 'boart' (diamond fragments).

The United States is the largest buyer of the world's diamonds, and now has an industry which turns out cut stones whose total value is greater than that for any other manufacturing centre. However, because of the high labour costs, it is uneconomic for New York cutters to handle relatively small stones (of $\frac{1}{4}$ carat or less). In terms of man-power, therefore, the American industry, which employs some 3,500 persons, is far smaller than that of Antwerp. There are also cutting and polishing centres in Puerto Rico and Arizona. The industry in Israel has grown rapidly, and now employs some 9,000 workers responsible for about one-third of the world trade in polished stones. Britain's industry is small but flourishing and owes a good deal to refugees who fled from Holland and Belgium during the 1930s and 1940s. There is now also a small industry in West Germany, and manufacturing has been re-established in Amsterdam. Finally, India, too, has a manufacturing industry in and around Navsari, Surat and Bombay. Some of the stones are mined at Panna, but the Indian Government now has an export promotion scheme whereby a proportion of the value of exported cut and polished diamonds, emeralds and rubies can be used to import rough diamonds. The world market in gem stones is, however, a competitive one. Moreover, because the C.S.O. charges uniform prices this competitiveness depends significantly upon costs at the processing end of the industry.

3. Some C.S.O. Problems

The Central Selling Organization has not existed since 1930 without encountering problems. Its control over the market has depended upon its near monopoly of sales, securely based upon the very considerable proportion of world diamond output directly under De Beers' control. The most serious threat to the C.S.O. was posed by Sierra Leone. In 1930 diamonds were discovered in the Gbobara River, as the result of which the Consolidated African Selection Trust sent a team and secured exclusive prospecting rights. Later, additional finds were made outside the concession area and so a Sierra Leone Selection Trust (S.L.S.T.) was negotiated in 1935 which was granted exclusive diamond mining rights over the whole country. After World War II the increase in demand for diamonds led to the establishment of a black market supplied by Sierra Leonians who started digging illegally in the remoter areas of the S.L.S.T. concession. By 1952 this digging had assumed the character of a rush. The number of diggers ran into thousands, and when they wished to dispose of their finds they simply set out through the jungle to Monrovia, the capital of Liberia, where they sold the stones with no questions asked. The turnover in Liberia was estimated to exceed £12 million a year at a time when total sales at the 'sights' in London were some £70. Eventually the S.L.S.T. agreed to surrender most of its concession to the government in return for compensation. The Sierra Leone government then legalized native operations by providing the diggers with licences provided they sold their diamonds to authorized traders. A De Beers company made its appearance, so that today a large proportion of the Sierra Leone production is sold through the C.S.O. in London. The problem is by no means entirely solved, however, for illicit diamond mining and dealing on the remaining S.L.S.T. concession is, it seems, booming. At present, though operations are illegal, they are difficult to control. Most of the stones are sold to Lebanese dealers, but a high proportion of them eventually find their way through the Diamond Corporation to the London market[3].

Other problems emerge from time to time as a by-product of the distaste felt for the policies of the South African government. Thus Nkrumah pulled out of the De Beers C.S.O. in 1954 and decreed that all Ghanian diamonds were henceforward to be sold in Accra, though the bulk still goes to London. The U.S.S.R. also announced, in 1963, that as part of its support of the boycott of trade with South Africa it would no longer market its diamonds through the C.S.O. These changes in the situation led H. F. Oppenheimer to state, in 1964, that political objections had imposed a measure of reorganization and that buying operations in newly independent African states 'are now undertaken by companies registered and managed outside the Republic of South Africa and which are not subsidiaries of De Beers'. Such changes are not in themselves enough to disrupt the De Beers organization, which nevertheless still markets 80 per cent of the 42 million or so carats of diamonds produced by the world every year. Such trends cannot fail to be disturbing to the C.S.O. for they could conceivably develop sufficiently to make its control over the trade less certain. However, the African continent seems to have been particularly well endowed with diamonds, as the accompanying tables 19.1 and 19.2 show. At present, for example, the richest diamond mine in the world is Consolidated Diamond Mines of South Africa, where the gems come from the marine terraces along the edge of the Namib desert. Moreover, since 1962,

TABLE 19.1

VALUES OF UNITED KINGDOM IMPORTS OF DIAMONDS FOR 1968 a
£ thousand

Imports From	
Sierra Leone	31,272·2
Ghana	3,763·6
Tanzania	9,416·0
Hong Kong	1,481·8
Irish Republic	22,200·2
Soviet Union	37,654·0
West Germany	1,512·3
East Germany	56·3
Netherlands	4,402·3
Belgium	25,748·1
France	2,029·2
Switzerland	2,062·6
Portugal	17,216·8
Congo (Brazzaville)	1,793·5
Congo (Kinshasa)	12,879·5
Republic of South Africa	95,979·2
Israel	7,868·4
United States of America	4,558·3
Others	9,637·2
Total	291,531·5

a. Includes undrilled industrial diamonds, diamond dust powder and boart.

Source: Annual Statement of Trade.

TABLE 19.2
WORLD EXPORTS OF ROUGH DIAMONDS BY VALUE, 1949–68
£ thousand

	1949-54e	1955-60e	1958	1965	1968
Sierra Leone a	1,357	6,960	7,184	18,480	23,140
Ghana	4,032	8,264	8,662	6,759	7,117
Tanzania	1,898	3,815	4,415	7,114	7,901
South Africa b	19,737	23,679	20,572	26,655	81,625
Congo (Kinshasa) c	4,927	10,750	12,055	14,000	14,800
Angola	3,384	5,727	6,885	11,273	16,872
Others	2,096	4,233	3,256	8,287	11,500
Estimated World Total d	33,400	63,400	63,030	92,800	163,000

a. Method of valuation changed from 1960.
b. Data refer to exports of natural gem diamonds: the values of synthetic diamonds from 1962 were as follows:

£ thousand	1962	1963	1964	1965	1968
	550	1156	810	194	2,083

c. Data from 1960 are estimated: from 1962 include diamonds mined illegally and exported through Congo (Brazzaville) and Burundi.
d. Excluding exports from the Soviet Union and Brazil for which complete figures are not available.
e. Annual averages.

In addition exports of rough diamonds are recorded by certain non-producing countries as follows:

	1949-54d	1955-60d	1958	1965	1968
Belgium	3,918	15,275	12,319	29,167	56,530
United States	91	424	361	3,719	2,895
West Germany	a	a	a	679	9,275
France	247	267	243	643	802
Sweden	20	66	97	64	242
Japan	15 b	39	19	c	c
United Kingdom	a	a	a	158,384	271,674
Netherlands	a	a	a	10,102	12,610

a. Figures not available.
b. Average 1953 and 1954.
c. From 1962 uncut diamonds are not separately distinguished in the Japanese Trade Returns.
d. Annual averages.
These figures should not be taken to imply any high degree of accuracy because of the increasing scale of smuggling.

Source: Commodities Division of the Commonwealth Secretariat and Non-Metallic Minerals, No. 2 (London, 1967).

diamonds have been won from the ocean bed off the coast of South Africa. The operation is now in the hands of De Beers, who sank a floating mine in 1964. Also, a 'pipe' mine (i.e. of kimberlite blue ground in which diamonds are found) near Postmasburg, known as the Finsch mine, was opened in 1967 – the first such mine to be opened since 1903 – in addition to which the original De Beers mine at

Kimberley has been re-opened. Finally, important new finds have recently been made in Botswana.

All the activities mentioned above are in the hands of the De Beers organization, the strength of whose present position is indicated by comparing the 20 per cent or so of world production for which the Republic of South Africa is responsible, with the 80 per cent, or thereabouts, of world production which it markets.

4. *Synthetic Diamonds*

Meanwhile, the growth of demand for both gems and industrial diamonds has led to the development of substitute materials. The oldest substitute for gems is, of course, 'paste'. This is simply a lead glass, which is still extensively used for costume jewellery. There are also natural stones, such as zircon, which resemble diamonds in poor light, and a synthetic white stone which can also be made to resemble diamond when it is step-cut. Probably the most successful substitute is a recent discovery now marketed as 'fabulite', which is a strontium titronate which has the same refractive index as diamond. Other synthetic gems include rutile, white sapphire and white spinel.

Attempts to produce synthetic gems which have all the brilliance and fire which are associated with first class diamonds are more recent than attempts to make synthetic industrial diamonds, which were first produced in 1955 by the General Electric Company. These are pale gold or pale black in colour and therefore useless as jewellery. While synthetic diamonds are by no means a complete substitute for natural diamonds they have, nevertheless, become an effective replacement in certain applications. The effect has been to release natural diamonds for other uses, for it was the scarcity of industrial diamonds which led to the search for a synthetic substitute in the first place. Since then there has been an enormous growth in the use of industrial diamonds and their substitutes. De Beers now have a factory for the production of synthetic stones in the Republic of South Africa. The production of synthetic diamonds was accompanied by a long and expensive dispute between De Beers and General Electric over patent rights. This was eventually resolved by an agreement (reported by H. F. Oppenheimer in his statement which accompanied the Annual Report and Accounts of De Beers Consolidated Mines Ltd for 1967) by which General Electric assigned to De Beers its patents in South Africa to produce synthetic diamonds. It also licensed De Beers to market and produce diamonds in a number of European countries including Ireland. At the same time, De Beers entered into agreements with the Swedish company, Allamanna Svenska Elekriska Aktiebolaget (A.S.E.A.), by which De Beers, through a subsidiary, acquired a 50 per cent interest in certain companies which were formed by A.S.E.A. to take over their synthetic diamond and diamond tool manufacturing.

All the synthetic diamonds manufactured by De Beers' associated companies are marketed through the Central Selling Organization. By this means it is hoped, obviously, to maintain the near monopoly position which has so far enabled this organization to control prices. As synthetic production expands to an ever-increasing circle of advanced industrial countries, the De Beers organization will doubtless seek to maintain control by means of further agreements. The prospect of belonging to an organization through which diamond prices can be governed will doubtless prove attractive to many, though in view of Russia's break with the C.S.O. in 1963 it is more doubtful whether De Beers will be able to interest Russia or other Communist-bloc countries in marketing synthetic output through the C.S.O.

Meanwhile the search for nature's diamonds continues and has been extended as far afield as the Arctic. It is reported,[4] moreover, that at least one anxious De Beers shareholder has written in asking what the company is doing to secure mining rights on the moon. He was told, apparently, that though at present the territorial status of the moon has yet to be decided, he could rest assured that shareholders' interests would be pursued at all times. Of that there can be little doubt, and probably for the foreseeable future, though the De Beers' grip is somewhat less secure than it once was, it is probably still firm enough to ensure the status quo in the face of all but major disruptions.

Chapter Twenty

THE RATIONALE OF THE MARKETS

1. *The Development of Central Markets*

TRADERS have always tended to congregate in order to transact business, for the presence of many sellers and a concourse of buyers ensure a market for the former and supplies for the latter. At a time when transport and communications were slow and uncertain, moreover, buyers needed to be assured of supplies, so that it was natural for stocks of commodities to be held at or near centres of consumption rather than at origin. For commodities produced at a distance, therefore, the chief centres of consumption became 'reservoirs' of commercial stock to which the produce was attracted. One of the best early examples of such a primary produce stockpile established near its market rather than its origin is that of the English wool staple at Calais. For this species of compulsory marketing board proximity to the Flemish manufacturing centres and the routes to the Italian cities was all-important. It was at these centres of consumption, therefore, that the goods changed hands.

An international market centre naturally develops as a focus of information concerning the likely state of future demand and supply. Thus, as the emphasis of English foreign trade shifted after the middle of the sixteenth century from the North Sea to the oceans which separated Europe from more distant lands, uncertainties multiplied and the need for centres of information increased. The coffee houses supplied this need, for it was by knowing something of the harvest prospects for important overseas crops and the details of shipping movements that buyers formed their judgements as to how much they ought to pay for goods, and sellers what they ought to fetch.

The risk and uncertainty involved in long-distance commerce at a time when transport and communications were rudimentary meant that merchants were loath to adventure a major portion of their capital upon one voyage, and yet large ventures were more likely to survive and prosper than small ones. This problem was solved by the monopolistic organizations established in the sixteenth century and later: enterprises such as the Dutch and the English East India Companies, the Muscovy Company, the Levant Company, and others. These organizations minimized risks by enabling merchants to limit their individual participation in enterprises which were on a comparatively large scale. Their monopolistic structure, moreover, ensured

410

the best possible prices for merchandise at the periodic markets held after the return of the ships. The ability to absorb merchandise was important in achieving good prices, and this the chartered companies were able to do because of their general opulence, for some of this wealth was used to build warehouses for the storage of commodities. There was thus very little piecemeal selling on thin markets. Even at their zenith, however, these companies accounted for no more than a portion of England's foreign trade. The question then arises as to how the remaining trade was organized and, indeed, how all overseas supplies were absorbed by the commodity markets when the day of the chartered companies was done.

The absorption of supplies by a market, whether it is a medium for transactions in produce from home or overseas, requires the development both of a physical and a financial organization appropriate to the volume of trade being handled. Fairs, for example, were held only periodically during medieval times in order to ensure the necessary concourse of buyers and sellers. Eventually the growth of the volume of trade in places such as Antwerp and later Amsterdam, turned these centres into what were virtually continuous fairs. Market organization became correspondingly complex and its system of brokers, dealers and financiers was one which we would have little difficulty in recognizing today. However, the actions of these figures were not always condoned either in England or on the continent, and the legitimacy of some of their functions remained a matter for legislation and of bitterness over many centuries. In brief, it took society many years to recognize that a free market requires intermediaries in order to fulfil efficiently its functions of registering variations in demand and supply pressures and of ensuring the release or absorption of additional supplies as prices rise and fall.

In England the early domestic produce markets shared with the overseas commodity markets the vicissitudes of the process of emancipation, for in essence their functioning was the same. Typically, on both markets produce came to be consigned to factors or brokers for sale 'on the spot' in the central markets. During early modern times the broggers and staplers took over much of the finance of the wool trade from the Italians and the large-scale 'woolmen', while the Blackwell Hall factors provide a fascinating example of how financial facilities developed in the cloth trade. The Mark Lane corn factor, too, was often a very important financier, and both he and his confrères in merchanting were prominent as early members of that hybrid species, the merchant banker. In the marketing of commodities from overseas the evidence points strongly to the vital role of the factors and brokers in financing the movement of goods. For this purpose they used the bill of exchange developed by the Italian bankers. In the financial field, therefore, there were no strict demarca-

tions of function between bankers on the one hand, and merchants and
agents on the other, especially before the nineteenth century. It was a
period of fluidity and growth in commerce and in spite of his oath the
broker, too, seldom felt obliged to deny himself the advantages of
dealing on his own account or on that of a nominee. Many brokers
built up fortunes by providing credit to clients, a dual function also
characteristic of many merchants, who doubled as factors when this
proved profitable. For both broker and factor provision of a channel of
finance was often the vital service provided to the overseas producer
and not infrequently – as in the early nineteenth century cotton trade –
to the domestic manufacturer as well.

In general, official intervention during the medieval and early
modern periods was inspired either by the threat of scarcity or else by
situations in which the bargaining power of buyer and seller was
unequal. Thus, though the ordinances against regrating, forestalling
and engrossing might appear to be merely doctrinaire from this
distance, their origin probably owed a great deal to society's concern
that flagrant injustice would result from the absence of intervention,
for monopolistic practices are much easier to adopt when transport
difficulties shelter the market from outside competition. A similar
concern for the consumer lay behind state intervention in the Tudor
period to ensure an adequate supply of essential grains for the metropolis. During the period of London's rapid expansion the Tudors felt
that its provisioning could not be entrusted to corn middlemen. This
resulted in legislation against the fraternity as the State turned in the
direction of a more solid-seeming section of the community – the
justices of the peace and the twelve livery companies – to perform the
task subsequently left to corn merchants, market dealers, brokers and
financiers. However, the notion that the market mechanism should be
set aside during abnormal periods when scarcity threatens is one which
has been espoused subsequently on a number of occasions, notably
during the two major wars of the present century.

The transition from official regulation to freedom, like most transi-
tions, was usually painful. There were frequent abuses, some of which
we have examined. Indeed, many appear upon first inspection to have
been so great as to render the net advantages of freedom suspect. Upon
closer examination, however, some seeming malpractices – such as
the purchase of cattle at one end of the market for subsequent re-sale
at the other – turn out to be no more than arbitrage-type operations
which made the markets more perfect by exerting pressures which
tended to establish uniform prices. Other practices, such as withholding supplies from purchasers in order to enhance the price, though
they appear more sinister, turn out to be doomed to futility in the long
run because of the limited time for which it was possible to deny
supplies to the market. Usually such actions merely tended to ensure

supplies when shortages threatened and prices started to rise. This was the obvious justification for the activities of the jobber who emerged as a prominent market intermediary during the eighteenth century. In the fish, meat and similar trades, keeping qualities were obviously a restraint upon the jobbers' attempts to manipulate the market, but finance could also be a factor. Clearly, the most fundamental consideration was monopoly power, especially when linked to financial resources. The East India Company and similar organizations, for example, could often afford to hold goods for long periods, while the power to make advances upon the basis of merchandise also entrenched the position of many factors and brokers in commodities from overseas. Though many other traders, such as the Mark Lane corn factors or the Smithfield jobbers, seemed to possess power over the market through their selling operations, it is doubtful whether they really had much influence on prices in the long run because, unlike the Committee of the Newcastle Coal Vend, they possessed no power to regulate output.

2. *The Decline of Auctions and the Growth of Forward Transactions*

Until the nineteenth century was well advanced, the predominant method of sale was of goods 'on the spot'. As we have seen, most commodities reached the central markets via the following three routes: the consignment of shipments by producers themselves, by commercial banks with a financial interest in the commodity, or by shipping firms which, for the most part, established their headquarters in the principal market centres. Inevitably the producer was separated from his market by middlemen since the alternative, not very realistic for most, was to provide the finance, and run the necessary risks, in order to market the commodity himself. In the market centres the stockholding function was performed by market dealers and substantial merchants, while the brokers provided the links between buyers and sellers. The link at one time was very frequently between selling and buying broker, with the auction chamber as the venue for purchase and sale. As already mentioned, the uncertainties of long distance transport meant that goods had for the most part to be sold after arrival; the other reason was that purchasers wished to examine commodities before buying them. Auctions in fact continued to be the method of distribution of most produce until accurate systems of grading developed, and for raw materials the demand for reliability in this respect became more insistent with industrialization, for quality is usually more critical in machine than in more primitive hand production. Examples of forward sales may, of course, be traced back to medieval times, but uncertainties surrounding delivery and quality militated against major developments in this direction until more reliable transport and communications had emerged.

Clearly, for domestically produced goods, improved internal communications exercised a considerable influence in enabling orders and samples to be sent by post Information was disseminated more quickly and, to the extent that links between markets were improved, they became less imperfect. An international postal service developed across Europe and its speed enabled forward sales of Russian wheat to be made on the Baltic and deliveries to be organized by the establishment of 'ports of call' at which the captains of vessels called for orders. However, the most profound revolution occurred with the introduction of the steamship and the electric telegraph, and with the opening of the Suez canal. These innovations resulted in a decisive shift of emphasis from the exporter of commodities to the importer at the central market, for the latter was henceforth able to order commodities for forward delivery in the reasonably secure knowledge that they would be delivered on the due date. With improvements in grading, moreover, he became increasingly confident of getting what he really wanted, as commodity trades evolved from sales by lot-sample to sales by description based upon standard samples.

This dramatic increase in the speed of communications killed the consignment trade in cotton and grain at an early date and, in time, forward trading became more general. In all trades the rapid and almost continuous links established between producer and consumer countries implied improved intelligence. The demand and supply pressures thus focussed upon the central market became a more accurate record of the world situation for that commodity. Local shortages were less able than formerly to give rise to substantial price increases when supplies existed elsewhere: news of scarcity and, accordingly, a hardening of prices henceforward resulted in the transmission of this intelligence to producer countries and the assurance of additional supplies. Central markets thus became more truly world markets than they had ever been before. Clearly, however, the trader's ability to order confidently from origin meant that the merchant's need to hold stocks was reduced. To the extent that this happened, it reduced the importance of the merchant, who tended from this time to be replaced by firms of brokers, with a consequent shortening in the channel of distribution between producer and consumer. In the sugar trade, for example, the chain of distribution through sugar factors and brokers to manufacturers gave way to the establishment of firms of international brokers, such as C. Czarnikow Ltd, who dealt directly with the producers, selling for them in London and on other markets. Despite the reduction in the stocks which needed to be held at international market centres, however, the ability to absorb and produce supplies according to changes in demand and supply pressures continued to be an essential feature of these markets. What happened after the introduction of steam and the cable was simply that the function of such markets as 'reservoirs' applied, not to the total flow of produce from producer to consumer, but only to that proportion which did not find direct final purchasers. The London Metal Exchange, for example, still performs this function though only some five per cent of the world's output of the metals concerned pass through this market.

The natural concomitant of more accurate grading and the growth of c.i.f. trading was a decline in sales by auction. In some commodity trades this tendency was encouraged by the brokers, who were often able to secure a double commission from private sales. In other trades, however, the difficulties of grading the produce accurately, and the fact that higher prices were frequently obtainable at public sales, resulted in the retention of the auction system. Thus, in London, tea, wool, furs and skins, ivory and bristles were still sold in this way, though the coffee auctions proved a failure when private trade was resumed after the 1939-45 war, despite efforts to re-establish them. The main London auctions (i.e. in tea, wool and furs) have their counterparts in some other major centres as the most satisfactory method of distributing these commodities, though misgivings are expressed by producers from time to time as to the efficacy of this method of sale.

The need for arrangements to arbitrate in disputes arising from commodity transactions has always existed and must have made up a considerable proportion of the work of the courts of 'piepowder' during the medieval fairs. With the growth of trade and the development of forward trading, however, the need for associations of traders responsible for the terms and conditions of trade, especially the drawing up of standard forms of contract for sales by description, the provision of arbitration machinery and the dissemination of information, became much more vital. This need coincided with the growth of specialization in particular commodities on the part of merchants and brokers and with the increase in competitive pressures. Trade associations established standard grades and kept – as they still do – standard samples. Committees of the various associations were formed to arbitrate in disputes, to draw up forms of contract and to keep them under review. This enabled commodity transactions to be reduced to their bare essentials of determining a mutually agreeable price, for the conditions governing delivery, quality and other pertinent matters were made uniform throughout the trade by the standard contract forms.

3. *The Development of Futures Trading*

Such refinements in forward trade by description were an essential pre-requisite to the development of modern futures trading. Markets in prices were by no means unknown even in sixteenth century Antwerp and seventeenth century Amsterdam, but in more recent times futures markets have evolved from the decisive shift in favour of forward trading in many major commodities. The development of significant markets in arrivals enabled traders to hedge their positions by entering into offsetting transactions. However, the fact that such transactions are for specific produce 'to arrive' imposes limitations upon traders because their ability to hedge then depends, as buyers, upon the availability of contracts which are suitable as to grade and date of maturity. Similarly, traders who wish to hedge by selling must depend upon finding buyers on the market prepared to take produce of a named grade and date of maturity. In brief, the limitations of forward markets as hedging media arise from the fact that they are markets in physical commodities. The solution therefore was to establish markets for contracts not subject to these limitations, that is, futures markets which are merely promises to deliver produce of a basis grade.[1] In establishing markets in prices the broker members of the trade associations concerned, therefore, took the evolution of commodity markets to their most refined stage. In their initial phase these markets were staples, reservoirs, or central storehouses for commodities at which goods were sold 'on the spot'. Next, with the development of reliable lot samples, it became possible to dispense with auctions of present goods in favour of private-treaty forward sales. The significance of commodity markets as international stockpiles thus declined, though the markets at these centres still maintained their function of registering prices, both in the present and for forward delivery. Modern futures markets evolved from these arrivals markets and, like forward markets, they are markets in 'rights' to the commodity rather than sales of the commodity itself. 'Rights' markets obviously enable traders to conclude transactions at a distance from the storehouses or wharves where shipments of commodities are landed. Indeed, the tendency for auctions to be superseded by private-treaty sales and for most commodities to be ordered for forward delivery set[3] the stage for a decline in markets defined as congregations of traders who meet to transact business. With the introduction of the telephone many brokers found that it was more convenient to marry up offers with requirements from their offices. However, this tendency operated most strongly only when the number of buyers and sellers dwindled with amalgamations. Thus, the actuals markets (variously known as spot, cash, physical and delivery markets) in many commodities – such as sugar and cocoa – though large, are now conducted almost entirely from brokers' offices rather than on a market floor. Many commodity exchanges (and an exchange is usually a centre at which transactions in a commodity are conducted in the absence of the good itself), therefore, have now evolved to the stage at which traders gather only to transact business in commodity futures. In Mincing Lane this applies to the examples of sugar and cocoa, given above, as well as to others previously mentioned.

4. *The Growth of Rival Markets*

Improvements in transport and communications, coupled with the growth in the importance of an increasing number of countries as consumers of commodities, have transformed patterns of trade and the relative importance of many market centres over the past hundred years or so. Among the industrial countries commodity markets of international importance have grown in continental Europe and America. In most cases the process was one of increasing demand for food and raw materials in countries other than the U.K. which, with improving transport and communications, made it progressively less worthwhile for ships to break bulk in U.K. ports. The development of regular shipping services to continental and North American ports, served by good internal railway systems, eventually took toll of the London and Liverpool markets, where the re-export trade declined, as indicated by Table 20.1. This change was encouraged by the discontinuity of the wars of 1914-18 and 1939-45 accompanied as they were by the closure of the U.K. markets. A good deal of the 'third country trade' associated with the commodity markets persists; indeed, this has been encouraged by the same development of rapid communications which has helped foreign centres to challenge the dominance of the U.K. markets.

The appearance of successful markets in countries of origin is a further development which has proceeded at an accelerated pace during the twentieth century, though in some cases this growth was already far advanced before the end of the nineteenth century. As has already been emphasized, the facilities afforded by the London money market were an important adjunct of the U.K. markets. Financial facilities enabled London factors to provide producers with immediate payments for their commodities, while the predominance of the U.K. as a centre helped producers to obtain good prices there. However, successful markets at producing centres developed once it was found possible to tap the resources of the London money market, as the well-documented history of the Australian wool trade makes abundantly clear. Here, too, the closure of the U.K. markets during the two major wars of the twentieth century created opportunities for producers to sell direct to consuming countries, and these were exploited and held. Ultimately, some of the markets now supplied direct from producing countries rather than via re-exports from London and Liverpool grew to be larger than those of the U.K. itself: Japan, for example, buys more wool than the U.K. at the Australian auctions, and the U.S.A. buys more rubber from the Eastern markets than the U.K. In consequence, these markets at origin are now larger than those of the U.K. while other producer markets – such as the tea auctions at Calcutta and Colombo, the tin market at Penang, and the fur auctions at Leningrad, Copenhagen, New York and elsewhere – are

TABLE 20.1

VALUES OF U.K. RE-EXPORTS FOR SELECTED COMMODITIES, 1854–1968 (Five-year annual averages)

£ million

Years	Grain	Coffee	Tea	Raw Cotton	Raw Wool	Oils, Oilseeds, Gums, Resins Tallow etc.	Hides Skins Furs	Non-ferrous Metals and Manufactures	Rubber
1854–58	0·4 a	0·7	0·6	3·1	2·0	2·0 b	1·1 b	0·4	0·1 c
59–63		1·7	1·3	10·4	3·1	2·3	1·4	0·7	0·1
64–68		3·1	2·5	16·6	5·6	2·3	1·3	1·5	0·2
69–73	0·7 a	4·5	2·7	9·3	7·6	2·9	2·1	1·8	0·5
74–78		5·3	2·5	5·1	11·6	2·7	2·2	2·2	0·6
79–83		4·5	2·5	5·3	15·2	3·2	2·3	2·4	1·3
84–88		2·8	2·1	5·0	13·8	3·1	2·8	2·9	1·2
89–93		2·5	1·6	4·7	15·2	3·5	3·2	3·0	1·6
94–98		2·1	1·4	3·9	12·9	3·8	3·3	2·2	2·7
99–1903		1·7	1·7	5·7	9·8	4·2	4·7	4·4	4·0
1904–08		1·8	2·0	7·6	11·7	4·7	5·4	6·2	5·9
09–13	1·1 a	1·2	2·5	9·6	14·3	6·0	7·4	7·7	13·7
14–18		1·2	2·3	8·6 b	6·0	4·7	4·3	4·7	12·8
19–23	2·4 b	2·5	3·3	13·2	26·8	6·4	10·8	5·0	9·4
24–28	1·3 b	1·8	7·7	8·5	29·0	2·9	14·0	3·5	15·3
29–33	1·0	1·8	5·9	2·5	15·6	1·1	9·0	2·1	2·6
34–38	1·1	0·6	4·5	2·0	12·8	0·7	9·2	6·8	3·6
1948	0·02	0·2	1·1	0·6	9·3	1·6	6·2	0·06	4·4
1958	0·2	0·9	8·6	0·7	6·3	1·3	18·9	0·4	32·0 d
1968	0·8	0·2	13·8	0·8	2·2	0·4	36·6	3·7	1·7

a. For the years 1854, 1874 and 1913 only.   b. 4 year average.   c. 2 year average.
d. For a number of years, starting in 1955, there was a considerable re-export trade to the Soviet Union which has now virtually ceased.

Sources: Mitchell, *Abstract of British Historical Statistics* and the *Annual Statement of Trade*.

of major international significance. Naturally, there is sometimes a division of function between the various centres. For example, for wool the London auctions have now become a marginal market in unsold Australian lots, whereas in coffee London is the chief centre for Robusta while New York predominates in Brazilian. Again, in the fur trade, London is the acknowledged world centre for Persian lambskins.

5. *Interventions*

In addition to facing competition from markets in producer countries and in other centres of consumption, the U.K. markets have also had to contend with interventions of various kinds since World War I. A rigid control over price can only be made effective provided that the controlling authority is prepared to offer, or to buy up, supplies. The interventions of metal producers, as we have seen, succeeded on a number of occasions since World War I in by-passing the London Metal Exchange and indeed in posing a threat to its very existence. However, the problem of stabilizing prices effectively is a considerable one and, if the market considers that too high a price has been fixed, stocks will be run down in anticipation of a collapse. The quantity to be hedged is thus reduced, while forward prices on futures markets will also reflect the expected break under these conditions. The backwardation which results will reduce the attraction of hedging, therefore, at the very time when, though the amount to be hedged may be reduced, stockholders will feel the need to insure most keenly. However, on the other side of the market, speculators willing to accommodate traders seeking to hedge stocks will be reluctant to enter the market, because any assessment of the likely future course of prices has to include guesswork as to the plans of the intervening agency. Surpluses from the American stockpile of strategic materials, sold through the General Services Administration – sometimes seemingly erratically – have frequently upset commodity markets. The influence of G.S.A. sales has thus been to increase traders' needs to hedge, in contrast with other forms of both official and private intervention which, by seeking to stabilize prices, have sometimes posed threats to the operation of free markets.

Official intervention in commodity trade may be unilateral or it may be international, embracing a number of countries, including consuming as well as producing countries. When a government intervenes in the market in order to fix the price, the repercussions are indistinguishable from the interventions of the producers themselves. For example, both the Canadian and Australian Wheat Boards are government agencies and their operation of a deferred pricing policy has made the hedging of wheat from these sources unnecessary for U.K. importers. The failure of the Liverpool cotton futures market is attributable to the same cause; that is, market intervention by a government agency (i.e. the U.S. Commodity Credit Corporation), and it is interesting to note a recent revival of activity in raw cotton futures in the U.K. following modifications in American pricing policy. The control of the export prices of shellac by the Indian government eventually proved inimical to the continuation of the London Shellac Terminal Market, which has now closed. More recently, the London Fishmeal Terminal Market failed to survive a number of influences adverse to its continuation, among the chief of which was price control by the Peruvian government.

International commodity agreements may attempt to stabilize prices, though this is not invariably true. The International Grains Arrangements treaty, the successor to a series of International Wheat Agreements, makes no attempt to regulate supply, and therefore price. Its aim is the less ambitious one of providing guaranteed markets for a proportion both of producers' output and of supplies for importing countries, at prices within an agreed range. It is nevertheless important for the successful continuation of the Arrangements to pitch the price range at a viable level, though this consideration is not of direct consequence for the operation of those grain markets, which are not affected by this type of agreement. By contrast with the Grains Arrangements, other types of international agreements seek to exert a direct influence upon world commodity prices by regulating supplies. This is accomplished either through output and/or export quotas (as for sugar and coffee) or else by means of export quotas coupled with buffer-stocks (as in the International Tin Agreement). The restriction of price movements for sugar and tin, however, has never been such as to stifle the operation of the markets in those commodities. Where agreements to intervene are operative, the ability of free markets to survive is largely governed by the range within which prices are allowed to move. The re-negotiated International Sugar Agreement of 1968, for example, obliges the Council to adjust export quotas so as to keep the price between $3\frac{1}{4}$ and $5\frac{1}{4}$ cents a lb, thus providing a very generous range equal to nearly half the mid-range price. The International Tin Council has found it necessary not only to shift the range of prices within which it is prepared to tolerate price fluctuations but also to widen this range. (The present band of £350 is about a quarter of the mid-range price of £1,350 a ton.) By contrast, the ranges established under the International Coffee Agreement were much narrower. (These varied with the type of coffee, but were worst for Colombian coffee for which it was only one-eleventh of the mid-range price in 1966 compared with one-eighth for Robusta coffee.) The consequence of such narrow permissible fluctuations was to inhibit the mechanism of the market to a very marked degree, besides making the Agreement a good deal more difficult to operate successfully. As we have already noted, the combination of the Agreement and a coffee glut virtually put paid to the New York futures market, while in London, which was affected to a lesser extent because the terminal market contract is for Robusta basis grade, turnover fell appreciably during the years following the conclusion of the Agreement.

6. Synthetic Substitutes

Meanwhile, the growth of synthetic substitutes has also been a major factor affecting turnover. It was calculated some time ago,[2] for example, that the increase in the consumption of substitutes has been at four times the rate of the various natural materials. One of the great advantages of synthetic materials is that price fluctuations are almost completely absent. Production is very frequently by large-scale enterprises which, even when short-term cost changes occur, are ready to absorb them in order to market the product at a stable price. Consequently, when synthetics become important substitutes for natural raw materials they not only prevent the sales of the latter from growing at the rate which world demand would otherwise make possible, but also exert an influence upon their prices. When the price of a primary commodity goes up, its synthetic substitute becomes increasingly competitive. The price increase of the former thus tends to weaken and fade out. Rubber producers have faced a considerable challenge from synthetic substitutes, the world production of which has been greater than that of the natural commodity since 1962. Thus, though no figures are available, it would appear that the turnover of rubber in London has been fairly steady for several years, although 'substantially less'[3] than during the 1950s, owing to the stabilizing influence which synthetic rubber has had on the price of the natural product. The growth of synthetic-fibre competition has probably contributed significantly to the declining turnover of the world's major futures markets in wool, though until recently the London terminal market turnover was probably adversely affected by an inappropriate basis contract. The situation is therefore a continuation of a trend which has always affected the commodity markets: the old-established hemp and tallow trades on the Baltic are now over-shadowed by nylon and electricity, just as the natural drugs and dyes sold in Mincing Lane have been largely overtaken by more modern manufactured substitutes. This trend, which appears to be accelerating, will doubtless continue to affect both delivery and futures markets, though it is obviously almost entirely confined to raw materials as opposed to foodstuffs.

7. Effects of Concentration among Buyers and Sellers

After the monopolistic chartered companies had had their day, prices on commodity markets were determined by a plurality of both buyers and sellers. During more recent times, however, the competitive picture has been modified very radically for some commodities. In some trades producers have joined forces to market their produce through a single channel. These marketing boards have varied in their ability to influence prices, as we have seen, from the cocoa marketing boards of West Africa to the Wheat Boards of Canada and Australia, and the U.S. Commodity Credit Corporation. Thus, whereas the West African boards cannot fix selling prices, though they do determine buying prices from producers, the Wheat Boards and the C.C.C. have much more power to do so. This departure from the competitive picture is matched in many trades by a trend towards larger manufacturing concerns in importing countries. The amalgamations which have taken place among the millers and the cotton spinners in the U.K. provide a clear example of these departures from competitive ideals, but many more instances may be cited: there are very large manufacturers in rubber, sugar, cocoa and vegetable oils, and in many other trades there has been much amalgamation though on a less spectacular scale.

The consequence of concentration among producers and manufacturers has been the tendency to by-pass traditional channels on the delivery markets. There has, in other words, been a major trend to 'buying direct' rather than through the market and this clearly affects the position of commodity brokers and dealers. In the U.K. grain trade, as we have seen, the broker and the port merchant have diminished greatly in importance as the large-scale millers have tended increasingly to deal with shippers. However, even when most of the physical trade in a commodity by-passes the market, it is still possible for that market to function efficiently as a register of prices, as the experience of the London Metal Exchange indicates. The L.M.E. is, of course, a delivery market as well as a medium for hedging and speculation, but, provided that price fluctuations persist, futures markets continue to indicate market conditions for the trade completely separately from the selling and handling of the commodities themselves.

The debate as to the relative efficiency of distribution via the markets compared with bulk purchase by the government appears in the United Kingdom at present to have been resolved decisively in favour of the former. Certainly such evidence as has been culled in the present study supports this conclusion. It is equally evident from the story of the markets and the course of prices during wartime, however, that abnormal conditions enable gains to be made from scarcities which high prices are quite unable to correct via the market mechanism. In these circumstances the government has every justification for imposing control over essential supplies in order to ensure that all sections of the populace are fed and able to wage war in the most efficient manner. By the same token, experience over many years indicates that futures markets also work most satisfactorily when commercial stocks are adequate. (It will be recalled that in market circles 'commercial stocks' mean supplies other than stocks held by government agencies or by manufacturers.) With adequate commercial stocks the market is able to function as a 'shock-absorber' of sudden increases in demand, so that no steep rise in prices occurs. Furthermore, when the market is in this balanced position forward futures contracts will be at a premium over spot prices (i.e. there will be a 'contango' as opposed to a 'backwardation'). These price relationships facilitate the hedging of stocks. Commercial stocks tend to be very low during abnormal conditions, such as obtain, for example, when war threatens. As we have seen, the early years following World War II were abnormal so that when the U.K. commodity markets were re-opened backwardation was a persistent problem, a condition which detracted from the usefulness of the U.K. futures markets for long periods.

In their most developed form, as we have seen, markets channelled commodities from producer to manufacturer through the intermediary of the market dealers and brokers. More recently the tendency has been to by-pass these traders in favour of direct purchases from shippers or producers' agents. However, an examination of markets in which these trends have manifested themselves reveals that what has triggered off the changes has been a breakdown at some point in the competitive pattern of numerous sellers and buyers. Suffice it to quote, in this connection, one major example, that is, the evolution of the grain trade, where there was an emergence of official selling agencies in some countries, matched ultimately by amalgamations among buyers in the U.K. The function of dealers and brokers was therefore reduced, though their usefulness in providing commercial stocks, splitting large parcels into smaller ones, and marrying up buyers and sellers when the structure of the trade was more competitive, remains undeniable. It thus seems extremely unlikely that the near-perfect atomistic competition, which obtained on the great organized commodity markets earlier this century, would have been accompanied by higher costs of distribution of produce than those which exist at present. In other words, the change in many markets from their former highly competitive structure was not caused by the shortcomings of competition, but by a reduction in the number of buyers or sellers or both.

8. The Changing Structure of the Markets

The tendency for erstwhile major market intermediaries – brokers and dealers – to diminish in number when they are by-passed is clear enough. A similar diminution in the numbers of these intermediaries has occurred with the decline in the importance of particular markets. In the London rubber market, for example, there are now only four firms whose major interest is in rubber even though there are some fourteen listed on the official prospectus of the Rubber Exchange. Similar rationalizations, moreover, have taken place on much stronger markets. On the London cocoa market, for example, which has been growing in size to vie with that of New York in recent years, though much of the supply is still bought from merchants by manufacturers, the tendency is increasingly to by-pass brokers in favour of dealers. The upshot of this has been to halve the number of broker firms over the past decade. Consequently, some of the firms have amalgamated, while others have turned to dealing in cocoa.

In addition to the need for a growth in size in order to cope with large-scale producers and manufacturers who wish to transact business in large parcels, there are a number of other reasons for the changes which have taken place among market intermediaries. Some markets, as we have seen, have been weakening and are dominated by the need to keep down overheads. Even on relatively strong markets, however, the need to keep down costs has become increasingly crucial, for the problems of financing commodity shipments have grown more acute for U.K. merchants. Interest rates have remained very high for many years and adequate credit has often been difficult to obtain. In addition, there has been an increase in the taxation of trading companies, while the increasing uncertainties experienced in the foreign exchange market over a prolonged period have led to a greater need to cover transactions in forward exchange markets, thus adding still more to costs.

The disappearance of some firms and the amalgamation of others also owes something to the complexity of communications, with its implications for capitalization, which is a necessary concomitant of the thrust now necessary to secure business in a world in which Britain is no longer the industrial hub. Private quarter-speed cables to principal clients half-way round the world are not unknown, in addition to direct Telex lines to major centres in North America and Europe. 'Quotation units' whereby users may obtain New York prices of literally a minute or two earlier by pressing a desk button are now commonplace. Closed circuit television, too, is often used. Some of the largest brokers have their own computers, while others make use of the London Produce Clearing House's computer facilities. The number of employees per firm to be found among the commodity market dealers and brokers ranges from as few as ten to as many as 170 or so.[4] Unlike the London Stock Exchange, where the demarcation of functions is quite clear, a fusion of functions to embrace broking and dealing in the physical commodity still occurs. Such firms also very frequently minister to their clients' needs in both delivery and futures markets. The small specialist firms continue to find a niche, though a number will be found on closer examination to be subsidiaries of other firms, for whom they provide a convenient channel to a terminal market for hedging physical transactions. However, for the reasons adumbrated, there are strong tendencies towards the growth of intermediaries which are large and operate on a near-global scale, both as brokers and often as stock-holders, in a number of commodities. This need for increased size and capitalization has meant that some firms have become owned by merchant bankers. Despite diversification, when firms are sufficiently large they are able to provide a complete service in the products in which they trade, a necessary characteristic for traders whose effectiveness ultimately depends upon their overall position on delivery and futures markets taken together. Clearly, large size is necessary to these brokers when they aim to transact business for clients both in the physical product itself and in the prices of those products on futures markets, especially when diversification into more than one commodity has taken place. Where brokers are floor members of a number of terminal markets they are in fact exploiting their skills as experts in the very specialized activity of transacting business on these markets; it is an expertise which is distinct from that needed in judging the qualities of a physical commodity, for the floor trading members of these firms are perfectly capable of switching from one terminal market floor to another according to the state of trade.

TABLE 20.2

ACTIVITIES OF COMMODITY BROKERS AS SHOWN BY
MEMBERSHIP OF TERMINAL MARKET ASSOCIATIONS
AT PLANTATION HOUSE 1970

No. of Firms who are Floor Members in:	Membership Totals	No. of Floor Members in Individual Markets	
1 Market = 68	68	Rubber Trade Association of London	11
2 Markets = 10	2 × 10 = 20	London Wool Terminal Market Association	10
3 Markets = 12	3 × 12 = 36	London Cocoa Terminal Market Association	46
4 Markets = 5	4 × 5 = 20	London Coffee Terminal Market Association	35
5 Markets = 7	5 × 7 = 35	United Terminal Sugar Market Association	19
6 Markets = 2	2 × 6 = 12	London Vegetable Oils Terminal Market Association	32
7 Markets = 2	2 × 7 = 14	Liverpool Cotton Futures Market	20
8 Markets = 0	0	London Metal Exchange	32
	205		205

Source: Compiled from the London Commodity Exchange, List of Members, with the cooperation of the London Produce Clearing House Ltd.

The pure commission houses on the commodity markets do not aim to provide a complete service in any commodity, though the right of any seller to tender actual produce in fulfilment of a futures contract means that these houses have to provide facilities to dispose of these deliveries on behalf of their clients. The commission houses are specialists in dealing on futures markets on behalf of clients and are commonly members of more than one such market. In addition, they may be members of a number of stock exchanges. Of recent years some large American commission houses, notably Bache and Co., and Merrill Lynch Pierce, Fenner and Smith Ltd, have appeared on the London commodity markets in response to an increase in interest by the general public. These commission houses are members of several commodity markets, as befits organizations of very large size in their field. As a result, a significant number of firms are now members of two or more markets, as the accompanying table (Table 20.2) shows. The evidence from the Mincing Lane markets, moreover, indicates a decline in the membership, of various categories, of the London Commodity Exchange, as Table 20.3 shows. The membership of the London Metal Exchange is at present thirty-two, and it exhibits a degree of separation from the Mincing Lane markets. To a considerable extent, dealers in metals are specialists in metals; possibly the high proportion of deliveries effected on the contracts has been instrumental in keeping out some of the large commission houses. The Baltic market in home-grown wheat and barley contracts is as yet too new and small to afford useful comparisons. It is evident, too, that the barrier separating the flow of funds into the stock and commodity exchanges respectively is now in process of being broken down, a process which will probably be accelerated by the rather more forceful publicity espoused by the American commission houses. The increase in the

TABLE 20.3

MEMBERSHIP OF THE LONDON COMMODITY EXCHANGE
ILLUSTRATING CONCENTRATION AMONG BROKERS, etc.

	1961	1964	1966	1970
Sponsor Members	237	192	178	160
Trading Members	372	319	286	258
Nominees	366	304	300	300

Note:

Sponsor members are firms which are shareholders in the Exchange Company, which runs the Exchange through a Board of Directors, assisted by a Floor Committee. Sponsor members have the right of representation in the Exchange. These representatives are members of the Sponsoring firms, and are known as Trading members. They, in turn, may appoint Nominees who also enjoy trading rights. The only other persons allowed on the Exchange floor are clerks who are registered by name, but not authorized to trade.

Source: Compiled from the London Commodity Exchange, *List of Members*, with the cooperation of the London Produce Clearing House Ltd.

movement of funds will undoubtedly prevent the markets from becoming too thin and therefore from establishing prices which may not be representative. Indeed, the danger is probably the opposite one of some distortion, in that the prices registered by the commodity exchanges will tend increasingly to move in sympathy with prices on the Stock Exchange. The financial resources available to the terminal markets are obviously of considerable importance to their success, and it is in this respect that their linkages with the City of London are of vital importance. It was for this reason more than any other that the wool terminal market was established in London in 1953 and, more recently, that a raw cotton futures contract was resuscitated in London rather than in Liverpool, its traditional home. In London, moreover, apart from the London Metal Exchange, all the terminal markets including the markets of the recently established London Oil Terminal Market Association are now located in Plantation House. (Before the war futures markets in vegetable oils were held on the floor of the Baltic, which continues to house the delivery market.) This close proximity of the markets enables the floor members to move from one to the other with the minimum waste of time, as is appropriate to a situation in which key personnel are skilled in market techniques rather than experts in the commodity in which futures are transacted. The other major reason for the establishment of these markets in London is clearly the common clearing facilities supplied by the London Produce Clearing House Ltd (of which some account has been given above in Chapter 8).

The commodity trade associations have played a prominent part in all facets of the organization of the markets during the past century or so, though many are able to trace a lineage which goes back even further. These associations have made themselves responsible for all matters affecting transactions in the commodity concerned. Many U.K. associations were pioneers in their field, so that today traders the world over are indebted to these organizations, which have drawn up forms of contract and thus cleared the way for transactions to take place both quickly and smoothly. The contracts of the U.K. associations are used far afield, even though the actual business does not pass through a British market, because the conditions of sale, the grade of the commodity, the conditions of freight, insurance and delivery are all carefully laid down, so that possible misunderstandings and disputes are reduced to a minimum. Moreover, when disputes do arise, the disputants frequently resort to the impartial machinery which has been evolved by the trade associations over the years. Thus, these panels are very frequently asked to arbitrate on disputes concerning transactions which have never passed through a U.K. commodity market, or, indeed, through any market at all. The contracts are copyright, and a charge is made for their use. Similarly, there is a scale of fees payable to the association concerned for the services of its arbitration panel. Finally, it should be mentioned in connection with the work of the associations that, because the trades were organized in this way, the difficulties surrounding the reopening of the markets after World War II were overcome through cooperation between these bodies and the Bank of England. The committees of the trade associations virtually supervised the special exchange control arrangements made for the benefit of their members. These arrangements allowed firms handling any of the so-called 'scheme' commodities to conduct business freely with overseas firms and on foreign markets, provided that they followed the broad trading rules laid down by the schemes, without needing to obtain confirmation that each transaction was permissible before making a contract. The arrangements made between the Bank and the associations provided for 'regular consultation regarding the general position, trading and condition of the Market', to be achieved by frequent liaison meetings between representatives of the Bank and of the executive committees of each market. With the easing of exchange control restrictions discussions have tended to centre far more, according to the Bank's testimony,[5] upon general questions affecting trade, commodity agreements and kindred subjects. More-over, these liaison meetings have now been broadened to cover certain market associations having no particular interest in special exchange control schemes.[6] Meanwhile, outside London, close relations also exist between the cotton market and the Bank's branches in Liverpool and Manchester, between the grain market and the Liverpool branch, and between the wool market and the Leeds branch.

9. *The Bank, and the Markets' Earnings*

The relations between the Bank and the commodity traders became somewhat strained following the devaluation of 1967, but the con-tinuing liaison established between the associations and the Bank then proved their usefulness. Following discussions with the associations the Bank resolved the worst difficulties of traders, who faced losses following the failure of certain countries to devalue along with sterling, by offering unsecured loans at 5 per cent to cover 80 per cent of the losses up to a total of £5 million. The episode was a painful demonstration for the markets of their changed role in the modern trading world and of the extent to which they had, for some years, been running currency risks. The difficulties were clearly serious and the Bank viewed its task not only as a problem of assisting traders over their difficulties, but also of preventing the possible development of a chain reaction which might have endangered the future of the markets concerned.

Attempts have been made of recent years, especially by the Com-mittee on Invisible Exports, to separate out the earnings of the various activities which contribute to Britain's invisible earnings.[7] The complete isolation of the items needed for an exact calculation of the earnings of the U.K. commodity markets is impossible, but it would appear from the available breakdown of items in the Balance of Payments 'Pink Book'[8] that earnings on 'third country trade' amount to about £20 million a year. Commissions on imports and exports come to some £45 million a year, but this figure also includes the earnings of some other city merchants. Terminal market earnings are omitted from official estimates both because of insufficient information and because they are subject to such wide variations. This contention is borne out by some figures made available to the Committee on Invisible Exports. In 1962, for example, the United Sugar Terminal Market Association of London registered a net debit on overseas earnings of some £50,000 and a £3.7 million credit in the – admittedly exceptional – year 1963. The coffee terminal market's net overseas earnings in 1964 were negative (a debit of £38,000) but in 1965 there was a credit of £104,000. For 1964 and 1965, the foreign earnings of the cocoa terminal market consisted of a credit of £40,000 and a debit of £186,000. Rubber transactions moved from a debit of £1,000 for 1963 to a credit on overseas earnings of £7,000 for 1965.

The Committee on Invisible Earnings obtained figures from certain markets for their overseas earnings in 1964 and 1965. The returns were voluntary and, therefore, incomplete, but they were, nevertheless, appreciably greater than official estimates. Members of the associations were asked to estimate their gross profit earned in trade with non-residents, the gross commissions paid to them by non-residents, and the total differences received from or paid to non-residents in respect of terminal market contracts. Unfortunately, the returns included earnings in respect of U.K. imports and there is no way of separating these. The results obtained are shown in Table 20.4.

The profits and commissions directly earned by the commodity

TABLE 20.4

OVERSEAS EARNINGS OF SOME COMMODITY MARKETS
£ million

	1964	1965
Coffee	0·3	0·5
Cocoa	0·9	1·6
Grain		0·3 a
Rubber	1·2	1·3
Sugar	3·7 b	(similar to 1964)
Copper ⎤		
Tin ⎬	3·2	4·3
Lead		
Zinc ⎦		
Cattle foods	1·8 c	

a. Returns from Baltic Exchange, 1966.
b. Figures refer to 1963 but estimated that results for 1964 were similar.
c. Average of 1963–4.

Source: Britain's Invisible Earnings, p. 107.

markets are only part of their total benefit to the United Kingdom balance of payments. When the contracts exchanged on the markets are executed, the traders bring into play British banking, insurance and shipping services, for these contracts are almost invariably c.i.f. In the past, therefore, when a greater proportion of the country's total imports passed through the markets, their function as world centres of commerce was obviously a major causal element in London's world supremacy as a financial centre. Foreigners who wished to buy in the markets found it convenient to have sterling bank balances, and this was a material factor in the emergence of sterling as an international currency.

10. *International Comparisons, and the Future of the Markets.*
During the more recent past the fortunes of the markets have been seen to be inextricably bound up with the state of the pound sterling. After the war the markets failed to re-open because the U.K. monetary authorities felt for many years that they had to circumscribe very closely indeed the convertibility of sterling into gold or dollars. Some of the business which was formerly transacted through the markets was permanently lost as a consequence, and Table 20.1 shows how, in general, the drift downward has continued. The effect of the devaluation of 1967 upon traders has already been referred to, but the effects of its likelihood upon the markets were evident well before the long-delayed devaluation was finally forced upon a reluctant administration. Many markets continue, nevertheless, to be of considerable importance in a global context, though when comparing relative size it is as well to remember that dramatic changes in significance can take place within a relatively short time. For example, after the New York No. 4 sugar contract became inappropriate during the early 1960s (its delivery terms were f.a.s. Cuba), the No. 2 contract on the London sugar terminal market gained enormously in importance and the two markets have subsequently remained of approximately equal size. In the coffee trade, following the International Coffee Agreement and the coffee glut, London is now the world's premier futures market. The cocoa terminal markets in both London and New York are very active and generate considerable arbitrage business. Statistics for rubber are scant, but it is known that the London futures market is a great deal larger than the New York futures market, on which the trading volume had fallen to less than 2,000 tons by the end of 1967.

As recently as 1963-64, the turnover on the London Wool Terminal Market was significantly greater than that of New York, though the Sydney market was much the largest. By 1968, however, the London market was appreciably smaller than that of New York, while the Sydney market, though it had lost half its former turnover, was still the largest market. The continental wool terminal markets remain small but comparatively stable. The relatively new London Vegetable Oil Terminal Market Association's markets are still small by comparison with the large American markets, but among the metals London makes a much braver showing. In 1964-65 the turnover in copper on the New York Commodity Exchange was about four times as large as the L.M.E. turnover. Subsequently, however, the New York turnover fell to some 1.2 million (short) tons, while the London turnover grew so as to be roughly comparable with this. The volume of business in tin on the New York Commodity Exchange is almost negligible, so that the L.M.E. contract leads the field, as it does to an even greater extent for lead. The New York turnover in zinc is also negligible compared with that of London.

It would thus appear that where terminal market facilities exist in London, the exchanges often vie with, and are indeed sometimes more significant than, their counterparts in the U.S.A., although it must be remembered that the range of markets in the U.S.A. is very much wider than in the U.K.[9] However, as recently remarked,[10] assessments based purely on volume of turnover are clearly unsatisfactory for judging the international significance of a particular market. One market may be larger than another, and yet serve almost purely domestic interests. The danger in many of America's markets is that fluctuations in domestic demand exercise too preponderant an influence and distort the prices registered as viewed in a true world perspective. The U.S.A. also has markets which it is very difficult for overseas traders to use as hedging media because of the price structures produced by the intervention of government agencies in the pricing of the commodity.

As to the future of the U.K. markets, it seems likely that the re-export trades, with which the markets are intimately bound up, will continue to dwindle. Direct trading by producers and manufacturers, too, will undoubtedly continue to make some inroads into the turnover of many delivery markets. Broadly speaking, it seems evident that the commodity market functions which should continue to be of importance in the United Kingdom are those concerned with contracts (that is, transactions in rights), rather than the handling of the physical commodity. Some small specialized firms serving the markets are likely to continue, but the large broking firms are probably destined to become increasingly important in a highly competitive world. The maintenance of turnover probably depends crucially upon their being able to keep brokerage charges low. As previously mentioned, many firms have experienced considerable difficulties in doing so in recent years when interest charges, rents and taxation have tended to increase to high levels. In the present, as in the past, the provision of finance plays an important part in the retention of business. Purchasers of tea in Mincing Lane, for example, can still obtain three months' credit despite the fact that growers in producing countries often receive payment for their crops before the produce has been dispatched. The same is true of the fur trade, and examples could be multiplied. A significant proportion of commodity trade is still financed by brokers' capital: their borrowing from the banks is for short periods and is covered by bills, bonds and storekeepers' warrants of entitlement.

In the longer run, it becomes very difficult to forecast a future for the markets. They obviously face a number of adverse influences. British-based intermediaries would no doubt survive entry into the European Economic Community, and here the London Metal Exchange has shown an aggressive leadership in the establishment of continental delivery points. A more real threat is posed by the possibility of further market interventions in an endeavour to harmonize and stabilize prices in such a community. Further threats would be presented by more global ambitions to try to stabilize primary product prices through international commodity agreements, not to mention the growth of trade with the communist bloc and other centrally planned economies, whose negotiators would prefer to barter, or to trade with fixed prices, rather than to use free markets. It is possible, furthermore, to point not only to the by-passing of the markets by large producers and large manufacturers in consuming countries, but also to the increasing trend in favour of processing produce at origin. The countries of the under-developed world are now clamouring for adjustments in tariff preferences which would provide greater encouragement to these changes. In the meantime, improvements in transport and even in communications continue to be made, which have the effect of removing the trading world increasingly from the situations of uncertainty which gave rise to the widespread adoption of futures trading. A smoother flow of commodities, suitably aided by producer stocks, will tend to dampen short-term price fluctuations and so ultimately reduce the demand for the facilities afforded by markets and their intermediaries.

However, should the day ever dawn when the markets are no longer needed, it is as yet a long way ahead. In the meantime it would be wrong to be fatalistic or defeatist about the future, for the developments described in this study reveal an impressive ability to generate and sell specialized skills concerned with the international trading of commodities. There is every reason to believe that this ability will be valued by its purchasers for a very considerable time to come.

POSTSCRIPT

Commodity Prices and Decimals

The change to decimal currency leaves many of the London commodity markets unaffected, since prices are already quoted in pounds and decimal fractions of a pound per long or metric ton. They are: base metals (copper, tin, lead, zinc), coffee, sugar, sunflower oil, soya-bean oil, coconut oil.

With decimalization, silver will be quoted in new pence and tenths of new pence per troy oz. Wool futures, cotton, rubber, tea and hides, previously quoted in pence per pound weight, will change to new pence per kilo.

Location of Plantation House Terminal Markets from 1972

Corn Exchange Company's press notice of 22 April 1971:—

The Directors of the Corn Exchange Company and of the London Commodity Exchange Co. Ltd are pleased to announce that satisfactory arrangements have been concluded and plans agreed, for the move to Mark Lane of markets comprising the membership of the London Commodity Exchange. These Markets include four Terminal Markets, viz., the Coffee Terminal Market Association of London, the London Cocoa Terminal Market Association, the London Vegetable Oil Terminal Market Association and the United Terminal Sugar Market Association, and there will also be facilities provided for members of the London Copra Association, the London Jute Association, the Rubber Trade Association of London, the London Shellac Trade Association, the General Produce Market and such other members. They will occupy the entire ground floor market area of the present London Corn Exchange and the Corn Market is to be rebuilt at first floor level to accommodate the members of the London Corn Exchange.

Rebuilding of the whole market area will commence shortly and will be completed during 1972, when the members of the London Commodity Exchange will move from Mincing Lane and commence to operate from Mark Lane.

433

APPENDIX I   FUTURES TRADING

1. *Offsetting Transactions in Forward Markets*

Most risks which arise in the ordinary business of life – as well, indeed, as those affecting life itself – can be insured against on the well-known principle of pooling the risks with others concerned to protect themselves against similar contingencies. Compensation can thus be paid from a fund assembled out of the premiums, calculated according to the degree of risk involved and collected from members of the pool. In business, for example, buildings, machinery and equipment are insured against fire and theft, while owners are protected from the loss of ships and cargoes by similar insurance policies. However, the list of risks for which this insurance principle provides protection does not include the considerable fluctuations in price to which primary produce is subject. No matter how well founded business plans might be, volatile prices can result in catastrophic losses unless some compensation is obtained. However, whereas fire, theft and natural disasters will only visit a small, statistically predictable minority over a given period, any price fluctuations which occur will be the common experience of all who handle the commodity concerned. Insurance against price risks must therefore be organized on an entirely different basis from that of pooling these other risks.

The possibility of organizing a market on which traders may protect themselves against the effects of price changes arises basically from the fact that, following any price change, there will be a distribution of gains and losses. A fall in price, for example, ordinarily entails a loss for those who hold stocks of the commodity the price of which has fallen, whereas merchants, manufacturers, and others who have committed themselves to supplying the commodity at the original price before they have made the purchases necessary to do so, will gain from a fall in price. The trader who wishes to avoid the possibility of loss from a fall in the price of goods which he has bought, and has to hold for some time, will, therefore, be able to do so by entering into an offsetting transaction promising to sell goods for delivery at a future date (if possible, coinciding with that at which he anticipates selling the stocks of the commodity he has bought). In brief, he purchases produce, simultaneously selling promises to deliver the same commodity at an appropriate date. In market parlance, he is 'long of the commodity because of his purchases on the 'spot' market, and, therefore, sells 'short' on the forward market, committing himself to supply the goods at a future date. Should the feared price fall occur when he is long of the commodity, he will obviously make a loss upon re-sale. However, it is equally obvious that, when it comes to buying claims to the commodity in order to honour his matured sales in the forward market, the fall in price will enable him to purchase more cheaply than he has sold. His loss from holding stocks of the commodity will therefore be offset by his forward sales. Similarly, should the trader's position be one of commitment to supply an amount of a commodity on some future date at a price determined when he enters into the transaction, he will need to 'hedge' against a rise in price, since subsequent purchases, nearer the date on which he has undertaken to deliver the goods, would entail losses. The trader's 'hedge' must, therefore, take the form of purchases in the forward market. In brief, when he signs a contract to supply on a future date at a certain price his action will be to enter into an offsetting contract to buy for forward delivery at this price. Should the feared price rise then occur the trader's obligation to supply will involve him in a loss, but this same price rise will also ensure a gain from the hedging transaction: upon maturity of the forward contract he receives claims to the commodity which he can dispose of at a profit.

2. *The Shortcomings of Forward Markets*

It will be evident from the above simplified version of how a trader may protect himself from price fluctuations that the *sine qua non* for hedging operations is the possibility of concluding forward transactions, which must necessarily depend upon description as opposed to inspection of the commodity concerned. (These forward sales are sometimes known as sales 'to arrive', and, by traders themselves, as c.i.f. trading. The use of the last named term stems from the fact that, in discussing forward transactions, the responsibility for insurance and freight charges must be dealt with in addition to the price of the good itself.) Sales by description have been made possible by the development of an accurate and widely recognized system of grades. When this has evolved, traders can be reasonably confident of the quality of commodity for which delivery has been contracted. Trade associations, with panels to arbitrate in cases of dispute, have frequently accompanied sales by description: these panels are, moreover, often assisted in their work by the existence of standard samples, or by procedures for sampling bulk shipments to establish the 'fair average quality' (f.a.q.) of the season's shipments. With some commodities (such as sugar or tin) the grade can be established by scientific analysis.

Sales by description thus constituted an enormous advance in that they enabled traders to hedge against price fluctuations. Because they enabled forward markets to emerge they also gave rise to a significant increase in speculation. As long as markets were confined to sales 'on the spot' (that is, of 'spot' or present goods) speculation was confined to buying in the expectation of a rise in price, that is, 'bull' speculation. Gains from a fall in price became possible only when speculators could sell forward goods which they did not possess at the time. Thus the 'bear' speculator, selling 'short' on forward markets, could emerge only when selling by description gave rise to arrivals markets.

For a number of reasons, however, forward markets were imperfect media for both hedging and speculation. The basic difficulty lay in the fact that forward markets are delivery markets for actual produce; their purpose is to ensure supplies for traders. Thus when speculators entered the markets, and concluded contracts to deliver produce at some future date, they needed to be reasonably sure of being able to secure produce in order to fulfil their commitments at the relevant time. Operations on the market were thus closely circumscribed by the particular collection of quantities, qualities, and delivery dates of available produce. Bear speculation, therefore, though possible, was fraught with risk and, for commodities for which the commercial stocks held were not normally very high, it was comparatively easy for other market operators to intervene in the market to 'squeeze the bears'. All that was necessary was for them to buy up a significant proportion of the stocks held. This created an artificial scarcity, and, when stocks could not be replenished quickly, the upshot was that the bears were compelled to pay high prices to secure the commodity in order to honour their commitments. Naturally the high prices paid made the operation a profitable one for the bear squeezers, provided that they could 'get rid of the corpse' satisfactorily. 'Getting rid of the corpse' was the market's vivid expression to describe the problem of disposing of the stocks which it was necessary to buy in order to drive the price up, for their release naturally tended to drive the price down again. Though market operators might successfully squeeze the bears, therefore, they were always faced subsequently with the problem of timing the disposal of their stocks if they were to retain a net profit from their interventions. Their problem was least acute when the commodity was shipped from distant sources of supply and therefore could not be replenished very quickly. (Tin provides a very good example of a commodity suitable for these operations, as normal commercial stocks were low, and most of it came from the other side of the world.)

Clearly the problems associated with the use of forward markets were not confined to speculators, for traders who wished to use forward markets to hedge were afflicted by precisely the same difficulties. When they entered the forward market, in order to conclude transactions to offset their normal trading business, they were often disappointed by being unable to match the particular qualities, quantities and delivery dates for which a hedge was required. However, in common with the bear speculators, traders who had sold 'short' in order to offset their risks as stockholders could be caught in a 'bear squeeze'. When the hedge sale happened to be an exact match, in terms of quality and delivery date with their unsold stocks, traders clearly had nothing to worry about. When this was not so, however, they stood to suffer along with the speculators from these manipulations of the market.

3. Futures Markets

The nature of the difficulties experienced in using forward markets as a medium for hedging and speculation serves to indicate the direction in which the solution lay. Would-be hedgers required a market on which they could be sure of being able to buy or sell a suitable contract. The ready supply which this implies was only possible when traders and speculators were able to draw up contracts which represented not specific produce, but merely a promise to deliver a commodity of a stated grade. (The Liverpool cotton trade during the American Civil War provides a clear example of this, when market operators began to deal in cotton 'yet to be shipped'.) When this happened, traders were no longer closely circumscribed by the number of contracts available at any one time on forward markets, but were free to draw up obligations according to need. By the same token, the market was enormously broadened by the vastly increased scope which this allowed for speculators both to take up contracts for sale issued by traders, and to utter their own.

Because futures markets are hedging and speculative media, rather than delivery markets, one of their obvious advantages to users is that, under normal circumstances, less than five per cent of the contracts result in delivery. Positions on the market are usually 'closed out', that is, traders liquidate their positions simply by entering into an obligation opposite to that which they already hold. (Sellers of futures therefore 'close out' their positions simply by buying futures for the same amount and delivery date.) Thus when all a trader's futures transactions are periodically offset against one another, in the clearing houses which the market associations set up for the purpose, settlements have to be made only in respect of the price differences of his several transactions. However, sellers of futures have the right to tender produce in discharge of their obligations, while buyers can always ensure obtaining produce simply by refraining from closing out their futures contracts. A delivery will then have to be made though this will not necessarily, or even probably, come from the trader who sold the futures. It is one of the functions, usually, of the clearing house to arrange such deliveries by marrying up any demand for the physical product, when futures contracts mature, with the supply. Obviously, the right to tender and to demand delivery links up futures markets with their delivery markets in a way which has important consequences for price relationships. These are discussed below.

Usually, the contracts evolved for use on futures markets are not very suitable media for transactions in the physical commodity. On actuals markets the primary concern of the market authorities must be to define standards of the commodity so that sales can be made by description on their contracts. Buyers, especially if they process the commodity with machinery which proves troublesome, or even impossible, to use when the quality is not suitable, will, therefore, often be extremely fastidious in their purchases. On the futures market, by contrast, other criteria determine the description of the grade on the contract. In order to reduce opportunities to corner physical supplies, the grade established for futures trading must be one for which actual supplies are adequate. For these reasons it is normal for terminal markets to permit the delivery of a whole range of grades against futures contracts and, because of this, such contracts are often referred to as 'basis' contracts. It frequently happens, therefore, that grades which may be delivered under the terms of a futures contract will not be suitable for the manufacturer. Normally, the existence of two separate markets – one for purchasing the physical commodity and the other for hedging – ensures that the manufacturer need not run the risk of having to use a contract for shipments which could turn out to be unsuitable, should the seller decide to deliver a grade permitted within the terms of the 'basis' contract. Attempts to combine delivery with hedging and speculation on one market are always subject to this very real difficulty, as the history of the London Metal Exchange makes abundantly clear.

Where more than one grade may be tendered in fulfilment of a futures contract the price differential which should obtain between the official contract grade and the one actually delivered within the range permitted by the 'basis' contract, is also an issue of some importance for traders. In practice there are two ways of settling this: the terminal market association may either adopt a system of 'fixed differences', which it determines and may review from time to time, or else it can use the differential established on the physical market. When the association follows the latter course it is said to be applying a system of 'commercial differences'. Of the two systems the latter is ideal when conditions allow its application, for when 'fixed differences' are in operation the seller's tendency is to deliver the grade most favourable to himself. In the early 1960s, for example, deliveries of copper on the London Metal Exchange were mostly of the fire-refined grade because the fixed discount was, for a long time, less than that which obtained generally. Buyers tend to react to this situation by attempting to discount their prospective losses through the offer of lower prices for futures contracts than they would be prepared to pay were these being dealt with on the basis of 'commercial differences' when the contracts terminate in delivery (and as much as 20 per cent of the copper contracts on the London Metal Exchange result in deliveries of the commodity). However, when the turnover on futures markets is low the system of 'commercial differences' becomes less reliable and manageable, which explains why U.K. market associations tend to operate on 'fixed differences'.

4. *The Problems of Incomplete Cover*

In practice the mere placing of a hedge on a terminal market does not necessarily ensure a 100 per cent risk cover,[1] and the tribulations associated with this fact have undoubtedly exercised a major influence on the view taken by many traders of the usefulness of these facilities. In fact the profit or loss on the actuals market will only be exactly compensated by transactions on the futures market (neglecting carrying and dealing costs, as well as profit margins) when prices in the two markets have moved in the same direction and by the same amount. Any change in the difference between the spot price and the forward futures price (that is, any change in what is known as 'basis') will give rise to over- or under-compensation.

When the forward futures price is higher than the spot price, the market's expression for the situation is that a 'contango' exists. Carrying costs (that is, the cost of warehousing and insuring stocks) normally set the limit to the premium of forward futures prices over spot prices, for, if forward prices were to rise above a level given by the spot price plus carrying costs, it would pay arbitrageurs to enter the market as sellers of futures and as buyers in the spot market. All they would need to do in order to make a profit would then be to bear the costs of storage and fulfil the contract upon maturity by delivering the goods. This action of the part of arbitrageurs will tend to drive spot prices up and weaken forward futures prices until an equilibrium relationship (i.e. forward futures prices which are not greater than the spot price plus carrying costs) is restored. In the absence of other influences, therefore, the actions of arbitrageurs would tend to lead to parallelism of prices in the delivery and the futures market. In practice, however, other forces also operate in other directions. For example, futures markets are more sensitive to relatively small changes in demand and supply, while different qualities of the commodity will, as has already been mentioned, also exert their influence upon price. Finally, it should be noted that arbitrage does not work nearly as well when the futures price is less than the spot price plus carrying costs, for then there is an evident inducement to sell the commodity on the spot market and so purchase forward futures contracts. However, only traders who hold stocks of the commodity can arbitrage in this way, and this limits the tendency. We must conclude, therefore, that, when the spot and the forward futures price are in a contango relationship, arbitrage is not certain to establish equilibrium price relationships except when the forward futures price is greater than the spot price plus carrying costs. When this happens the actions of arbitrageurs will reduce the difference. Moreover, because carrying costs decline with the approach of the forward date, the normal tendency will be for the approach of the maturity date of the futures contract to result in a reduction in the spread, or 'basis' between the spot and the forward price.

Contango price relationships stand in contrast to those which reveal a 'backwardation', that is, a spot price which is higher than the price of futures for some forward date. A backwardation may develop in a number of situations even in normal times. For example, should stocks of an agricultural commodity happen to be low, then the scramble to cover 'short' sales drives spot prices up, while quotations for relatively distant months will remain low if there are prospects of a good harvest to follow. A strong demand for spot supplies is often associated with war scares, but the possible causes are numerous, and include strikes, lock-outs and changes in foreign exchange regulations. Keynes argued[2] that the normal state of markets was likely to be one of persistent backwardation because futures markets would naturally be dominated by traders wishing to hedge stocks. This demand would give rise to a heavy sale of forward futures contracts and so depress their price in relation to spot prices. It was left to Kaldor to point to the fact that on some markets traders would quite conceivably be entering the market on the 'long' rather than on the 'short' side. In other words, some markets might be characterized by a preponderance of traders wishing to hedge commitments rather than stocks, while others might also show characteristics other than that of 'normal backwardation' when they are dominated by speculators.[3]

For a merchant or manufacturer holding stocks of the commodity and therefore wishing to sell futures, a backwardation on the markets is likely to be very frustrating, especially in view of the fact that, unlike contango, there is no corresponding limit to the possible extent of backwardation. Assuming that the spread, or 'basis', between spot and forward futures prices reduces to zero with the approach of the forward date, the loss suffered on a short hedge when there is a backwardation may be illustrated as follows. Suppose an importer of tin buys ten tons from Penang and wishes to hedge this on the London Metal Exchange. If we ignore carrying and dealing costs together with profits, the initial and final transactions can be tabulated as below.

Month 1—
   (a) Purchase 10 tons of tin at £900 per ton   £9,000
   (b) Sale 10 tons of 3 months tin £880 per ton   £8,800

Month 4—
    (c) Sale 10 tons of tin at £950 per ton   £9,500
    (d) Purchase 10 tons current month's tin at £950   £9,500

The rise in the price of tin between its purchase and sale (a and c) provides the importer with a windfall gain of £500, while his short hedge, when closed out (b and d), gives rise to a loss of £700. The difference between these two sums is equal to the backwardation of £20 per ton (a and b) on ten tons. The undercompensation of the hedge is unaffected by the direction in which market prices change from month 1 to month 4, as may readily be ascertained by working out the example for a fall rather than a rise in prices. The significance of the demonstration lies in the inadequacy of terminal markets to provide complete protection for important trading interests when there is a backwardation.[4] Many of the United Kingdom markets underwent a difficult prolonged period of backwardation when they reopened after the 1939-45 war. These price relationships operated to the detriment of their turnover and, obviously, any return to comparable conditions of scarcity and great instability will work against their continued existence.

5. *Arbitrage*
As has already been observed, the normal tendency will be for the 'spread' or 'basis' between forward futures and spot prices to disappear as the former approach maturity. This market trend will also tend, usually, to be buttressed by arbitrage activity on the part both of hedgers and of speculators. At its simplest this will take the form of a demand for deliveries of the commodity by holders of matured futures contracts when the spot price of the produce is higher than the market price of the futures. When the spot price is below that of the matured futures, on the other hand, the sellers of these contracts will tender the commodity rather than liquidate their positions by closing out on the terminal market. These actions exert pressures towards an equalization of the spot and the matured futures contract prices. In the latter case, moreover, these equilibrating pressures would be reinforced by a tendency to accumulate stocks and to sell futures. When cash prices are above matured futures prices, by contrast, in addition to the demand for actual deliveries in discharge of the contracts on the terminal market, there would also be some liquidation of stocks, attempts to defer commodity purchases and a buying pressure for futures contracts.

Moreover, these arbitrage activities need not be confined to the delivery month. When the forward price in the futures market is higher than the forward price in the physical market, arbitrageurs will then find it profitable to sell forward in the futures market and buy forward in the delivery market. Then, when the forward date comes round, these arbitrageurs discharge their obligations in the terminal market with deliveries of produce. However, it has already been observed that, whereas arbitrage ensures that a forward futures price cannot exceed the current spot price plus marginal carrying costs, such (risk-free) dealings cannot ensure that the spot price does not exceed the forward futures price plus carrying costs. In other words, though there is a limit to contango there can be no symmetrical limit to backwardation, for holders of futures will obviously be unable to turn these contracts into stocks for re-sale at the cash price until the future date arrives – and by that time there will be no advantage in holding stocks.

When two or more terminal markets trade in similar contracts, market operators have the opportunity to engage in arbitrage activities between these markets, that is, in the activity known on American markets as 'spreading'. The most elementary form of arbitrage activity consists in buying in one market where the price is relatively low, and reselling in another where the price is relatively high. This process, however, entails the transport of produce, so the technique has been evolved of buying futures in one market and selling in another when the price is low on the one, and high on the other. Each contract is then closed out on the market on which it was made. Because organized produce markets will normally register prices which, in the absence of government interference, will differ only by the cost of transporting produce from the one to the other, arbitrage will be profitable whenever prices on different markets do not stand in this relationship to each other.

6. *Privileges*
On American futures markets, the practice of 'privileges' is known as dealing in 'options'. Privileges or options on the commodity markets are confined to futures trading. In fact they were traditionally regarded on continental markets as a futures transaction with the special proviso that, in return for a cash payment, one of the parties concerned could exercise his privilege or option to withdraw from his obligation to buy or to sell, within a stipulated time period.[5] However, though their use is so largely speculative, privileges are perhaps best regarded as very temporary insurance against price fluctuation. Privileges consist, essentially, of the option of claiming a sale, or else a purchase, at some previously agreed price, often based upon the previous day's official closing price. A 'put' is the right to claim a sale, and a 'call' the right to claim a purchase. Evidently, privileges are bought at a price, or rather two prices, for the price settled for the right to purchase or to sell is often different from the price settled for withdrawing from a transaction. The 'double option', the American term for which is a 'straddle', combines both 'put' and 'call' privileges, that is, it confers

upon the trader the right, within the stipulated time period, to either buy or sell, or to do neither.

7. *Evidence of the Effectiveness of Hedging*

The theory of futures markets indicates very clearly that these markets should be useful to the trader as a means of reducing his risk of loss from fluctuating prices. Moreover, the continued use of these markets by traders over many years tends to bear out the contention that they have been found useful. Recently, however, some economists have also turned their attention to the task of examining the evidence to discover whether it is likely that hedging does reduce risks. Obviously, it is not possible within the compass of the present essay to give more than an indication of the work in this field, which has been progressing with increasing sophistication. Professor B. S. Yamey's investigation into the effects of hypothetical hedging operations on the Liverpool Cotton Exchange from 1930 to 1932, and 1938 to 1940, is a classic.[6] Yamey concludes that, during these two periods of fluctuating cotton prices, hedging was, on the whole, an effective means of reducing price risks in the cotton trade, except for the smallest spot price changes. In other words, the degree of cover provided seemed to vary directly with the magnitude of the spot price change. The hedges which aggravated the problem of price risks for traders amounted to only seven per cent in all, and were limited to spot price changes of less than 1d. per lb. Some subsequent students have been less sanguine as to the proportion of hedging transactions which aggravated price risks. In his study of the sugar futures market, embracing almost 1,100 hypothetical hedging transactions, R. H. Snape[7], for example, concluded that about 23 per cent of these were worse than useless to the trader seeking to reduce price risks. Like Yamey, Snape also discovered that the success of hedging in reducing price risks varied directly with the magnitude of the spot price change. One of the most reassuring conclusions of the study, from the trader's viewpoint, is that the 'cover' provided by hedging proved most effective in the contracts where it was most important.

8. *Speculation*

Traders use futures markets in order to protect their profit margins from being eroded by price fluctuations; in principle, hedging enables them to do this at the expense of also denying them the possibility of achieving windfall gains from price changes. (For example, if a trader holds stocks and hedges against a fall in price by selling futures, a rise in price will result in a gain from sales in the delivery market, and an offsetting loss in the futures market.) While traders seek to avert risks arising from price fluctuations, speculators are the market operators who are prepared to assume these risks in the hope of making gains. Thus, because there is unlikely to be a balance between hedgers on the short and on the long side of the market, terminal markets cannot do without speculators. Furthermore, these financial interests broaden markets which would otherwise be extremely thin and so register distorted prices. (On some very active futures markets the turnover is often many times the volume of the physical trade in the commodity over the same period.) The usefulness of speculative activity, provided it is kept under supervision by the market authorities concerned, is thus clear enough. To the extent that traders hedge with one another or with speculators, the uncertainty due to price fluctuations is removed from the trade and borne by financial interests. The pursuit of gain by commodity speculators thus provides a useful economic service in transferring price risks from those who do not wish to bear them to those who do. A market in prices – which, in essence, is the purpose of futures trading – is thus ultimately beneficial to society because traders are enabled through its use to charge lower prices. In other words, traders would require rather higher margins in the absence of futures markets because of the greater risk of losses entailed by fluctuating prices. The greatest fallacy is to believe that the elimination of speculative markets would abolish speculation, when in reality it would merely shift the incidence onto other shoulders. When, for example, the State interposes an organization (such as the post-war Raw Cotton Commission) into the channel of distribution which absorbs price changes, it, in effect, assigns to the taxpayer the role of risk bearer for the trade concerned. Where no market or institution acts as the risk bearer for price changes, the trader himself perforce assumes the role of speculator. Viewed in this light, therefore, the speculator is a middleman who provides insurance against the risk of price fluctuations. His operations on markets in prices thus expedite the passage of the good to the ultimate consumer in a way which is no different, in principle, from that of other middlemen, be they bankers, insurance companies, acceptance houses, warehouse-keepers or shipping agents.

It is often claimed that speculators exercise a steadying influence on the market by selling at times of rising prices and by buying when prices are down, for their aim is to make profits rather than to ensure stocks. However, the difficulty with this view is that it implies that speculators are better informed than dealers. Clearly, only a detailed investigation of each case can reveal whether speculators have in particular instances exercised a dampening influence upon price movements, or whether they have destabilized markets. It is undoubtedly true that outside operators do sometimes cause embarrassment by building up considerable uncovered positions when a price trend looks particularly strong. When the price movement eventually weakens the resulting panic sales will send prices plunging. (The behaviour of sugar prices in 1963, as described in Chapter 10, provides a pattern consonant with a surge of outside buying and selling.)

Clearly, the speculator can be differentiated from other market interests only conceptually, for it is impossible to tell without detailed investigation whether particular contracts are speculative. Traders do not as a rule maintain a completely balanced position on the market, except perhaps during periods of great uncertainty. Most of the time the amount of cover taken on a futures market will vary according to the view taken of the market and, when the individual trader's opinion is widely shared, this will obviously be registered in forward futures prices on the terminal market. Thus, in addition to serving as a medium for hedging and speculation, when an active and broadly-based futures market is functioning it provides an extremely sensitive barometer for registering what the market considers to be the appropriate price for the commodity, for positions which range into the future sometimes for as long as a year or more ahead.

APPENDIX 2

MAJOR BRITISH COMMODITY TRADE ASSOCIATIONS

Commodity	Associations	Futures Market Associations (where applicable)
Animal feeding-stuffs	London Cattle Food Trade Association	
Chemicals and dyestuffs	British Chemical and Dyestuff Traders Association Ltd	
Cocoa	Cocoa Association of London Association of U.K. Intermediaries (Brokers and Dealers) in Cocoa and Cocoa Products	London Cocoa Terminal Market Association
Coffee	Coffee Trade Federation comprising: Coffee Brokers' Association of London Coffee Merchants' and Roasters' Association Ltd United Kingdom Coffee Association Ltd Coffee Importers and Exporters Association of London Ltd	Coffee Terminal Market Association of London Ltd
Copra	London Copra Association	
Cork	Cork Importers and Merchants Association	
Cotton	Liverpool Cotton Association Ltd	Liverpool Cotton Futures Market Ltd
Diamonds	Diamond Trading Co. Industrial Distributors (Sales) Ltd	
Dried Fruit	London Dried Fruit Trade Association United Kingdom Association of Independent Importers of Dried and Evaporated Fruit	
Edible Nuts	Federation of Edible Nuts Associations	
Flour	National Association of Flour Importers Ltd.	
Furs	British Fur Trade Association Incorporated London Fur Trade Association Incorporated	
Grains	National Federation of Corn Trade Associations, comprising: London Corn Trade Association Ltd Liverpool Corn Trade Association Ltd and other associations throughout the United Kingdom	London Grain Futures Association Ltd Liverpool Corn Trade Association Ltd
Hides and Skins	Hide and Skin Shippers' Agents Association	
Jute	London Jute Association	
Kapok	Kapok Trade Association	
Non-ferrous metals	London Metal Exchange	London Metal Exchange Co. Ltd.
Rice	London Rice Brokers Association	
Rubber	Rubber Trade Association of London	London Rubber Exchange Co. Ltd
Shellac	London Shellac Trade Association	
Sisal	London Sisal Association	

Commodity	Associations	Futures Market Associations (where applicable)
Sugar	Sugar Association of London	United Terminal Sugar Market Association of London
	Refined Sugar Association	
	Sugar Traders Association of the United Kingdom	
	London Sugar Brokers Association	
Tea	Tea Buyers' Association	
	Tea Brokers' Association of London	
	Tea Buying Brokers' Association of London	
Timber	Timber Trade Federation of the United Kingdom	
	Timber Agents and Brokers Association of the United Kingdom	
Vegetable oils and oilseeds, animal fats and marine oils	Federation of Oils, Seeds and Fats Associations, comprising: Incorporated Oil Seed Association London Copra Association London Oil and Tallow Trades Association Seed, Oil, Cake and General Produce Association	London Vegetable Oil Terminal Market Association
Wool	British Wool Federation	London Wool Terminal Market Association
	London Wool Brokers Ltd	
	London Wool Importers Association	
	Associated London Selling Wool Brokers	
	Committee of London Wool Brokers	
	Association of West Africa Merchants	
General	British Federation of Commodity Associations	
	Federation of Empire Producers Agents Associations	
	Foreign Produce Importers Federation	
	General Produce Brokers Association of London	
	Institute of Chartered Shipbrokers	
	Liverpool United Warehouse Keepers Conference	
	London Association of Public Wharfingers Ltd	
	Member Associations of the British Federation of Commodity and Allied Trade Associations Ltd	

NOTES

CHAPTER ONE   Medieval Commodity Trade

1. See E. M. Carus Wilson and O. Coleman, *England's Export Trade 1275-1547* (Oxford 1963), pp. 13 and 41.
2. The Champagne fairs were already past their zenith by the end of the thirteenth century, but the development of other commercial areas subsequently gave rise to new land routes, and so to other fairs such as those of Geneva and Frankfurt. For a complete account of these developments, see O. Verlinden's Chapter on 'Markets and Fairs in' the *Cambridge Economic History of Europe* Vol. III (Cambridge, 1963).
3. The voyages of the Venetian state galleys are presented in a series of maps in A. Tenenti et C. Vivanti, 'Les grandes trafics d'état à Venise: les galères da mercato, 1332-1534', *Annales: Économies, Sociétés, Civilisations*, Vol. 16 (1961).
4. I am indebted to Dr. E. B. Fryde for this information.
5. A. A. Ruddock, *Italian Merchants and Shipping in Southampton 1270-1600* (Southampton, 1951), p. 97.
6. The anonymous author of the notorious *Libelle of Englysche Polycye*, written in 1436, alludes scornfully to the commodities brought especially by the Venetian and Florentine galleys as follows:

    > The grete galees of Venees and Florence
    > Be wel ladene wyth thynges of complacence
    > All spicerye and other grocers ware
    > Wyth swete wynes, all manere of chaffare
    > Apes and japes and marmusettes taylede,
    > Nifles, trifles, that litell have availed.

    (O.U.P. Edition, 1926, p. 18, Ed. Sir George Warner).
7. H. L. Gray, 'English Foreign Trade from 1446 to 1482', in *Studies in English Foreign Trade in the Fifteenth Century*, edited E. Power and M. Postan (London, 1933).
8. The name is a corruption of *staalhof* meaning sample yard: the steelyard used for weighing takes its name from a device used for this purpose at the time by the Hanse merchants at their headquarters.
9. *Bulletin de la Commission Royale d'Histoire CXVIII* (Brussels, 1953), cited by E. M. Carus Wilson in *Medieval Merchant Venturers* (London, 1954), p. xiii.
10. G. Unwin, 'London Tradesmen and their Creditors', in *Studies in Economic History* (London, 1927), p. 100 et seq.
11. Arnold's *Chronicle*, p. 97, cited by L. F. Salzman, *English Trade in the Middle Ages* (Oxford, 1931), p. 113. In medieval usage 'forayn' meant a person outside the franchise, while stranger was synonymous with alien.
12. A. R. Bridbury, *England and the Salt Trade in the Later Middle Ages* (Oxford, 1955), p. 119.
13. An account of weights and measures, together with regulations governing the weighing of imports and exports, may be found in L. F. Salzman, *English Trade in the Middle Ages* Chapter III; also Postan and Power, op. cit., p. 257, et seq.
14. S. Thrupp, 'The Grocers of London, A Study of Distributive Trade' in *Studies in English Foreign Trade in the Fifteenth Century*, ed. E. Power and M. Postan, p. 247.
15. Ibid, p. 262.
16. Ibid, p. 261. The nearest modern equivalent of 'mistery' is probably mastery. The word comes from the French *maîtresse*.
17. Bridbury, op. cit., p. 146.
18. For a history of Stourbridge fair, see C. Walford, *Fairs Past and Present* (London, 1883) pp. 54-163.
19. Walford, op. cit., p. 73.
20. E. Lipson, *The Economic History of England* (London, 1957 edn) Vol. 1, p. 241.
21. Davis, *Regesta Regum Anglo-Normanorum* i, p. 16, cited by Lipson, op. cit., p. 251.
22. Sir John Clapham, *A Concise Economic History of Britain from the Earliest Times to 1750* (Cambridge, 1949), p. 151.
23. M. M. Postan, 'Credit in Medieval Trade, *Economic History Review*, Vol. I (1928) No. 2, reprinted in *Essays in Economic History*, Vol. I, ed. E. M. Carus-Wilson (London, 1954) p. 65.

24. Jacques Heers, *Gênes au XVᵉ Siècle* (École Practique des Hautes Études – VIᵉ Section Centre de Recherches Historiques, Paris, 1961), p. 460.
25. R. de Roover, 'The Organization of Trade', in the *Cambridge Economic History of Europe*, Vol. III (Cambridge, 1963), p. 95.
26. See for example M. K. James, 'The Fluctuations of the Anglo-Gascon Wine Trade during the Fourteenth Century', *Economic History Review*, Second Series, Vol. IV 1951.
27. M. E. Mallett, 'Anglo-Florentine Commercial Relations 1465-1491', *Economic History Review*, Second Series, Vol. XV No. 2 (1962), p. 254.
28. F. Sargeant, 'The Wine Trade with Gascony', in *Finance and Trade under Edward III*, ed. G. Unwin (London, 1918).
29. For a full account of William de la Pole's activities, which sheds considerable light on the activities of the major English merchants of the day, see E. B. Fryde, *The Wool Accounts of William de la Pole* (York, 1964).
30. *Studies in English Foreign Trade in the Fifteenth Century*, ed. E. Power and M. Postan, p. 151.
31. For an account of the development of regular facilities for overland transport, see W. Brulers, 'L'exportation des Pays Bas vers l'Italie par voie de Terre au milieu du XVIᵉ siècle', *Annales: Économies, Sociétés, Civilisations*, Vol. 14 (1959).

CHAPTER TWO   The Royal Exchange and the Coffee Houses

1. The early history of the Royal Exchange may be found in Maitland's *London* (London, 1756), Vol. I pp. 256-7, Vol. II pp. 878-902, in *Stow's Survey of London*, ed. C. L. Kingsford (Oxford, 1927), and in W. Besant, *London in the Time of the Tudors* (London, 1904), pp. 219-222.
2. See, for example, R. B. Westerfield, *Middlemen in English Business 1660-1760* (New Haven, 1915), p. 348.
3. Maitland, op. cit., Vol. II, p. 998.
4. *The Spectator* No. 69, 19 May 1711, cited by H. R. Fox Bourne, *English Merchants* (London, 1886), p. 206.
5. G. D. Ramsay, *English Overseas Trade during the Centuries of Emergence* (London, 1957), p. 16.
6. R. Van der Wee, *The Growth of the Antwerp Mart* (The Hague, 1963) Vol. II, p. 127.
7. R. H. Tawney, introduction to *A Discourse upon Usury* by Dr. Thomas Wilson (London, 1925), p. 62.
8. G. Malynes, *Lex Mercatoria* (London, 2nd Edn, 1686), p. 144, cited by Violet Barbour in *Capitalism in Amsterdam in the Seventeenth Century* (Baltimore, 1950), p. 74.
9. Violet Barbour, op. cit., p. 75, citing evidence in Ricard, *Le Négoce d'Amsterdam*, 1722.
10. R. H. Tawney, op. cit., p. 80.
11. A. E. Feaveryear, *The Pound Sterling; A History of English Money*, ed. E. V. Morgan (Oxford, 1963), p. 64.
12. F. J. Fisher, 'Commercial Trends and Policy in Sixteenth Century England', *Economic History Review*, Vol. X (1940), No. 2, p. 104.
13. J. Wheeler, *A Treatise of Commerce* (London, 1601), p. 9.
14. See, especially M. Ashley, *Financial and Commercial Policy under the Cromwellian Protectorate* (London, 1962), p. 133 (First Edn 1934).
15. Charles Knight, *London* (London, 1843) Vol. V, p. 59.
16. A. Pulling, *A Practical Treatise on the Laws, Customs, Usages, and Regulations of the City and Port of London* (London, 1849), p. 463.
17. K. G. Davies, *The Royal African Company* (London, 1957), p. 183.
18. E. B. Schumpeter, *English Overseas Trade Statistics 1697-1808* (Oxford, 1960).
19. Ibid. Introduction, p. 11.
20. Ibid.
21. R. Pares, *A West India Fortune* (London, 1950), Chapter IX.
22. See for example J. M. Price, 'The Rise of Glasgow in the Chesapeake Tobacco Trade 1707-1775', *William and Mary Quarterly* (1954) Vol. XI, No. 2.
23. An Appendix to the *Report from the Committee appointed to Enquire into . . . Providing Sufficient Accommodation for the increased Trade and Shipping of the Port of London* (1796) contains some figures of charges on imports, from which the following table has been constructed to show Liverpool's advantage over the Port of London at this time.

	Total London	Total Liverpool	In Liverpool's Favour
Hogshead of Sugar 16 cwt Gross	7s. 3d.	3s. 4d.	3s. 11d.
Bag of Cotton 3 cwt	2s. 8d.	8¾d.	1s. 11¼d.
Hogshead of Coffee 7 cwt	6s. 10d.	2s. 0d.	4s. 10d.
Barrel of Ashes 3 cwt	1s. 10½d.	8½d.	1s. 2d.

24. E. Victor Morgan and W. A. Thomas, *The Stock Exchange, its History and Functions* (London, 1962), p. 36 and pp. 52-53.
25. D. Morier Evans, *City Men and City Manners* (London, 1852), pp. 132-3.
26. J. A. Findlay, *The Baltic Exchange* (London, 1927), p. 33.
27. G. Findlay, the *Public Ledger* Supplement 15 December 1950, p. 4.
28. W. Tate, *The Elements of Commercial Calculations* (etc.) (London, 1819), pp. 116-120.
29. From an advertisement in the *Public Ledger* of 9 June 1760.
30. Pulling, op. cit., p. 364.
31. W. Tate, op. cit., p. 116.
32. Pulling, op. cit., p. 426.
33. See for example L. J. Ragatz, 'The Fall of the Planter Class in the British Caribbean 1763-1833', *American Historical Association*, 1928, p. 100.
34. R. Pares, *A West-India Fortune*, p. 187.
35. S. G. Checkland, 'American versus West India Traders in Liverpool 1793-1815', *Journal of Economic History* Vol. XVIII No. 2 (1958).
36. *Select Committee on Commercial Distress*, Q. 677; Q. 965, 996; Q. 965, 966.
37. 1845 Vol. XII.
38. *Select Committee on the Law relating to Merchants, Agents or Factors*, 1823, Vol. IV, p. 11.
39. *Minutes of Evidence*, Vol. IV, p. 36. Evidence of John Bannatyne, general merchant, partner in the house of Findlay, Bannatyne.
40. J. R. McCulloch, *A Dictionary of Commerce* (London, 1834 Edn), p. 532.
41. By 6 George IV c. 94; 5 & 6 Victoria c. 39: 40 & 41 Victoria c. 39. The main provision of the 1889 Act are conveniently summarized in Halsbury's *Statutes of England* 2nd Edn, Vol. 1 (1948), pp. 27-35.
42. W. Tate, op. cit, p. 116. See also the *Report from the Committee on Laws Relating to the Manufacture, Sale, and Assize of Bread, 1814-15 Sessional Papers*, Vol. V, p. 36. Evidence of Robert Wilson.
43. Op. cit., p. 159.
44. *The Economist* 15 May 1847.
45. 29 Charles II c. 3.
46. Pulling, op. cit., p. 429.
47. Anon. *The City* (London, 1844), p. 177.
48. *Minutes of Evidence of the Select Committee on Commercial Distress 1847-48* XIII, Pt. I, p. 1.
49. R. Campbell, *The London Tradesman* 3rd edition (London, 1747), p. 296.
50. See for example, Pulling, op. cit., especially pp. 465-468.
51. Manuscripts Nos. 8188-8199 at the Guildhall Muniment Room (Accession No. 119338), deposited there in 1954, and cited by W. M. Stern, 'The London Sugar Refiners around 1800', *Guildhall Miscellany* No. 3, February 1954.
52. *Merchant Banking Co. v. Phoenix Bessemer Steel Co.* 1877, cited by J. G. Smith, *Organized Produce Markets* (London, 1922), p. 11.

CHAPTER THREE Early Domestic Produce Markets

1. *Calendar of Letter Books of London*, Vol. C, p. 18 (1293), cited by N. S. B. Gras, *The Evolution of the English Corn Market* (Cambridge, Mass., 1915), p. 71n.
2. *Acts of the Privy Council*, Vol. VII, p. 280; *Calendar of State Papers Domestic*, Elizabeth, Vol. 1, p. 259 (6 October 1565).
3. The various regulations embodying the Tudor corn policy were eventually consolidated and published in a document called the *Book of Orders*, in 1587.
4. F. J. Fisher, 'The Development of the London Food Market 1540-1640', *Economic History Review*, Vol. V (1935), No. 2.
5. *Statutes of the Realm*, Vol. V, p. 685.
6. Ibid, Vol. V, p. 781.
7. Cannan Edn. (London, 1930), Vol. II, p. 34.
8. Sir William Petty, *A Treatise of Taxes and Contributions* (London, 1662), p. 11.
9. *Essay against Forestallers*, 1718, p. 27.
10. Defoe, *The Complete English Tradesman* (Edn 1727), Vol. II, part ii, pp. 43-6; *Annals of Agriculture*, Vol. XXV, pp. 427-428, cited by Lipson, *The Economic History of England*, Vol. II, pp. 420-421.
11. See, for example, the evidence of William Smiton in the *Seventh Report of the (House of Commons) Committee appointed to Consider the Present High Price of Provisions*, 1801, also evidence of Wm. Gray Fearnside to the House of Commons *Select Committee on the Sale of Corn*, 1834, Vol. VII, p. 75.
12. Evidence of Wm. Gray Fearnside to the *Select Committee on the Sale of Corn*, 1834, Vol. VII, p. 75.

13. The mealman was a seller of meal, i.e. the ground edible portion of grains other than wheat.
14. See A. B. Robertson, 'The Foundation of Mark Lane Corn Exchange', *Guildhall Miscellany* No. 2, February 1953.
15. *Seventh Report of the (House of Commons) Committee appointed to consider the present High Price of Provisions*, 1801, Vol. 2, p. 174.
16. Ibid., Vol. 2, p. 4.
17. Ibid., p. 42.
18. Pulling, *A Practical Treatise on the Laws, Customs, Usages and Regulations of the City and Port of London*, p. 470. The *del credere* commission, it will be recalled, is the additional brokerage payable when a broker guarantees a transaction for his client.
19. C. R. Fay, *Great Britain from Adam Smith to the Present Day* (London, 1928), p. 228.
20. Report from the *Committee on the Laws Relating to the Manufacture, Sale, and Assize of Bread* (1814-1815), Vol. V, p. 26. Evidence of George Scholey, Alderman, and former Mayor of London.
21. J. H. Clapham, *An Economic History of Modern Britain*, Vol. I, 'The Early Railway Age' (Cambridge, 1926), Ch. XI, p. 232.
22. Pulling, op. cit., p. 470.
23. 12 Geo. III c. 71.
24. *House of Commons Journals*, Vol. 30, p. 763; *The Gentlemen's Magazine*, 1751, p. 474, p. 509-10; and *Abuses Relative to Provisions*, p. 28.
25. At a somewhat later date, the Report from the *Select Committee on Petitions Complaining of Agricultural Distress*, II, 1820, explains how the corn averages of the day were computed. It notes that there were great differences between actual prices ruling on the Mark Lane Exchange and the letters from the factors which purported to report prices upon which the opening or closing of the ports was determined.
26. John Lord Sheffield (J. B. Holroyd), *Observations on the Corn Bill (etc.)*, (London, 1791), p. 53.
27. Public Record Office, *BT6/130 Report to Lord Mayor and Court of Aldermen of a Committee appointed to consider the corn regulations, and the manner of collecting prices*, 24 March 1789.
28. *The High Price of Provisions*, Vol. II, p. 129.
29. C. Smith, *A Short Essay on the Corn Trade and the Corn Laws* (London, 1758), p. 17.
30. G. Unwin, *Industrial Organization in the Sixteenth and Seventeenth Centuries* (Oxford, 1904), Appendix A (ii), quoting *State Papers Domestic*, James I, Vol. LXXX, p. 13.
31. G. Unwin, op. cit., Appendix A (ii).
32. Commons *Debates*, 1621, Vol. V, p. 468-9; p. 486-8; 503-7.
33. *Statutes of the Realm*, 21 James I c. 28.
34. P. J. Bowden, 'The Home Market in Wool 1500-1700', *Yorkshire Bulletin of Economic and Social Research*, Vol. VIII (1956), p. 134, and M. E. Finch, *The Wealth of Five Northamptonshire Families: the Spencers of Althorp*, Northants Record Society, Vol. 19 (1956).
35. Daniel Defoe, *A Tour through England and Wales*, Vol II (London, 1927), p. 33.
36. See for example A. Ure, *The Cotton Manufacture of Great Britain Systematically Investigated*, Vol. I (London, 1836).
37. 10 William III c. 16.
38. J. Stow, *A Survey of London*, Morley ed. (London, 1890), pp. 277-9.
39. R. B. Westerfield, *Middlemen in English Business between 1660 and 1760* (Yale, 1915), p. 337.
40. The contents of this Act are given in W. Maitland's *History and Survey of London*, Vol. I, p. 462-7.
41. J. Smith, *Chronicum Rusticum Commerciale, or Memoirs of Wool, Woollen Manufacture and Trade etc.*, Vol. II (London, 1747) p. 310-12.
42. See for example C. Gill, 'Blackwell Hall Factors, 1795-1799', *Economic History Review*, Second Series, Vol. VI, No. 3 (1954), p. 268.
43. 8 and 9 William III c. 9.
44. *House of Commons Journals*, Vol. XII, p. 277.
45. A Newcastle chaldron held 53 cwt, while a London chaldron was 36 cwt. J. U. Nef, *The Rise of the British Coal Industry* (London, 1932), Vol. II, p. 368, states, however, that the weight of the Newcastle chaldron increased continually until 1678.
46. Ibid., pp. 279-82.
47. R. Smith, *Sea-Coal for London* (London, 1961), p. 10.
48. Sir William Petty, *Another Essay in Political Arithmetick concerning the growth of the City of London* (London, 1683), p. 99, also cited by R. B. Westerfield, op. cit., p. 222.
49. 9 Anne c. 28, Section 2.
50. A. Anderson, *An Historical and Chronological Deduction of the Origin of Commerce from the Earliest Accounts* (London, 1801), Vol. IV, Appendix, pp. 701-2.
51. 3 George II c. 26, Section 1.
52. Ibid., Section 3. The brokers' acts did not cover coal factors.

53. Anderson, op. cit., Vol. IV, p. 701.
54. Westerfield, op. cit., p. 233.
55. *The Frauds and Abuses of the Coal-Dealers Detected and Exposed*, etc. (London, 1743-4), p. 7.
56. Anderson, op. cit., p. 701.
57. *Journal of the House of Commons*, Vol. 56, p. 284: proprietors' evidence given in 1801.
58. *Report of the Committee appointed to consider the Coal Trade*, June 1800.
59. Evidence of Mr John Read, Receiver of the groundage of colliers and baillage of sea-coal, submitted in 1793 to the City Lands Committee of the Corporation, cited by R. Smith, op. cit., p. 89.
60. Apart from the evidence of Select Committees and accounts from other sources cited by Nef, Smith, Westerfield and others, interesting material on this aspect of the market exists, for example, in the Public Record Office, BT6/116, for 1787.
61. 28 George III c. 53.
62. Robert Edington, *Historical Account of the Various Coal Mines of South Wales* (London, 1824).
63. Insole's day book, Item 69, 20 April 1830. I am indebted for this, as well as for other unpublished information on the marketing of South Wales coal, to Dr. E. D. Lewis, author of *The Rhondda Valleys* (London, 1959). Dr. Lewis was fortunately permitted to peruse the Insole Company's papers shortly before they were destroyed. 'Wain Wilt' is, of course, a corruption of the Welsh term 'waun wyllt'.
64. J. H. Morris and L. J. Williams, *The South Wales Coal Industry 1841-1875* (Cardiff, 1958), p. 34.
65. S. W. Dowling, *The Exchanges of London* (London, 1929), p. 130.
66. R. B. Westerfield, op. cit., p. 189.
67. 5 – 6 Edward VI c. 14, Section 16.
68. 22 and 23 Charles II c. 19.
69. R. O. Roberts, 'Bank Advances for Welsh Drovers in the Early Nineteenth Century', *The Bankers' Magazine*, June 1959.
70. See for example the *Gentleman's Magazine*, 1755, p. 294.
71. *Essay against Forestallers*, p. 14.
72. *House of Commons Journals*, Vol. 30, p. 787-8; Vol. 51, p. 637. *Essay against Forestallers*, p. 14.
73. Evidence of Daniel Sharpe, clerk at Smithfield Market. *House of Commons Journals*, Vol. 51, 1796, p. 640.
74. Maitland, op. cit., Vol. II, p. 757.
75. *Select Committee on the State of Smithfield Market* (etc.), 1828, Vol. VIII, p. 213.
76. Ibid., p. 197.
77. Ibid., p. 50.
78. Ibid., p. 207. See for example the evidence of Joseph Pockington, on money taken and banked at Smithfield.
79. Westerfield, op. cit., p. 197.
80. 25 Charles II, c. 4.
81. 22 and 23 Charles II c. 19.
82. The Acts concerned were 4 and 5 William and Mary c. 24: 11 and 12 William III c. 13: 5 Anne c. 34. The 1670 statute also prohibited the reselling of fat cattle in Smithfield, and abolished the ancient custom of 'foreign bought and foreign sold' on that market.
83. W. J. Passingham, *London's Markets. Their Origin and History* (London, 1935), p. 13. The London Central Poultry Market gradually acquired most of the wholesale poultry business of Leadenhall Market (an ancient Corporation market) which has since grown in size as a retail poultry centre. This market was divested of its hide and meat sections in 1871 by the City Corporation.
84. *The Marketing of Meat and Livestock*, 1965, Cmnd. 2737.
85. R. Campbell, *The London Tradesman*, p. 279.
86. William Horsely, *The Universal Merchant* (etc.) (London, 1753), p. 19, Section XLI.
87. See, for example, the *Gentlemen's Magazine* (1755), p. 129.
88. *Billingsgate Market Redevelopment; Layout and Material Handling*, November 1966.

CHAPTER FOUR   The Liverpool Cotton Market to 1914

1. S. Dumbell, 'The Organization of the Cotton Market in the Eighteenth Century', *Economic Journal*, Vol. XXXIII (1923), p. 362; also A. P. Wadsworth and J. de L. Mann, *The Cotton Trade and Industrial Lancashire 1600-1780* (Manchester, 1931), p. 185.
2. The terms 'bag', 'package' and 'bale', were used very loosely during this early period. In 1790 the American 'bale' or 'bag' was computed at 200 lbs. By 1824, all the bales imported into Liverpool averaged 266 lbs, and they increased in size yearly until in 1832 they weighed on an average 319 lbs. N. S. Buck, *The Development of the Organisation of Anglo-American Trade, 1800-1850* (Yale, 1925), p. 31n, provides a full list of references, and a discussion of this great confusion.

3. Figures for 1823 are given by Henry Smithers, *Liverpool, its Commerce, Statistics and Institutions, etc.* (Liverpool, 1825), p. 143. Figures for 1833 are quoted in E. Baines, *History of the Cotton Manufacture in Great Britain* (London, 1835), p. 318.
4. T. Ellison, *The Cotton Trade of Great Britain* (London, 1886), p. 279, and G. Von Schulze-Gaevernitz, *The Cotton Trade in England and on the Continent* (London, 1895), p. 55.
5. *Select Committee on Commercial Distress,* Q. 2007.
6. F. E. Hyde, B. B. Parkinson and S. Marriner, 'The Cotton Broker and the Rise of the Liverpool Cotton Market', *Economic History Review,* Second Series, Vol. VIII (1955-56), p. 75.
7. Op. cit., Vol. VIII, p. 386.
8. T. Ellison, op. cit., p. 176.
9. Report of Evidence, taken before the *Select Committee on Manufactures, Commerce, and Shipping* (1833), Vol. VI, p. 247.
10. *Liverpool Exchanges Yearbook,* 1908-9, p. 159.
11. T. Ellison, *The Cotton Trade of Great Britain,* p. 175.
12. Ibid., p. 179.
13. The peak price for 1857 was 9¼d. per lb for Uplands cotton, a level which caused considerable excitement, as the market reports of the period make plain. See for example G. L. Rees *Reports on the Cotton Market 1848-1863* in the series 'British reports relating to America' (Micro-Methods, Ed. W. E. Minchinton) (York, 1965).
14. W. O. Henderson, *The Lancashire Cotton Famine 1861-1865* (Manchester, 1934), p. 36, relates the story of John Bright's activities in this connection.
15. M. Williams, *Seven Years' History of the Cotton Trade of Europe* (Liverpool, 1868), p. 51. Henderson, op. cit., pp. 16-17, quotes a letter from *The Times* of 12 November 1863 which makes clear that selling short was taking place for much longer periods than had been customary until then.
16. Ellison, *The Cotton Trade of Great Britain,* p. 279.
17. Ibid., p. 280.
18. S. Dumbell, 'The Origin of Cotton Futures', *Economic History,* 1926-1929, Vol. I, p. 261.
19. A. R. Marsh, 'Cotton Exchanges and their Economic Function', *Annals of the American Academy of Political and Social Science,* Vol. XXXVIII, 1911.
20. See Appendix I, p. 434.
21. This liquidation of the hedge – relinquishing cover – is frequently referred to as the 'closing out' of the position.
22. For early descriptions of the actual operations of the markets, see P. E. J. Hemelryk, *Forty Years' Reminiscences of the Cotton Market* (Liverpool, 1916), p. 16, and C. W. Smith's evidence to the *Royal Commission on Agriculture 1894,* S.P. XVI, Part II, Q. 15, 590 and Q. 15, 620.
23. *Liverpool Exchanges Yearbook,* 1908-9, p. 161.
24. *Royal Commission on Agriculture,* 1894, Q. 15, 590.
25. Ibid., Q. 15, 592-94. Smith quotes the case of *Cooke v. Eshelby,* in which an action was brought against a Liverpool broker and ultimately went for settlement to the House of Lords. In spite of Smith's apparently positive role in the development of futures markets, he was in fact a noted anti-optionist, as the remainder of his answers to some shrewd questions indicate.
26. J. G. Smith, *Organized Produce Markets* (London, 1922), p. 57-58.
27. W. F. Machin, 'A Short History of the Liverpool Cotton Market', *The Liverpool Raw Cotton Annual* (1958), p. 108.
28. *Royal Commission on the Depression of Trade and Industry,* 1886, Vol. XXI, Appendix to the Second Report, pp. 294-5.
29. Sir W. B. Forward, *Recollections of a Busy Life* (Liverpool, 1910), pp. 42-4.
30. The initials c.i.f. stand for cost, insurance and freight. With the growth of orders to origin by cable, the term c.i.f. trade became the term used by brokers, etc., to describe orders for shipment by producers and their agents from overseas. Insurance and freight charges then required explicit mention, as opposed to 'spot' trade in which the goods are already 'on the spot'.
31. See Appendix I, p. 434.
32. In American market usage, the term 'straddle' is used for what on English markets is called a 'put and call option'; that is, a double privilege. These activities are discussed in the Appendix.
33. 'Imperfect' hedges are discussed in the Appendix, p.   .
34. The lowest price in cotton futures was reached on 31st January 1895. This was 2 31/32 d. per lb for February-March delivery. The same day also saw the lowest spot price on record, of 2 31/32 d. J. L. Watkins, *King Cotton, A Historical and Statistical Review 1790 to 1908* (New York, 1908), p. 24.
35. 'Corners' and 'squeezes' are discussed in the Appendix. The details of Rangers' activities are given by that invaluable eye-witness to the development of the cotton market, Thomas Ellison, in his *Gleanings and Reminiscences* (Liverpool, 1905).

36. Practices of this type were prevalent on some of the markets at Antwerp and Amsterdam at an early date, as we saw from Malynes' description, quoted above in Chapter 2, p.35. Privileges are generally referred to as 'options' on American markets, and the term was adopted on this side of the Atlantic in some quarters, especially in Liverpool, whose markets were from the outset closely linked with the development of their American counterparts. Unfortunately, futures contracts themselves are also sometimes referred to as 'options', particularly in relation to a particular delivery month (e.g. 'July option'). This has come about simply because the actual day of delivery of produce in fulfilment of a futures contract (should delivery be chosen), is at the seller's option within the given month, or, in the case of cotton at the time, two months.

CHAPTER FIVE   The Cotton Market since 1914

1. S. J. Chapman, *The War and the Cotton Trade* (Oxford Pamphlets, 1915).
2. H. D. Henderson, *The Cotton Control Board* (Oxford, 1922), p. 14. It was only for cotton lying in U.K. warehouses that licences were required, merchants and spinners being permitted to purchase as much as they could get hold of from abroad.
3. As W. F. Machin points out in *The Liverpool Raw Cotton Annual*, (1958), p. 26, high though this price was, it failed to equal the 31¼d. reached in July 1864 for Middling Orleans. The latter was for cotton on the spot, and of a superior quality to that represented on the futures contract of February 1920.
4. Mitchell, *Abstract of British Historical Statistics*, p. 181.
5. The Rules of the Liverpool Cotton Association defined a 'straddle' as a transaction in cotton for future delivery in which contracts are made either:
   '(a)   For the purchase of a certain number of bales of one growth for a certain period of delivery, and for the sale of an equal number of bales of the same growth for another period of delivery.
   (b)   For the purchase of a certain number of bales of one growth for a certain period of delivery, and the same of a contract or contracts of the nearest equivalent in weight of another growth for the same or another period of delivery.'
   In other words, the English concept of a 'straddle' is that of a gamble on the difference in price of the same grade at different dates, or a bet on the difference in price of different grades at the same or different dates. What was a 'straddle' in the Liverpool parlance was classified as an arbitrage transaction in the U.S.A.
6. The U.S. Agricultural Marketing Act of 1929 created a Federal Farm Relief Board which was responsible for getting the farmers' co-operative to form a central organization through which it afterwards worked to lend money to individual members.
7. The world's carry-over of American cotton had increased by almost 2 million bales to 6¼ million bales in 1930-31, and reached a peak of 12⅖ million bales for the season 1932-33. John A. Todd, *The Marketing of Cotton* (London, 1934), Statistical Appendix, Table IX.
8. R. Robson, *The Cotton Industry in Britain* (London, 1957), p. 260.
9. *Liverpool Cotton Gazette*, 24 June 1939.
10. Ibid., 23 December 1939. In Alexandria the market authorities tried to exercise some control over speculation by imposing daily maximum and minimum prices, while options dealings were forbidden on the Bombay market.
11. 10 & 11, Geo. VI, c.26.
12. Details of the Commission's purchasing activities are contained in its Annual Reports.
13. This is indicated by the *Annual Report* of 1948 para. 18, 19; the *Annual Report* for 1949, para. 11, and that for 1950, para. 11. Modifications subsequently became possible, so that by 1952-53 all requirements of Egyptian cotton were met by shippers' agents in Liverpool.
14. See, for example, the arguments quoted by W. Robertson in 'The Raw Cotton Commission: an Experiment in State Trading', *Journal of Industrial Economics*, Vol. IV (1955-56), p. 225.
15. J. Wiseman and B. S. Yamey, The Raw Cotton Commission 1948-52, *Oxford Economic Papers*, N.S. Vol. VIII (1956), pp. 9-12.
16. Ibid., pp. 18-19.
17. In fact, with effect from 1 April 1948 (*Annual Report* 1948, paragraph 52).
18. Annual Reports; see also W. Robertson, op. cit., p. 227. The dollar was, of course, the scarce currency par excellence, but others, such as the Belgian franc, were also 'hard' at their existing exchange rates, given the flow of bilateral trade under arrangements concluded under the conditions of inconvertibility of currencies prevailing at the time. For an account of the trade and currency arrangements of the period, see G. L. Rees, *Britain and the Post War European Payments Systems* (University of Wales Press, 1963).

19. Wiseman and Yamey, *The Raw Cotton Commission*, pp. 23-24.
20. That is, enterprises which control operations involved in the production and sale of a commodity from the purchase of its raw materials to the marketing of the finished good.
21. See chapter 4, and the Appendix on Futures Trading below.
22. The Commission's accounts at the end of the last year's trading in August 1954 showed a deficit of £7 million. In addition to this the reserve fund of £31 million, which it received from the Board of Trade at the outset, had already disappeared. Since this amount arose from the last year's profitable trading of the Cotton Control (including stocks), however, it could be argued that the net effect of state operations was a loss of £7 million. Whichever way one looks at it, the result was an unsatisfactory one for a period in which prices were rising.
23. This generally happens, as in the present instance, when large new crops are expected, but when spot supplies are scarce at the end of the season. Prices of forward supplies then show a considerable discount, and the process of carrying cotton 'into the discount' is, therefore, one in which stocks continue to be held in spite of falling prices.
24. In spite of a decline in the share of textiles in world trade in manufactures from 33¼ per cent to 17½ per cent between 1900 and 1950, Japan increased its share in world trade in manufactures by expanding its share of the declining world textile market and its exports of other consumer goods. Over the relevant period (1948-1952) Japan was, with American aid, making a strong industrial recovery. See, for example, H. Tyszynski, 'World Trade in Manufactured Commodities', *Manchester School of Economic and Social Studies*, Vol. 19, No. 3, September, 1951, pp. 272-298.
25. The Commission did not finally disappear until 1954. Price comparisons at the beginning of 1948 and 31 August 1954 for leading cottons are as follows:

	d. per lb.	
	1/1/1948	31/8/1954
American Middling 15/16 inch ...	21·50	33·38
Brazilian Sao Paulo	20·65	31·74
Egyptian Ashmouni	22·25	43·59
Egyptian Karnak	25·25	52·74

(*Liverpool Raw Cotton Annual* 1958, p. 75).
26. *Report of the Cotton Import Committee*, April 1952, Cmnd. 8510.
27. The *Public Ledger*, 30 January 1954.
28. The climax to a period of great transformation on this side of the trade took place in the summer of 1964, when Viyella, Courtaulds, Carrington and Dewhurst and English Sewing Cotton between them absorbed six other major companies, including Lancashire Cotton. See, for example, the *Financial Times*, 20 August 1965, p. 10.
29. The *Public Ledger*, 31 January 1953.
30. B. S. Yamey, 'Cotton Futures Trading in Liverpool', *The Three Banks Review*, No. 49 (March 1959), p. 27.
31. See above note 5, p. 454, for a description of straddling operations.
32. That is, the British Commonwealth (except Canada), Eire, British Trust Territories, British Protectorates and Protected States, Burma, Iraq, Iceland, Jordan and Libya.
33. For a discussion of these accounts and their re-organization, see G. L. Rees, op. cit., especially pp. 57-66 and pp. 159-61.
34. W. B. Hutchinson, 'Is There a Future for Futures?', *Liverpool Raw Cotton Annual* (1959), p. 43.
35. American and Nigerian basis cottons were tenderable at par; East African at a premium of 3 per cent; while Mexican and Syrian were assessed at discounts of 2 and 3 per cent respectively. The system worked as followed: when, for example, American cotton was relatively cheap – say, at a discount of more than 3 per cent in relation to East African growths – then the effective basis became American cotton. On the other hand, should the spot price of East African be cheap relative to American, the price of near months of the contract would be determined by this cotton rather than American.
36. W. B. Hutchinson, 'Price Risk Insurance for Cotton', *Liverpool Raw Cotton Annual* (1962), p. 41.
37. The *Public Ledger*, 30 October 1954.
38. In 1958 some 44 per cent of U.K. cotton supplies came from the U.S.A. These cost almost £31 million, of a total cotton import of £71.6 million. Supplies from the Sudan for the same year cost almost £10 million. By 1962 the U.K. cotton cheque to the U.S.A. had dropped to £13.4 million out of a total import of £59.7 million. Brazil was next in importance, sending supplies for which it received £4.4 million.
39. Karnak and Menoufi from good to fully good cotton, were tenderable for the long-staple (i.e. the former) contract, each futures contract representing 33 bales of 720 lbs each, totalling 24,000 lbs in all. Ashmouni and Giza No. 30 grades from good fair and upwards were deliverable against the 1956 contract (the medium staple contract), at price differentials fixed by a committee.

40. S. S. Brand, 'The Decline in the Cotton Futures Market', *Stanford Food Research Institute Studies*, Vol. IV, No. 3 (1964), pp. 305-315.
41. *Financial Times*, 1 February 1966.
42. An account of the organization of the Mincing Lane markets is given in Chapter 8 below.
43. The work of the London Produce Clearing House Ltd, is also discussed in Chapter 8 below.
44. There is a cotton market at Bremen, though no terminal market facilities are available there at present.

CHAPTER SIX   The Organization of the Grain Markets to 1914

1. Evidence of Wm. Mellish, M.P., a general merchant, before the House of Lords *Select Committee respecting Grain and the Corn Laws*, 1814-15, Vol. V, p. 53.
2. 33 George III c. 27.
3. 55 George III c. 26.
4. Select Committee on the *Laws Relating to the Manufacture, Sale, and Assize of Bread*, Vol. V, p. 21. Evidence of John Gear Jones.
5. Ibid., p. 58. Evidence of John Fothergill, a corn and flour factor.
6. See, an undated folio on a *Proposed Corn Exchange* B.M.M.S.S. 8223.e, 10f125, and a *Prospectus for a New Corn Exchange*, B.M. M.S.S., 8223.e, 10f100.
7. *Royal Commission on Agriculture* (1882), Vol. XIV, p. 345. Evidence of Wm. J. Harris, of Harris Brothers, Corn Brokers, and a Director of London Docks.
8. *Select Committee on Petitions Complaining of Agricultural Distress* (1821), Vol. II.
9. C. R. Fay, *Great Britain from Adam Smith to the Present Day* (London, 1928), p. 65.
10. *Select Committee on Commercial Distress*, 1848, Minutes of Evidence, p. 5.
11. D. Morier Evans, *The Annual Commercial Register and General Record of Prices in the Year 1849* (London, 1850), p. 225.
12. R. W. Hidy, *The House of Baring in American Trade and Finance* (Camb., Mass., 1949), p. 357.
13. R. Findlay, *The Baltic Exchange* (London, 1927), p.16.
14. S. E. Fairlie, *The Anglo-Russian Grain Trade, 1815-1861*, an unpublished Ph.D. thesis, University of London, 1959, pp. 251-63.
15. Ibid., p. 341.
16. See, the evidence of W. J. Harris to the *Royal Commission on Agriculture* 1882, Vol. XIV, p. 345 (Q. 66317) and to the *Royal Commission on the Depression of Trade and Industry*, 1886, Vol. XXI, 3rd Report, p. 85 (Q. 9629). Though Harris's evidence was given in the 1880s, he appears to have been thinking of the system of trade as it was in its heyday some twenty years earlier.
17. G. Fridlizias, *Swedish Corn Export in the Free Trade Era; Patterns in the Oats Trade 1850-1880* (Institute of Economic History, Lund University, 1957), p. 177.
18. *Select Committee on Commercial Distress* 1847-48, 3rd Report, p. 227. Evidence of A. H. Wylie.
19. G. R. Porter, *Progress of the Nation* (London, 1851), p. 143.
20. G. J. S. Broomhall and John H. Hubback, *Corn Trade Memories* (Liverpool, 1930), p. 35.
21. R. W. Paul, 'The Wheat Trade between California and the United Kingdom', *The Mississippi Valley Historical Review*, Vol. XLV, No. 3, December 1958, p. 412.
22. *Shipping World*, Vol. VIII, 1 September 1890, p. 151.
23. *The Liverpool Corn Trade Association 1853-1953* (Liverpool, 1953), p. 14.
24. *Royal Commission on Agriculture*, 1894, Vol. XVI, Pt. II, p. 50.
25. H. C. Emery, *Speculation on the Stock and Produce Exchanges of the U.S.A.* (New York, 1896), p. 46.
26. F. Hecht, *Die Warrants* (Stuttgart, 1884), cited by Emery, op. cit., p. 36.
27. See the Appendix for a discussion of the way in which transactions in forward contracts restrict traders' ability to hedge.
28. H. C. Emery, op. cit., p. 40.
29. W. E. Baer and L. Woodruff, *Commodity Exchanges* (New York, 1929), p. 3.
30. B. L. Pierce, *A History of Chicago, Vol. I, The Beginning of a City, 1673-1848* (New York, 1937), p. 130.
31. New York Produce Exchange, *Annual Report*, 1881.
32. *Royal Commission on Agriculture* 1882, Vol. XIV, Q66347.
33. *Royal Commission on the Depression of Trade and Industry* 1886, Vol. XXI, 3rd Report, Q9628
34. *First series of Memoranda (on) . . . British and Foreign Trade* 1903 (Cd. 1761), p. 130, quoted by Sir John Clapham, *Economic History of Modern Britain*, Vol. III (London, 1951), p. 72.

35. S. Marriner, *Rathbones of Liverpool 1845-1873* (Liverpool, 1961), p. 115.
36. A. C. Stevens, 'Futures in the Wheat Market', *Quarterly Journal of Economics*, Vol. II (1887), p. 37.
37. J. H. Hubback, 'Some Aspects of the International Grain Trade', *Economic Journal*, Vol. XXI, 1911, pp. 121-31.
38. *Liverpool Corn Trade Association 1853-1953*, p. 12.
39. *Royal Commission on Agriculture*, Q15620.
40. Broomhall and Hubback, op. cit., pp. 28-30.
41. C. W. Smith, *International Gambling in Futures and Fictitious Agricultural Produce* (Prague 1898).
42. See above, Chapter 3, p. 62ff.
43. P. T. Dondlinger, *The Book of Wheat: An Economic History and Practical Manual of the Wheat Industry* (New York, 1908), p. 251.
44. Pierce, *A History of Chicago*, Vol. II, p. 79.
45. Taylor, *The History of the Chicago Board of Trade*, cited by Pierce, op. cit., p. 80.
46. W. E. Baer, 'Market Wrecking', *The Fortnightly Review*, Vol. 61, N.S. (April 1897), pp. 546-55.
47. J. D. Whelply, 'An International Wheat Corner', *The Fortnightly Review*, Vol. 68, N.S. (July 1900), pp. 208-16.
48. *Liverpool Exchanges Yearbook*, 1908-9, p. 266.
49. W. E. Baer, 'Market Gambling', *Contemporary Review*, Vol. LXV (June 1894), p. 791.
50. Bank of England Bristol 17 (B-L) 1 January 1886. I am indebted to Mr. R. O. Roberts for this information.
51. A. A. Hooker, *The International Grain Trade*, Second Edition (London, 1939), p. 21 et seq.
52. Ibid., p. 39.
53. *Royal Commission on Agriculture*, 1894, Q. 15,592.
54. Hubback, *Economic Journal*, 1911, op. cit., p. 127.
55. See the Appendix on Futures Trading for a discussion of 'differences'.
56. C. Chattaway, 'Arbitration in the Foreign Corn Trade of London', *Economic Journal*, Vol. XVII (1907), pp. 428-31.
57. The background to these changes is given in V. Fowke, *Canadian Agricultural Policy* (Toronto, 1947), pp. 241-50.
58. D. A. MacGibbon, *The Canadian Grain Trade* (Toronto, 1932), p. 33.
59. A. Barker, *The British Corn Trade from the Earliest Times to the Present Day* (London, 1920), p. 90.
60. Hubback, *Economic Journal*, 1911, p. 130.
61. It was estimated in 'Speculation, Short selling, and the Price of Wheat', *Stanford Wheat Studies*, Vol. VII, No. 4 (February 1931), p. 251, that the volume of wheat futures speculation in Chicago was then at least ten times, and probably more than twenty times, as much as in Liverpool.
62. One circular, known as the *Exley, Dimsdale, and Hopkinson's Corn Exchange Circular* was published in London as early as 1824. A *Corn Trade Circular* also appeared on 24 October 1825. There were other non-specialist journals in existence before this, of course, the oldest extant daily being the *Public Ledger*, started on 12 January 1760. *Dornbusch's Floating Cargoes Evening List* was started, according to Barker (op. cit., pp. 85-7), in the 1850s. This, the *Morning List* and *Beerbohm's Corn Trade List* (which was started in 1869) were amalgamated with the *London Grain, Seed, and Oil Reporter* in 1914. This last named in turn suffered the same fate in 1945, being incorporated in the *Public Ledger*. There were, in addition, other early publications, such as the short-lived *Corn Exchange and Mark Lane Register* and the *London Corn Circular*, the last named of which is still running.

In Liverpool, the most notable publication remains Broomhall's *Corn Trade News*, published in a daily, a weekly and an American edition, together with a Yearbook.
63. *Stanford Wheat Studies*, op. cit., p. 247.
64. The tramp ship owner will let out his ships, voyage by voyage, to trade in any direction in which the most profitable cargo is available. The cargo liner, on the other hand, runs in a regular service on a regular route, carrying whatever cargo is available at the scheduled loading ports.

CHAPTER SEVEN   The Grain Markets since 1914

1. More than 40 million metric tons of grains, flour, rice and pulse were bought by the Allied Wheat Executive during the two years eight months beginning 1 January 1917. A full account of operations is given in the *Royal Commission on Wheat Supplies*, Cmd. 1544, 1921. See especially pp. 29-44; Appendices 32-8, and Appendices 42-3.
2. F. M. Surface, *The Grain Trade during the World War* (New York, 1928), p. 34.

3. No. 1 Northern Manitoba spot delivery prices at Fort William fell from $2.73½ per bushel for September, to $1.15½ for October of the following year. V. C. Fowke, *The National Policy and the Wheat Economy* (Toronto, 1957), p. 177.
4. *Report of the Royal Grain Inquiry Commission*, 1925; *Report of the Commission to Enquire into Trading in Grain Futures*, 1931; *Report of the Royal Grain Inquiry Commission*, 1938.
5. G. L. Wood, 'Wheat Pools, with Special Reference to Australia', *Economic Record* (February 1928) Supplement, p. 22.
6. 'Speculation, Short Selling, and the Price of Wheat', *Stanford Wheat Studies*, p. 249.
7. A pre-war load was 1,000 quarters. At present a load on the physical market is 250 tons, but on the futures market a load is 125 tons, i.e. the minimum quantity for which it is possible to deal.
8. E. Staley, *Raw Materials in Peace and War*, Appendix C, p. 311.
9. V. C. Fowke, *The National Policy and Wheat Economy*, pp. 198-9.
10. For a full account, see the International Labour Office, *Inter-governmental Commodity Control Agreements* (Montreal, 1943), pp. 1-24; W. Malenbaum, *The World Wheat Economy 1885-1939* (Camb., Mass., 1953), pp. 205-11; & J. W. F. Rowe, *Markets & Men* (Cambridge, 1936), pp. 51-73.
11. For an account of the operations of this body, see E. Roll, *The Combined Food Board, A Study in Wartime International Planning* (Stanford, 1956), especially pp. 141-7.
12. This section is based upon the present author's article, 'Britain's Grain Markets', *National Provincial Bank Review* (November 1966).
13. *The Public Ledger*, 15 August 1953.
14. U.N. Food and Agriculture Organization (F.A.O.), *National Grain Policies* (1959), p. 59.
15. Report of Restrictive Practices Cases, Vol. 1, pp. 387-472.
16. D. K. Britton and associates, *Cereals in the United Kingdom* (London, 1969), p. 350.
17. At present the position is as follows:

	Preferential Tariff	Full Duty
Wheat in grain	free	free
Wheat flour	free	10% ad valorem
Maize in grain other than flat white	free	free
Oats in grain ... 3s.	free	3s. per cwt.
Rye in grain	free	10% ad valorem
Barley in grain	free	10% ad valorem

18. U.N. International Wheat Conference 1967.
19. See e.g. International Wheat Council *Review of the World Grains Situation* (1968-9), p. 36.

CHAPTER EIGHT   The Organization of the Mincing Lane Markets

1. A c.i.f. contract, it will be recalled, implies a sale of produce which has yet to be shipped from origin, the price being made up of its cost, insurance and freight. Goods at origin may of course be priced f.o.b. (free on board), while other formulae may specify f.a.v. (free alongside vessel), f.o.r. (free on rail), and c. & f. (cost and freight). In the case of c.i.f. contracts, insurance and freight are to a named port, but it remains the buyer's task to claim insurance in the event of loss or damage: the seller of goods c.i.f. is, in other words, entitled to payments upon the delivery of the appropriate documents.
2. Whereas the American term 'futures' found favour in Liverpool, where the markets had close connections with Chicago, New York, New Orleans and other towns, the older continental term was adopted in London. The French equivalent for example is *marché à terme*, while the Dutch expression is *termijnhandel*, and the German, *Termingeschafte*.
3. F. H. B. Williams, *The Tea Trade* (unpublished M.Sc. thesis, University of London, 1938), p. 66.
4. See e.g. Port of London Authority *Annual Report and Accounts*, 31 March 1964.
5. The market in physical produce has various appellations. It is sometimes known simply as the 'physical market', or the market in 'actuals'. Sometimes it is referred to as the 'delivery market', the 'cash market', or even the market in 'real transactions'. When trade was predominantly in produce already in warehouses, it was often referred to as the 'spot' market. With the growth of c.i.f. trading it is becoming increasingly referred to as the 'shipment market'. Continental usage seems to be more settled, the French term being *en disponible*, the Dutch, *op levering*, and the German, *effektiv*.

6. It is estimated in the *Report of the Committee on Invisible Earnings* (London, 1967), p. 106, that 'third country trade' amounted to some £20 million for 1965.
7. See the Appendix on Futures Trading.
8. The records of these transactions were kindly placed at the author's disposal by the London Produce Clearing House Ltd. The turnover of these early markets will be found in the chapters on the relevant commodities.
9. 'Options' or 'privileges' are explained in the Appendix on Futures Trading page 434.
10. For a fuller account, see G. L. Rees, *Britain and the Postwar European Payments System*, Chapter 3.
11. When transactions in 'non-scheme' commodities did require permission and registration, this was effected on the Bank of England's exchange control forms EC(G) 60 and EC(G) 68.

CHAPTER NINE   The Tea Trade

1. 12 Charles II c.23. Curiously enough, the system first devised was to tax the liquid rather than the dry leaf (at 8d. a gallon).
2. 24 George III c.38.
3. J. R. McCulloch, 'Some Observations on the Trade with China', *Edinburgh Review*, January 1824, p. 463.
4. Quoted by John Phipps, *A Practical Treatise on the China and Eastern Trade* (1836), p. xxxviii.
5. *The Times*, 17 December 1834. M. Greenberg, *British Trade and the Opening of China 1800-1842* (Cambridge University Press, 1951), p. 187, also mentions Hull and Falmouth in this connection, and adds a fourth ship, the *Pyramus*.
6. Braithwaite Poole, *The Commerce of Liverpool* (1854), p. 77, put average annual tea imports 'a short time ago', at 18,000 tons into London, compared with 4,000 tons into Liverpool. The total import into the United Kingdom was then 23,500 tons.
7. *Harrisons and Crosfield, 1844-1943*, One Hundred Years as East India Merchants (London, 1943), pp. 16-17.
8. S. Marriner, *Rathbones of Liverpool 1845-73* (Liverpool University Press, 1961), pp. 68-72.
9. See for example G. C. Allen and A. Donnithorne, *Western Enterprise in Far Eastern Economic Development, China and Japan* (1954, London), p. 54.
10. *The Economist*, 30 January 1847.
11. See for example the *Mining Journal and Commercial Gazette* for 12 December 1835, or *The Economist's* London Market Report for 1 June 1845.
12. D. Morier Evans, *Speculative Notes and Notes on Speculation* (London, 1864), pp. 117-18.
13. For a discussion of these matters, see, for example, N. A. Pelcovits, *Old China Hands and the Foreign Office* (New York, 1948); the *Report of the Select Committee on Commercial Relations with China*, 1848; and S. Marriner, op. cit., pp. 26-32.
14. Imperial Economic Committee, *Eighteenth Report on Tea* (London, 1931), p. 24.
15. J. A. Fairlie, 'The Economic Effects of Ship Canals', *Annals of the American Academy of Political and Social Science*, Vol. II, 1898, p. 63-4.
16. Ibid., p. 61.
17. For the history of wartime control, see, for example, Sir William Beveridge's *British Food Control* (Oxford University Press, 1928).
18. Graham, 'A Review of Tea Market Conditions between 1918-1933', in *I.T.C. Review of the Tea Regulation Scheme, 1933-1943*, p. 29, quoted by V. D. Wickizier, *Tea under International Regulation* (Stanford University Press, 1944), p. 60.
19. Board of Trade, *Report by the Food Council to the President of the Board of Trade on Wholesale Tea Prices*, 1926, pp. 20-1.
20. International Tea Committee *Report* for 1933-34 (London, 1934), p. 5.
21. J. W. F. Rowe, *Primary Commodities in International Trade* (Cambridge, 1965), p. 149.
22. Commonwealth Economic Committee, *Plantation Crops* (London, 1948), p. 28.
23. V. D. Wickizier, *Coffee, Tea and Cocoa* (Stanford, 1951), pp. 239-40.
24. The *Public Ledger*, 14 April 1950.
25. Harrisons and Crosfield Ltd, *Report and Accounts* for 1963 emphasize the fact that whereas before World War II average supply and offtake were in balance at about 980 million lbs annually, by 1962 the figure was as much as 1,628 million lbs. – a 65 per cent increase over pre-war and a 40 per cent increase over 1952. Virtually the whole of the increase has been absorbed by India, the U.S.S.R., Egypt and other Near East markets.

26. As a selling broker explained to the *Report of the Plantation Inquiry Commission 1956 – Tea* (para 10, p. 172), 'The term "Broker" when used in connection with tea brokers is rather a misnomer. We are a number of things. We are auctioneers and valuers. We are consultants on tea manufacture and market prospects. We are financiers and we deal in Real Estate. We provide the basis of tea documentation and statistics'. Cited by H. Roy, *Tea Price Stabilisation – The Indian Case* (Calcutta, 1965), p. 32.

27. The Monopolies and Restrictive Practices Commission *Report on the Supply of Tea*, H.M.S.O., 1955.

28. Chests differ in weight according to origin: Indian chests are normally 118 lbs, while those from Ceylon are 106 lbs, and from Indonesia, 110 lbs.

29. An interesting item in the *Shipping World*, Vol. I (August 1883), p. 152, describes the introduction of a 'revolutionary' method of bulking tea. The old method consisted simply in turning the 'break' out on the warehouse floor, mixing it with shovels to ensure uniformity, and returning it into the chests: the warehousemen compressed the tea by treading it down with their boots. The new method eliminated this, together with the loss of flavour involved in mixing in the open air, by employing a mixing drum, and a hydraulic iron 'presser'.

30. U.N. Food and Agriculture Organization, *Tea Trends and Prospects*, No. 30 (Rome, 1960), p. 3. It is interesting in this connection to note that the introduction of a method of speeding up the process of manufacture introduced in Northern India, known as 'crush, tear, and curl', results in the absence of 'leaf' grades of tea from this part of the world.

31. This limit was put at some 90,000 chests by the trade in its submissions to the Commission (op. cit., p. 29) and a figure of some 70,000 chests as the amount which 'could reasonably be handled week after week'.

32. Ibid., p. 40.

33. Ibid., p. 41. The trade urged upon the Commission that without uniformity, a buyer would have to adjust his bid for any particular type of tea to meet changes in the conditions under which it was sold, and that with sales conducted at high speed the situation would become chaotic for all concerned.

34. *Report by the Food Council to the President of the Board of Trade on wholesale Tea Prices*, 1926, para. 22, p. 21.

35. Ibid., p. 11.

36. Imperial Economic Committee, *Eighteenth Report on Tea*, p. 21.

37. Commonwealth Economic Committee, *Plantation Crops*, 1958, p. 147-8.

38. 'Cess' is archaic in England by this time, but the word appears to have survived in Scotland, Ireland and India. In the present context, the use of this word seems to be a convenient way of distinguishing one export tax from another. The proceeds of the Ceylon cess are used to finance its Tea Research Institute and other schemes.

39. F.A.O., *Tea Trends and Prospects*, p. 18.

CHAPTER TEN   The U.K. Sugar Market

1. T. Tooke, *The History of Prices*, Vol. II, pp. 391 & 412-14, quoted by J. H. Clapham, *The Early Railway Age*, p. 244. The estimate was for a common quality of sugar, namely 'East India, Brown, in Bond'.

2. Ragatz, *The Fall of the Planter Class in the British Caribbean 1763-1833*, p. 100.

3. An interesting account of the details of the procedure, together with the changes in the routine after the establishment of the wet docks and their related warehouses, is contained in *The Attorney General v. the London Dock Company before the Lord Chief Baron in the Court of the Exchequer* (London, 1851), pp. 2-10.

4. R. Pares, 'Merchants and Planters', *Economic History Review*, Supplement No. 4, 1960, p. 27.

5. J. M. Hutcheson, *Notes on the Sugar Industry* (Greenock, 1901), p. 76.

6. See above, p. 40.

7. The details of the many changes in tariff rates, together with an account of the various Parliamentary debates, are given by N. Deer, *The History of Sugar* (London, 1949 and 1950, 2 Vols.). See especially Vol. II, Chapter 27, 'Sugar Duties in England'.

8. S. J. Hurwitz, *State Intervention in Great Britain, A Study of Economic Control and Social Response 1914-1919* (New York, 1949), p. 72.

9. B. C. Swerling, *International Control of Sugar, 1918-1941* (Stanford Commodity Policy Studies, No. 7, 1949), p. 23.

10. Report of the *Committee on the Sugar Industry in the U.K.*, Cmd. 4871 (London, 1935), known as the Greene Committee Report.

11 K. Stahl, *The Metropolitan Organisation of British Colonial Trade* (London, 1951), p.37

12. 'Free-market exports' were defined as all exports excluding those which were part of trade within a colonial empire, exports to the U.S.A. under its quota system, exports from the U.S.S.R. to Mongolia, Sin-Kiang and Tannu Tuva, and exports from Belgium to Luxembourg. The U.K. market was specifically allocated between home beet production, its colonies, Australia, South Africa and the free market.
The 1937 Agreement also gave birth to the formation of the International Sugar Council, the balance of voting power on which was 35 per cent to the eighteen exporting countries, and 45 per cent to the four importers (China, India, the U.K. and U.S.A.).

13. In his contribution to V. P. Timoshenko and B. C. Swerling, *The World's Sugar* (Stanford U.P., 1957), pp. 19-22.

14. The International Sugar Council *Sugar Yearbook* provides the annually revised quota figures. Thus the overall quota agreed for 1967 was 2,780,000 long tons, of which the negotiated-price quota was 1,742,500 long tons.

15. The term 'dollar good' was applied not only to a commodity originating in the dollar area, but often to goods which were scarce enough in parts of the non-dollar world to command dollars in payment for them, or else a 'soft-currency' premium which betrayed the falsity of most exchange rates in relation to the dollar.

16. The *Public Ledger*, 4 October 1952.

17. Ministry of Agriculture, Fisheries and Food, *Future Arrangements for the Marketing of Sugar* (Cmd. 9519, 1955).

18. Commonwealth Economic Committee, *Plantation Crops* (1967), p. 206.

19. C. Czarnikow Ltd, *Sugar Review*, No. 63, 31 January 1952, p. 2.

20. The terms non-centrifugal and centrifugal sugar are used to distinguish between primitively produced sugars and modern sugars.

21. C.E.C., *Plantation Crops*, op. cit., p. 98.

22. A. D. Webb, 'The Relation between Wholesale and Retail Prices of Sugar', *Economic Journal*, Vol. XXIV, 1914.

23. Some of the most valuable sources of information on the world's sugar exchanges is provided by C. Czarnikow's house journal *Sugar* (but variously titled over the years), and Farr, Whitlock's and Co.'s *Manual of Sugar Companies* (New York). The present author has also benefited considerably from Dr. R. H. Snape's unpublished Ph.D. thesis, *Protection and Stabilization in the World Sugar Industry*, submitted to the University of London in 1962.

24. This gives an indication of the purity of the sugar. The origin of the term lies in the behaviour of a beam of polarised light when passing through a solution of sugar. A solution of sucrose will turn such a beam to the right whereas a solution of an invert sugar will turn it to the left. The extent of the movement is a measure of the strength of the solution.

25. *Report of the Committee on Invisible Exports* (London, 1967), p. 107.

CHAPTER ELEVEN   The Coffee Market

1. *Select Committee on Import duties*, 1840, p. 201.
2. R. Porter, *Progress of the Nation*, p. 448.
3. J. W. F. Rowe, *Primary Commodities in International Trade* (Cambridge, 1965), p. 124.
4. R. J. Hammond, *History of the Second World War, Vol. I*, 'Food, The Growth of Policy' (1951), p. 43.
5. The *Public Ledger*, 30 January, 3 and 7 February 1951.
6. The *Public Ledger*, 3 January 1952.
7. For a full description of the preparation of coffee for the London market prior to World War II see, for example, B. B. Keale, *Coffee, from Grower to Consumer* (London, 1933), pp. 76-7. According to G. C. Schulter, 'The Coffee Industry with special Reference to the Dominions and Colonies', *Journal of the Royal Society of Arts*, Vol. LXXXVI, 1937, pp. 148-66', the pre-war auctions were held 'two, three, or four times a week, according to arrivals'. Samples were exhibited previously in the brokers' salerooms and were roasted and tasted by prospective buyers before purchase.
8. F.A.O. Commodity Series, *The World Coffee Economy*, No. 33 (Rome, 1961).
9. See, e.g., 'Coffee as a Cold War Commodity', *National and Grindlay's Bank Review*, October 1962.
10. F.A.O. *Commodity Review and Outlook*, 1968-69, p. 58.

CHAPTER TWELVE   The Cocoa Market

1. Historicus, *Cocoa; all about it*, (London, 1892), and R. Whymper, *Cocoa and Chocolate* (London, 1921).
2. A detailed account of the price changes between 1953 and 1963 is given in F. Helmut Weymar, *The Dynamics of the World Cocoa Market* (Cambridge, Mass., 1968).
3. *The Economist*, 5 March 1960, 12 November 1960.
4. *The Economist*, 4 February 1961, 18 February 1961 and 4 November 1961.
5. *The Economist*, 14 October 1967.
6. *The Economist*, 23 December 1967.
7. *The Economist*, 3 June 1970 and 16 June 1970.

CHAPTER THIRTEEN   The Rubber Market

1. W. Woodruff, *The Rise of the British Rubber Industry during the Nineteenth Century* (Liverpool, 1955), p. 8.
2. Dowling, *The Exchanges of London*, p. 104.
3. H. N. Whitford, 'The Crude Rubber Situation' in W. S. Culbertson (Ed.), 'Raw Materials in Commercial Policies', *The Annals of the American Academy of Political and Social Science*, Vol. CXII, No. 201, March 1924, p. 150.
4. Woodruff, *The Rise of the British Rubber Industry during the Nineteenth Century*, p. 45.
5. Between 1922 and 1924 futures contracts were cleared by the London Produce Clearing House Ltd.
   Futures Transactions in Rubber, 1922-1924
   1922 – 495 tons   1923 – 450 tons   1924 – 225 tons
   Source: London Produce Clearing House Ltd.
6. *General Regulations relating to the Constitution of the Rubber Trade Association of London* (1966 reprint).
7. L. R. H. Procter, 'The Rubber Trade Association of London', *Financial Times*, 6 March 1964.
8. 'Selling Futures in the Rubber Trade', *India Rubber World* (New York), 15 September 1892.
9. See, for example, L. R. H. Procter in the *Financial Times*, 6 March 1964.
10. Dowling, op. cit., p. 105 and p. 112.
11. Sir A. McFadyean, *The History of Rubber Regulation, 1934-1943* (London, 1949), pp. 30-5.
12. Agreement . . . to Regulate Production and Export of Rubber. Cmd. 4583, XXVII. May 1934.
13. Declaration . . . recording the . . . Agreement of 7 May 1934 regarding the Regulation of the Production and Export of Rubber. Cmd. 5901, XXVII, 1938-39.
14. P. T. Bauer, *The Rubber Industry* (London, 1948), pp. 154-72.
15. *The Economist*, 9 October 1954, p. 145.
16. *The Economist*, 10 December 1955, pp. 959-61.
17. P. W. Bidwell, *Raw Materials: A Study of American Policy* (New York, 1958), p. 271.
18. See also the *Review of the current situation in specific commodities subject to competition from synthetics and substitutes. Case study on natural rubber.* Note by the U.N.C.T.A.D. Secretariat, 7 July 1967.
19. Ibid., p. 48.

CHAPTER FOURTEEN   Jute, Shellac and General Produce

1. The *Dundee Advertiser* of 6th February 1835, cited by Sir Alexander Murray, 'The Jute Industry', *Journal of the Royal Society of Arts*, Vol. LXXXII, August 1934, pp. 977-96.
2. Alex J. Warden, *The Linen Trade, Ancient and Modern* (London, 1864), pp. 62-5.
3. Ibid. The control over the number of City brokers is discussed, Chapter 2, p. 47.
4. See, *Reports of Restrictive Practices*, Vol. 4, March 1963 (Restrictive Practices Court, Scotland), pp. 406-7.
5. At a Conference held in Dacca in November 1967 under the auspices of the Pakistan Jute Board, in which the principal jute importing interests participated, the multiplicity of traditional jute grades and marks were re-classified as follows: P.W. (Pakistan White) Special, A, B, C, D and E; and P.T. (Pakistan Tossa) Special, A, B, C, D and E. The former well known terms, such as 'Export Firsts' and 'Lightnings', have thus disappeared.

6. *Reports of Restrictive Practices*, Vol. 4, pp. 401-2.
7. In 1939 futures transactions in Shellac amounted to 23,250 bags and/or cases. Source: London Produce Clearing House Ltd.
8. *Hansard Reports*, Vol. 298, 1934-5, pp. 2155-63.
9. *Public Ledger*, 30 April 1955, and 23 June 1956.
10. Hale & Son, *Market Review*, 1963.
11. The U.N. Food and Agriculture Organization point out in their Commodity Bulletin Series No. 34, *Spices, Trends in World Markets* (Rome, 1962) that for spices as a whole, the peak price as a percentage of the low price works out at 593 compared with 246 for the average of other primary products. Moreover, though this percentage was as much as 670 for rubber, individual spices easily outstripped this swing; for example, on the same reckoning, cloves worked out at 1120.

CHAPTER FIFTEEN   The Vegetable Oil, Oil-Seed and Oil-Cake Market

1. H. W. Brace, *History of Seed Crushing in Great Britain* (London, 1960), p. 15.
2. International Institute of Agriculture, *Oleaginous Products and Vegetable Oils* (Rome, 1923), p. 88.
3. For details, see the *Report of the Committee on Edible and Oil-Producing Nuts and Seeds* (Cd. 8247). Appendix C.
4. *Reports on Oil-Seeds* (Imperial Institute, London, 1920). See especially pp. 8-24.
5. Re-exports consist of material landed which usually changes hands in the reexporting country while transit trade is conducted mostly on through bills of lading.
6. Commonwealth Secretariat, *Vegetable Oils and Oilseeds* (London, 1968), p. 24.
7. *Public Ledger*, 23 June 1956 and 21 December 1957.
8. F.A.O. *Commodity Review, 1968* (Rome, 1968), p. 66.

CHAPTER SIXTEEN   Marketing Dominion Wool

1. Evidence of John Ellman and Richard Healy to the *Select Committee of the House of Lords on the State of the British Wool Trade*, 1828, Vol. VIII, pp. 18, 34.
2. Ibid., p. 319.
3. S. MacArthur Onslow, *Early Records of the Macarthurs of Camden* (Sydney, 1912), p. 434.
4. *Select Committee on the State of the British Wool Trade*, Vol. VIII, pp. 40, 287.
5. S. MacArthur Onslow, p. 414.
6. R. Montgomery Martin, *History of the British Colonies* (London, 1835), Vol. IV, p. 360.
7. A. Barnard, *The Australian Wool Market 1840-1900* (Melbourne, 1958), p. 133, cites Crawley and Smith in this connection as being willing to consign to either Antony Gibbs and Co. of London, or to Gibbs, Bright and Co. in Liverpool.
8. Ibid., p. 55.
9. Du Plessis, *The Marketing of Wool* (London, 1931), Chapter VII.
10. S. MacArthur Onslow, op. cit., pp. 409-10.
11. Quoted by E. Lipson, *A Short History of Wool and its Manufacture* (London, 1953), pp. 8-9.
12. Barnard, op. cit., p. 153.
13. Dalgety & Co. Ltd, *A Souvenir to Commemorate the Jubilee Year*, 1884, p. 29.
14. See, for example, the evidence of W. R. Price, a shipowner and an underwriter at Lloyds, to the *Royal Commission on the Depression of Trade and Industry, 1886*, Third Report Minutes of Evidence, Q.10072.
15. H. Munz, *The Australian Wool Industry* (Sydney, 1950).
16. A. Sharp, 'Wool and the Wool Trade', *Bradford Textile Society Journal 1952-53*.
17. See *U.K. – Dominion Wool Disposals Ltd* (Joint Organization) July 1946, Cmd. 6855; also *Origin, History and Operations of the U.K. – Dominion Wool Disposals Ltd*, August 1951, Cmd. 8329.
18. The *Public Ledger*, 2 May 1953.
19. Prices are given in the Monopolies Commission Report, *Man-made Cellulosic Fibres* (London, 1968), and the Commonwealth Secretariat publication *Plantation Crops*, No. 11.
20. L. Briscoe, 'The Demand for Wool', *Westminster Bank Review*, August 1968, p. 77.
21. *Financial Times*, 30 June 1968.

CHAPTER SEVENTEEN   The London Metal Exchange

1. The early history of the tin trade has been recounted at length in Carew's *Survey of Cornwall* (London, 1602), and in C. Welch, *History of the Worshipful Company of Pewterers* (London, 1902).
2. An account of the rise of the re-export trade is given in D. Lardner, *A Treatise on the Progressive Improvement and Present State of the Manufactures in Metal*, 2 Vols (London, 1831-33).
3. Economist Intelligence Unit, *The London Metal Exchange* (London, 1958), p. 12.
4. For a detailed account of this system, see W. Henderson, 'Remarks on Statistics relating to Swansea Usages and Customs as they Affect the Sellers of Foreign or Colonial Copper Ores'. *Transactions*, British Association for the Advancement of Science, Section F (Swansea, 1880), pp. 681-686.
5. D. B. Barton, *A History of Copper Mining in Cornwall and Devon* (Truro, 1961), p. 16.
6. R. O. Roberts, 'The development and decline of the non-ferrous metal smelting industries in South Wales', *Industrial South Wales, 1750-1914*, ed. W. E. Minchinton (London, 1969), pp. 150-3.
7. The terms 'matte' and 'blister' copper refer to stages in the smelting process. 'Copper matte' has not been completely smelted whereas 'blister copper' has been smelted but not refined.
8. W. O. Alexander, 'The Copper, Zinc and Brass Industries in Great Britain', *Murex Review*, I, 15 (1955), p. 419.
9. *The Cambrian*, 21 October 1892, p. 5, cited by R. O. Roberts, in an unpublished paper.
10. See, for example, J. B. Baer and G. P. Woodruff, *Commodity Exchanges* (New York, 1929), p. 204; J. C. Carr and W. Taplin, *History of the British Steel Industry* (Oxford, 1962), pp. 8-9. For accounts of speculation in pig-iron warrants, see, for example, *Shipping World*, Vol. VI, 1 July 1888, p. 65, Vol. II, 1 March 1890, pp. 336-7, and Vol. IX, 1 March 1892.
11. See the Appendix on Futures Trading.
12. *Shipping World*, 1 March 1890, pp. 336-7.
13. Dowling, *The Exchanges of London*, p. 141.
14. J. E. Spurr and F. E. Wormser, *The Marketing of Metals and Minerals* (New York, 1925), p. 57.
15. Economist Intelligence Unit, *The Metal Exchange*, p. 106.
16. The principal movements in commodity prices from 1913 to 1931 are described in *Commodity Prices and Markets*, by Austral Developments Ltd (London, 1931).
17. Klaus Knorr, *Tin under Control* (London, 1945).
18. Economist Intelligence Unit, *The London Metal Exchange*, p. 130.
19. J. Hurstfield, *The Control of Raw Materials* (in the series, *The History of the Second World War*) (London, 1953), p. 146.
20. *The Economist*, 2 March 1946.
21. *The Economist*, 20 April 1946.
22. See Chapter 5.
23. For a commentary, see British Metal Corporation, *Review of Base Metal Conditions 1954*.
24. *The Economist*, 16 July 1949.
25. G. L. Rees, *Britain and the Postwar European Payments Systems*, Chapter 3.
26. 'Commodity shunting' became worthwhile when the weakness of sterling gave rise to exchange rate quotations against the U.S. dollar, in unofficial markets, appreciably below the officially declared range of $2.78–$2.82 to the £. This 'cheap sterling' was bought by importers in the dollar area through the intermediacy of foreign agents, in whose names the purchases had to be made because American residents were not allowed to hold inconvertible sterling. The cheap sterling was then employed to purchase any commodities for which its use was permitted. The difficulty presented by the ultimate dollar area destination of such goods – for they were ostensibly bought by a resident from a transferable or bilateral account country – was met either by falsifying the shipping documents, or else by 'shunting' the goods from their first destination outside the dollar area to their ultimate destination inside it. If by means of this device the American importer succeeded in buying his supplies more cheaply than the conversion of his dollars at the official rate would have implied, the aim of the subterfuge was served. The sale of cheap sterling would also be worthwhile to the vendors provided that they obtained a sufficient number of dollars in exchange to enable them to resell at a profit in unofficial currency markets. G. L. Rees, op. cit., pp. 54-55.
27. *Public Ledger*, 20 September 1952.
28. *Public Ledger*, 22 November 1952.
29. *Public Ledger*, 1 August 1953.
30. See the Appendix on Futures Trading for a demonstration of this point.
31. B. S. Yamey, 'The London Metal Exchange', *The Three Banks Review*, No. 30, June 1956, p. 33.

32. *Public Ledger*, 7 May 1955.
33. S. D. Strauss, 'Marketing of Nonferrous Metals and Ores', Part I, *Economics of the Mineral Industries* (New York, 1959), p. 282.
34. *Public Ledger*, 12 January 1957.
35. *Public Ledger*, 12 October 1957.
36. The British Metal Corporation, *Review of Non-Ferrous Metals*, 1966, p. 5.
37. C. D. Rogers, 'Consumer Participation in the International Tin Agreements', *The Malayan Economic Review*, Vol. XIV, No. 2, October 1969, p. 121.
38. British Metal Corporation Ltd, *Review of Non-Ferrous Metals in 1969*, p. 19.
39. M. Desai, 'An Econometric Study of the World Tin Economy, 1948-61', *Econometrica*, Vol. XXXIV, No. 1, January 1966, pp. 105-134.
40. *Financial Times*, 12 October 1966.
41. *The Economist*, 17 August 1968.
42. Paul Jeanty of Samuel Montagne and Co. Ltd, *Financial Times*, 5 May 1969.
43. G. L. Rees and J. Wiseman, 'London's Commodity Markets', *Lloyds Bank Review*, No. 91, January 1969, pp. 38-39.
44. In 1970 Metallgesellschaft Ag. opened a London office and were elected ring members of the L.M.E. This company produces about one-sixth of the E.E.C.'s non-ferrous metals and contributes as much as 40 per cent of West Germany's copper production.
45. *The Economist*, 7 March 1970, p. 71.
46. M. C. Brackenbury and Co., *Dealing on the London Metal Exchange* (London, 1968), p. 8

CHAPTER EIGHTEEN   The Hudson's Bay Fur Auctions

1. *Encyclopaedia Britannica*, 1962, Vol. 9, p. 935.
2. For a résumé of these laws, see e.g. E. Veale, *The English Fur Trade in the Later Middle Ages* (Oxford, 1966), pp. 1-21.
3. E. E. Rich, *The History of the Hudson's Bay Company, 1670-1870* (London, 1958), Vol. I, pp. 1-3.
4. H. A. Innes, 'Fur Trade and Industry', *Encyclopaedia of the Social Sciences*, Vol. VI, p. 531.
5. W. J. Passingham, *London's Markets*, p. 38.
6. E. E. Rich, 'Russia and the Fur Trade', *Economic History Review*, Vol. VII, 1955, p. 323.
7. M. G. Lawson, *Fur, a Study in English Mercantilism 1700-1775* (Toronto, 1943), p. 70.
8. Report from the *Select Committee on the Hudson's Bay Company* . . . (London, 1857).
9. W. J. Passingham, *op. cit.*, p. 243.
10. *Financial Times* reports, 19 June 1966 and 1 May 1967.
11. *Financial Times*, 14 July 1967. Cancellations of entire sales series do take place sometimes at various centres. Thus the Consortium of Scandinavian Fur Auctions cancelled its June 1966 series because most of the consignments had already been sold.

CHAPTER NINETEEN   The London Diamond Market

1. See e.g. P. J. Oppenheimer's remarks in *The Times Supplement on the Diamond Industry*, 7 October 1964, p. V.
2. A full account is given in the Commonwealth Economic Committee publication *Non-Metallic Minerals* for 1967.
3. *The Times*, 20 March 1969.
4. *The Times*, 27 June 1969.

CHAPTER TWENTY   The Rationale of the Markets

1. An account of how futures markets operate will be found in the Appendix on Futures Trading.
2. A. Maizels, 'Trade and Development Problems of the Under-developed Countries', *National Institute Economic Review*, No. 28, May 1964, p. 33.
3. *Bank of England Bulletin*, Vol. 9, No. 2, June 1969, p. 207.
4. G. L. Rees and J. Wiseman, *London's Commodity Markets*, January 1969, p. 41.
5. *Bank of England Bulletin*, Vol. 4, No. 3, September 1964, p. 195.
6. *Bank of England Bulletin*, Vol. 9, No. 2, June 1969, p. 205.
7. The Report of the Committee on Invisible Exports, *Britain's Invisible Earnings*, directed by W. M. Clarke (London, 1967).
8. Central Statistical Office, *U.K. Balance of Payments* (H.M.S.O., 1948).
9. See for example the *Commodity Yearbook* of the U.S. Commodity Research Bureau Inc.
10. Rees and Wiseman, *London's Commodity Markets*, p. 39.

APPENDIX ONE   Futures Trading

1. A dealer's position is described as 'open', or 'uncovered', when the amount of his total stocks, forward purchases and futures purchases is greater than the total of his forward sales and futures sales.
2. J. M. Keynes, *Treatise on Money* (London, 1930), Vol. II, pp. 142-144.
3. N. Kaldor, 'Speculation and Economic Stability', *Review of Economic Studies*, Vol. 7, No. 1, October 1939, pp. 1-27.
4. G. L. Rees, 'The Future of Futures', *The Bankers' Magazine*, April 1965, p. 256.
5. A description of their use on very early continental markets is given in Chapter 2.
6. B. S. Yamey, 'An Investigation of Hedging on an Organised Produce Exchange', *Manchester School of Economic and Social Studies*, Vol. XIX, No. 3, September 1951, pp. 305-319.
7. R. H. Snape, *Protection and Stabilization in the World Sugar Industry*. Unpublished Ph.D. thesis, University of London, 1962.

Select Bibliography

PARLIAMENTARY PAPERS etc.

1565   Public Record Office, *Calendar of State Papers, Domestic, of the reign of Elizabeth I,* 6 October 1565, Vol. I.

1796   'Report from the Select Committee on the best mode of Providing accommodation for the increased Trade and Shipping of the Port of London', 1796, First Series, Vol. XIV.

1800   'Two Reports from the Select Committee on the present state of the Coal Trade of this Kingdom', 1800, First Series, Vol. X.

1801   'Seventh Report from the House of Commons Committee appointed to consider the present High Price of Provisions', 1801, First Series, Vol. IX.

1814-15   'Report of the Select Committee on the Laws Relating to the Manufacture, Sale and Assize of Bread', 1814-15, Vol. V.

1814-15   'Reports from the Lords Committees on the State of the Growth, Commerce and Consumption of Grain and all the laws relating thereto', 1814-15, Vol. V.

1821   'Report from the Select Committee on the Petitions Complaining of the depressed state of the Agriculture of the United Kingdom', 1821, Vol. IX.

1823   'Report of the Select Committee on the Law relating to Merchants, Agents or Factors', 1823, Vol. IV.

1828   'Report from the Select Committee of the House of Lords on the State of the British Wool Trade', 1828, Vol. VIII.

1828   'Report from the Select Committee on the State of Smithfield Market', 1828, Vol. VIII.

1833   'Report from the Select Committee on the present state of Manufactures, Commerce and Shipping in the United Kingdom', 1833, Vol. VI.

1834   'Report from the Select Committee on the present Practices of selling corn throughout the United Kingdom with a view to the better Regulation thereof', 1834, Vol. VII.

1840   'Select Committee on Import Duties', 1840, Vol. V.

1845   'Report of the Select Committee of the House of Lords appointed to enquire into the effects of alterations made in the law regulating the interest on money', 1845, Vol. XII.

1847   'Report of the Select Committee on Commercial relations with China', 1848, Vol. V.

1847-48   'Secret Committee on Commercial Distress (How far has it been affected by the issue of Bank Notes Payable on Demand)', 1847-48, Vol. VIII, Parts 1, 2 and 3.

1857   'Report from the Select Committee on the Hudson's Bay Company . . .' 1857, Vol. XV.

1882   'Royal Commission on the Depressed Condition of Agricultural Interests.' (c. 3309) 1882, Vol. XIV.

1886   'Royal Commission on the Depression of Trade and Industry', (c. 4797) 1886, Vol. XXIII.

1894   'Royal Commission on Agricultural Depression', (c. 7400) 1894, Vol. XVI, Part 2.

1916   'Report of the Committee on Edible and Oil-producing Nuts and Seeds', Cd. 8247, 1916, Vol. IV.

1921   'First Report of the Royal Commission on Wheat Supplies' Cmd. 1544, 1921, Vol. XVIII.

1925   'Report of the Royal Grain Inquiry Commission', Cmd. 2462, 1925, Vol. XV.

1935   'Report on the Sugar Industry in the United Kingdom' (Greene Committee Report), Cmd. 4871, 1935, Vol. XI.

1946   'United Kingdom Dominion Wool Disposals Ltd. (Joint Organisation)', Cmd. 6855, July 1946, Vol. XX.

1948-49   'First Annual Report and Statement of Accounts of the Raw Cotton Commission', 1949, Vol. XXI.

1951   'Origin, History and Operations of the existing Joint Organisation', Cmd. 8329, August 1951, Vol. XXVII.

1952   'Report of the Cotton Import Committee', Cmd. 8510, April 1952, Vol. IX.
1955   Ministry of Agriculture, Fisheries and Food: Future Arrangements for the Marketing of Sugar, Cmd. 9519, 1955.
1957   Monopolies and Restrictive Practices Commission: Report on the Supply of Tea, 1956-57, Vol. XVII.
1963   Reports of Restrictive Practices Cases (Restrictive Practices Court, Scotland), March 1963, Vol. IV.
1965   'The Marketing of Meat and Livestock', Cmd. 2737, 1965, Vol. XXIX.
1968   'Monopolies Commission Report: A Report on the supply of man-made cellulosic fibres', 1967-68, Vol. XXVI.

JOURNALS

Alexander, W. O., 'The Copper, Zinc and Brass Industries in Great Britain', *Murex Review*, Vol. 1, No. 15, 1955.
Baer, W. E., 'Market Gambling', *Contemporary Review*, Vol. LXV, June 1894.
Baer, W. E., 'Market Wrecking', *The Fortnightly Review*, Vol. 61, N.S. April 1897.
Bowden, P. J., 'Movements in Wool Prices, 1490-1610', *Yorkshire Bulletin of Economic and Social Research*, Vol. IV, No. 2, 1952.
Bowden, P. J., 'Movements in Wool Prices – a Reply', *Yorkshire Bulletin of Economic and Social Research*, Vol. VIII, No. 2, 1956.
Brand, S. S., 'The Decline in the Cotton Futures Market', *Stanford Food Research Institute Studies*, Vol. IV, No. 3, 1964.
Briscoe, L., 'The Demand for Wool', *Westminster Bank Review*, August 1968.
Brulers, W., 'L'exportation des Pays Bas vers L'Italie par voie de Terre au milieu du XVIᵉ siècle', *Annales: Économies, Sociétés, Civilisations*, Vol. 14, 1959.
Chattaway, C., 'Arbitration in the Foreign Corn Trade of London', *Economic Journal*, Vol. XVII, 1907.
Checkland, S. G., 'American versus West India Traders in Liverpool 1793-1815', *Journal of Economic History*, Vol. XVIII, No. 2, 1958.
Culbertson, W. S. (ed.), 'Raw Materials in Commercial Policies', *Annals of the American Academy of Political and Social Science*, Vol. CXII, No. 201, March 1924.
Desai, M., 'An Econometric Study of the World Tin Economy 1948-1961', *Econometrica*, Vol. XXXIV, No. 1, January 1966.
Dumbell, S., 'The Organization of the Cotton Market in the Eighteenth Century', *Economic Journal*, Vol. XXXIII, 1923.
Dumbell, S., 'The Origin of Cotton Futures', *Economic Journal Supplement, Economic History*, Vol. 1, 1926-29.
Fairlie, J. A., 'The Economic Effects of Ship Canals', *Annals of the American Academy of Political and Social Science*, Vol. II, 1898.
Fisher, F. J., 'The Development of the London Food Market 1540-1640', *Economic History Review*, Vol. V, No. 2, 1935.
Fisher, F. J., 'Commercial Trends and Policy in Sixteenth Century England', *Economic History Review*, Vol. X, No. 2, 1940.
Gill, C., 'Blackwell Hall Factors 1795-1799', *Economic History Review*, second series, Vol. VI, No. 3, 1954.
Hubback, J. H., 'Some Aspects of the International Grain Trade', *Economic Journal*, Vol. XVI, 1911.
Hutchinson, W. B., 'Is There a Future for Futures?', *Liverpool Raw Cotton Annual*, 1959.
Hutchinson, W. B., 'Price Risk Insurance for Cotton', *Liverpool Raw Cotton Annual*, 1962.
Hyde, F. E., Parkinson, B. B., and Marriner, S., 'The Cotton Broker and the Rise of the Liverpool Cotton Market', *Economic History Review*, second series, Vol. VIII, 1955-56.
James, M. K., 'The fluctuations of the Anglo-Gascon wine trade during the 14th Century', *Economic History Review*, Vol. IV, second series, 1951.
Jeanty, Paul (of Samuel Montagu and Co. Ltd), *Financial Times*, 5 May 1969.
Kaldor, N., 'Speculation and Economic Stability', *Review of Economic Studies*, Vol. 7, No. 1, October 1939.
McCulloch, J. R., 'Some Observations on the Trade with China', *Edinburgh Review*, January 1824.
Machin, W. F., 'A Short History of the Liverpool Cotton Market', *The Liverpool Raw Cotton Annual*, 1958.
Maizels, A., 'Trade and Development Problems of the Under-developed Countries', *National Institute Economic Review*, No. 28, May 1964.
Mallett, M. E., 'Anglo-Florentine Commercial Relations 1465-1491', *Economic History Review*, second series, Vol. XV, No. 2, 1962.

Marsh, A. R., 'Cotton Exchanges and their Economic Function', *Annals of the American Academy of Political and Social Science*, Vol. XXXVIII, 1911.

Murray, Sir Alexander, 'The Jute Industry', *Journal of the Royal Society of Arts*, Vol. LXXXII, August 1934.

Oppenheimer, P. J., *The Times* supplement on the Diamond Industry, 7 October, 1964.

Pares, R., 'Merchants and Planters', *Economic History Review*, Supplement No. 4, Cambridge, 1960.

Paul, R. W., 'The Wheat Trade between California and the United Kingdom, *The Mississippi Valley Historical Review*, Vol. XLV, No. 3, December 1958.

Postan, M. M., 'Credit in Medieval Trade', *Economic History Review*, Vol. 1, No. 2, 1928.

Price, J. M., 'The Rise of Glasgow in the Chesapeake Tobacco Trade 1707-1775', *William and Mary Quarterly*, Vol. XI, No. 2, 1954.

Proctor, L. R. H., 'The Rubber Trade Association of London', *Financial Times*, 6 March 1964.

Rees, G. L., 'The Future of Futures', *The Bankers' Magazine*, April 1965.

Rees, G. L., 'Britain's Grain Markets', *National Provincial Bank Review*, November 1966.

Rees, G. L. and Wiseman, J., 'London's Commodity Markets', *Lloyds Bank Review*, January 1969.

Rich, E. E., 'Russia and the Fur Trade', *Economic History Review*, Vol. VII, 1955.

Robertson, A. B., 'The Foundation of Mark Lane Corn Exchange', *Guildhall Miscellany* No. 2, February 1953.

Robertson, W., 'The Raw Cotton Commission: an Experiment in State Trading', *Journal of Industrial Economics*, Vol. VI, 1955-56.

Rogers, C. D., 'Consumer Participation in the International Tin Agreements', *The Malayan Economic Review*, Vol. XIV, No. 2, October 1969.

Schulter, G. C., 'The Coffee Industry with Special Reference to the Dominions and Colonies', *Journal of the Royal Society of Arts*, Vol. LXXXVI, 1937.

Sharp, A., 'Wool and the Wool Trade', *Bradford Textile Society Journal*, 1952-53.

Stern, W. M., 'The London Sugar Refiners around 1800', *Guildhall Miscellany*, No. 3, February 1954.

Stevens, A. C., 'Futures in the Wheat Market', *Quarterly Journal of Economics*, Vol. II, 1887.

Tenenti, A. and Vivanti, C., 'Les grandes trafics d'état à Venise: les galères da mercato, 1332-1534', *Annales: Économies, Sociétés, Civilizations*, Vol. 16, 1961.

Tyszynski, H., 'World Trade in Manufactured Commodities, 1899-1950', *Manchester School of Economic and Social Studies*, Vol. XIX, No. 3, 1951.

Webb, A. D., 'The Relation between Wholesale and Retail Prices of Sugar', *Economic Journal*, Vol. XXIV, 1914.

Whitford, H. N., 'The Crude Rubber Situation', in W. S. Culbertson (ed.), 'Raw Materials in Commercial Policies', *The Annals of the American Academy of Political and Social Science*, Vol. CXII, No. 201, March 1924.

Whelply, J. D., 'An International Wheat Corner', *The Fortnightly Review*, Vol. 68, N.S. July 1900.

Wiseman, J. and Yamey, B. S., 'The Raw Cotton Commission 1948-52', *Oxford Economic Papers*, N.S. Vol. VIII, 1956.

Wood, G. L., 'Wheat Pools with special Reference to Australia', *Economic Record*, Supplement, February 1928.

Wyse, R. C., 'The Selling and Financing of the American Cotton Crop', *Economic Journal*, Vol. XXX, 1920.

Yamey, B. S., 'An Investigation of Hedging on an Organized Produce Exchange', *Manchester School of Economic and Social Studies*, Vol. XIX, No. 3, 1951.

Yamey, B. S., 'The London Metal Exchange', *Three Banks Review*, No. 30, June 1956.

Yamey, B. S., 'Cotton Futures Trading in Liverpool', *Three Banks Review*, No. 49, March 1959.

BOOKS

Albion, R. G., *The Rise of New York Port*, New York, 1939.

Allen, G. C. and Donnithorne, A., *Western Enterprise in Far Eastern Economic Development: China and Japan*, London, 1954.

Anderson, A., *An Historical and Chronological Deduction of the Origin of Commerce from the Earliest Accounts*, Vol. IV, London, 1801.

Ashley, M., *Financial and Commercial Policy under the Cromwellian Protectorate*, London, 1962.

Baer, W. E. and Woodruff, L., *Commodity Exchanges*, New York, 1929.

Baines, E., *History of the Cotton Manufacture in Great Britain*, London, 1835.

Barbour, Violet, *Capitalism in Amsterdam in the Seventeenth Century*, Baltimore, 1950.

Barnard, A., *The Australian Wool Market*, 1840-1900, Melbourne, 1958.

Barker, A., *The British Corn Trade from the Earliest Times to the Present Day*, London, 1920.

Barnes, E., *History of the Cotton Manufacture in Great Britain*, London, 1835.
Barton, D. B., *A History of Copper Mining in Cornwall and Devon*, Truro, 1961.
Bauer, P. T., *The Rubber Industry*, London, 1948.
Besant, W., *London in the Time of the Tudors*, London, 1904.
Beveridge, Sir William, *British Food Control*, Oxford, 1928.
Bidwell, P. W., *Raw Materials: A Study of American Policy*, New York, 1958.
Boyle, J. E., *Cotton and the New Orleans Cotton Exchange*, New York, 1934.
Brace, H. W., *History of Seed Crushing in Great Britain*, London, 1960.
Bridbury, A. R., *England and the Salt Trade in the later Middle Ages*, Oxford, 1955.
Britton, D. K. and Associates, *Cereals in the United Kingdom*, London, 1969.
Broomhall, G. J. S. and Hubback, John H., *Corn Trade Memories*, Liverpool, 1930.
Buck, N. S., *The Development of the Organization of Anglo-American Trade*, 1800-1850, Yale, 1925.
Burn, Richard, *Statistics of the Cotton Trade*, London, 1847.
Campbell, R., *The London Tradesman*, third edition, London, 1747.
Carew, R. *Survey of Cornwall*, London, 1602.
Carr, J. C. and Taplin, W., *History of the British Steel Industry*, Oxford, 1962.
Carus-Wilson, E. M., *Medieval Merchant Venturers*, London, 1954.
Carus-Wilson, E. M. (ed.), *Essays in Economic History*, Vol. 1, London, 1954.
Carus-Wilson, E. M. and Coleman, O., *England's Export Trade* 1275-1547, Oxford, 1963.
Chapman, S. J., *The War and the Cotton Trade*, Oxford, 1915.
The City, London, 1844.
Clapham, J. H., *An Economic History of Modern Britain*, Vol. I, 1926; Vol. II, 1932; Vol. III, 1938. Cambridge
Clapham, Sir John, *A Concise Economic History of Modern Britain from the Earliest Times to 1750*, Cambridge, 1949.
Davies, K. G., *The Royal African Company*, London, 1957.
Deerr, N., *The History of Sugar*, 2 vols., London, 1949 & 1950.
Defoe, Daniel, *The Complete English Tradesman*, 2nd Edition London, 1727.
Defoe, Daniel, *A Tour through England and Wales*, Vol. 2, London, 1927.
Dondlinger, P. T., *The Book of Wheat: An Economic History and Practical Manual of the Wheat Industry*, New York, 1908.
Donnell, E. J., *The History of Cotton*, New York, 1872.
Dowling, S. W., *The Exchanges of London*, London, 1929.
Du Plessis, A. F., *The Marketing of Wool*, London, 1931.
Edington, Robert, *Historical Account of the Various Coal Mines of South Wales*, London, 1824.

Ellis, Arthur, *The Rationale of Market Fluctuation*, London, 1879.
Ellison, T., *The Cotton Trade of Great Britain*, London, 1886.
Ellison, T., *Gleanings and Reminiscences*, Liverpool, 1905.
Emery, H. C., *Speculation on the Stock and Produce Exchanges of the U.S.A.*, New York, 1896.
Essay against Forestallers, London, 1718 (Anon).
Evans, D. Morier, *The Annual Commercial Register and General Record of Prices in the year 1849*, London, 1850.
Evans, D. Morier, *City Men and City Manners*, London, 1852.
Evans, D. Morier, *Speculative Notes and notes on Speculation*, London, 1864.
Fairlie, S. E., *The Anglo-Russian Grain Trade 1815-1861*. Unpublished Ph.D. thesis, University of London, 1959.
Fay, C. R., *Great Britain from Adam Smith to the Present Day*, London, 1928.
Feaveryear, A. E., *The Pound Sterling: a History of English Money*, ed. E. Victor Morgan, Oxford, 1963.
Findlay, J. A., *The Baltic Exchange*, London, 1927.
Fitton, R. S. and Wadsworth, A. P., *The Strutts and the Arkwrights 1758-1830*, Manchester, 1958.
Forward, Sir W. B., *Recollections of a Busy Life: Being the Reminiscences of a Liverpool Merchant, 1840-1910*, Liverpool, 1910.
Fowke, V. C., *Canadian Agricultural Policy*, Toronto, 1947.
Fowke, V. C., *The National Policy and the Wheat Economy*, Toronto, 1957.
Fox Bourne, H. R., *English Merchants*, London, 1886.
The Frauds and Abuses of the Coal-Dealers Detected and Exposed, London, 1743-4. (Anon.)
Fridlizias, G., *Swedish Corn Export in the Free Trade Era: Patterns in the Oats Trade, 1850-1880*, Lund University, Sweden, 1957.
Fryde, E. B., *The Wool Accounts of William de la Pole*, York, 1964.
Gras, N. S. B., *The Evolution of the English Corn Market*, Cambridge, Mass., 1915.
Gray, H. L., 'English Foreign Trade from 1446 to 1482; in *Studies in English Foreign Trade in the Fifteenth Century*, ed. E. Power & M. Postan, London, 1933.
Greenberg, M., *British Trade and the Opening of China 1800-1842*, Cambridge, 1951.

Hammond, R. J., *Food, Vol. I, The Growth of Policy* in the series *The History of the Second World War*, ed. W. K. Hancock, London, 1951.

Hecht, F., *Die Warrants*, Stuttgart, 1884.

Hemelryk, P. E. J., *Forty Years' Reminiscences of the Cotton Market*, Liverpool, 1916.

Henderson, H. D., *The Cotton Control Board*, Oxford, 1922.

Henderson, W., 'Remarks on Statistics relating to Swansea Usages and Customs as they affect the sellers of Foreign or Colonial Copper Ores', *Transactions British Association for the Advancement of Science*, Section F, Swansea, 1880.

Henderson, W. O., *The Lancashire Cotton Famine 1861-1865*, Manchester, 1934.

Hidy, R. W., *The House of Baring in American Trade and Finance*, Cambridge, Mass., 1949.

Historicus (R. Cadbury), *Cocoa: all about it*, London, 1892.

Hooker, A. A., *The International Grain Trade*, second edition, London, 1939.

Horsely, William, *The Universal Merchant etc.*, London, 1753.

Hurstfield, J., *The Control of Raw Materials*, in the series *The History of the Second World War*, ed. W. K. Hancock, London, 1953.

Hurwitz, S. J., *State Intervention in Great Britain. A study of Economic Control and Social Response 1914-1919*, New York, 1949.

Hutcheson, John M., *Notes on the Sugar Industry*, Greenock, 1901.

Innes, H. A., *Fur Trade and Industry*, Encyclopaedia of the Social Sciences, Vol. VI, New York, 1931.

Keale, B. B., *Coffee from Grower to Consumer*, London, 1933.

Keynes, J. M., *Treatise on Money*, Vol. II, London, 1930.

Kingsford, C. L. (ed.), *Additional Notes to a Survey of London by John Stow*, Oxford, 1927.

Knight, Charles, *London*, Vol. V, London, 1843.

Knorr, Klaus, *Tin Under Control*, London, 1945.

Lardner, D. (ed.), *A Treatise on the Progressive Improvement and Present State of the Manufactures in Metal . . . Iron and Steel*, 2 Vols., London, 1831-33.

Lawson, M. G., *Fur, a Study in English Mercantilism 1700-1775*, Toronto, 1943.

Lewis, E. D., *The Rhondda Valleys*, London, 1959.

Lipson, Ephraim, *The Economic History of England*, Vol. I, *The Middle Ages*, & Vol. II, *The Age of Mercantilism*, London, 1937.

Lipson, Ephraim, *A Short History of Wool and its Manufacture*, London, 1953.

Macarthur Onslow, S., *Early Records of the Macarthurs of Camden*, Sydney, 1912.

McCulloch, J. R., *A Dictionary of Commerce*, London, 1834.

McFadyean, Sir A., *The History of Rubber Regulation, 1934-1943*, London, 1949.

MacGibbon, D. A., *The Canadian Grain Trade*, Toronto, 1932.

Maitland, W. and others, *History and Survey of London*, London, 1756.

Malenbaum, W., *The World Wheat Economy 1885-1939*, Cambridge, Mass., 1953.

Marriner, Sheila, *Rathbones of Liverpool 1845-1873*, Liverpool, 1961.

Mathias, Peter, *Brewing Industry in England 1700-1830*, Cambridge, 1959.

Minchinton, W. E. (ed.), *Industrial South Wales, 1750-1914*, London, 1969.

Mitchell, B. R., *Abstract of British Historical Statistics*, Cambridge, 1962.

Morgan, E. Victor, and Thomas, W. A., *The Stock Exchange, its History and Functions*, London, 1962.

Montgomery Martin, R., *History of the British Colonies*, Vol. IV, London, 1835.

Morris, J. H. and Williams, L. J., *The South Wales Coal Industry*, Cardiff, 1958.

Munz, H., *The Australian Wool Industry*, Sydney, 1950.

Nef, J. U., *The Rise of the British Coal Industry*, London, 1932.

Pares, R., *A West India Fortune*, London, 1950.

Passingham, W. J., *London's Markets, their Origin and History*, London, 1935.

Pelcovits, N. A., *Old China Hands and the Foreign Office*, New York, 1948.

Petty, Sir William, *Another Essay in Political Arithmetick concerning the Growth of the city of London*, London, 1683.

Petty, Sir William, *A Treatise of Taxes and Contributions*, London, 1662.

Phipps, John, *A Practical Treatise on the China and Eastern Trade*, London, 1836.

Pierce, B. L., *A History of Chicago*, Vol. I, *The Beginning of a City 1673-1848*, New York, 1937.

Poole, Braithwaite, *The Commerce of Liverpool*, London, 1854.

Porter, G. B., *Progress of the Nation*, London, 1851.

Power, E. and Postan, M., (Eds.) *Studies in English Foreign Trade in the Fifteenth Century*, London, 1933.

Pratt, Edward Ewing, *International Trade in Staple Commodities*, New York, 1928.

Pulling, A., *A Practical Treatise on the Laws, Customs, Usages, and Regulations of the City and Port of London*, London, 1849.

Ramsay, G. D., *English Overseas Trade during the Centuries of Emergence*, London, 1957.

Ragatz, L. J., 'The Fall of the Planter Class in the British Caribbean 1763-1833', *American Historical Association*, 1928.

Rees, G. L., *Britain and the Postwar European Payments Systems*, University of Wales Press, 1963.

Rees, G. L., *Reports on the Cotton Market, 1843-1863*, in the series *British Reports relating to America*, ed. W. E. Minchinton, York, 1965.

Ricard, J. P., *Le Négoce d'Amsterdam*, Amsterdam, 1722.

Rich, E. E., *The History of the Hudson's Bay Company, 1670-1870*, Vol. I, London, 1958.

Roberts, R. O., *The Development and decline of the non-ferrous metal smelting industries in South Wales*, in *Industrial South Wales, 1750-1914*, ed. W. E. Minchinton, London, 1969.

Robson, R., *The Cotton Industry in Britain*, London, 1957.

Roll, E., *The Combined Food Board: a study in wartime International Planning*, Stanford, 1956.

Rowe, J. W. F., *Markets and Men*, Cambridge, 1936.

Rowe, J. W. F., *Primary Commodities in International Trade*, Cambridge, 1965.

Roy, H., *Tea Price Stabilization – The Indian Case*, Calcutta, 1965.

Ruddock, A. A., *Italian Merchants and Shipping in Southampton 1270-1600*, Southampton, 1951.

Salzman, L. F., *English Trade in the Middle Ages*, Oxford, 1931.

Sargeant, F., *The Wine Trade with Gascony* in *Finance and Trade under Edward III*, ed. G Unwin, London, 1918.

Schulze-Gaevernitz, G. Von, *The Cotton Trade in England and on the Continent*, London, 1895.

Schumpeter, E. B., *English Overseas Trade Statistics, 1697-1808*, Oxford, 1960.

Sheffield, Lord (J. B. Holroyd), *Observations on the Corn Bill*, London, 1791.

Smith, Adam, *Wealth of Nations*, Cannan edition, London, 1930.

Smith, C., *A Short Essay on the Corn Trade and the Corn Laws*, London, 1758.

Smith, C. W., *International Gambling in Futures and Fictitious Agricultural Produce*, Prague, 1897.

Smith, J., *Chronicum Rusticum Commerciale or Memoirs of Wool, Woollen Manufacture and Trade etc.*, Vol. II, London, 1747.

Smith, J. G., *Organized Produce Markets*, London, 1922.

Smith, R., *Sea-Coal for London*, London, 1961.

Smithers, Henry, *Liverpool, its Commerce, Statistics and Institutions etc.*, Liverpool, 1825.

Snape, R. H., *Protection and Stabilization in the World Sugar Industry*, Unpublished Ph.D. thesis, University of London, 1962.

Spurr, J. E. and Wormser, R. E., *The Marketing of Metals and Minerals*, New York, 1925.

Stahl, K. M., *The Metropolitan Organization of British Colonial Trade*, London, 1951.

Staley, E., *Raw Materials in Peace and War*, New York, 1937.

Staveacre, F. W. F., *Tea and Tea Dealing*, London, 1929.

Stow, J., *A Survey of London*, Morley edition, Oxford, 1890.

Stow, J., *Survey of London*, ed. C. L. Kingsford, London, 1908.

Strauss, S. D., *Marketing of Non-ferrous Metals and Ores*, Part I, *Economics of the Mineral Industries*, New York, 1959.

Surface, F. M., *The Grain Trade during the World War*, New York, 1928.

Swerling, B. C., 'International Control of Sugar, 1918-1941', *Stanford Commodity Policy Studies*, No. 7, 1949.

Tate, W., *The Elements of Commercial Calculations etc.*, London, 1819.

Thrupp, S., 'The Grocers of London. A Study of Distributive Trades', in *Studies in English Foreign Trade in the Fifteenth Century*, ed. E. Power and M. Postan, London, 1933.

Timoshenko, V. P. and Swerling, B. C., *The World's Sugar*, Stanford, 1957.

Todd, J. A., *The Marketing of Cotton*, London, 1934.

Unwin, G., *Industrial Organization in the Sixteenth and Seventeenth Centuries*, Oxford, 1904.

Unwin, G. (ed.), *Finance and Trade under Edward III*, London, 1918.

Unwin, G., *London Tradesmen and their Creditors*, London, 1927.

Ure, A., *The Cotton Manufacture of Great Britain Systematically Investigated*, Vol. I, London, 1836.

Veale, E., *The English Fur Trade in the Later Middle Ages*, Oxford, 1966.

Wadsworth, A. P. and Mann, J. de L., *The Cotton Trade and Industrial Lancashire 1600-1780*, Manchester, 1931.

Walford, C., *Fairs Past and Present*, London, 1883.

Warden, Alex. J., *The Linen Trade, Ancient and Modern*, London, 1864.

Warner, Sir George (ed.), *Libelle of Englysche Polycye etc.*, Oxford, 1926.

Watkins, J. L., *King Cotton: A Historical and Statistical Review, 1790-1908*, New York, 1908.

Wee, R. Van der, *The Growth of the Antwerp Mart.*, Vol. II, The Hague, 1963.

Welch, C., *History of the Worshipful Company of Pewterers of the City of London etc.*, London, 1902.

Westerfield, R. B., 'Middlemen in English Business between 1660-1760', in *Transactions of the Connecticut Academy of Arts and Sciences*, Vol. XIX, Yale, 1915.

Weymar, F. Helmut, *The Dynamics of the World Cocoa Market*, Cambridge, Mass., 1968.

Wheeler, J., *A Treatise of Commerce*, London, 1601.

Whymper, R., *Cocoa and Chocolate*, London, 1921.

Wickizier, V. D., *Coffee, Tea and Cocoa*, Stanford, 1951.

Wickizier, V. D., *Tea under International Regulation*, Stanford, 1944.

Williams, F. H. B., *The Tea Trade*, Unpublished M.Sc. thesis, University of London, 1938.

Williams, M., *Seven Years History of the Cotton Trade of Europe*, Liverpool, 1868.

Wilson, Dr. Thomas, *A Discourse upon Usury*, London, 1925.
Woodruff, W., *The Rise of the British Rubber Industry during the Nineteenth Century*, Liverpool, 1955.

OTHER PUBLICATIONS
Bank of England, *Quarterly Bulletin*.
Brackenbury, M. C. and Co., *Dealing on the London Metal Exchange*, London, 1968.
British Metal Corporation, *Review of Base Metal Conditions*.
British Metal Corporation, *Review of Non-Ferrous Metals*.
Bulletin of the Wool Manufacturers.
Committee on Invisible Exports (Director of Study, W. C. Clarke), published for the
    Financial Advisory Panel on Exports, London, 1967.
Commissioners of H.M. Customs and Excise, *Annual Statement of the Trade of the United
    Kingdom*.
Commodity Research Bureau, *Commodity Year Books*, New York.
Commonwealth Economic Committee, *World Trade in Wool and Wool Textiles*.
Commonwealth Secretariat (Commonwealth Economic Committee),
                        Industrial Fibres
                        Non-Metallic Minerals
                        Non-Ferrous Metals
                        Plantation Crops
                        Vegetable Oils and Oilseeds
Czarnikow Ltd, C., *Sugar Reviews*.
Dalgety and Co. Ltd, *A Souvenir to Commemorate the Jubilee Year*, London 1884.
Department of Trade and Industry, *Overseas Trade Statistics of the United Kingdom* (previously
    Overseas Trade Accounts of the United Kingdom).
The Economist.
Economist Intelligence Unit, *The London Metal Exchange*, London, 1958.
Empire Marketing Board, *Fibres*, London, July 1933.
The *Financial Times*.
Gentlemen's Magazine.
Hale and Son, *Market Reviews*.
Harrisons and Crosfield Ltd, *Report and Accounts*, London.
Harrisons and Crosfield Ltd, *One Hundred Years as East India Merchants 1844-1943*, London,
    1943.
Imperial Economic Committee, *Wool Production and Trade 1928-1934*, London, 1935.
Imperial Economic Committee, *Eighteenth Report on Tea*, London, 1931.
Imperial Institute, *Indian Trade Enquiry – Reports on Oil Seeds*, London, 1920.
International Institute of Agriculture, *Oleaginous Products and Vegetable Oils*, Rome, 1923.
International Labour Office, *Intergovernmental Commodity Control Agreements*, Montreal, 1943.
International Sugar Organization, *Sugar Yearbook*, London.
International Tea Committee, *Report 1933-1934*, London, 1934.
International Tea Committee, *Annual Bulletin of Statistics*, London.
International Wheat Council, *Review of the World Grains Situation, 1968-69*, London, 1970.
Liverpool Cotton Gazette, June 24 and 23 December, 1939.
The Liverpool Corn Trade Association, *The Liverpool Corn Trade Association 1853-1953*,
    Liverpool, 1953.
Liverpool Exchanges Yearbook.
Liverpool Raw Cotton Annual, 1958.
Mining Journal and Commercial Gazette, 12 December 1835.
New York Produce Exchange, *Annual Report*, 1881.
Port of London Authority, *Annual Report and Accounts*.
Rubber Statistical Bulletin.
Shipping World.
The *Times*, various dates.
United Nations, Food and Agriculture Organization, *National Grain Policies*, Rome, 1959.
United Nations, Food and Agriculture Organization, *The World Sugar Economy in Figures
    1880-1959*, Rome, 1961.
United Nations, Food and Agriculture Organization, Commodity Bulletin Series, *Tea
    Trends and Prospects*, No. 30, Rome, 1960.
United Nations, Food and Agriculture Organization, Commodity Bulletin Series, *The
    World Coffee Economy*, No. 33, Rome, 1961.
United Nations, Food and Agriculture Organization, Commodity Bulletin Series, *Spices:
    Trends in World Markets*, No. 34, Rome, 1962.
United Nations, Food and Agriculture Organization, *Commodity Review 1968*, Rome, 1968.
United Nations, Food and Agriculture Organization, *Commodity Review and Outlook, 1968-69*,
    Rome, 1969.
United Nations, *International Wheat Conference*, New York, 1967.

INDEX